MATTERHORN
THE QUINTESSENTIAL MOUNTAIN

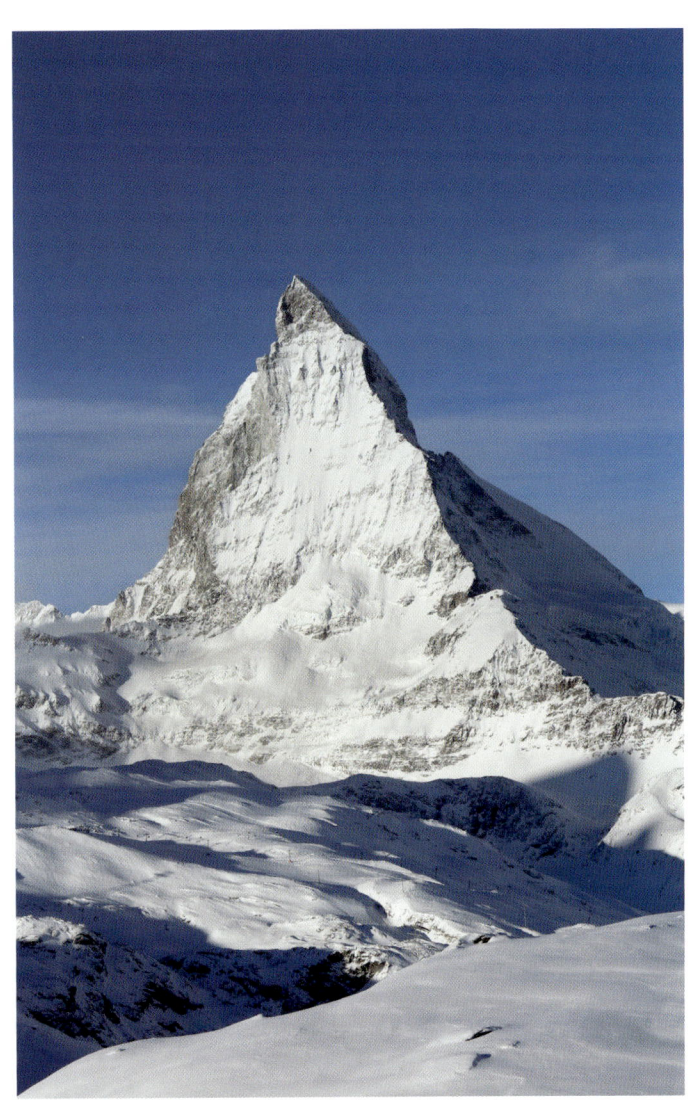

GRAEME WALLACE

With extracts from
THE ASCENT OF THE MATTERHORN
EDWARD WHYMPER

First published in Great Britain 2015

Text and photography copyright © Graeme Wallace

The rights of Graeme Wallace to be identified as the author and photographer of this work has been asserted by him in accordance with the Copyright, Designs and Patents Act 1988

All rights reserved. No part of this publication may be reproduced, stored in a retrieval system or transmitted in any form by any means electronic, mechanical, photocopy or otherwise without the prior permission in writing of the copyright owner.

Photograph of Edward Whymper
copyright © Archives départementales des Hautes-Alpes
Photographs on pages 248, 249 and 250 by John McCune.
Photograph on page 252 by Sandy Allan

Extract text and illustrations copyright © 1871 Edward Whymper

In 1871 Edward Whymper wrote and illustrated his book *Scrambles Amongst the Alps*. Nine years later, in 1880, the book was revised and re-released as *The Ascent of the Matterhorn*. Extracts from the later book are presented here. Note: any inconsistencies or misspellings in the quoted text are as they appear in the original.

Designed by Mark Bennett

Printed in Poland

Published by
GW Publishing
PO Box 15070
Dunblane
FK15 5AN

www.gwpublishing.com
Blog **thematterhorn4478.com**

ISBN 978-0-9570844-9-0

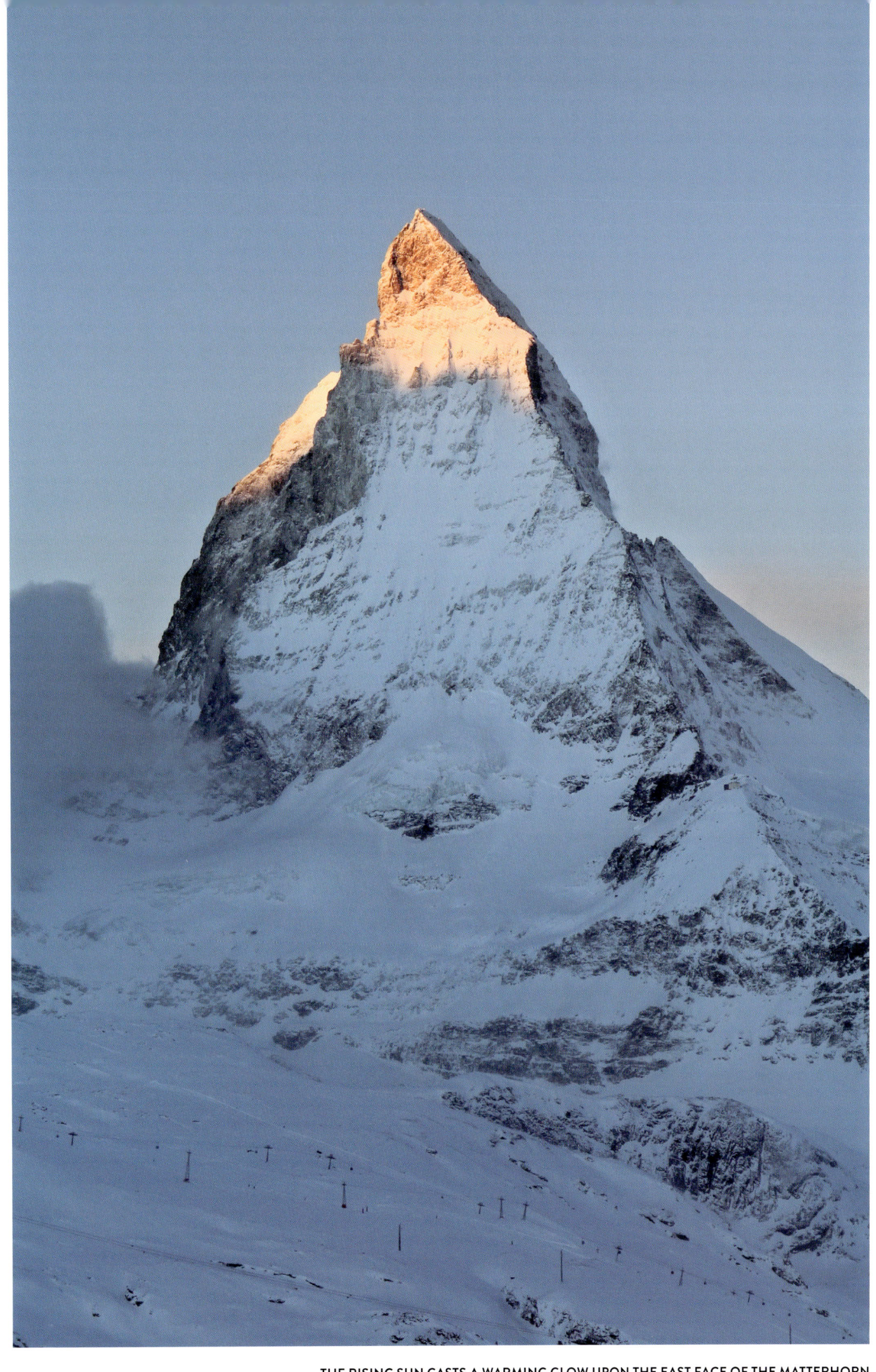

THE RISING SUN CASTS A WARMING GLOW UPON THE EAST FACE OF THE MATTERHORN

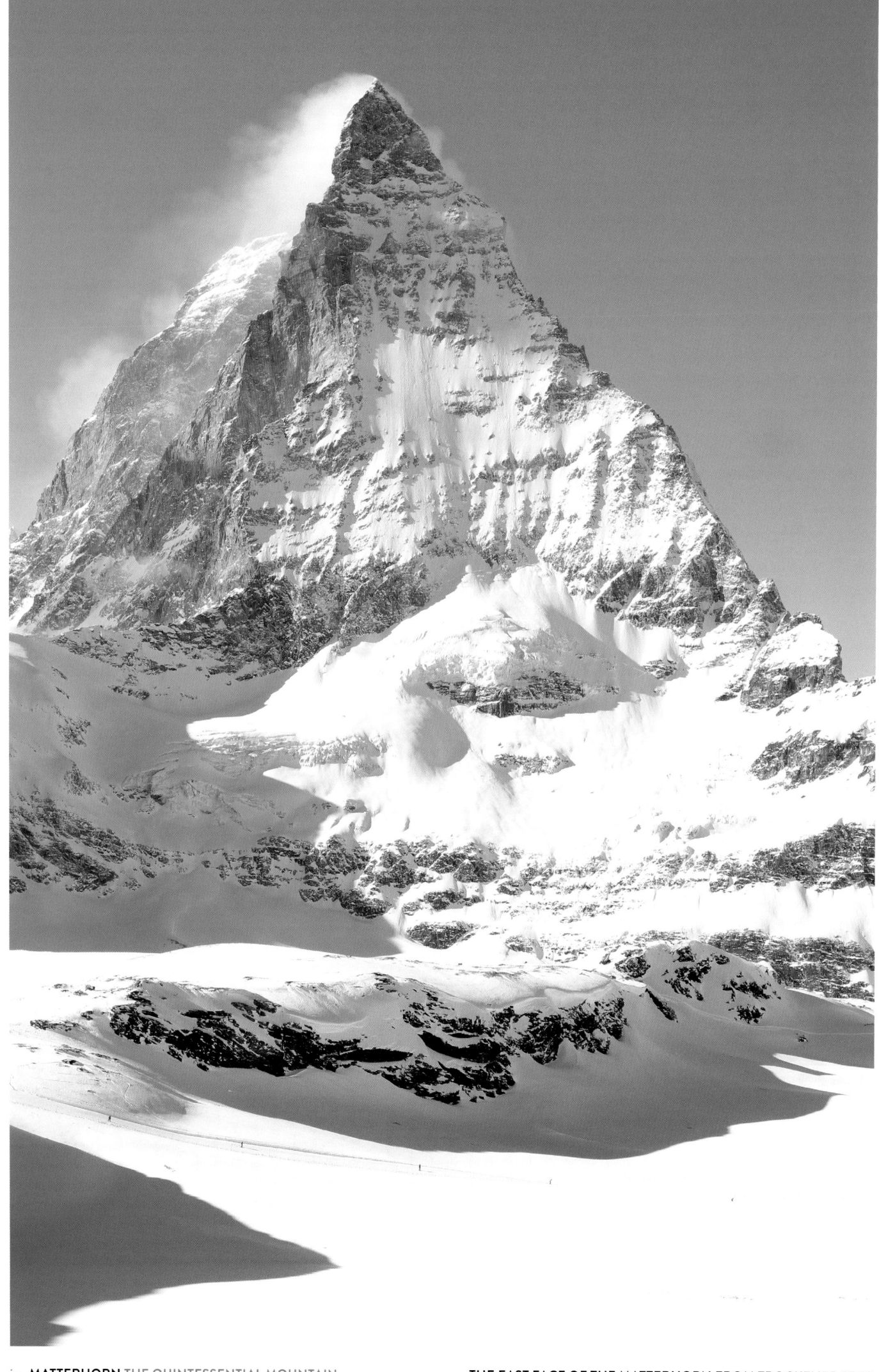

THE EAST FACE OF THE MATTERHORN FROM TROCKENER STEG

PREFACE

In 1880, English mountaineer, Edward Whymper wrote the book *The Ascent of the Matterhorn*, in which he describes his six years mountain scrambling in the Alps between 1860 and 1865, culminating in his eighth attempt to ascend the Matterhorn. His work was descriptive, graphic and captivating and was supported by wood-engraved illustrations, created by Whymper himself. The book graphically relays the challenges, emotions and decisions that Whymper and his companions faced, and highlights the same considerations that today's' mountaineers still confront. *The Ascent of the Matterhorn* was published in 1880 and was a revised copy of his earlier book, *Scrambles Amongst the Alps*, which was first published in 1871. *Scrambles Amongst the Alps* is now currently available as part of the *National Geographic* Adventure Classics series.

Sadly, it is often the failures, mistakes and tragedies that grab our attention and in his text, Whymper never shies away from highlighting his own poor judgements or, indeed, the mistakes and shortcomings of others.

There were mistakes made, not only by Whymper, but also by a great many of the pioneering mountaineers; so much so that Queen Victoria questioned the viability of the sport and consulted her Lord Chamberlain as to whether mountain climbing should be made illegal. However, men and women were by then hooked and it would have been impossible to reverse the tide of English 'tourists' wanting to set foot on the lofty peaks of the Alps. *The Times* newspaper was particularly questioning with an editorial on 27th July, 1865:

> *What is the use of scaling precipitous rocks, and being for half an hour at the top of the terrestrial globe? There is use in the feats of sailors, of steeple-climbers, vane-cleaners, chimney sweepers, lovers, and other adventurous professions. A man may be content to die in such a cause, for it is his life's battle. But in the few short moments a member of the Alpine Club has to survey his life when he finds himself slipping, he had but a sorry account to give of himself. What is he doing there, and what right has he to throw away the gift of life?*

Throughout his book, and particularly toward the end, Whymper gave his own more convincing response and reasoning for climbing, and frequently relays some of the emotion and elation upon reaching a summit or success. Simply put: 'a panorama extending over as much ground as the whole of England is one worth taking some trouble to see'. It is true that the views are often breathtaking: more so than words and pictures can relay. But there is more that drives people to take up the relatively high-risk sport. The sense of accomplishment at having pitted oneself against the elements and attaining a difficult goal provides lasting character traits that make us more fulfilled and better able to deal with everyday decisions and challenges.

Whymper goes on to say in his Preface: 'The ablest pens have failed, and I think must always fail, to give a true idea of the grandeur of the Alps. The most minute descriptions of the greatest writers do nothing more than convey impressions that are entirely erroneous-the reader conjures up visions, it may be magnificent ones, but they are infinitely inferior to the reality'.

There is certainly truth in this statement, but Whymper deserves particular recognition for doing an outstanding job in portraying the grandeur of the Alps and his time amongst the many soaring peaks.

In this book, tribute is paid to Edward Whymper, not only for his climbing achievements, but also for his artistic talent and literary work. To commemorate the 150th anniversary of Whymper's crowning achievement, this book combines substantial extracts and illustrations from *The Ascent of the Matterhorn* interwoven with my own story and photography, as I walk in some of the footsteps of this pertinacious pioneering mountaineer.

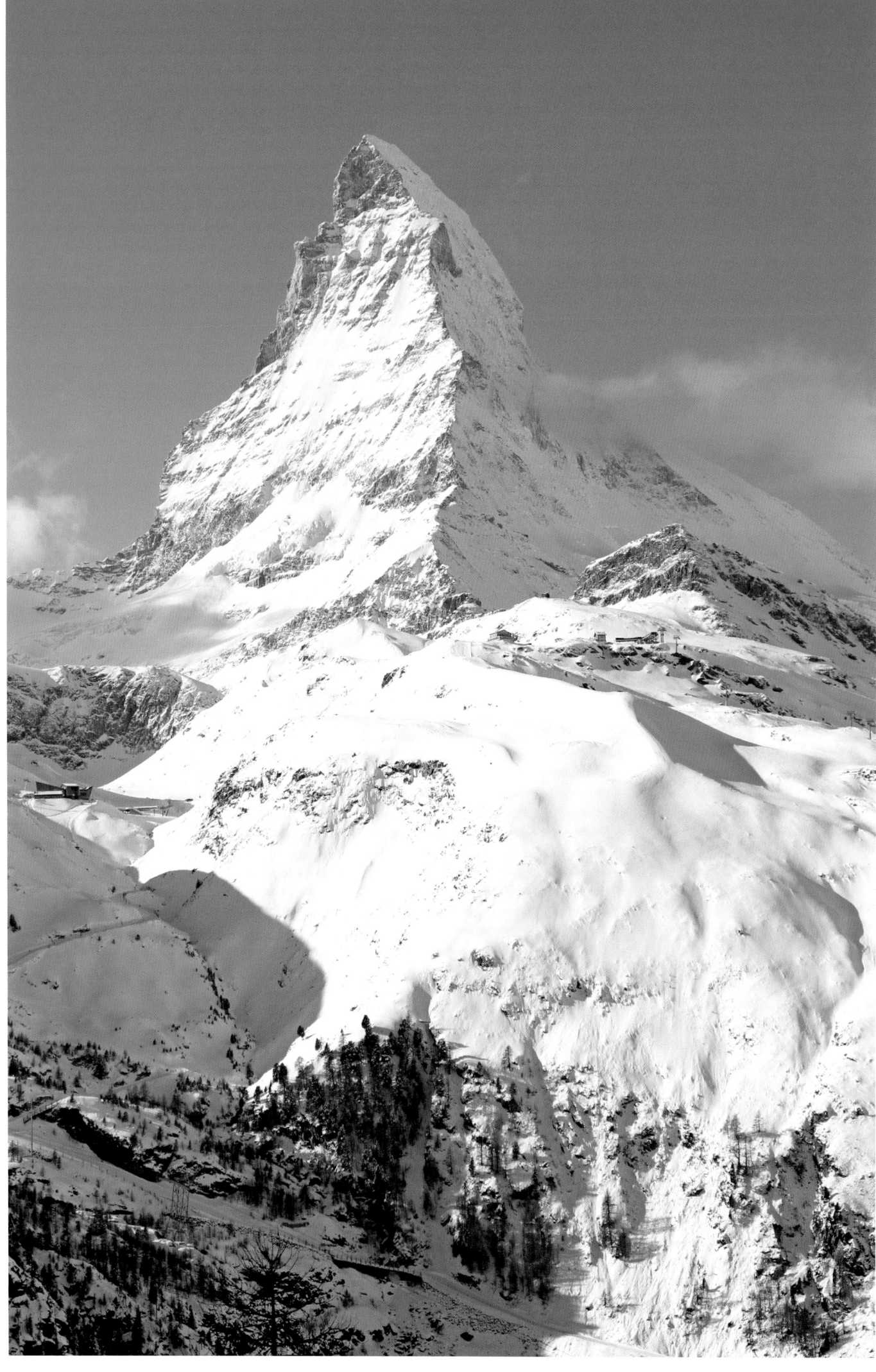

CONTENT

Preface v

Introduction 12

Chapter One
    Edward Whymper 13

Chapter Two
    The Matterhorn 15

Chapter Three
    Mountaineering 17

Chapter Four
    From the Preface of *The Ascent of the Matterhorn* 19

Chapter Five
    1860: First Explorations 20

Chapter Six
    1861: Mont Pelvoux and the Matterhorn 57

Chapter Seven
    1862: Renewed Attempts on the Matterhorn 91

Chapter Eight
    1863: Dent d'Hérens, Grand Tournalin and the Matterhorn 124

Chapter Nine
    1864: The Aiguilles d'Arves, Barre des Écrins, Mont Dolent, Aiguille de Tré-la-Tête and Aiguille d'Argentiére 154

Chapter Ten
    1865: Grand Cornier, Dent Blanche, Grandes Jorasses, Aiguille Verte, La Ruinette and the Matterhorn 189

Afterword 253

Author's Log
    Preparations and Training 23
    Winter 2015 24
    Spring 2015 69
    Summer 2015 (Week One) 99
    Summer 2015 (Week Two) 131
    Summer 2015 (Week Three) 169
    Summer 2015 (Nadelhorn 4,327m) 213
    Summer 2015 (Matterhorn 4,478m) 233

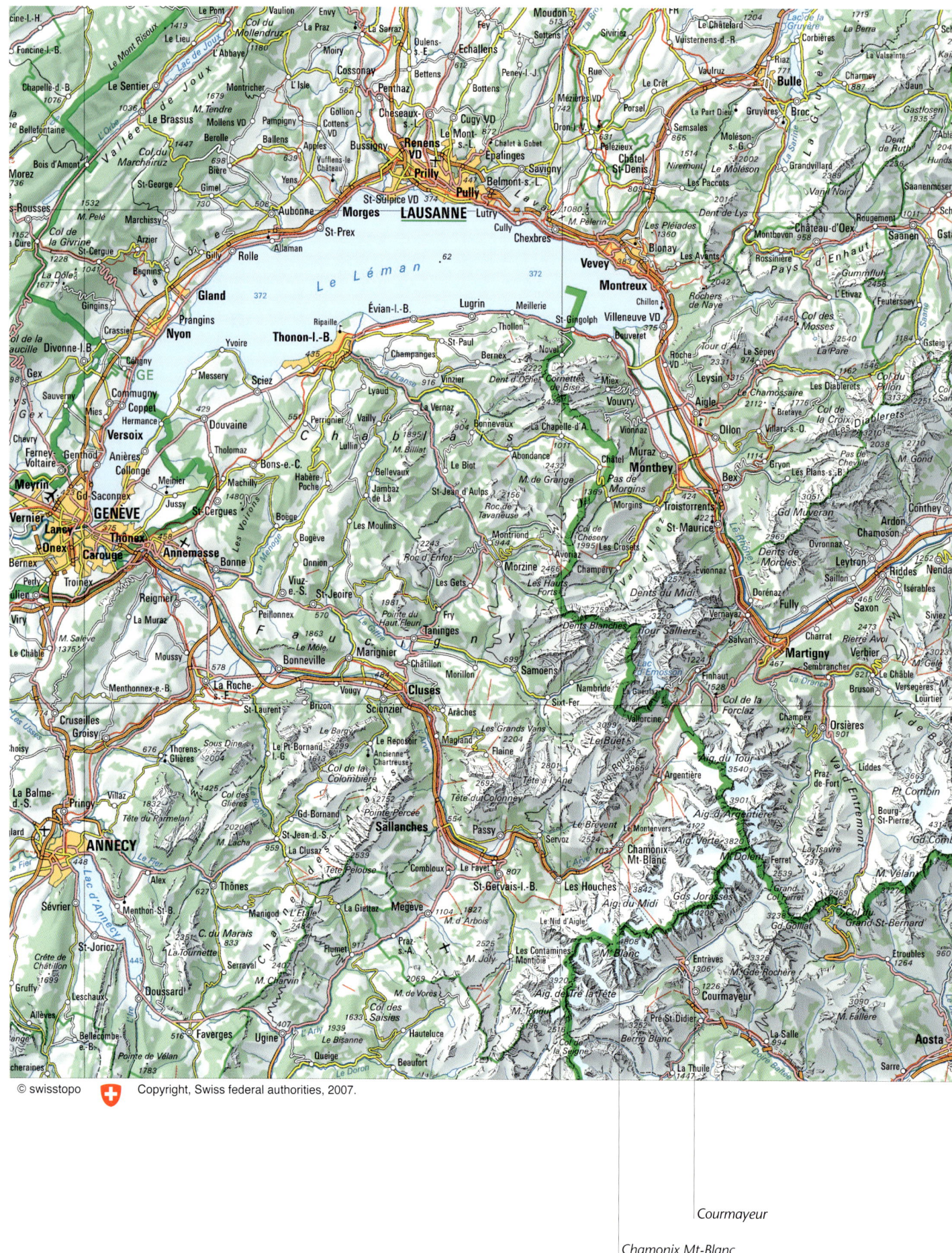

Courmayeur

Chamonix Mt-Blanc

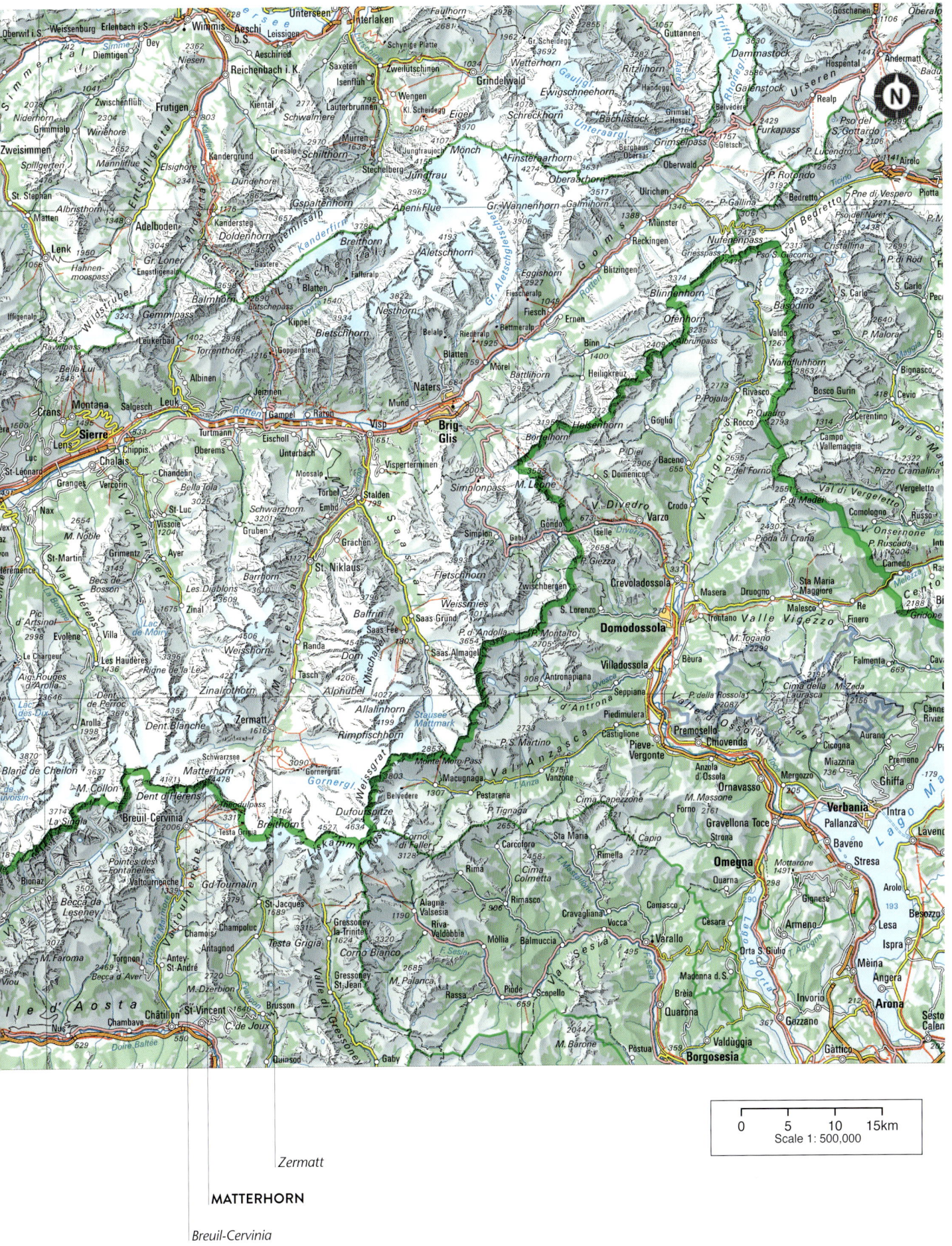

Zermatt

MATTERHORN

Breuil-Cervinia

PENNINE ALPS

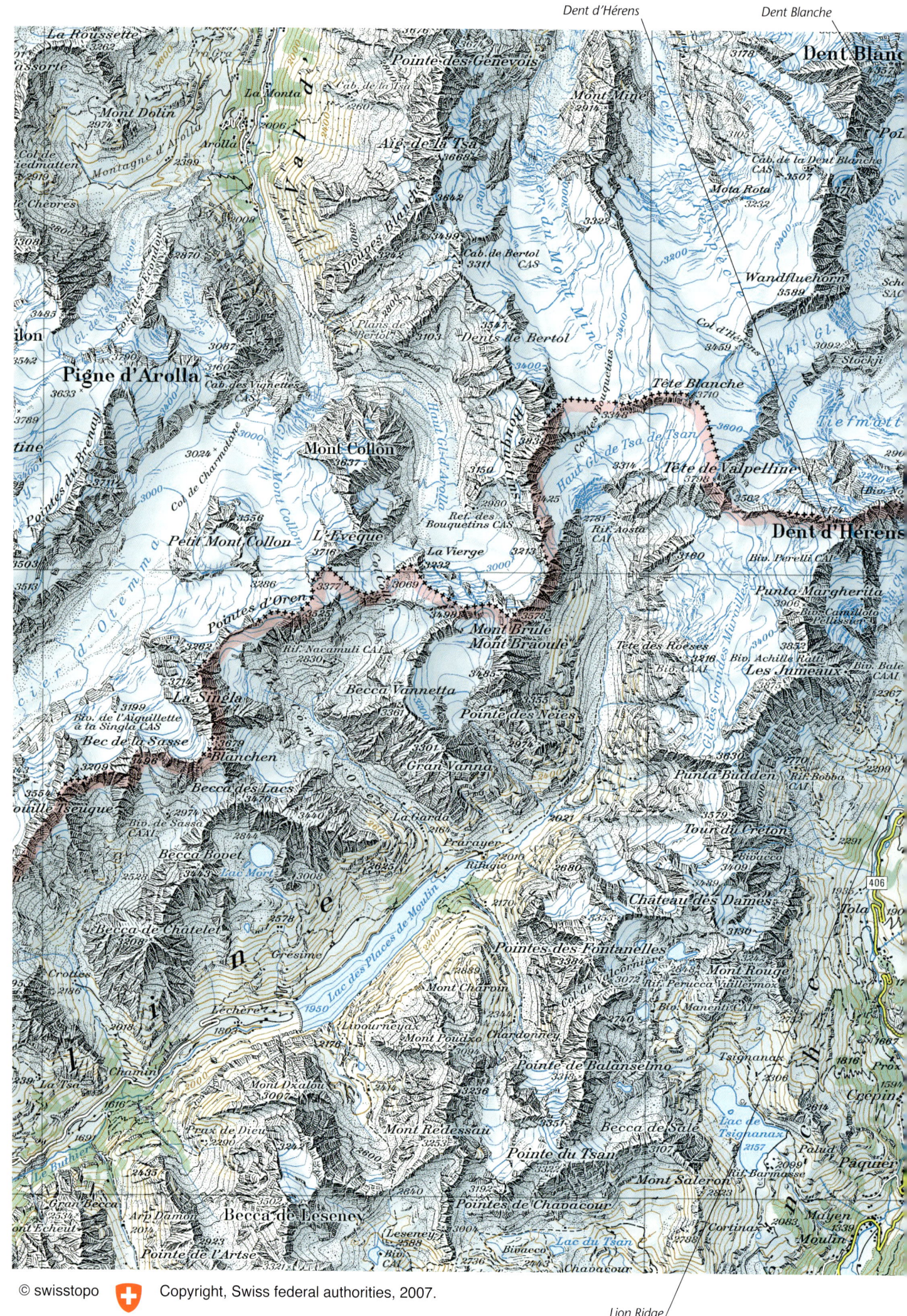

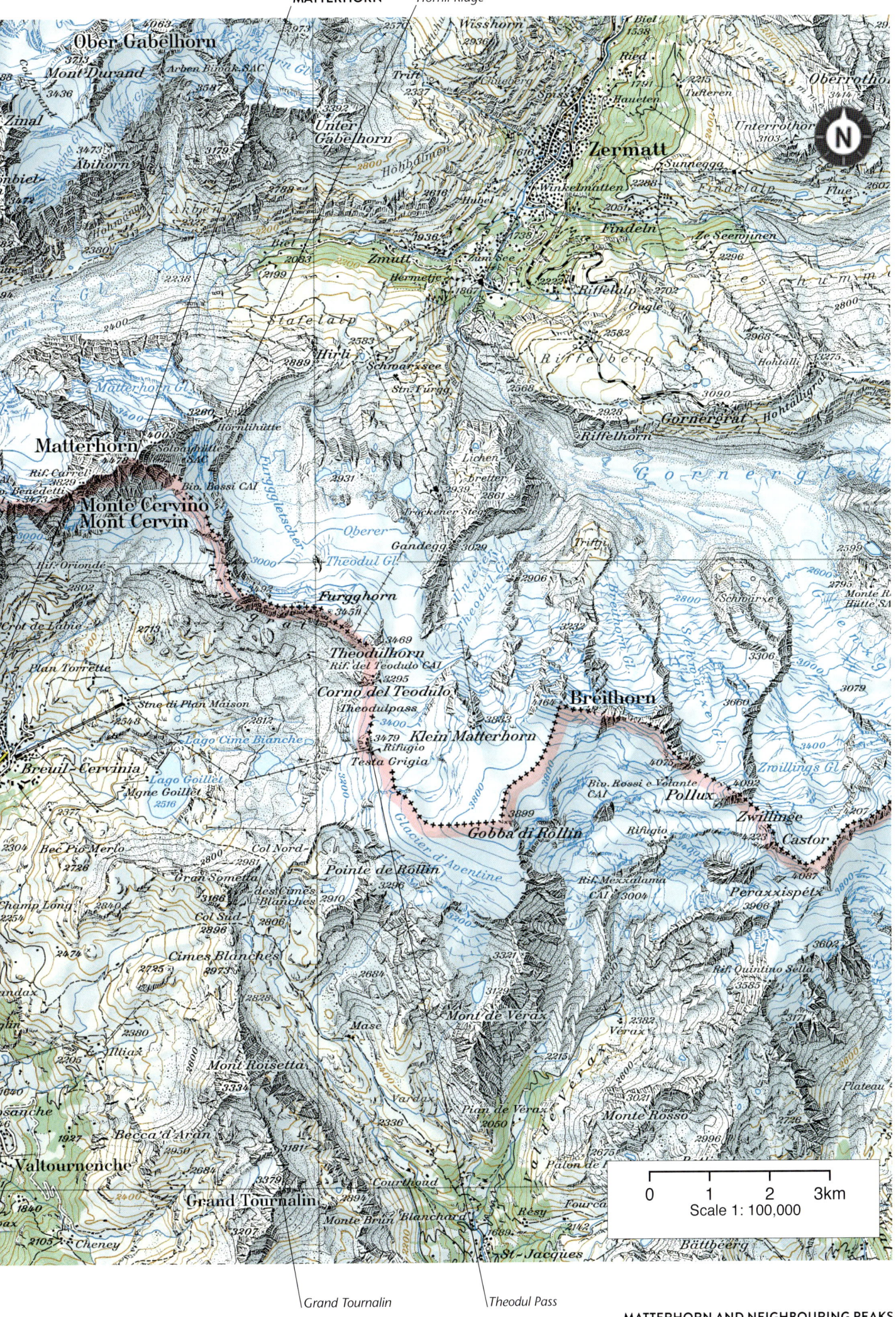

MATTERHORN AND NEIGHBOURING PEAKS

INTRODUCTION

During one of our regular mountaineering trips in the Highlands of Scotland, my climbing partner Mat Tams recounted the details of the story he had learned as a child about the first ascent of the Matterhorn, the most recognisable and iconic mountain in the world. It was in the Golden Age of Mountaineering, dominated by proud, self-assured and intrepid characters from the British Isles, who were still enjoying their Victorian perspective of being superior and invincible. Exciting and daring, they were pioneering men, trail-blazing and seeking to be amongst the first, if not *the* first to scale the Alpine peaks.

Perhaps it was inevitable that our conversation would lead to us considering scaling the Matterhorn, and soon a date was set to make our dream a reality. Mat had, in fact, made two previous trips to climb the infamous peak, but on both occasions was unable to make the attempt, owing to unsuitable weather. I was determined not to suffer the same fate and so the planning started for how to maximise our chances of success. At this time, we had not appreciated that the year we had planned to climb was also the 150th anniversary of the first summit in 1865.

The weather-window for climbing the more challenging Alpine peaks is mid-July to early September. Our experience was that later would be better, so we agreed on the last week in August and first week in September for our trip. We subsequently learnt that in 2014, no guides went up on the Matterhorn until mid-August, which reaffirmed our reasoning and belief that our planning was sound. Nevertheless, allowing for some acclimatisation and knowing that an early snowfall would halt our plans, we did everything possible to keep our options open, in order to catch a good calm and clear two-day period.

Edward Whymper made a total of eight attempts to climb the Matterhorn, most of them from the Italian Liongrat (Lion) Ridge to the south-west, as any other route was considered impossible. Whymper's one and only attempt from the Swiss, Hörnli Ridge to the north-east resulted in success, and this route has subsequently become the normal ascent for most climbers. However, in order to best experience some of Whymper's ordeals, our plan was to climb to the summit via the Lion Ridge and to then descend the Hörnli Ridge. It was hoped that this would also provide a more interesting and challenging trip.

Upon learning that 2015 would be the 150th anniversary of Edward Whymper's and his party's first ascent of the Matterhorn, I felt it would be only fitting to produce this book in commemoration of their success, and in recognition of Whymper's wider achievements in the Alps. This, in turn, meant numerous additional trips would be required in order to understand and portray the Alps as Whymper saw them.

Details of our experiences are recorded throughout the book, indicated by a light blue background to the page. A more detailed account can be read on the blog *www.thematterhorn4478.com*

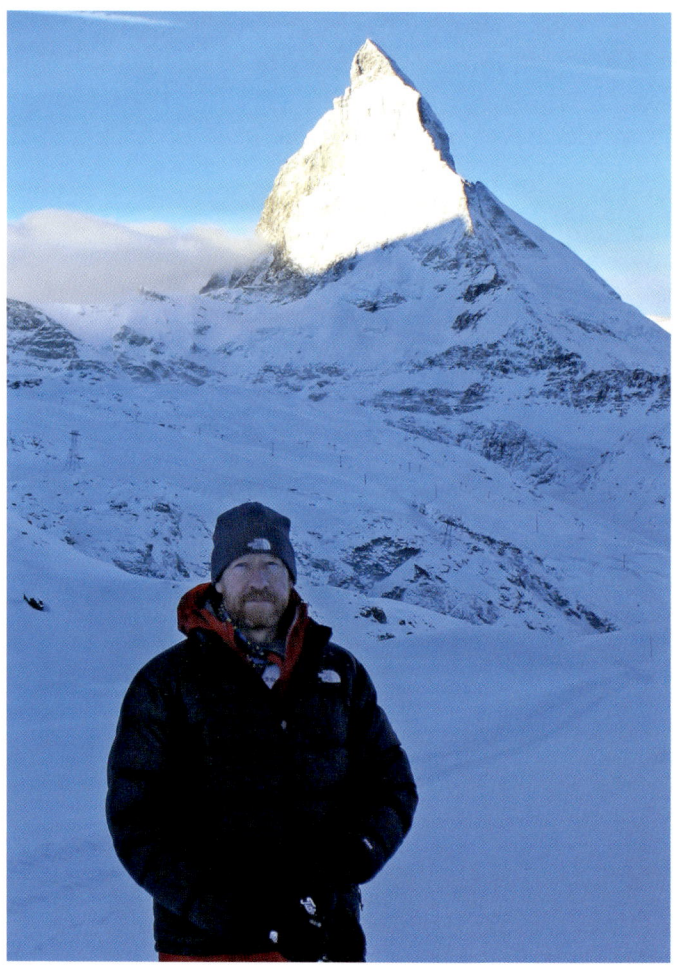

CHAPTER ONE
EDWARD WHYMPER

14th July, 1865. This is the day that marked the end of the Golden Age of Alpine Climbing and Britain's greatest mountaineering achievement to date. Brought about by the events that took place on the Matterhorn, it was the end of one age but the beginning of a new one. Prior to this date, Edward Whymper had been mountaineering — or more aptly 'mountain-scrambling' — for a mere five years, and yet by comparative standards, had quickly become one of the most experienced mountain men of the age. He was a natural: strong, fit and fearless, with a willingness to accept discomfort for the greater reward. He was quick to learn the skills, was prepared to push boundaries, and crucially, was unafraid of what the unknown might hold and of what deadly hurdle might lie ahead. He had a good sense of direction and was resourceful, determined, tactical and skilful. He attacked the Alps with a vengeance, and was not simply there for recreational or social reasons, which was the case with most other English Alpinists. He was there to conquer and, in particular, to conquer the most invincible of mountains: the Matterhorn.

Whymper never fully gained the level of respect that he very much deserved from the Victorian public and among the English climbing community. He did, however, earn the respect and friendship of some of the best European mountain guides of the day ,and as is so often the case with the British, was more highly regarded overseas than at home.

One characteristic that was an essential attribute to all Victorian mountaineers was wealth. In addition to the time away from work and the various travel costs, guides and porters were needed, and as the typical excursion was effectively an expedition, costs quickly escalated. Thus, the poor did not climb in the Alps. The sport was generally considered to be a pastime for men with power and heritage, and men held in high esteem. And so, it was the aristocracy, successful merchants and businessman that first climbed the Alps, along with scholarly men, such as scientists and men of the cloth!

Born in 1840, Edward Whymper was neither poor nor particularly wealthy, but had just sufficient capital to pay for his passion. He was the second of eleven children born to Josiah Whymper. His father had left the security of the family in Suffolk, which had fallen into financial hardship, and settled in London, making his own way as an artist, illustrator and wood-engraver; his company eventually becoming one of the most highly regarded firms in London's publishing arena. Edward was trained by his father as a wood draughtsman, and by the age of twenty had mastered his skill and was receiving commissions.

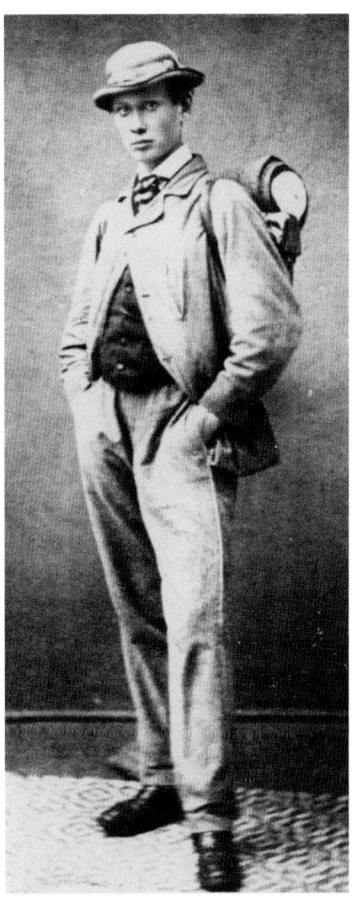

Clearly, Edward Whymper inherited the pioneering spirit from his father and his grandfather, Nathaniel Whymper, who had established a brewery in Ipswich. Nathaniel's cousin was Sir William Whymper, a notable physician in his day, who became Surgeon-Major to the Coldstream Guards and Physician to the Duke of

Cambridge. With somewhat distant aristocratic family connections, and certainly a respectable upbringing and education, Edward Whymper would not have felt particularly out of place among his peers of The Alpine Club, established just a few years earlier, in 1857.

And yet he appears not to have sought their favour, remaining somewhat of an outsider. A man with his own mission, working to his own agenda, but with no obvious reason for setting out on his conquests other than for the satisfaction of his achievement.

Focused and single-minded, solitary and reserved, he was not the easiest man to relate to; preferring the company of a few close friends by a campfire over a gaggle of loud men in a cramped bar. He was not a man to climb with unless you were of a similar outlook and of equal stamina. Few men were. Some have concluded from this that Whymper struggled with relationships, and maybe so. However, he did bond with those of similar determination, and won the respected of the mountaineers and guides who climbed with him.

Leading French, Italian and German guides of the time, climbed with Whymper on numerous occasions, and he quickly developed a particularly strong bond with Frenchman Michel Croz, who summed Whymper up as 'above the range of ordinary mortals' and 'the impetuous man after his own heart'.

Although Whymper's driving force was unquestionably to be the first man to summit some of the remaining unconquered Alpine peaks — and this goal became an obsession with the Matterhorn — he clearly enjoyed being on the mountains, taking in the vast scenery and drawing inspiration from being out amongst the raw elements of nature.

As a boy, Whymper dreamed of becoming a polar explorer but it was an artistic commission to produce wood engravings of the Alps for a leading London publisher that set Whymper on his course to become one of the greatest mountaineers ever. Some of his accomplishments may not appear that impressive by today's standards, but it must always be remembered that he usually went where no man had been before, venturing into the unknown, with little if any reference material to guide him. He had to figure things out for himself: routes, techniques and ideas from which subsequent mountaineers would greatly benefit.

Among his achievements, he made the first ascent of dozens of Alpine peaks, more than any other Englishman, and clocked up over 30,000 vertical metres (100,000 ft) in 18 days in his most prodigious year. He was the first known European to climb above 6,000m (20,000 ft), being the first man to summit Chimborazo in the Ecuadorian Andes in 1880. There was some doubt as to whether he actually reached the summit when he climbed it with brothers Jean-Antoine and Louise Carrel, so he proceeded to climb it a second time in the same year. Owing to the earth being slightly oval in shape, Chimborazo is considered to be the furthest point from the centre of the earth, and until the beginning of the nineteenth century, was considered the highest mountain on earth.

Key to his successes were his fitness and stamina that enabled his body to equal his mind in pushing on beyond the apparent boundaries. Although he had never seen a mountain before his first trip to the Alps in 1860, he was an ardent walker, regularly walking up to forty miles per day. Even in his fifties he remained active, once walking from London to Edinburgh at an average rate of fifty-five miles per day.

Whymper was certainly a man with idiosyncrasies and a product of his time, with traits which some have held against him. He may have been somewhat haughty, demanding and opinionated, but Whymper was a remarkable and brave man and his successes deserve to be seen alongside those of the world's greatest explorers and adventurers.

CHAPTER TWO
THE MATTERHORN

Straddling Italy and Switzerland, the Matterhorn is unquestionably the king of the Alps, although at 4,478m (14,692 ft) it is not the tallest. It is, in fact, the sixth highest mountain in the Alps, and as part of the Pennine Alps, is the eleventh highest peak in the range, of which 32 are above 4,000m (13,123 ft). Its solitary position and symmetrical pyramid shape make it appear particularly lofty and indomitable when viewed from the north and north-east, while from the south it emerges as a menacing hulk.

From the Italian side to the south, it appears less uniform and acute, but still foreboding, dominating the scattered dwelling at its feet. So imperious was it that only a handful of Italians and Swiss who lived in its shadow, believed it could be climbed, or was worth the attempt. It was considered by many of the locals as a place where only spirits dwelt and that anyone who tried to scale it was mad and would suffer its wrath.

To the north of the Matterhorn lies the bustling Swiss town of Zermatt in the district of Visp, which is in the canton of Valais. At an elevation of 1,620m (5,310 ft), this has traditionally been, and still is, the hub and starting point for people visiting the mountain from the north. To the south lies the small Italian town of Breuil-Cervinia in the *comune* of Valtournenche, which has a town of the same name 9km (5.6 miles) further to the south. Simply referred to as 'Breil' by Whymper, it sits 2,006m (6,581 ft) above sea level, yet still enjoys a lush meadow setting.

The quickest way to travel on foot between Zermatt and Breuil-Cervinia was over the Theodul Pass, a glacier pass at 3,295m (10,810 ft) to the east of the Matterhorn. Whymper and his fellow 'tourists' relied on this ancient pass to transfer between the two towns. Few travellers today would consider taking this direct route of 19km (12 miles), and will take the 228km (141 mile) road trip instead. However, the novelty of skiing over the border between Switzerland and Italy attracts keen skiers to the Theodul, benefitting from the cable-car points on either side.

Today, it would appear odd to hear of someone that did not consider the Matterhorn as an object of beauty, and for the mountaineering fraternity to ever think there was a time when man did not want to climb it. But this is precisely the case. The earliest shepherds and brave pilgrims considered it to be the throne of a god, or home to a demon that would hurl rocks down upon these simple people. Not until 1789 was it written about in admirable terms. Swiss botanist Horace Saussure had climbed Mont Blanc in 1787, the year following the first successful ascent, and noted of the Matterhorn: 'Its precipitous sides which give no hold to the very snows, are such as to afford no means of access'.

In 1818, Johann Gottfried Ebel's primitive guidebook was translated into English. In it the mountain has three names: Silvius, Mont Cervin and Matterhorn. The guide, which referred to it as 'one of the most splendid and wonderful obelisks in the Alps', no doubt played a major part in ushering tourism in to the area, with the affluent English arriving to actually admire or study the mountain first hand. These first 'tourists' will have seen the mountain in a way we can only imagine: peaceful, simple, isolated, magnificent.

In 1825, William Brockendon described it as 'a spectacle of indescribable grandeur', while Lord Minto, during a visit in 1830, claimed, 'It is impossible for words to convey any idea of the immensity of this pyramid, regular and symmetrical in form, as if it had been designed by an architect'.

Eminent philosopher and seasoned traveller James David Forbes went on to note, in 1841, 'the most wonderful peak in the Alps, unscaled and unscalable'. And so, like a red rag to a bull, the stage was set for men, primarily English gentry, to dream of its ascent.

Italians can take pride in knowing that the first

believers and first recorded attempt to climb Monte Cervino — as it was, and still is known on that side — was by three of their countrymen in 1857. Armed with little more than a hatchet and some morsels of food, hunter Jean Jacques Carrel led young Jean-Antoine Carrel and a somewhat nonconformist young priest called Amé Gorret up to reach the Téte du Lion. There, an impassable drop forced their retreat at that time.

Their adventure appeared subsequently in an English book published in 1858, resulting in the best climbers of the day visiting Valtournenche to assess the feasibility of climbing the Matterhorn. E.S. Kennedy visited in 1858 and considered it impossible, while in 1859, Vaughan Hawkins considered it 'a different sort of affair from Mont Blanc or Monte Rosa, or any of the other of the thousand and one summits which nature has kindly opened to man'. Hawkins returned the following year with guide J.J. Bennen and John Tyndall, employing Jean Jacques Carrel as simply their porter. Climbing a little higher than the Col du Lion, they were also forced to retreat, with Hawkins noting, 'The mountain, too, has a sort of prestige of invincibility which is not without its influence on the mind, and almost leads one to expect to encounter some new and unheard-of source of peril upon it'.

While having a respect for danger is healthy, a fear of the unknown is often the greatest challenge for us to overcome, and rarely more so on the Matterhorn. Enter Edward Whymper. Fearless and defiant, he was about to become the new demon of the Matterhorn.

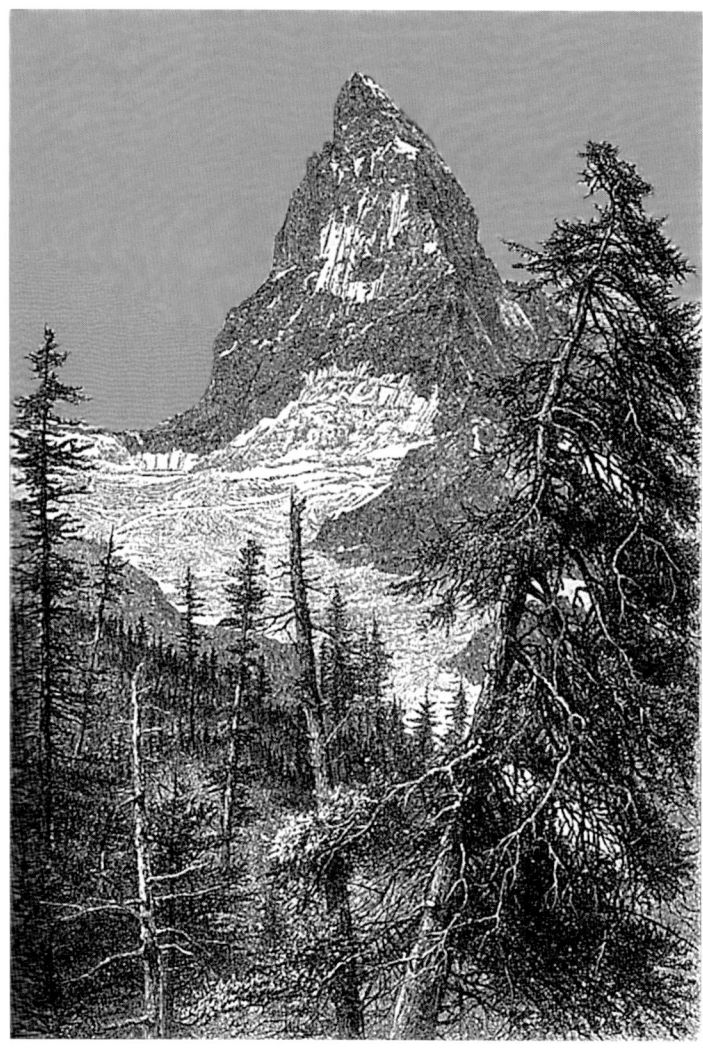

The Matterhorn from the Riffelberg

CHAPTER THREE
MOUNTAINEERING

Times have changed for mountaineers as they have for travellers. The intrepid Victorian mountaineer had few pieces of specialist equipment and, of course, did not have guidebooks and reference materials that those who travel in their footsteps so easily take for granted: no satellite navigation and GPS; no detailed maps; and, in the case of 'first ascents', absolutely no knowledge of what lay ahead. They did not have hard helmets to protect against rockfall or lightweight waterproof and wind-resistant clothing to wick away moisture while allowing the garment to breathe, keeping the wearer dry, warm and comfortable.

Whymper often slept in a 'blanket bag', or bivi bag, which was no more than a blanket sewn up along the base and sides, and invented his own mountain tent that could be erected on narrow cliffs. He also developed various pieces of his own equipment, including the 'claw' (a type of grappling hook) with a rope attached to it, for getting up or down otherwise impassable cliffs. The modern ice axe is far removed from what was used then, reduced from a clumsy chest-high walking staff to the considerably lighter and shorter ergonomic tool utilised today. Finally, instead of specially made stiff waterproof boots, which can accept the addition of spiked crampons, these early adventures wore simple boots — and in some cases shoes — that would be just as suitable in the streets and rolling hills of England; the only addition being 'hobnails', metal studs. A form of crampon spike had become available but was considered too cumbersome by most.

One invaluable piece of equipment the early Alpinists did use was rope. Whymper certainly appreciated the advantage of roping up together with his guides or fellow climbers, and appears to have always had rope with him. However, not all guides, or indeed English climbers, valued the use of rope, and many of the best practices of how to use it were still to be established.

While Edward Whymper created a number of 'tent platforms', where he would leave a tent to return to, he invariably spent many nights sleeping under the stars with just his blanket to protect him from the elements. Today's climbers can take advantage of the huts (refuges) strategically placed throughout the Alps, allowing for an invaluable early start and providing an emergency shelter if caught out by weather or time. On both the Hörnli Ridge and the Lion Ridge, there is a hut providing overnight accommodation, and at the Hörnli hut, dinner is also catered for.

Finally, modern-day mountaineers benefit from a team standing by to pluck stricken climbers off the mountain with the aid of a helicopter that can be scrambled and in-situ within as little as an hour, giving considerable reassurance, albeit no guarantee of rescue.

Despite all the modern conveniences, the Matterhorn remains a true challenge, with people still dying in their attempt to reach its summit. Over 500 deaths have occurred on the mountain in the past 150 years. Fortunately, with increased knowledge, most climbers that attempt the summit return safely.

There is simply no substitute for care and common sense. Being brave does not mean taking silly risks and this is just as relevant now as ever before. Taking great care in the descent, particularly so on the Matterhorn, cannot be overemphasised. Having had little sleep overnight, followed by numerous hours in a high state of alertness, and having climbed for many hours in the previous days, it is natural and good to relax and enjoy the time on the summit. However, as the descent is generally more dangerous than the ascent, owing to the difficulty in seeing holds and maintaining balance, greater vigilance is required, just as the mind and body start to switch off as a result of fatigue and apathy – having already attain the 'goal'.

The illustrations on the next page provide examples of equipment used then and now.

EARLY EQUIPMENT # THE MODERN EQUIVALENT

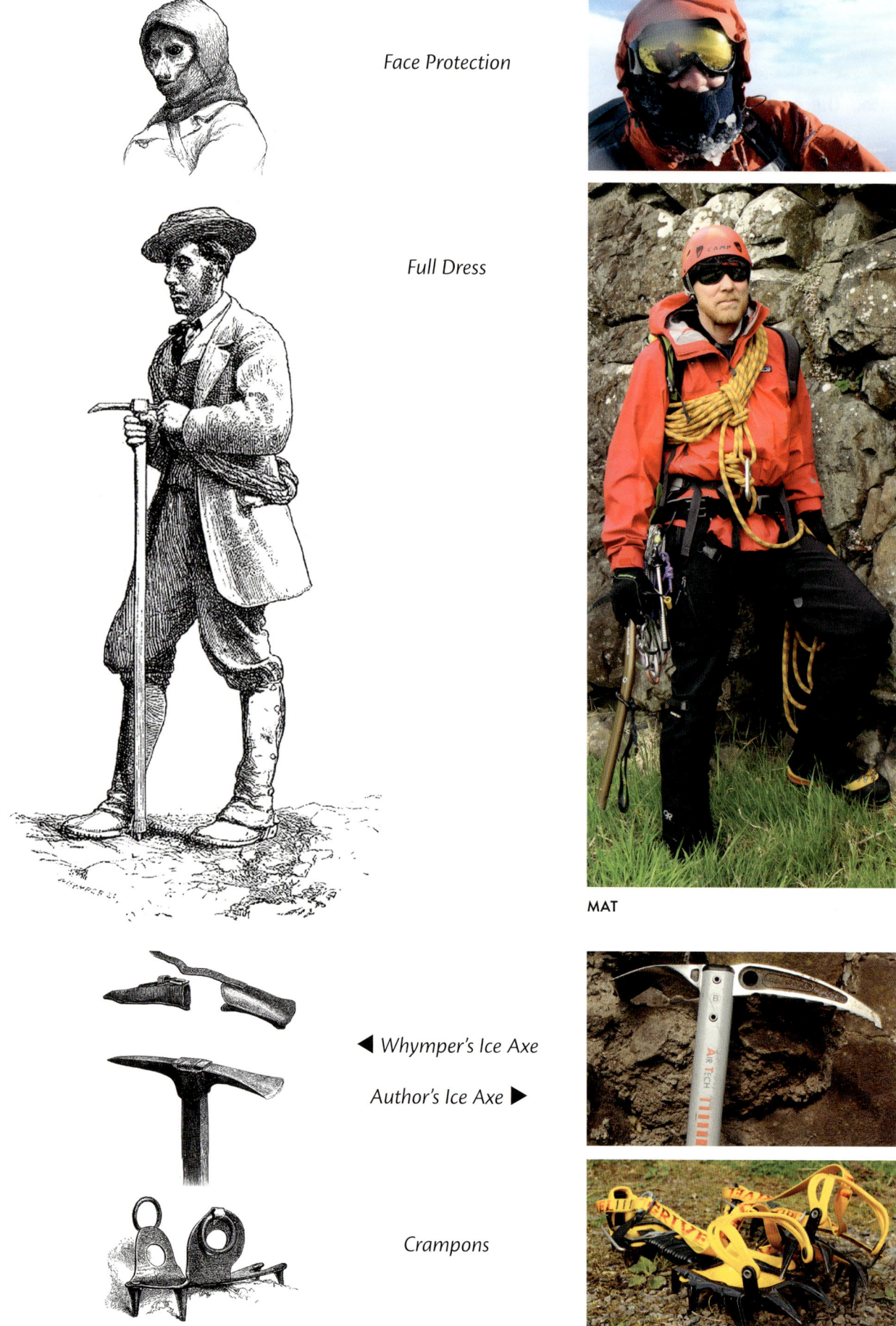

Face Protection

Full Dress

MAT

◀ *Whymper's Ice Axe*

Author's Ice Axe ▶

Crampons

CHAPTER FOUR
FROM THE PREFACE OF
The Ascent of the Matterhorn by Edward Whymper

Edward Whymper was an eager and fresh-faced young man of just twenty years when he first visited the Alps. It was love at first sight and he was instantly smitten. Captivated, there would be no turning back, his future path into history now set in motion.

In the year 1860, shortly before leaving England for a long continental tour, a certain eminent London publisher requested me to make for him some sketches of the great Alpine peaks. At that time I had only a literary acquaintance with mountain-climbing, and had not even seen-much less set foot upon-a mountain. Among the peaks which were upon the list was Mont Pelvoux, in Dauphiné [**in south-east France**]. The sketches that were required of it were to celebrate the triumph of some Englishman who intended to make its ascent. They came — they saw — but they did not conquer.

By a mere chance I fell in with a very agreeable Frenchman who accompanied this party, and was pressed by him to return to the assault. In 1861 we did so, with my friend Macdonald — and we conquered.

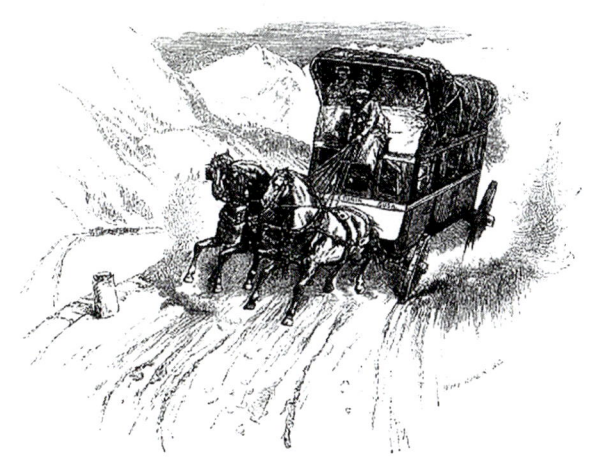

Crossing Mont Cenis (1861)

The ascent of Mont Pelvoux (including the disagreeables) was a very delightful scramble. The mountain air did *not* act as an emetic; the sky did *not* look black, instead of blue; nor did I feel tempted to throw myself over precipices. I hastened to enlarge my experience, and went to the Matterhorn. I was urged toward Mont Pelvoux by those mysterious impulses which cause men to peer into the unknown. This mountain was reputed to be the highest in France, and on that account was worthy of attention; and it was believed to be the culminating point of a picturesque district of great interest, which was then almost entirely unexplored! The Matterhorn attracted me simply by its grandeur. It was considered to be the most completely inaccessible of all mountains, even by those who ought to have known better. Stimulated to make fresh exertions by one repulse after another, I returned, year after year, as I had opportunity, more and more determined to find a way up it, or to prove it to be really inaccessible.

In endeavouring to make the book of some use to those who may wish to go mountain-scrambling, whether in the Alps or elsewhere, prominence has been given to our mistakes and failures; and to some it may seem that our practice must have been bad if the principles which are laid down are sound, or that the principles must be unsound if the practice was good. The principles which are brought under the notice of the reader are, however, deduced from long experience, which experience had not been gained at the time that the blunders were perpetrated; and, if it had been acquired at an earlier date, there would have been fewer failures to record.

(From The Ascent of the Matterhorn, pp.v-vi)

CHAPTER FIVE
1860 FIRST EXPLORATIONS

Commissioned by London publisher Longman, Green, Longman, and Roberts to produce a series of engravings of the central and western alpine region between Switzerland, France and Italy for a book titled *Peaks, Passes and Glaciers*, Edward Whymper set out on a journey that would lead to guaranteeing him a place in history.

On the 23rd of July, 1860, I stared for my first tour in the Alps. As we steamed out into the Channel, Beachy Head came into view, and I recalled a scramble of many years ago. With the impudence of ignorance, my brother and I, schoolboys both, had tried to scale the great chalk cliff. Not the head itself — where sea-birds circle, and where the flints are ranged in orderly parallel lines — but a place more to the east, where a pinnacle called the Devil's Chimney had fallen down. Since then we have been often in dangers of different kinds, but never have we more nearly broken our necks than upon that occasion.

After stopping off in Paris and visiting Notre Dame, Whymper arrives in Zermatt and embarks upon a steep learning curve of how, or rather, how not, to travel in the Alps.

At Zermatt I wandered in many directions, but the weather was bad, and my work was much retarded. One day, after spending a long time in attempts to sketch near the Hörnli, and in futile endeavours to seize the forms of the peaks as they for a few seconds peered out from above the dense banks of woolly clouds, I determined not to return to Zermatt by the usual path, and to cross the Gorner glacier to the Riffel hotel. After a rapid scramble over the polished rocks and snowbeds which skirt the base of the Théodule glacier, and wading through some of the streams which flow from it, at that time much swollen by the late rains, the first difficulty was arrived at, in the shape of a precipice about three hundred feet high. It seemed that it would be easy enough to cross the glacier if the cliff could be descended; but higher up, and lower down, the ice appeared, to my inexperienced eyes, to be impassable for a single person. The general contour of the cliff was nearly perpendicular, but it was a good deal broken up, and there was little difficulty in descending by zigzagging from one mass to another. At length there was a long slab, nearly smooth, fixed at an angle of about forty degrees between two wall-sided pieces of rock. Nothing, except the glacier, could be seen below. It was an awkward place, but I passed it at length by lying across the slab, putting the shoulders stiffly against one side, and the feet against the other, and gradually wriggling down, by first moving the legs and then the back. When the bottom of the slab was gained a friendly crack was seen, into which the point of the baton could be stuck, and I dropped down to the next piece. It took a long time coming down that little bit of cliff, and for a few seconds it was satisfactory to see the ice close at hand. In another moment a second difficulty presented itself. The glacier swept round an angle of the cliff, and as the ice was not of the nature of treacle or thin putty, it kept away from the little bay, on the edge of which I stood. We were not widely separated, but the edge of the ice was higher than the opposite edge of rock; and worse, the rock was covered with loose earth and stones which had fallen from above. All along the side of the cliff, as far as could be seen in both directions, the ice did not touch it, but there was this marginal crevasse, seven feet wide, and of unknown depth.

All this was seen at a glance, and almost at once I concluded that I could not jump the crevasse, and began to try along the cliff lower down; but without success, for the ice rose higher and higher, until at last further progress was stopped by the cliffs becoming perfectly smooth. With an axe it would have been possible to cut up the side of the ice; without one I saw there was no alternative but to return and face the jump.

Night was approaching, and the solemn stillness of the High Alps was broken only by the sound of rushing water or of falling rocks. If the jump should be successful — well; if not, I fell into that horrible chasm, to be frozen in, or drowned in that gurgling, rushing water. Everything depended on that jump. Again I asked myself, 'Can it be done?' It *must* be. So, finding my stick was useless, I threw it and the sketch-book to the ice, and first retreating as far as possible, ran forward with all my might, took the leap, barely reaching the other side, and fell awkwardly on my knees.

The glacier was crossed without further trouble, but the Riffel, which was then a very small building, was crammed with tourists, and could not take me in. As the way down was unknown to me, some of the people obligingly suggested getting a man at the chalets, otherwise the path would be certainly lost in the forest. On arriving at the chalets no man could be found, and the lights of Zermatt, shining through the trees, seemed to say, 'Never mind a guide, but come along down, I'll show you the way;' so off I went through the forest, going straight towards them. The path was lost in a moment, and was never recovered. I was tripped up by pine-roots, tumbled over rhododendron bushes, fell over rocks. The night was pitch dark, and after a time the lights of Zermatt became obscure, or went out altogether. By a series of slides, or falls, or evolutions more or less disagreeable, the descent through the forest was at length accomplished; but torrents of formidable character had still to be passed before one could arrive at Zermatt. I felt my way about for hours, almost hopelessly; by an exhaustive process at last discovering a bridge, and about midnight, covered with dirt and scratches, re-entered the inn which I had quitted in the morning.

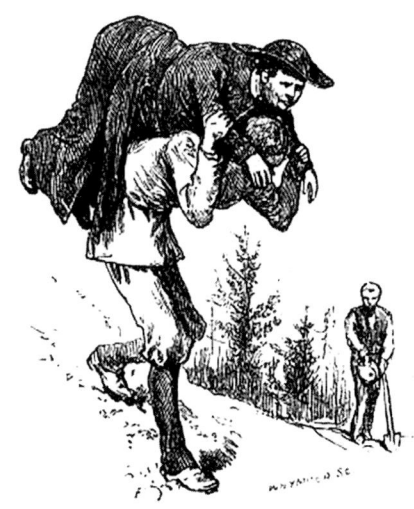

Others besides tourists get into difficulties. A day or two afterwards, when on the way to my old station, near the Hörnli, I met a stout *curé* who had essayed to cross the Théodule pass. His strength or his wind had failed, and he was being carried down, a helpless bundle and a ridiculous spectacle, on the back of a lanky guide; while the peasants stood by, with folded hands, their reverence for the church almost overcome by their sense of the ludicrous.

Relentless, and undeterred by misadventures and unfavourable weather, Whymper made his way around Switzerland in search of scenery worthy of sketching for his project. He then turned south to Italy, seeking out a guide to see him over the pass.

… the old woman, now convinced of my respectability, busied herself to find a guide. Presently she introduced a native, picturesquely attired in high-peaked hat, braided jacket, scarlet waistcoat, and indigo pantaloons, who agreed to take me to the village of Val Tournanche [**now Valtournenche**]. We set off early on the next morning, and got to the summit of the pass without difficulty. It gave me my first experience of considerable slopes of hard steep snow, and, like all beginners, I endeavoured to prop myself up with my stick, and kept it outside, instead of holding it between myself and the slope, and leaning upon it, as should have been done. The man enlightened me; but he, had, properly, a very small opinion of his employer, and it is probably on that account that, a few minutes after we had passed the summit, he said he would not go any further and would return to Biona … Being rather nervous about descending some long snow-slopes, which still intervened between us and the head of the valley, I offered more pay, and he went on a little way. Presently there were some cliffs down which we had to scramble. He called to me to stop, then shouted that he would go back, and beckoned to me to come up. On the contrary, I waited for him to come down; but instead of doing so, in a second or two he turned round, clambered deliberately up the cliff, and vanished … This was rather embarrassing, for he carried off my knapsack. The choice of action lay between chasing him and going on to Breil [**now Breuil-Cervinia**], risking the loss of my knapsack. I chose the latter course, and got to Breil the same evening. The landlord of the inn, suspicious of a person entirely innocent of luggage, was doubtful if he could admit me, and eventually thrust me into a kind of loft, which was already occupied by guides and by hay.

My sketches from Breil were made under difficulties, for my materials had been carried off. Nothing better than fine sugar-paper could be obtained … However, they *were* made, and the pass was again crossed, this time alone. By the following evening the old woman of Biona again produced the faithless guide. The knapsack was recovered after the lapse of several hours, and then I poured forth all the terms of abuse and reproach of which I was master. The man smiled when called a liar, and shrugged his shoulders when referred to as a thief, but drew his knife when spoken of as a pig.

Clocking up hundreds of miles, Whymper journeyed to Chamonix, France, up to Geneva, Switzerland, back down to Turin, Italy, and back in to France to climb a peak in the Cottian Alps. Despite unpleasant weather, he made the summit and enjoyed a magnificent cloud inversion; a spectacle that truly makes one feel on top of the world.

… after a battle with a snow-slope of excessive steepness, I reached the summit. The scene was extraordinary, and, in my experience, unique. To the north there was not a particle of mist, and the violent wind coming from that direction blew one back staggering. But on the side of Italy, the valleys were completely filled with dense masses of cloud to a certain level; and there — where they felt the influence of the wind — they were cut off as level as the top of a table, the ridges appearing above them.

At last, making his way north-west through France, Whymper arrived at Mont Pelvoux, the mountain which he had been commissioned to illustrate. It would appear that he arrived too late, although the time was not completely wasted, as he met two amenable Frenchmen with whom he would climb numerous peaks.

… by chance I walked into a cabaret where a Frenchman was breakfasting, who, a few days before, had made an unsuccessful attempt to ascend that mountain with three Englishmen and the guide Michel Croz of Chamounix; a right good fellow, by name Jean Reynaud.

The 1860 tour of the Alps was concluded with yet more eventful and testing days; all par for the course for a nineteenth-century walking traveller.

I slept at Briançon, intending to take the courier on the following day to Grenoble; but all places had been secured several days beforehand, so I set out at two P.M. on the next day for a seventy-mile walk. The weather was again bad; and on the summit of the Col de Lautaret I was forced to seek shelter in the wretched little hospice. It was filled with workmen who were employed on the road, and with noxious vapours which proceeded from them. The inclemency of the weather was preferable to the inhospitality of the interior. Outside, it was disagreeable, but grand; inside, it was disagreeable and mean. The walk was continued under a deluge of rain, and I felt the way down — so intense was the darkness — to the village of La Grave, where the people of the inn detained me forcibly. It was perhaps fortunate that they did so; for, during that night, blocks of rock fell at several places from the cliffs on to the road with such force that they made large pits in the macadam. I resumed the walk at half-past five the next morning, and proceeded, under steady rain, through Bourg d'Oysans to Grenoble, arriving at the latter place soon after seven P.M., having accomplished the entire distance from Briançon in about eighteen hours of actual walking.

This was the end of the Alpine portion of my tour of 1860, on which I was introduced to the great peaks, and acquired the passion for mountain-scrambling …

(Ibid., pp. 1–13)

PREPARATIONS AND TRAINING

AUTHOR'S LOG

Climbing the Matterhorn requires a combination of skills and abilities. No one should be on the mountain if they are not comfortable on exposed ridges, in climbing with ropes and ice axes, or in walking and climbing on crampons. The mountain is very steep and icy in places, while the summit ridge is narrow, with immense precipices on both sides. With a European climbing grade of AD III, it is far from the most technical of routes; rather, it is the ever present danger of the crumbling rock and difficulty in navigation that present the greatest challenges. Additionally, in order to reach the summit and to be back off the mountain before mid-afternoon when rock fall becomes an increased risk, a high level of fitness and stamina is vital.

Both Mat and I felt that climbing the Matterhorn was comfortably within our abilities, but were keen to get in as much preparation as possible; in particular, to be as fit as we could reasonably expect to be. Our training consisted of two main activities, the first of which was to undertake long hikes and to climb as frequently as we could in the Scottish Mountains, particularly along ridges and in winter conditions. That said, Scotland is well known for its inclement weather and many planned trips were cancelled as a result of severe wind or heavy rain. Nevertheless, enjoying some flexibility in our work schedules, we were able to clock up a good number of ridge climbs, including in the Cuillin hills on Skye, on the north face of Ben Nevis and in our much loved Glencoe, which is a relatively convenient 1½ hours from home.

Even with the relative flexibility of our free days and the close proximity of Glencoe, we needed an alternative, more convenient form of regular exercise. The solution was to buy a couple of road bikes at the beginning of 2014. With rugged Stirlingshire and rolling Perthshire on our doorstep, we clocked up thousands of scenic miles during the intervening period, eventually, feeling as ready as we could have hopped to be by the time of our trip.

While the most popular route to climb the Matterhorn is via the Hörnli Ridge from Zermatt — which is the route Edward Whymper took on his eighth attempt — we decided to traverse the summit by going up the Liongrat Ridge on the Italian side, which is the route Whymper attempted on all but one of his earlier attempts, and to then descend the Hörnli Ridge. In doing so, we could better experience the challenges, as well as the highs and lows that he and his fellow climbers faced 150 years before. It also offered a less busy ascent route and, particularly for me, a better evening location for taking pictures from the Carrel mountain hut.

An ascent via the Lion Ridge involves two long days, starting with an initial six hour hike to the Carrel hut at 3,836m (12,585 ft). Then with a pre-dawn start, another four hours of climbing is required to reach the 4,478m (14,692 ft) summit. The summit is only halfway, of course, so another six hours of focused down climbing to the Hörnli hut must be undertaken before being able to relax. Not for too long though, as the return journey still includes two gondola rides back up to the Klein Matterhorn station, followed by a hike across the Rosa Plateau and a further two cable cars down to Breuil-Cervinia. If the cable cars are closed then it's an additional 1500m decent on foot!

Although, climbing the Matterhorn was within our ability, we opted to take guides on the Matterhorn; primarily, to ensure that we kept to the safest route and made good time. Our research had shown overwhelmingly that the vast majority of incidents had resulted from people losing their way while climbing unguided.

Whymper made the first ascent of numerous Alpine peaks and commented frequently on the particularly fine views from many of them. Some of the mountains he climbed were chosen specifically for their views of the surrounding landscape, and in particular, of the Matterhorn. Therefore, in addition to climbing the Matterhorn, we had a list of other mountains to climb, with the aim of photographing some of the scenes by which Whymper was so captivated.

WINTER 2015

AUTHOR'S LOG

The Matterhorn is a stunning mountain, arguably the finest mountain on our planet, and my first sighting of it from Zermatt on 13th January, did not disappoint. In fact, it far exceeded my expectation, simply for its overwhelming dominance. Despite having previously reviewed hundreds of photographs to determine its form; when I viewed it with my own eyes, I was taken back with its magnificence which all but defied words.

My goal during those two weeks in January was to capture the sense of scale and awe of the mountain; something that is quite simply impossible to do in one photograph. From Zermatt, one gets an uninterrupted view to the Matterhorn's summit, towering almost 3,000m (9,500 ft) above the village, giving some sense of scale. However, cameras tend to distort the perspective, foreshortening the mountain, and presenting it squatter than it appears to be with the naked eye. Thus, it is hoped that a series of images will serve better.

The following selection of photographs were all taken during the January trip, and together present the most dramatic aspects of the Matterhorn, including the north-east ridge viewed from Zermatt, the full eastern face and around to the south-east ridge seen from the Klein Matterhorn gondola station. The image on page 25 shows the Hörnli Ridge with the Solvay and Hörnli Huts highlighted to give a better sense of scale. The Hörnli Hut has just been renovated and downsized from 170 beds to sleep 130 people in great comfort. The images on pages 26 and 56 show the Matterhorn's position as it dominates the bustling modern town, while many of the other photographs highlight its solitary position.

Keen to capture an image of the alpenglow (pre-sunrise) and the first light catching the peak, I chose what promised to be a clear morning to make an early start up above the town. The tracks through the forest were closed due to icy conditions, which hampered my initial plan somewhat, but fortunately I learnt that there was an early departure of the Gornergrat cog train, which could whisk me up to the viewpoint I had in mind before sunrise. I was the only one to get off at the Rotenboden Station and as the inky-blue sky lightened, I hurriedly scoped out a vantage point from which to set up the camera. The result was a pleasing success and a wonderful selection of images were captured as the sun's rising was signalled on the face of the Matterhorn like a giant sun clock. Shortly after the sun was fully in the sky I became aware that my 'trigger' finger had become totally numb, having been in and out of my glove a few too many times, in something below -15 degrees Celsius. Not being the first time this had happened, although probably the most severe incident, I reverted to the trick of sucking my finger, where it gradually regained feeling. It was a timely reminder of how quickly the cold can become disabling, and I took the warning as time to move on and find a new location that benefitted from some warmth from the sun.

My plan for the last good day was to stay overnight at a high mountain hut, in order to catch the first light once again. Unfortunately, the warden could not open up for me so I reverted to taking the earliest gondola up to the Klein Matterhorn station at 3,888m (12,756 ft). This meant I would not be on location as the sun rose, but it did allow me to stop off at the various stations along the way. While it was largely a fine clear day, clouds were stubbornly fixed around the highest station, making my ultimate objective look doubtful. After waiting for over an hour at the Trockener Steg station so that I could see what was happening with the weather, I anxiously squeezed into one of the large gondola cars, just as the clouds appeared to be thinning above.

The final station was still heavily shrouded in cloud when I arrived, but after watching, waiting and standing around in the icy cold conditions for twenty minutes at a time, I eventually caught a ten-minute clearing to capture the south-east of the Matterhorn protruding above the low shifting cloud. Mission accomplished, the cloud returned as quickly as it had cleared, swallowing up the mountain once again and ushering in the end of my trip.

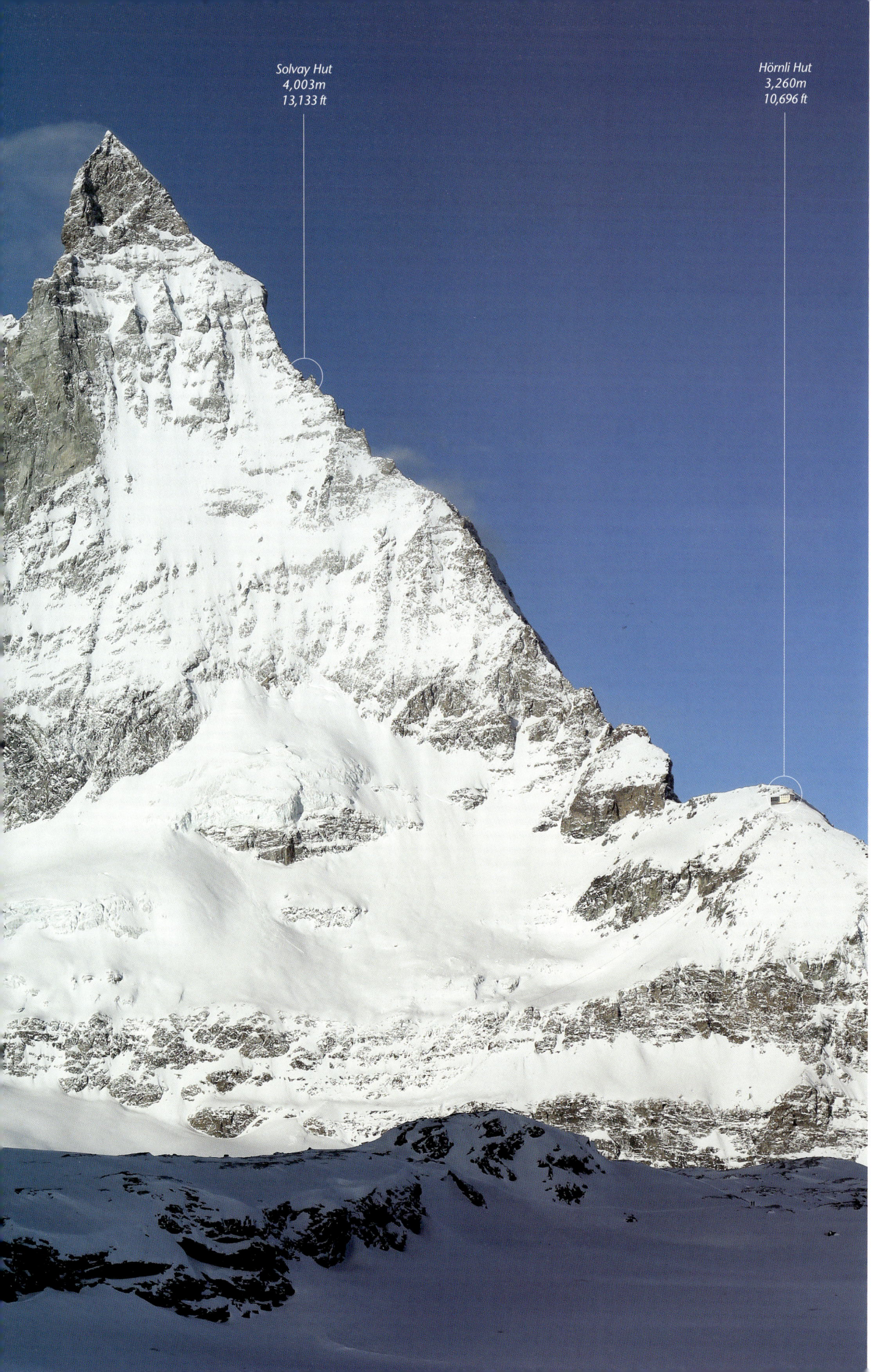

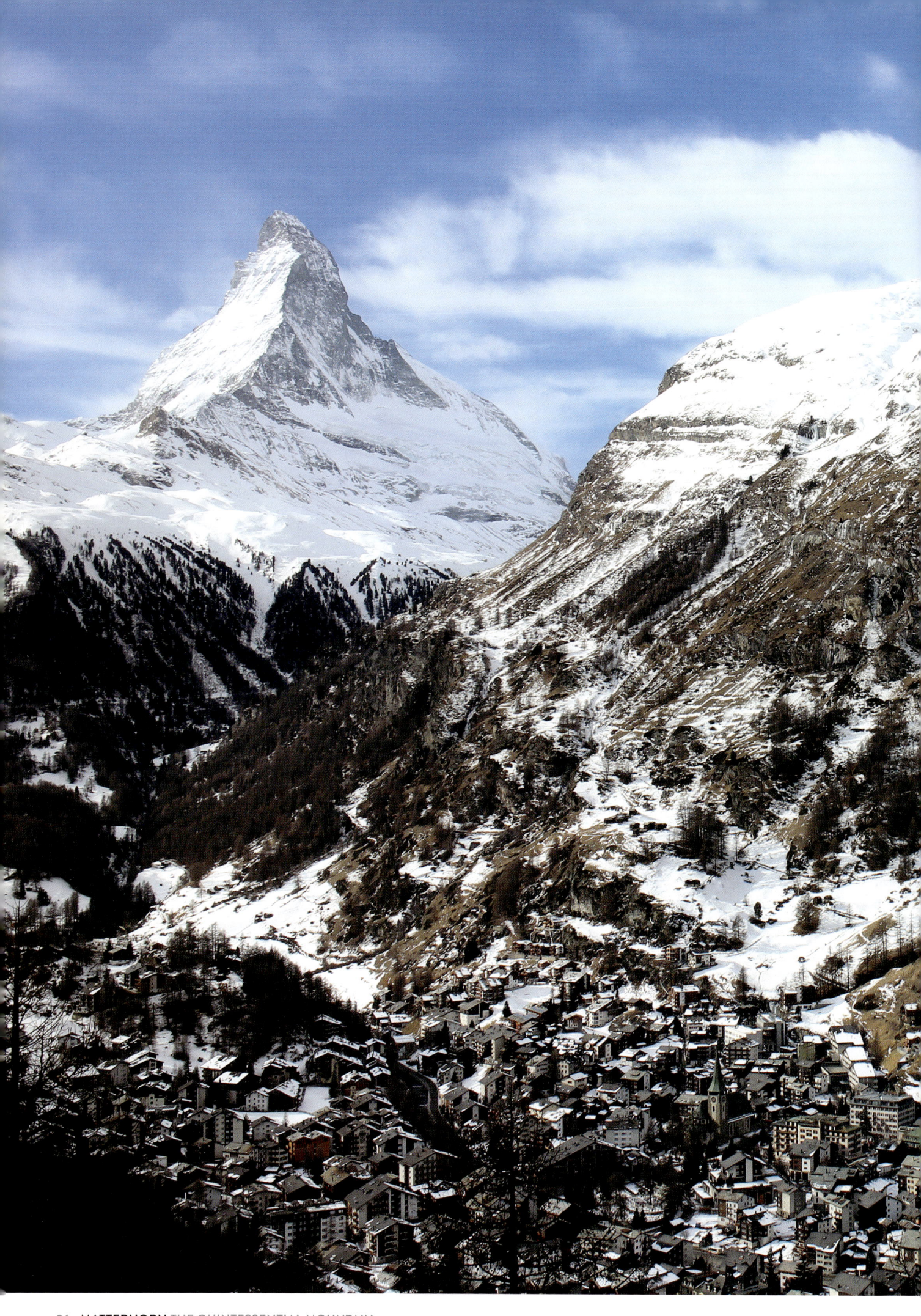

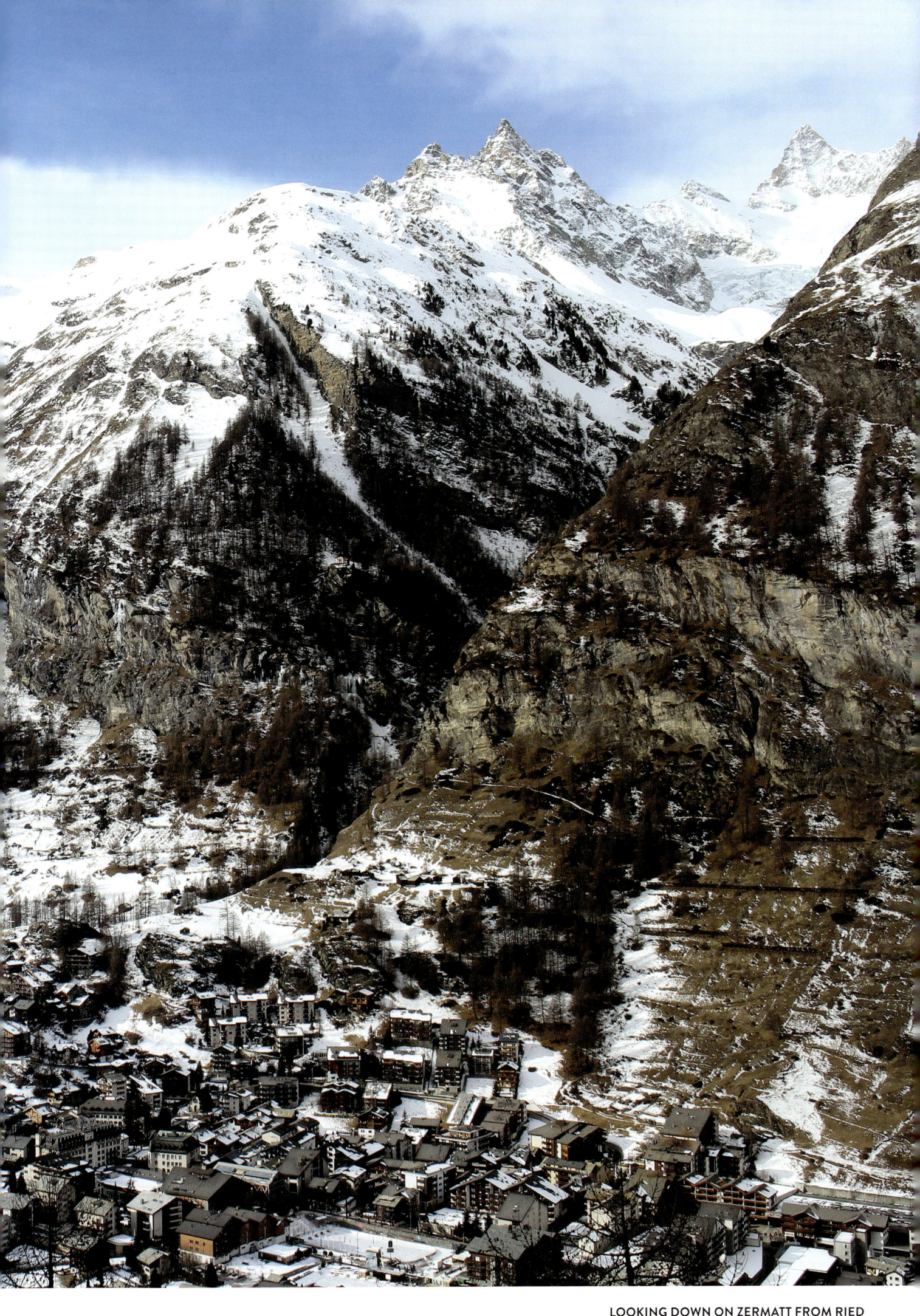

LOOKING DOWN ON ZERMATT FROM RIED

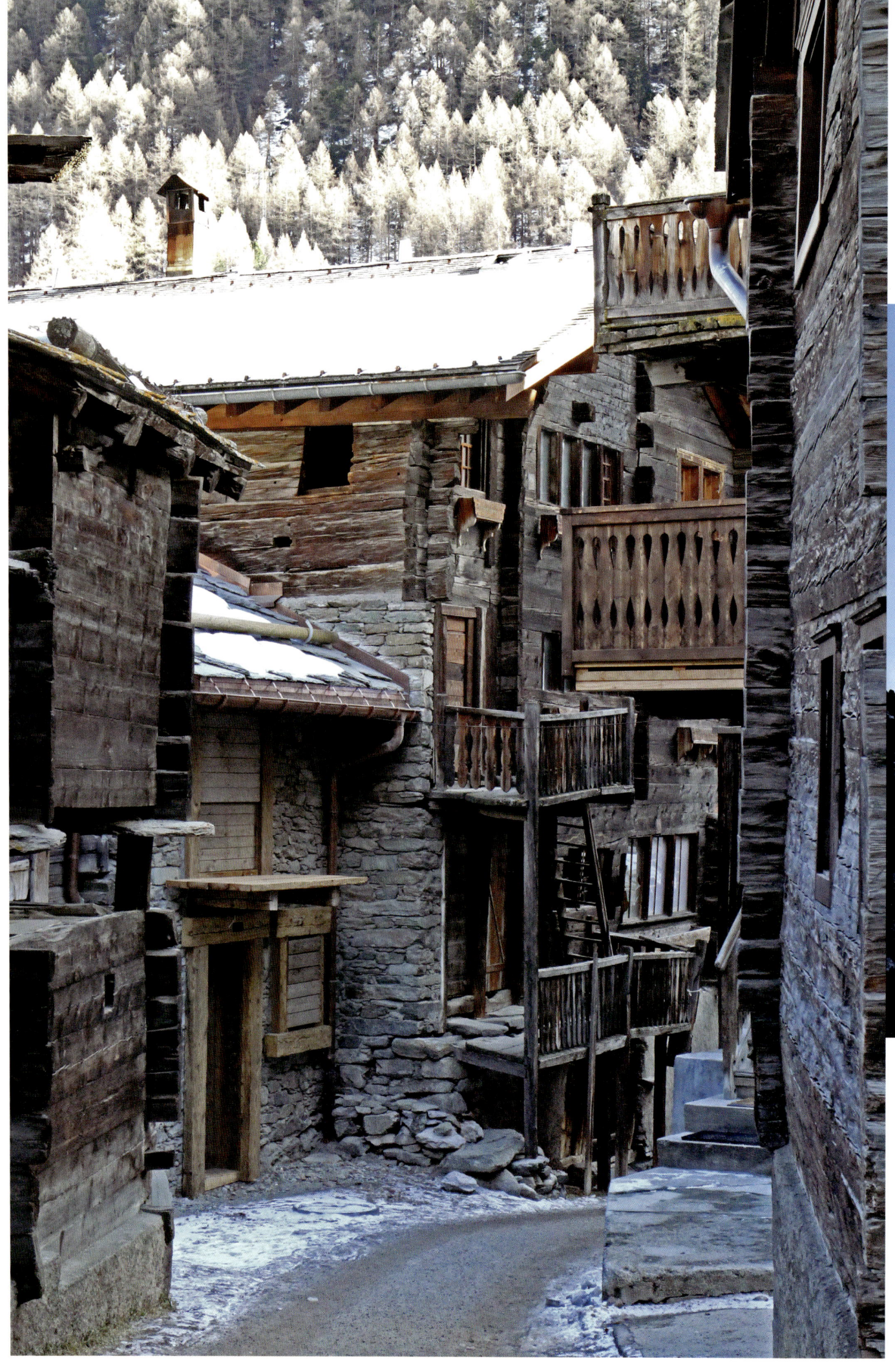

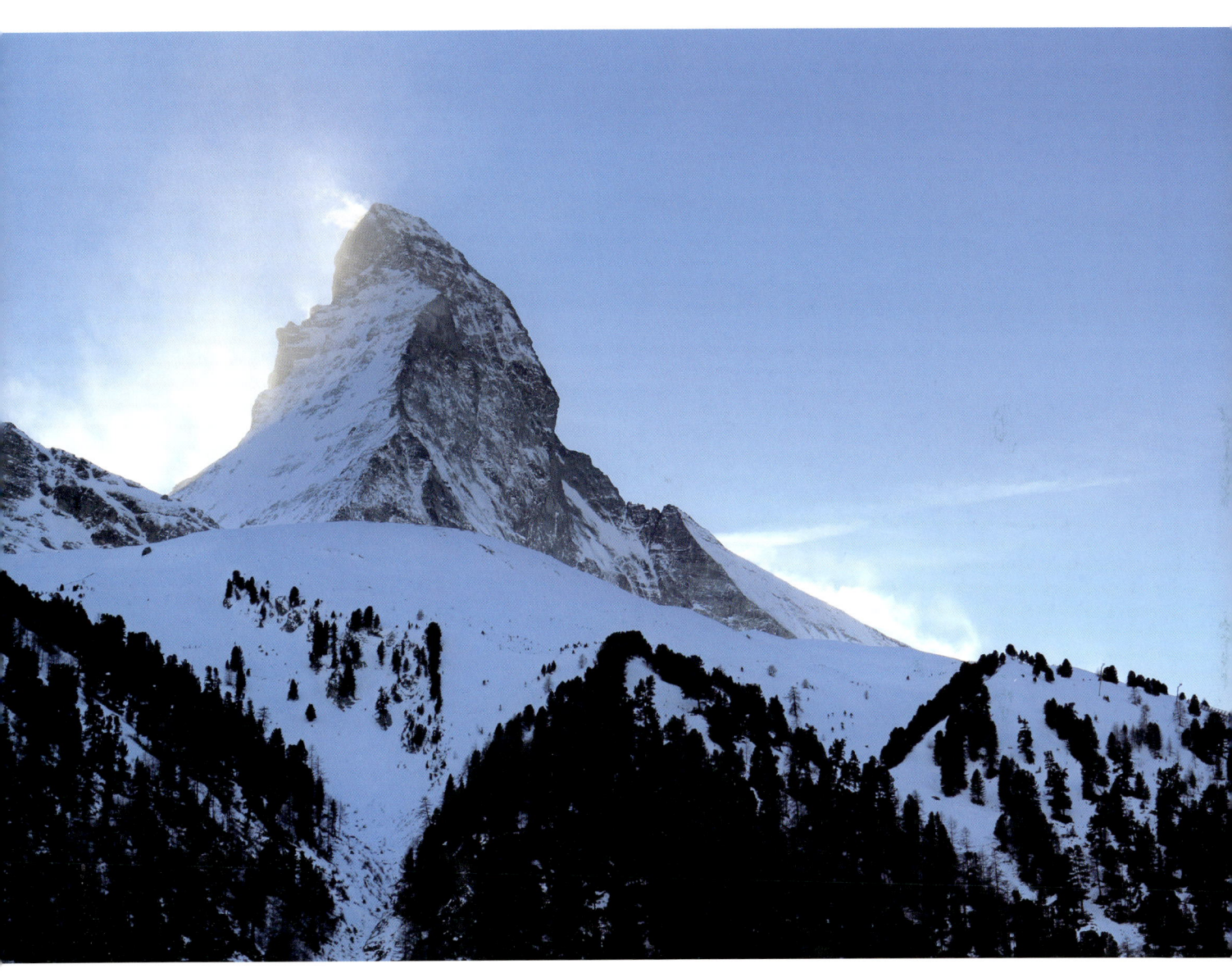

THE MATTERHORN FROM ZMUTT AS THE SUN BEGINS TO SET BEHIND IT

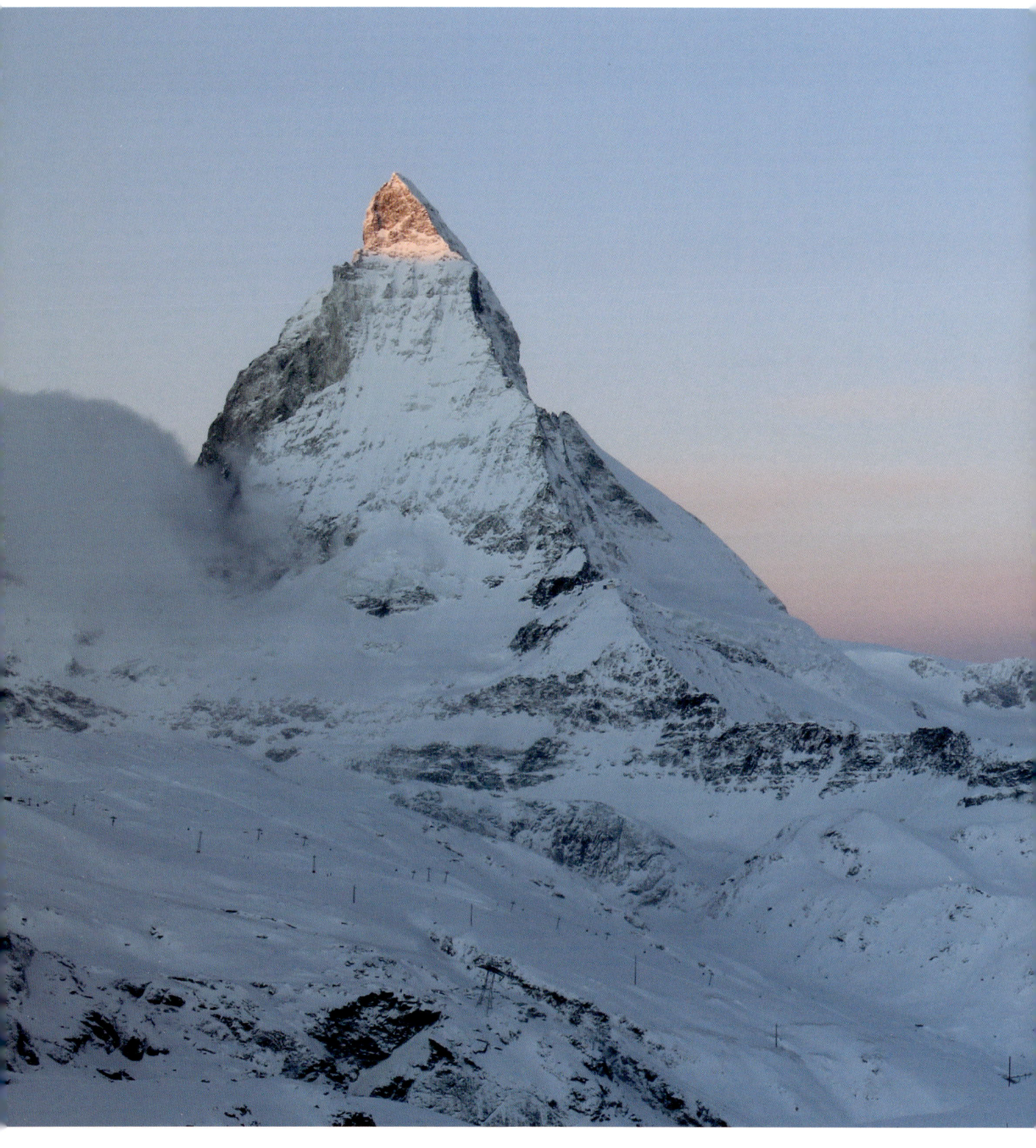

ALPENGLOW ON THE MATTERHORN

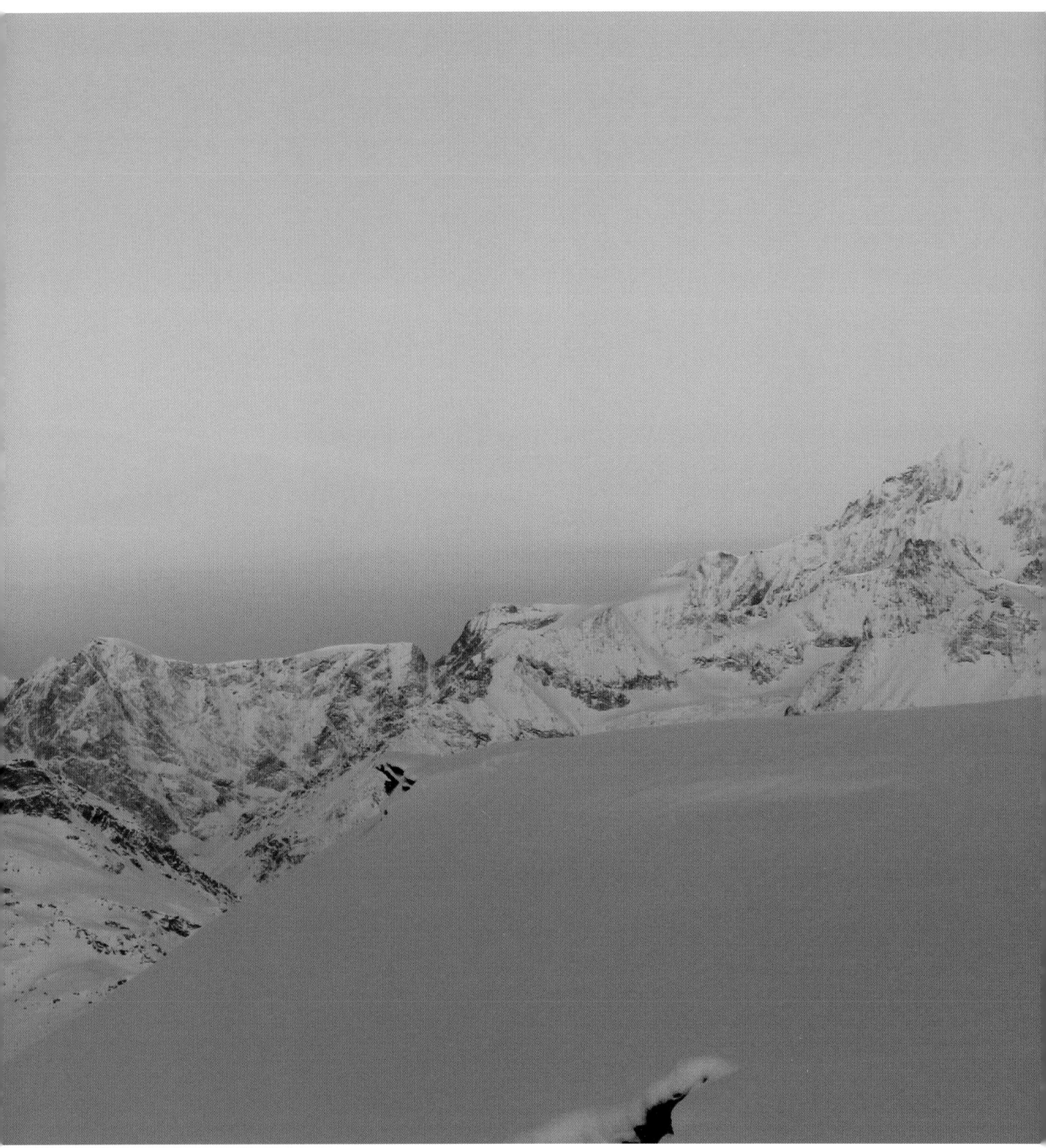

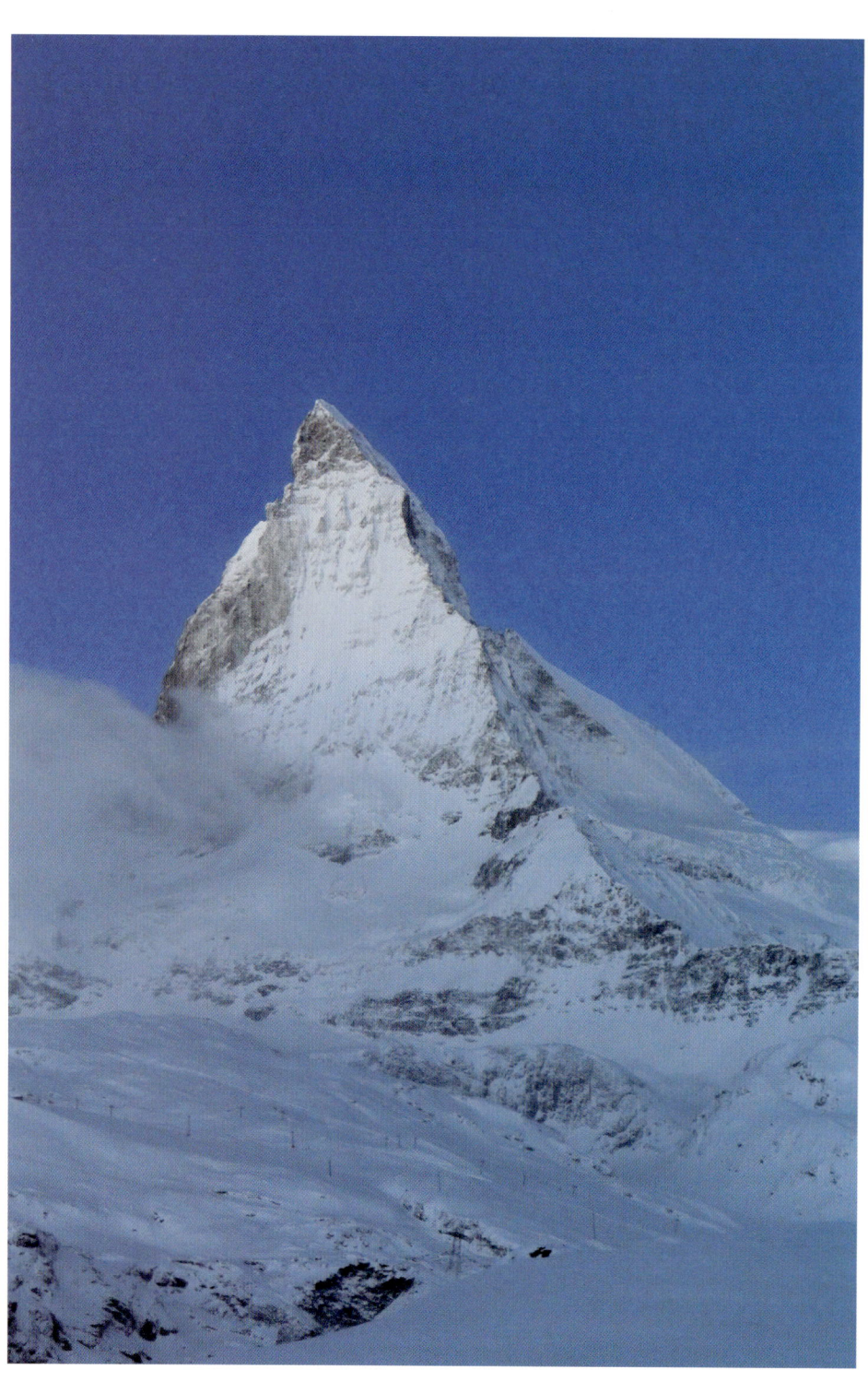

(Above) **THE MATTERHORN BEFORE DAWN**

(Opposite) **THE RISING SUN CASTS A WARMING GLOW UPON THE EAST FACE OF THE MATTERHORN**

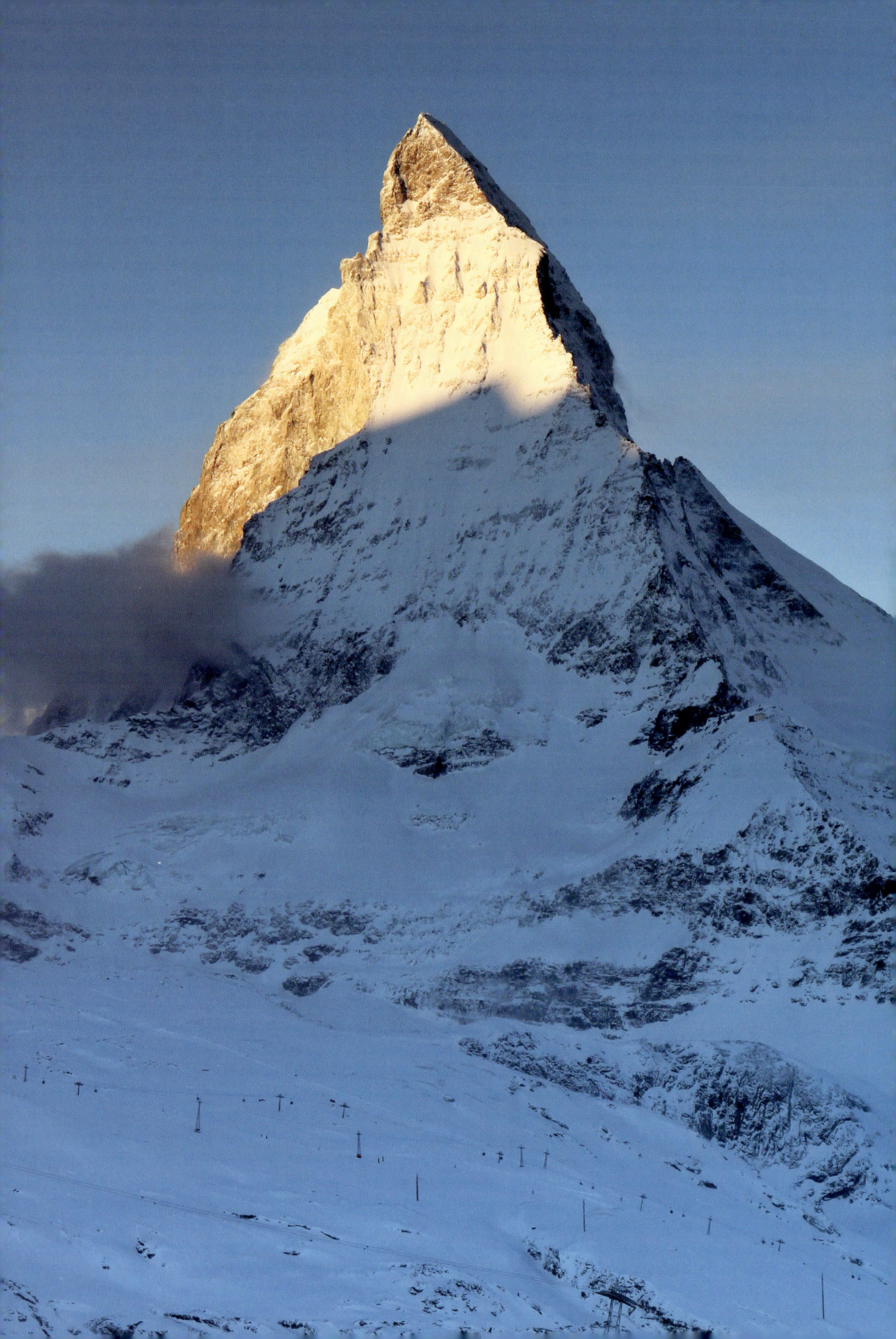

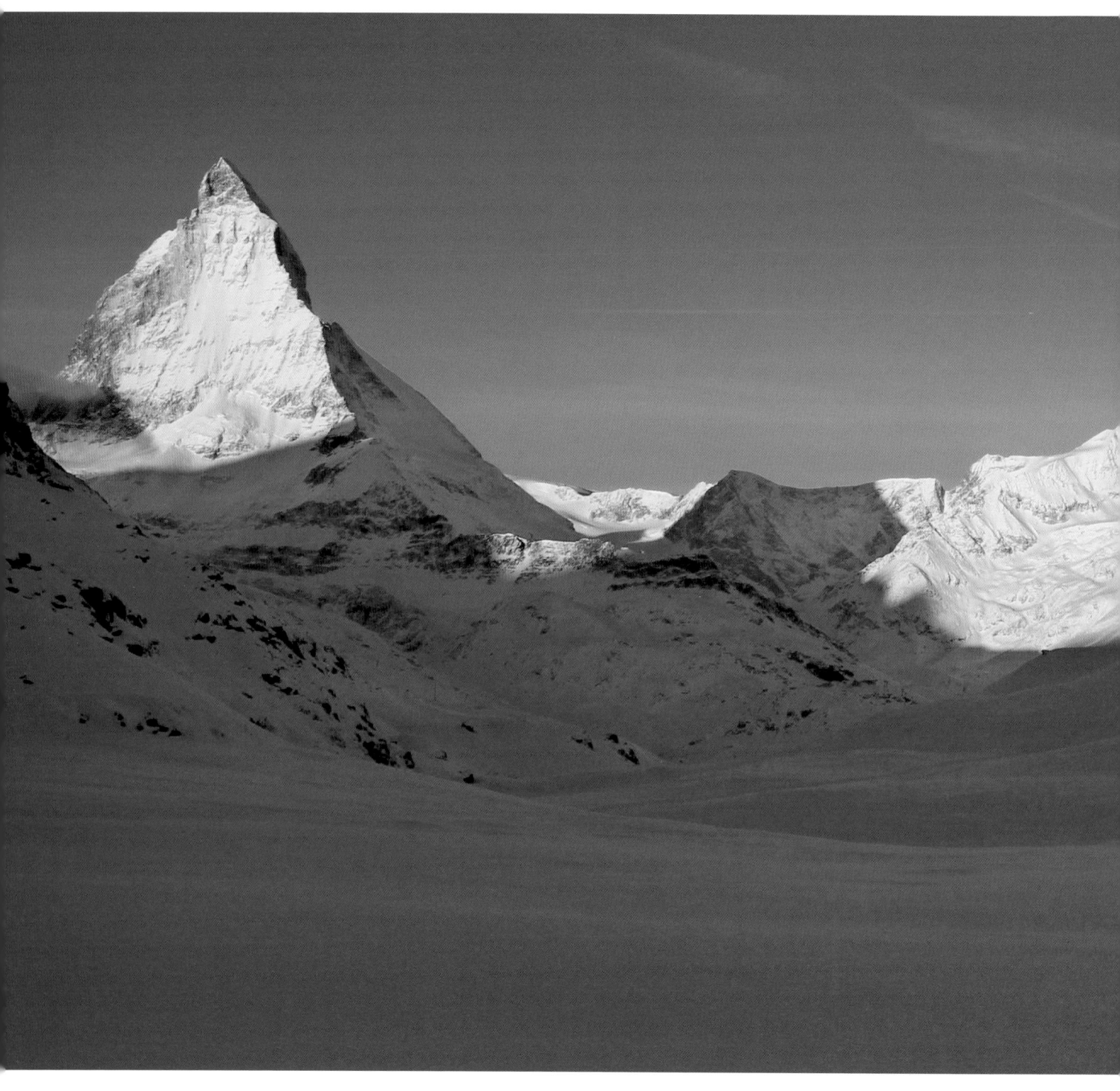
THE MATTERHORN AND WESTERNLY PEAKS FROM ROTENBODEN

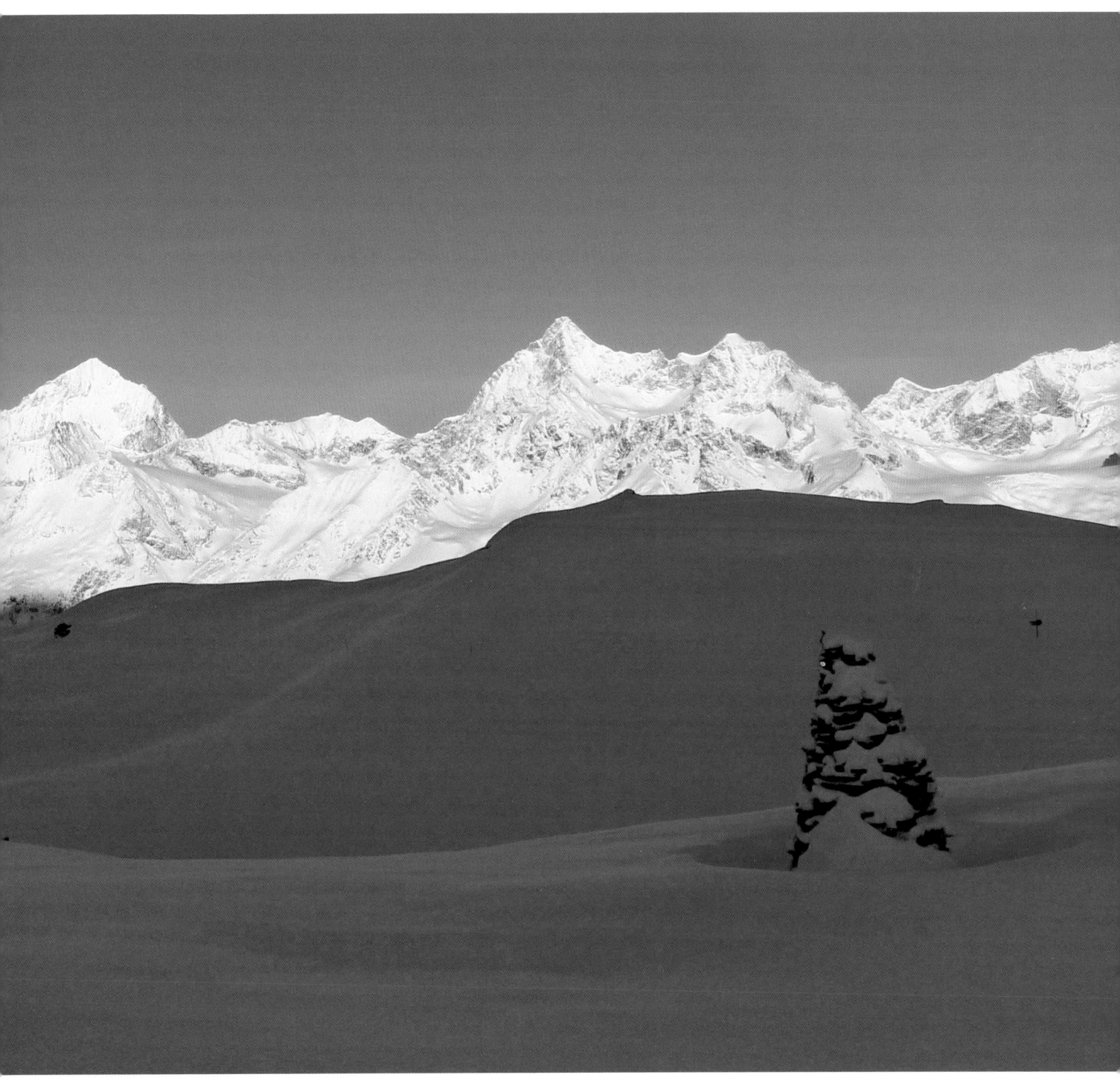

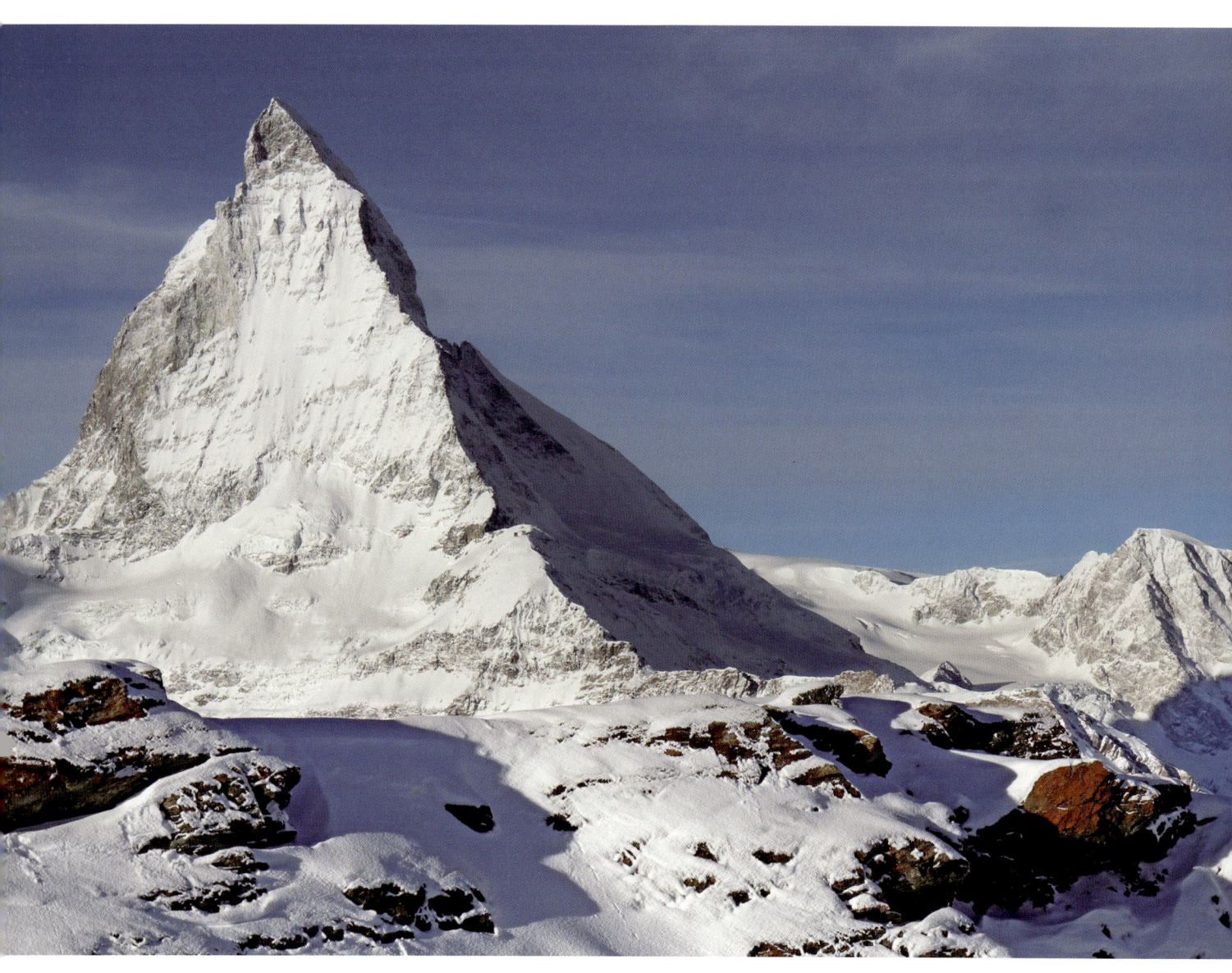

THE SHARP HÖRNLI (NORTH-EAST) RIDGE OF THE MATTERHORN

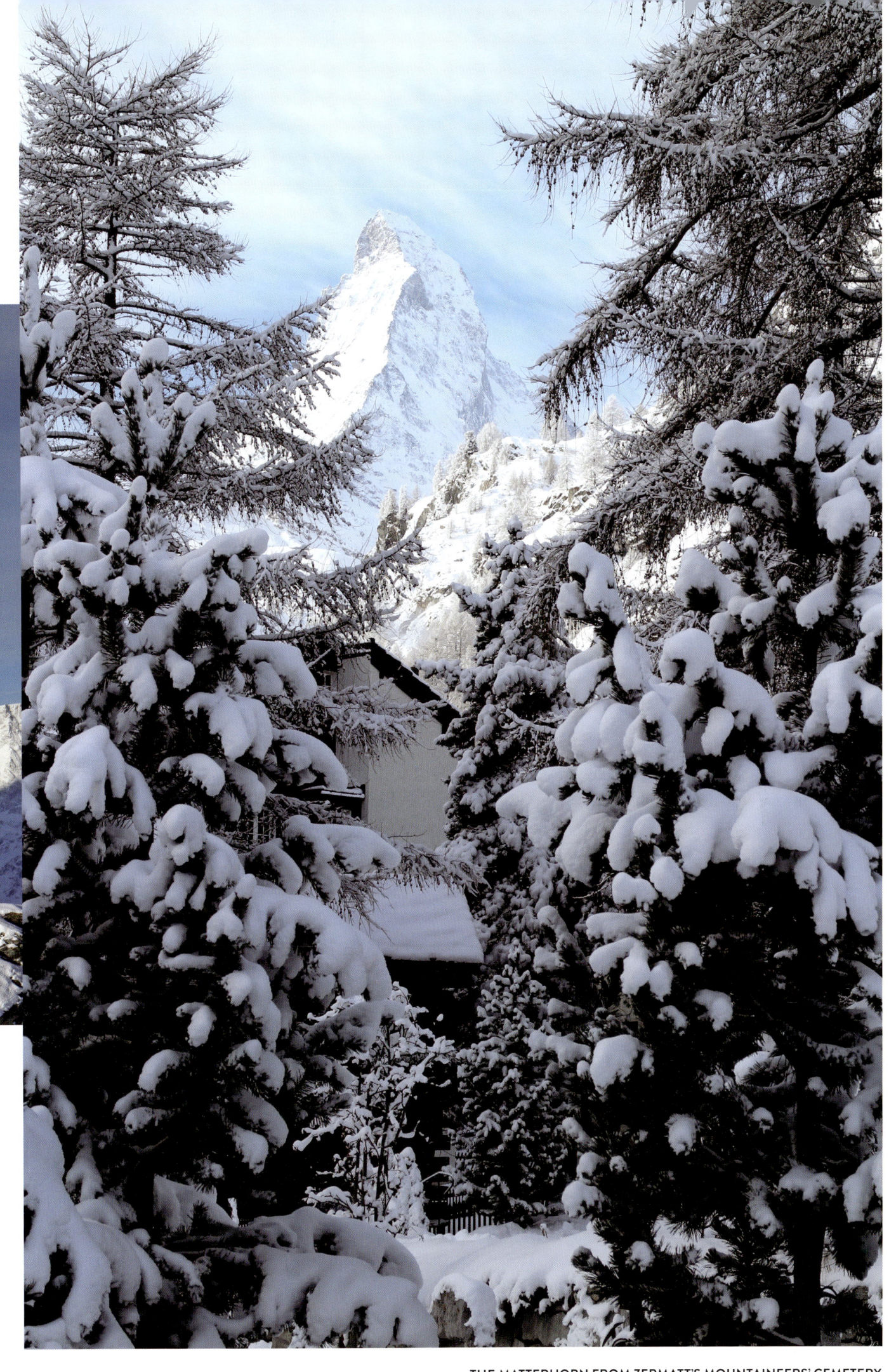

THE MATTERHORN FROM ZERMATT'S MOUNTAINEERS' CEMETERY

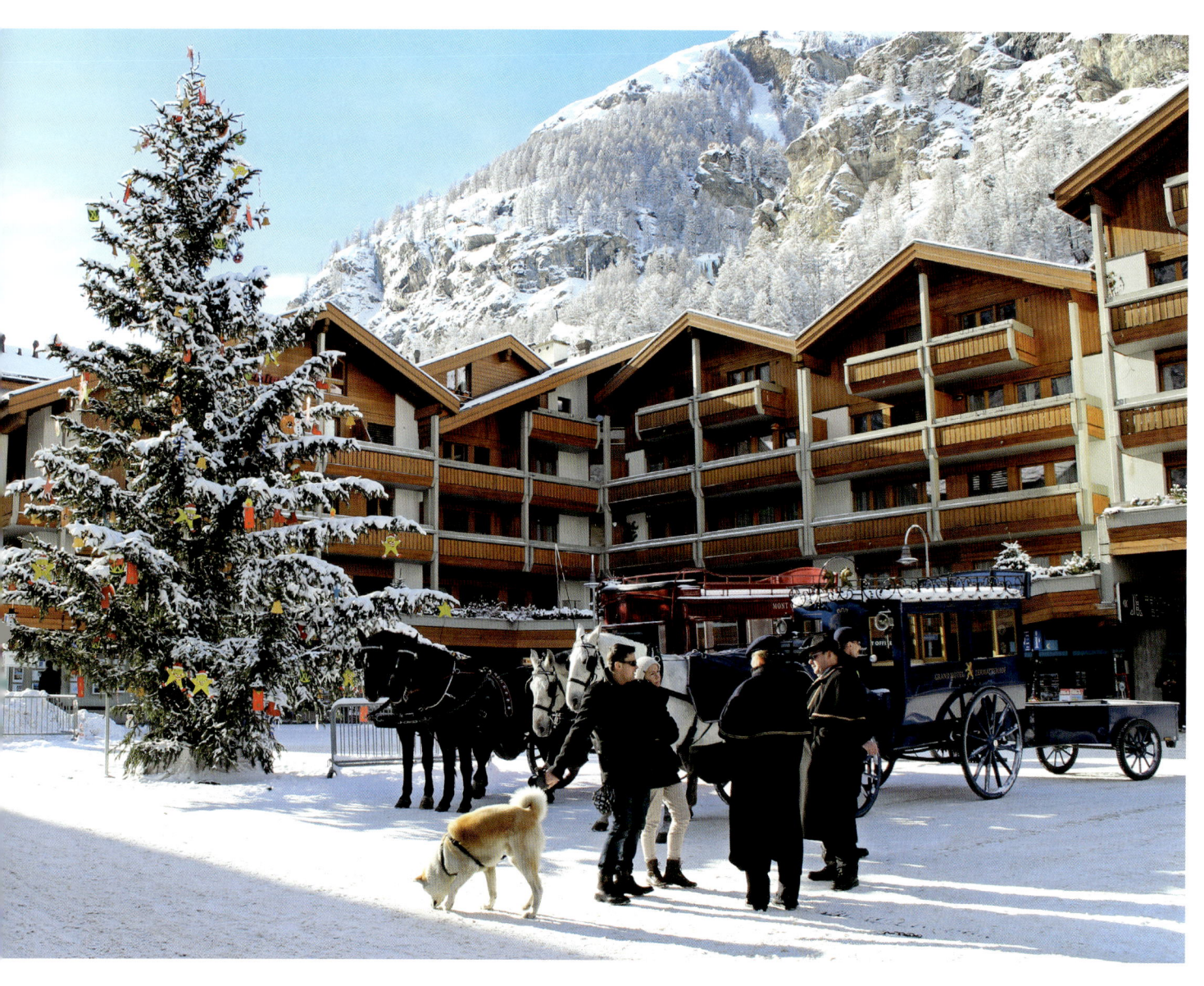

(Above) **THE STATION SQUARE IN ZERMATT**

(Opposite) **A HORSE-DRAWN CARRIAGE TRANSFERS GUESTS TO AND FROM THE MONT CERVIN PALACE HOTEL. (MONT CERVIN IS FRENCH FOR MATTERHORN)**

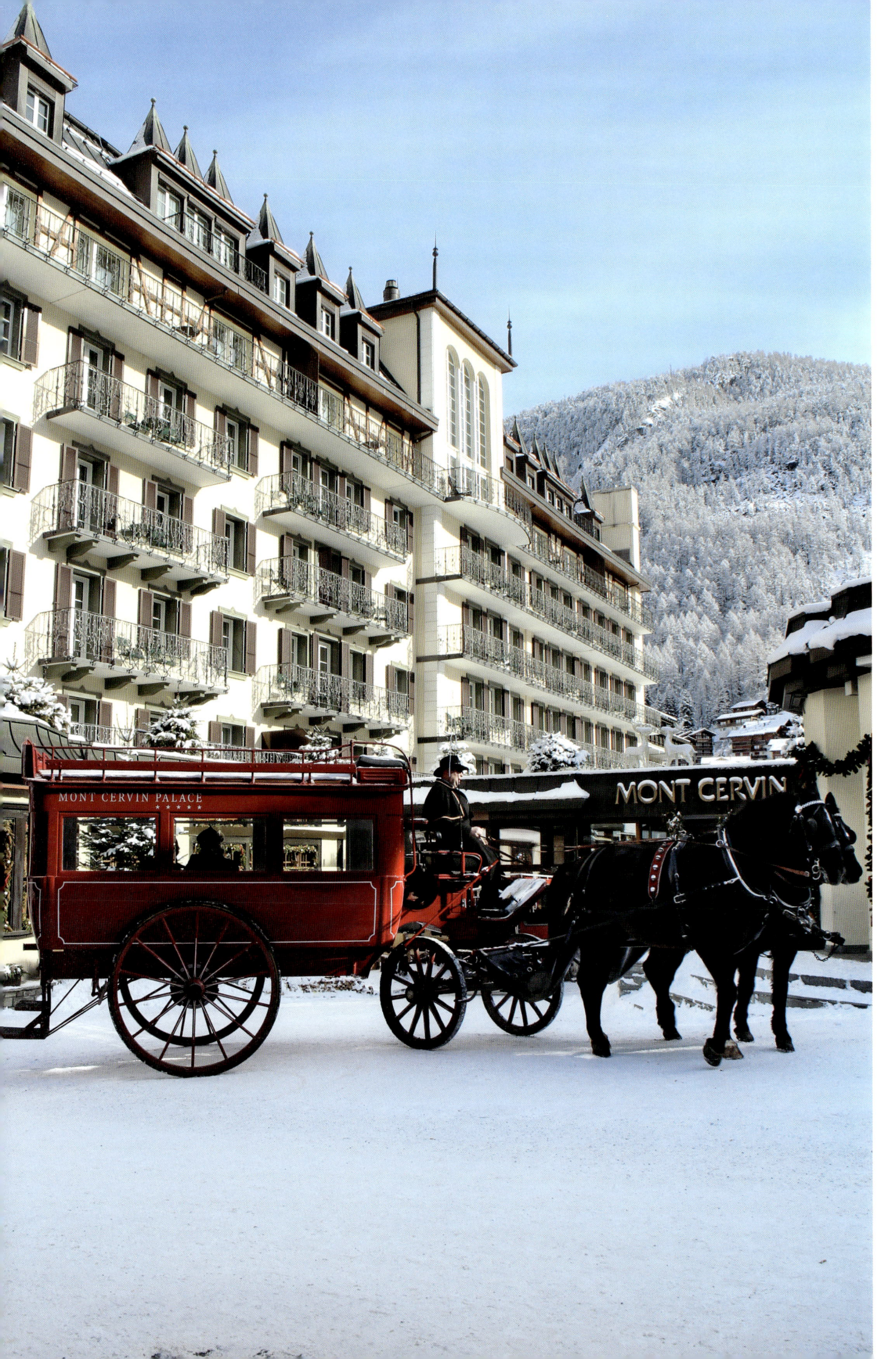

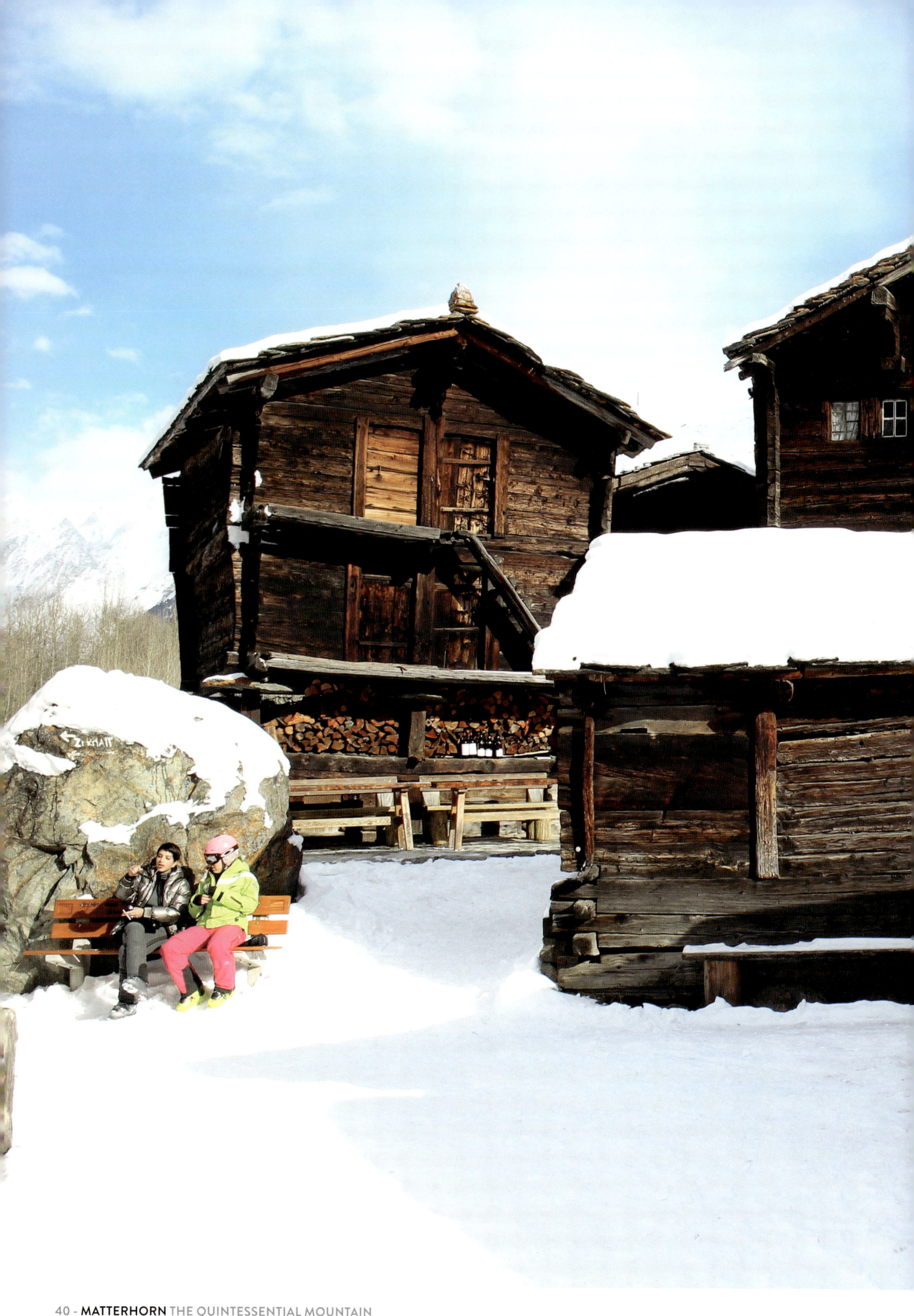

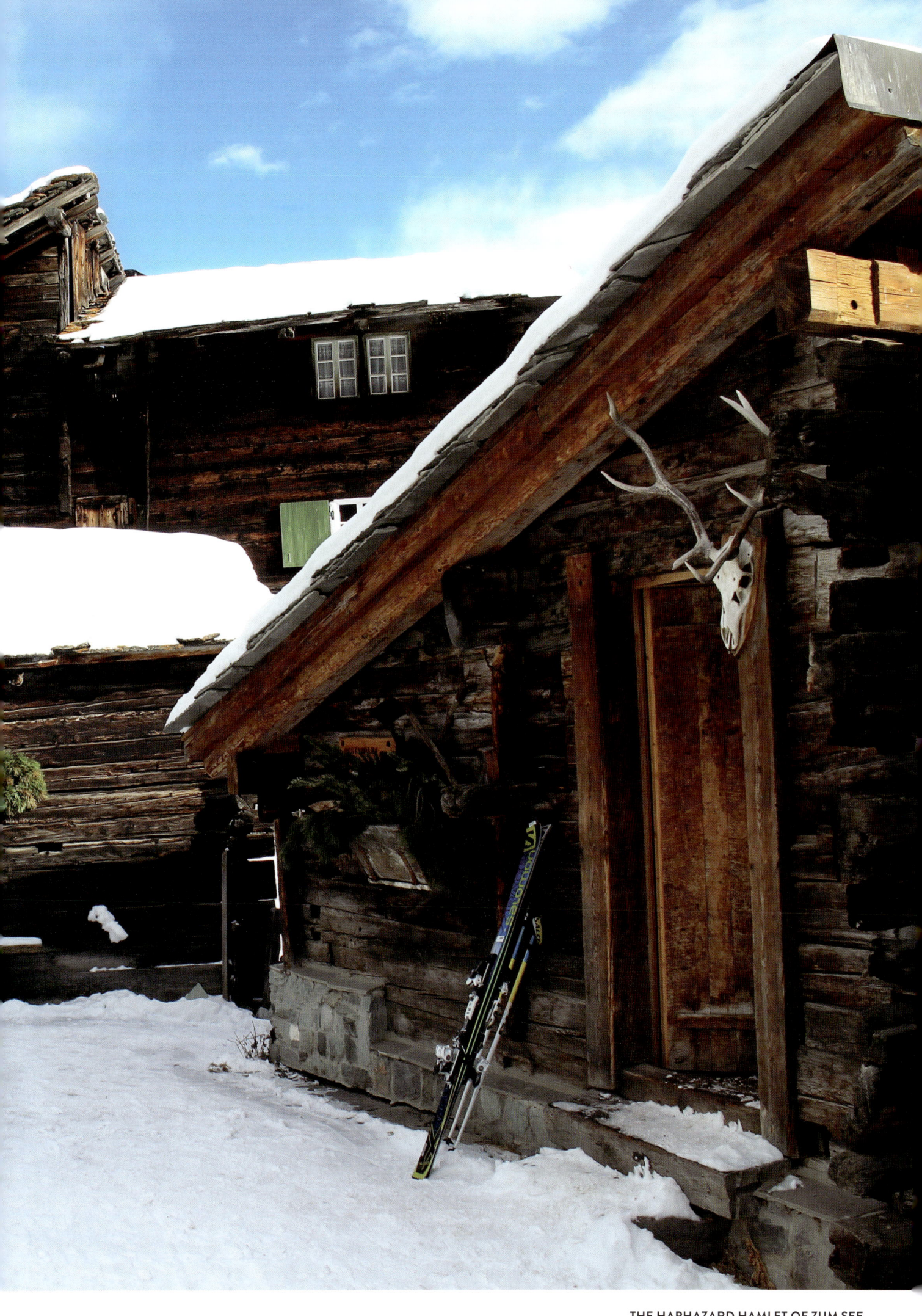

THE HAPHAZARD HAMLET OF ZUM SEE

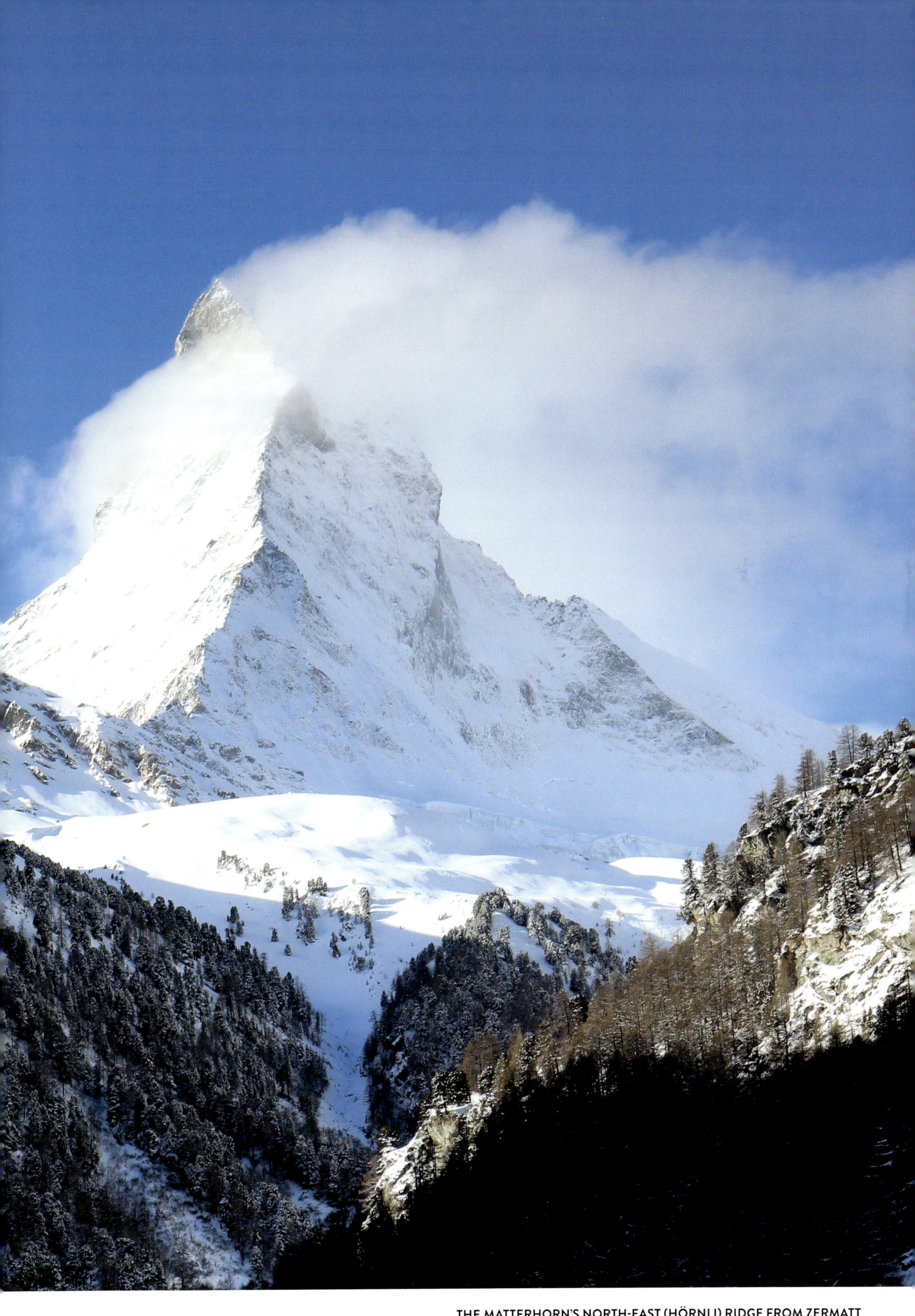
THE MATTERHORN'S NORTH-EAST (HÖRNLI) RIDGE FROM ZERMATT

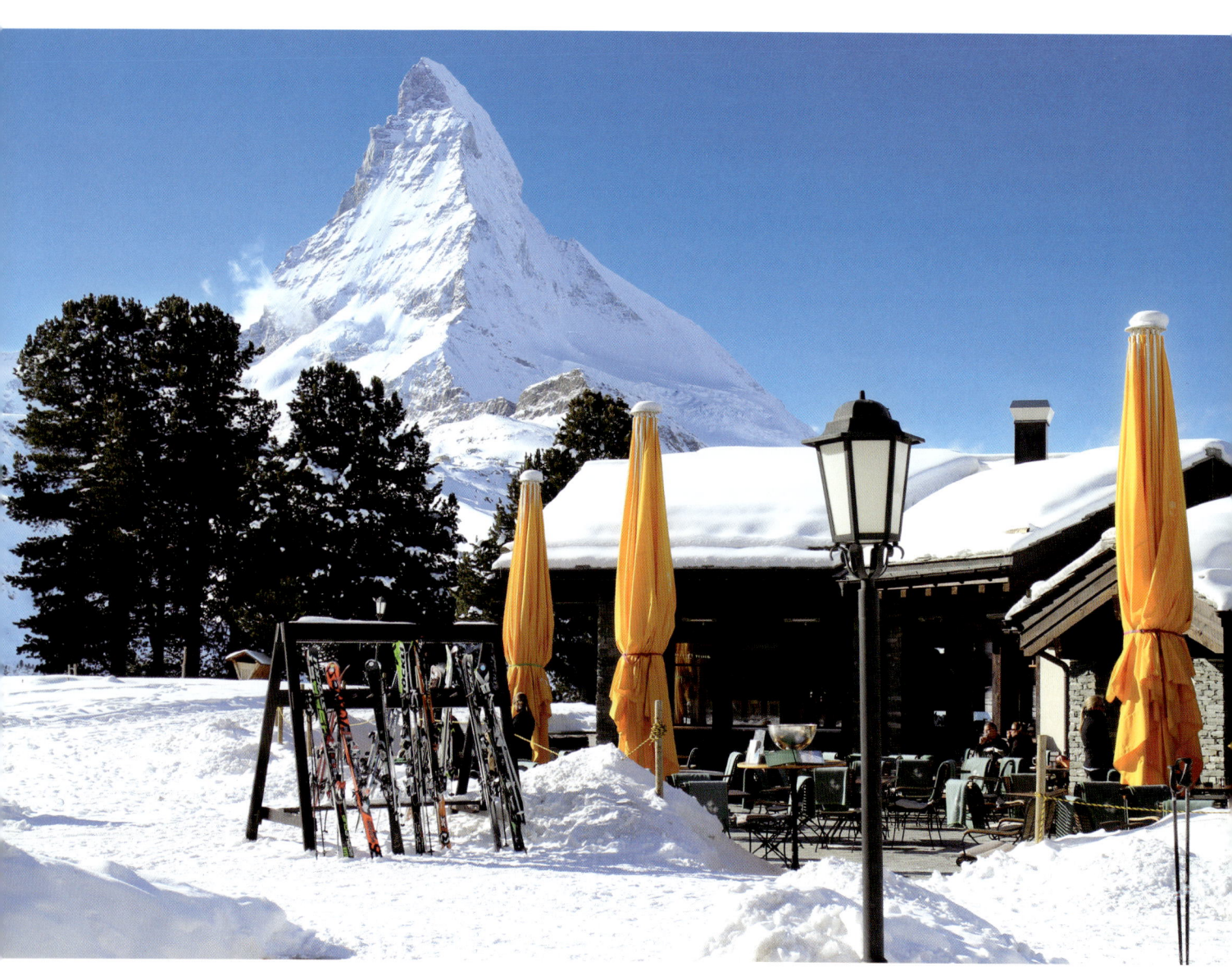

FROM THE HOTEL RIFFELALP (2,222M), ABOVE ZERMATT

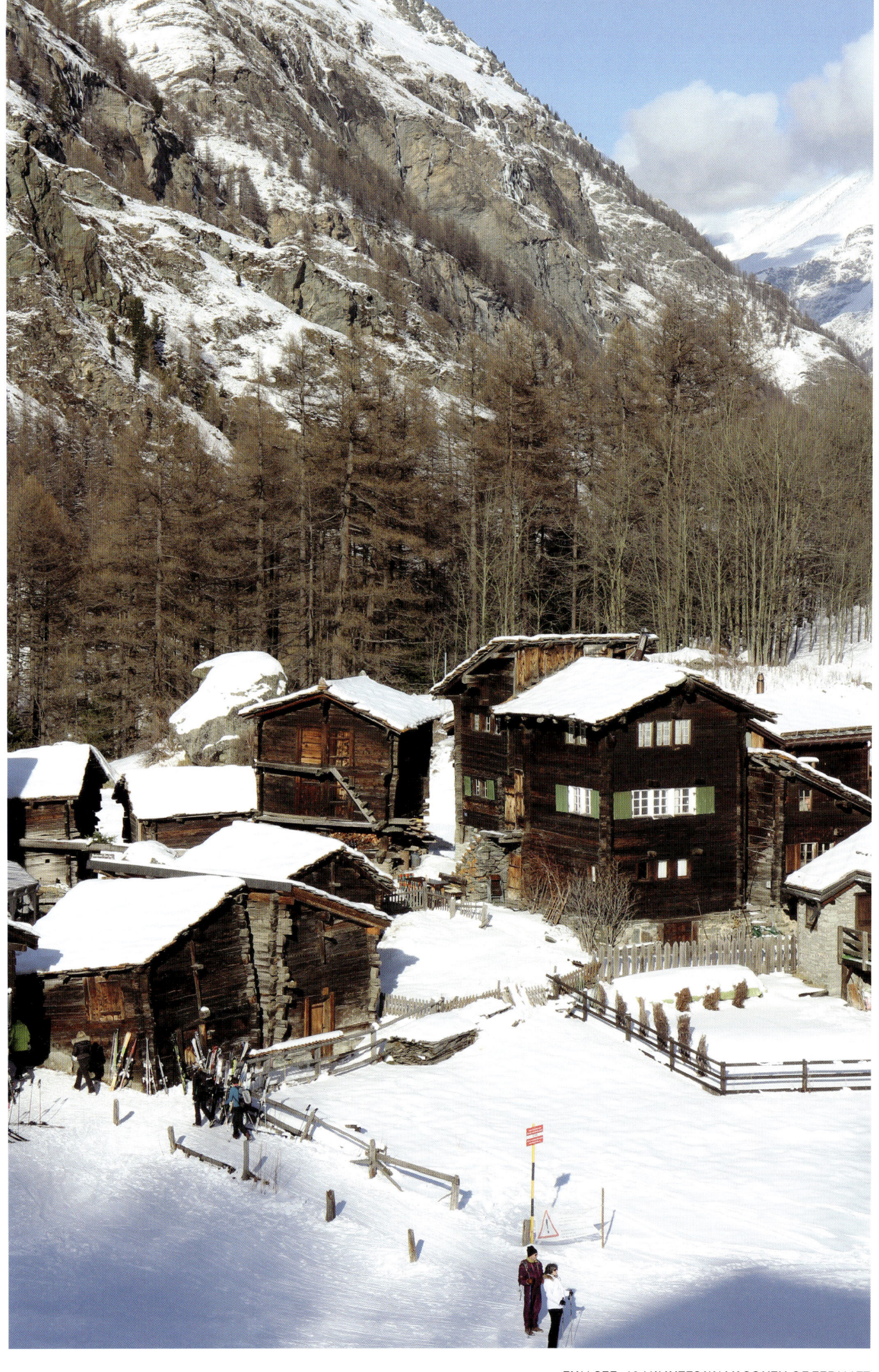

ZUM SEE, 40 MINUTES WALK SOUTH OF ZERMATT

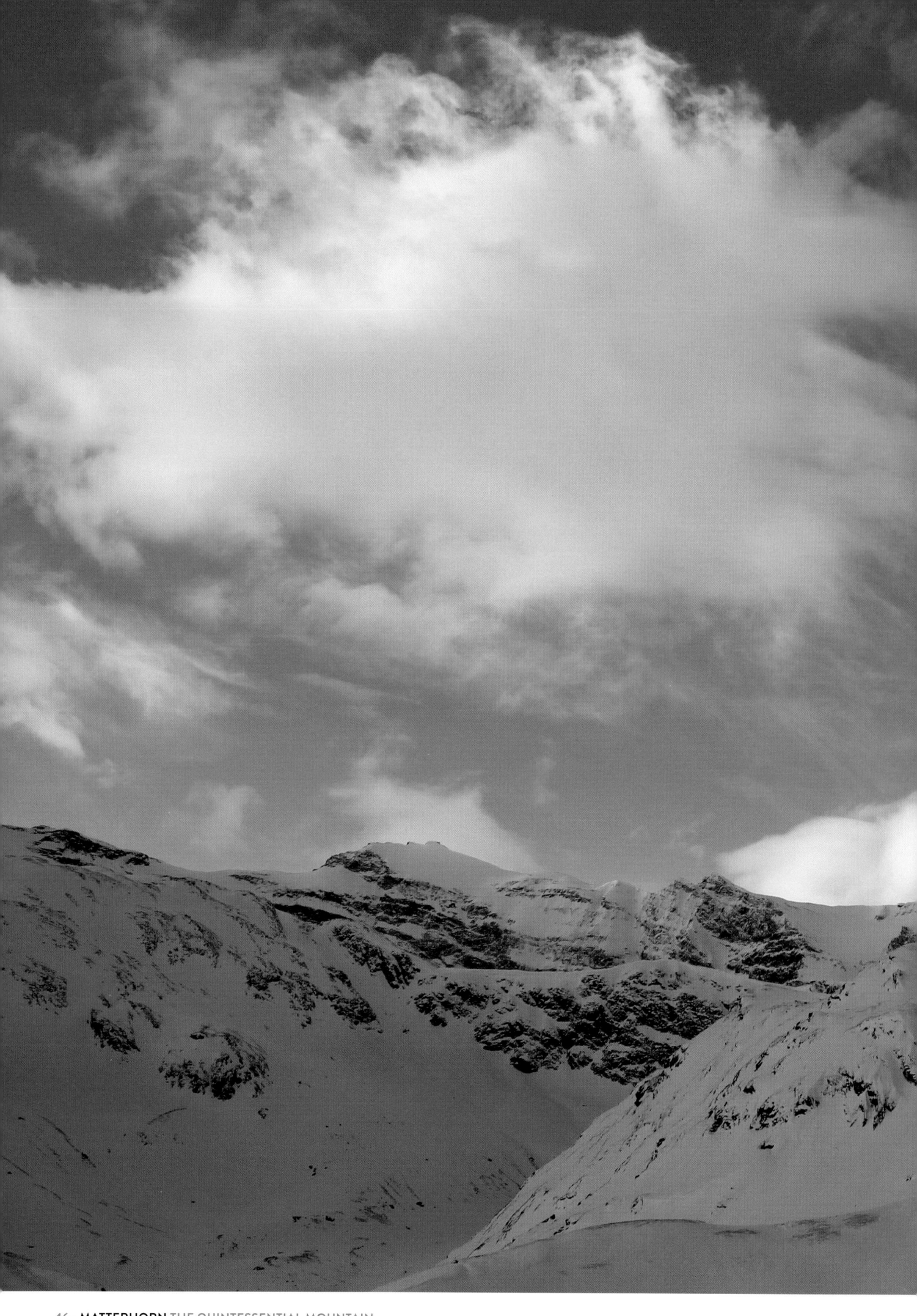

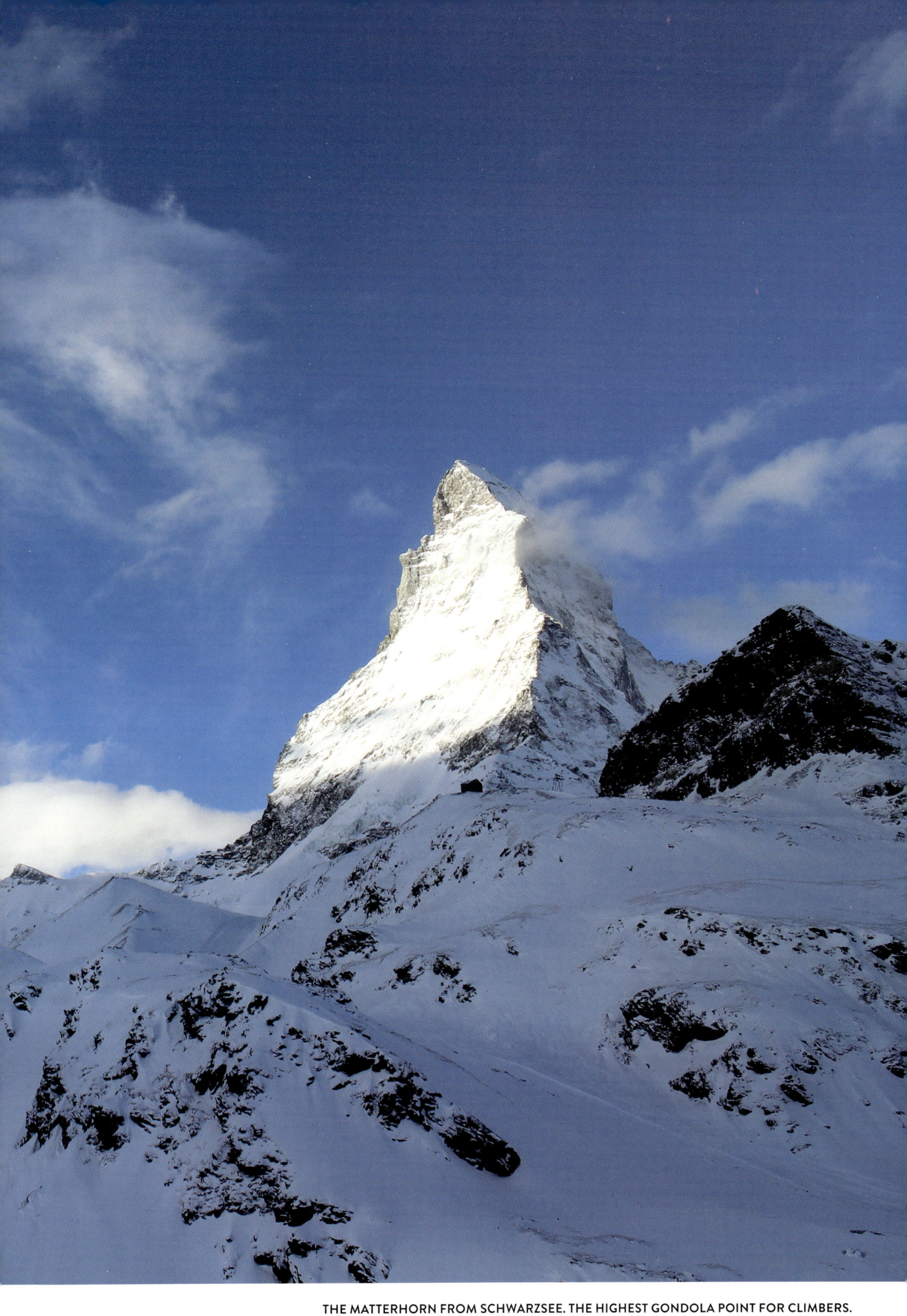

THE MATTERHORN FROM SCHWARZSEE. THE HIGHEST GONDOLA POINT FOR CLIMBERS.
FROM HERE IT IS A TWO HOUR WALK TO THE HÖRNLI HUT

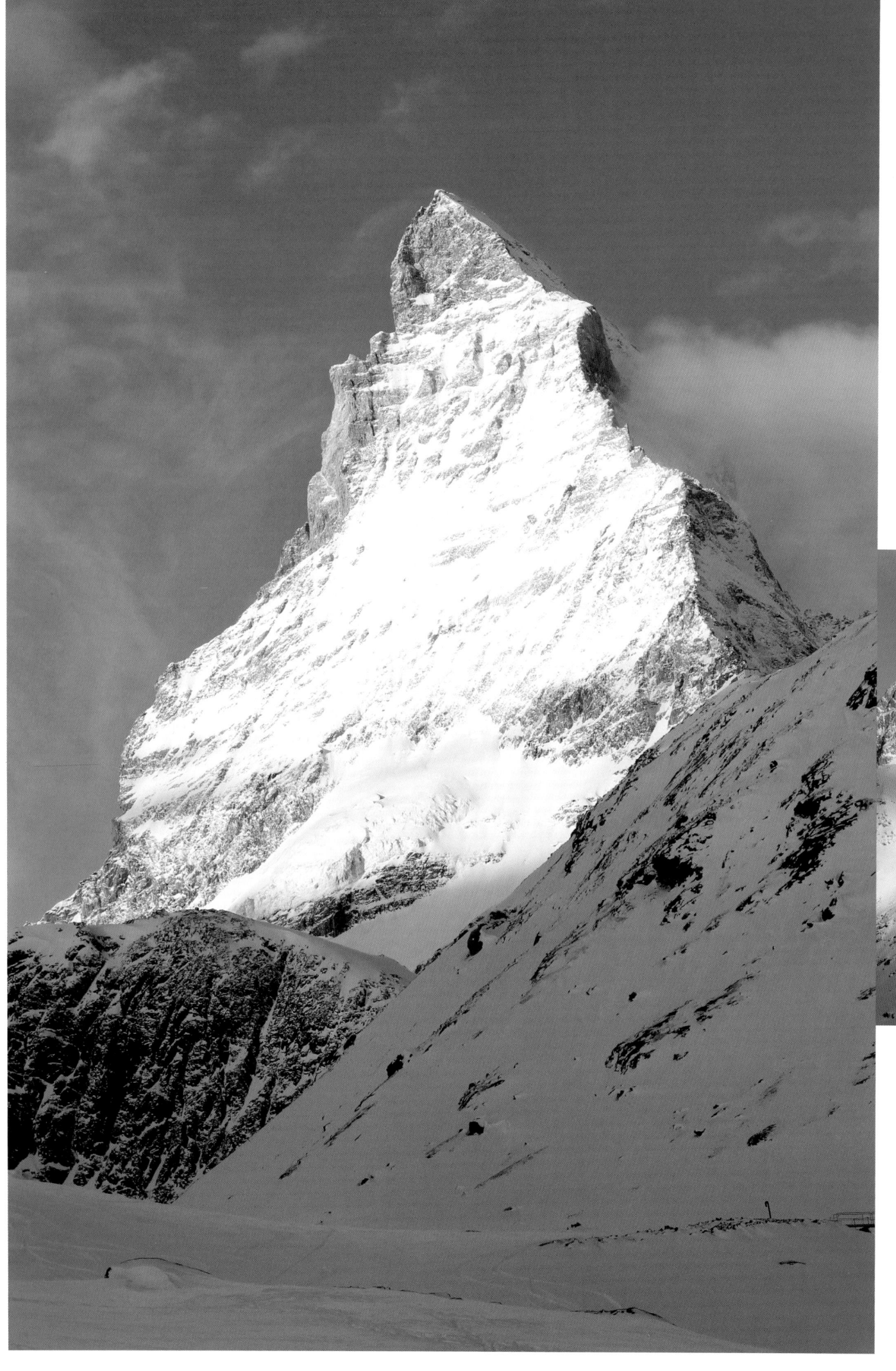

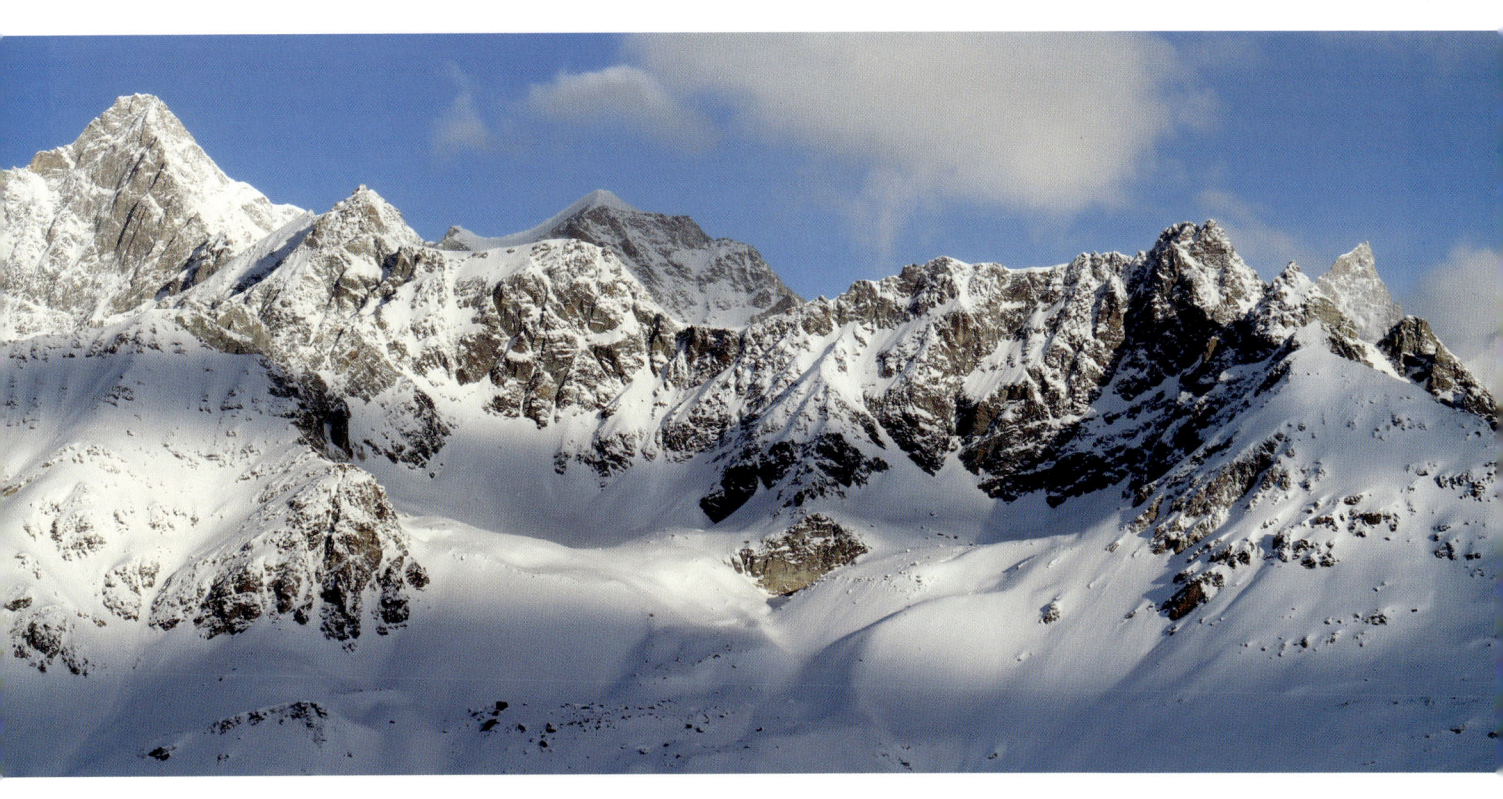

DENT BLANCHE 4,356M TO ZINALROTHORN 4,221M FROM SCHWARZSEE

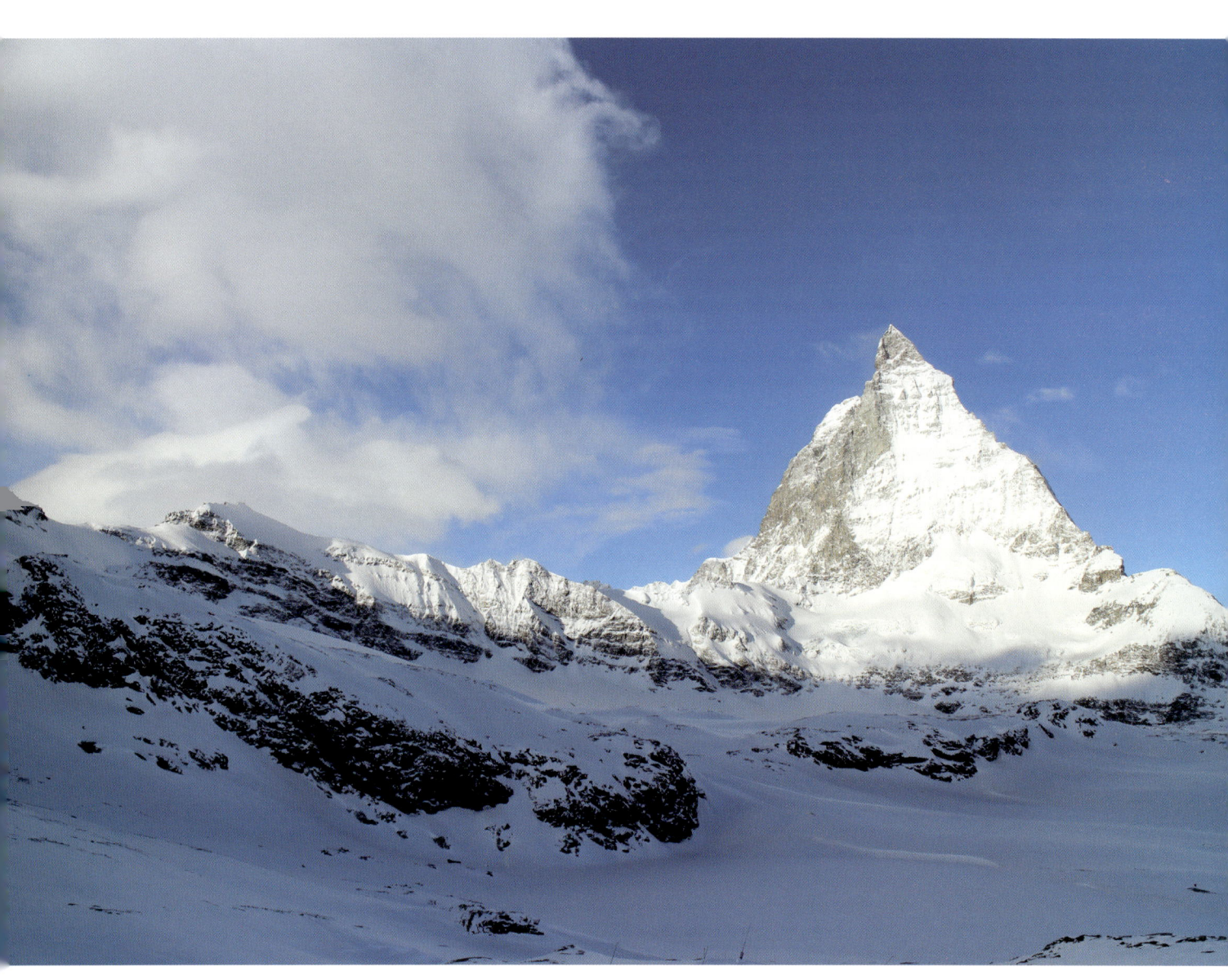

(Above) **THE EAST FACE OF THE MATTERHORN FROM TROCKENER STEG**

(Opposite) **A PROFILE OF THE HÖRNLI RIDGE FROM TROCKENER STEG. THE MOST COMMON ROUTE UP THE MATTERHORN**

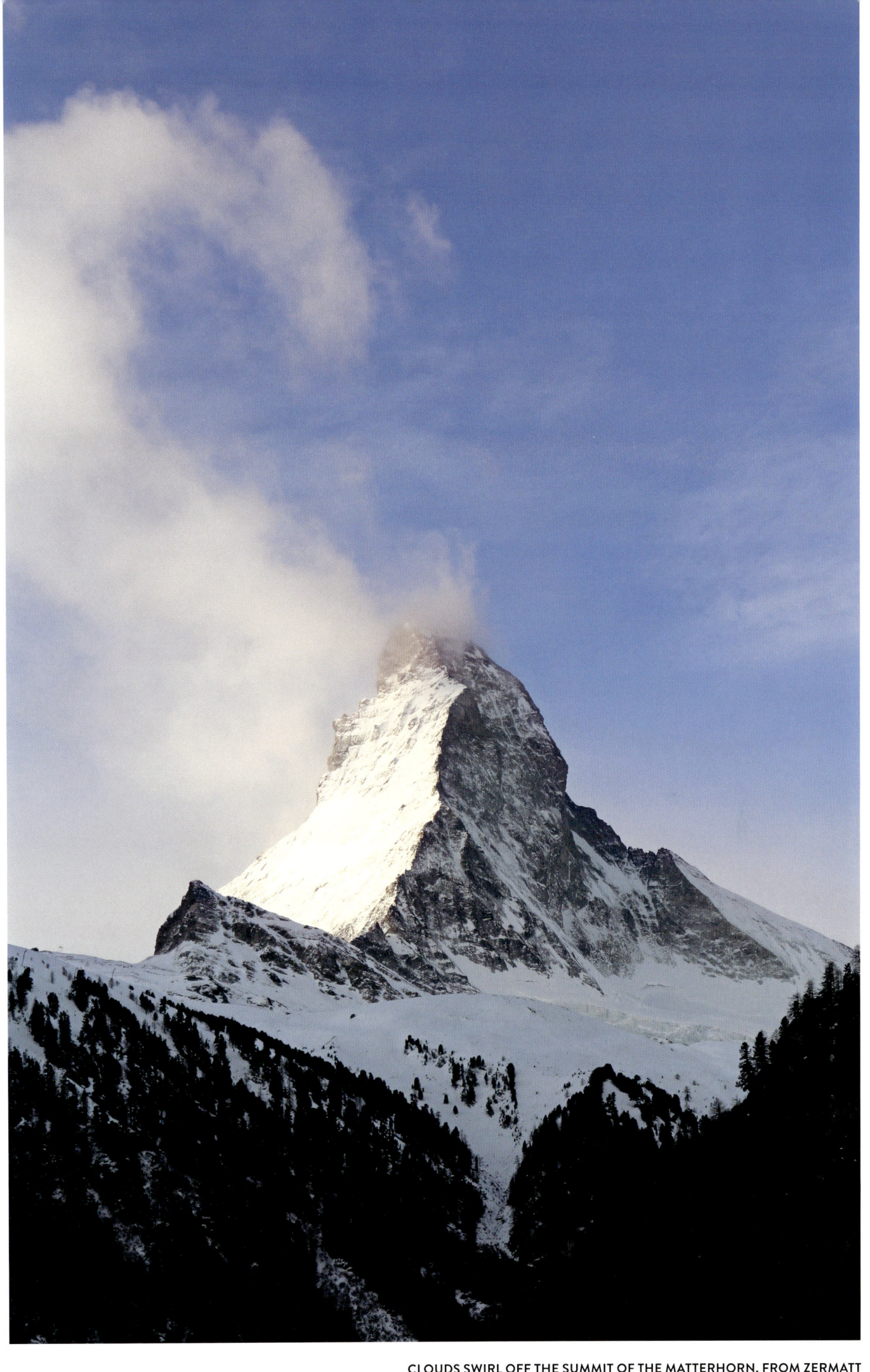

CLOUDS SWIRL OFF THE SUMMIT OF THE MATTERHORN, FROM ZERMATT

Dent d'Hérens 4,171m   *Matterhorn 4,478m*   *Dent Blanche 4,357m*

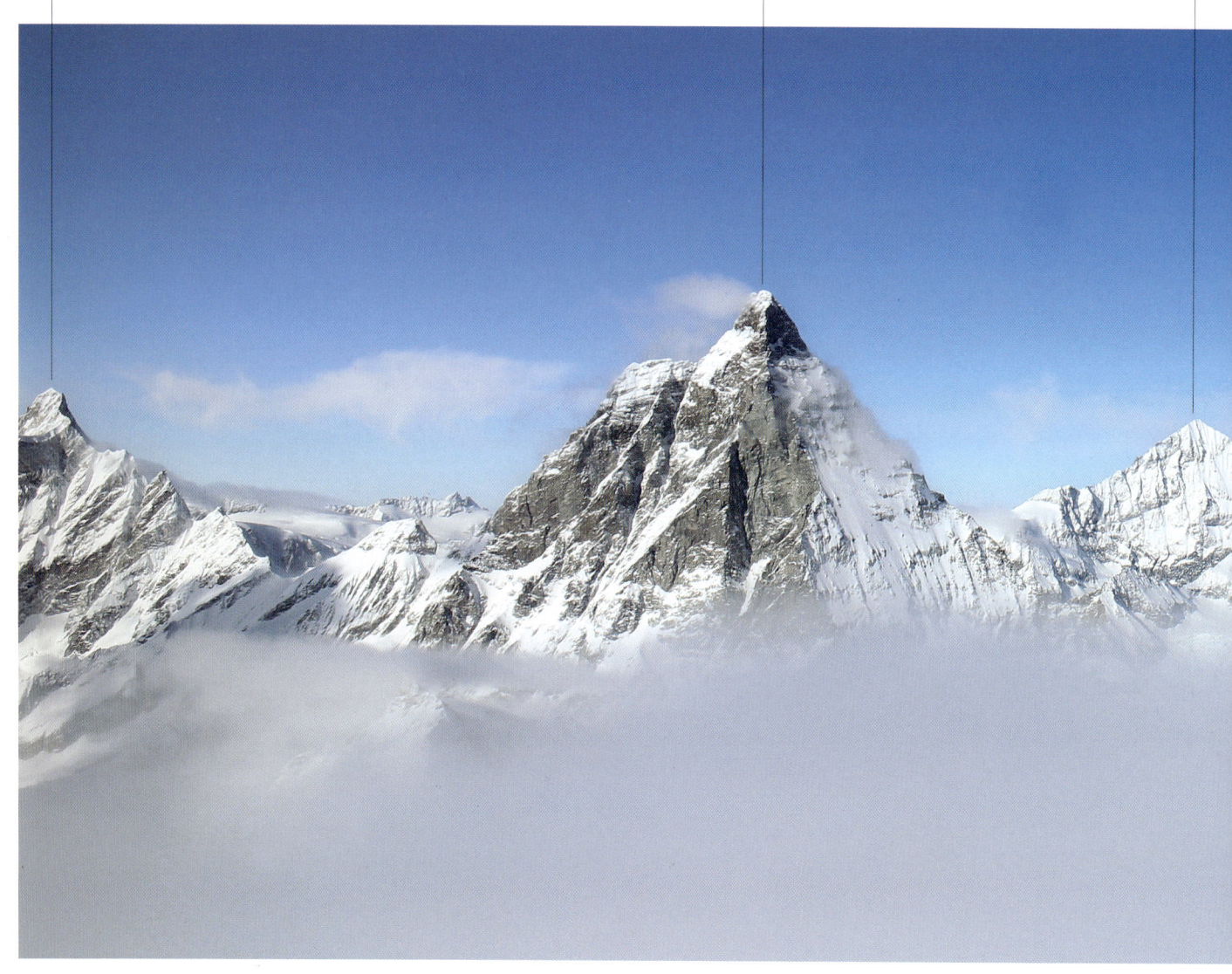

THE MATTERHORN AND SURROUNDING PEAKS FROM KLEIN MATTERHORN

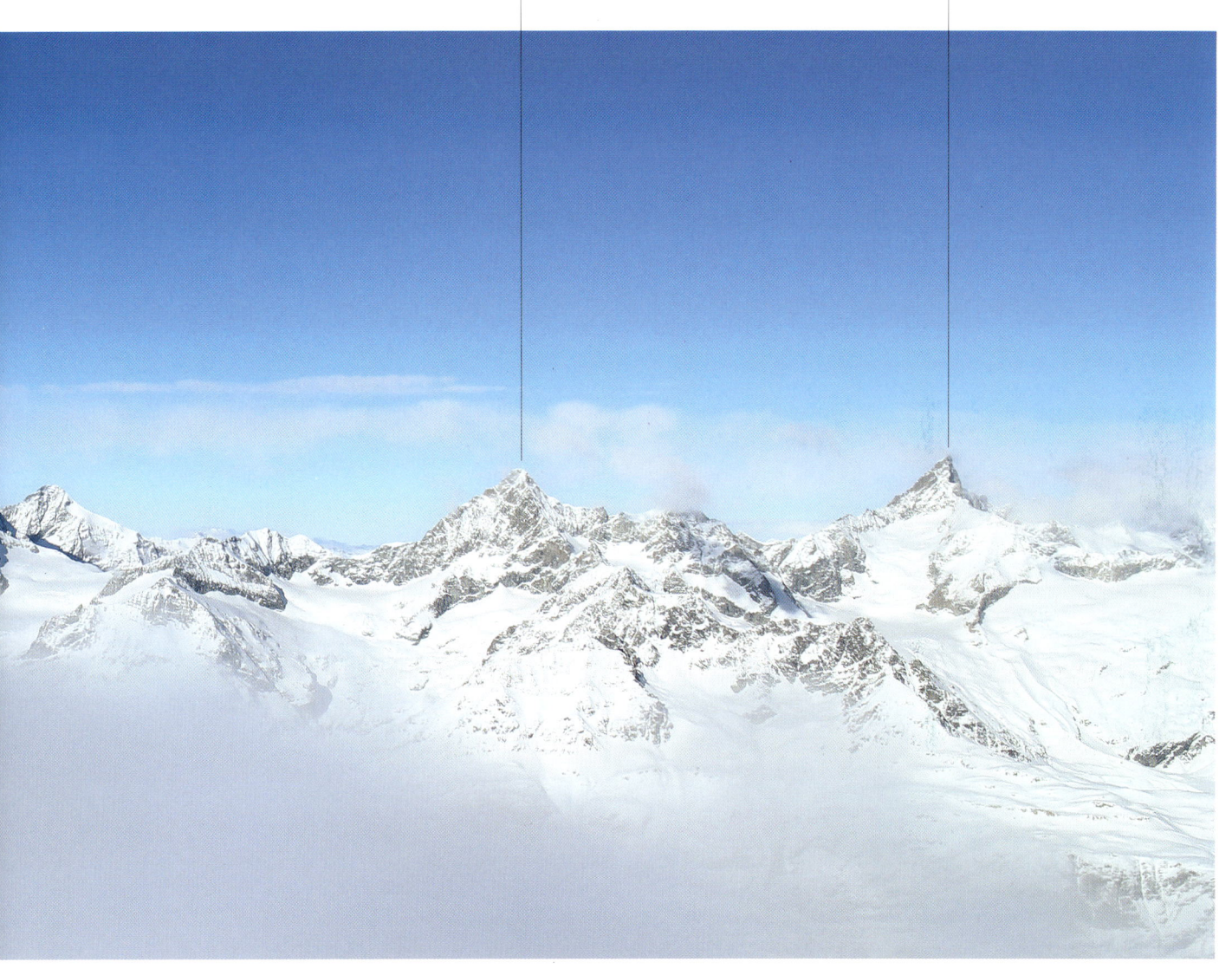

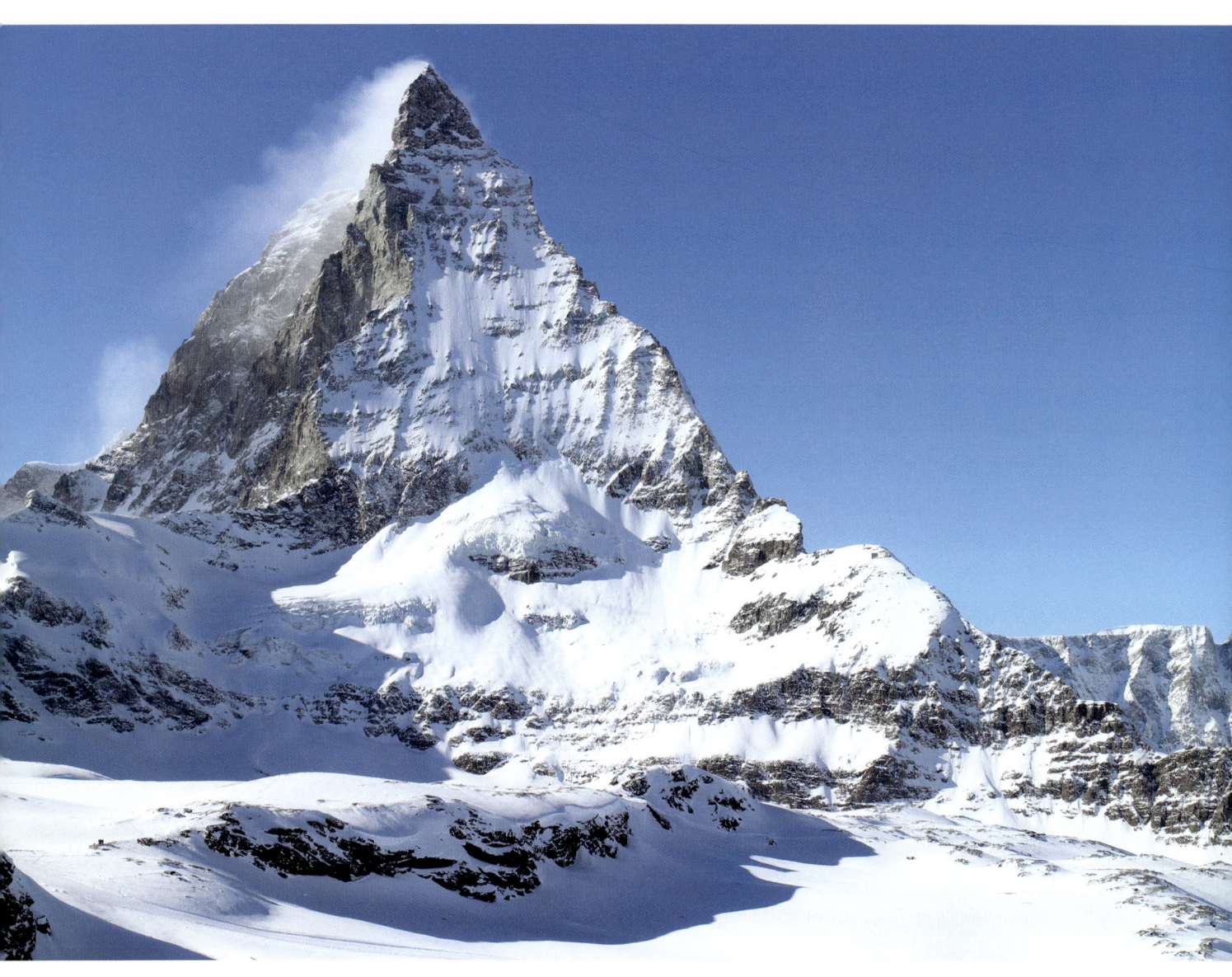

THE MATTERHORN FROM TROCKENER STEG

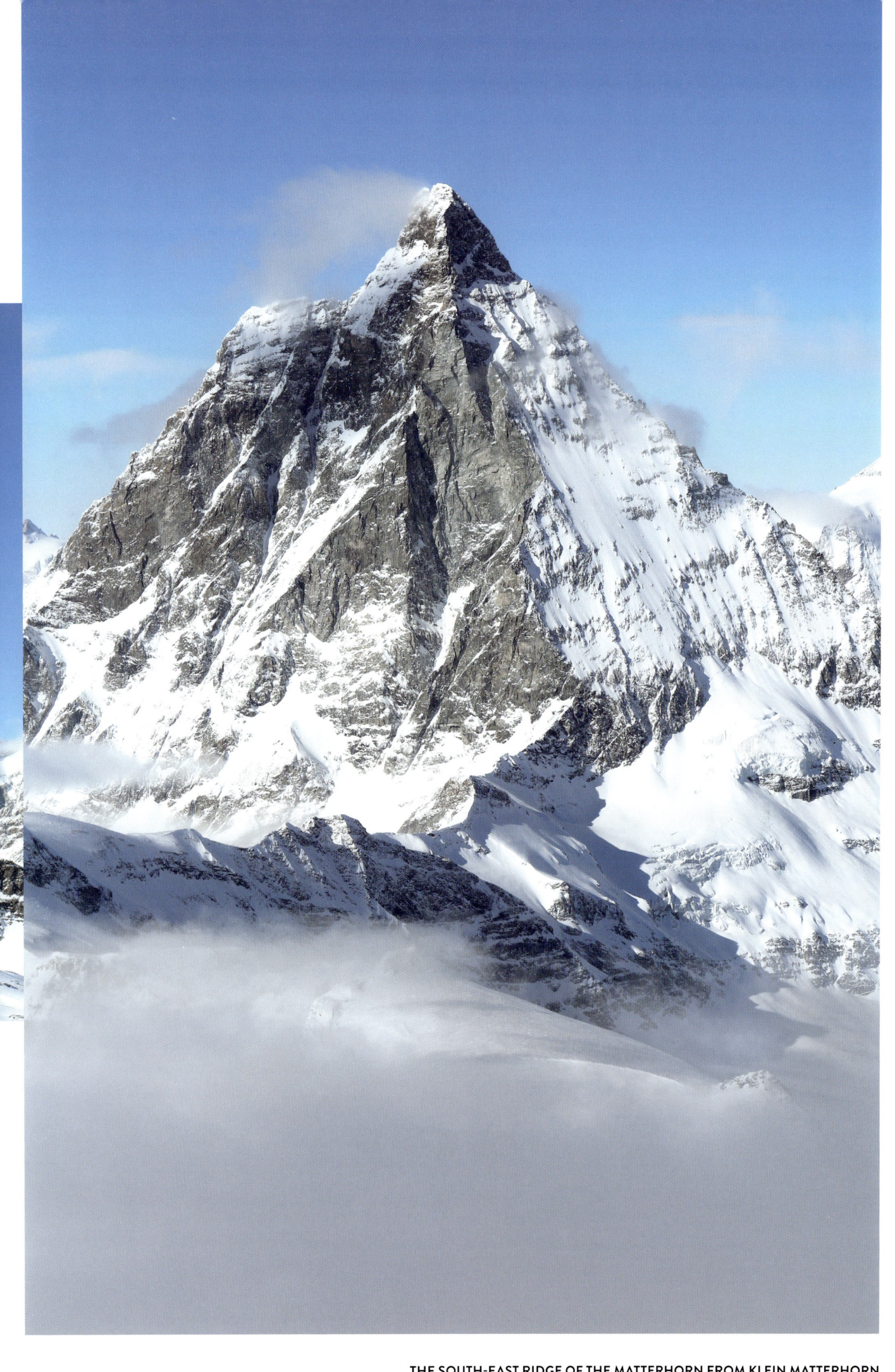

THE SOUTH-EAST RIDGE OF THE MATTERHORN FROM KLEIN MATTERHORN

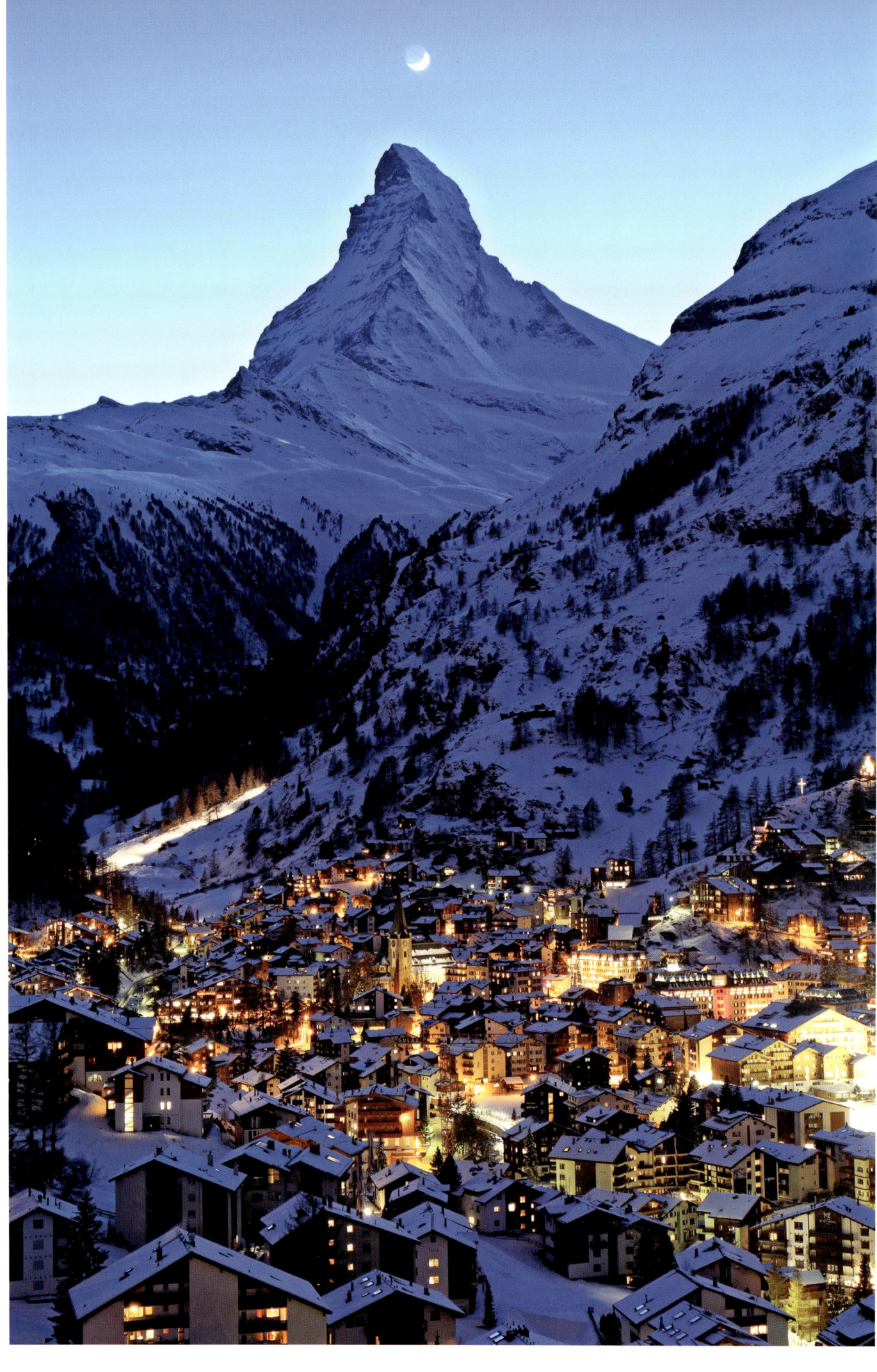

A WINTER'S EVENING IN ZERMATT WITH A LOW MOON OVER THE MATTERHORN

CHAPTER SIX
1861: MONT PELVOUX AND THE MATTERHORN

TWO ATTEMPTS TO ASCEND MONT PELVOUX: THE FOURTH HIGHEST PEAK OF THE DAUPHINÉ ALPS

At 3,946m (12,946 ft), Mont Pelvoux was believed, erroneously, to be the highest mountain in the Massif des Écrins range within the Dauphiné Alps in south-eastern France. When Edward Whymper set out to climb it in 1861, he believed it was the highest mountain in France and that it had never been climbed.

This district contains the highest summits in France, and some of its finest scenery. It has not perhaps the beauties of Switzerland, but has charms of its own; its cliffs, its torrents, and its gorges are unsurpassed; its deep and savage valleys present pictures of grandeur, and even sublimity, and it is second to none in the boldness of its mountain forms.

Few Englishmen had ventured this far off the beaten path and Whymper really was exploring the unknown. The little information he did have to hand, including any rough mapping, could not be relied upon, either owing to a lack of detail or incorrect information.

The district is still very imperfectly known; there are probably many valleys, and there are certainly many summits which have never been trodden by the feet of tourists or travellers; but in 1861 it was even less known. Until quite recently there was, practically, no map of it; General Bourcet's, which was the best that was published, was completely wrong in its delineation of the mountains, and was frequently incorrect in regard to paths or roads.

The mountainous regions of Dauphiné, moreover, are not supplied, like Switzerland, Tyrol, or even the Italian valleys, with accommodation for travellers. The inns, when they exist, are often filthy beyond description; rest is seldom obtained in their beds, or decent food found in their kitchens, and there are no local guides worth having. The tourist is thrown very much on his own resources, and it is not therefore surprising that these districts are less visited and less known than the rest of the Alps.

The 'right good fellow' Jean Reynaud, who Whymper had met at the end of his 1860 trip, had accompanied Messrs Bonney, Hawkshaw and Mathews, with the guide Michael Croz, in an attempt on Mont Pelvoux that year. They failed to make the summit, but Reynaud had proposed to Whymper that they try the following year.

The proposition was a tempting one, and Reynaud's cordial and modest manner made it irresistible, although there seemed small chance that we should succeed where a party such as that of Mr. Mathews had been beaten.

At the beginning of July 1861, I despatched to Reynaud from Havre, blankets (which were taxed as 'prohibited fabrics'), rope, and other things desirable for the excursion, and set out on the tour of France; but, four weeks later, at Nîmes, found myself completely collapsed by the heat, then 94° Faht. in the shade, and took a night train at once to Grenoble.

Grenoble is a town upon which a volume might be written. Its situation is probably the finest of any in France, and the views from its high forts are superb. I lost my way in the streets of this picturesque and noisome town, and having but a half-hour left in which to get a dinner and take a place in the diligence, was not well pleased to hear that an Englishman wished to see me. It turned out to be my friend Macdonald, who confided to me that he was going to try to ascend a mountain called Pelvoux in the course of ten days. On hearing of my intentions, he agreed to join us at La Bessée on the 3rd of August. In a few moments more I was perched in the banquette *en route* for Bourg d'Oysans, in a miserable vehicle which took nearly eight hours to accomplish less than 30 miles.

At five on a lovely morning I shouldered my knapsack and started for Briançon. Gauzy mists clung to the mountains, but melted away when touched by the sun … revealing the wonderfully bent and folded strata in the limestone cliffs behind the town. Then I entered the Combe de Malval … and passed on to Le Dauphin, where the first glacier came into view, tailing over the mountain-side on the right. From this place until the summit of the Col de Lautaret was passed, every gap in the mountains showed a glittering glacier or a soaring peak; the finest view was at La Grave, where the Meije rises by a series of tremendous precipices 8000 feet above the road.

All the peaks of Mont Pelvoux are well seen from La Bessée — the highest point, as well as that upon which the [French] engineers [led by Captain Durand in 1828 had] erected their cairn ... The natives knew only that the engineers had ascended one peak, and had seen from that one a still higher point, which they called the Pointe des Arcines or des Ecrins [now Barre des Écrins]. They could not ... tell the peak upon which the cairn had been erected ... They confidently asserted that the highest point of Mont Pelvoux had not been attained by any one. It was this point we wished to reach.

The 3rd of August came, and Macdonald did not appear, so we started for the Val Louise; our party consisting of Reynaud, myself, and a porter, Jean Casimir Giraud ... An hour and a half's smart walking took us to La Ville de Val Louise, our hearts gladdened by the glorious peaks of Pelvoux shining out without a cloud around them.

Reynaud kindly undertook to look after the commissariat, and I found to my annoyance, when we were about to leave, that I had given tacit consent to a small wine-cask being carried with us, which was a great nuisance from the commencement. It was excessively awkward to handle; one man tried to carry it, and then another, and at last it was slung from one of our batons ...

At 'La Ville' ... we moved steadily forwards to the village of La Pisse, where Pierre Sémiond lived, who was reputed to know more about the Pelvoux than any other man. He looked an honest fellow, but unfortunately he was ill and could not come. He recommended his brother, an aged creature, whose furrowed and wrinkled face hardly seemed to announce the man we wanted; but having no choice, we engaged him and again set forth. Walnut and a great variety of other trees gave shadow to our path and fresh vigour to our limbs; while below, in a sublime gorge, thundered the torrent, whose waters took their rise from the snows we hoped to tread on the morrow.

The Pelvoux could not be seen at La Ville, owing to a high intervening ridge; we were now moving along the foot of this to get to the châlets of Alefred ... where the mountain actually commences. From these châlets the subordinate, but more proximate, peaks appear considerably higher than the loftier ones behind, and sometimes completely conceal them. But the whole height of the peak, which in these valleys goes under the name of the 'Grand Pelvoux,' is seen at one glance from its summit to its base, six or seven thousand feet of nearly perpendicular cliffs.

We rested a minute to purchase some butter and milk, and Sémiond picked up a disreputable-looking lad to assist in carrying, pushing, and otherwise moving the wine-cask.

Our route now turned sharply to the left, and all were glad that the day was drawing to a close, so that we had the shadows from the mountains. A more frightful and desolate valley it is scarcely possible to imagine; it contains miles of boulders, débris, stones, sand, and mud; few trees, and they placed so high as to be almost out of sight; not a soul inhabits it; no birds are in the air, no fish in its waters; the mountain is too steep for the chamois, its slopes too inhospitable for the marmot, the whole too repulsive for the eagle. Not a living thing did we see in this sterile and savage valley during four days, except some few poor goats which had been driven there against their will.

We rested a little at a small spring, and then hastened onwards ... and clambered for half-an-hour through scattered firs and fallen boulders. Then evening began to close in rapidly, and it was time to look for a resting-place. There was no difficulty in getting one, for all around there was a chaotic assemblage of rocks. We selected the under side of a boulder which was more than fifty feet long by twenty high, cleared out the rubbish, and then collected wood for a fire.

The wine-cask had got through all its troubles; it was tapped, and the Frenchmen seemed to derive some consolation from its execrable contents. Reynaud chanted scraps of French songs, and each contributed his share of joke, story, or verse. The weather was perfect, and our prospects for the morrow were good ... One by one our party dropped off to sleep, and at last I got into my blanket-bag. It was hardly necessary, for although we were at a height of at least 7000 feet, the minimum temperature was above 40° Fahrenheit.

We mounted the slopes and quickly got above the trees, then had a couple of hours' clambering over bits of precipitous rock and banks of débris, and, at a quarter to seven, got to a narrow glacier ... which streamed out of the plateau on the summit ... We worked as much as possible to the right, in hopes that we should not have to cross it, but were continually driven back, and at last we found that over we must go. Old Sémiond had a strong objection to the ice, and made explorations on his own account to endeavour to avoid it; but Reynaud and I preferred to cross it ... It was narrow — in fact, one could throw a stone across — and it was easily mounted on the side; but in the centre swelled into a steep dome, up which we were obliged to cut.

Old Sémiond of course came after us when we got across. We then zigzagged up some snow-slopes, and shortly afterwards commenced to ascend the interminable array of buttresses which are the great peculiarity of the Pelvoux. They were very steep in many places, yet on the whole afforded good hold, and no climbing should be called difficult which does that. Gullies abounded among them, sometimes of great length and depth. *They* were frequently rotten, and would have been difficult for a single man to pass. The uppermost men were continually abused for dislodging rocks and for harpooning those below with their bâtons. However, without these incidents the climbing would have been dull — they helped to break the monotony.

We went up chimneys and gullies by the hour together, and always seemed to be coming to something, although we never got to it ... Up we mounted, and reached the pinnacles; but, lo! another set was seen, — and another, — and yet more — till at last we reached the top, and found it was only a buttress, and that we must descend 40 or 50 feet before we could commence to mount again. When this operation had been performed a few dozen times, it began to be wearisome, especially as we were in the dark as to our whereabouts. Sémiond, however, encouraged us, and said he knew we were on the right route, — so away we went once more.

It was now nearly mid-day, and we seemed no nearer the summit of the Pelvoux than when we started. At last we all joined together and held a council. 'Sémiond, old friend, do you know where we are now?' 'Oh yes, perfectly, to a yard and a half.' 'Well, then, how much are we below this plateau?' He affirmed we were not half-an-hour from the edge of the snow. 'Very good; let us proceed.' Half-an-hour passed, and then another, but we were still in the same state, — pinnacles, buttresses, and gullies were in profusion, but the plateau was not in sight. So we called him again — for he had been staring about latterly, as if in doubt — and repeated the question. 'How far below are we now?' Well, he thought it might be half-an-hour more. 'But you said that just now; are you sure we are going right?' Yes, he believed we were. Believed! that would not do. 'Are you sure we are going right for the Pic des Arcines?' 'Pic des Arcines!' he ejaculated in astonishment, as if he had heard the words for the first time. 'Pic des Arcines; no! but for the pyramid, the celebrated pyramid he had helped the great Capitaine Durand,' [ascend].

Here was a fix; — we had been talking about it to him for a whole day, and now he confessed he knew nothing about it. I turned to Reynaud, who seemed thunderstruck. 'What did he suggest?' He shrugged his shoulders. 'Well,' we said, after explaining our minds pretty freely to Sémiond, 'the sooner we turn back the better, for we have no wish to see your pyramid.'

We halted for an hour, and then commenced the descent. It took us nearly seven hours to come down to our rock; but I paid no heed to the distance, and do not remember anything about it. When we got down we made a discovery which affected us as much as the footprint in the sand did Robinson Crusoe: a blue silk veil lay by our fireside. There was but one explanation, — Macdonald had arrived; but where was he? We soon packed our baggage, and tramped in the dusk, through the stony desert, to Alefred, where we arrived about half-past nine.

We passed that night in a hay-loft, and in the morning, after settling with Sémiond, posted down to catch Macdonald. We had already determined on the plan of operation, which was to get him to join us, return, and be independent of all guides, simply taking the best man we could get as a porter.

I rushed after [Macdonald], turned angle after angle of the road, but could not see him; at last, as I came round a corner, he was also just turning another, going very fast. I shouted, and luckily he heard me. We returned, reprovisioned ourselves at La Ville, and the same evening saw us passing our first rock, *en route* for another. I have said we determined to take no guide; but, on passing La Pisse, old Sémiond turned out and offered his services. He went well, in spite of his years and disregard of truth. 'Why not take him?' said my friend. So we offered him a fifth of his previous pay, and in a few seconds he closed with the offer. This time he came in an inferior position, — we were to lead, he to follow. Our second follower was a youth of twenty-seven years, who was not all that could be desired. He drank Reynaud's wine, smoked our cigars, and quietly secreted the provisions when we were nearly starving.

We had another merry evening with nothing to mar it; the weather was perfect, and we lay backward in luxurious repose, looking at the sky spangled with its ten thousand brilliant lights.

We retired at last, but I was too excited to sleep. At a quarter-past four every man once more shouldered his pack and started. This time we agreed to keep more to the right, to see if it were not possible to get to the plateau without losing any time by crossing the glacier … We mounted steadily for an hour and a half, sometimes walking, though more frequently climbing, and then found, after all, that it was necessary to cross the glacier. The part on which we struck came down a very steep slope, and was much crevassed. The word crevassed hardly expresses its appearance — it was a mass of formidable séracs. We found, however, more difficulty in getting on than across it; and, thanks to the rope, it was passed in safety. Then the interminable buttresses began again. Hour after hour we proceeded upwards, frequently at fault, and obliged to descend … When twelve o'clock came we lunched, and contemplated the scene with satisfaction; all the summits in sight, with the single exception of [Monte] Viso, had given in, and we looked over an immense expanse — a perfect sea of peaks and snow-fields. Still the pinnacles rose above us, and opinions were freely uttered that we should see no summit of Pelvoux that day … We came at last to a very bad piece, rotten and steep, and no hold. Here Reynaud and Macdonald confessed to being tired, and talked of going to sleep. A way was discovered out of the difficulty; then some one called out, 'Look at the Viso!' and we saw that we almost looked over it. We worked away with redoubled energy … This gave us fresh hopes; we were not deceived; and with a simultaneous shout we greeted the appearance of our long-wished-for snows. A large crevasse separated us from them; but a bridge was found; we tied ourselves in line, and moved safely over it. Directly we got across, there rose before us a fine snow-capped peak. Old Sémiond cried, 'The pyramid! I see the pyramid!' 'Where, Sémiond, where?' 'There; on the top of that peak.'

There, sure enough, was the cairn he had helped to erect more than thirty years before. Where was the Pic des Arcines? … Somewhat sadly we moved towards the pyramid, sighing that there was no other to conquer; but hardly had we gone two hundred paces, before there rose a superb white cone on the left, which had been hidden before by a slope of snow. We shouted, 'The Pic des Arcines!' and inquired of Sémiond if he knew whether that peak had been ascended. As for him, he knew nothing, except that the peak before us was called the pyramid … and that it had not been ascended since … We immediately turned at right angles for the cone, [Sémiond] making faint struggles for his beloved pyramid. Our progress was stopped … by the edge of the ridge connecting the two peaks, and we perceived that it curled over in a lovely volute. We involuntarily retreated. Sémiond, who was last in the line, took the opportunity to untie himself, and refused to come on; said we were running dangerous risks, and talked vaguely of crevasses. We tied him up again, and proceeded. The snow was very soft; we were always knee-deep, and sometimes floundered in up to the waist; but a simultaneous jerk before and behind always released one. By this time we had arrived at the foot of the final peak. The left-hand ridge seemed easier than that upon which we stood, so we curved round to get to it. Some rocks peeped out 150 feet below the summit, and up these we crawled, leaving our porter behind, as he said he was afraid … The rocks led to a short ridge of ice — our plateau on one side, and a nearly vertical precipice on the other. Macdonald cut up it, and at a quarter to two we stood shaking hands on the loftiest summit of the conquered Pelvoux.

The day still continued everything that could be desired, and, far and near, countless peaks burst into sight, without a cloud to hide them. The mighty Mont Blanc, full seventy miles away, first caught our eyes, and then, still farther off, the Monte Rosa group; while, rolling away to the east, one unknown range after another succeeded in unveiled splendour; fainter and fainter in tone, but still perfectly defined, till at last the eye was unable to distinguish sky from mountain, and they died away in the far-off horizon. Monte Viso rose up grandly, but it was less than forty miles away, and we looked over it to a hazy mass we knew must be the plains of Piedmont. Southwards a blue mist seemed to indicate the existence of the distant Mediterranean; to the west we looked over to the mountains of Auvergne. Such was the panorama; a view extending in nearly every direction for more than one hundred miles. It was with some difficulty we wrenched our eyes from the more distant objects to contemplate the nearer ones. Mont Dauphin was very conspicuous, but La Bessée was not readily perceived. Besides these places not a habitation could be seen; all was rock, snow, or ice; and, large as we knew were the snow-fields of Dauphiné, we were surprised to find that they very far surpassed our most ardent imagination. Nearly in a line between us and Viso, immediately to the south of Chateau Queyras, was a splendid group of mountains of great height. More to the south an unknown peak seemed still higher; while close to us we were astonished to discover that there was a mountain which appeared even higher than that on which we stood. At least this was my opinion; Macdonald thought that it was not so high, and Reynaud that it was much about the same elevation as our own peak.

Thrilled to have been the first to reach the true summit of Mont Pelvoux, but disappointed to learn it was not the highest mountain in mainland France, Whymper was correct in identifying that the peak to the south — Ailefroide 3,954m (12,972 ft) — was slightly higher by a mere 8 metres (26 ft), and that there was a closer, even higher mountain to the north, which was Barre des Écrins 4,102m (13,458 ft). He would go on to attempt to climb the latter in 1864.

We left the summit at last, and descended to the rocks … where I boiled some water, obtained by melting snow. After we had fed, and smoked our cigars (lighted without difficulty from a common match), we found it was ten minutes past three, and high time to be off. We dashed, waded, and tumbled for twenty-five minutes through the snow, and then began the long descent of the rocks. It was nearly four o'clock, and, as it would be dark at eight, it was evident that there was no time to be lost, and we pushed on to the utmost. Nothing remarkable occurred going down. We kept rather closer to the glacier, and crossed at the same point as in the morning. Getting *off* it was like getting *on* it — rather awkward. Old Sémiond had got over — so had Reynaud; Macdonald came next, but, as he made a long stretch to get on to a higher mass, he slipped, and would have been in the bowels of a crevasse in a moment had he not been tied.

It was nearly dark by the time we had crossed, yet I still hoped that we should be able to pass the night at our rock. Macdonald was not so sanguine, and he was right; for at last we found ourselves quite at fault, and wandered helplessly up and down for an hour, while Reynaud and the porter indulged in a little mutual abuse. The dreary fact that, as we could not get down, we must stay where we were, was now quite apparent.

We were at least 10,500 feet high, and if it commenced to rain or snow, as the gathering clouds and rising wind seemed to threaten, we might be in a sore plight. We were hungry, having eaten little since 3 A.M., and a torrent we heard close at hand, but could not discover, aggravated our thirst.

A more detestable locality for a night out of doors it is difficult to imagine. There was not shelter of any kind; it was perfectly exposed to the chilly wind which began to rise, and it was too steep to promenade. Loose rubbly stones covered the ground, and had to be removed before we could sit with any comfort.

Thunder commenced to growl, and lightning to play among the peaks above, and the wind, which had brought the temperature down to nearly freezing-point, began to chill us to the bones. We examined our resources. They were six and a half cigars, two boxes of vesuvians [matches], one-third of a pint of brandy-and-water, and half-a-pint of spirits of wine: rather scant fare for three fellows who had to get through seven hours before daylight. The spirit-lamp was lighted, and the remaining spirits of wine, the brandy and some snow, were heated by it. It was a strong liquor, and we wished for more of it. When it was consumed, Macdonald endeavoured to dry his socks by the lamp, and then the three lay down under my plaid to pretend to sleep. Reynaud's woes were aggravated by toothache; Macdonald somehow managed to close his eyes.

The longest night must end, and ours did at last. We got down to our rock in an hour and a quarter, and found the lad not a little surprised at our absence. He said he had made a gigantic fire to light us down, and shouted with all his might; we neither saw the fire nor heard his shouts. He said we looked a ghastly crew, and no wonder; it was our fourth night out.

We feasted at our cave, and performed some very necessary ablutions. The persons of the natives are infested by certain agile creatures — rapid of motion, numerous, and voracious. It is dangerous to approach too near, and one has to study the wind, so as to get on their weather-side. In spite of all such precautions my unfortunate companion and myself were being rapidly devoured alive. We only expected a temporary lull of our tortures, for the interiors of the inns are like the exteriors of the natives, swarming with this species of animated creation.

It is said that once, when these tormentors were filled with an unanimous desire, an unsuspecting traveller was dragged bodily from his bed! This needs confirmation. One word more, and I have done with this vile subject. We returned from our ablutions, and found the Frenchmen engaged in conversation. 'Ah!' said old Sémiond, 'as to fleas, I don't pretend to be different to anyone else, — *I have them.*' This time he certainly spoke the truth.

I have not attempted to conceal that the ascent of Mont Pelvoux is of a rather monotonous character; the view from its summit can, however, be confidently recommended. A glance at a map will show that, with the single exception of the Viso, whose position is unrivalled, it is better situated than any other mountain of considerable height for viewing the whole of the Western Alps.

It has been observed by others that it is improbable the French surveyors should have remained for several days upon the Pic de la Pyramide without visiting the other and loftier summit. If they did, it is strange that they did not leave some memorial of their visit. The natives who accompanied them asserted that they did not pass from one to the other; we therefore claimed to have made the ascent of the loftiest point for the first time. The claim, however, cannot be sustained, on account of the ascent of M. Puiseux. It is a matter of little moment; the excursion had for us all the interest of a first ascent; and I look back upon this, my first serious mountain scramble, with more satisfaction, and with as much pleasure as upon any that is recorded in this volume.

A few days later, I left Abries to seek a quiet bundle of hay at Le Chalp — a village some miles nearer to the Viso. On approaching the place, the odour of sanctity became distinctly perceptible; and on turning a corner the cause was manifested — there was the priest of the place, surrounded by some of his flock. I advanced humbly, hat in hand, but almost before a word could be said, he broke out with, 'Who are you?' 'What are you?' 'What do you want?' I endeavoured to explain. 'You are a deserter; I know you are a deserter; go away, you can't stay here; go to Le Monta, down there; I won't have you here,' and he literally drove me away. The explanation of his strange behaviour was that Piedmontese soldiers who were tired of the service had not unfrequently crossed the Col de la Traversette into the valley, and trouble had arisen from harbouring them. However, I did not know this at the time, and was not a little indignant that I, who was marching to the attack, should be taken for a deserter.

So I walked away, and shortly afterwards, as it was getting dark, encamped in a lovely hole — a cavity or kind of basin in the earth, with a stream on one side, a rock to windward, and some broken fir branches close at hand. Nothing could be more perfect: rock, hole, wood, and water. After making a roaring fire, I nestled in my blanket bag (an ordinary blanket sewn up double round the legs, with a piece of elastic riband round the open end), and slept, but not for long. I was troubled with dreams of the Inquisition; the tortures were being applied — priests were forcing fleas down my nostrils and into my eyes — and with red-hot pincers were taking out bits of flesh, and then cutting off my ears and tickling the soles of my feet. This was too much; I yelled a great yell and awoke, to find myself covered with innumerable crawling bodies. They were ants; I had camped by an ant-hill, and, after making its inhabitants mad with the fire, had coolly lain down in their midst.

The night was fine, and as I settled down in more comfortable quarters, a brilliant meteor sailed across full 60° of the cloudless sky, leaving a trail of light behind which lasted for several seconds. It was the herald of a splendid spectacle. Stars fell by hundreds; and not dimmed by intervening vapours, they sparkled with greater brightness than Sirius in our damp climate.

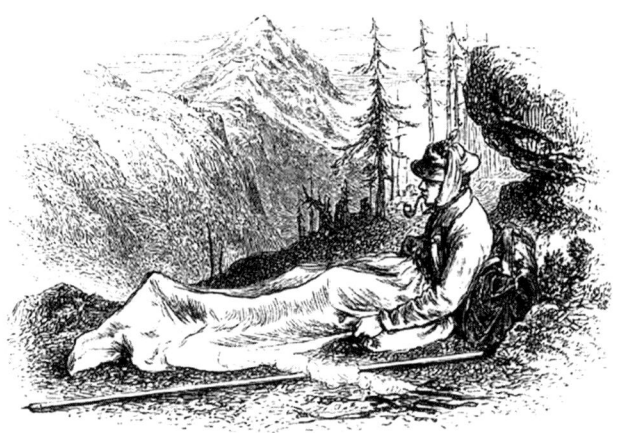

The Blanket Bag

(Ibid., pp. 14–41)

Whymper, then attempted to climb and become the first man to summit Monte Viso which he had viewed so prominently from Mont Pelvoux. Approaching from the north, he reached an impasse, forcing him to return. Two weeks later, another party summited successfully from the south.

FIRST ATTEMPT TO ASCEND THE MATTERHORN

By 1861, many of the Alpine peaks had already been summited so Whymper made somewhat of a late arrival to the party. Not too late, however, as the race to be the first to summit the crowning jewel was still on, although the question was: for how much longer. The most prominent English climber trying to make the first assent of the Matterhorn was Professor John Tyndall. Twenty years Whymper's senior and a pioneering physicist, Tyndall was more typical of the Victorian 'hobbyist' alpinist climber, and had visited the Alps each summer of the previous five years. He tackled the mountains with a considerable support team and had his sights firmly set on the two remaining big prizes.

However, it was Whymper who attracted the attention as the man most determined to succeed. Italian mountaineer, Guido Rey who was born in this year, 1861, romantically wrote in his book *Il Monte Cervino*, **published in 1946, 'Now Edward Whymper came upon the scene. Into the bullring ... the** *espada* **[matador] steps forth eager and brave; the eyes of all are fixed on him.' 'The struggle is to be terrible, unceasing, full of daring stratagems; one of the two must fall.'**

'Here too, as in the arena at Seville, it is not the bull which seeks the encounter: the man attacks, the bull defends himself, dies or kills; and in the duel the Matterhorn had all the material advantages of its enormous strength, of its fits of brutal rage; the man's weapon was his iron will.'

'The history of the contest between this man, young, strong, and confident, and the hoary, cold, and unresponsive rock is perhaps one of the finest and most telling in the whole history of mountaineering, and, apart from mountaineering, it is not an unimportant episode in the hard-won conquest of unknown territory.'

Two summits amongst those in the Alps which yet remained virgin had especially excited my admiration. One of these had been attacked numberless times by the best mountaineers without success; the other, surrounded by traditional inaccessibility, was almost untouched. These mountains were the Weisshorn **[page 85]** and the Matterhorn.

Rumours were floating about that the former had been conquered, and that the latter was shortly to be attacked, and they were confirmed on arrival at Chatillon, at the entrance of the Val Tournanche. My interest in the Weisshorn consequently abated, but it was raised to the highest pitch on hearing that Professor Tyndall was at Breil, and intending to try to crown his first victory by another and still greater one.

Up to this time my experience with guides had not been fortunate, and I was inclined, improperly, to rate them at a low value. They represented to me pointers out of paths, and large consumers of meat and drink, but little more; and, with the recollection of Mont Pelvoux, I should have greatly preferred the company of a couple of my countrymen to any number of guides.

When walking up towards Breil, we inquired for another man of all the knowing ones, and they, with one voice, proclaimed that Jean-Antoine Carrel, of the village of Val Tournanche, was the cock of his valley. We sought, of course, for Carrel; and found him a well-made, resolute-looking fellow, with a certain defiant air which was rather taking. Yes, he would go. Twenty francs a day, whatever was the result, was his price. I assented. But I must take his comrade. 'Why so?' Oh, it was absolutely impossible to get along without another man. As he said this, an evil countenance came forth out of the darkness and proclaimed itself the comrade. I demurred, the negotiations broke off, and we went up to Breil. This place will be frequently mentioned in subsequent chapters, and was in full view of the extraordinary peak, the ascent of which we were about to attempt.

Those by whom this book is likely to be read will know that that peak is nearly 15,000 feet high, and that it rises abruptly, by a series of cliffs which may properly be termed precipices, a clear 5000 feet above the glaciers which surround its base. They will know too that it was the last great Alpine peak which remained unscaled, — less on account of the difficulty of doing so, than from the terror inspired by its invincible appearance. There seemed to be a *cordon* drawn around it, up to which one might go, but no farther. Within that invisible line gins and effreets were supposed to exist — the Wandering Jew and the spirits of the damned. The superstitious natives in the surrounding valleys (many of whom still firmly believe it to be not only the highest mountain in the Alps, but in the world) spoke of a ruined city on its summit wherein the spirits dwelt; and if you laughed, they gravely shook their heads, told you to look yourself to see the castles and the walls, and warned one against a rash approach, lest the infuriate demons from their impregnable heights might hurl down vengeance for one's derision. Such were the traditions of the natives. Stronger minds felt the influence of the wonderful form, and men who ordinarily spoke or wrote like rational beings, when they came under its power seemed to quit their senses, and ranted, and rhapsodised, losing for a time all common forms of speech.

The Matterhorn looks equally imposing from whatever side it is seen; it never seems commonplace; and in this respect, and in regard to the impression it makes upon spectators, it stands almost alone amongst mountains. It has no rivals in the Alps, and but few in the world.

The seven or eight thousand feet which compose the actual peak have several well-marked ridges and numerous others. The most continuous is that which leads towards the north-east; the summit is at its higher, and the little peak, called the Hörnli, is at its lower end. Another one that is well-pronounced descends from the summit to the ridge called the Furgen Grat. The slope of the mountain that is between these two ridges will be referred to as the eastern face. A third, somewhat less continuous than the others, descends in a south-westerly direction, and the portion of the mountain that is seen from Breil is confined to that which is comprised between this and the second ridge. This section is not composed, like that between the first and second ridge, of one grand face; but it is broken up into a series of huge precipices, spotted with snow-slopes, and streaked with snow-gullies. The other half of the mountain, facing the Z'Mutt glacier, is not capable of equally simple definition. There are precipices, apparent, but not actual;

there are precipices absolutely perpendicular; there are precipices overhanging: there are glaciers, and there are hanging glaciers; there are glaciers which tumble great séracs over greater cliffs, whose débris, subsequently consolidated, becomes glacier again; there are ridges split by the frost, and washed by the rain and melted snow into towers and spires: while, everywhere, there are ceaseless sounds of action, telling that the causes are still in operation which have been at work since the world began; reducing the mighty mass to atoms, and effecting its degradation.

Most tourists obtain their first view of the mountain either from the valley of Zermatt or from that of [Val] Tournanche. From the former direction the base of the mountain is seen at its narrowest, and its ridges and faces seem to be of prodigious steepness. The tourist toils up the valley, looking frequently for the great sight which is to reward his pains, without seeing it (for the mountain is first perceived in that direction about a mile to the north of Zermatt), when, all at once, as he turns a rocky corner of the path, it comes into view; not, however, where it is expected; the face has to be raised up to look at it; it seems overhead … The view of the mountain from Breil, in the Val Tournanche, is not less striking than that on the other side; but, usually, it makes less impression, because the spectator grows accustomed to the sight while coming up or down the valley. From this direction the mountain is seen to be broken up into a series of pyramidal wedge-shaped masses; on the other side it is remarkable for the large, unbroken extent of cliffs that it presents, and for the simplicity of its outline. It was natural to suppose that a way would more readily be found to the summit on a side thus broken up than in any other direction. The eastern face, fronting Zermatt, seemed one smooth, inaccessible cliff, from summit to base. The ghastly precipices which face the Z'Mutt glacier forbade any attempt in *that* direction. There remained only the side of Val Tournanche; and it will be found that nearly all the earliest attempts to ascend the mountain were made upon the southern side.

My guide and I arrived at Breil on the 28th of August 1861, and we found that Professor Tyndall *had* been there a day or two before, but had done nothing. I had seen the mountain from nearly every direction, and it seemed, even to a novice like myself, far too much for a single day. I intended to sleep out upon it, as high as possible, and to attempt to reach the summit on the following day. We endeavoured to induce another man to accompany us, but without success … A sturdy old fellow — Peter Taugwalder by name — said he would go! His price? 'Two hundred francs.' 'What, whether we ascend or not?' 'Yes — nothing less.' The end of the matter was that all the men who were more or less capable showed a strong disinclination, or positively refused, to go … or else asked a prohibitive price. This, it may be said once for all, was the reason why so many futile attempts were made upon the Matterhorn. One first-rate guide after another was brought up to the mountain, and patted on the back, but all declined the business. The men who went had no heart in the matter, and took the first opportunity to turn back. For they were, with the exception of one man, to whom reference will be made presently, universally impressed with the belief that the summit was entirely inaccessible.

We resolved to go alone, and anticipating a cold bivouac, begged the loan of a couple of blankets from the innkeeper. He refused them … We did not require them that night, as it was passed in the highest cow-shed in the valley, which is about an hour nearer to the mountain than is the hotel. The cowherds, worthy fellows, seldom troubled by tourists, hailed our company with delight, and did their best to make us comfortable; brought out their little stores of simple food, and, as we sat with them round the great copper pot which hung over the fire, bade us in husky voice, but with honest intent, to beware of the perils of the haunted cliffs. When night was coming on, we saw, stealing up the hillside, the forms of Jean-Antoine Carrel and the comrade. 'Oh ho!' I said, 'you have repented?' 'Not at all; you deceive yourself.' 'Why then have you come here?' 'Because we ourselves are going on the mountain to-morrow.' 'Oh, then it is *not* necessary to have more than three.' 'Not for *us*.' I admired their pluck, and had a strong inclination to engage the pair; but, finally, decided against it.

His comrade, was in fact his cousin, Jean-Jacques Carrel, the 'mighty hunter' who had lead Jean-Antoine

on the first recorded attempt to climb the Matterhorn in 1857. There was probably no better a man to have taken with them.

Jean-Antoine Carrel was born in Valtournenche in 1829 in the Aosta Valley below the Matterhorn. He grew up working as a shepherd and was considered a good hunter. This later skill was to come in useful when he spent time in the army, earning the nickname of Bersagliere (Marksman) for his accuracy with a gun. In 1859, he won a medal for defending his home country against Austria.

The first attempt by Carrel to climb the Matterhorn was in 1857. Not surprisingly, he considered it his own territory and held the view that no one could climb it without him. He and Whymper would get to know each other well and climbed together on numerous occasions during the next few years. Having their own ambitions, and both being proudly independent men, they formed a competitive but healthy relationship; crucially, one of mutual respect and cooperation.

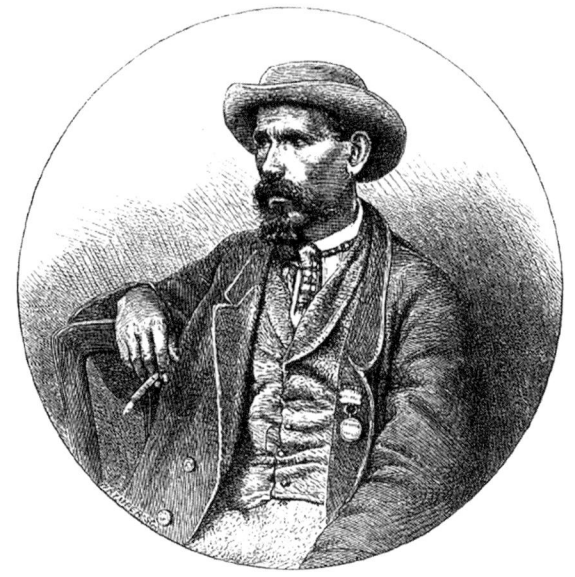

Jean-Antoine Carrel (1869)

Both [Carrels] were bold mountaineers; but Jean-Antoine was incomparably the better man of the two, and he is the finest rock-climber I have ever seen. He was the only man who persistently refused to accept defeat, and who continued to believe, in spite of all discouragements, that the great mountain was not inaccessible, and that it could be ascended from the side of his native valley.

The two Carrels crept noiselessly out before daybreak, and went off. We did not start until nearly seven o'clock, and followed them leisurely, leaving all our properties in the cow-shed; sauntered over the gentian-studded slopes which intervene between the shed and the Glacier du Lion, left cows and their pastures behind, traversed the stony wastes, and arrived at the ice. Old, hard beds of snow lay on its right bank (our left hand), and we mounted over them on to the lower portion of the glacier with ease. But, as we ascended, crevasses became numerous, and we were at last brought to a halt by some which were of very large dimensions; and, as our cutting powers were limited, we sought an easier route, and turned, naturally, to the lower rocks of the Tête du Lion, which overlook the glacier on its west. Some good scrambling took us in a short time on to the crest of the ridge which descends towards the south; and thence, up to the level of the Col du Lion, there was a long natural staircase, on which it was seldom necessary to use the hands. We dubbed the place 'The Great Staircase.' Then the cliffs of the Tête du Lion, which rise above the Couloir, had to be skirted. This part varies considerably in different seasons, and in 1861 we found it difficult; for the fine steady weather of that year had reduced the snow-beds abutting against it to a lower level than usual, and the rocks which were left exposed at the junction of the snow with the cliffs, had few ledges or cracks to which we could hold. But by half-past ten o'clock we stood on the Col, and looked down upon the magnificent basin out of which the Z'Mutt glacier flows. We decided to pass the night upon the Col, for we were charmed with the capabilities of the place, although it was one where liberties could not be taken. On one side a sheer wall overhung the Tiefenmatten glacier. On the other, steep, glassy slopes of hard snow descended to the Glacier du Lion, furrowed by water and by falling stones. On the north there was the great peak of the Matterhorn, and on the south the cliffs of the Tête du Lion.

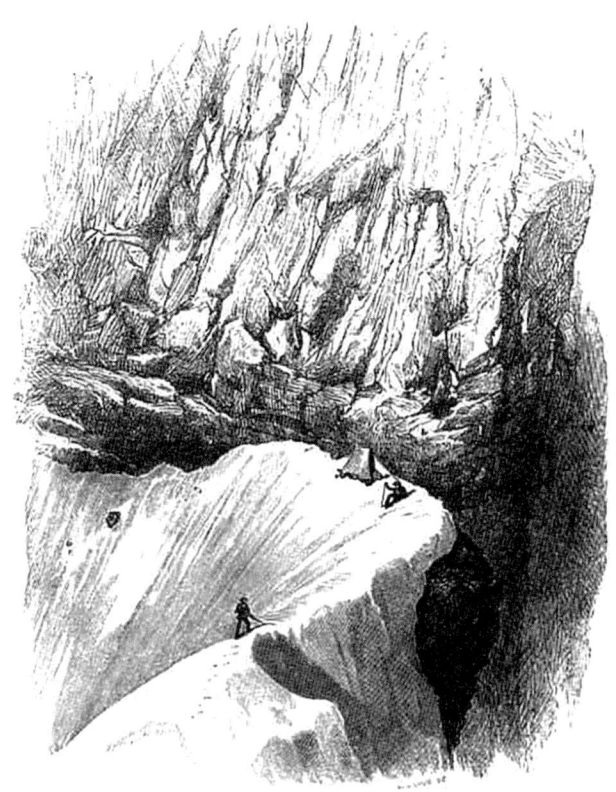

The Col du Lion: Looking Towards The Tête du Lion

We waited for a while, basked in the sunshine, and watched or listened to the Carrels, who were sometimes seen or heard, high above us, upon the ridge leading towards the summit; and, leaving at mid-day, we descended to the cow-shed, packed up the tent and other properties, and returned to the Col, although heavily laden, before six o'clock. This tent was constructed on a pattern suggested by Mr. Francis Galton, and it was not a success. It looked very pretty when set up in London, but it proved thoroughly useless in the Alps … The wind, which playfully careered about the surrounding cliffs, was driven through our gap with the force of a blow-pipe; the flaps of the tent would not keep down, the pegs would not stay in, and it exhibited so marked a desire to go to the top of the Dent Blanche, that we thought it prudent to take it down and to sit upon it. When night came on we wrapped ourselves in it, and made our camp as comfortable as the circumstances would allow. The silence was impressive. No living thing was near our solitary bivouac; the Carrels had turned back and were out of hearing; the stones had ceased to fall, and the trickling water to murmur.

The Carrels had reached a height of 4,032m (13,200 ft) and possessively, Jean-Antoine carved his name in the rock of his mountain. Whymper would do the same in the following year, defiantly, adding his own name above that of Carrel's.

It was bitterly cold. Water froze hard in a bottle under my head. Not surprising, as we were actually on snow, and in a position where the slightest wind was at once felt. For a time we dozed, but about midnight there came from high aloft a tremendous explosion, followed by a second of dead quiet. A great mass of rock had split off, and was descending towards us. My guide started up, wrung his hands, and exclaimed, 'O my God, we are lost!' We heard it coming, mass after mass pouring over the precipices, bounding and rebounding from cliff to cliff, and the great rocks in advance smiting one another. They seemed to be close, although they were probably distant, but some small fragments, which dropped upon us at the same time from the ledges just above, added to the alarm, and my demoralised companion passed the remainder of the night in a state of shudder, ejaculating 'terrible,' and other adjectives.

We put ourselves in motion at daybreak, and commenced the ascent of the south-west ridge. There was no more sauntering with hands in the pockets; each step had to be earned by downright climbing. But it was the most pleasant kind of climbing. The rocks were fast and unencumbered with débris; the cracks were good, although not numerous, and there was nothing to fear except from one's-self. So we thought, at least, and shouted to awake echoes from the cliffs. Ah! there is no response. Not yet; wait a while, everything here is upon a superlative scale; count a dozen, and then the echoes will return from the walls of the Dent d'Hérens, miles away, in waves of pure and undefiled sound; soft, musical, and sweet. Halt a moment to regard the view! We overlook the Tête du Lion, and nothing except the Dent d'Hérens, whose summit is still a thousand feet above us, stands in the way. The ranges of the Graian Alps — an ocean of mountains — are seen, at a glance, governed by their three great peaks, the Grivola, Grand Paradis, and Tour de St. Pierre. How soft, and yet how sharp, they look in the early morning! The mid-day mists have not begun to rise; nothing is obscured; even the pointed Viso, all but a hundred miles away, is perfectly defined.

Turn to the east, and watch the sun's slanting rays coming across the Monte Rosa snow-fields. Look at the shadowed parts, and see how even they — radiant with reflected light — are more brilliant than man knows how to depict. See, how — even there — the gentle undulations give shadows within shadows; and how — yet again — where falling stones or ice have left a track, there are shadows upon shadows, each with a light and a dark side, with infinite gradations of matchless tenderness. Then, note the sunlight as it steals noiselessly along, and reveals countless unsuspected forms; — the delicate ripple-lines which mark the concealed crevasse, and the waves of drifted snow; producing each minute more lights and fresh shadows; sparkling on the edges and glittering on the ends of the icicles; shining on the heights and illuminating the depths, until all is aglow, and the dazzled eye returns for relief to the sombre crags.

Hardly an hour had passed since we left the Col before we arrived at the 'Chimney' ... a smooth, straight slab of rock was fixed, at a considerable angle, between two others equally smooth. My companion essayed to go up, and, after crumpling his long body into many ridiculous positions, he said that he would not, for he could not, do it. With some little trouble I got up it unassisted, and then my guide tied himself on to the end of our rope, and I endeavoured to pull him up. But he was so awkward that he did little for himself, and so heavy that he proved too much for me, and after several attempts he untied himself, and quietly observed that he should go down. I told him he was a coward, and *he* mentioned his opinion of me. I requested him to go to Breil, and to say that he had left his 'monsieur' on the mountain, and he turned to go; whereupon I had to eat humble pie and ask him to come back; for, although it was not very difficult to go up, and not at all dangerous with a man standing below, it was quite another thing to come down, as the lower edge overhung in a provoking manner.

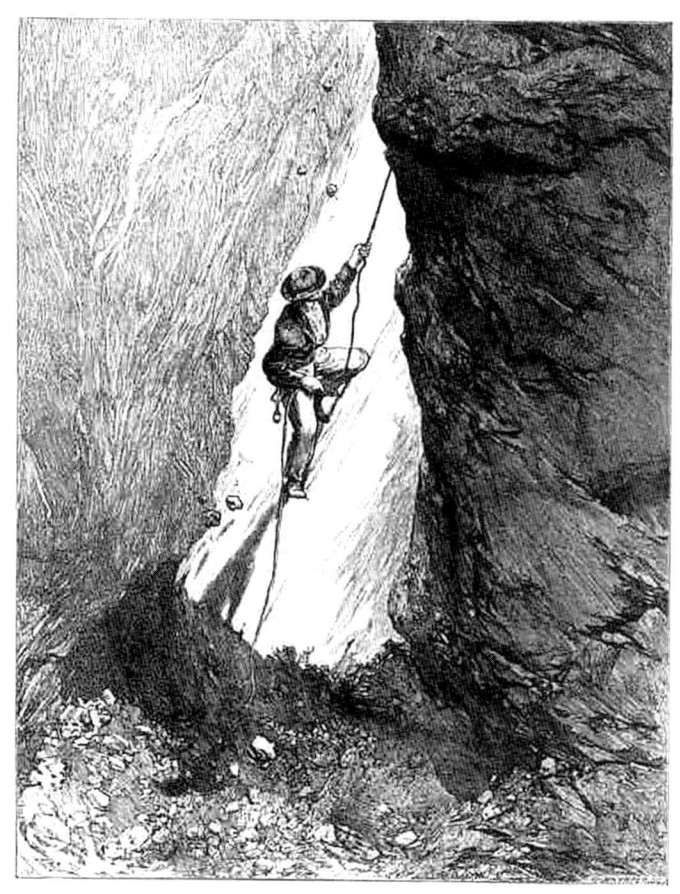

'The Chimney'

The day was perfect; the sun was pouring down grateful warmth; the wind had fallen; the way seemed clear, no insuperable obstacle was in sight; yet what could one do alone? I stood on the top, chafing under this unexpected contretemps, and remained for some time irresolute; but as it became apparent that the Chimney was swept more frequently than was necessary ... I turned at last, descended with the assistance of my companion, and returned with him to Breil, where we arrived about mid-day.

I left Breil with the conviction that it was little use for a single tourist to organise an attack upon it, so great was its influence on the morals of the guides, and persuaded that it was desirable at least two should go, to back each other when required: and departed with my guide over the Col Théodule, longing, more than before, to make the ascent, and determined to return, if possible with a companion, to lay siege to the mountain until one or the other was vanquished.

(*Ibid.*, pp. 42–57)

SPRING 2015

AUTHOR'S LOG

I returned to the Alps in May, with the intention of capturing some images that reflected the season. While blankets of snow undoubtedly present a clean and enchanting landscape, I believe an image is more engaging with additional colour. Snow-capped peaks also appeal more than a mountain without any remaining snow, so the hope was that May would provide the perfect balance.

While Edward Whymper is best known for making the first ascent of the Matterhorn, and while the Matterhorn is the focus of this book, he also made the first ascent of dozens of other Alpine peaks. His book, *The Ascent of the Matterhorn* covers some of these other mountains in great detail. It was therefore felt that this book would be incomplete without looking at and visiting some of those other peaks.

With the aim of visiting various regions, the logical location to base myself was Chamonix for the most part, and this is where I settled. Chamonix is located at the foot of Mont Blanc, which at 4,810 m (15,781 ft) is the highest mountain in the Alps, and therefore a very popular tourist destination. Visiting between the winter and summer seasons meant that it was particularly quiet, which suited me, and would allow me to make changes to my plans at short notice.

Whymper spent quite a bit of time in the Mont Blanc massif, particularly in 1864 and 1865. The pictures I took of the area during my trip appear in chapters 9 and 10.

No visit to Chamonix would be complete without a gondola ride to the top of the Aiguille du Midi 3,842m (12,605 ft), the Needle of the South, and this was high on my agenda, as it provided the ideal viewpoint from which to photograph Grandes Jorasses 4,208m (13,806 ft), an unusually formed mountain with peaks at either end, rather like a set of horns. As Grandes Jorasses was east of Aiguille du Midi, I needed to photograph it later in the day and, having relatively quick access to the summit, I decided to wait for a partly cloudy sky. After several days, the conditions seemed right and I made my way up, with two hours in which to work before the final car was scheduled to descend. From my vantage point, the peaks of Grandes Jorasses made only the briefest of appearances and, frustratingly, it continued like this for an hour and a half.

Anxious that I had miscalculated the weather, I scanned through what I'd photographed thus far, hoping that one of the images would do the mountain justice. Then, with less than half an hour to go, an increasing amount of clear sky appeared, and within a few more minutes, both ends of Grandes Jorasses could be seen at once, with swirling cloud to the left, right and below: perfect! I was certain that I had the photograph I had envisaged and believed I could not have achieved better when, suddenly, half-a-dozen climbers appeared in the bottom of the view, adding a real sense of scale and drama. With time to compose just two photographs, I got what I felt was a truly unique picture and could then turn my attention to my next objective.

As Edward Whymper had made most of his attempts to climb the Matterhorn from Italy, I was keen to include some photographs from that direction, and to do so while there was still sufficient snow to highlight the rugged south face. A very early start and a breathtaking drive up the Valtournenche Valley took me to Breuil-Cervinia shortly after sunrise on a lovely warm, sunny day. Excited to visit the hamlet about which Whymper had written so frequently, and which had been the setting for the anxious days immediately before the final race for the summit, I sought out the small lake, Lac Bleu, which I felt offered the finest viewpoint of the Matterhorn from the south.

A clear, emerald-blue lake, Lac Bleu is sheltered from the wind and perfectly positioned to reflect the Matterhorn across its still surface. Unsurprisingly, I returned there several times throughout the day. I reconnoitred and photographed the Matterhorn from various other locations, although some viewpoints that I had had in mind were still cut of by snow and would have to wait until the summer.

My next assignment was to head south to the Dauphiné Alps and, in particular, to the Écrins National Park, established in 1973. The highlight of Whymper's 1861 trip had been his two challenging attempts to climb Mont Pelvoux 3,946m (12,946 ft), considered at that time to be the highest mountain in the whole of France. The account of his visit to that region sums up better than anywhere else in his writings the somewhat estranged relationship between the British mountaineers and the native people.

Mont Pelvoux is an attractive mountain and, as on each previous trip, I had tried to determine the ideal viewpoint before setting off. With plans in place to photograph three mountains over two days, I made my way to the park. The journey ended up taking more than double the estimated four hours, as a result of having to double-back twice after finding closed mountain passes. Knowing I would not reach the park in time, I shelved my plans to hike up to the high mountain hut, and resolved to stay at the accommodation at the start of the trail instead. However, it was after 11 p.m. when I eventually arrived, and the lodge was already closed for the night. I had no alternative other than to spend the night on the back seat of the very small rental car.

After a better night's sleep than anticipated — no doubt helped by being particularly tired after the long drive — I was awake an hour before dawn, and made my way up the mountainside towards the mountain hut where I'd originally planned to spend the night. As always it was wonderful to be out at the start of the day and to witness my surroundings come to life. Seeing the mountains change from cold blue shadows, to warm orange, then a yellow glow in the crisp, clear air is enough to reward the weariest spirit. Eventually, after two hours, I reached a great viewpoint for Mont Pelvoux and photographed it just as envisaged.

From there, I wandered for another four hours, capturing a number of images that had not been planned, but which I believed would give an admirable impression of the views Whymper had enjoyed so much.

My final destination for this trip was Zermatt, with six days allocated and two primary objectives in mind: to photograph the north face of the Matterhorn from the Zmutt Valley; and to obtain an aerial view by taking to the sky in a tandem paraglider.

Planning is an important aspect of photography, but time and chance certainly play their part. Having just spent several days in a balmy 31 degrees Celsius, the temperature and conditions changed dramatically with snowfall on the day I relocated, leaving up to twelve inches on the ground at Zermatt. This provided an unexpected bonus, and with clearing skies, a wonderful tree-shrouded photograph of the Matterhorn was taken early the next morning along its north-east ridge.

Unlike Scotland, the Alps often appear against a cloudless blue sky and, as I mentioned earlier, I prefer some cloud in my photographs. So, in what appeared to be the most ideal conditions, I set off up the Zmutt Valley in the late afternoon, with the aim of photographing the full north face at the end of the day … hopefully, with the last of the sunlight or with a partly cloudy sky; maybe even both.

Arriving at my destination, I set up the camera and stationed myself there for an hour or so, photographing every fifteen minutes as the sun descended, the haze cleared and the shadows lengthened. With less than half an hour before the sun was due to set, I started to head back down the track, keeping the camera on the tripod, poised over my shoulder, ready to capture the view if conditions improved further.

And improve they did. With the Matterhorn behind me, it was difficult to walk down the track without stumbling, as every time I looked over my shoulder the mountain had changed, taking on a warmer, more orange appearance, with low cloud building ever so gradually. Stopping and photographing every five minutes, thinking each time would be the last, I was sure the cloud would swallow up the mountain or that the sun would be lost behind the cloud. Reaching a viewpoint I'd noted on the way up, I stopped again, this time until the sunlight was finally snuffed out. I could not have been more content, and with the combined images produced from the trip, felt particularly satisfied with my two weeks in May.

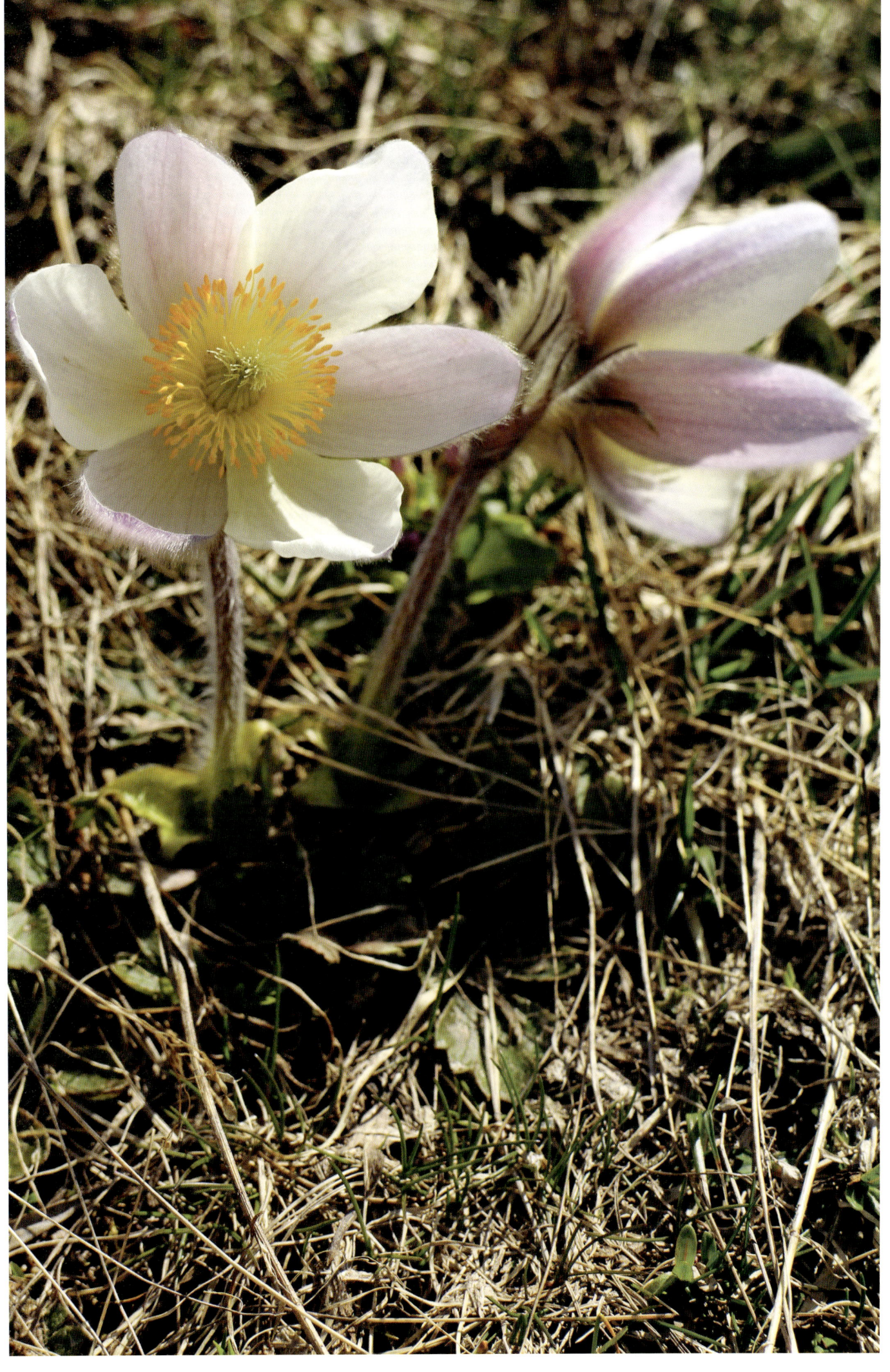

ANEMONE ALPINE

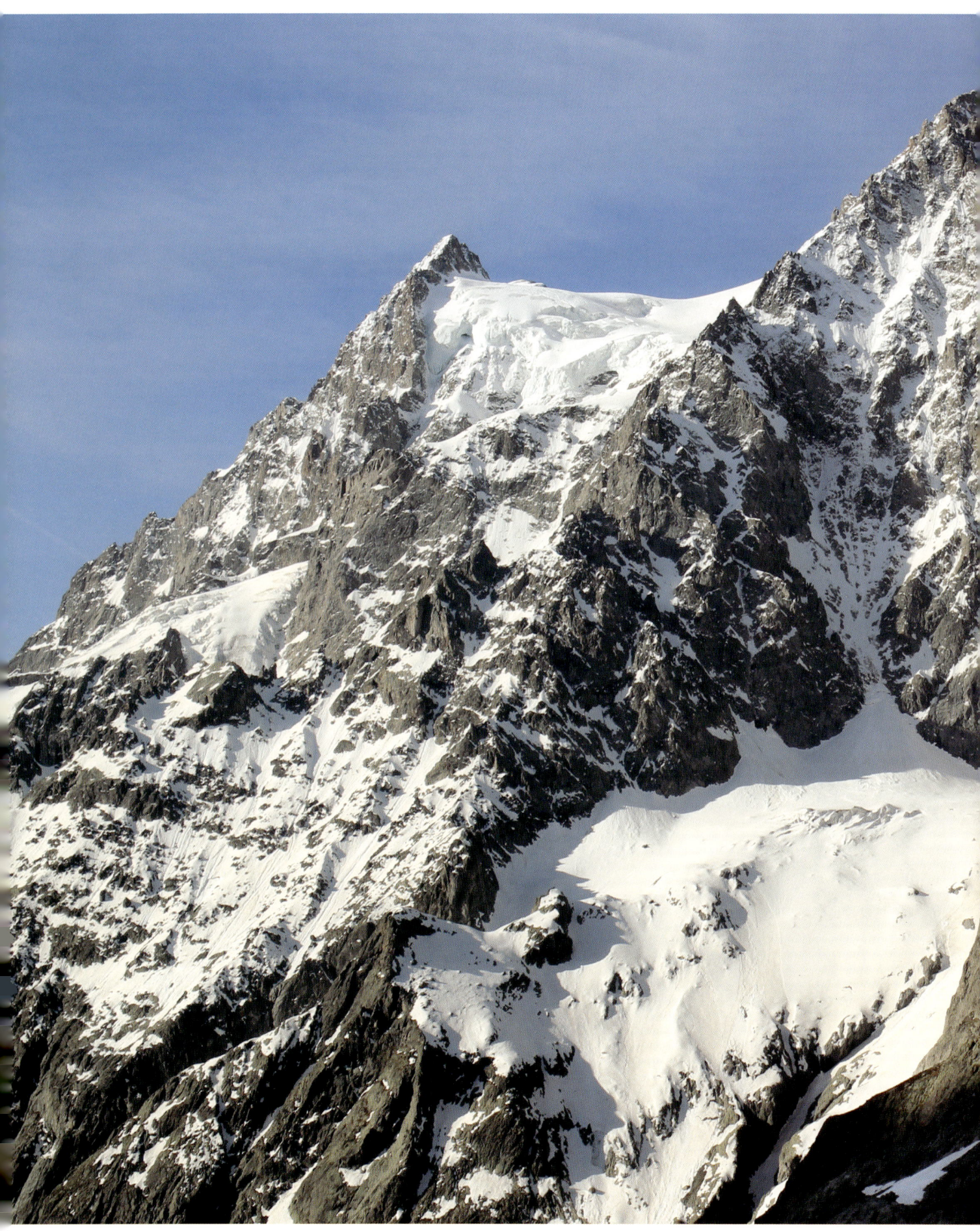
MONT PELVOUX 3,946M, MASSIF DES ÉCRINS, DAUPHINÉ ALPS

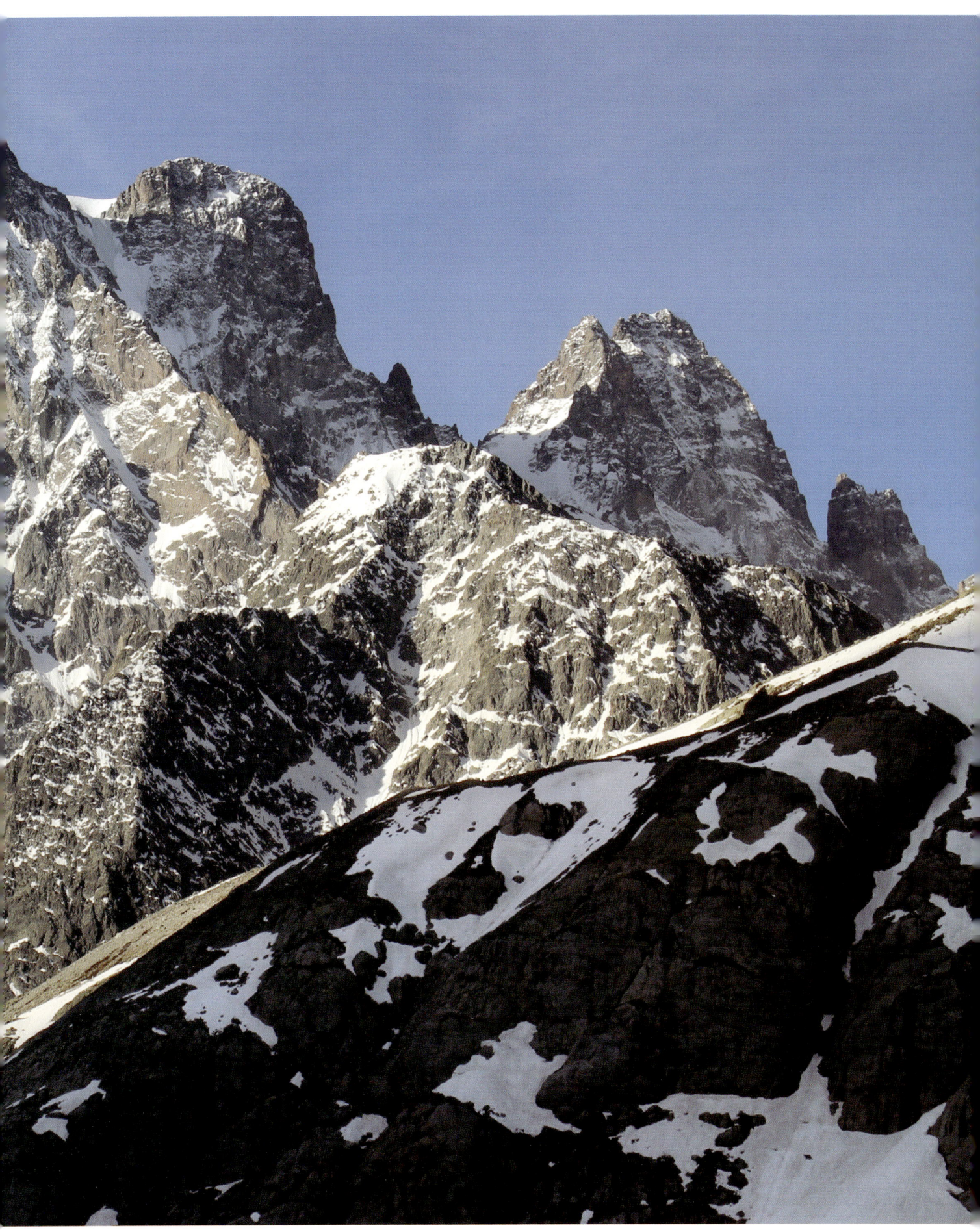

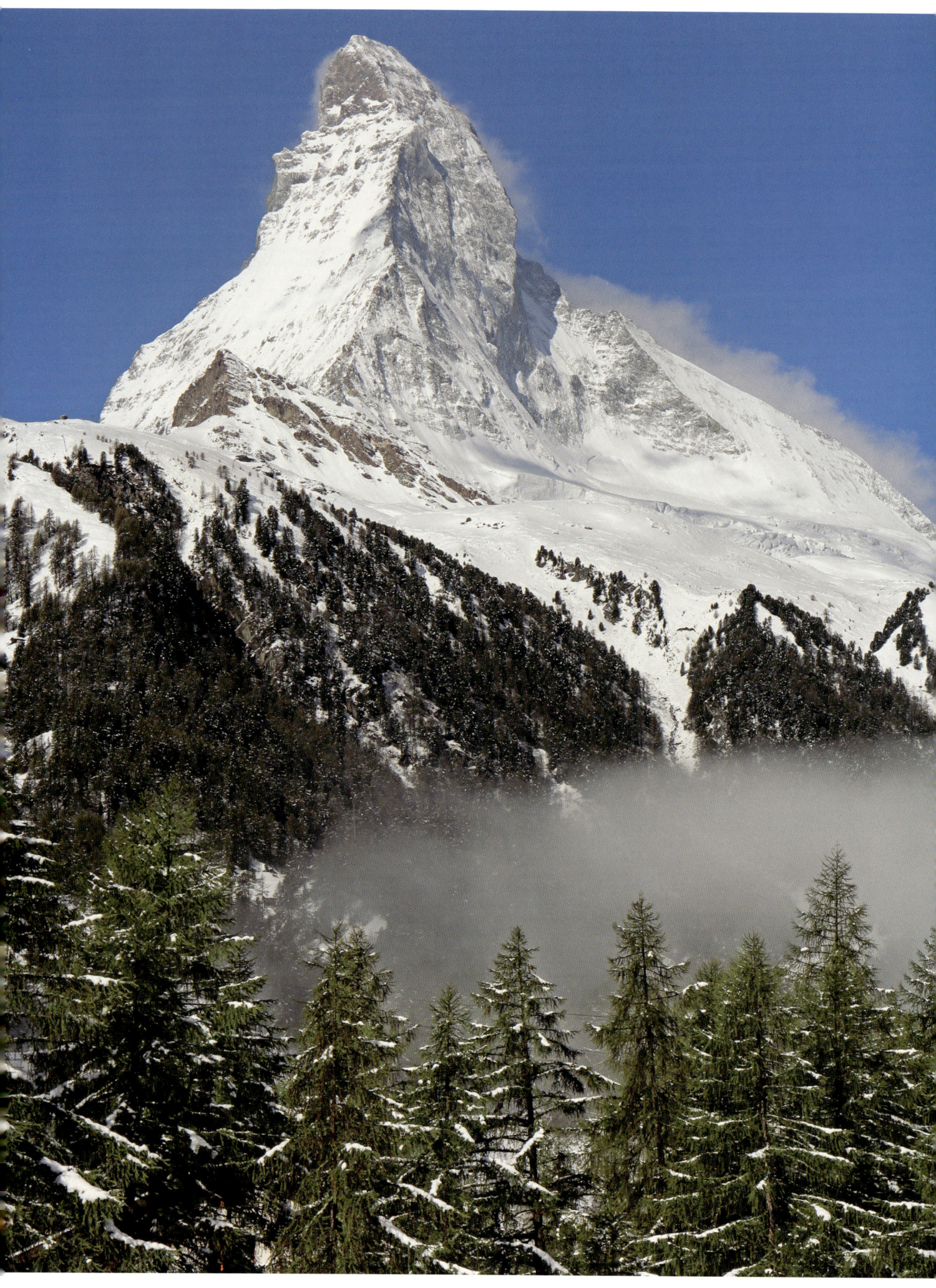

A LATE SNOWFALL IN SPRING AS TEMPERATURES PLUMMETED

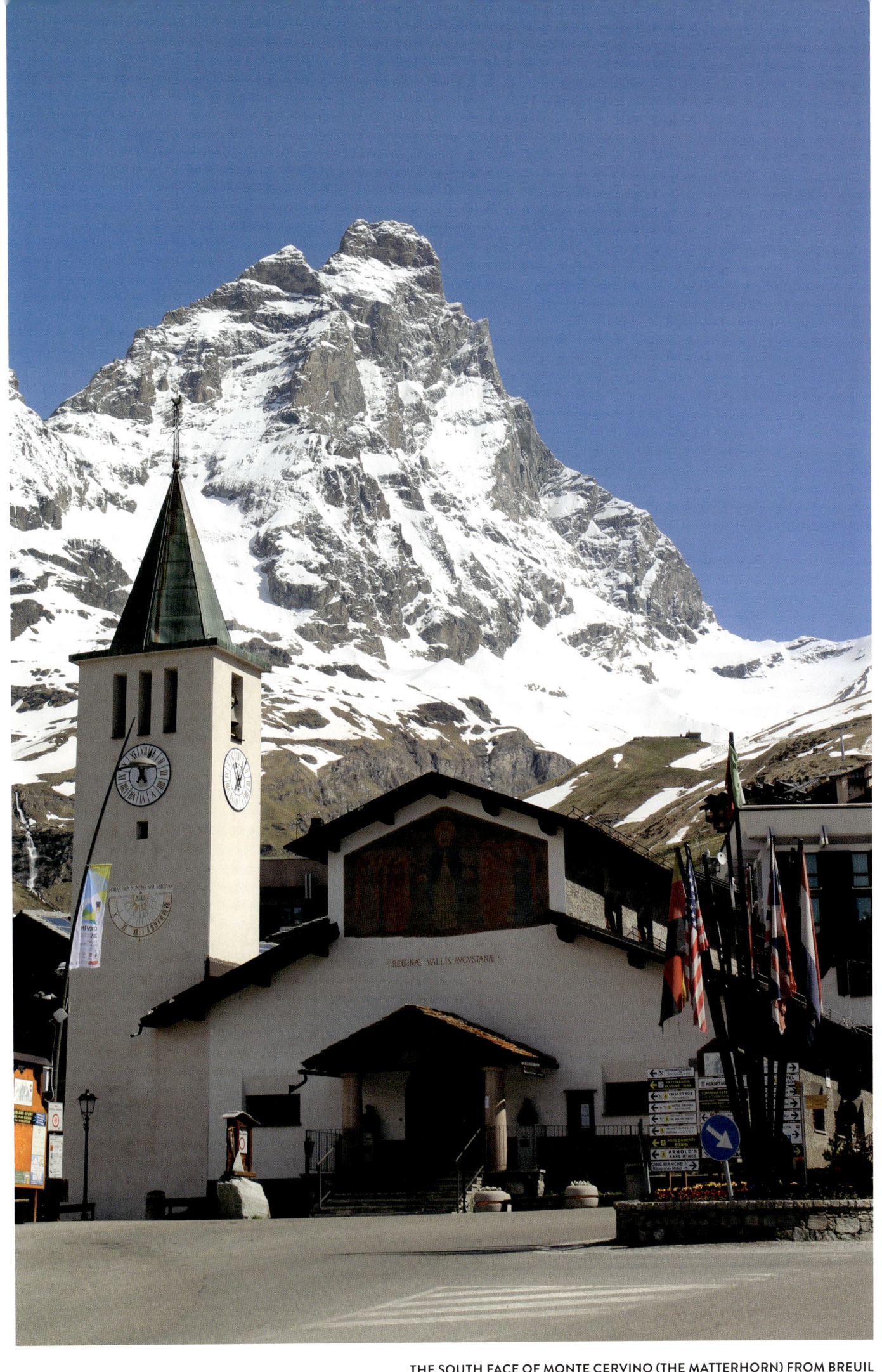

THE SOUTH FACE OF MONTE CERVINO (THE MATTERHORN) FROM BREUIL

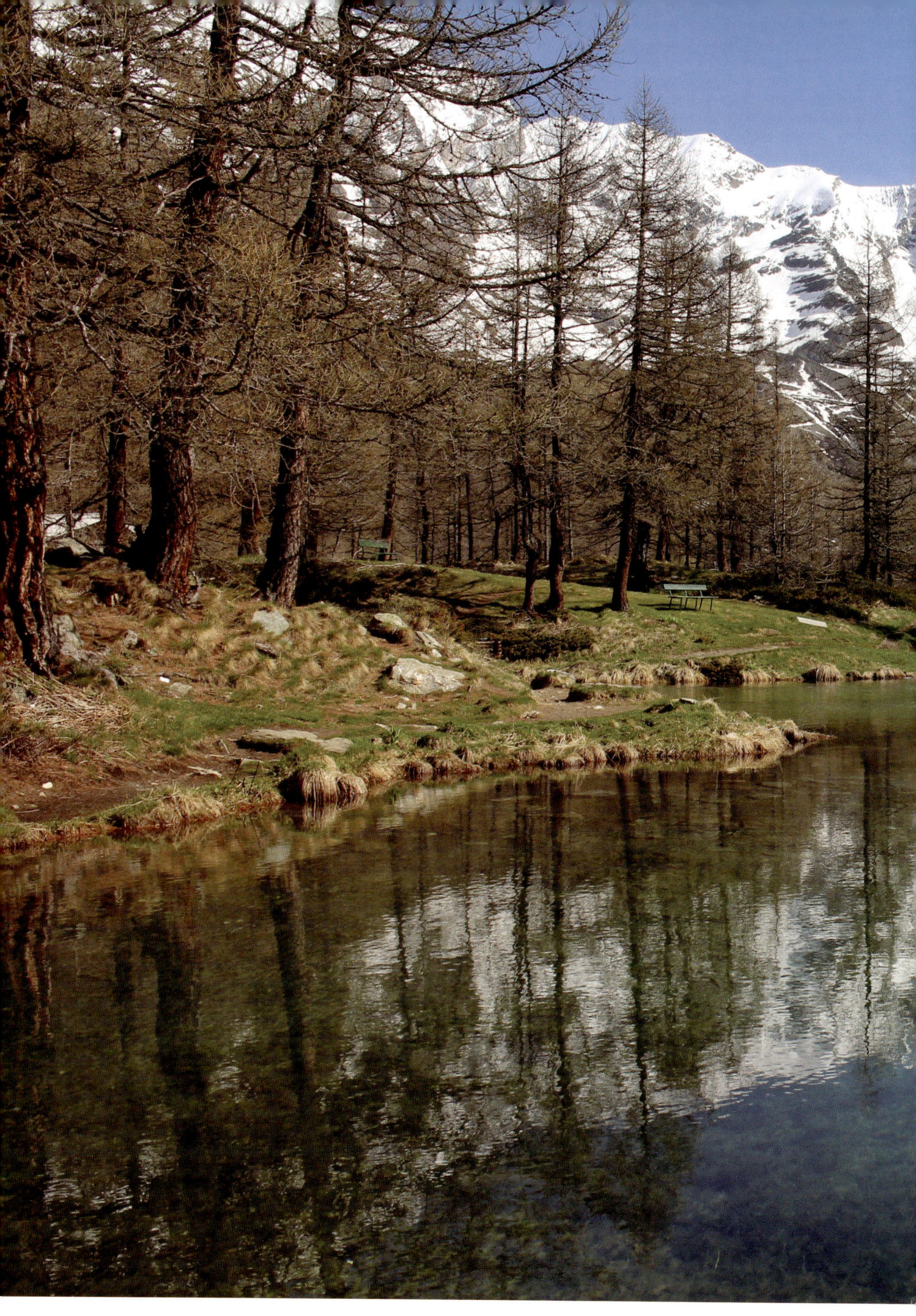

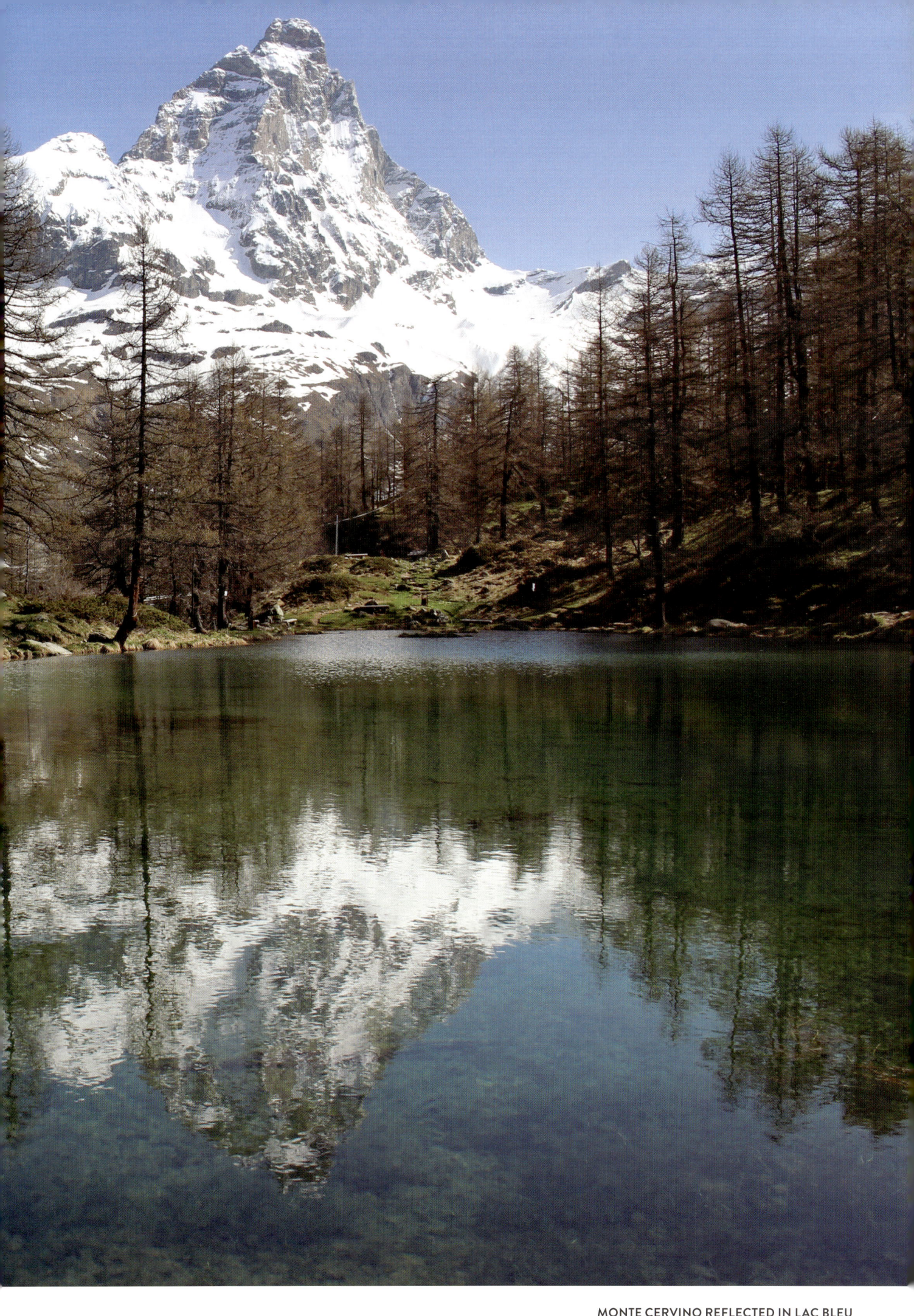

MONTE CERVINO REFLECTED IN LAC BLEU

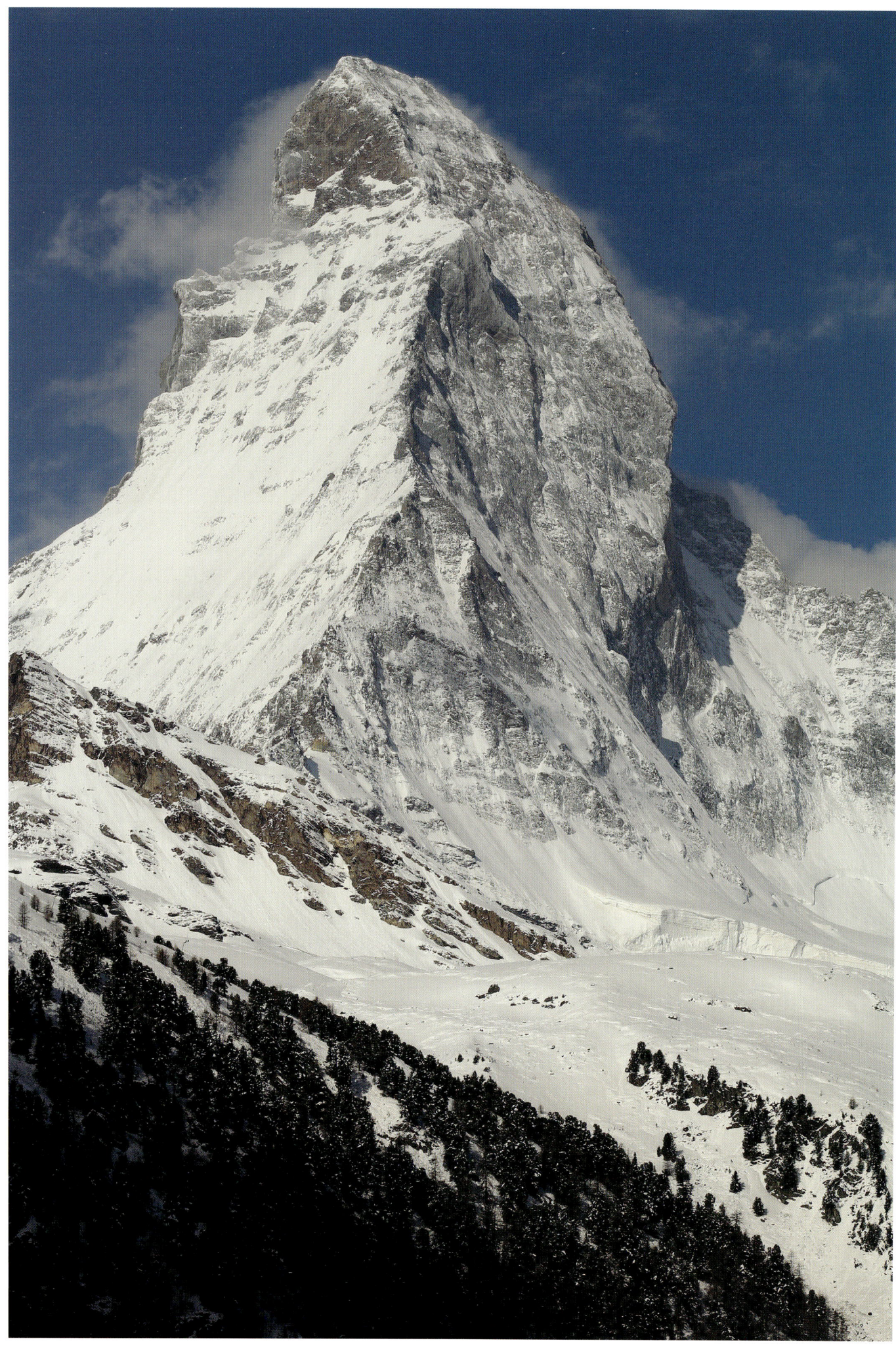

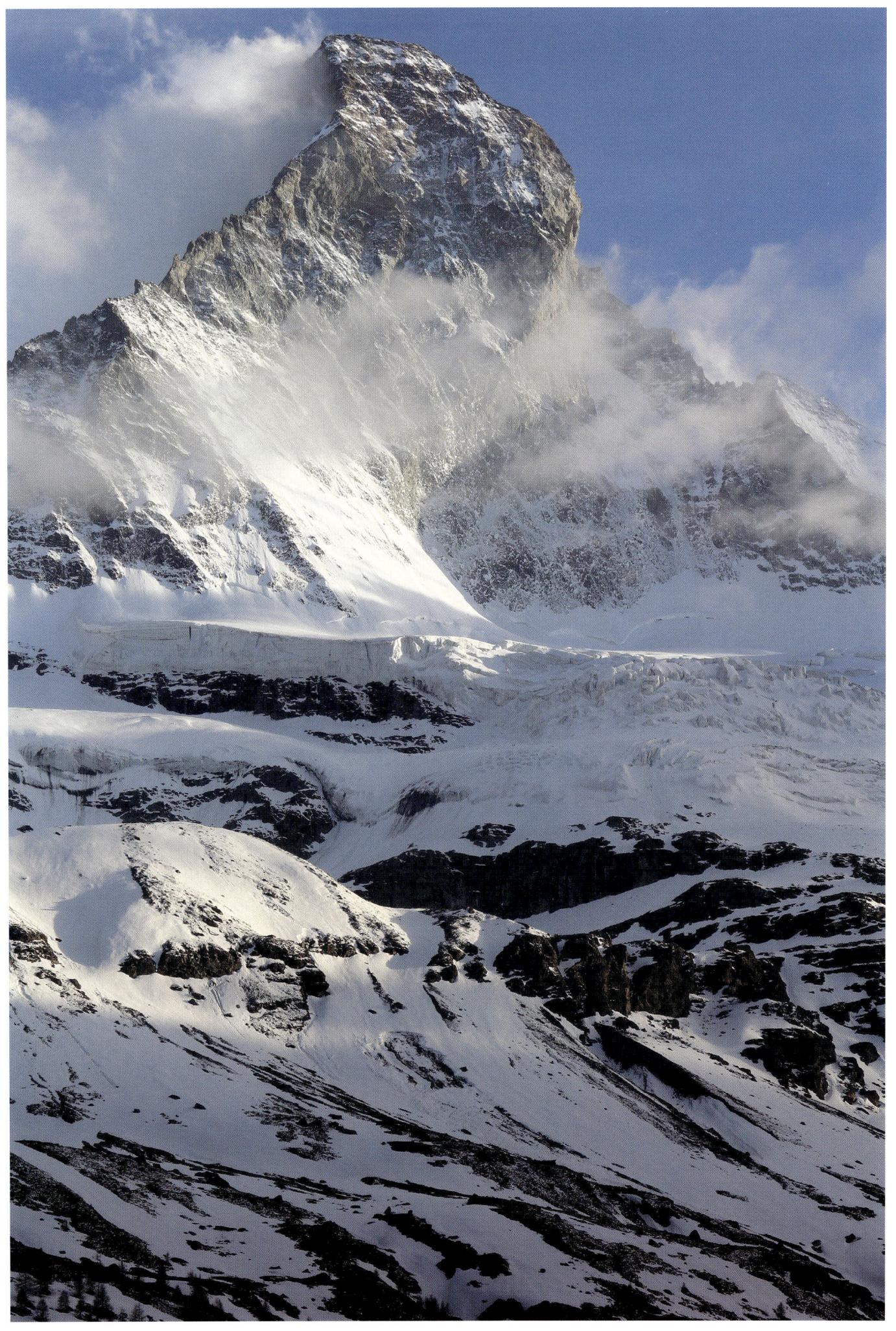

THE NORTH FACE OF THE MATTERHORN FROM THE ZMUTT VALLEY

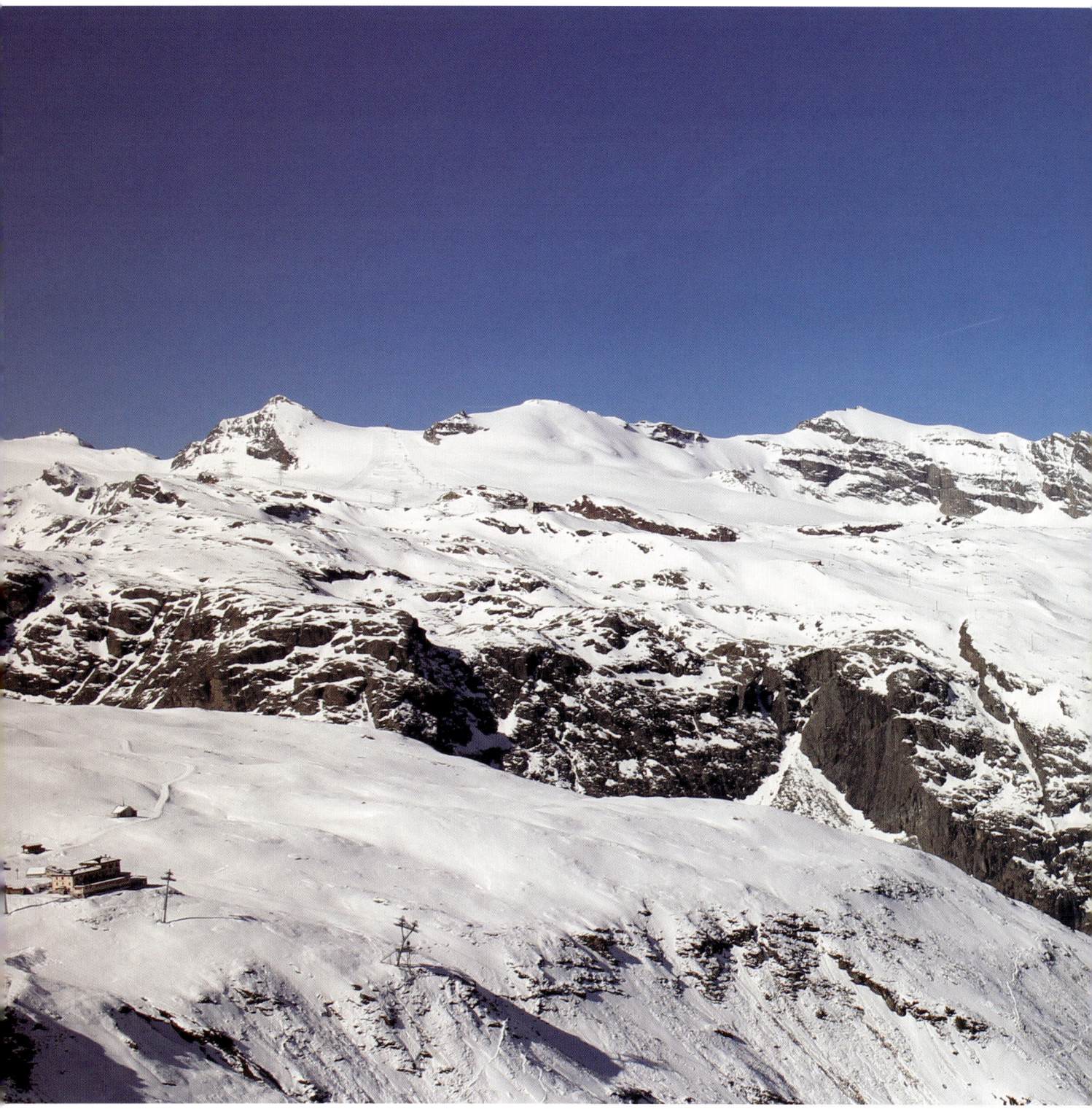

THE MATTERHORN FROM GORNERGRAT

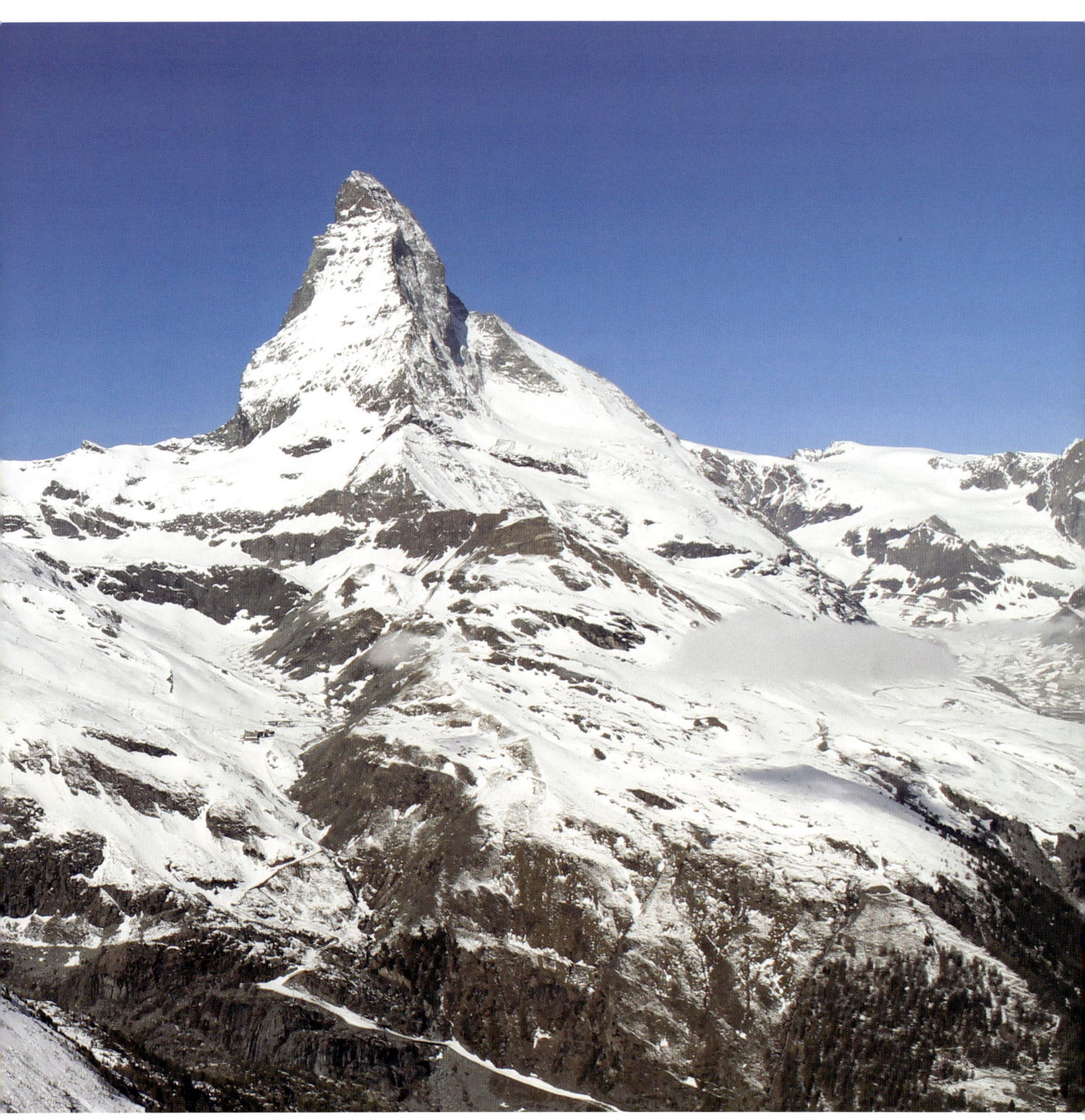

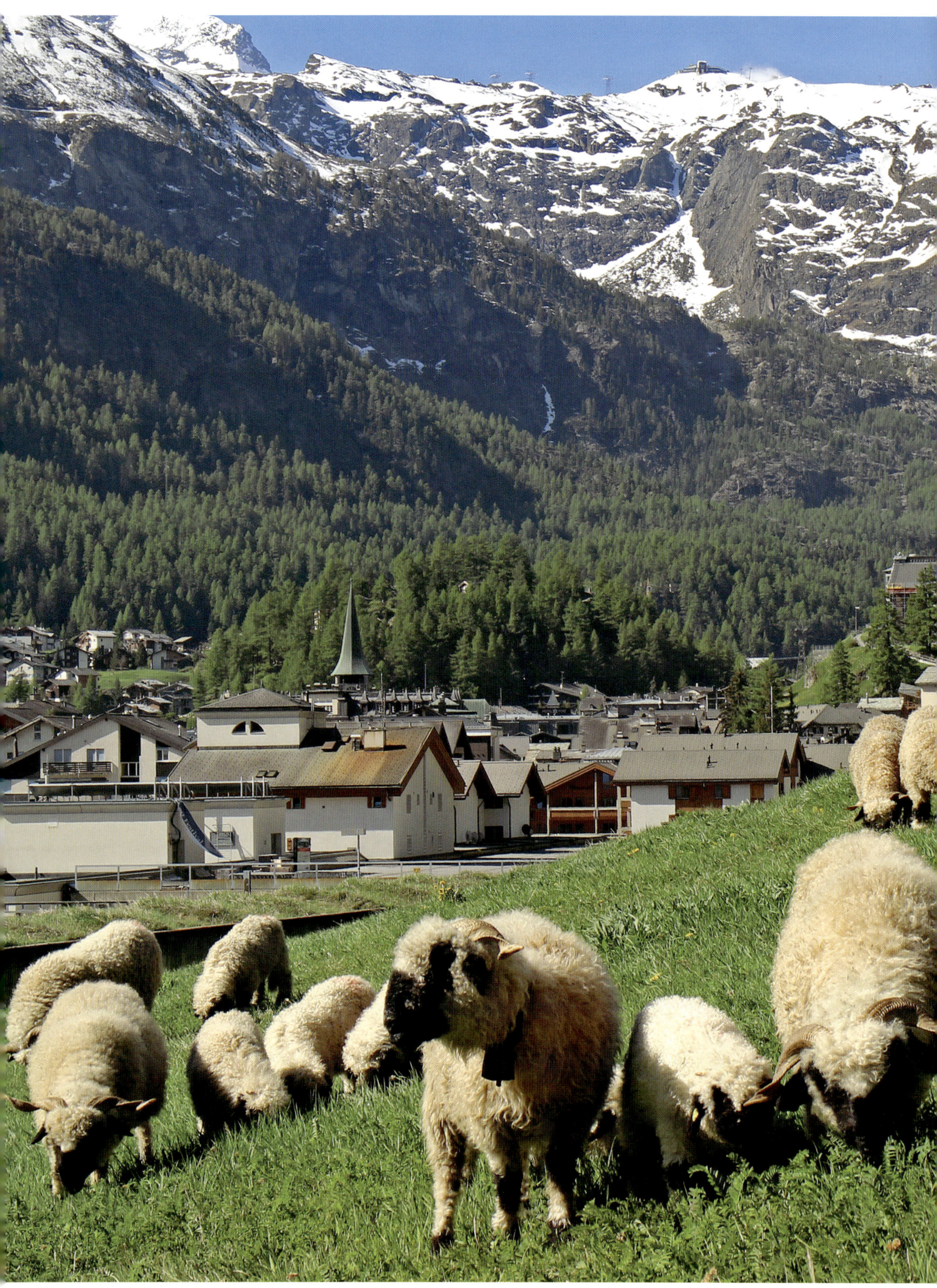

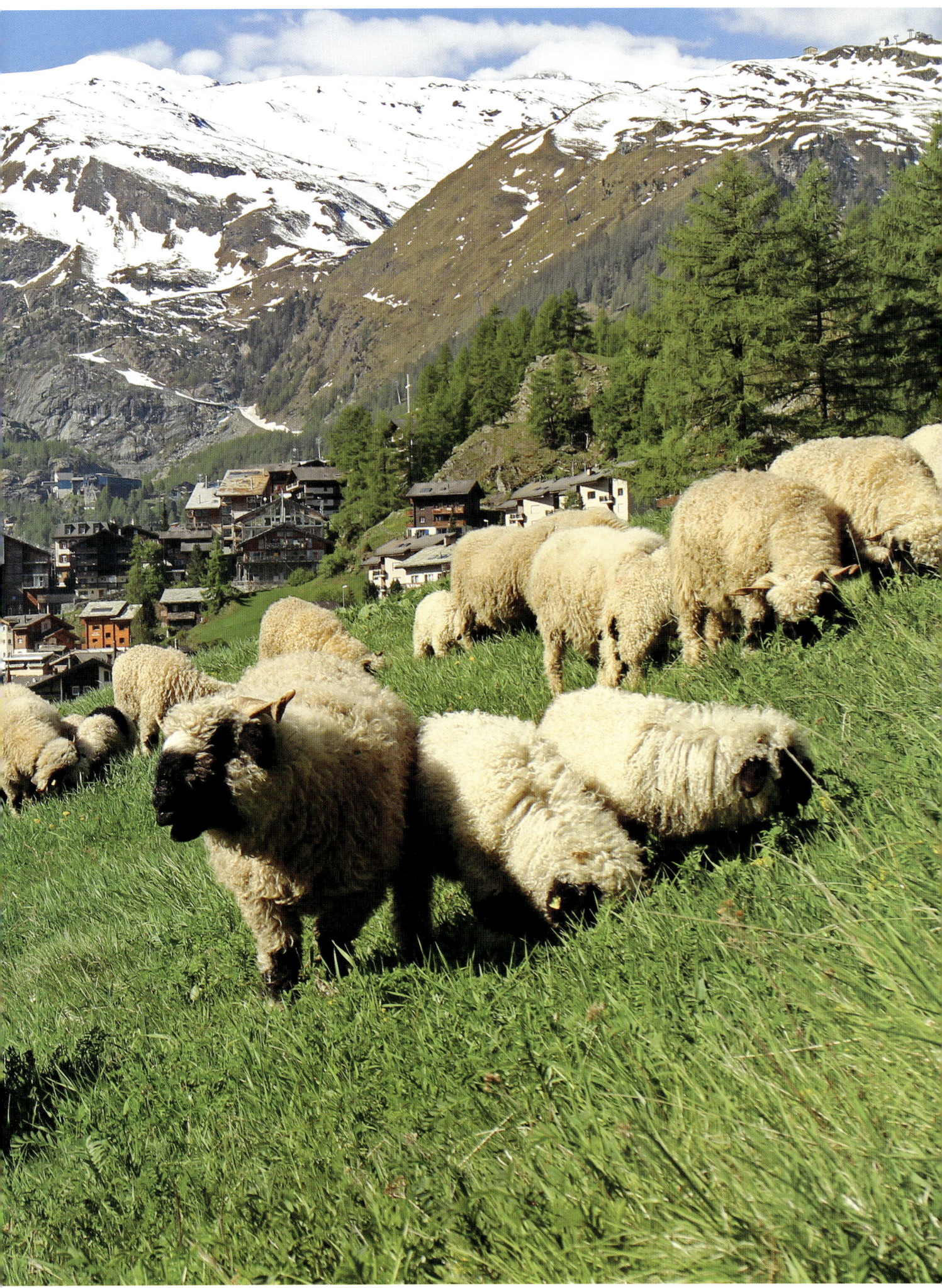

VALAIS BLACKNOSE SHEEP

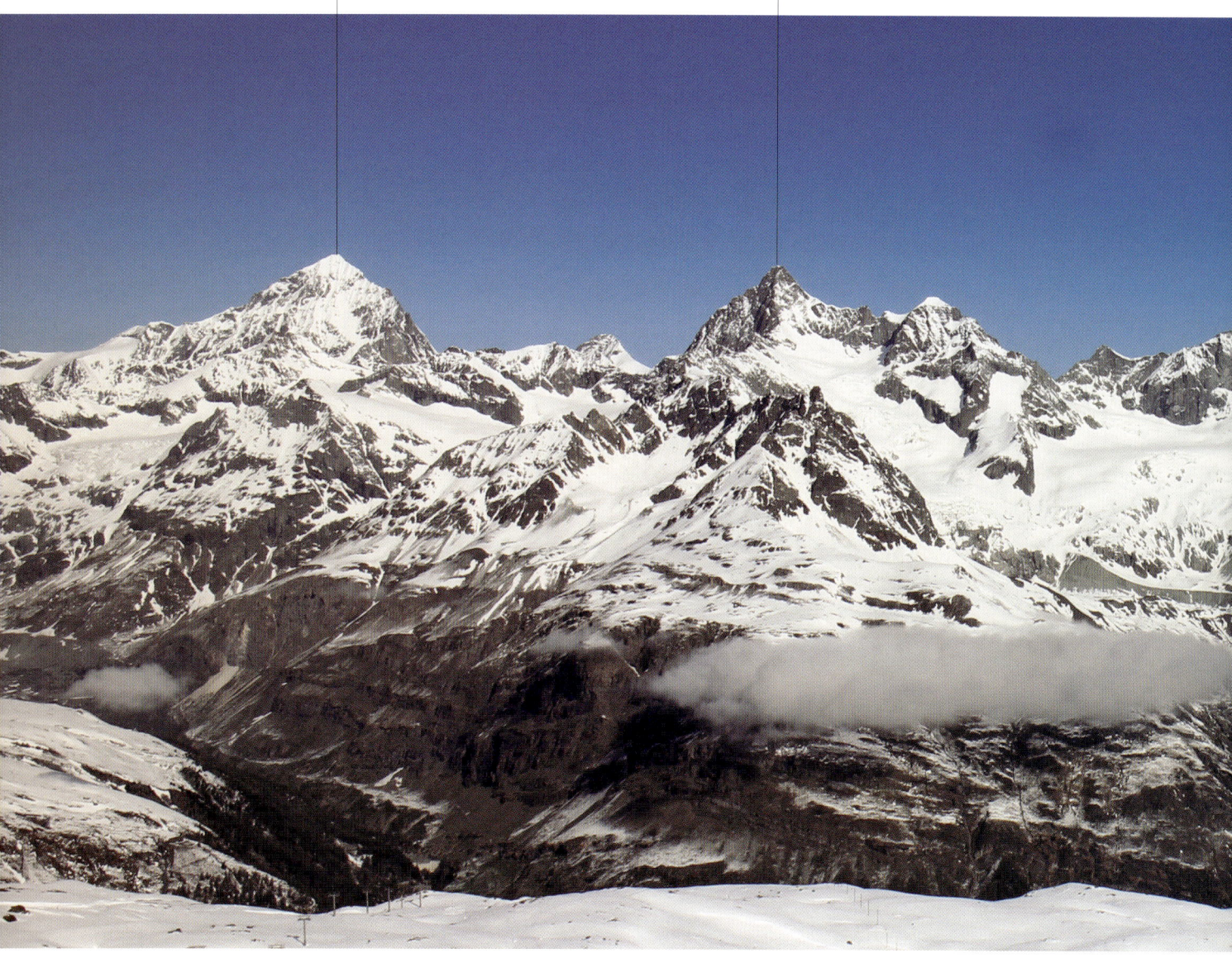

Dent Blanche 4,357m *Ober Gabelhorn 4,063m*

THE 4,000M NORTHERNLY PEAK ABOVE ZERMATT

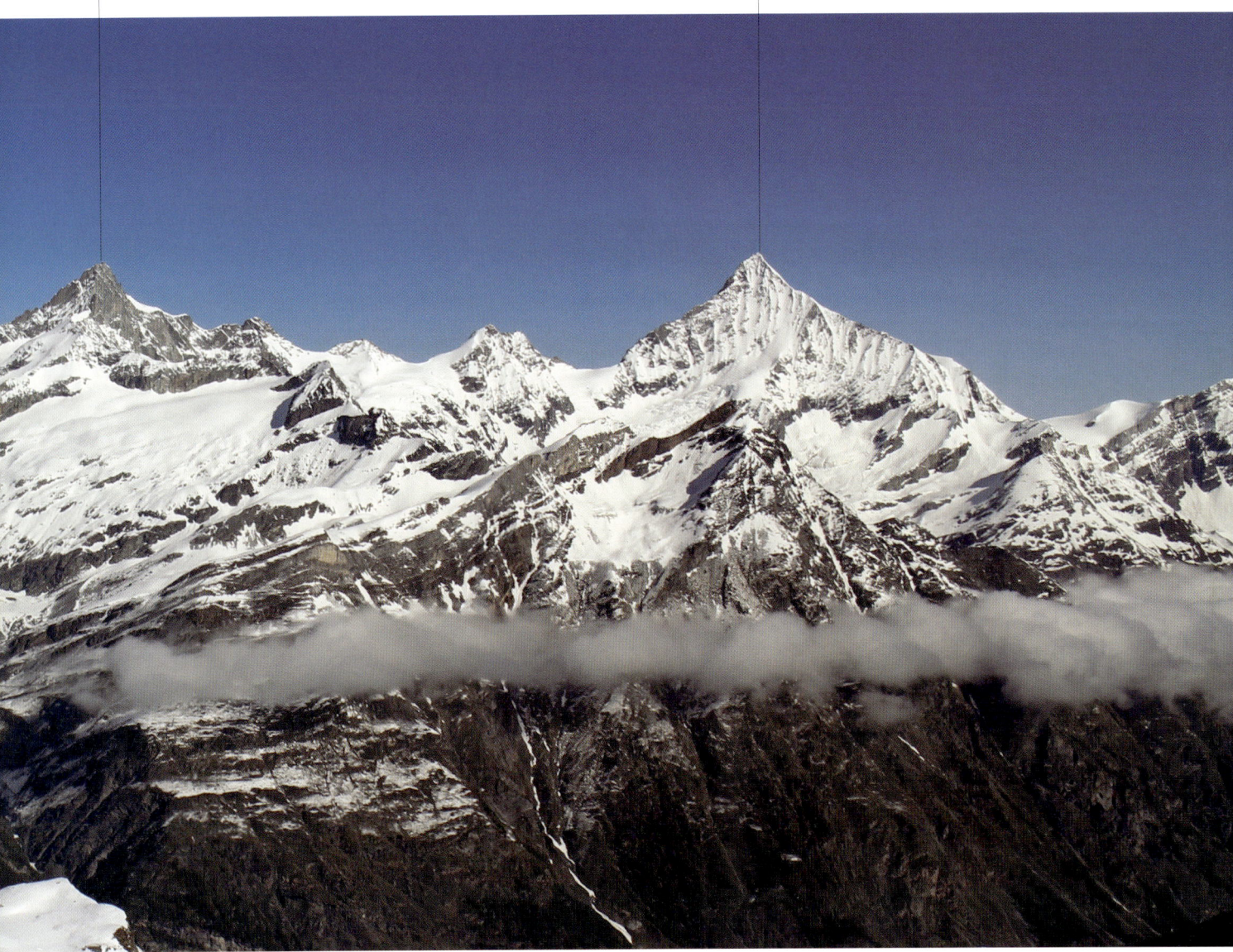

Zinalrothorn 4,221m

Weisshorn 4,506m

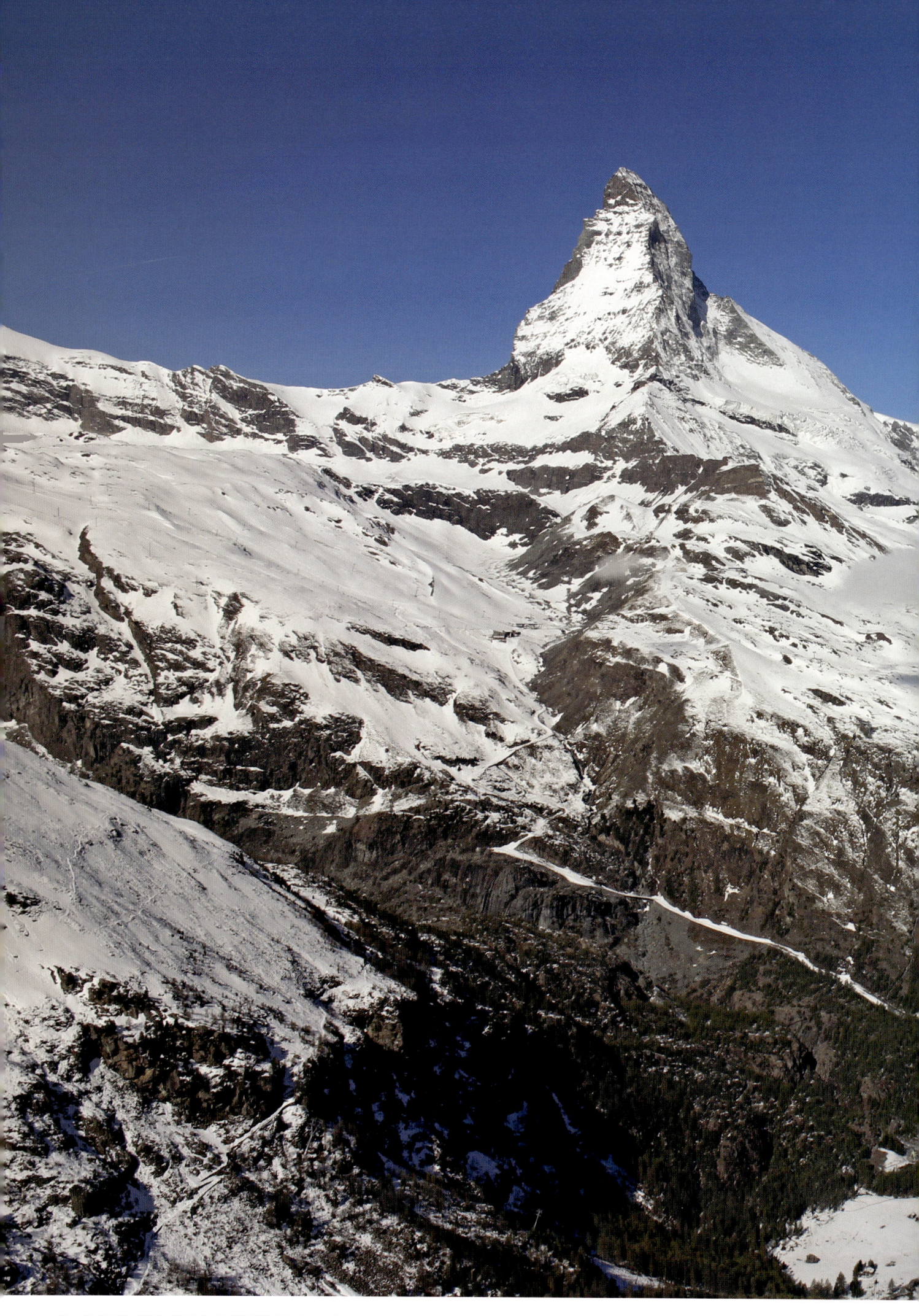

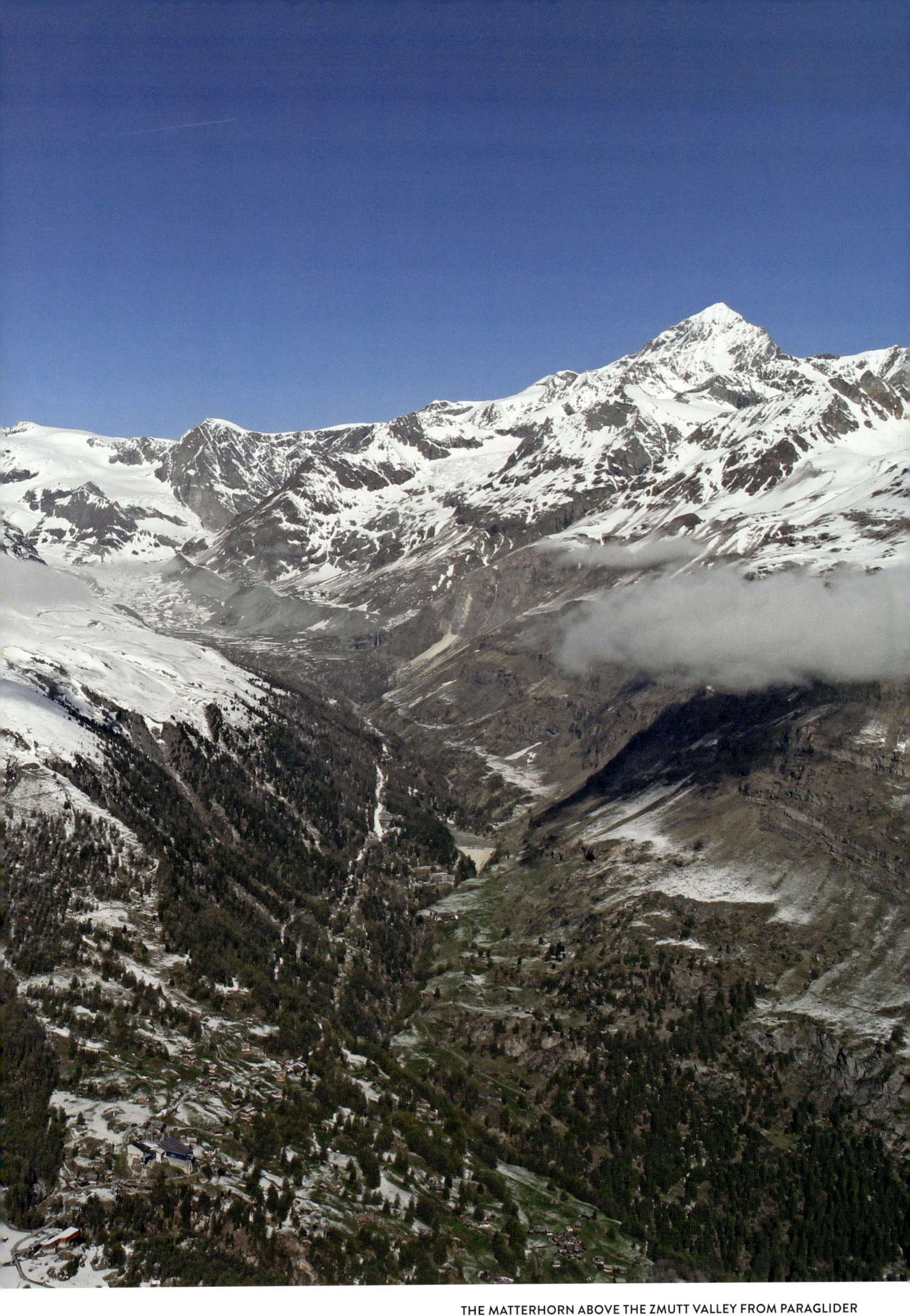

THE MATTERHORN ABOVE THE ZMUTT VALLEY FROM PARAGLIDER

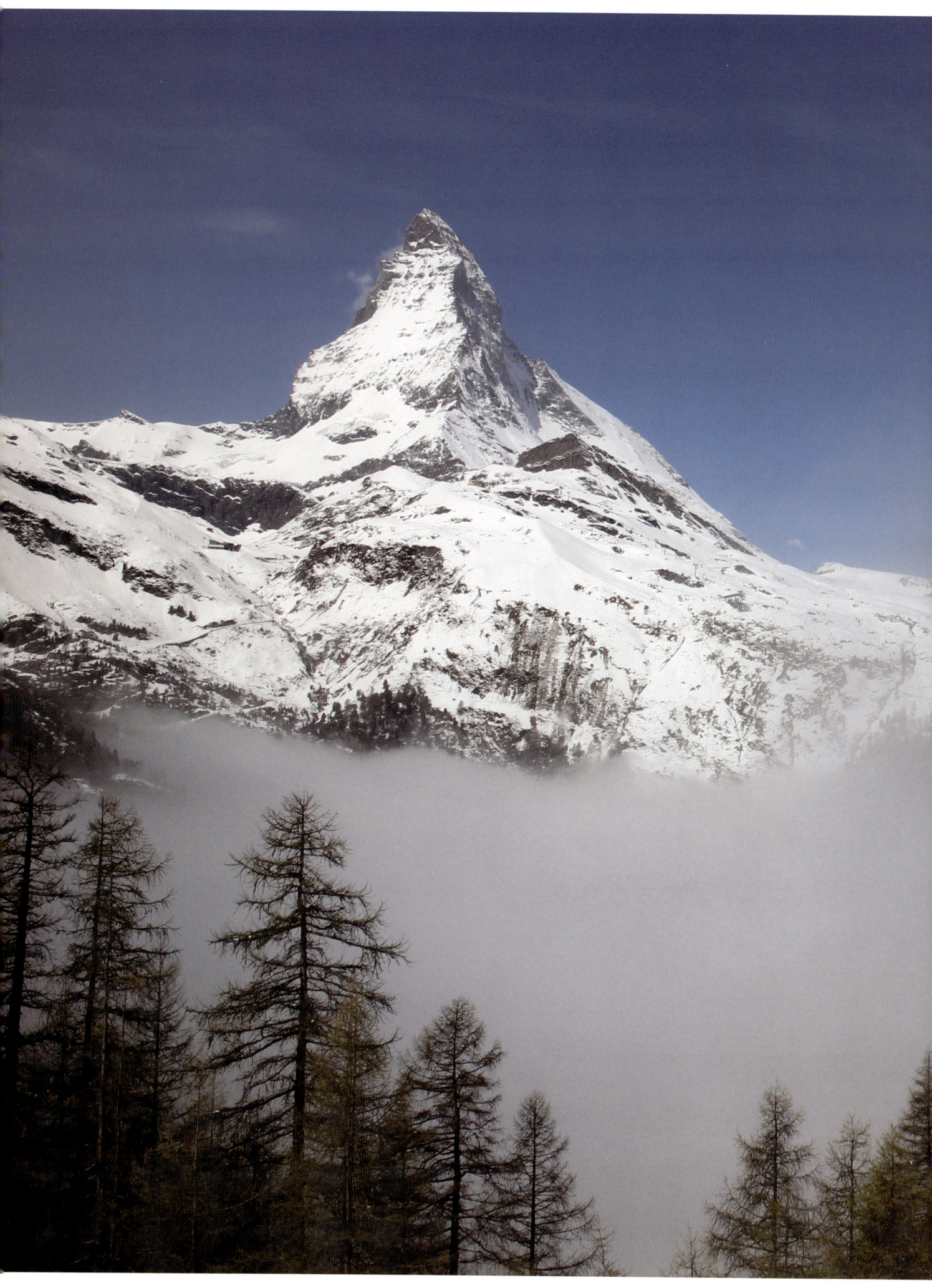

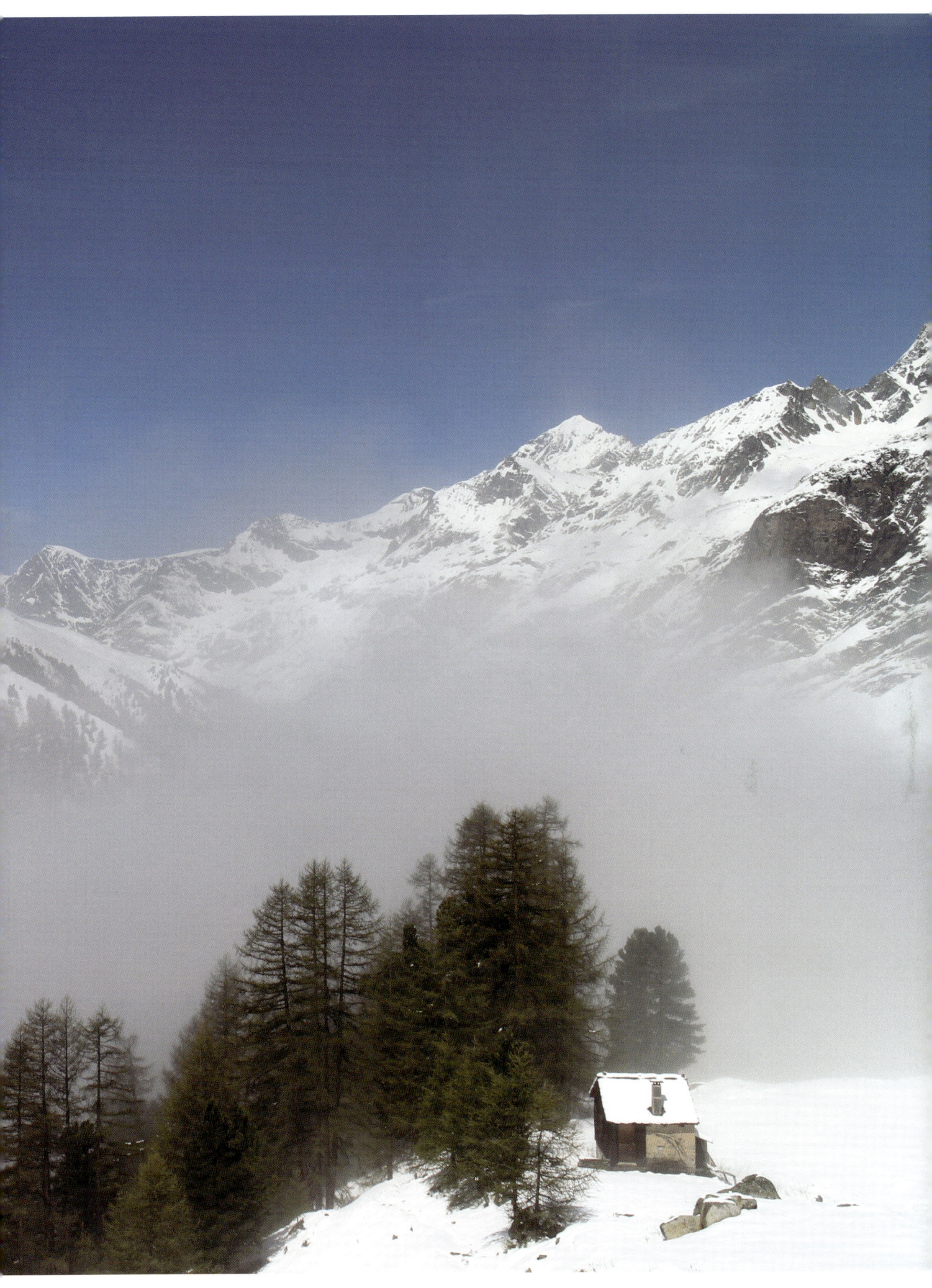

THE MATTERHORN RISING BEYOND THE VALLEY MIST

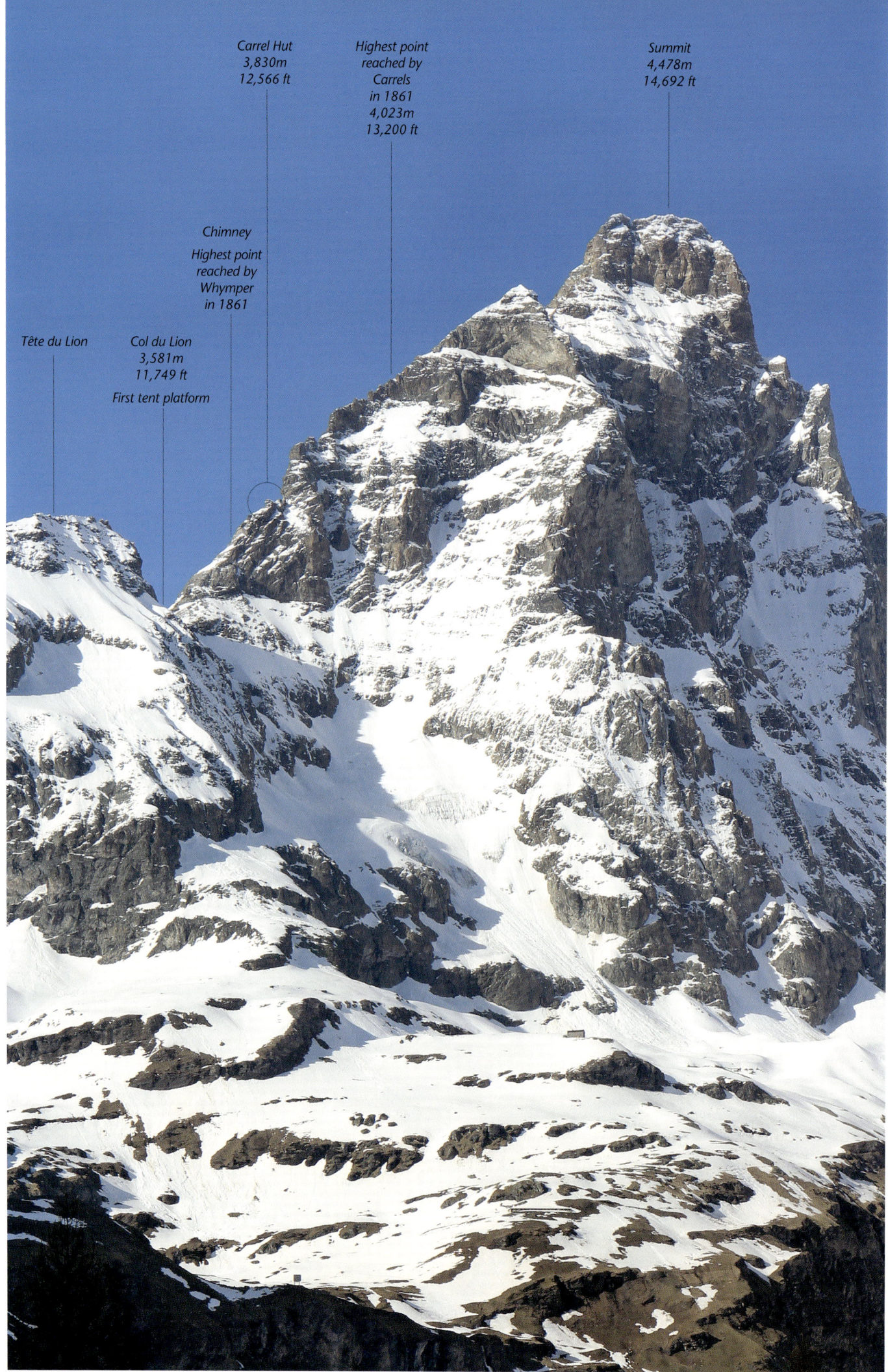

90 - **MATTERHORN** THE QUINTESSENTIAL MOUNTAIN   **THE LION (SOUTH-WEST) RIDGE OF MONTE CERVINO**

CHAPTER SEVEN
1862: RENEWED ATTEMPTS ON THE MATTERHORN

SECOND ATTEMPT

The year 1862 was still young, and the Matterhorn, clad in its wintry garb, bore but little resemblance to the Matterhorn of the summer, when a new force came to do battle with the mountain, from another direction. Mr. T. S. Kennedy of Leeds conceived the extraordinary idea that the peak might prove less impracticable in January than in June, and arrived at Zermatt in the former month to put his conception to the test. With stout Peter Perrn and sturdy Peter Taugwalder he slept in the little chapel at the Schwarzensee, and on the next morning … followed the ridge between the peak called Hörnli and the great mountain. But they found that snow in winter obeyed the ordinary laws, and that the wind and frost were not less unkind than in summer. 'The wind whirled up the snow and spiculæ of ice into our faces like needles, and flat pieces of ice a foot in diameter, carried up from the glacier below, went flying past. Still no one seemed to like to be the first to give in, till a gust fiercer than usual forced us to shelter for a time behind a rock. Immediately it was tacitly understood that our expedition must now end; but we determined to leave some memento of our visit, and, after descending a considerable distance, we found a suitable place with loose stones of which to build a cairn. In half-an-hour a tower six feet high was erected; a bottle, with the date, was placed inside, and we retreated as rapidly as possible.' This cairn was placed at the spot marked upon Dufour's Map of Switzerland 10,820 feet (3298 metres) and the highest point attained by Mr. Kennedy was not, I imagine, more than two or three hundred feet above it.

Shortly after this Professor Tyndall gave, in his little tract *Mountaineering in 1861*, an account of the reason why he had left Breil, in August 1861, without doing anything. It seems that he sent his guide Bennen to reconnoitre, and that the latter made the following report to his employer: —'Herr, I have examined the mountain carefully, and find it more difficult and dangerous than I had imagined. There is no place upon it where we could well pass the night. We might do so on yonder Col upon the snow, but there we should be almost frozen to death, and totally unfit for the work of the next day.'

I was more surprised than discouraged by this report by Bennen. One half of his assertions I knew to be wrong. The Col to which he referred was the Col du Lion, upon which we had passed a night less than a week after he had spoken so authoritatively; and I had seen a place not far below the 'Chimney,' — a place about 500 feet above the Col — where it seemed possible to construct a sleeping-place … Not dismayed by this, my friend Mr. Reginald Macdonald, our companion on the Pelvoux — to whom so much of our success had been due, agreed to join me in a renewed assault from the south … We crossed the Col Théodule on the 5th, in thoroughly unsettled weather — rain was falling in the valleys, and snow upon the mountains. Shortly before we gained the summit we were made extremely uncomfortable by hearing mysterious, rushing sounds, which sometimes seemed as if a sudden gust of wind was sweeping along the snow, and, at others, almost like the swishing of a long whip: yet the snow exhibited no signs of motion, and the air was perfectly calm. The dense, black storm-clouds made us momentarily expect that our bodies might be used as lightning-conductors, and we were well satisfied to get under shelter of the inn at Breil, without having submitted to any such experience.

We had need of a porter, and, by the advice of our landlord, descended to the chalets of Breil in search of one Luc Meynet. We found his house a mean abode, encumbered with cheese-making apparatus, and tenanted only by some bright-eyed children; but as they said that uncle Luc would soon be home, we waited at the door of the little chalet and watched for him … We saw an ungainly, wobbling figure stoop down and catch up the little ones … the hunchback of Breil bore traces of trouble and sorrow, and there was more than a touch of sadness in his voice when he said that he must look after his brother's children. All his difficulties were, however, at length overcome, and he agreed to join us to carry the tent.

In the past winter I had turned my attention to tents, and that which we had brought with us was the result of experiments to devise one which should be sufficiently portable to be taken over the most difficult ground, and which should combine lightness with stability. Its base was just under six feet square, and a cross-section perpendicular to its length was an equilateral triangle, the sides of which were six feet long. It was intended to accommodate four persons … Such a tent costs about four guineas, and its weight is about twenty-three pounds; or, if the lightest kind of forfar is used, it need not exceed twenty pounds … it could be unrolled and set up by two persons in three minutes; a point of no small importance during extreme weather.

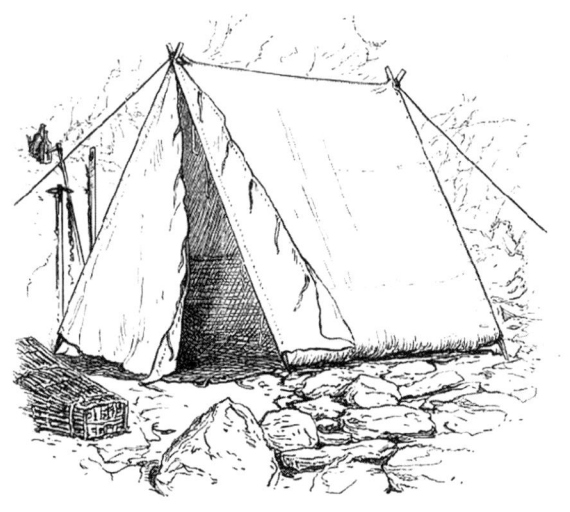

The Author's Mountain Tent

Sunday, the 6th of July, was showery, and snow fell on the Matterhorn, but we started on the following morning with our three men, and pursued my route of the previous year. I was requested to direct the way, as none save myself had been on the mountain before. I did not distinguish myself upon this occasion, and led my companions nearly to the top of the small peak before the mistake was discovered. The party becoming rebellious, a little exploration was made towards our right, and we found that we were upon the top of the cliff overlooking the Col du Lion … While descending a small snow-slope, to get on to the right track, Kronig slipped on a streak of ice, and went down at a fearful pace. Fortunately he kept on his legs, and, by a great effort, succeeded in stopping just before he arrived at some rocks that jutted through the snow, which would infallibly have knocked him over. When we rejoined him a few minutes later, we found that he was incapable of standing, much less of moving, with a face corpse-like in hue, and trembling violently. He remained in this condition for more than an hour, and the day was consequently far advanced before we arrived at our camping-place on the Col. Profiting by the experience of last year, we did not pitch the tent actually on the snow, but collected a quantity of débris from the neighbouring ledges, and after constructing a rough platform of the larger pieces, levelled the whole with the dirt and mud.

Meynet had proved invaluable as a tent-bearer; for … although he seemed to be built on principle with no two parts alike … we quickly found he had spirit of no common order, and that few peasants are more agreeable companions, or better climbers, than little Luc Meynet, the hunchback of Breil. He now showed himself not less serviceable as a scavenger, and humbly asked for gristly pieces of meat, rejected by the others, or for suspicious eggs; and seemed to consider it a peculiar favour, if not a treat, to be permitted to drink the coffee-grounds. With the greatest contentment he took the worst place at the door of the tent, and did all the dirty work which was put upon him by the guides, as gratefully as a dog — who has been well beaten — will receive a stroke.

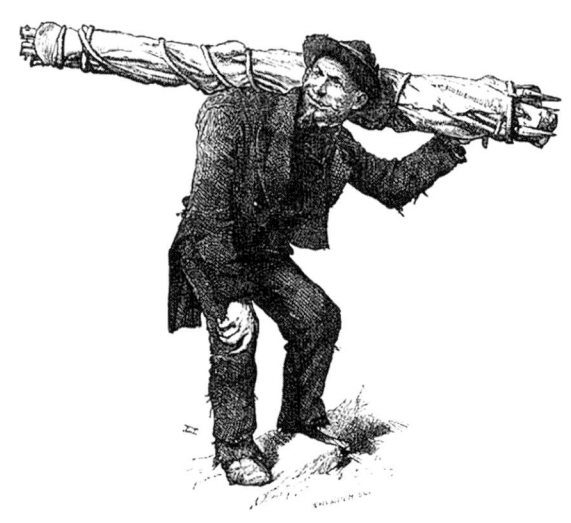

My Tent-Bearer, The Hunchback

A strong wind sprang up from the east during the night, and in the morning it was blowing almost a hurricane. The tent behaved nobly, and we remained under its shelter for several hours after the sun had risen, uncertain what it was best to do. A lull tempted us to move, but we had scarcely ascended a hundred feet before the storm burst upon us with increased fury. Advance or return was alike impossible; the ridge was denuded of its débris; and we clutched our hardest when we saw stones as big as a man's fist blown away horizontally into space. We dared not attempt to stand upright, and remained stationary, on all fours, glued, as it were, to the rocks. It was intensely cold, for the blast had swept along the main chain of the Pennine Alps, and across the great snow-fields around Monte Rosa. Our warmth and courage rapidly evaporated, and at the next lull we retreated to the tent; having to halt several times even in that short distance. [**The guides**] then declared that they had had enough, and refused to have anything more to do with the mountain. Meynet also informed us that he would be required down below for important cheese-making operations on the following day. It was therefore needful to return to Breil, and we arrived there at 2.30 P.M., extremely chagrined at our complete defeat.

(Ibid., pp. 58–65)

THIRD ATTEMPT

Jean-Antoine Carrel, attracted by rumours, had come up to the inn during our absence, and after some negotiations agreed to accompany us, with one of his friends named Pession, on the first fine day. We thought ourselves fortunate; for Carrel clearly considered the mountain a kind of preserve, and regarded our late attempt as an act of *poaching*. The wind blew itself out during the night, and we started again, with these two men and a porter, at 8 A.M. on the 9th, with unexceptionable weather. Carrel pleased us by suggesting that we should camp even higher than before; and we accordingly proceeded, without resting at the Col, until we overtopped the Tête du Lion. Near the foot of the 'Chimney,' a little below the crest of the ridge, and on its eastern side, we found a protected place; and by building up from ledge to ledge … we at length constructed a platform of sufficient size and of considerable solidity. Its height was about 12,550 feet above the sea; and it exists, I believe, at the present time. We then pushed on, as the day was very fine, and, after a short hour's scramble, got to the foot of the Great Tower upon the ridge … and afterwards returned to our bivouac. We turned out again at 4 A.M., and at 5.15 started upwards once more, with fine weather and the thermometer at 28°. Carrel scrambled up the Chimney, and Macdonald and I after him. Pession's turn came, but when he arrived at the top he looked very ill, declared himself to be thoroughly incapable, and said that he must go back. We waited some time, but he did not get better, neither could we learn the nature of his illness. Carrel flatly refused to go on with us alone. We were helpless. Macdonald, ever the coolest of the cool, suggested that we should try what we could do without them; but our better judgment prevailed, and, finally, we returned together to Breil. On the next day my friend started for London.

Three times I had essayed the ascent of this mountain, and on each occasion had failed ignominiously. I had not advanced a yard beyond my predecessors. Up to the height of nearly 13,000 feet there were no extraordinary difficulties; the way so far might even become 'a matter of amusement.' Only 1800 feet remained; but they were as yet untrodden, and might present the most formidable obstacles. No man could expect to climb them by himself. A morsel of rock only seven feet high might at any time defeat him, if it were perpendicular … It was evident that a party should consist of three men at least. But where could the other two men be obtained? Carrel was the only man who exhibited any enthusiasm in the matter; and he, in 1861, had absolutely refused to go unless the party consisted of at least *four* persons. Want of men made the difficulty, not the mountain.

(Ibid., pp. 66f)

FOURTH ATTEMPT

The weather became bad again, so I went to Zermatt on the chance of picking up a man, and remained there during a week of storms. Not one of the better men, however, could be induced to come, and I returned to Breil on the 17th, hoping to combine the skill of Carrel with the willingness of Meynet on a new attempt, by the same route as before; for the Hörnli Ridge, which I had examined in the meantime, seemed to be entirely impracticable. Both men were inclined to go, but their ordinary occupations prevented them from starting at once.

My tent had been left rolled up at the second platform, and whilst waiting for the men it occurred to me that it might have been blown away during the late stormy weather; so I started off on the 18th to see if this were so or not. The way was by this time familiar, and I mounted rapidly, astonishing the friendly herdsmen … But more deliberation was necessary when the pastures were passed, and climbing began, for it was needful to mark each step, in case of mist, or surprise by night. It is one of the few things which can be said in favour of mountaineering alone … that it awakens a man's faculties, and makes him observe. When one has no arms to help, and no head to guide him except his own, he must needs take note even of small things, for he cannot afford to throw away a chance …

The tent was safe, although snowed up; and I turned to contemplate the view, which, when seen alone and undisturbed, had all the strength and charm of complete novelty … most splendid of all, came the Dent Blanche (14,318), soaring above the basin of the great Z'Muttgletscher. Such a view is hardly to be excelled in the Alps, and *this* view is very rarely seen, as I saw it, perfectly unclouded.

Time sped away unregarded, and the little birds which had built their nests on the neighbouring cliffs had begun to chirp their evening hymn before I thought of returning. Half mechanically I turned to the tent, unrolled it, and set it up; it contained food enough for several days, and I resolved to stay over the night. I had started from Breil without provisions, or telling Favre — the innkeeper, who was accustomed to my erratic ways — where I was going. I returned to the view. The sun was setting, and its rosy rays, blending with the snowy blue, had thrown a pale, pure violet far as the eye could see; the valleys were drowned in purple gloom, whilst the summits shone with unnatural brightness: and as I sat in the door of the tent, and watched the twilight change to darkness, the earth seemed to become less earthy and almost sublime; the world seemed dead, and I, its sole inhabitant. By and by, the moon as it rose brought the hills again into sight, and by a judicious repression of detail rendered the view yet more magnificent. Something in the south hung like a great glow-worm in the air; it was too large for a star, and too steady for a meteor; and it was long before I could realise the incredible fact that it was the moonlight glittering on the great snow-slope on the north side of Monte Viso, at a distance, as the crow flies, of 98 miles. Shivering, at last I entered the tent and made my coffee. The night was passed comfortably, and the next morning, tempted by the brilliancy of the weather, I proceeded yet higher in search of another place for a platform.

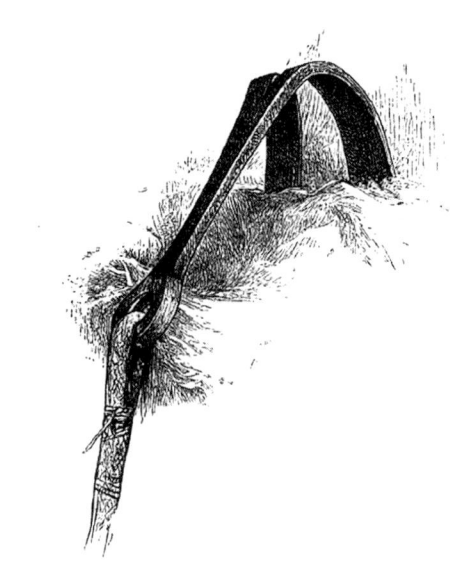

Solitary scrambling over a pretty wide area had shown me that a single individual is subjected to many difficulties which do not trouble a party of two or three men, and that the disadvantages of being alone are more felt while descending than during the ascent. In order to neutralise these inconveniences, I devised two little appliances, which were now brought into use for the first time. One was a claw — a kind of grapnel — about five inches long, made of shear steel, one-fifth of an inch thick. This was of use in difficult places, where there was no hold within arm's length, but where there were cracks or ledges some distance higher. The claw could be stuck on the end of the alpenstock and dropped into such places, or, on extreme occasions, flung up until it attached itself to something. The edges that laid hold of the rocks were serrated, which tended to make them catch more readily: the other end had a ring to which a rope was fastened. It must not be understood that this was employed for hauling one's-self up for any great distance, but that it was used in ascending, at the most, for only a few yards at a time. In descending, however, it could be prudently used for a greater distance at a time, as the claws could be planted firmly …

With these home made aids, Whymper climbed alone beyond the point Hawkins & Tyndall reached in 1860 and the point the Carrels reached in 1861.

This Great Tower is one of the most striking features of the ridge. It stands out like a turret at the angle of a castle … I found here a suitable place for the tent; which, although not so well protected as the second platform, possessed the advantage of being 300 feet higher up; and fascinated by the wildness of the cliffs, and enticed by the perfection of the weather, I went on to see what was behind.

The first step was a difficult one. The ridge became diminished to the least possible width — it was hard to keep one's balance — and just where it was narrowest, a more than perpendicular mass barred the way. Nothing fairly within arm's reach could be laid hold of; it was necessary to spring up, and then to haul one's-self over the sharp edge by sheer strength. Progression directly upwards was then impossible. Enormous and appalling precipices plunged down to the Tiefenmatten glacier on the left, but round the right-hand side it was just possible to go. One hindrance then succeeded another, and much time was consumed in seeking the way. I have a vivid recollection of a gully of more than usual perplexity … with arms and legs divergent, fixed as if crucified, pressing against the rock, and feeling each rise and fall of my chest as I breathed; of screwing my head round to look for hold, and not seeing any, and of jumping sideways on to the other side … The non-mountaineering reader cannot feel this, and his interest in descriptions of such places is usually small, unless he supposes that the situations are perilous. They are not necessarily perilous, but I think that it is impossible to avoid giving such an impression if the difficulties are particularly insisted upon.

… here, all was decay and ruin. The crest of the ridge was shattered and cleft, and the feet sank in the chips which had drifted down; while above, huge blocks, hacked and carved by the hand of time, nodded to the sky, looking like the grave-stones of giants.

The Tower was now almost out of sight, and I looked over the central Pennine Alps to the Grand Combin, and to the chain of Mont Blanc. My neighbour, the Dent d'Hérens, still rose above me, although but slightly, and the height which had been attained could be measured by its help. So far, I had no doubts about my capacity to descend that which had been ascended; but, in a short time, on looking ahead, I saw that the cliffs steepened, and I turned back … exulting in the thought that … I had, without assistance, got nearly to the height of the Dent d'Hérens, and considerably higher than any one had been before. My exultation was a little premature.

About 5 P.M. I left the tent again, and thought myself as good as at Breil. The friendly rope and claw had done good service, and had smoothened all the difficulties. I lowered myself through the Chimney, however, by making a fixture of the rope, which I then cut off, and left behind, as there was enough and to spare. My axe had proved a great nuisance in coming down, and I left it in the tent … the head or the handle of the weapon caught frequently against the rocks, and several times nearly upset me. So, out of laziness if you will, it was left in the tent. I paid dearly for the imprudence.

I found that the heat of the two past days had nearly obliterated the steps which had been cut when coming up. The rocks happened to be impracticable just at this corner, so nothing could be done except make the steps afresh. The snow was too hard to beat or tread down, and at the angle it was all but ice. Half-a-dozen steps only were required, and then the ledges could be followed again. So I held to the rock with my right hand, and prodded at the snow with the point of my stick until a good step was made, and then, leaning round the angle, did the same for the other side. So far well, but in attempting to pass the corner (to the present moment I cannot tell how it happened) I slipped and fell.

The slope was steep on which this took place, and was at the top of a gully that led down through two subordinate buttresses towards the Glacier du Lion — which was just seen, a thousand feet below. The gully narrowed and narrowed, until there was a mere thread of snow lying between two walls of rock, which came to an abrupt termination at the top of a precipice that intervened between it and the glacier. Imagine a funnel cut in half through its length, placed at an angle of 45 degrees, with its point below and its concave side uppermost, and you will have a fair idea of the place.

The knapsack brought my head down first, and I pitched into some rocks about a dozen feet below; they caught something and tumbled me off the edge, head over heels, into the gully; the bâton was dashed from my hands, and I whirled downwards in a series of bounds, each longer than the last; now over ice, now into rocks; striking my head four or five times, each time with increased force. The last bound sent me spinning through the air, in a leap of fifty or sixty feet, from one side of the gully to the other, and I struck the rocks, luckily, with the whole of my left side. They caught my clothes for a moment, and I fell back on to the snow with motion arrested. My head fortunately came the right side up, and a few frantic catches brought me to a halt, in the neck of the gully, and on the verge of the precipice. Bâton, hat, and veil skimmed by and disappeared, and the crash of the rocks — which I had started — as they fell on to the glacier, told how narrow had been the escape from utter destruction. As it was, I fell nearly 200 feet in seven or eight bounds. Ten feet more would have taken me in one gigantic leap of 800 feet on to the glacier below.

The situation was sufficiently serious. The rocks could not be left go for a moment, and the blood was spirting out of more than twenty cuts. The most serious ones were in the head, and I vainly tried to close them with one hand, whilst holding on with the other. It was useless; the blood jerked out in blinding jets at each pulsation. At last, in a moment of inspiration, I kicked out a big lump of snow, and stuck it as a plaster on my head. The idea was a happy one, and the flow of blood diminished. Then, scrambling up, I got, not a moment too soon, to a place of safety, and fainted away. The sun was setting when consciousness returned, and it was pitch dark before the Great Staircase was descended; but, by a combination of luck and care, the whole 4800 feet of descent to Breil was accomplished without a slip, or once missing the way. I slunk past the cabin of the cowherds, who were talking and laughing inside, utterly ashamed of the state to which I had been brought by my imbecility, and entered the inn stealthily, wishing to escape to my room unnoticed. But Favre met me in the passage, demanded 'Who is it?' screamed with fright when he got a light, and aroused the household. Two dozen heads then held solemn council over mine, with more talk than action. The natives were unanimous in recommending that hot wine mixed with salt, should be rubbed into the cuts. I protested, but they insisted. It was all the doctoring they received. Whether their rapid healing was to be attributed to that simple remedy, or to a good state of health, is a question; they closed up remarkably quickly, and in a few days I was able to move again.

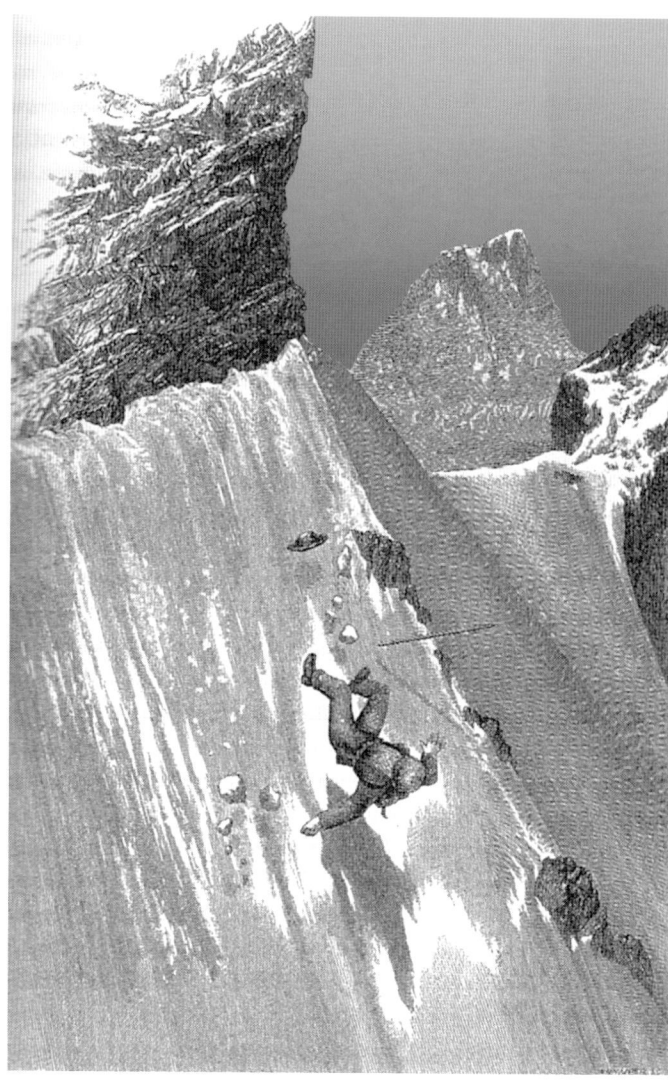

'In Attempting To Pass The Corner I Slipped And Fell'

(Ibid., pp. 67–79)

FIFTH ATTEMPT

The news of the accident brought Jean-Antoine Carrel up to Breil, and, along with the haughty chasseur, came one of his relatives, a strong and able young fellow named Cæsar. With these two men and Meynet I made another start on the 23rd of July. We got to the tent without any trouble, and on the following day had ascended beyond the Tower, and were picking our way cautiously over the loose rocks behind ... in lovely weather, when one of those abominable and almost instantaneous changes occurred, to which the Matterhorn is so liable on its southern side. Mists were created out of invisible vapours, and in a few minutes snow fell heavily. We stopped ... and, unwilling to retreat, remained on the spot several hours, in hopes that another change would occur; but, as it did not, we at length went down to the base of the Tower, and commenced to make a third platform, at the height of 12,992 feet above the sea. It still continued to snow, and we took refuge in the tent. Carrel argued that the weather had broken up, and that the mountain would become so glazed with ice as to render any attempt futile; and I, that the change was only temporary, and that the rocks were too hot to allow ice to form upon them. I wished to stay until the weather improved, but my leader would not endure contradiction, grew more positive, and insisted that we must go down. We went down, and when we got below the Col his opinion was found to be wrong; the cloud was confined to the upper 3000 feet, and outside it there was brilliant weather.

Carrel was not an easy man to manage. He was perfectly aware that he was the cock of the Val Tournanche, and he commanded the other men as by right. He was equally conscious that he was indispensable to me, and took no pains to conceal his knowledge of the fact ... But, let me repeat, he was the only first-rate climber I could find who believed that the mountain was not inaccessible. With him I had hopes, but without him none; so he was allowed to do as he would. His will on this occasion was almost incomprehensible. He certainly could not be charged with cowardice, for a bolder man could hardly be found ... It seemed to me that he was spinning out the ascent for his own purposes, and that although he wished very much to be the first man on the top, and did not object to be accompanied by any one else who had the same wish, he had no intention of letting one succeed too soon, — perhaps to give a greater appearance of *éclat* when the thing was accomplished.

Vexed at having my time thus frittered away, I was still well pleased when he volunteered to start again on the morrow, if it should be fine. We were to advance the tent to the foot of the Tower, to fix ropes in the most difficult parts beyond, and to make a push for the summit on the following day.

The next morning (Friday the 25th) when I arose, good little Meynet was ready and waiting, and he said that the two Carrels had gone off some time before, and had left word that they intended marmot-hunting, as the day was favourable for that sport. My holiday had nearly expired, and these men clearly could not be relied upon; so, as a last resort, I proposed to the hunchback to accompany me alone, to see if we could not get higher than before, though of reaching the summit there was little or no hope. He did not hesitate, and in a few hours we stood — for the third time together — upon the Col du Lion. It was the first time Meynet had seen the view unclouded. The poor little deformed peasant gazed upon it silently and reverently for a time, and then, unconsciously, fell on one knee in an attitude of adoration, and clasped his hands, exclaiming in ecstasy, 'Oh, beautiful mountains!' His actions were as appropriate as his words were natural, and tears bore witness to the reality of his emotion.

Our power was too limited to advance the tent, so we slept at the old station, and starting very early the next morning, passed the place where we had turned back on the 24th, and, subsequently, my highest point on the 19th. We found the crest of the ridge so treacherous that we took to the cliffs on the right, although most unwillingly. Little by little we fought our way up, but at length we were both spread-eagled on the all but perpendicular face, unable to advance, and barely able to descend. We returned to the ridge. It was almost equally difficult, and infinitely more unstable; and at length, after having pushed our attempts as far as was prudent, I determined to return to Breil, and to have a light ladder made to assist us to overcome some of the steepest parts. I expected, too, that by this time Carrel would have had enough marmot-hunting, and would deign to accompany us again.

Meynet was always merriest on the difficult parts, and, on the most difficult, kept on enunciating the sentiment, 'We can only die once,' which thought seemed to afford him infinite satisfaction. We arrived at the inn early in the evening, and I found my projects summarily and unexpectedly knocked on the head.

Professor Tyndall had arrived while we were absent, and he had engaged both Cæsar and Jean-Antoine Carrel … They had a ladder already prepared, provisions were being collected, and they intended to start on the following morning (Sunday) … I was astonished at the faithlessness of Carrel, and attributed it to pique at our having presumed to do without him. It was useless to compete with the Professor and his four men, who were ready to start in a few hours, so I waited to see what would come of their attempt.

Everything seemed to favour it, and they set out on a fine morning in high spirits, leaving me tormented with envy and all uncharitableness. If they succeeded, they carried off the prize for which I had been so long struggling; and if they failed, there was no time to make another attempt, for I was due in a few days more in London. When this came home clearly to me, I resolved to leave Breil at once; but, when packing up, found that some necessaries had been left behind in the tent. So I went off about midday to recover them; caught the army of the Professor before it reached the Col, as they were going very slowly; left them there (stopping to take food), and went on to the tent.

I waited at the tent to welcome the Professor, and when he arrived went down to Breil. Early next morning some one ran to me saying that a flag was seen on the summit of the Matterhorn. It was not so, however, although I saw that they had passed the place where we had turned back on the 26th. I had now no doubt of their final success, for they **[with the aid of a rope ladder,]** had got beyond the point which Carrel, not less than myself, had always considered to be the most questionable place on the whole mountain.

My knapsack was packed, and I had taken a parting glass of wine with Favre, who was jubilant at the success which was

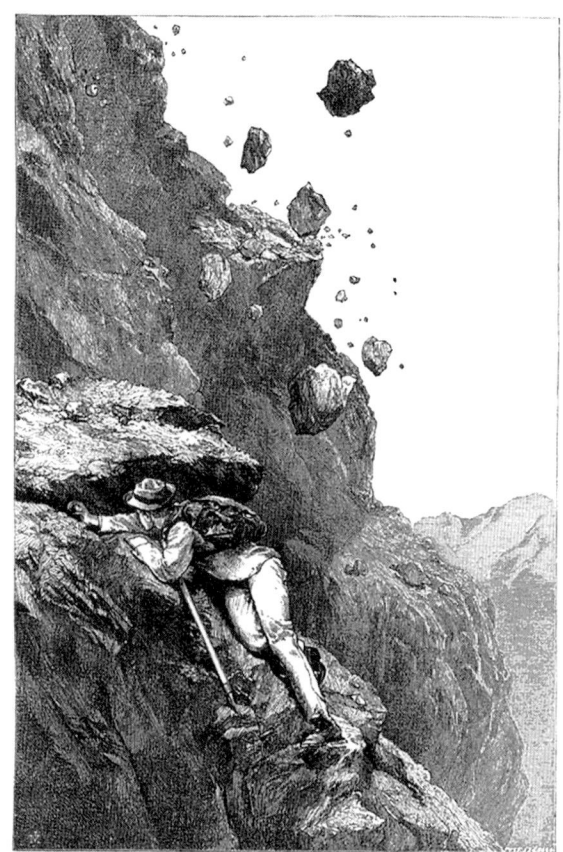

A Cannonade On The Matterhorn (1862)

to make the fortune of his inn; but I could not bring myself to leave until the result was heard, and lingered about, as a foolish lover hovers round the object of his affections, even after he has been contemptuously rejected. The sun had set before the men were descried coming over the pastures. There was no spring in their steps — they, too, were defeated. The Carrels hid their heads, and the others said, as men will do when they have been beaten, that the mountain was horrible, impossible, and so forth. Professor Tyndall told me they had arrived *within a stone's throw of the summit*, and admonished me to have nothing more to do with the mountain. I understood him to say that he should not try again, and ran down to the village of Val Tournanche, almost inclined to believe that the mountain was inaccessible; leaving the tent, ropes, and other matters in the hands of Favre, to be placed at the disposal of any person who wished to ascend it, more, I am afraid, out of irony than from generosity. There may have been those who believed that the Matterhorn could be ascended, but, anyhow, their faith did not bring forth works. No one tried again in 1862.

(Ibid., pp. 80–87)

SUMMER 2015 (WEEK ONE)

AUTHOR'S LOG

Just over 150 years ago on 14th July 1865, Edward Whymper and his party reached the summit of the Matterhorn. Three days later, Jean-Antoine Carrel's contingent made the first ascent from the Italian side. At last, the unrelenting determination of both Whymper and Carrel had paid off and speculation began over which side would benefit most from tourists wanting to see the 'tamed giant'. Now, in this 150th anniversary year, both towns on either side of the mountain were commemorating those first ascents. I had held off my visit until a few weeks after these events to give the towns some time to settle down, and in turn, to increase my chances of staying at mountain huts at short notice.

For this trip, I decided to drive down through France and into Switzerland, with the first week designated for gradual altitude acclimatisation and, more importantly, creating images from some key locations I had not yet visited.

The weather had been particularly dry and sunny and was set to continue fine for the next few days, which I was naturally delighted about. It was good news for mountaineering and photography, but it did mean that the east face of the Matterhorn was virtually bare of snow, making it look rather grey. There was a little rain forecast and I wondered if that would add some fresh snow to the peaks and tried to factor that into my planning. However, with high pressure dominating the weather, it was unlikely.

No book on the Matterhorn would be complete without a view of it reflected in either Stellisee or Riffelsee lake which are high up, to the east of Zermatt. My intention was to photograph views from both locations over a three-day period, but as there was an imminent possibility of a little low cloud and rain, I decided to first hike up the Zmutt Valley, west of Zermatt, to photograph the north-west ridge.

Back in 1863, with poor weather keeping them off the Matterhorn, Whymper and Carrel travelled up the Zmutt Valley together in a full re-contour of the mountain and were impressed by the views of the Matterhorn's various ridges. As a result, Whymper believed increasingly that the Hörnli ridge was the easiest way to reach the summit, while Carrel was more convinced that his Liongrat (Lion) ridge was the better way. During their circumnavigation, they were forced to also go around Dent d'Hérens; the Matterhorn's nearest neighbour, and in so doing attempted to be the first to climb it too.

At 2,700m, the Schönbiel mountain hut made an ideal stopover for me, both for acclimatisation and viewpoint. The last few hundred metres of the 1,100m hike up to the hut proved demanding enough, but after a quick rest and refuel, I headed on to a wonderful viewpoint at just over 3,000m. The thinner air made the last 200 metres a real challenge and I was happy to rest at the top for a few hours as the sun slowly lowered. From there I was able to photograph the Matterhorn's rather haphazard north-west ridge, alongside the north face of Dent d'Hérens.

Highlighting the uniformity of the Matterhorn, both the Hörnli and Lion ridges could be viewed simultaneously from the north-west ridge, and both the Solvay and Carrel huts were clearly visible. Back at my hut, there was no room to spare, with mountaineers and hikers crammed into the bunk beds like sardines in a can. Consequently, I got no more than a couple of hours' sleep, although that may have been more to do with the altitude, or my brain unable to shut down, rather than the cramped conditions.

Some cloud had moved in as forecast, so the next day was spent hiking back down to Zermatt so that I could prepare for the three-day lake sortie. While there are mountain huts within an hour of each lake, I wanted to camp right on the shore to be ready to catch the first light and fully enjoy the magnificent settings. With camera gear, three days of camping supplies and all my regular equipment, I knew my pack would be heavy and a considerable burden. I endeavoured to take only what I considered essential but, as time would prove, I had underestimated the challenge.

Full of enthusiasm and excited to visit the lakes, I set out just after midday for the four-hour hike up to Stellisee lake at 2,537m. This meant ascending the 1,000 metres in 25 degrees Celsius, the heat quickly proving all too evident, and I was glad to take my first break. It was edifying to work up the mountainside, passing through hamlets with their enterprising and busy restaurants. However, I was not there for the culinary experience and made do with water and a snack bar. My trek continued, and after another four hours of walking, I reached my destination. The lighting was not right for photographs and as I was particularly thirsty, I continued past the lake to the nearby mountain hut at Fluhalp.

A cold beer and a bottle of water were quickly consumed, then after lazing in the sun, I reneged on my camping plans and booked a bed in the dorm. As it turned out, it was an extremely damp night by the lake, so despite having carried the camping gear, the soft bed and dry room were particularly appreciated.

The following morning, an easy walk back down to the lake before sunrise resulted in some wonderful photographs of the sun gradually illuminating the mountains while reflected in a near-still lake: a very satisfying beginning and a spur to continue.

Resentfully, I shouldered my heavy pack and set off to Riffelsee lake, which was a little higher, at 2,757m. The undulating walk was very pleasant, and passed several smaller lakes along the way. However, after making my way up a particularly steep 300m track in the midday heat, I felt I had all but reached my limit. Truly exhausted, a long rest and rehydration were vital before making the final hour's journey to the lake.

Riffelsee lake is only about half the size of Stellisee and at first sight, it seemed doubtful whether it could produce the stunning panorama I had hoped for. The lake was particularly low, owing to the long dry spell, and just did not seem large enough to reflect the mountain range beyond. This time, I did pitch my tent and made the most of the tranquillity of the location, with nothing but a couple of crows and the ringing of sheep bells to break the silence.

After a welcome and very sound night's sleep, I awoke to find the lake mirror-calm, and with a perfect reflection of the landscape upon it. With plenty of time to pick my vantage point and set up, I watched the spectacle of the leisurely rising sun. The light changed from a deep orange to a bright yellow as it chased the shadows from the face of the Matterhorn and the neighbouring peaks.

I considered myself very fortunate and was in no hurry to leave the lake, staying there well after the sun had risen, and only moving on when hikers appeared and broke my solitude.

I had been extremely fortunate with my timing and had succeeded in my objectives for the first week. However, after six days of almost unbroken sunshine, the weather changed and for the next two days, the heavens opened in a near-relentless downpour: almighty rumbles of thunder up to a minute long sounded almost angry and vengeful; a warning to anyone foolhardy enough to venture out. Fortunately for me, it provided valuable time to review the images and my log for the book.

Earlier in the week I had learnt that the Lion Ridge (our planned route) up the Matterhorn had been closed due to rockfall that had damaged part of the roof of the Carrel Hut where we intended to stay, and had broken a section of fixed rope below it. Highlighting the primary and ever-present danger of the Matterhorn, this news brought into question how successful we might be. The only hope was that colder conditions might arrive, helping to freeze the mountain back together again!

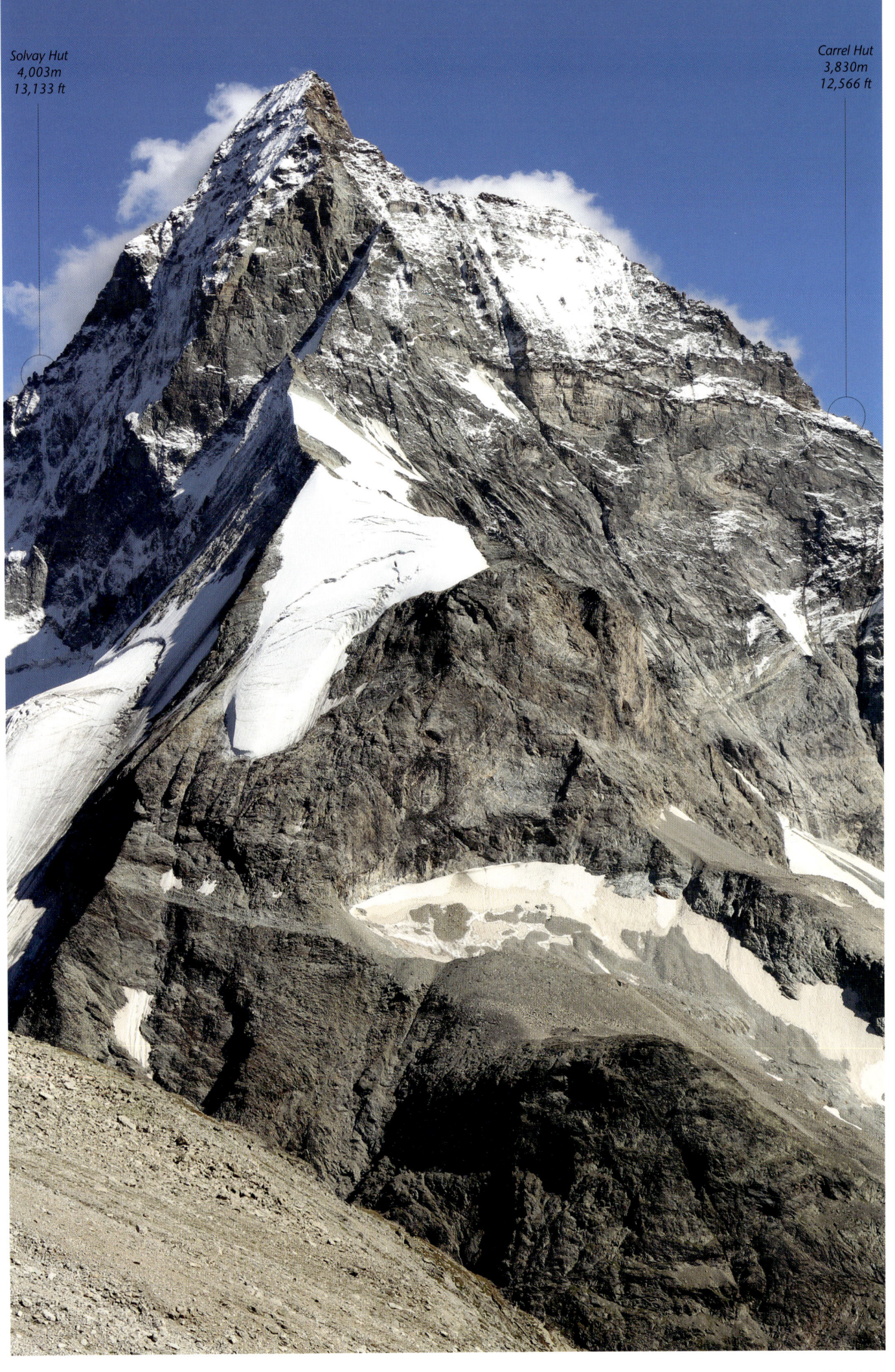

THE NORTH-WEST RIDGE OF THE MATTERHORN

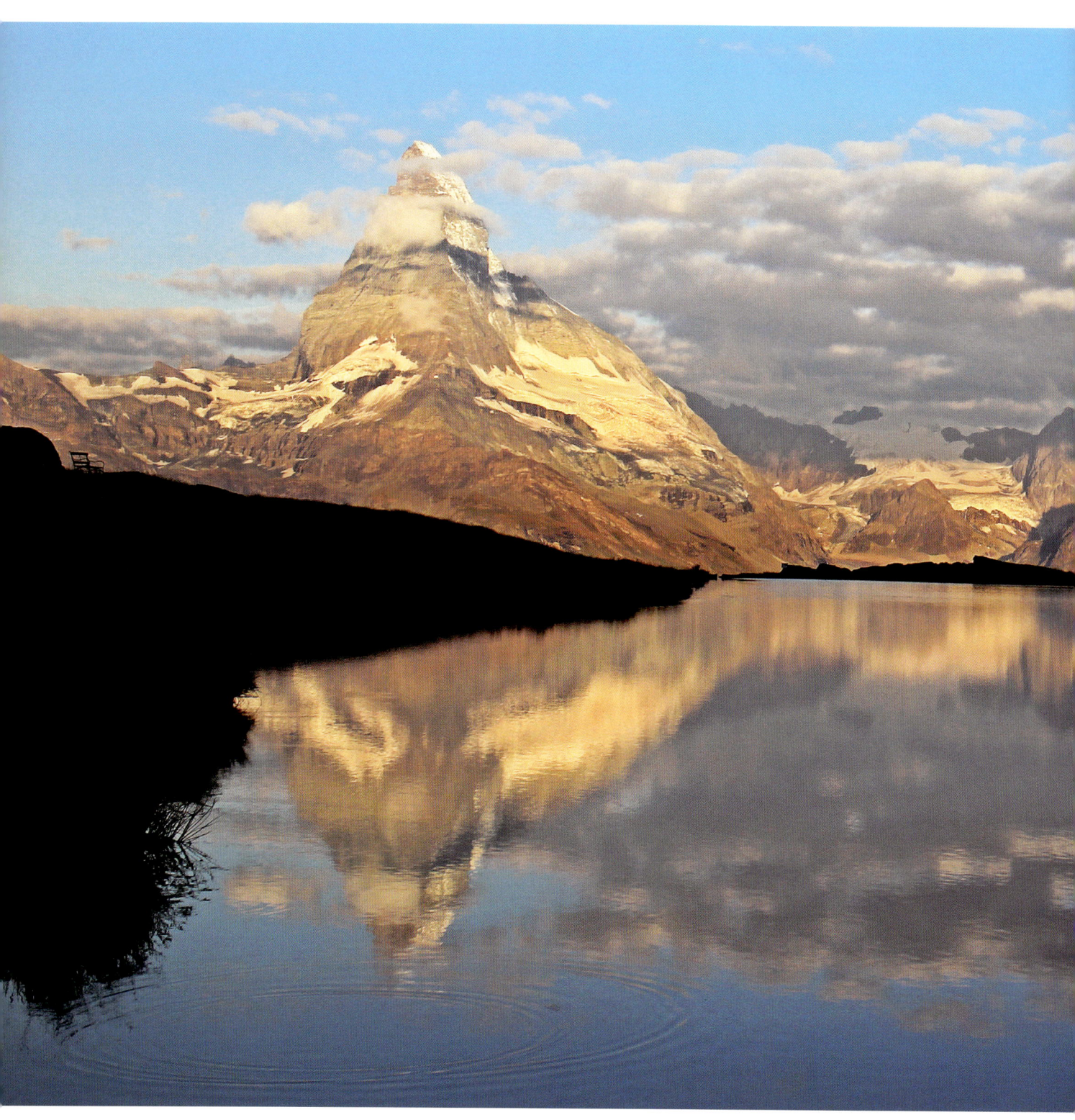

STELLISEE LAKE SUNRISE 2,537M

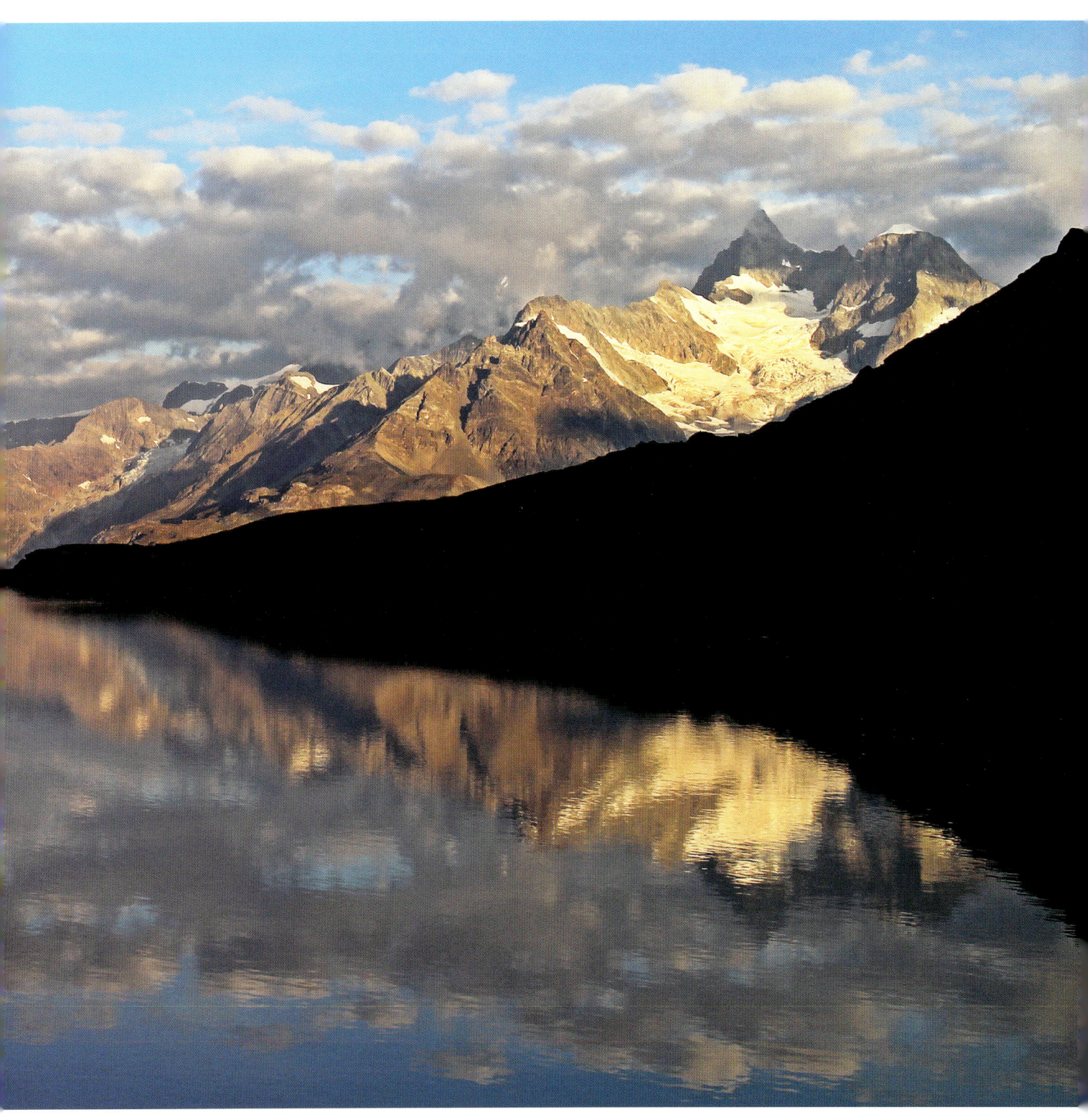

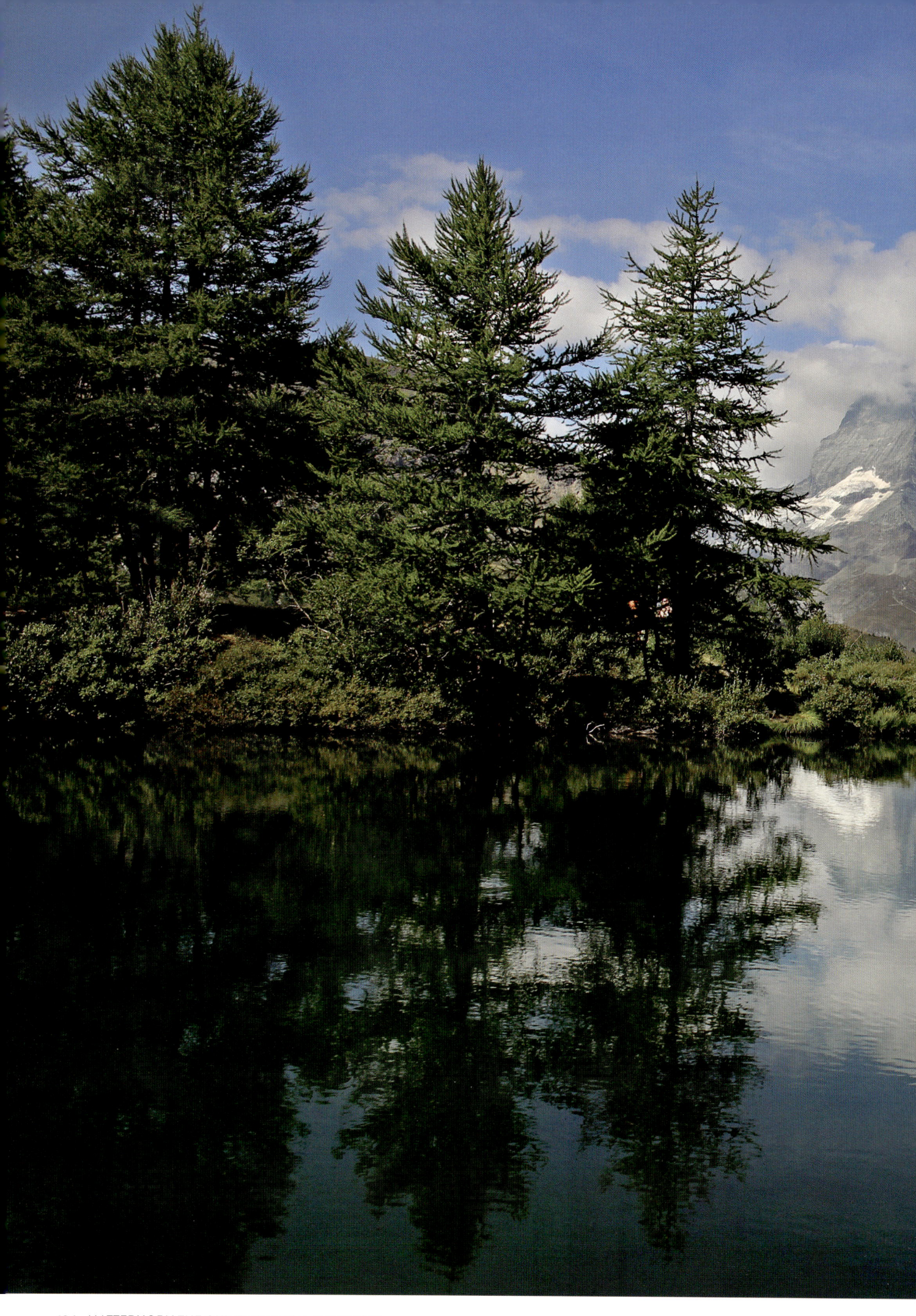

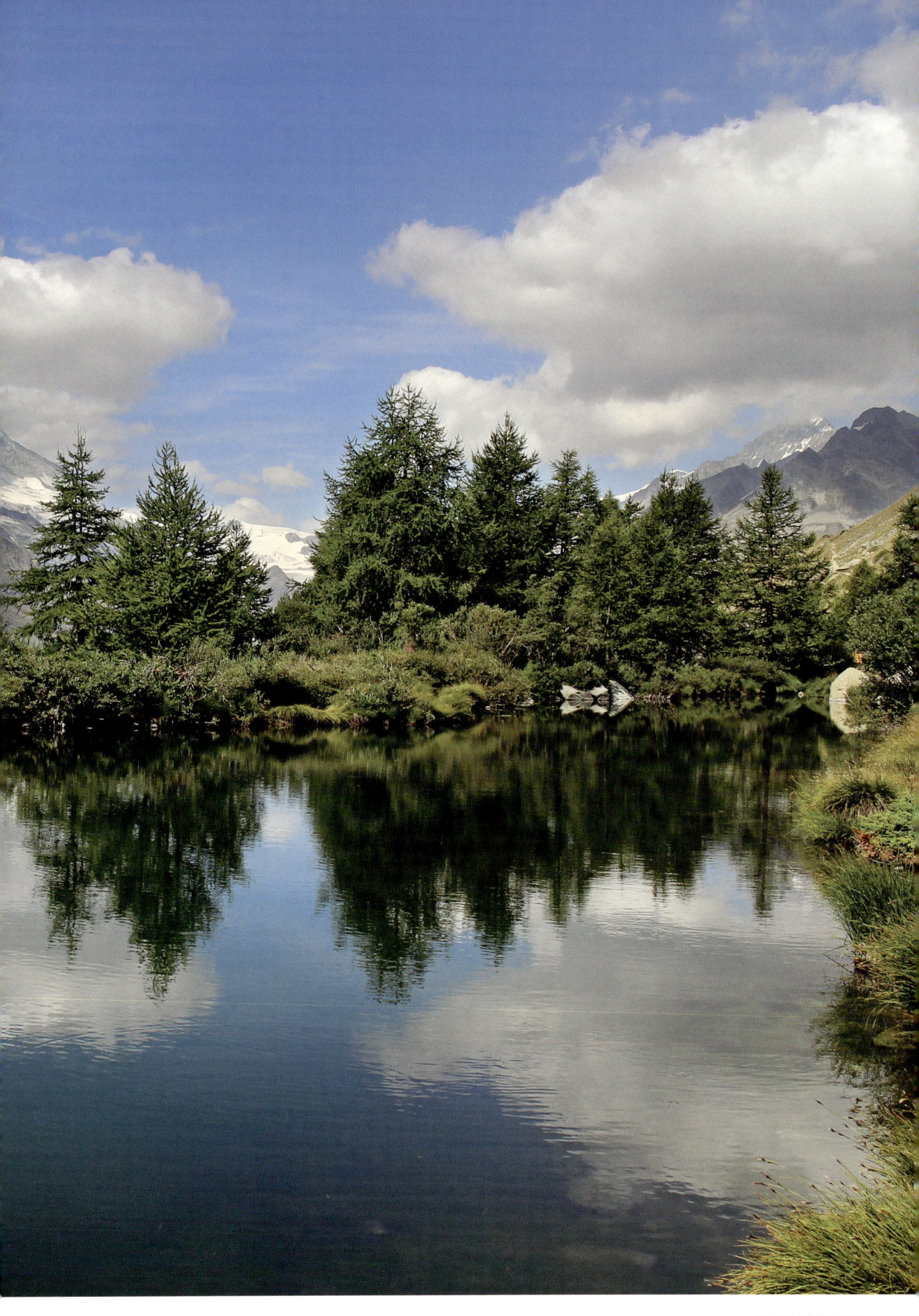

GRINDJISEE LAKE

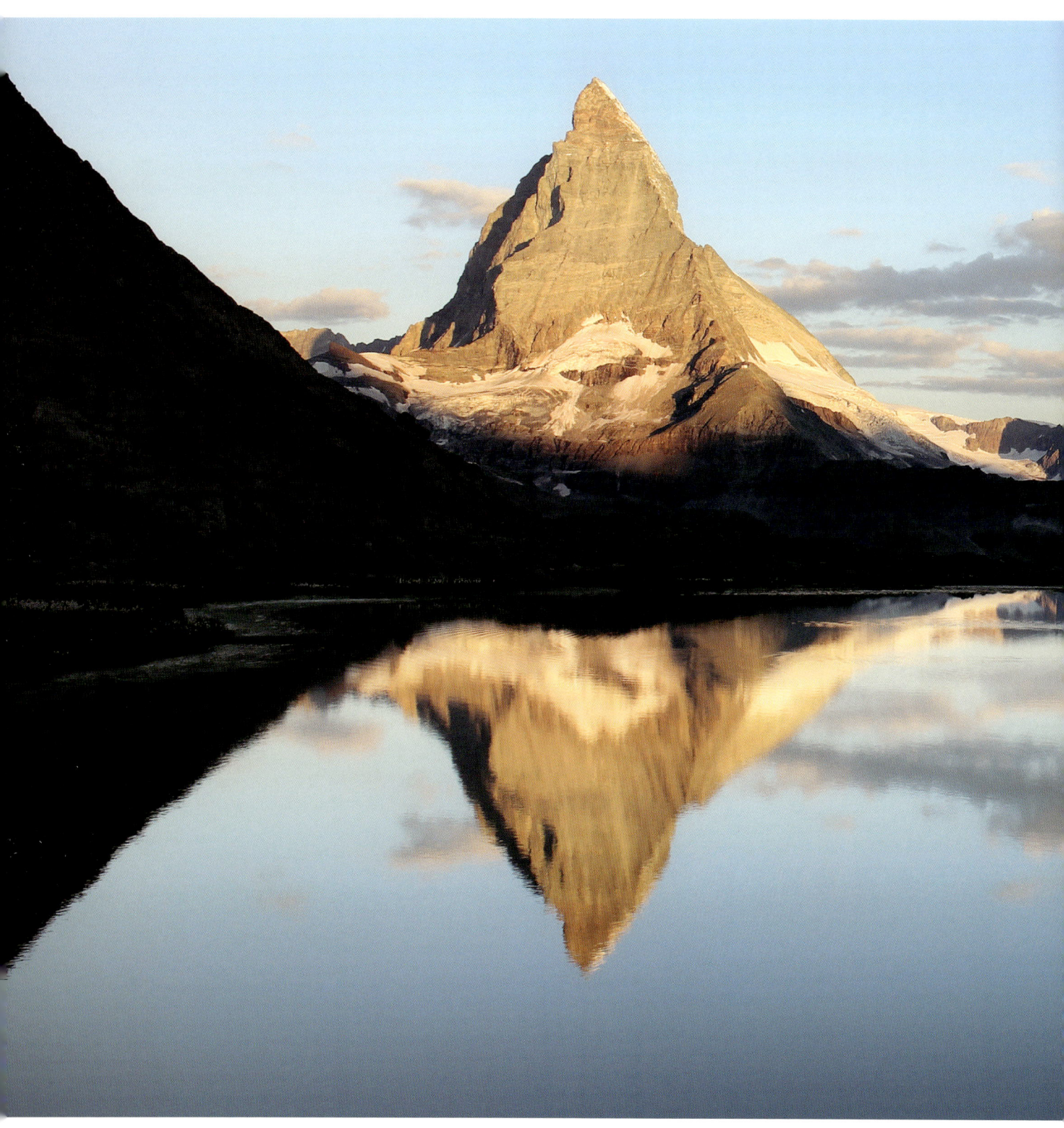

RIFFELSEE LAKE SUNRISE 2,757M

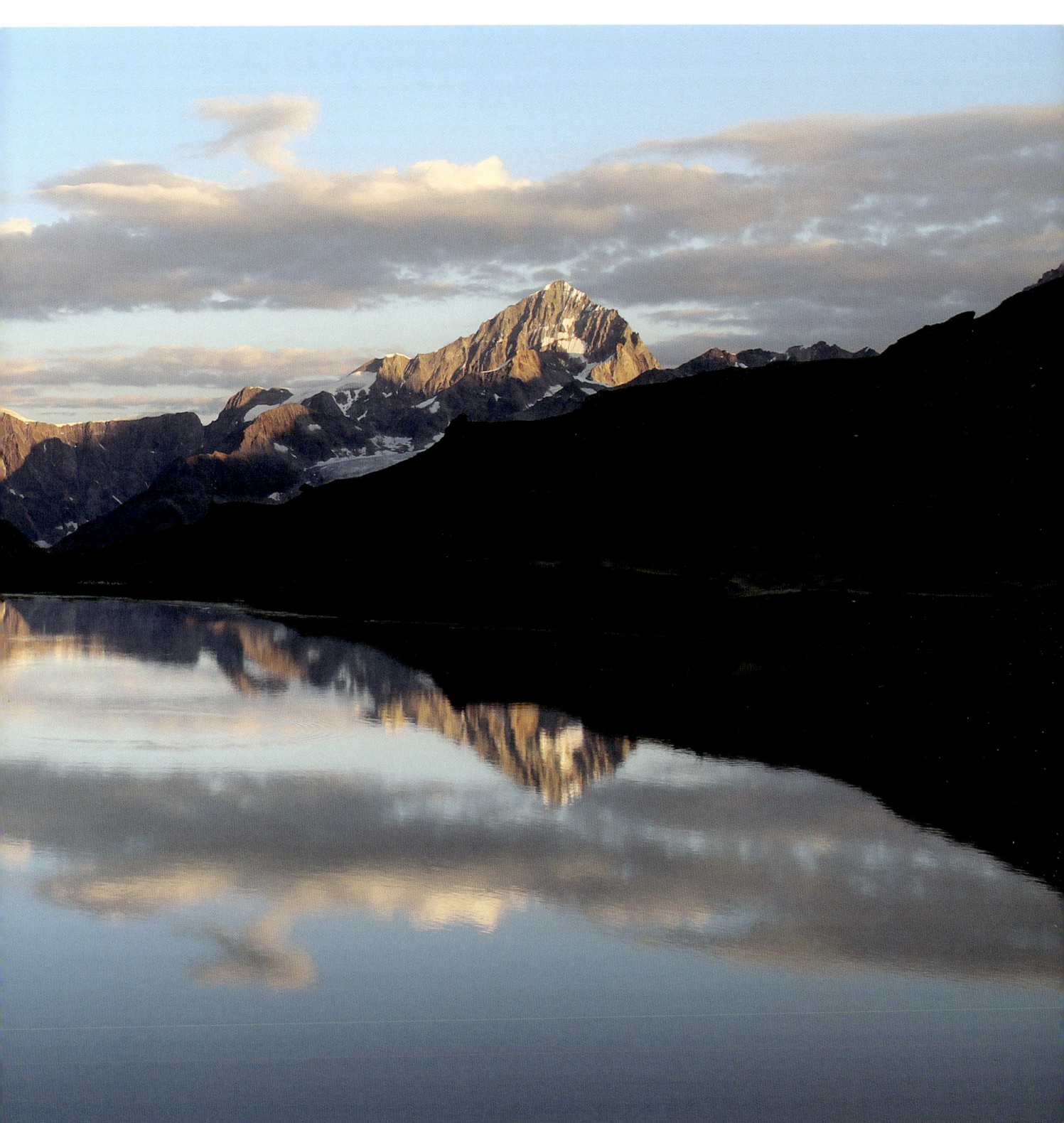

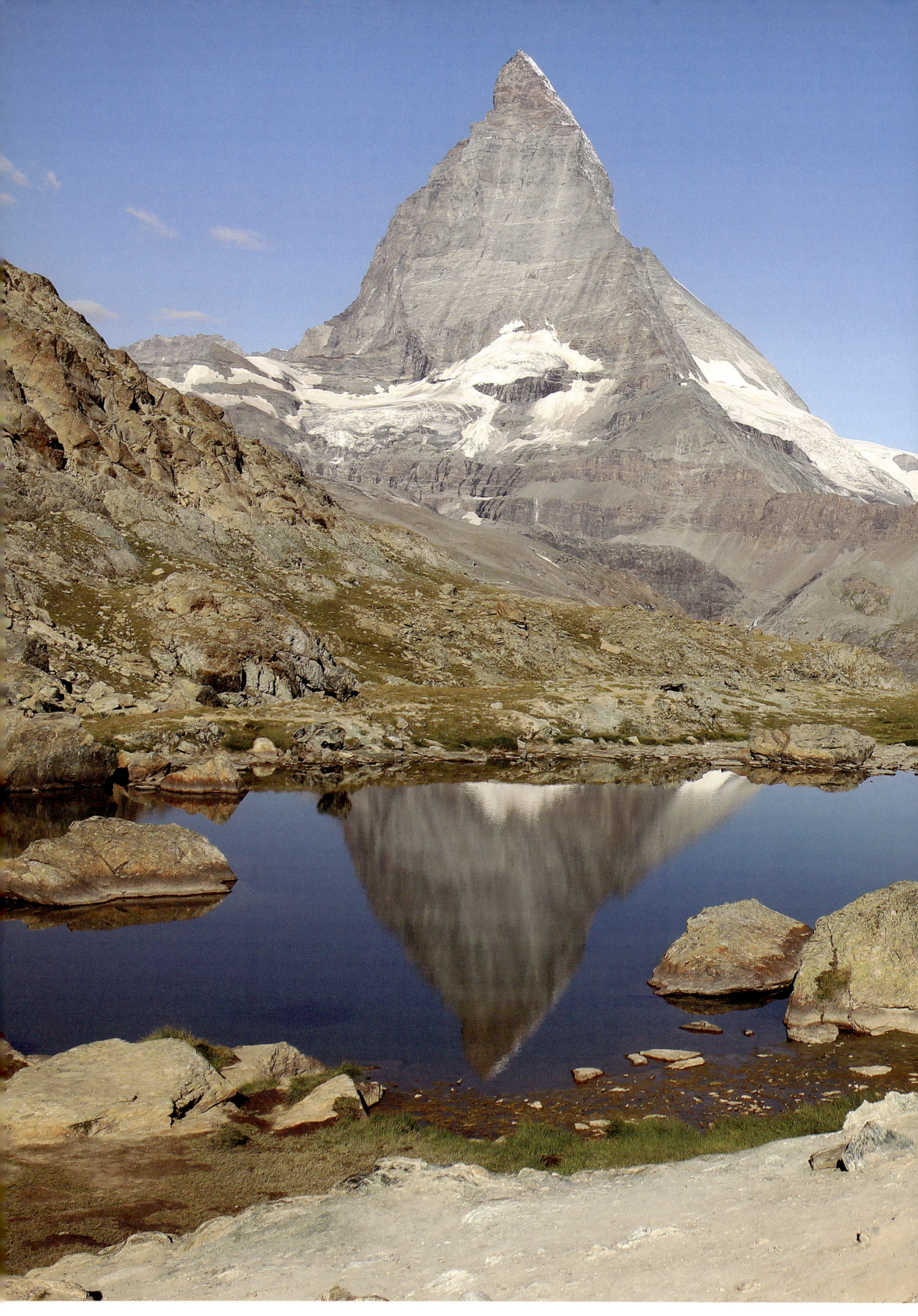

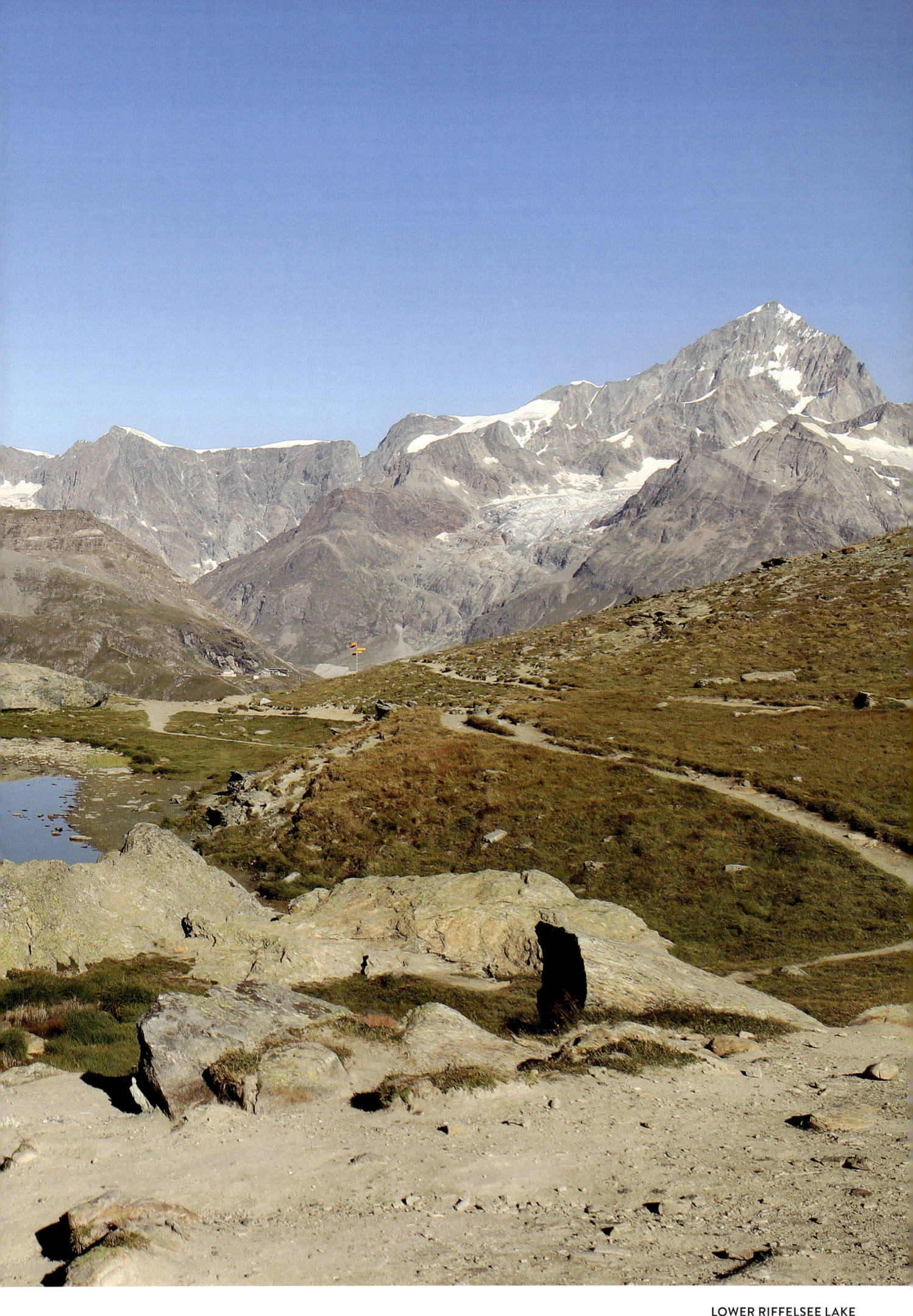

LOWER RIFFELSEE LAKE

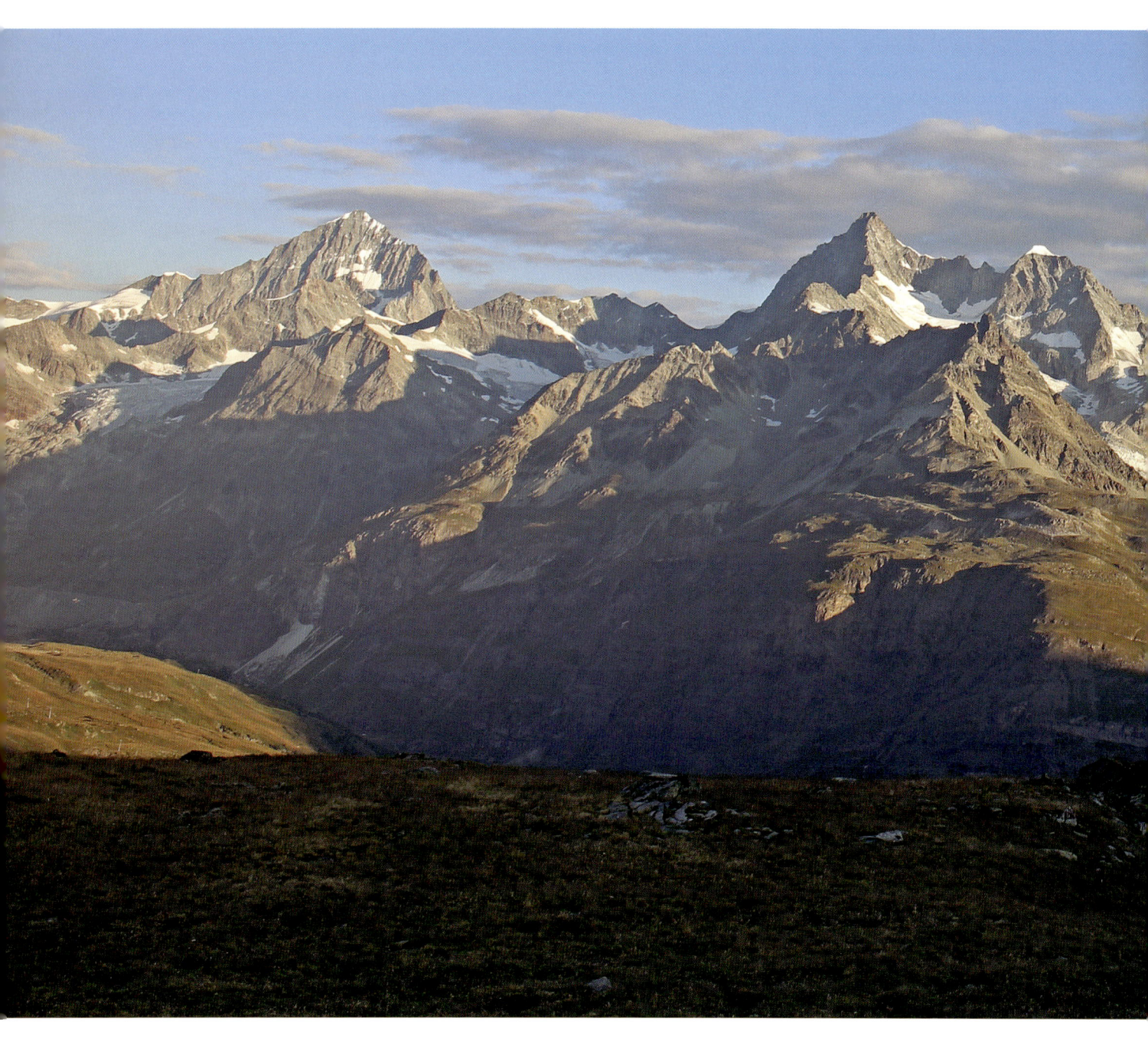

DENT BLANCHE 4,356m, OBER GABELHORN 4,063m, ZINALROTHORN 4,221m AND WEISSHORN 4,506m

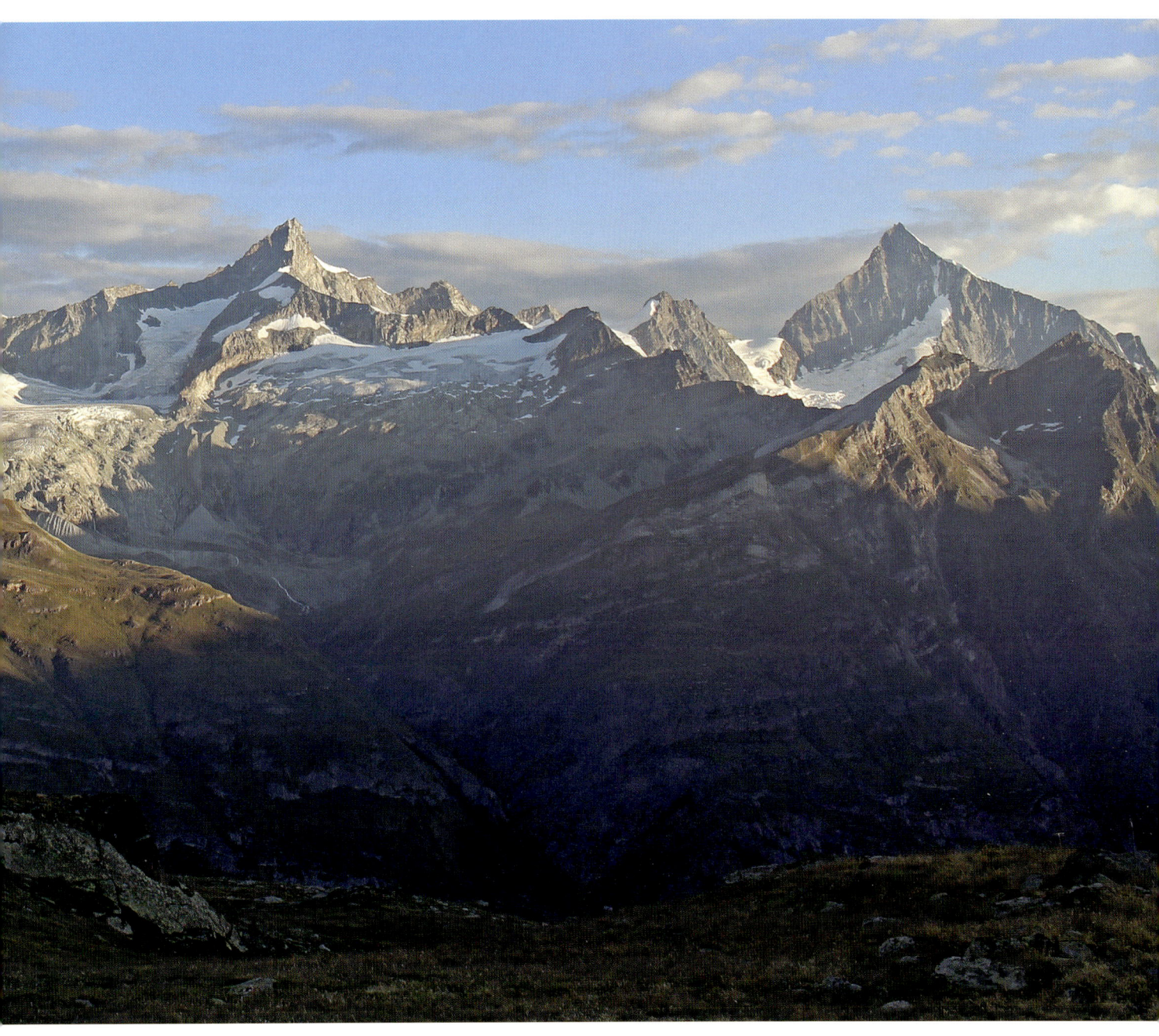

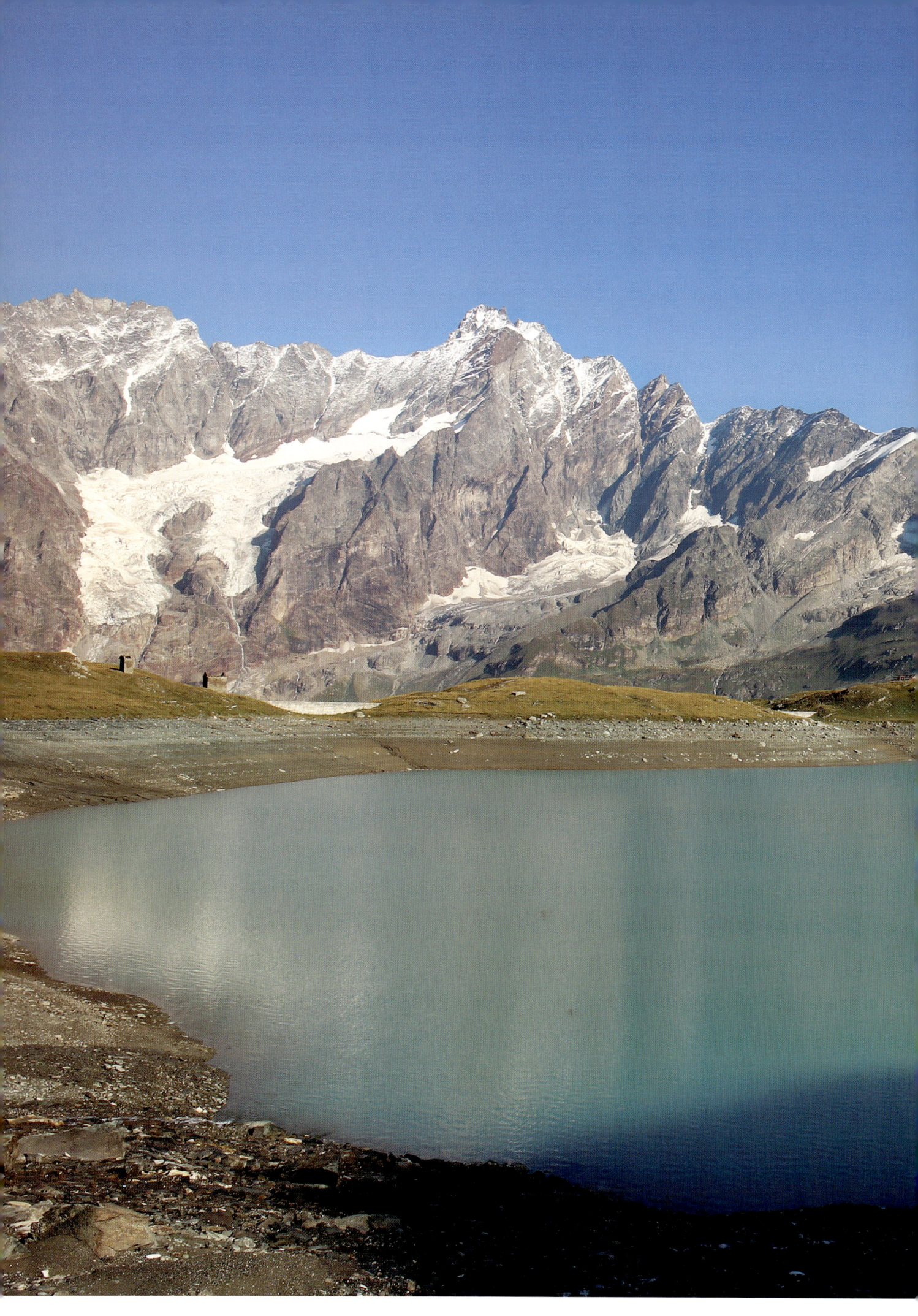

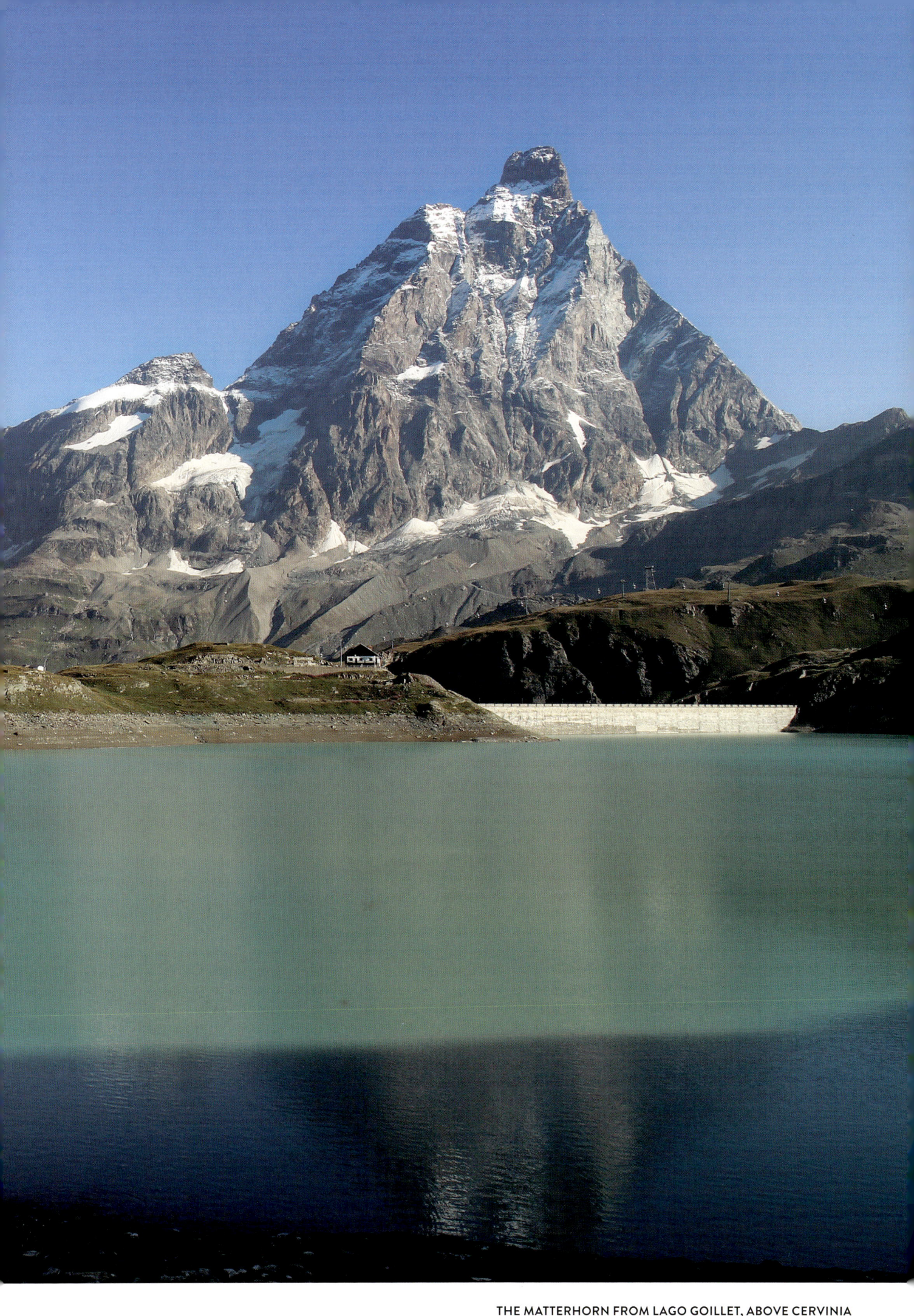

THE MATTERHORN FROM LAGO GOILLET, ABOVE CERVINIA

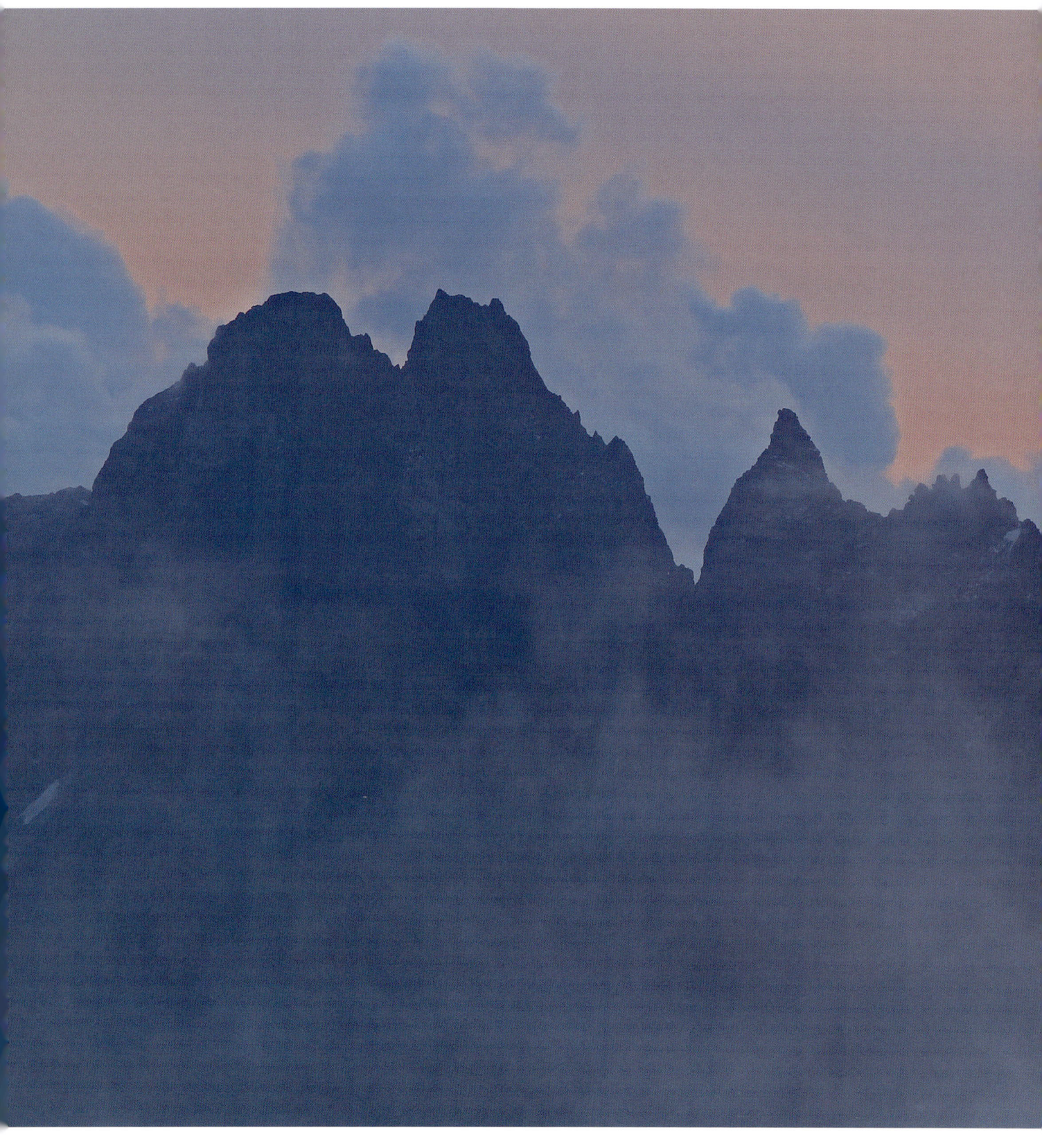

THE PEAKS OF GRANDES MURAILLES ADJOINING DENT D'HERENS

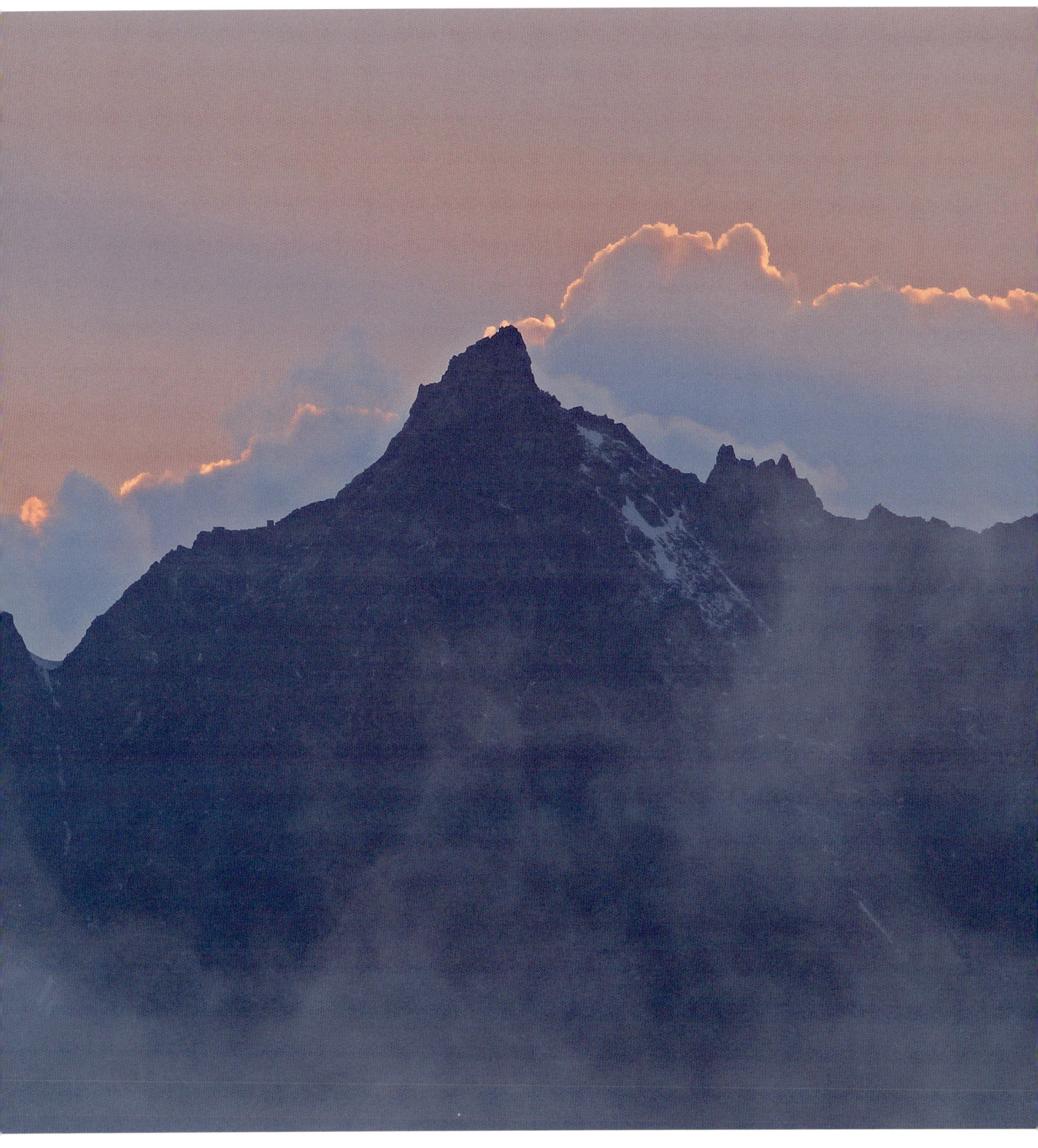

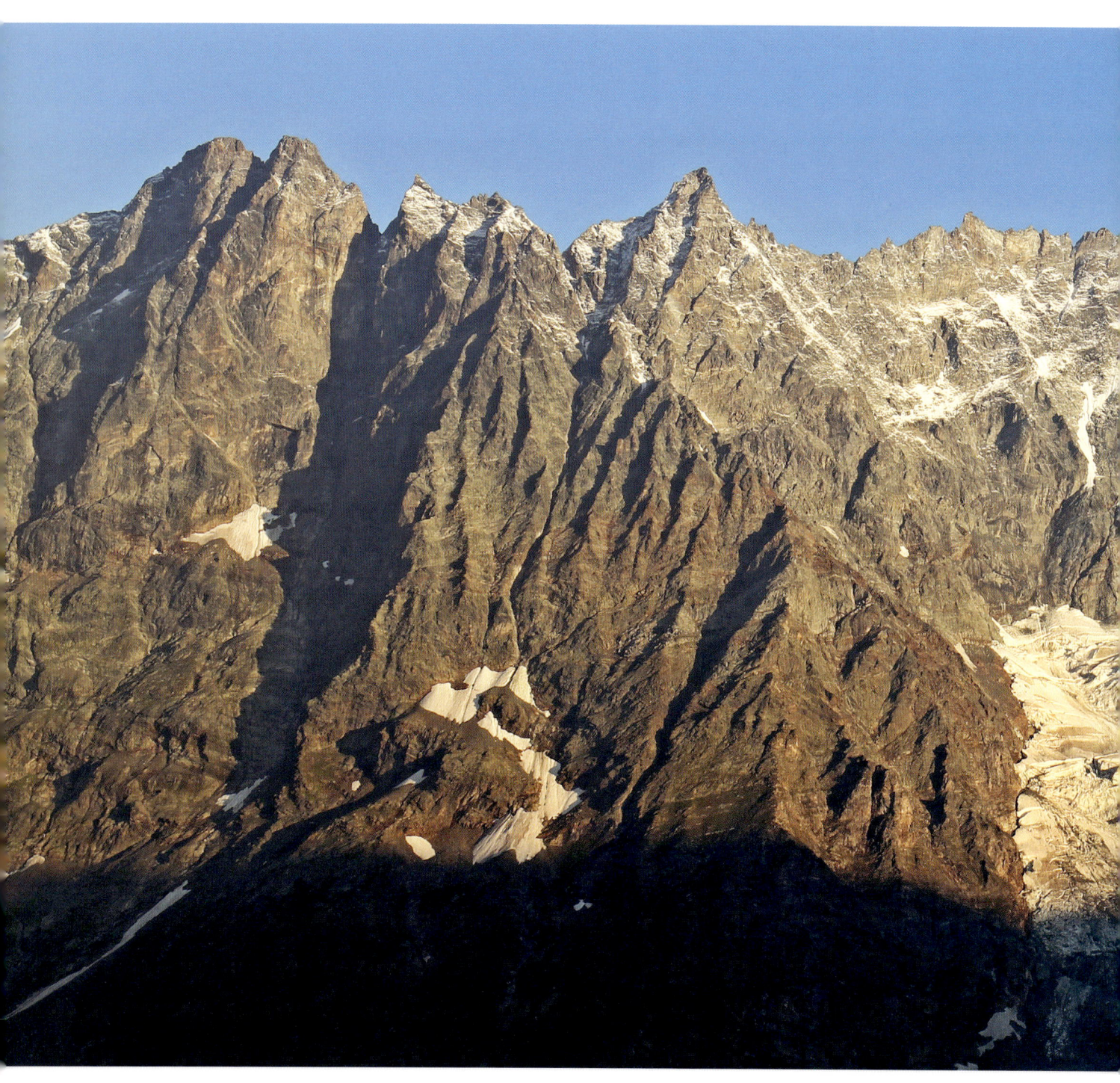

DENT D'HERENS 4,171m FROM LAGO GOILLET, ABOVE CERVINIA

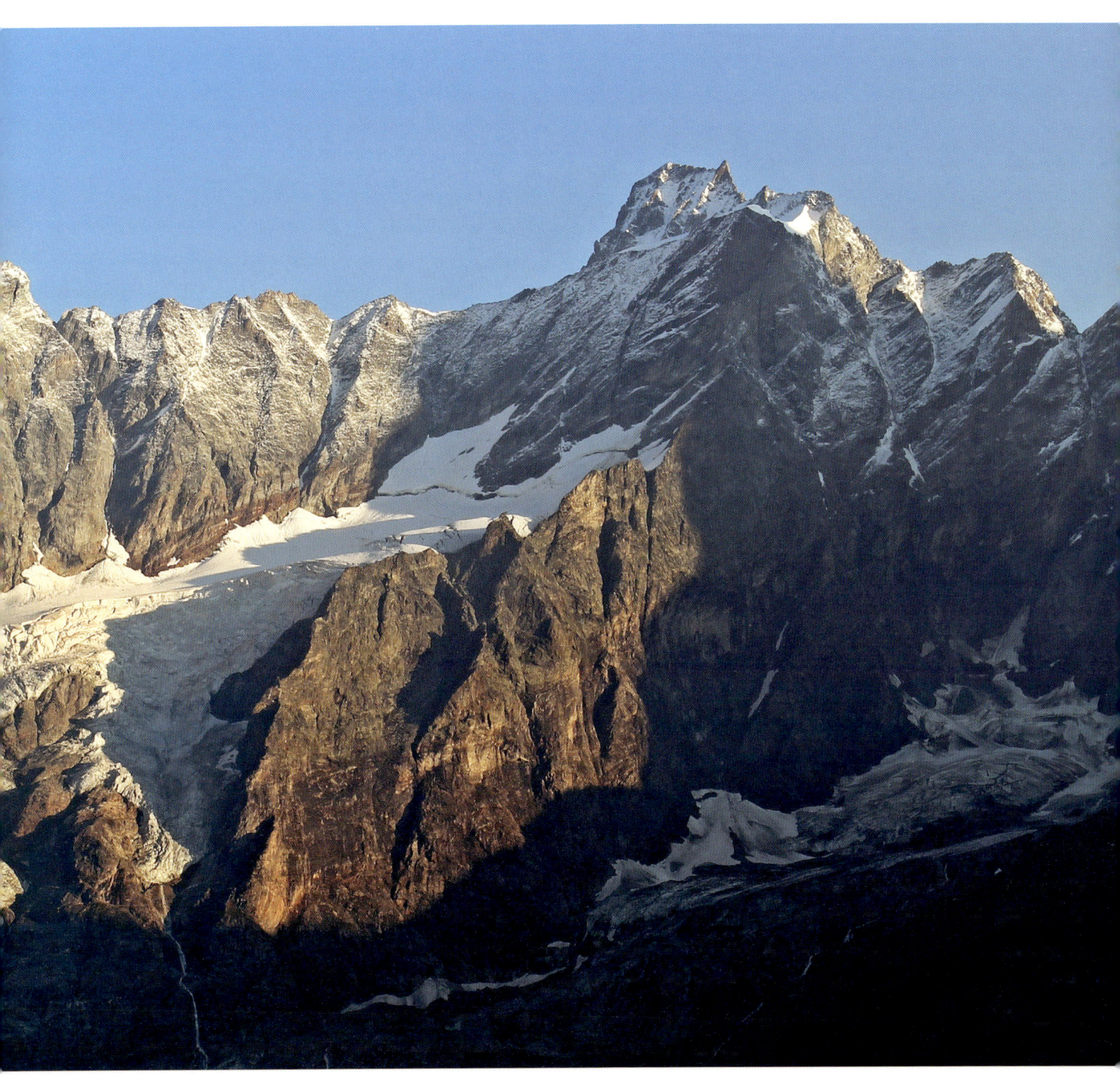

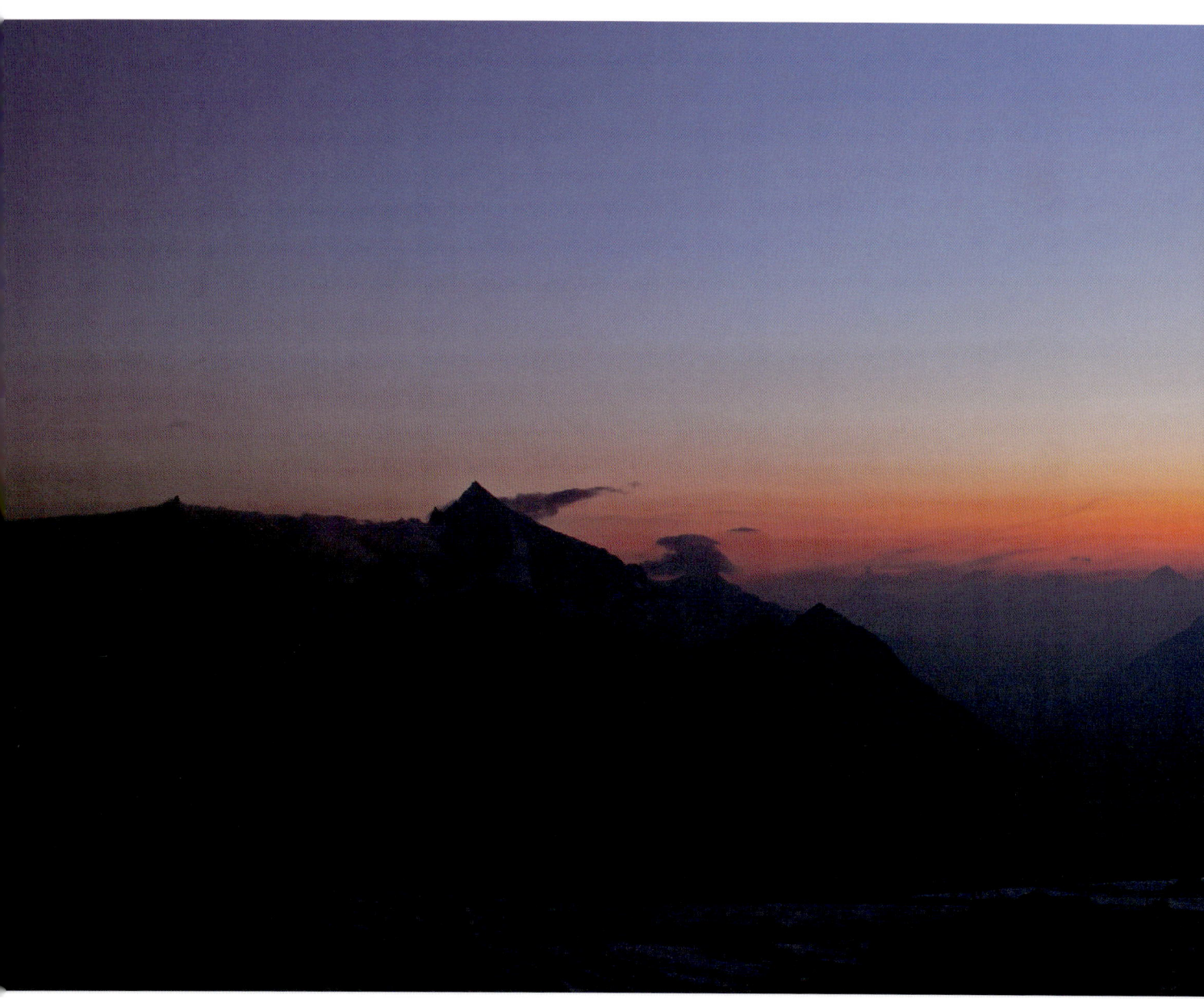

ALPENGLOW ABOVE ZERMATT

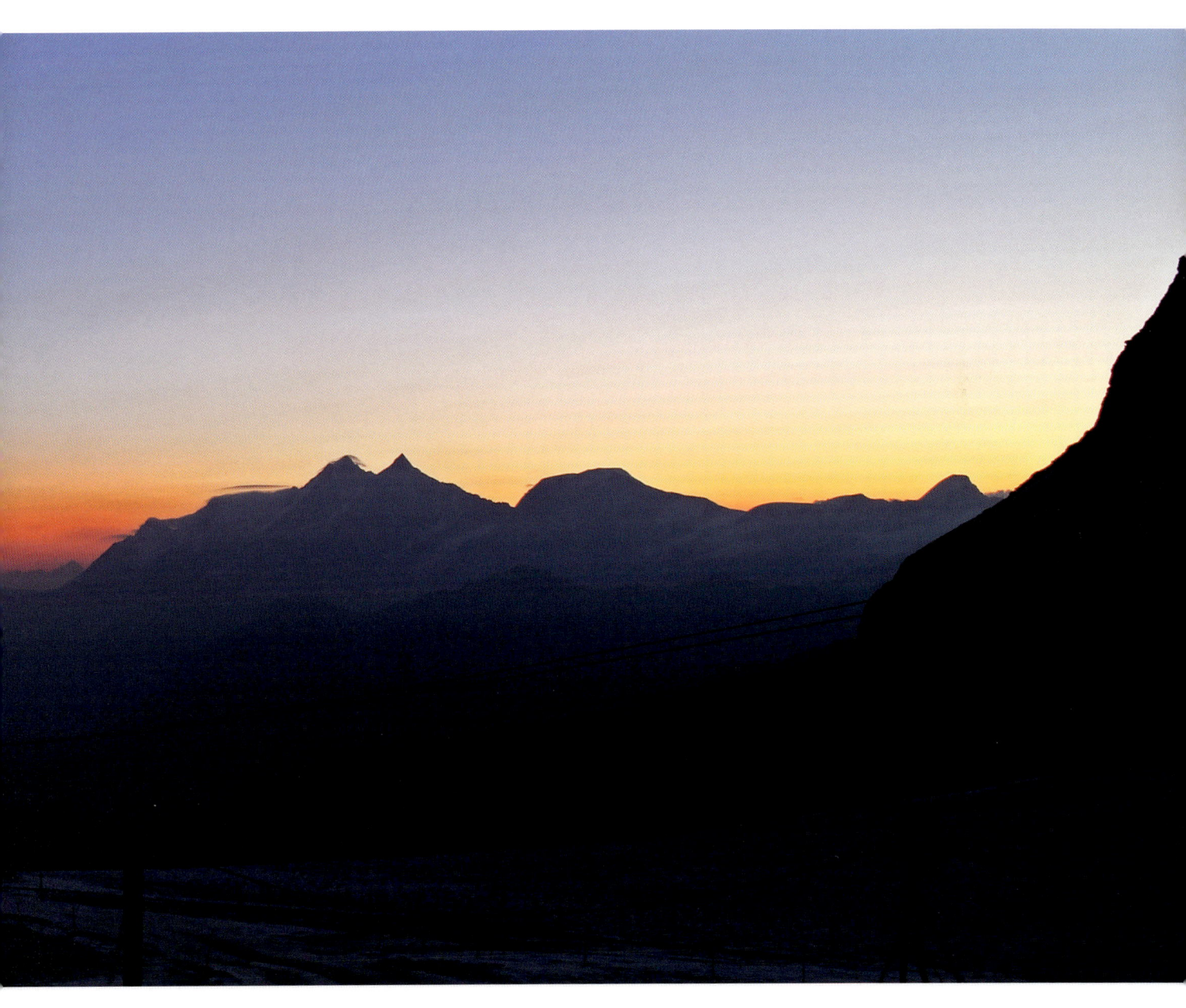

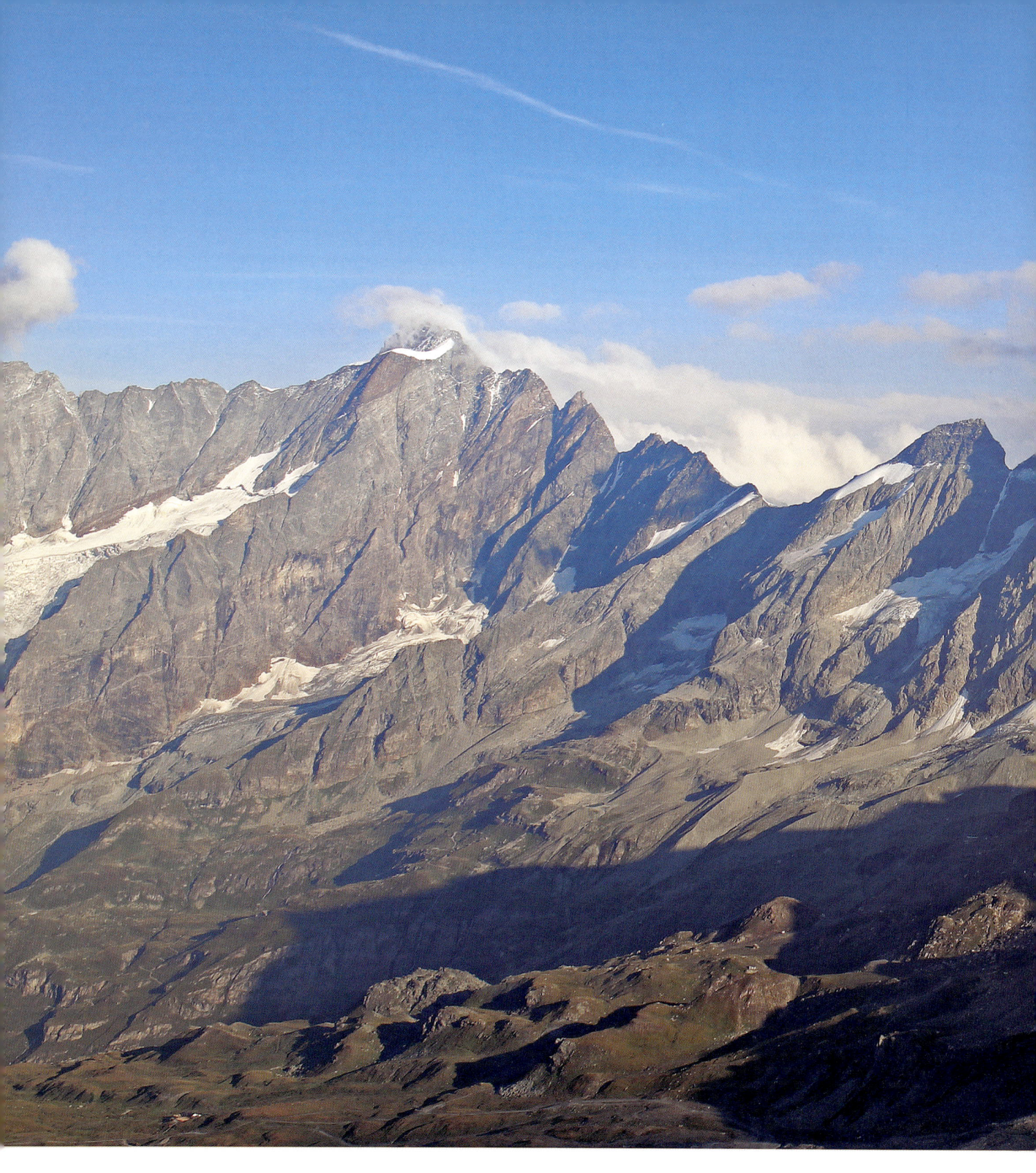

THE MATTERHORN LEADING TO DENT D'HERENS, FROM THEODUL PASS

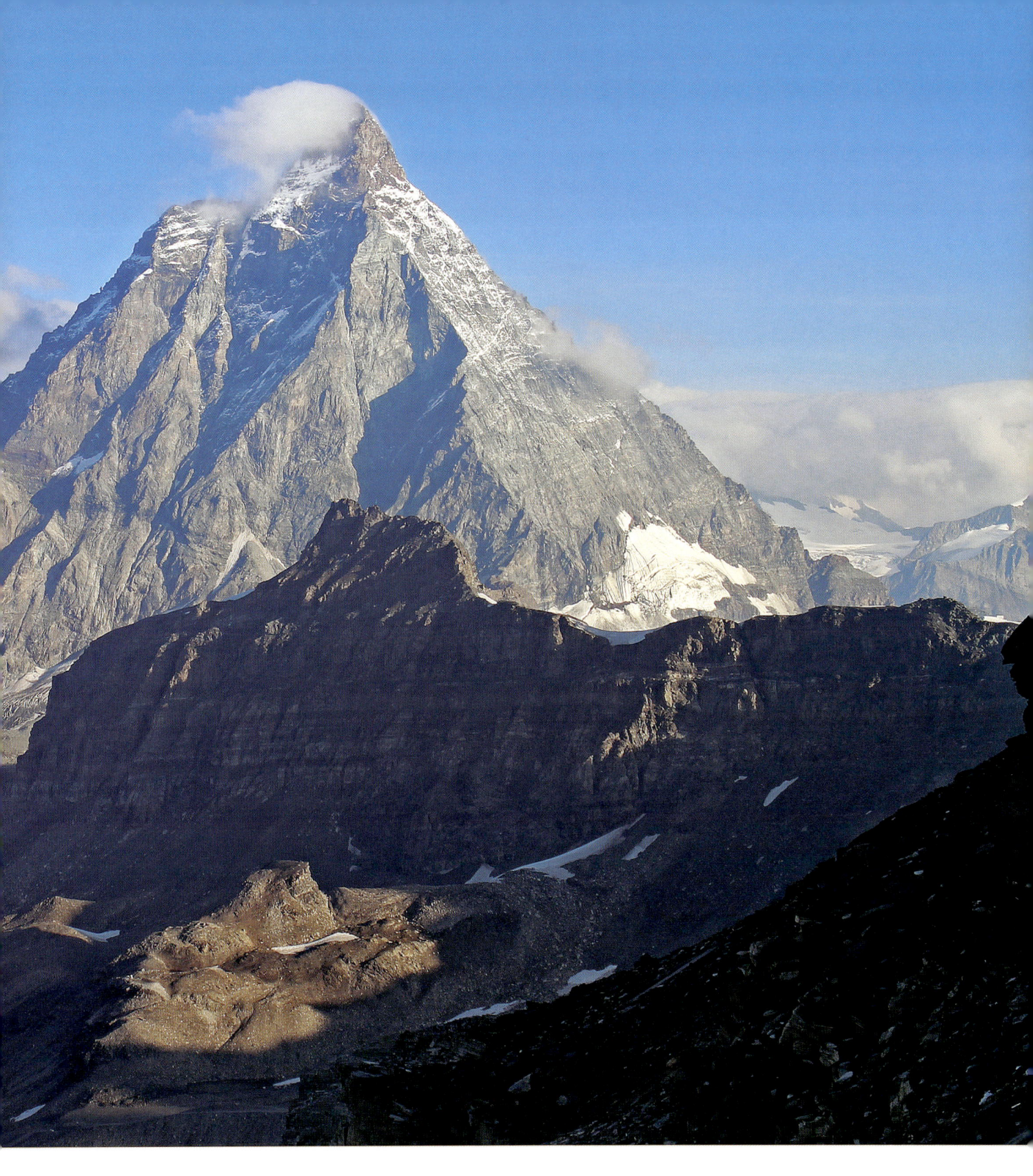

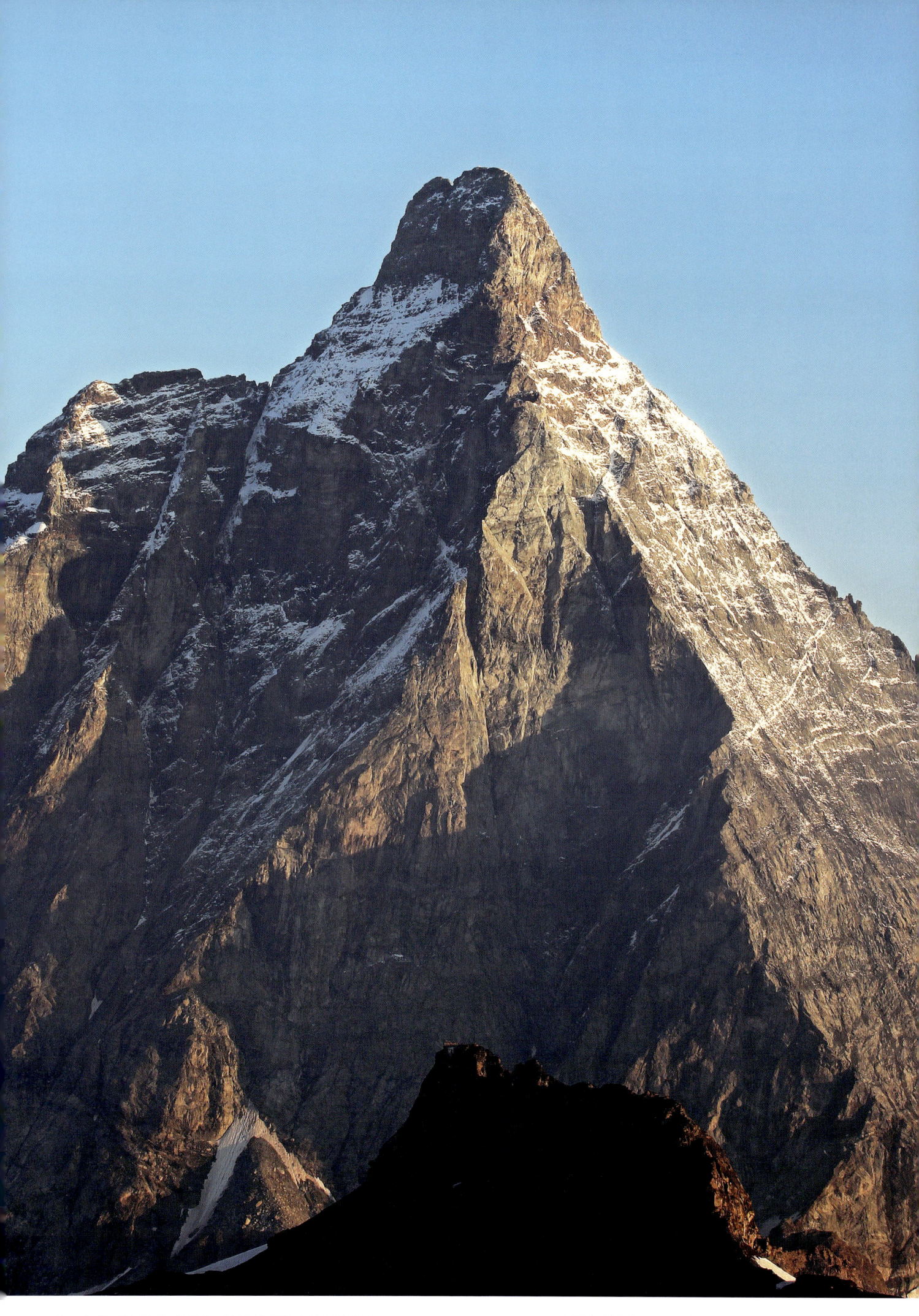

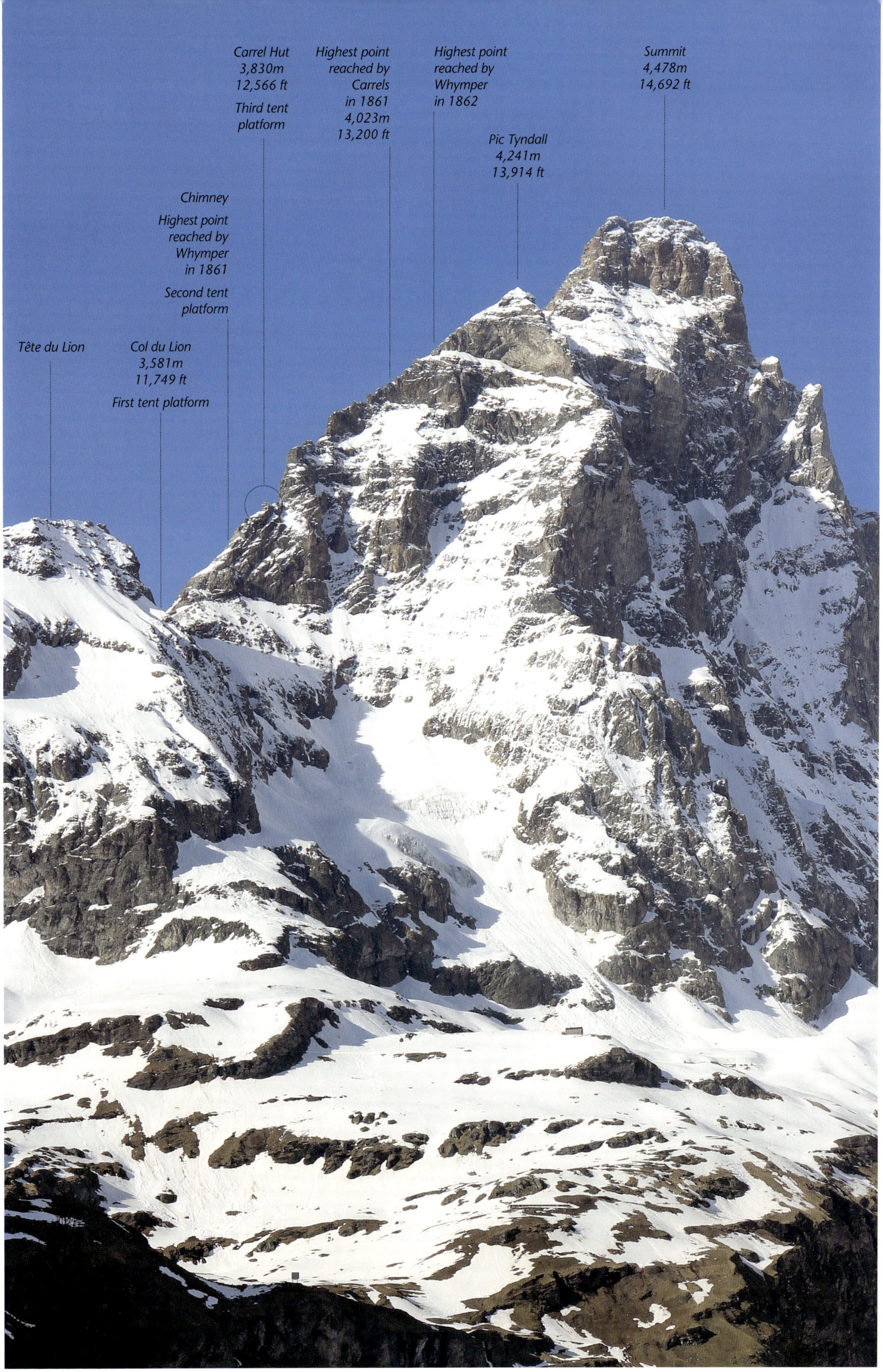

Carrel Hut
3,830m
12,566 ft

Third tent platform

Highest point reached by Carrels in 1861
4,023m
13,200 ft

Highest point reached by Whymper in 1862

Summit
4,478m
14,692 ft

Pic Tyndall
4,241m
13,914 ft

Chimney

Highest point reached by Whymper in 1861

Second tent platform

Tête du Lion

Col du Lion
3,581m
11,749 ft

First tent platform

THE LION (SOUTH-WEST) RIDGE OF MONTE CERVINO

CHAPTER EIGHT
1863: DENT D'HÉRENS, GRAND TOURNALIN AND THE MATTERHORN

In the preface to the first volume of the London *Alpine Journal*, published in 1863, the editor, Mr H. B. George announced 'While even if all the other objects of interest in Switzerland should be exhausted, the Matterhorn remains (who shall say for how long?) unconquered and apparently invincible.'

Meanwhile, in Italy, a gathering of eminent men met in the Valentino Castle with the aim of establishing their own Alpine Society. The English had deprived them of the first summit of so many of their mountains and it was time to set the record straight. Italians should be the first to reach the summit of the Matterhorn and national pride was at stake. Among these men were Quintino Sella and Felice Giordano, the latter was to oversee the mission. According to Giordano, 'In order to complete the ascent it would be necessary to cut steps and do other work in the rock for a height of about a hundred feet; eight or ten days, and three or four stone-cutters at twenty francs a day would be required.' Jean-Antoine Carrel was their obvious choice to lead the party and after succeeding to convince him to take part in their secret mission, a relatively loose agreement was made. Carrel would support the endeavour but was still free to climb the Matterhorn with others.

I crossed the Channel on the 29th of July 1863, embarrassed by the possession of two ladders, each twelve feet long, which joined together like those used by firemen, and shut up like parallel rulers. My luggage was highly suggestive of housebreaking, for, besides these, there were several coils of rope, and numerous tools of suspicious appearance, and it was reluctantly admitted into France, but it passed through the custom-house with less trouble than I anticipated, after a timely expenditure of a few francs.

My real troubles commenced at Susa. The officials there, more honest and more obtuse than the Frenchmen, declined at one and the same time to be bribed, or to pass my baggage until a satisfactory account of it was rendered; and, as they refused to believe the true explanation, I was puzzled what to say, but was presently relieved from the dilemma by one of the men, who was cleverer than his fellows, suggesting that I was going to Turin to exhibit in the streets; that I mounted the ladder and balanced myself on the end of it, then lighted my pipe and put the point of the bâton in its bowl, and caused the bâton to gyrate around my head. The rope was to keep back the spectators, and an Englishman in my company was the agent. 'Monsieur is acrobat then?' 'Yes, certainly.' 'Pass the effects of Monsieur the acrobat!'

I was once more *en route* for the Matterhorn, for I had heard in the spring of 1863 the cause of the failure of Professor Tyndall, and learnt that the case was not so hopeless as it appeared to be at one time … The guide … said it was impossible to proceed, and the Carrels, appealed to for their opinion (this is their own account), gave as an answer, 'We are porters; ask your guides' … Tyndall had nevertheless accomplished an advance of about 400 feet over one of the most difficult parts of the mountain.

We sauntered up the [**Valtournenche**] valley, and got to Breil when all were asleep. A halo round the moon promised watery weather, and we were not disappointed, for, on the next day (August 1), rain fell heavily, and when the clouds lifted for a time, we saw that new snow lay thickly over everything higher than 9000 feet. J.A. Carrel was ready and waiting (as I had determined to give the bold cragsman another chance); and he did not need to say that the Matterhorn would be impracticable for several days after all this new snow, even if the weather were to arrange itself at once. Our first day together was accordingly spent upon a neighbouring summit, the Cimes Blanches; a degraded mountain, well known for its fine panoramic view. It was little that we saw; for, in every direction except to the south, writhing masses of heavy clouds obscured everything; and to the south our view was intercepted by a peak higher than the Cimes Blanches, named the Grand Tournalin. But we got some innocent pleasure out of watching the gambollings of a number of goats, who became fast friends after we had given them some salt; in fact, too fast, and caused us no little annoyance when we were descending. 'Carrel,' I said, as a number of stones whizzed by which they had dislodged, 'this must be put a stop to.' 'Diable!' he grunted, 'it is very well to talk, but how will you do it?' I said that I would try; and, sitting down, poured a little brandy into the hollow of my hand, and allured the nearest goat with deceitful gestures. It was one who had gobbled up the paper in which the salt had been carried — an animal of enterprising character — and it advanced fearlessly and licked up the brandy. I shall not easily forget its surprise. It stopped short, and coughed, and looked at me as much as to say, 'Oh, you cheat!' and spat and ran away; stopping now and then to cough and spit again. We were not troubled any more by those goats.

(Ibid., pp. 88–93)

ATTEMPT TO ASCEND DENT D'HÉRENS

Snow continued to fall and believing there would be no chance of climbing the Matterhorn for some time, Whymper, with Carrel and Meynet, made their way over the Théodule Glacier to Zermatt. After a day exploring the mountainside and glaciers of Zermatt, they planned an exploratory trip around the northern and western base of the Matterhorn in order to better understand their adversary. In due course, they arrived at Dent d'Hérens 4,171m (13,694 ft), immediately west of the Matterhorn, and proceeded in a brave attempt to be the first to scale it.

At 4 A.M. we left [the] Monte Rosa Hotel, and were soon pushing our way through the thickets of grey alder that skirt the path up the right bank of the exquisite little valley which leads to the Z'Muttgletscher.

Nothing can well seem more inaccessible than the Matterhorn upon this side; and even in cold blood one holds the breath when looking at its stupendous cliffs. There are but few equal to them in size in the Alps, and there are none which can more truly be termed *precipices*. Greatest of them all is the immense north cliff, — that which bends over towards the Z'Muttgletscher. Stones which drop from the top of that amazing wall fall for about 1500 feet before they touch anything; and those which roll down from above, and bound over it, fall to a much greater depth, and leap well-nigh 1000 feet beyond its base. This side of the mountain has always seemed sombre — sad — terrible; it is painfully suggestive of decay, ruin, and death; and it is now, alas! more than terrible by its associations.

The desolate, outside pines of the Z'Mutt forests, stripped of their bark, and blanched by the weather, are a fit foreground to a scene that can hardly be surpassed in solemn grandeur. It is a subject worthy of the pencil of a great painter, and one which would tax the powers of the very greatest.

Higher up the glacier the mountain appeared less savage although not less inaccessible; and, about three hours later, when we arrived at the island of rock, called the Stockje (which marks the end of the Z'Muttgletscher proper, and which separates its higher feeder, the Stockgletscher, from its lower and greater one, the Tiefenmatten), Carrel himself, one of the least demonstrative of men, could not refrain from expressing wonder at the steepness of its faces, and at the audacity that had prompted us to camp upon the south-west ridge; the profile of which is seen very well from the Stockje. Carrel then saw the north and north-west sides of the mountain for the first time, and was more firmly persuaded than ever that an ascent was possible *only* from the direction of Breil.

Crossing down into Prerayan they rested there for the night, making a change of plan instead of continuing their circumnavigation.

The hill-tops were clouded when we rose from our hay on the 5th of August. We decided not to continue the tour of our mountain immediately … with the intention of attacking the Dent d'Erin [**now Dent d'Hérens**] on the next morning. We were interested in this summit, more on account of the excellent view which it commanded of the south-west ridge and the terminal peak of the Matterhorn, than from any other reason.

The Dent d'Erin had not been ascended at this time, and we had diverged from our route on the 4th, and had scrambled some distance up the base of Mont Brulé, to see how far its south-western slopes were assailable. We were divided in opinion as to the best way of approaching the peak. Carrel, true to his habit of sticking to rocks in preference to ice, counselled ascending by the long buttress of the Tête de Bella Cia ... I, on the other hand, proposed to follow the Glacier de Zardesan itself throughout its entire length, and from the plateau at its head ... to make directly towards the summit. The hunchback, who was accompanying us on these excursions, declared in favour of Carrel's route, and it was accordingly adopted.

The first part of the programme was successfully executed; and at 10.30 A.M. on the 6th of August, we were sitting astride the western ridge, at a height of about 12,500 feet, looking down upon the Tiefenmatten glacier. To all appearance another hour would place us on the summit; but in another hour we found that we were not destined to succeed. The ridge (like all of the principal rocky ridges of the great peaks upon which I have stood) had been completely shattered by frost, and was nothing more than a heap of piled up fragments. It was always narrow, and where it was narrowest it was also the most unstable and the most difficult. On neither side could we ascend it by keeping a little below its crest ... Forced, therefore, to keep to the very crest of the ridge, and unable to deviate a single step either to the right or to the left, we were compelled to trust ourselves upon unsteady masses, which trembled under our tread, which sometimes settled down, grating in a hollow and ominous manner, and which seemed as if a little shake would send the whole roaring down in one awful avalanche.

I followed my leader, who said not a word, and did not rebel until we came to a place where a block had to be surmounted which lay poised across the ridge. Carrel could not climb it without assistance, or advance beyond it until I joined him above; and as he stepped off my back on to it, I felt it quiver and bear down upon me. I doubted the possibility of another man standing upon it without bringing it down. Then I rebelled. There was no honour to be gained by persevering, or dishonour in turning from a place which was dangerous on account of its excessive difficulty. So we returned to Prerayen, for there was too little time to allow us to re-ascend by the other route, which was subsequently shown to be the right way up the mountain.

Four days afterwards a party of Englishmen (including my friends, W. E. Hall, Craufurd Grove, and Reginald Macdonald), arrived in the Valpelline, and (unaware of our attempt) on the 12th, under the skilful guidance of Melchior Anderegg, made the first ascent of the Dent d'Erin by the route which I had proposed. This is the only mountain which I have essayed to ascend, that has not, sooner or later, fallen to me. Our failure was mortifying, yet I am satisfied that we did wisely in returning, and that if we had persevered, by Carrel's route, another Alpine accident would have been recorded. Other routes have been since discovered up the Dent d'Erin. The ascent ranks amongst the more difficult ones which have been made in the Alps.

(Ibid., pp. 99–105)

ATTEMPT TO ASCEND GRAND TOURNALIN

The Grand Tournalin 3,379m (11,085 ft) was Valtournenche's mountain, due east of the town. Isolated, it enjoyed superb views of the surrounding peaks, non more so than of the Matterhorn. Despite this, there was no recorded of anyone having climbed its summit.

On the 7th of August we crossed the Va Cornère pass, and had a good look at the mountain named the Grand Tournalin as we descended the Val de Chignana. This mountain was seen from so many points ... and (as the weather continued unfavourable for the Matterhorn) I arranged with Carrel to ascend it the next day, and despatched him direct to the village of Val Tournanche to make the necessary preparations ... I rejoined Carrel the same evening at Val Tournanche, and we started from that place at a little before 5 A.M. on the 8th, to attack the Tournalin.

Meynet was left behind for that day, and most unwillingly did the hunchback part from us, and begged hard to be allowed to come. 'Pay me nothing, only let me go with you;' 'I shall want but a little bread and cheese, and of that

I won't eat much;' 'I would much rather go with you than carry things down the valley.' Such were his arguments, and I was really sorry that the rapidity of our movements obliged us to desert the good little man.

Carrel led over the meadows on the south and east of the bluff upon which the village of Val Tournanche is built, and then by a zig-zag path through a long and steep forest, making many short cuts, which showed he had a thorough knowledge of the ground. After we came again into daylight, our route took us up one of those little, concealed, lateral valleys which are so numerous on the slopes bounding the Val Tournanche.

After Ceneil is passed [**Grand Tournalin**] comes into view, rising above a cirque of cliffs (streaked by several fine waterfalls) … To avoid these cliffs the path bends somewhat to the south, keeping throughout to the left bank of the valley, and at about 3500 feet above Val Tournanche, and 1500 feet above Ceneil and a mile or so to its east, arrives at the base of some moraines … and here the path ends and the way steepens.

… in little more than half-an-hour [**we**] stood upon the Col, which commanded a most glorious view of the southern side of Monte Rosa, and of the ranges to its east, and to the east of the Val d'Ayas.

The ridge that led from the Col towards the summit was singularly easy, although well broken up by frost … but when we arrived on the summit we found ourselves separated from the very highest point by a cleft which had been concealed up to that time: its southern side was nearly perpendicular, but it was only fourteen or fifteen feet deep. Carrel lowered me down, and afterwards descended on to the head of my axe, and subsequently on to my shoulders, with a cleverness which was almost as far removed from my awkwardness as his own efforts were from those of the chamois. A few easy steps then placed us on the highest point. It had not been ascended before, and we commemorated the event by building a huge cairn, which was seen for many a mile … Its ascent (including halts) occupied us only four hours.

I advise the ascent of this mountain not on account of its height, or from its accessibility or inaccessibility, but simply for the wide and splendid view which may be seen from its summit. Its position is superb, and the list of the peaks which can be seen from it includes almost the whole of the principal mountains of the Cottian, Dauphiné, Graian, Pennine, and Oberland groups. The view has, in the highest perfection, those elements of picturesqueness which are wanting in the purely panoramic views of higher summits. There are three principal sections, each with a central or dominating point, to which the eye is naturally drawn. All three alike are pictures in themselves; yet all are dissimilar.

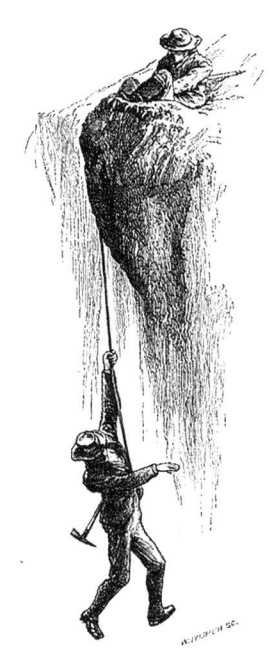

'Carrel Lowered Me Down'

Those who would, but cannot, stand upon the highest Alps, may console themselves with the knowledge that they do not usually yield the views that make the strongest and most permanent impressions. Marvellous some of the panoramas seen from the greatest peaks undoubtedly are; but they are necessarily without those isolated and central points which are so valuable pictorially.

No views create such lasting impressions as those which are seen but for a moment, when a veil of mist is rent in twain, and a single spire or dome is disclosed. The peaks which are seen at these moments are not, perhaps, the greatest or the noblest, but the recollection of them outlives the memory of any panoramic view, because the picture, photographed by the eye, has time to dry, instead of being blurred, while yet wet, by contact with other impressions. The reverse is the case with the bird's-eye panoramic views from the great peaks, which sometimes embrace a hundred miles in nearly every direction. The eye is confounded by the crowd of details, and is unable to distinguish the relative importance of the objects which are seen. It is almost as difficult to form a just estimate (with the eye) of the respective heights of a number of peaks from a very high summit, as it is from the bottom of a valley. I think that the grandest and the most satisfactory standpoints for viewing mountain scenery are those which are sufficiently elevated to give a feeling of depth, as well as of height, which are lofty enough to exhibit wide and varied views, but not so high as to sink everything to the level of the spectator. The view from the Grand Tournalin is a favourable example of this class of panoramic views.

We descended from the summit by the northern route, and found it tolerably stiff clambering as far as the Col. Thence, down the glacier, the way was straightforward, and we joined the route taken on the ascent at the foot of the ridge leading towards the east. In the evening we returned to Breil.

(Ibid., pp. 105–110)

SIXTH ATTEMPT TO ASCEND THE MATTERHORN

We rested on Sunday, August 9th, eagerly watching the lessening of the mists around the great peak, and started just before dawn upon the 10th, on a still and cloudless morning, which seemed to promise a happy termination to our enterprise.

By going always, though gently, we arrived upon the Col du Lion before nine o'clock. Changes were apparent. Familiar ledges had vanished; the platform, whereupon my tent had stood, looked very forlorn, its stones had been scattered by wind and frost, and had half disappeared: and the summit of the Col itself, which in 1862 had always been respectably broad, and covered by snow, was now sharper than the ridge of any church roof, and was hard ice. Already we had found that the bad weather of the past week had done its work. The rocks for several hundred feet below the Col were varnished with ice. Loose, incoherent snow covered the older and harder beds below, and we nearly lost our leader through its treacherousness. He stepped on some snow which seemed firm, and raised his axe to deliver a swinging blow, but, just as it was highest, the crust of the slope upon which he stood broke away, and poured down in serpentine streams, leaving long, bare strips, which glittered in the sun, for they were glassy ice. Carrel, with admirable readiness, flung himself back on to the rock off which he had stepped, and was at once secured. He simply remarked, 'It is time we were tied up,' and, after we had been tied up, he went to work again as if nothing had happened.

We had abundant illustrations during the next two hours of the value of a rope to climbers. We were tied up rather widely apart, and advanced, generally, in pairs. … This manner of progression was slow, but sure. One man only moved at a time, and if he slipped (and we frequently did slip) he could slide scarcely a foot without being checked by the others. The certainty and safety of the method gave confidence to the one who was moving, and not only nerved him to put out his powers to the utmost, but sustained nerve in really difficult situations. For these rocks (which, it has been already said, were easy enough under ordinary circumstances) were now difficult in a high degree. The snow-water which had trickled down for many days past in little streams, had taken, naturally, the very route by which we wished to ascend; and, refrozen in the night, had glazed the slabs over which we had to pass, — sometimes with a fine film of ice as thin as a sheet of paper, and sometimes so thickly that we could almost cut footsteps in it. The weather was superb, the men made light of the toil, and shouted to rouse the echoes from the Dent d'Hérens.

We went on gaily, passed the second tent platform, the Chimney, and the other well-remembered points, and reckoned, confidently, on sleeping that night upon the top of 'the shoulder;' but, before we had well arrived at the foot of the Great Tower, a sudden rush of cold air warned us to look out.

It was difficult to say where this air came from; it did not blow as a wind, but descended rather as the water in a shower-bath! All was tranquil again; the atmosphere *showed* no signs of disturbance; there was a dead calm, and not a speck of cloud to be seen anywhere. But we did not remain very long in this state. The cold air came again, and this time it was difficult to say where it did *not* come from. We jammed down our hats as it beat against the ridge, and screamed amongst the crags. Before we had got to the foot of the Tower, mists had been formed above and below. They appeared at first in small, isolated patches (in several places at the same time), which danced and jerked and were torn into shreds by the wind, but grew larger under the process. They were united together, and rent again, — showing us the blue sky for a moment, and blotting it out the next; and augmented incessantly, until the whole heavens were filled with whirling, boiling clouds. Before we could take off our packs, and get under any kind of shelter, a hurricane of snow burst upon us from the east. It fell very heavily, and in a few minutes the ridge was covered by it. 'What shall we do?' I shouted to Carrel. 'Monsieur,' said he, 'the wind is bad; the weather has changed; we are heavily laden. Here is a fine *gîte*; let us stop! If we go on we shall be half-frozen. That is *my* opinion.' No one differed from him; so we fell to work to make a place for the tent, and in a couple of hours completed the platform which we had commenced in 1862. The clouds had blackened during that time, and we had hardly finished our task before a thunderstorm broke upon us with appalling fury. Forked lightning shot out at the turrets above, and at the crags below. It was so close that we quailed at its darts. It seemed to scorch us, — we were in the very focus of the storm. The thunder was simultaneous with the flashes; short and sharp, and more like the noise of a door that is violently slammed, multiplied a thousandfold, than any noise to which I can compare it.

When I say that the thunder was *simultaneous* with the lightning, I speak as an inexact person. My meaning is that the time which elapsed between seeing the flash and hearing the report was inappreciable to me. I wish to speak with all possible precision, and there are two points with regard to this storm upon which I can speak with some accuracy. The first is in regard to the distance of the lightning from our party. We *might* have been 1100 feet from it if a second of time had elapsed between seeing the flashes and hearing the reports; and a second of time is not appreciated by inexact persons. It was certain that we were sometimes less than that distance from the lightning, because I saw it pass in front of well-known points on the ridge, both above and below us, which were less (sometimes considerably less) than a thousand feet distant.

The thunderstorm lasted nearly two hours, and raged at times with great fury; and the prolonged rollings from the surrounding mountains, after one flash, had not usually ceased before another set of echoes took up the discourse, and maintained the reverberations without a break.

The wind during all this time seemed to blow tolerably consistently from the east. It smote the tent so vehemently (notwithstanding it was partly protected by rocks) that we had grave fears our refuge might be blown away bodily, with ourselves inside; so, during some of the lulls, we issued out and built a wall to windward. At half-past three the wind changed to the north-west, and the clouds vanished. We immediately took the opportunity to send down one of the porters (under protection of some of the others, a little beyond the Col du Lion), as the tent would accommodate only five persons. From this time to sunset the weather was variable. It was sometimes blowing and snowing hard, and sometimes a dead calm. The bad weather was evidently confined to the Mont Cervin, for when the clouds lifted we could see everything that could be seen from our gîte. Monte Viso, a hundred miles off, was clear, and the sun set gorgeously behind the range of Mont Blanc. We passed the night comfortably — even luxuriously — in our blanket-bags, but there was little chance of sleeping, between the noise of the wind, of the thunder, and of the falling rocks. I forgave the thunder for the sake of the lightning. A more splendid spectacle than its illumination of the Matterhorn crags I do not expect to see.

The greatest rock-falls always seemed to occur in the night, between midnight and daybreak. This was noticeable on each of the seven nights which I passed upon the south-west ridge, at heights varying from 11,800 to 13,000 feet.

We turned out at 3.30 A.M. on the 11th, and were dismayed to find that it still continued to snow. At 9 A.M. it ceased to fall, and the sun showed itself feebly, so we packed up our baggage, and set out to try to get upon 'the shoulder.' We struggled upwards until eleven o'clock, and then it commenced to snow again. We held a council; the opinions expressed at it were unanimous against advancing, and I decided to retreat. For we had risen less than 300 feet in the past two hours, and had not even arrived at the rope which Tyndall's party left behind, attached to the rocks, in 1862. At the same rate of progression it would have taken us from four to five hours to get upon 'the shoulder.' Not one of us cared to attempt to do so under the existing circumstances; for besides having to move our own weight, which was sufficiently troublesome at this part of the ridge, we had to transport much heavy baggage, tent, blankets, and provisions, ladder, and 450 feet of rope, besides many other smaller matters. These, however, were not the most serious considerations. Supposing that we got upon 'the shoulder,' we might find ourselves detained there several days, unable either to go up or down. I could not risk any such detention, being under obligations to appear in London at the end of the week.

We returned to Breil in the course of the afternoon. It was quite fine there, and the tenants of the inn received our statements with evident scepticism. They were astonished to learn that we had been exposed to a snow-storm of twenty-six hours' duration. 'Why,' said Favre, the innkeeper, '*we* have had no snow; it has been fine all the time you have been absent, and there has been only that small cloud upon the mountain.' Ah! that small cloud! None except those who have had experience of it can tell what a formidable obstacle it is.

I conceive that we should look to differences of temperature rather than to the height or isolation of the mountain for an explanation. I am inclined to attribute the disturbances which occur in the atmosphere of the southern sides of the Matterhorn on fine days, principally to the fact that the mountain is a *rock* mountain; that it receives a great amount of heat, and is not only warmer itself, but is surrounded by an atmosphere of a higher temperature than such peaks as the Weisshorn and the Lyskamm, which are eminently *snow* mountains.

Provided that the temperature was uniform, or nearly so, on all sides of the Matterhorn, and to a considerable distance above its summit, no clouds would be likely to form upon it. But if the atmosphere immediately surrounding it is warmer than the contiguous strata, a local 'courant ascendant' must necessarily be generated; and portions of the cooler superincumbent (or circumjacent) air will naturally be attracted towards the mountain, where they will speedily condense the moisture of the warm air in contact with it.

This opinion is borne out to some extent by the behaviour of the neighbouring mountains. The Dom (14,935 feet) and the Dent Blanche (14,318) have both of them large cliffs of bare rock upon their southern sides, and against those cliffs clouds commonly form (during fine, still weather) at the same time as the cloud on the Matterhorn; whilst the Weisshorn (14,804) and the Lyskamm (14,889), (mountains of about the same altitude, and which are in corresponding situations to the former pair) usually remain perfectly clear.

I arrived at Chatillon at midnight on the 11th, defeated and disconsolate; but, like a gambler who loses each throw, only the more eager to have another try, to see if the luck would change: and returned to London ready to devise fresh combinations, and to form new plans.

(Ibid., pp. 114–123)

SUMMER 2015 (WEEK TWO)

AUTHOR'S LOG

The Matterhorn divides two very different countries, and from the extremely structured, almost militarily organised Swiss town of Zermatt, I travelled nearly full-circle through France, to the more easy-going town of Breuil-Cervinia, in Italy.

The general goal was the same: more acclimatisation at higher altitude and a trip to some locations not previously visited. There would be no wild camping this week, so I pitched my larger tent at a campsite just outside the village of Valtournenche, a little further down from Cervinia, in the captivating Aosta valley. This is, of course, where Carrel lived and where Whymper spent so many days preparing or resting from his forays. Today, as it was then, Valtournenche is a reasonably large town, while Cervinia remains somewhat more sleepy, albeit expanding with ever more holiday homes. It has become a thriving ski town and even in mid-summer, the cable cars were busy transporting skiers up to the Theodul Glacier.

Following several days of wet and thundery weather, another warm, dry spell was imminent, so with no time to waste, and before first light I headed up to Lake Goillet, at 2,516m. A huge glacier-fed, dammed lake, it not only provides the water and hydroelectricity for Cervina, but also provides the water needed for the artificial snow to keep the ski industry going throughout the year. The forecast was for near-zero wind, so I hiked up to the lake in the hope of another perfect reflection of the Matterhorn on its surface.

As finding the start of the trail in the dark was harder than anticipated, I ended up walking along the service track, which made the 500m ascent more manageable. Disappointingly, the lake was not mirror-like, so there were no reflective shots on this occasion. As compensation, however, the lake was an eye-catching turquoise-green as a result of the rock silt suspended in the water. The tiny particles cause the water to reflect rather than absorb the spectrum of light from the sun.

On another cloudless and peaceful morning, the full south face of the Matterhorn dominated the skyline above the colourful lake, while the Lion Ridge defined the monolith's western profile, which carried on along the lengthy ridgeline to Dent d'Hérens and beyond.

Having waited for the sun to rise sufficiently to illuminate the lake, I headed further on up the mountainside toward the Plateau Rosa, along the Theodul Pass. It was not possible to hike the whole way, so I took a gondola for the last section and arrived at the Rifugio delle Guide del Cervino by late afternoon. The temperature was a good 15 degrees cooler and I was instantly reminded of just where I was: 3,500m above sea level on a small rocky outcrop surrounded by glaciers. It was a pleasant enough afternoon but I could only imagine how many times the hut had provided a welcome, if not life-saving sanctuary for climbers that may have found themselves in difficulty in such a barren and inhospitable place.

The clouds had rolled in and the sun made only the briefest of appearances before I sat down to a very large bowl of pasta, following which I braved the increasing cold to photograph the sun as it set. Billowing clouds hid the setting sun but it did just manage to highlight any breaks above the jagged peaks of the Dent d'Hérens ridgeline.

Early to bed, and somewhat apprehensive about whether I would have a clear view of the Matterhorn the following morning, I settled down in the very small but perfectly adequate five-berth bunkroom. Alas, another night went by with what felt like no sleep. Throughout the night I was repeatedly aware of needing to take an extra gasp of air and was glad I was experiencing the phenomenon then, rather than halfway up the Matterhorn.

Another pre-dawn start to the day began with a warming coffee, which was just as well as the wind had picked up overnight and it was particularly chilly when stepping out on the frozen snow. Instantly, I was captured by the vivid alpenglow beyond the mountains above Zermatt and Sass-Fee; an awe-inspiring view that only early birds get to enjoy. With just enough time to photograph the vivid colours, I headed around the building and set up to photograph the rising sun against the east face and south-west ridge of the Matterhorn. To witness another sunrise in so unique a place, on the mountain that I've thought about daily for the past two years, was an incomparable and memorable moment. Then, having enjoyed my moment, skiers started to arrive to catch the freshly ploughed snow and I slipped away in the opposite direction, content with my last twenty-four hours on the Matterhorn (see chapter seven for photographs).

Once back at the campsite, I checked the forecast, which continued to predict a gradual deterioration in the conditions. There was little for it but to head straight back out and attempt to climb the first mountain of which Whymper made the initial ascent. After a brief catnap and shower, I packed as lightly as possible to head up Grand Tournalin; a four-hour hike to the summit. At 3,379m (11,086 ft), it is the highest peak above Valtournenche, and yet, despite this accolade, I had struggled to find any details ahead of time about the difficulty it posed. All I knew was that it was very well signposted to a height of about 2,400m, then well marked with rock cairns from there.

With little knowledge of the climb I started out from the isolated hamlet of Cheneil at 2,088m. Thronging with tourists, the few scattered dwellings in the upper valley basin marked the starting point for a great variety of walks. From here, Grand Tournalin looked little more than a long stroll and was graded a fairly moderate 'EE' on the signpost. Setting out under partly cloudy skies and with a spring in my step, I was excited to be climbing one of Whymper's mountains, although doubtful of getting the views about which he wrote so eloquently in 1863. But this outing was more about the climb and less about the photography. After two hours, I left the signposts and followed the cairns towards a col between Grand and Petit Tournalin. The mountainside was extremely fragmented and I doubt I would have reached the col without the frequent markers.

From the col, the way became a little clearer, although no less fragmented. Ever willing to turn back, by the time I reached a small section of fixed rope I was beginning to question whether I would succeed in reaching the summit alone. However, a little further on I saw the obligatory crucifix marking the summit with no further apparent difficulty ahead.

Unfortunately, it appeared to not quite indicate the summit and looking further north I could see a series of points which resembled several man-made piles of rocks along a narrow arête. Leaving my bag at the cross, I made my way over three of the individually coloured rock mounds before arriving a short distance from the final one. Sadly, this was the turning point for me as a deep drop separated it from where I stood. Alone, with no knowledge of the difficulty, and what appeared like nothing holding the rock piles together, I retreated to what I believed to be nine metres shy of the summit. Disappointed but largely content, I made a fairly rapid descent beneath increasingly darkening skies, certain I had made the correct decision.

Once again the week drew to a close with heavy rain and violent thunderstorms that lasted three days. And, just as Whymper fearfully described a night in the middle of a titanic thunderstorm during his sixth attempt on the Matterhorn, I was equally sure I was as close as I would ever wish to be to thunder during a ferocious long night in my tent.

A visit to the Guide Office in Cervinia confirmed that the Lion Ridge and Carrel hut were still closed, but I remained hopeful that the repairs would be made and the colder weather would freeze the rock. More anxious days lay ahead!

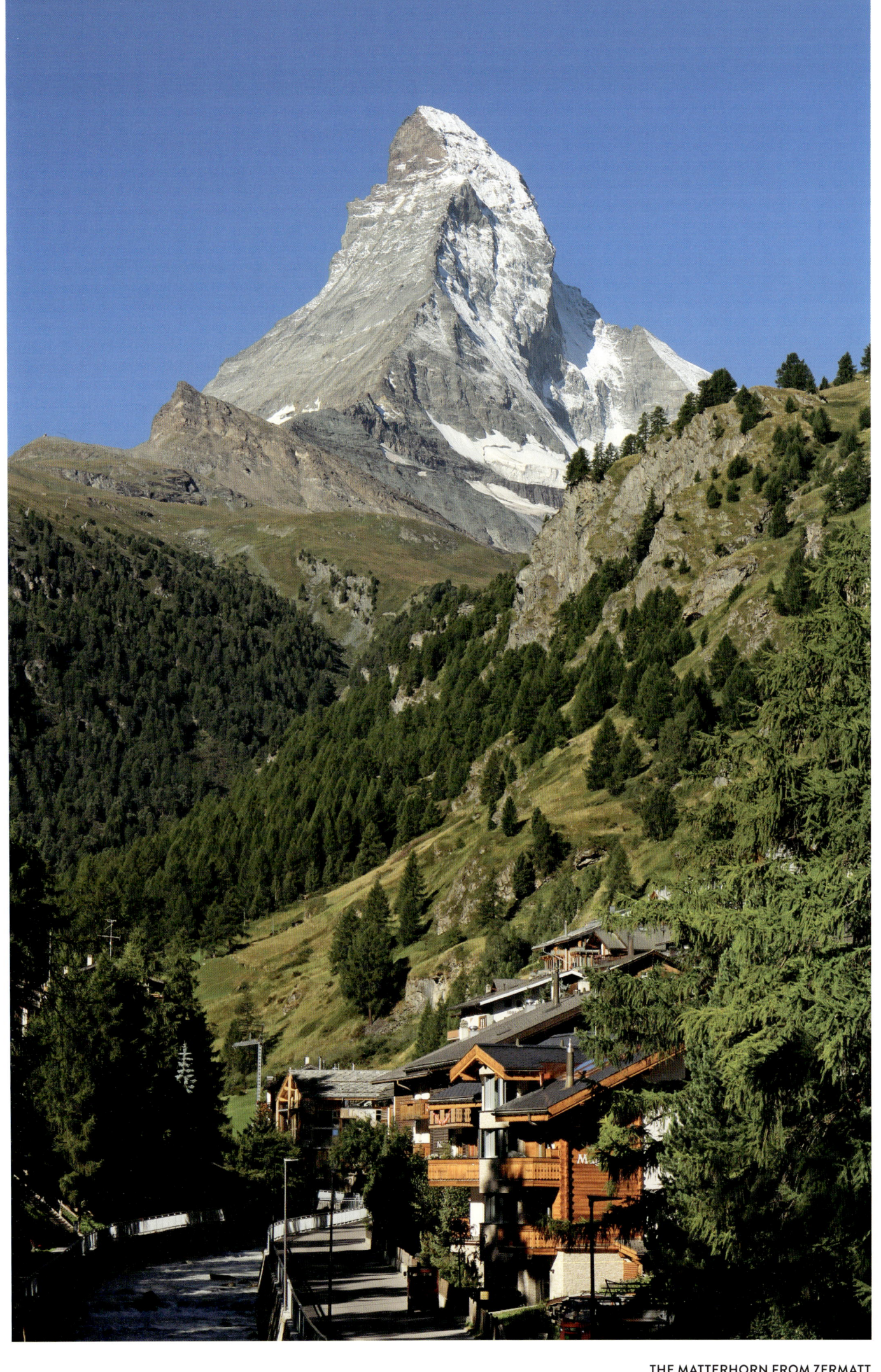

THE MATTERHORN FROM ZERMATT

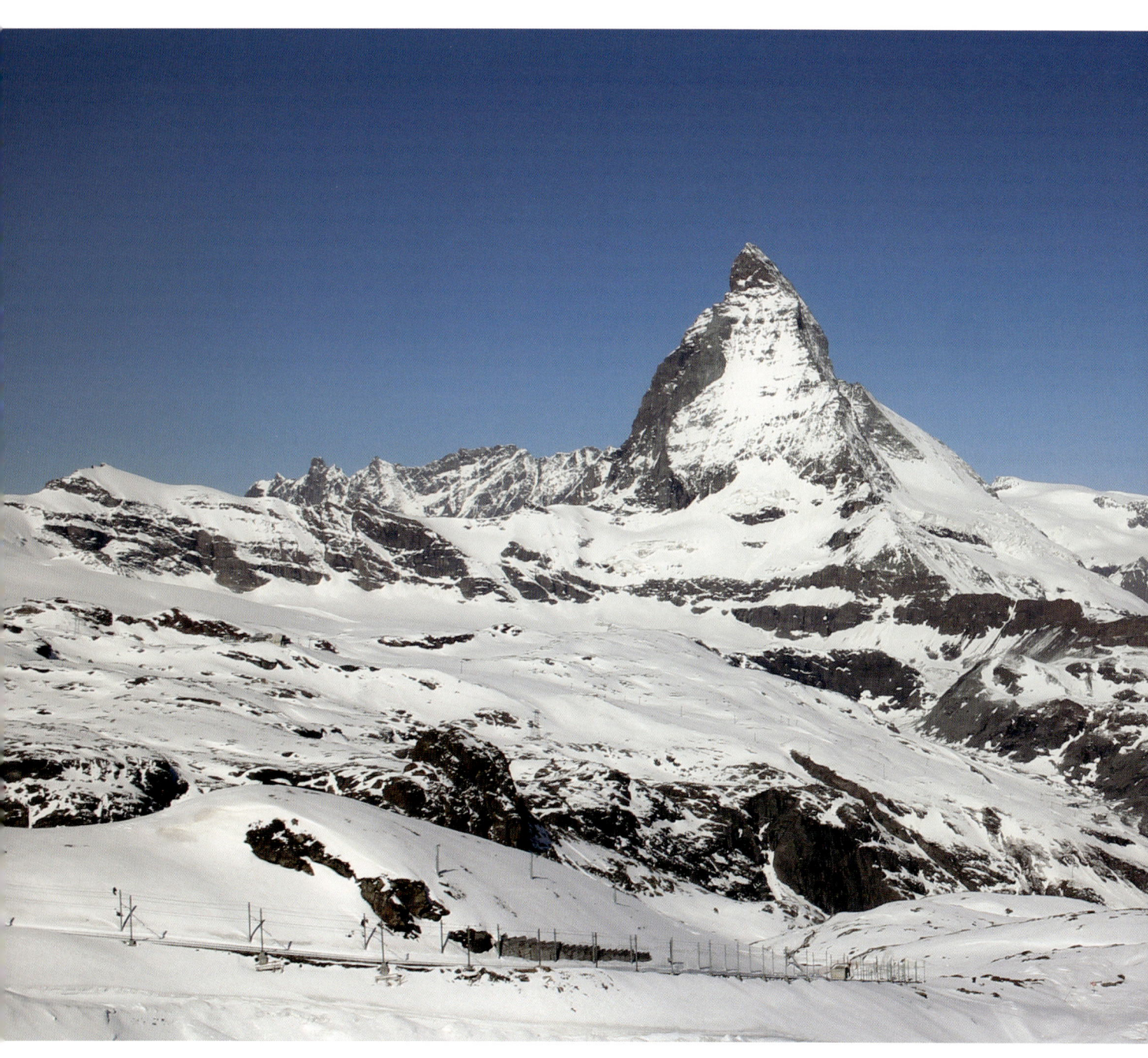

THE MATTERHORN AND ZMUTT VALLEY FROM GORNAGRAT

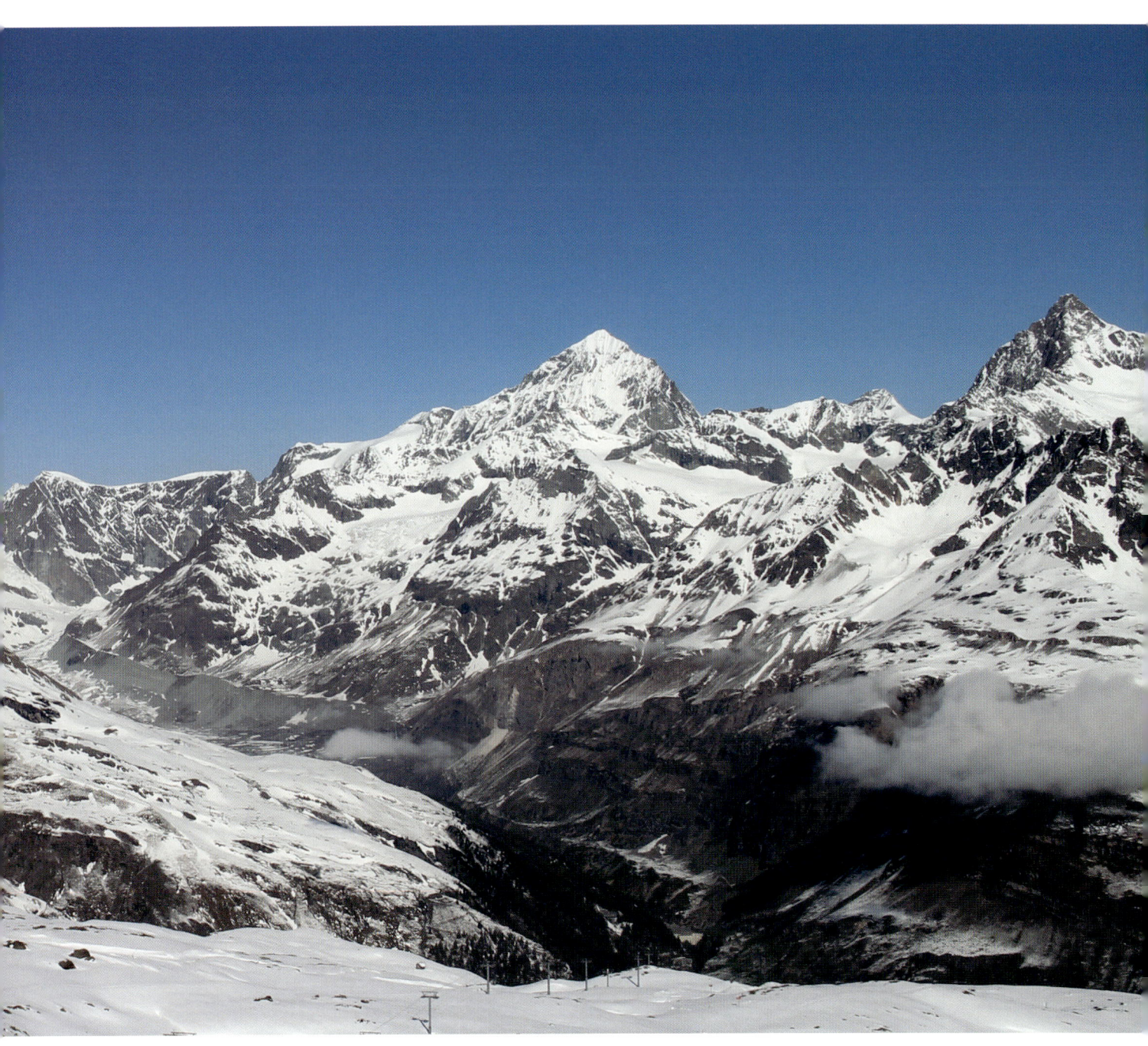

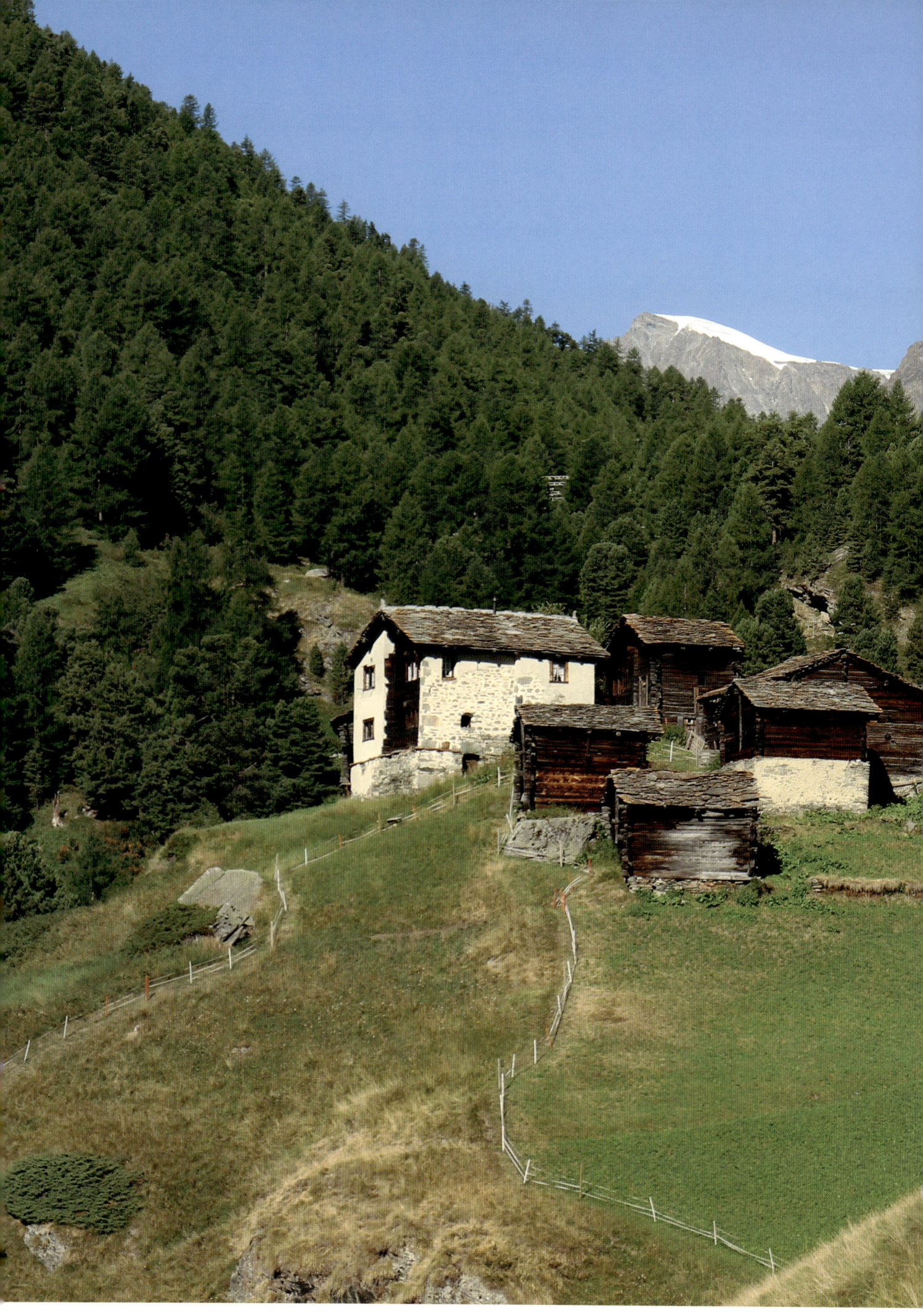

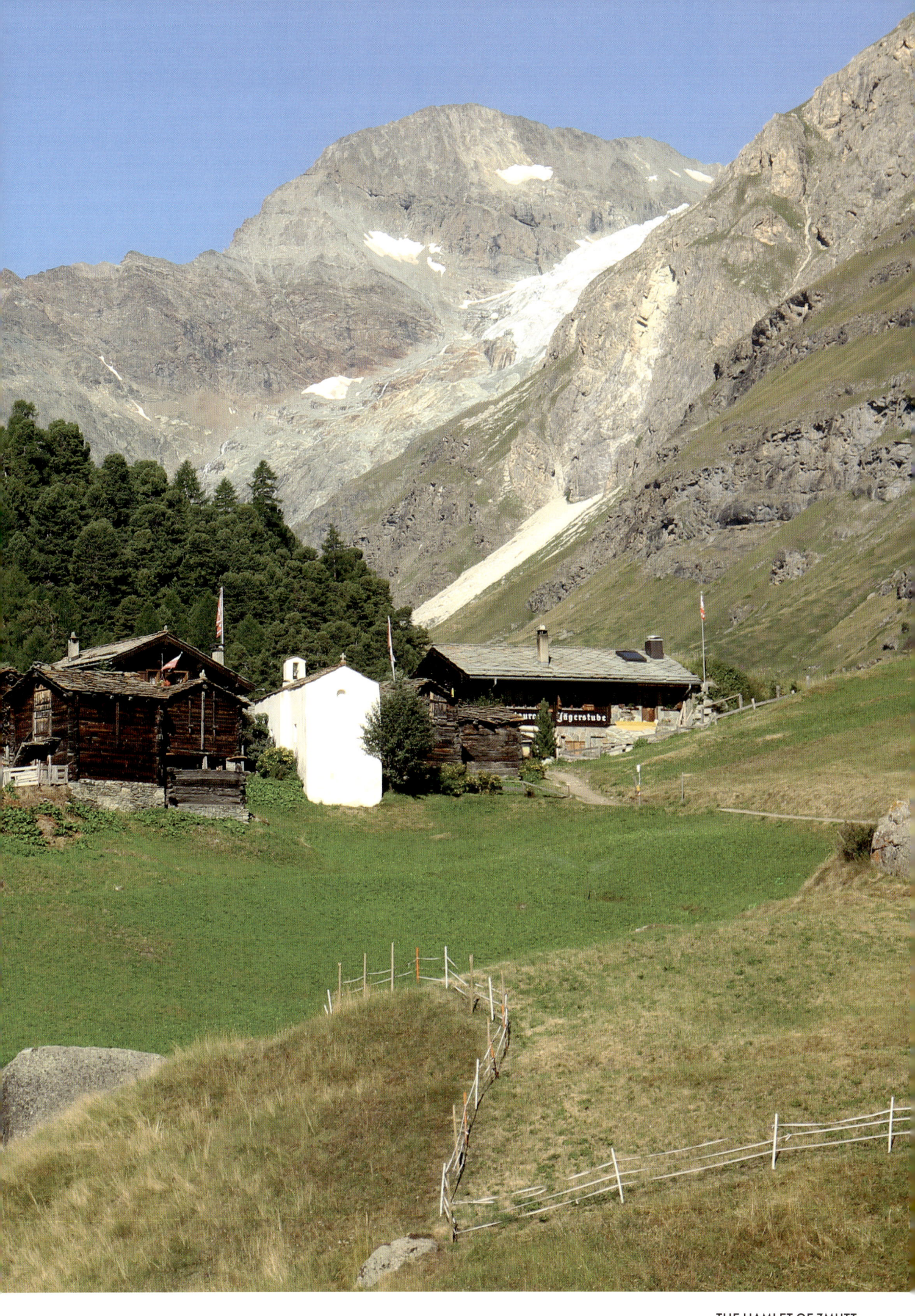
THE HAMLET OF ZMUTT

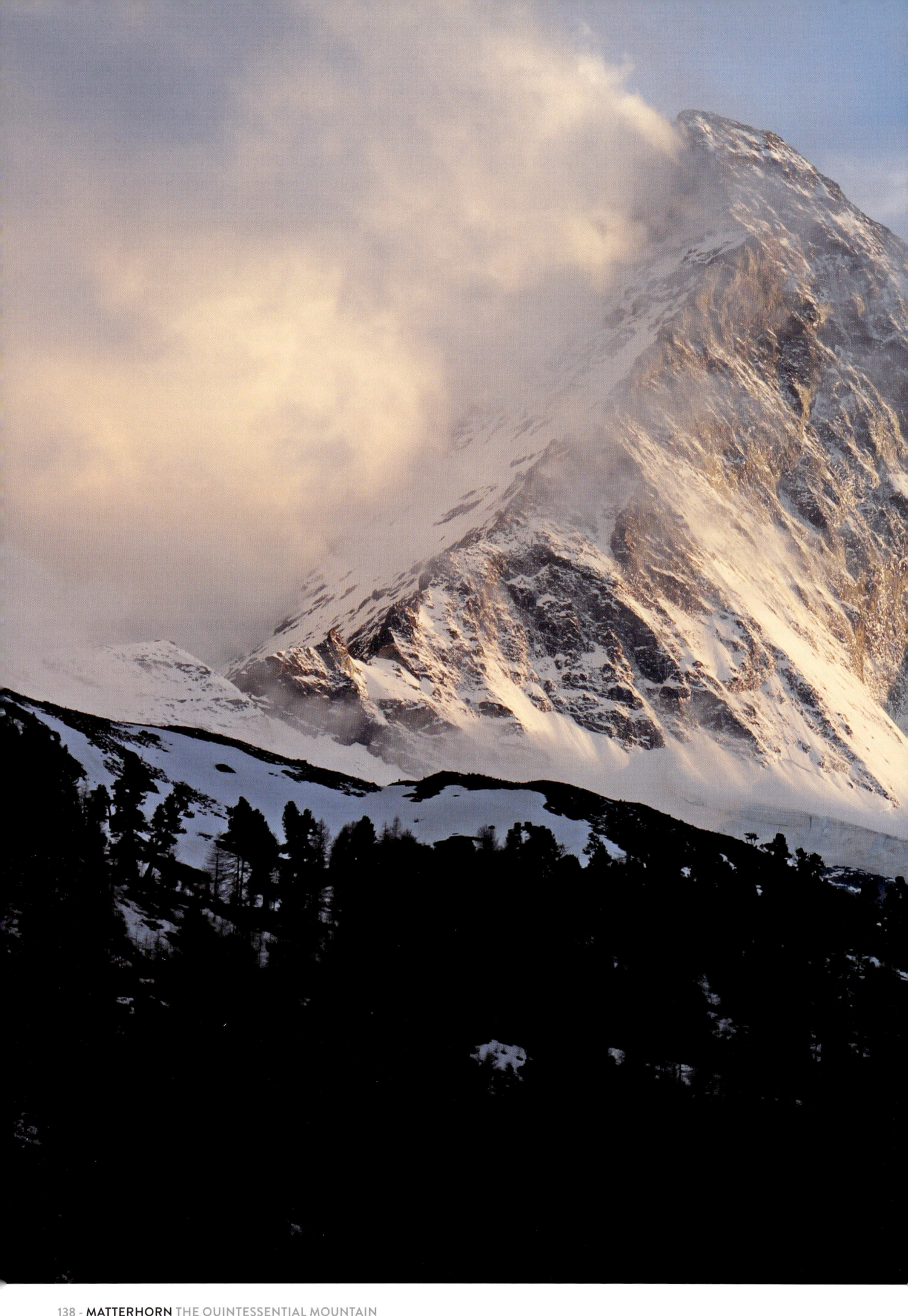

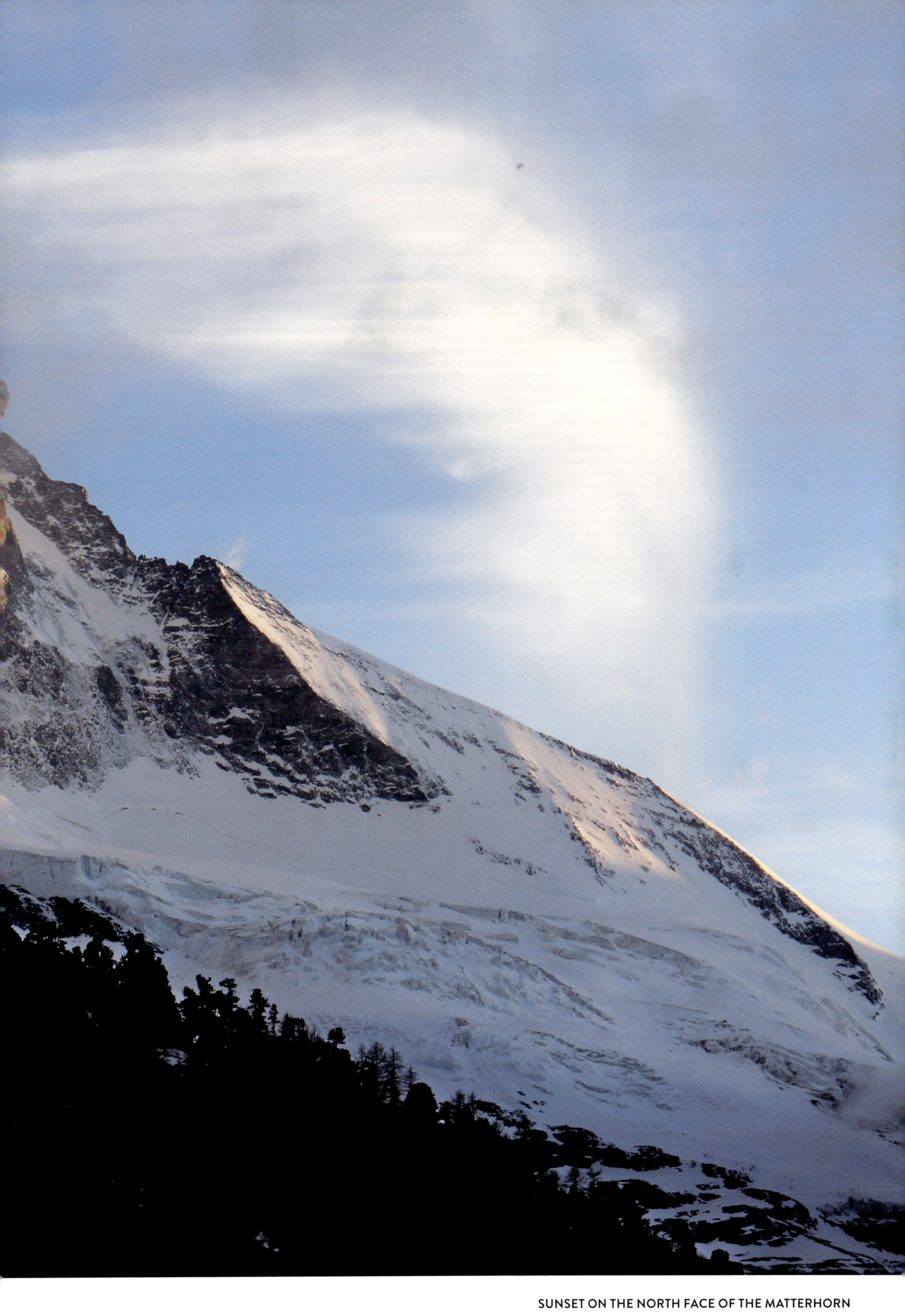

SUNSET ON THE NORTH FACE OF THE MATTERHORN

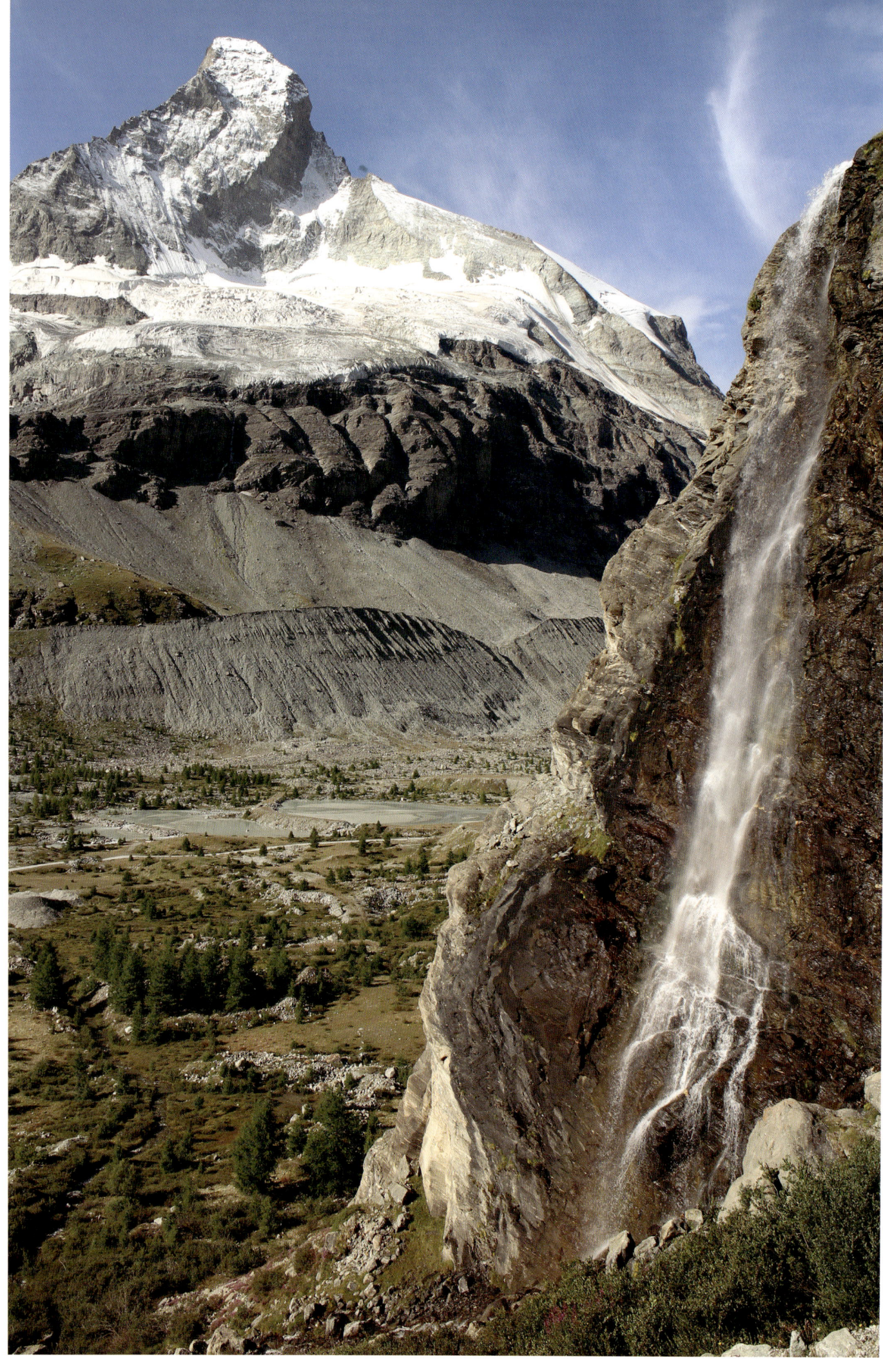

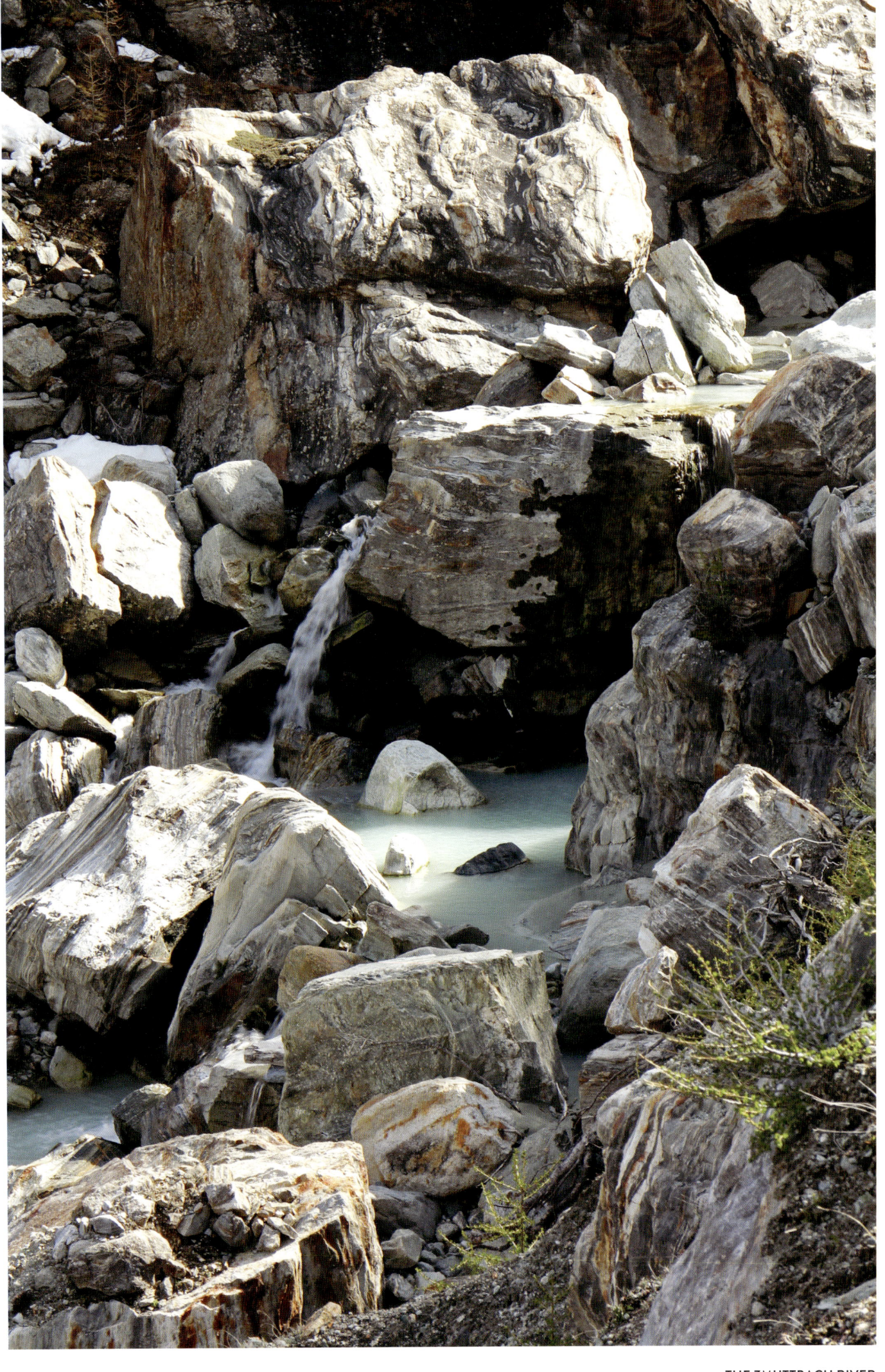

THE ZMUTTBACH RIVER

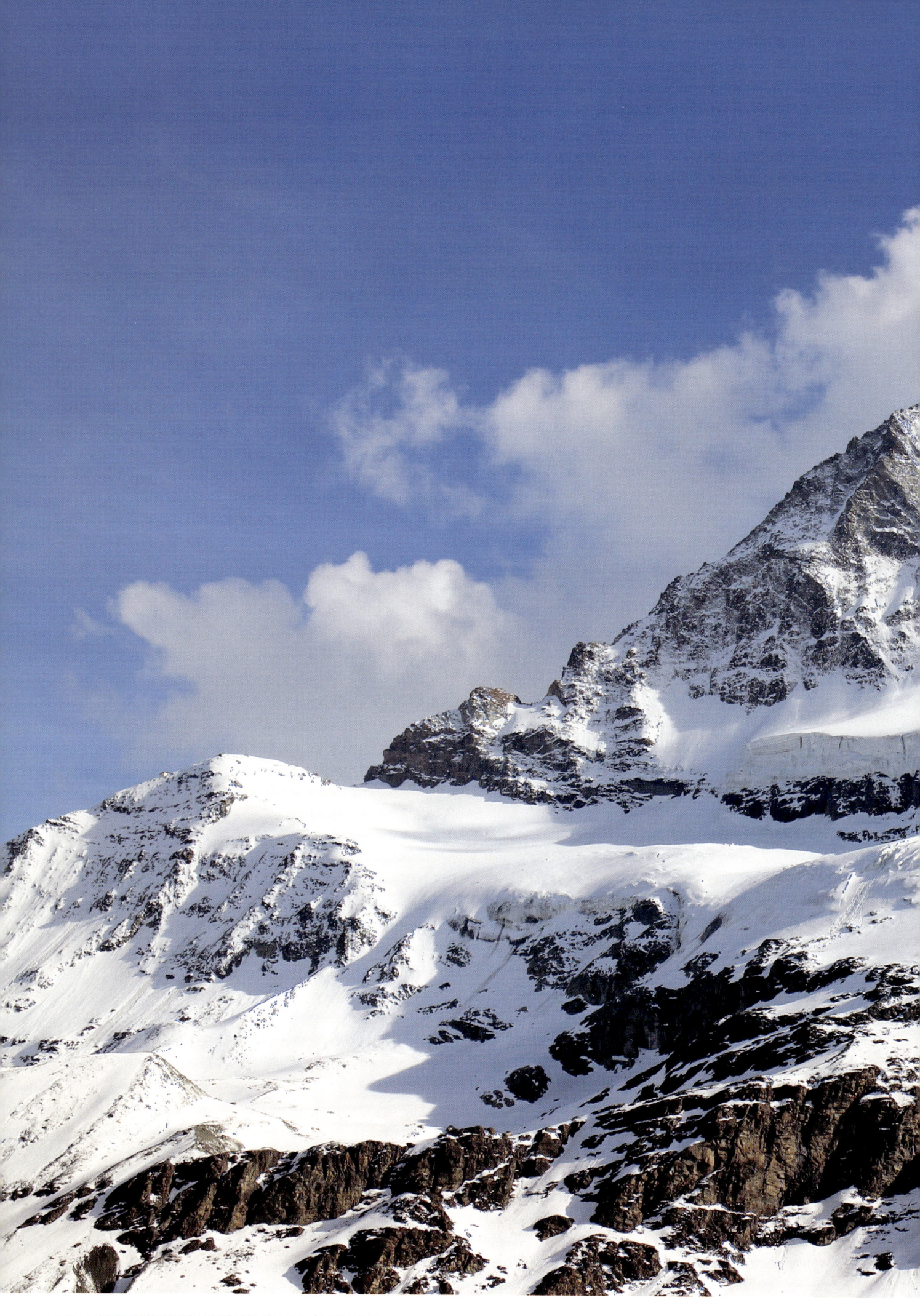

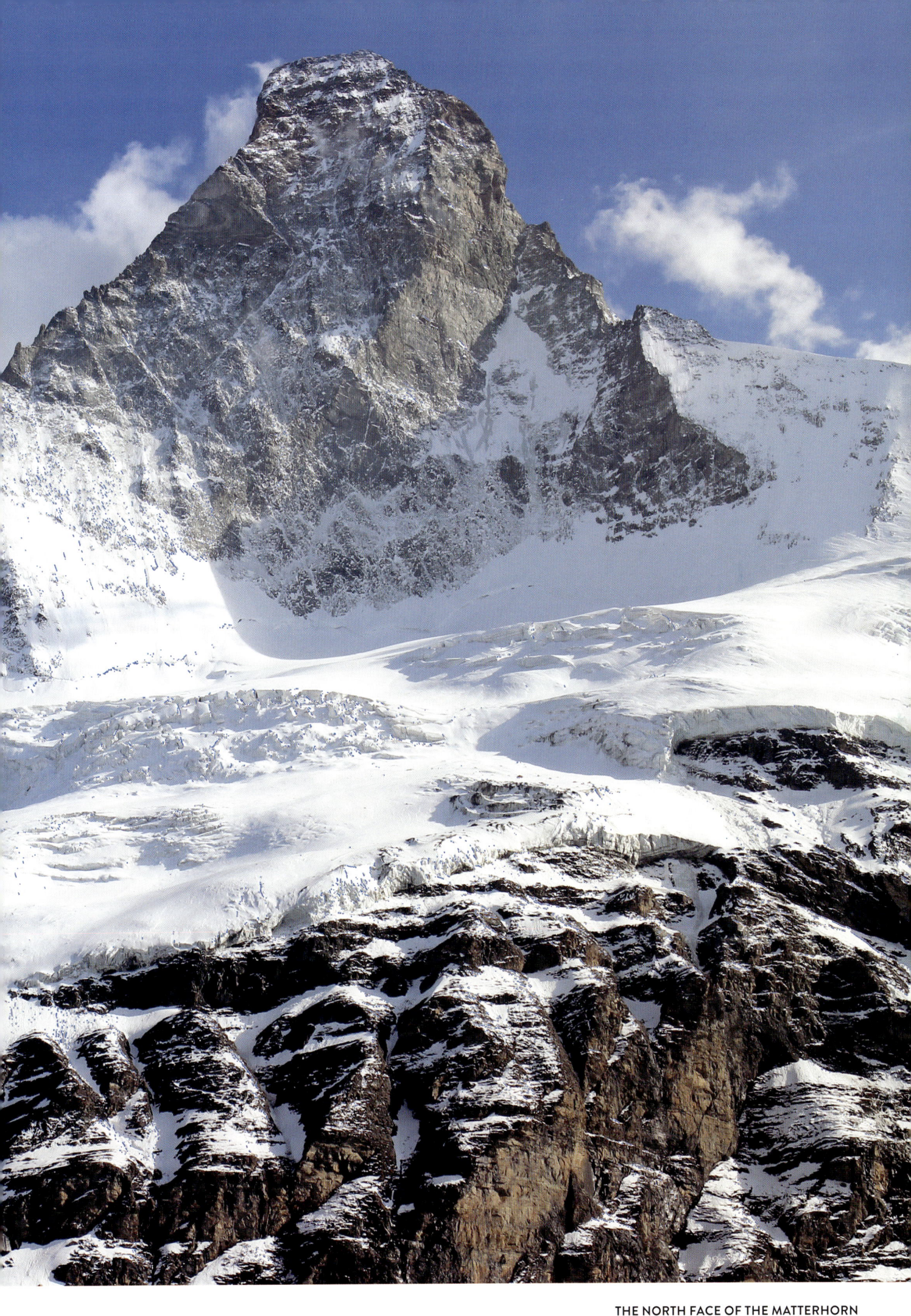

THE NORTH FACE OF THE MATTERHORN

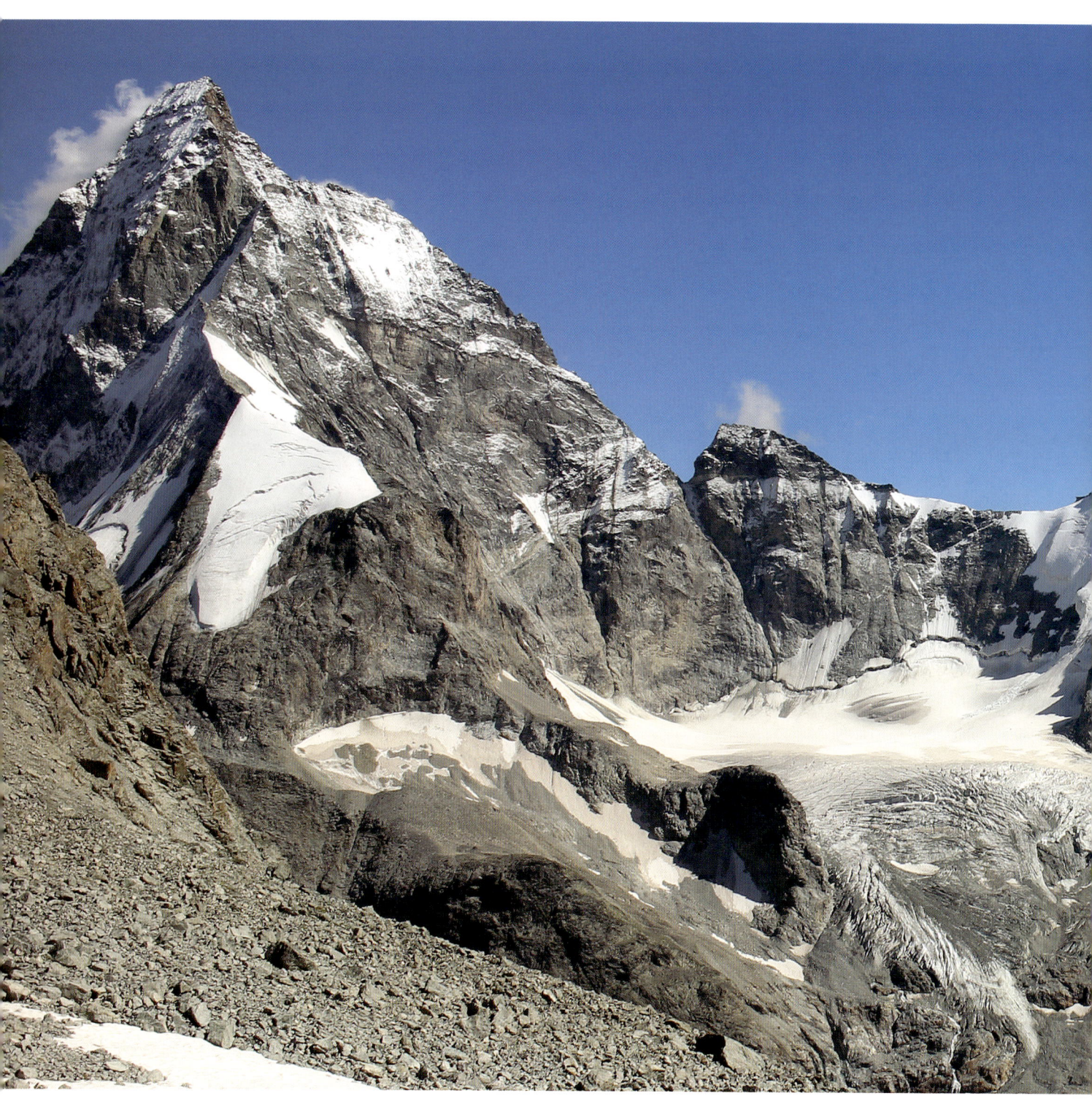

THE MATTERHORN AND DENT D'HERENS FROM POINTE DE ZINAL

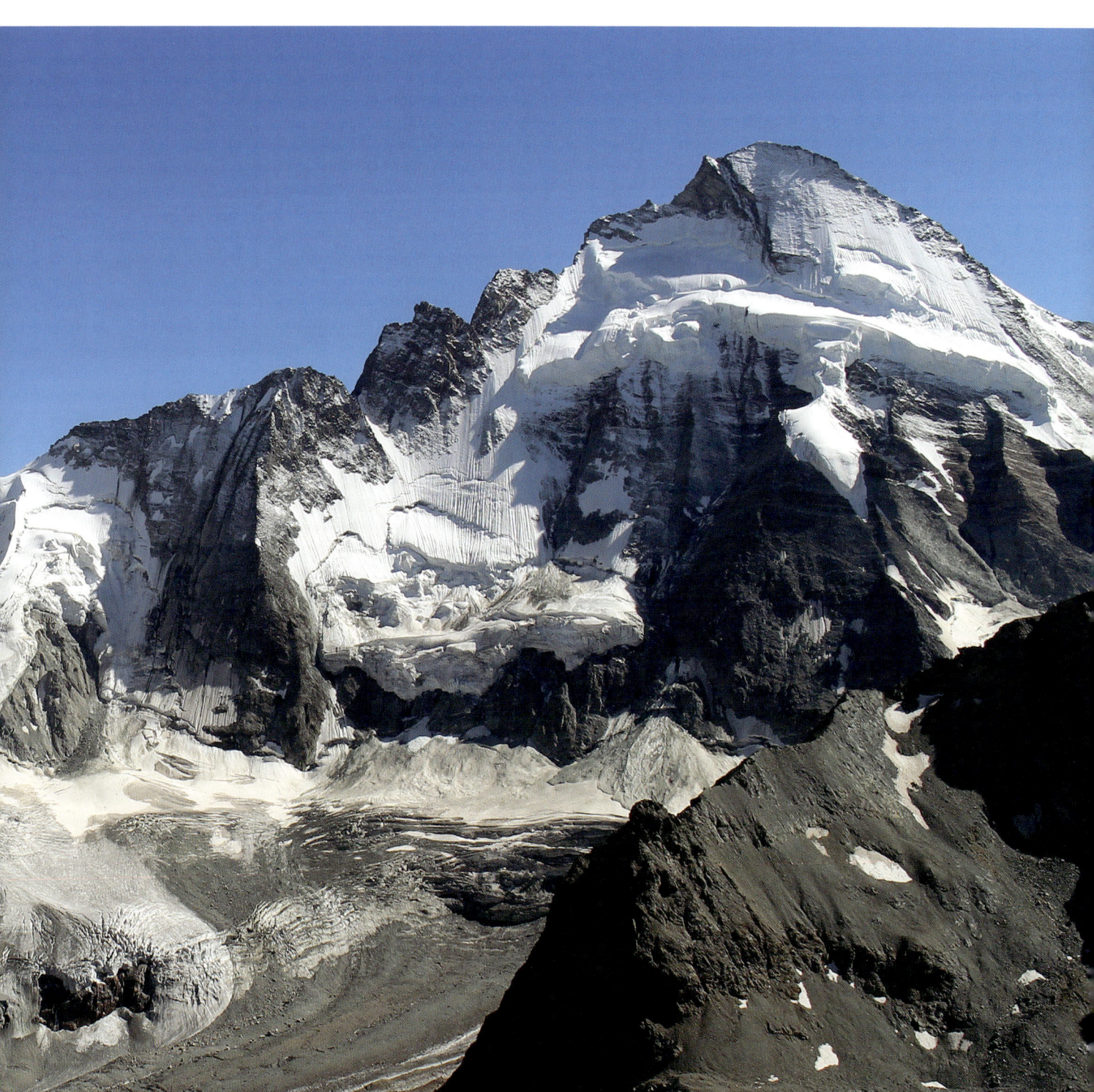

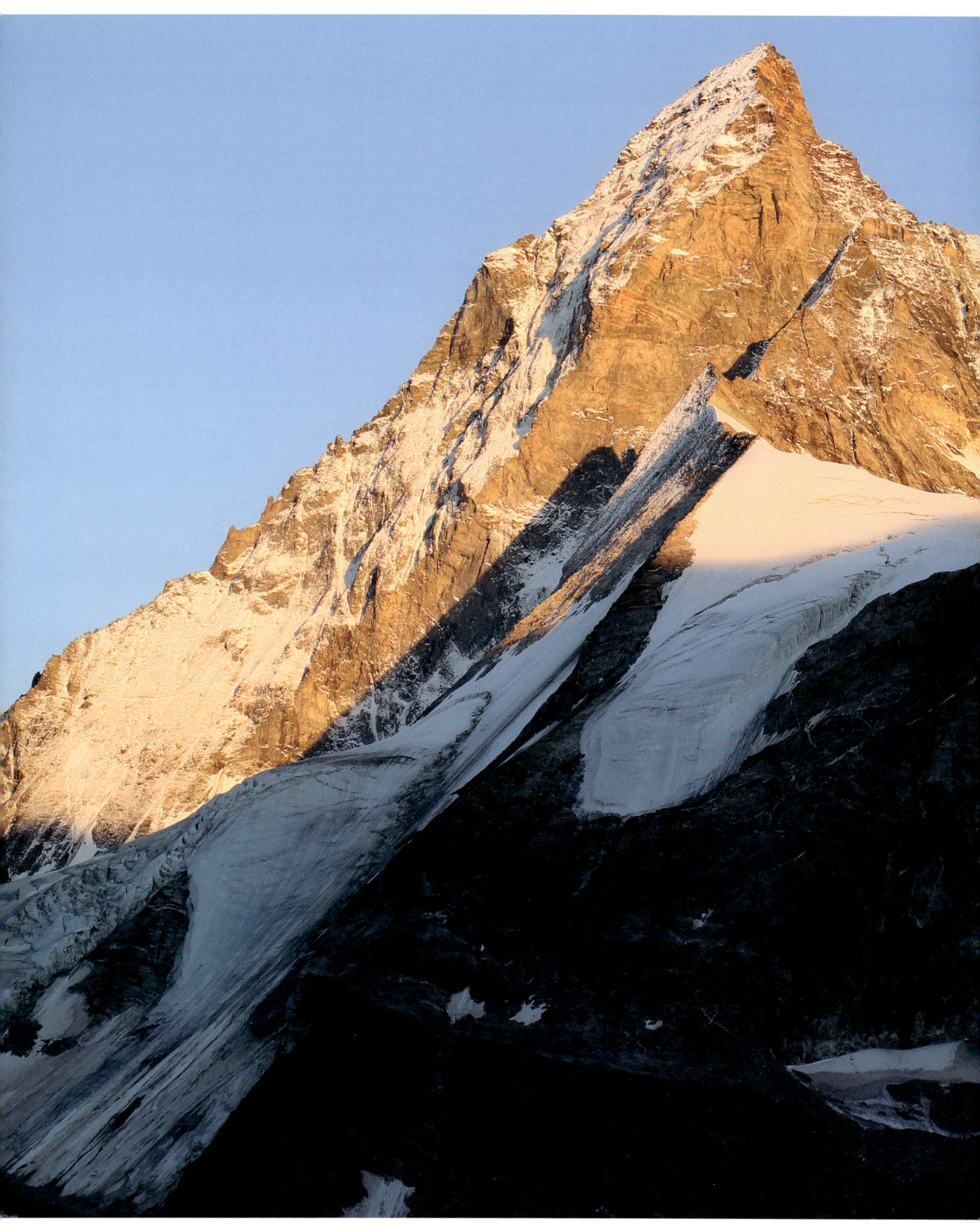

THE NORTH-WEST RIDGE OF THE MATTERHORN

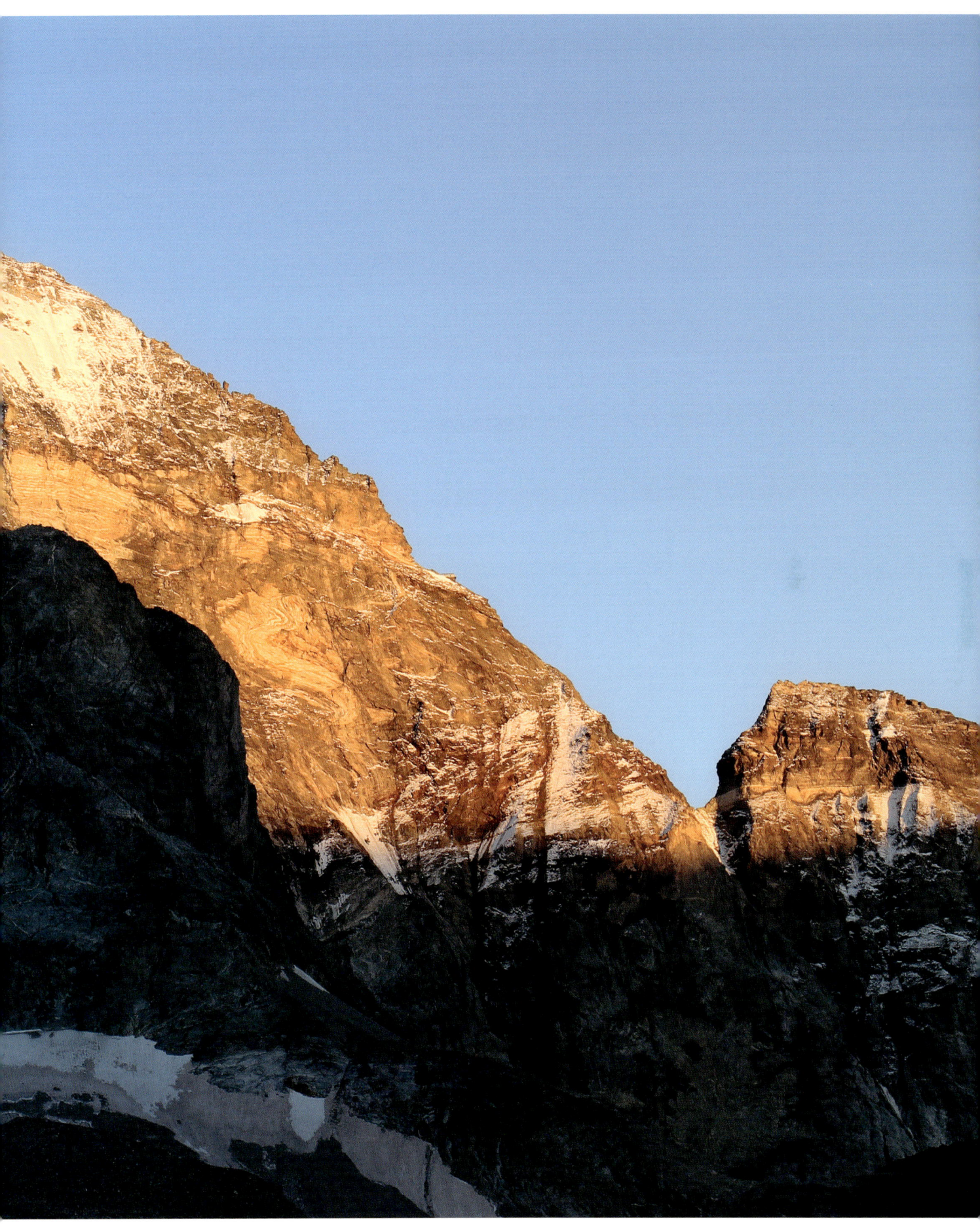

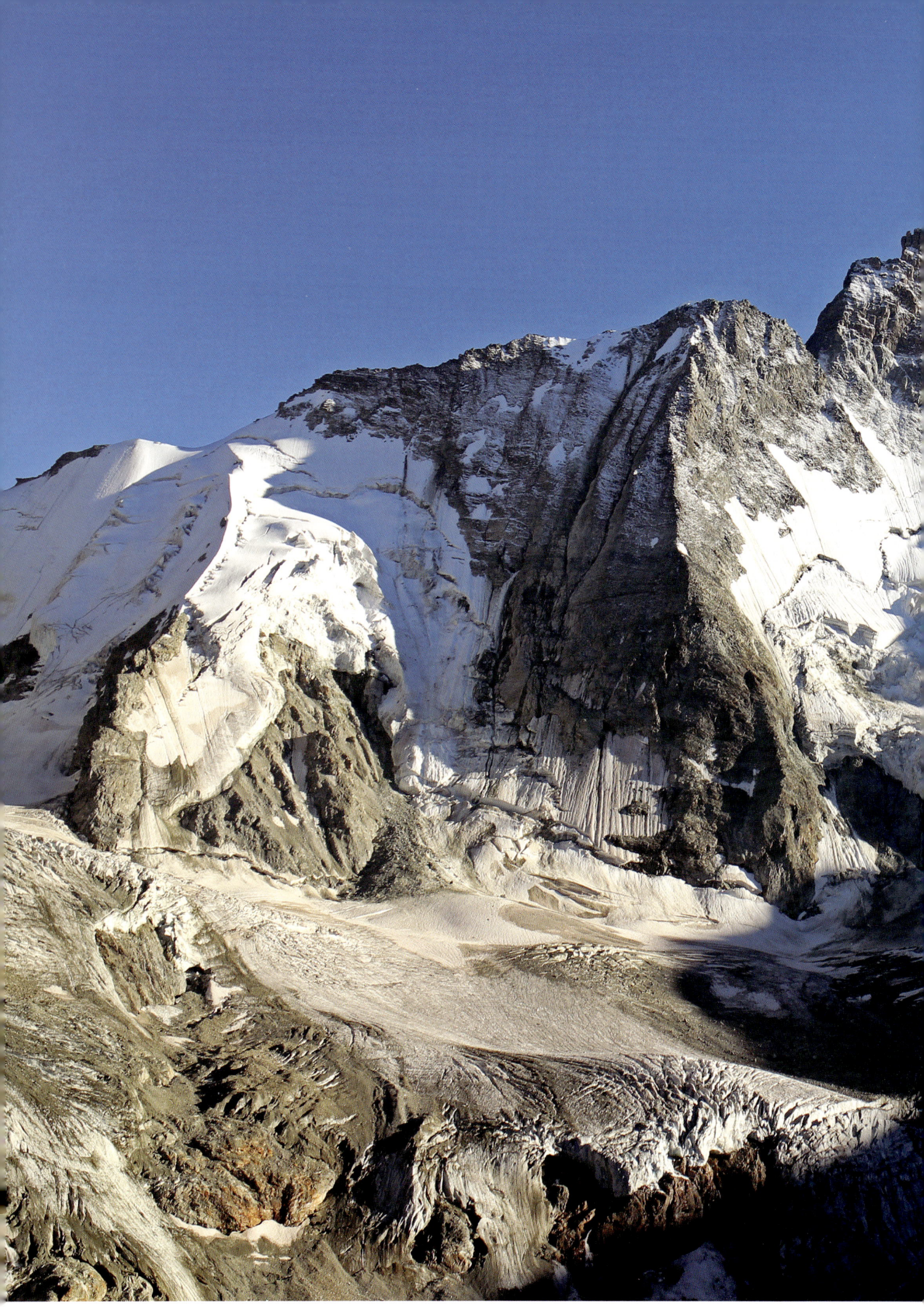

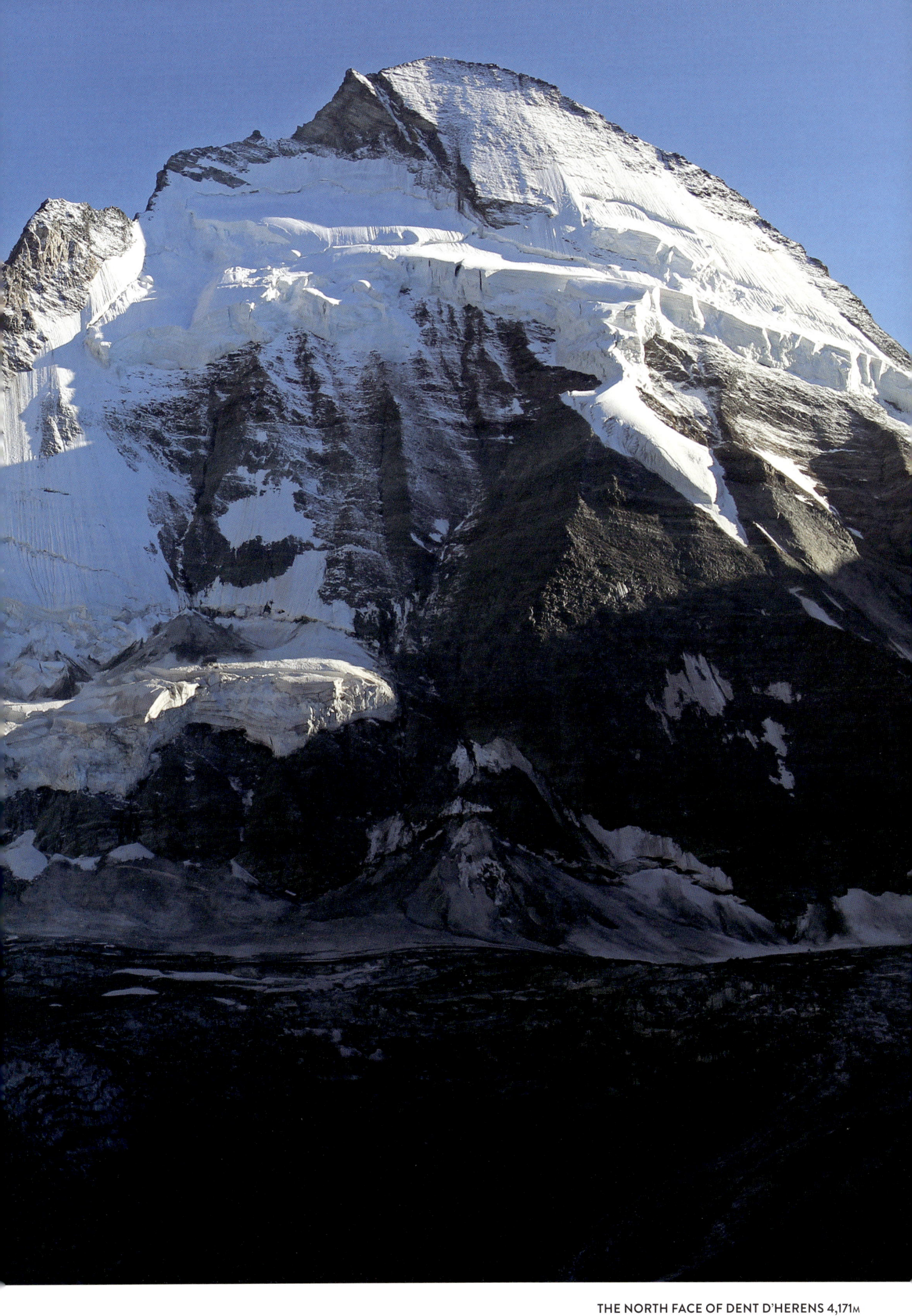

THE NORTH FACE OF DENT D'HERENS 4,171M

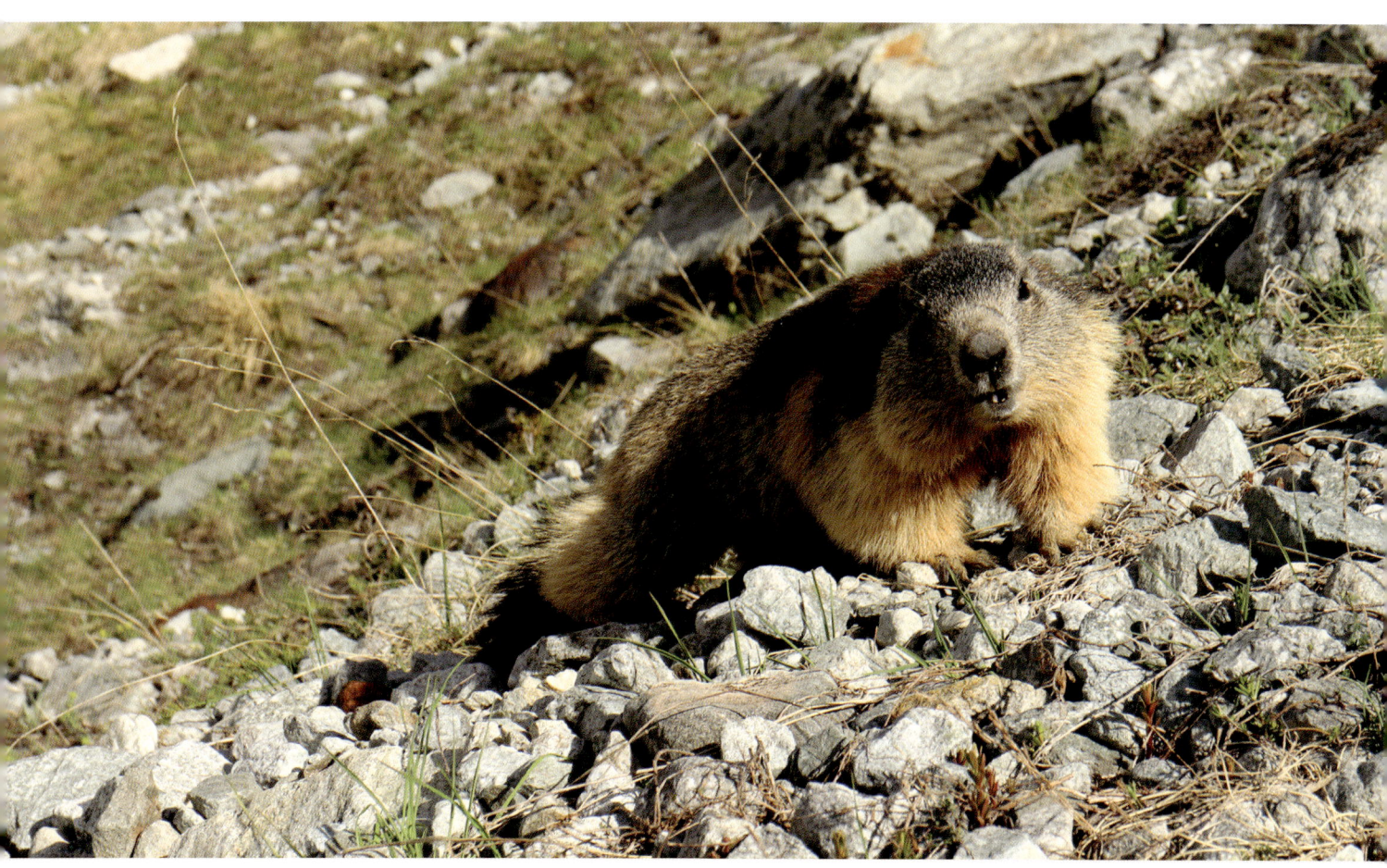

MARMOTT

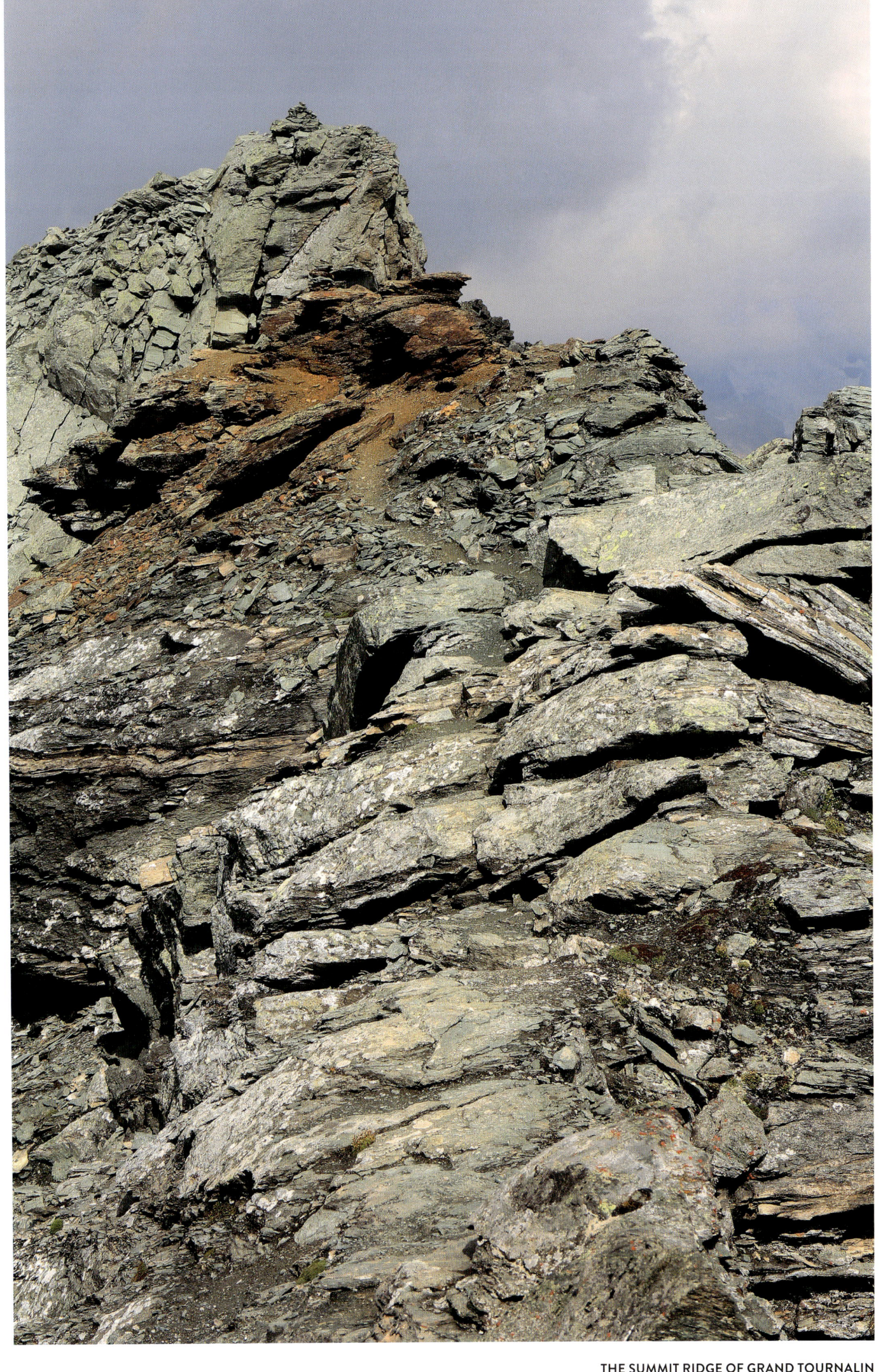

THE SUMMIT RIDGE OF GRAND TOURNALIN

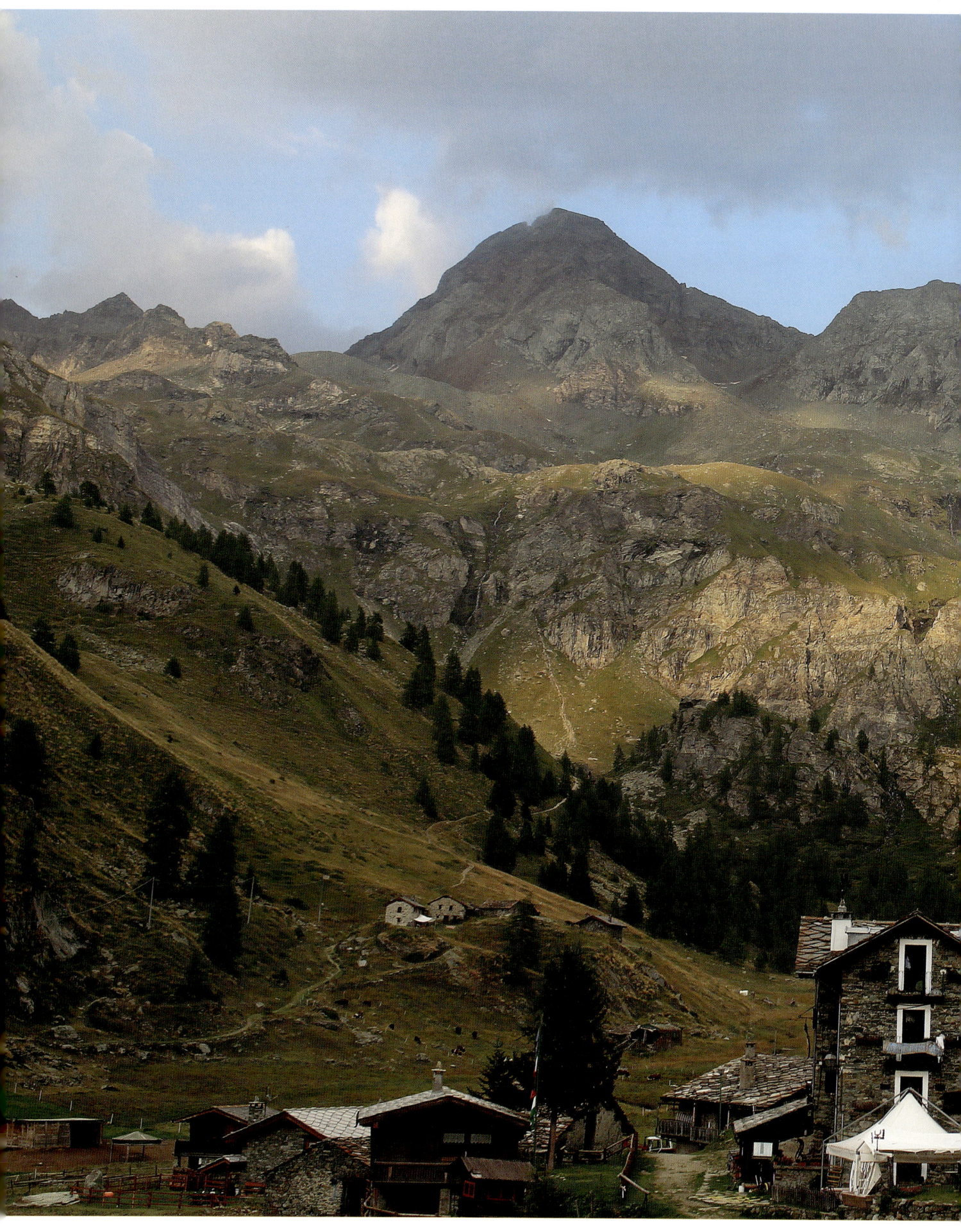

GRAND TOURNALIN 3,379m FROM CHENEIL

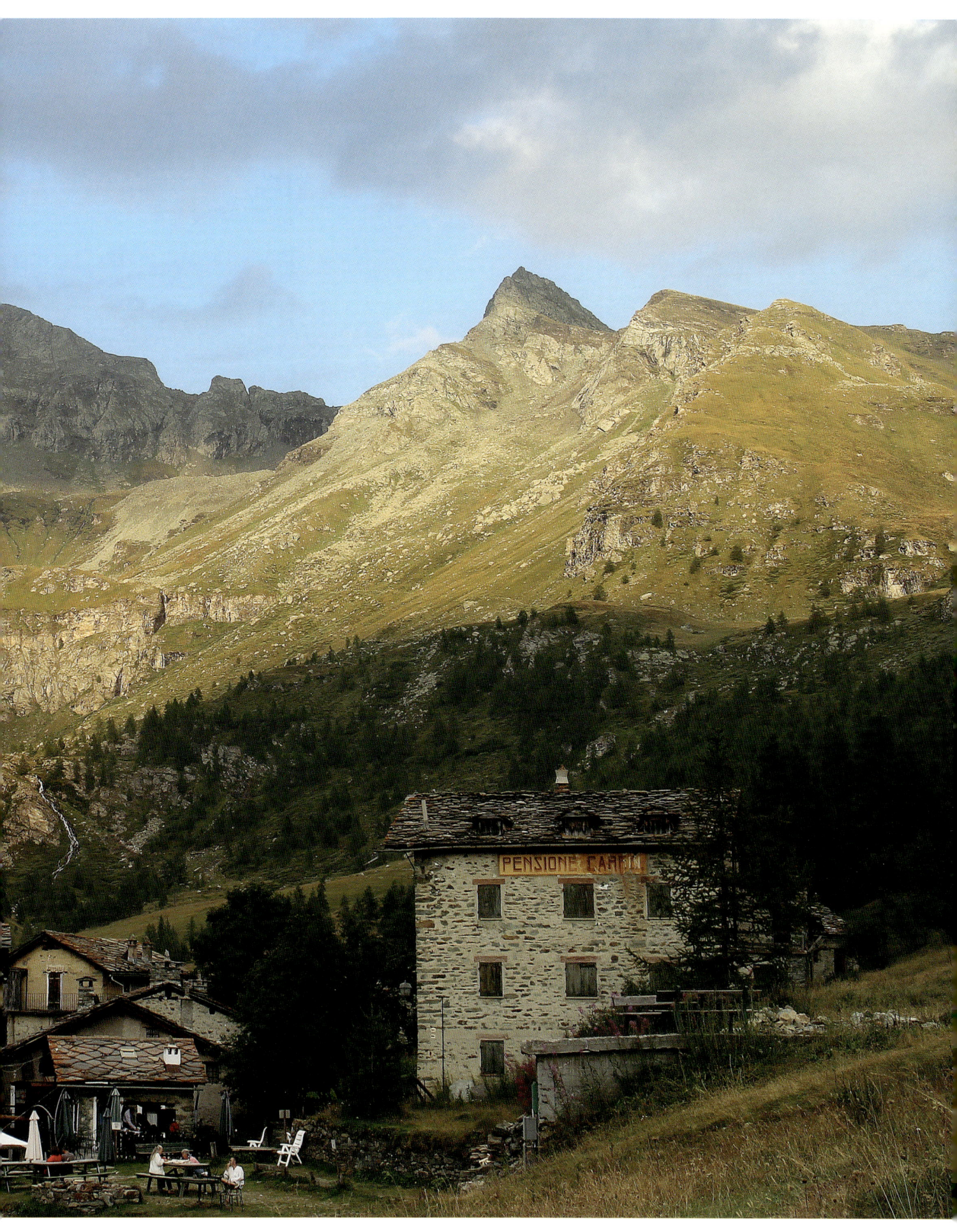

CHAPTER NINE
1864: THE AIGUILLES D'ARVES, BARRE DES ÉCRINS, MONT DOLENT, AIGUILLE DE TRÉ-LA-TÊTE AND AIGUILLE D'ARGENTIÉRE

When we arrived upon the highest summit of Mont Pelvoux, in Dauphiné, in 1861, we saw, to our surprise and disappointment, that it was not the culminating point of the district; and that another mountain — distant about a couple of miles, and separated from us by an impassable gulf — claimed that distinction. I was troubled in spirit about this mountain, and my thoughts often reverted to the great wall-sided peak, second in apparent inaccessibility only to the Matterhorn. It had, moreover, another claim to attention — it was the highest mountain [entirely] in France.

The year 1862 passed away without a chance of getting to it, and my holiday was too brief in 1863 even to think about it; but in the following year it was possible, and I resolved to set my mind at rest by completing the task which had been left unfinished in 1861.

In the meantime others had turned their attention to Dauphiné. First of all (in 1862) came Mr. F. Tuckett — that mighty mountaineer, whose name is known throughout the length and breadth of the Alps — with the guides Michel Croz, Peter Perrn, and Bartolommeo Peyrotte, and great success attended his arms. But Mr. Tuckett halted before the Pointe des Ecrins, and, dismayed by its appearance, withdrew his forces to gather less dangerous laurels elsewhere.

His expedition, however, threw some light upon the Ecrins. He pointed out the direction from which an attack was most likely to be successful, and Mr. William Mathews and the Rev. T. G. Bonney (to whom he communicated the result of his labours) attempted to execute the ascent, with the brothers Michel and J. B. Croz, by following his indications. But they too were defeated …

The guide Michel Croz had thus been engaged in both of these expeditions in Dauphiné, and I naturally looked to him for assistance. Mr. Mathews (to whom I applied for information) gave him a high character, and concluded his reply to me by saying, 'he was only happy when upwards of 10,000 feet high.'

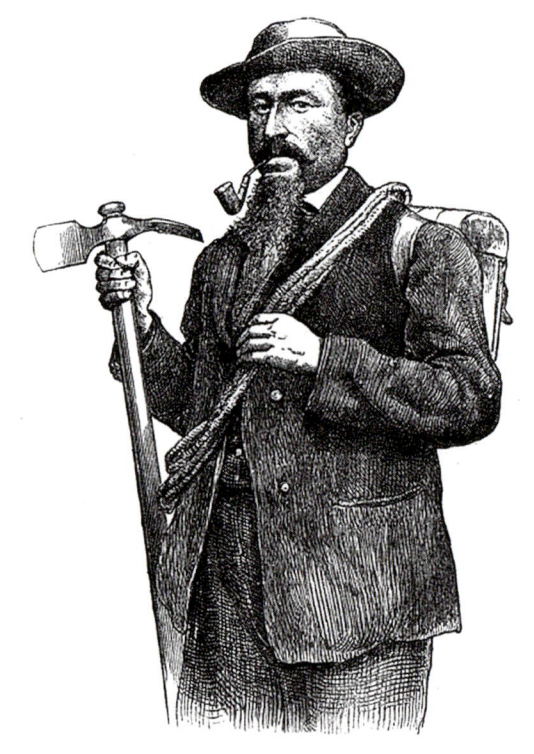

Michel-Auguste Croz (1865)

I know what my friend meant. Croz was happiest when he was employing his powers to the utmost. Places where you and I would 'toil and sweat, and yet be freezing cold,' were bagatelles to him, and it was only when he got above the range of ordinary mortals, and was required to employ his magnificent strength, and to draw upon his unsurpassed knowledge of ice and snow, that he could be said to be really and truly happy.

Of all the guides with whom I travelled, Michel Croz was the man who was most after my own heart. He did not work like a blunt razor, and take to his toil unkindly. He did not need urging, or to be told a second time to do anything. You had but to say *what* was to be done, and *how* it was to be done, and the work *was* done, if it was possible. Such men are not common, and when they are known they are valued. Michel was not widely known, but those who did know him employed him again and again. The inscription that is placed upon his tomb truthfully records that he was 'beloved by his comrades and esteemed by travellers.'

At the time that I was planning my journey, my friends Messrs. A. W. Moore and Horace Walker were also drawing up their programme; and, as we found that our wishes were very similar, we agreed to unite our respective parties.

Our united programme was framed so as to avoid sleeping in inns, and so that we should see from the highest point attained on one day a considerable portion of the route which was intended to be followed on the next. This latter matter was an important one to us, as all of our projected excursions were new ones, and led over ground about which there was very little information in print.

My friends had happily secured Christian Almer of Grindelwald as their guide. [**Almer had made many first ascents including of the Eiger in 1858**]. The combination of Croz and Almer was a perfect one. Both men were in the prime of life; both were endued with strength and activity far beyond the average; and the courage and the knowledge of each was alike undoubted. The temper of Almer it was impossible to ruffle; he was ever obliging and enduring, — a bold but a safe man. That which he lacked in fire …. was supplied by Croz, who, in his turn, was kept in place by Almer.

(Ibid., pp. 124–127)

ATTEMPT TO ASCEND AIGUILLES D'ARVES

Prior to attempting to climb the Barre des Écrins 4,102m (13,548 ft), the companions made an attempt to climb the highest peak of the Aiguilles d'Arve 3,514m (11,529 ft); an impressive three-fingered rock formation. With an inaccurate map of the area they ventured up into the unknown, but after almost five hours, and upon reaching a gap just below the main peak, they were faced with the reality of having to retreat.

We then studied the northern face of our intended peak, and finally arrived at the conclusion that it was 'relatively' impracticable. Croz shrugged his big shoulders, and said, 'My faith! I think you will do well to leave it to others.' Almer was more explicit, and volunteered the information that a thousand francs would not tempt him to *try* it. We then turned to the northernmost peak, but found its southern faces even more hopeless than the northern faces of the central one. We enjoyed accordingly the unwonted luxury of a three-hours' rest on the top of our pass; for pass we were determined it should be.

All mountaineers know that it is often harder to descend than to ascend and this knowledge was learned first-hand when Walker slipped while they made their way down a snow slope.

Our friend, however, started off at a standing glissade, and advanced for a time very skilfully; but after a while he lost his balance, and progressed downwards and backwards with great rapidity, in a way that seemed to us very much like tumbling head over heels. He let go his axe, and left it behind, but it overtook him and batted him heartily. He and it travelled in this fashion for some hundreds of feet, and at last subsided into the rocks at the bottom. In a few moments we were reassured as to his safety, by hearing him ironically request us not to keep him waiting down there.

Guided by the sound of a distant 'moo,' we speedily found the highest chalets in the valley, named Rieu Blanc. They were tenanted by three old women (who seemed to belong to one of the missing links sought by naturalists), destitute of all ideas except in regard to cows …

With the hospitality of the old women, the group spent the next couple of nights there, while exploring and gaining a better understanding of the area.

All mountaineers know how valuable it is to study beforehand an intended route over new ground from a height at some distance. None but blunderers fail to do so, if it is possible; and one cannot do so too thoroughly. As a rule, the closer one approaches underneath a summit, the more difficult it is to pick out a path with judgment. Inferior peaks seem unduly important, subordinate ridges are exalted, and slopes conceal points beyond; and if one blindly undertakes an ascent, without having acquired a tolerable notion of the relative importance of the parts, and of their positions to one another, it will be miraculous if great difficulties are not encountered.

(Ibid., pp. 129–140)

ATTEMPT TO ASCEND BARRE DES ÉCRINS: THE HIGHEST PEAK IN THE DAUPHINÉ ALPS

Before 5 o'clock on the afternoon of June 23, we were trotting down the steep path that leads into La Bérarde …

to watch for the arrival of one Alexander Pic, who had been sent overnight with our baggage *via* Freney and Venos. But when the night fell, and no Pic appeared, we saw that our plans must be modified; for he was necessary to our very existence — he carried our food, our tobacco, our all. So, after some discussion, it was agreed that a portion of our programme should be abandoned, that the night of the 24th should be passed at the head of the Glacier de la Bonne Pierre, and that, on the 25th, a push should be made for the summit of the Ecrins. We then went to straw.

Our porter Pic strolled in next morning with a very jaunty air, and we seized upon our tooth-brushes; but, upon looking for the cigars, we found starvation staring us in the face. 'Hullo! Monsieur Pic, where are our cigars?' 'Gentlemen,' he began, 'I am desolated!' and then, quite pat, he told a long rigmarole about a fit on the road, of brigands, thieves, of their ransacking the knapsacks when he was insensible, and of finding them gone when he revived! 'Ah! Monsieur Pic, we see what it is, you have smoked them yourself!' 'Gentlemen, I never smoke, *never!*' Whereupon we inquired secretly if he was known to smoke, and found that he was. However, he said that he had never spoken truer words, and perhaps he had not, for he is reported to be the greatest liar in Dauphiné!

We were now able to start, and set out at 1.15 P.M. to bivouac upon the Glacier de la Bonne Pierre, accompanied by Rodier, who staggered under a load of blankets. Many slopes had to be mounted, and many torrents to be crossed, all of which has been described by Mr. Tuckett. We, however, avoided the difficulties he experienced with the latter by crossing them high up, where they were subdivided. But when we got on to the moraine on the right bank of the glacier (or, properly speaking, on to one of the moraines, for there are several), mists descended, to our great hindrance; and it was 5.30 before we arrived on the spot at which it was intended to camp.

Each one selected his nook, and we then joined round a grand fire made by our men. Fortnum and Mason's portable soup was sliced up and brewed, and was excellent; but it should be said that before it *was* excellent, three times the quantity named in the directions had to be used. Art is required in drinking as in making this soup, and one point is this — always let your friends drink first; not only because it is more polite, but because the soup has a tendency to burn the mouth if taken too hot, and one drink of the bottom is worth two of the top, as all the goodness settles.

While engaged in these operations, the mist that enveloped the glacier and surrounding peaks was becoming thinner; little bits of blue sky appeared here and there, until suddenly, when we were looking towards the head of the glacier, far, far above us, at an almost inconceivable height, in a tiny patch of blue, appeared a wonderful rocky pinnacle, bathed in the beams of the fast-sinking sun. We were so electrified by the glory of the sight that it was some seconds before we realised what we saw, and understood that that astounding point, removed apparently miles from the earth, was one of the highest summits of Les Ecrins; and that we hoped, before another sun had set, to have stood upon an even loftier pinnacle. The mists rose and fell, presenting us with a series of dissolving views of ravishing grandeur, and finally died away, leaving the glacier and its mighty bounding precipices under an exquisite pale blue sky, free from a single speck of cloud.

The night passed over without anything worth mention, but we had had occasion to observe in the morning an instance of the curious evaporation that is frequently noticeable in the High Alps. On the previous night we had hung up on a knob of rock our mackintosh bag containing five bottles of Rodier's bad wine. In the morning, although the stopper appeared to have been in all night, about four-fifths had evaporated. It was strange; my friends had not taken any, neither had I, and the guides each declared that they had not seen any one touch it. In fact it was clear that there was no explanation of the phenomenon, but in the dryness of the air. Still it is remarkable that the dryness of the air (or the evaporation of wine) is always greatest when a stranger is in one's party — the dryness caused by the presence of even a single Chamounix porter is sometimes so great, that not four-fifths but the entire quantity disappears. For a time I found difficulty in combating this phenomenon, but at last discovered that if I used the wine-flask as a pillow during the night, the evaporation was completely stopped.

On each [**previous**] occasion the parties slept out at, and started from, a considerable elevation, and arrived at the base of the final peak of the Ecrins early in the day, and with plenty of superfluous energy. Guides and travellers alike, on each occasion, were exceptional men, experienced mountaineers, who had proved their skill and courage on numerous antecedent occasions, and who were not accustomed to turn away from a thing merely because it was difficult. On each occasion the attempts were abandoned because the state of the snow on and below the final peak was such that avalanches were anticipated; and, according to the judgment of those who were concerned, there was such an amount of positive danger from this condition of things, that it was unjustifiable to persevere.

The reader need scarcely be told, after all that has been said about the variableness of weather in the High Alps, the chance was small indeed that we should find upon the 25th of June, or any other set day, the precise condition of affairs that was deemed indispensable for success. We had such confidence in the judgment of our friends, that it was understood amongst us the ascent should be abandoned, unless the conditions were manifestly favourable.

By five minutes to six we were at the top of the gully (a first-rate couloir, about 1000 feet high), and within sight of our work. Hard, thin, and wedge-like as the Ecrins had looked from afar, it had never looked so hard and so thin as it did when we emerged from the top of the couloir through the gap in the ridge. No tender shadows spoke of broad and rounded ridges, but sharp and shadowless its serrated edges stood out against the clear sky. It had been said that the route must be taken by one of the ridges of the final peak, but both were alike repellent, hacked and notched in numberless places. They reminded me of my failure on the Dent d'Hérens in 1863, and of a place on a similar ridge, from which advance or retreat was alike difficult. But, presuming one or other of these ridges or arêtes was practicable, there remained the task of getting to them, for completely round the base of the final peak swept an enormous bergschrund, almost separating it from the slopes which lay beneath. It was evident thus early that the ascent would not be accomplished without exertion, and that it would demand all our faculties and all our time. In more than one respect we were favoured. The mists were gone, the day was bright and perfectly calm; there had been a long stretch of fine weather beforehand, and the snow was in excellent order; and, most important of all, the last new snow which had fallen on the final peak, unable to support itself, had broken away and rolled in a mighty avalanche, over schrund, névé, séracs, over hills and valleys in the glacier (levelling one and filling the other), completely down to the summit of the Col des Ecrins, where it lay in huge jammed masses, powerless to harm us; and had made a broad track, almost a road, over which, for part of the way at least, we might advance with rapidity.

We took in all this in a few minutes, and seeing there was no time to be lost, despatched a hasty meal, left knapsacks, provisions, and all incumbrances by the Col, started again at half-past six, and made direct for the left side of the schrund, for it was there alone that a passage was practicable. We crossed it at 8.10.

Thus far there was no trouble, but the nature of the work changed immediately. If we regard the upper 700 feet alone of the final peak of the Ecrins, it may be described as a three-sided pyramid. One face is towards the Glacier Noir, and forms one of the sheerest precipices in the Alps. Another is towards the Glacier du Vallon, and is less steep, and less uniform in angle than the first. The third is towards the Glacier de l'Encula, and it was by this one we approached the summit. Imagine a triangular plane, 700 or 800 feet high, set at an angle exceeding 50°; let it be smooth, glassy; let the uppermost edges be cut into spikes and teeth, and let them be bent, some one way, some another. Let the glassy face be covered with minute fragments of rock, scarcely attached, but varnished with ice; imagine this, and then you will have a very faint idea of the face of the Ecrins on which we stood. It was not possible to avoid detaching stones, which, as they fell, cause words unmentionable to rise. The greatest friends would have reviled each other in such a situation. We gained the eastern arête, and endeavoured for half-an-hour to work upwards towards the summit; but it was useless (each yard of progress cost an incredible time); and having no desire to form the acquaintance of the Glacier Noir in a precipitate manner, we beat a retreat, and returned to the schrund. We again held a council, and it was unanimously decided that we should be beaten if we could not cut along the upper edge of the schrund, and, when nearly beneath the summit, work up to it. So Croz took off his coat and went to work; — on ice, — not that black ice so often mentioned and so seldom seen, but on ice as hard as ice could be. Weary work for the guides. Croz cut for more than half-an-hour, and we did not seem to have advanced at all. Some one behind, seeing how great the labour was, and how slow the progress, suggested that after all we might do better on the arête. Croz's blood was up, and indignant at this slight on his powers, he ceased working, turned in his steps, and rushed towards me with a haste that made me shudder: 'By all means let us go there, the sooner the better.' No slight was intended, and he resumed his work, after a time being relieved by Almer. Half-past ten came; an hour had passed; they were still cutting. Dreary work for us, for no capering about could be done here; hand as well as foot holes were necessary; the fingers and toes got very cold; the ice, as it boomed in bounding down the bergschrund, was very suggestive; conversation was very restricted, separated as we were by our tether of 20 feet apiece. Another hour passed. We were now almost immediately below the summit, and we stopped to look up. We were nearly as far off it (vertically) as we had been more than three hours before. The day seemed [to be] going against us. The only rocks near at hand were scattered; no bigger than tea-cups, and most of these, we found afterwards, were glazed with ice. Time forbade cutting right up to the summit, even had it been possible, which it was not. We decided to go up to the ridge again by means of the rocks; but had we not had a certain confidence in each other, it unquestionably would not have been done; for this, it must be understood, was a situation where not only *might* a slip have been fatal to every one, but it would have been so beyond doubt: nothing, moreover, was easier than to make one. It was a place where all had to work in unison, where there must be no slackening of the rope, and no unnecessary tension. For another hour we were in this trying situation, and at 12.30 we gained the arête again at a much higher point, close to the summit. Our men were, I am afraid, well-nigh worn out. Cutting up a couloir 1000 feet high was not the right sort of preparation for work of this kind. Be it so or not, we were all glad to rest for a short time, for we had not sat down a minute since leaving the col six hours before. Almer, however, was restless, knowing that midday was past, and that much remained to be accomplished, and untied himself, and commenced working towards the summit. Connecting the teeth of rock were beds of snow, and Almer, only a few feet from me, was crossing the top of one of these, when suddenly, without a moment's warning, it broke away under him, and plunged down on to the glacier. As he staggered for a second, one foot in the act of stepping, and the other on the falling mass, I thought him lost; but he happily fell on to the right side and stopped himself. Had he taken the step with his right instead of the left foot, he would, in all probability, have fallen several hundred feet without touching anything, and would not have been arrested before reaching the glacier, a vertical distance of at least 3000 feet.

Small, ridiculously small, as the distance was to the summit, we were occupied nearly another hour before it was gained. Almer was a few feet in front, and he, with characteristic modesty, hesitated to step on the highest point, and drew back to allow us to pass. A cry was raised for Croz, who had done the chief part of the work, but he declined the honour, and we marched on to the top simultaneously; that is to say, clustered round it, a yard or two below, for it was much too small to get upon.

Did space permit me, I could give a very poor idea of the view, but it will be readily imagined that a panorama extending over as much ground as the whole of England is one worth taking some trouble to see, and one which is not often to be seen even in the Alps. No clouds obscured it, and a list of the summits that we saw would include nearly all the highest peaks of the chain. I saw the Pelvoux now — as I had seen the Ecrins from it three years before — across the basin of the Glacier Noir.

We could stay on the summit only a short time, and at a quarter to two prepared for the descent. Now, as we looked down, and thought of what we had passed over in coming up, we one and all hesitated about returning the same way. Moore said, no. Walker said the same, and I too; the guides were both of the same mind: this, be it remarked, although we had considered that there was no chance whatever of getting up any other way. But those 'last rocks' were not to be forgotten. Had they only protruded to a moderate extent, or had they been merely glazed, we should doubtless still have tried: but they were not reasonable rocks, — they would neither allow us to hold, nor would do it themselves. So we turned to the western arête, trusting to luck that we should find a way down to the schrund, and some means of getting over it afterwards. Our faces were a tolerable index to our thoughts, and apparently the thoughts of the party were not happy ones. Had any one then said to me, 'You are a great fool for coming here,' I should have answered with humility, 'It is too true.' And had my monitor gone on to say, 'Swear you will never ascend another mountain if you get down safely,' I am inclined to think I should have taken the oath. In fact, the game here was not worth the risk. The guides felt it as well as ourselves, and as Almer led off, he remarked, with more piety than logic, 'The good God has brought us up, and he will take us down in safety,' which showed pretty well what *he* was thinking about.

The ridge down which we now endeavoured to make our way was not inferior in difficulty to the other. Both were serrated to an extent that made it impossible to keep strictly to them, and obliged us to descend occasionally for some distance on the northern face and then mount again. Both were so rotten that the most experienced of our party, as well as the least, continually upset blocks large and small. Both arêtes were so narrow, so thin, that it was often a matter for speculation on which side an unstable block would fall.

At one point it seemed that we should be obliged to return to the summit and try the other way down. We were on the very edge of the arête. On one side was the enormous precipice facing the Pelvoux, which is not far from perpendicular; on the other a slope exceeding 50°. A deep notch brought us to an abrupt halt. Almer, who was leading, advanced cautiously to the edge on hands and knees, and peered over; his care was by no means unnecessary, for the rocks had broken away from under us unexpectedly several times. In this position he gazed down for some moments, and then, without a word, turned his head and looked at us. His face *may* have expressed apprehension or alarm, but it certainly did not show hope or joy. We learned that there was no means of getting down, and that we must, if we wanted to pass the notch, jump across on to an unstable block on the other side. It was decided that it should be done, and Almer, with a larger extent of rope than usual, jumped. The rock swayed as he came down upon it, but he clutched a large mass with both arms and brought himself to anchor. That which was both difficult and dangerous for the first man was easy enough for the others, and we got across with less trouble than I expected; stimulated by Croz's perfectly just observation, that if we couldn't get across there we were not likely to get down the other way.

Before long we were close to the schrund, but unable to see what it was like at this part, as the upper edge bent over. Two hours had already passed since leaving the summit, and it began to be highly probable that we should have to spend a night on the Glacier Blanc. Almer, who yet led, cut steps right down to the edge, but still he could not see below; therefore, warning us to hold tight, he made his whole body rigid, and (standing in the large step which he had cut for the purpose), had the upper part of his person lowered out until he saw what he wanted. He shouted that our work was finished, made me come close to the edge and untie myself, advanced the others until he had rope enough, and then with a loud *jödel* jumped down on to soft snow. Partly by skill and partly by luck he had hit the crevasse at its easiest point, and we had only to make a downward jump of eight or ten feet.

We had been more than eight hours and a half accomplishing the ascent of the final peak ... During this period we had not stopped for more than half-an-hour, and our nerves and muscles had been kept at the highest degree of tension the whole time. It may be imagined that we accepted the ordinary conditions of glacier travelling as an agreeable relief, and that that which at another time might have seemed formidable we treated as the veriest bagatelle. Late in the day as it was, and soft as was the snow, we put on such pace that we reached the Col des Ecrins in less than forty minutes. We lost no time in arranging our baggage, for we had still to traverse a long glacier, and to get clear of two ice-falls before it was dark; so, at 5.35 we resumed the march, adjourning eating and drinking, and put on a spurt which took us clear of the Glacier Blanc by 7.45 P.M. We got off the moraine of the Glacier Noir at 8.45, just as the last remnant of daylight vanished. Croz and myself were a trifle in advance of the others, and fortunately so for us; for as they were about to commence the descent of the snout of the glacier, the whole of the moraine that rested on its face peeled off, and came down with a tremendous roar.

We had now the pleasure of walking over a plain that is known by the name of the Pré de Madame Carle, covered with pebbles of all sizes, and intersected by numerous small streams or torrents. Every hole looked like a stone, every stone like a hole, and we tumbled about from side to side until our limbs and our tempers became thoroughly jaded. My companions, being both short-sighted, found the travelling especially disagreeable; so there was little wonder that when we came upon a huge mass of rock as big as a house, which had fallen from the flanks of Pelvoux, a regular cube that offered no shelter whatever, Moore cried out in ecstasy, 'Oh, how delightful! the very thing I have been longing for. Let us have a perfectly extemporaneous bivouac.' This, it should be said, was when the night threatened thunder and lightning, rain, and all other delights.

The pleasures of a perfectly extemporaneous bivouac under these circumstances not being novelties to Croz and myself, we thought we would try for the miseries of a roof; but Walker and Almer, with their usual good nature, declared it was the very thing that they, too, were longing for; so the trio resolved to stop. We generously left them all the provisions (a dozen cubic inches or thereabouts of bacon fat, and half a candle), and pushed on for the chalets of Aléfroide, or at least we thought we did, but could not be certain. In the course of half-an-hour we got uncommonly close to the main torrent, and Croz all at once disappeared. I stepped cautiously forward to peer down into the place where I thought he was, and quietly tumbled head over heels into a big rhododendron bush. Extricating myself with some trouble, I fell backwards over some rocks, and got wedged in a cleft so close to the torrent that it splashed all over me.

The colloquy which then ensued amid the thundering of the stream was as follows: —

'Hullo, Croz!' 'Eh, Monsieur.' 'Where *are* you?' 'Here, Monsieur.' 'Where *is* here?' 'I don't know; where are *you*?' 'Here, Croz;' and so on.

The fact was, from the intense darkness, and the noise of the torrent, we had no idea of each other's situation. In the course of ten minutes, however, we joined together again, agreed we had had quite enough of that kind of thing, and adjourned to a most eligible rock at 10.15.

How well I remember the night at that rock, and the jolly way in which Croz came out! We were both very wet about the legs, and both uncommonly hungry, but the time passed pleasantly enough round our fire of juniper, and until long past midnight we sat up recounting, over our pipes, wonderful stories of the most incredible description, in which I must admit, my companion beat me hollow. Then throwing ourselves on our beds of rhododendron, we slept an untroubled sleep, and rose on a bright Sunday morning as fresh as might be, intending to enjoy a day's rest and luxury with our friends at La Ville de Val Louise.

I have failed to give the impression I wish if it has not been made evident that the ascent of the Pointe des Ecrins was not an ordinary piece of work. There is an increasing disposition now-a-days amongst those who write on the Alps, to underrate the difficulties and dangers which are met with, and this disposition is, I think, not less mischievous than the old-fashioned style of making everything terrible. Difficult as we found the peak, I believe we took it at the best, perhaps the only possible, time of the year. The great slope on which we spent so much time was, from being denuded by the avalanche of which I have spoken, deprived of its greatest danger. Had it had the snow still resting upon it, and had we persevered with the expedition, we should almost without doubt have ended with calamity instead of success. The ice of that slope is always below, its angle is severe, and the rocks do not project sufficiently to afford the support that snow requires, to be stable, when at a great angle. So far am I from desiring to tempt any one to repeat the expedition, that I put it on record as my belief, however sad and however miserable a man may have been, if he is found on the summit of the Pointe des Ecrins after a fall of new snow, he is likely to experience misery far deeper than anything with which he has hitherto been acquainted.

(Ibid., pp. 145–165)

THE COL DE PILATTE

After only a day's rest, and having fled from the hustle and bustle of the busy town, preparations were made for their next excursion to establish a new mountain pass and a shorter route across the central Dauphiné Alps.

We meant the 26*th* to be a day of rest, but it was little that we found in the *cabaret* of Claude Giraud, and we fled before the babel of sound which rose in intensity as men descended to a depth which is unattainable by the beasts of the field, and found at the chalets of Entraigues the peace that had been denied to us at Val Louise.

Early the next morning, they were met by their good friend Reynaud and set off, making quick progress up a fine snow couloir.

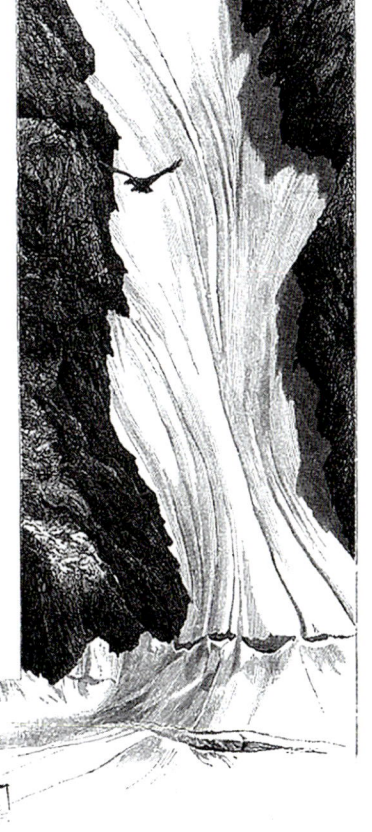

A Snow Couloir

Couloirs look prodigiously steep when seen from the front, and, so viewed, it is impossible to be certain of their inclination within many degrees. Snow, however, does actually lie at steeper angles in couloirs than in any other situations; — 45° to 50° degrees is not an uncommon inclination. Even at such angles, two men with proper axes can mount on snow at the rate of 700 to 800 feet per hour. The same amount can only be accomplished in the same time on steep rocks when they are of the very easiest character, and four or five hours may be readily spent upon an equal height of difficult rocks. Snow couloirs are therefore to be commended because they economise time.

At 9.30 A.M. we commenced the ascent of the couloir leading from the nameless glacier to a point in the ridge, just to the east of Mont Bans. So far the route had been nothing more than a steep grind in an angle where little could be seen, but now views opened out in several directions, and the way began to be interesting.

Croz cut the way with unflagging energy throughout the whole of the ascent, and at 10.45 we stood on the summit of our pass, intending to refresh ourselves with a good halt. Unhappily, at that moment a mist, which had been playing about the ridge, swooped down and blotted out the whole of the view on the northern side. Croz was the only one who caught a glimpse of the descent, and it was deemed advisable to push on immediately, while its recollection was fresh in his memory.

We commenced to descend towards the Glacier de Pilatte by a slope of smooth ice, the face of which, according to the measurement of Mr. Moore, had an inclination of 54°! Croz still led, and the others followed at intervals of about 15 feet, all being tied together, and Almer occupying the responsible position of last man. The two guides were therefore about 70 feet apart. They were quite invisible to each other from the mist, and looked spectral even to us. But the *strong* man could be heard by all hewing out the steps below, while every now and then the voice of the *steady* man pierced the cloud, — 'Slip not, dear sirs; place well your feet: stir not until you are certain.'

For three quarters of an hour we progressed in this fashion. The axe of Croz all at once stopped. 'What is the matter, Croz?'

'Bergschrund, gentlemen.' 'Can we get over?' 'Upon my word, I don't know; I think we must jump.' The clouds rolled away right and left as he spoke. The effect was dramatic! It was a *coup de théâtre*, preparatory to the 'great sensation leap' which was about to be executed by the entire company.

Some unseen cause, some cliff or obstruction in the rocks underneath, had caused our wall of ice to split into two portions, and the huge fissure which had thus been formed extended, on each hand, as far as could be seen. We, on the slope above, were separated from the slope below by a mighty crevasse. No running up and down to look for an easier place to cross could be done on an ice-slope of 54°; the chasm had to be passed then and there.

A downward jump of 15 or 16 feet, and a forward leap of 7 or 8 feet had to be made at the same time. That is not much, you will say. It was not much; it was not the quantity, but it was the quality of the jump which gave to it its particular flavour. You had to hit a narrow ridge of ice. If that was passed, it seemed as if you might roll down for ever and ever. If it was not attained, you dropped into the crevasse below; which, although partly choked by icicles and snow that had fallen from above, was still gaping in many places, ready to receive an erratic body.

Croz untied Walker in order to get rope enough, and warning us to hold fast, sprang over the chasm. He alighted cleverly on his feet; untied himself and sent up the rope to Walker, who followed his example. It was then my turn, and I advanced to the edge of the ice. The second which followed was what is called a supreme moment. That is to say, I felt supremely ridiculous. The world seemed to revolve at a frightful pace, and my stomach to fly away. The next moment I found myself sprawling in the snow, and then, of course, vowed that *it was nothing*, and prepared to encourage my friend Reynaud.

He came to the edge and made declarations. I do not believe that he was a whit more reluctant to pass the place than we others, but he was infinitely more demonstrative, — in a word, he was French. He wrung his hands, 'Oh! what a *diable* of a place!' 'It is nothing, Reynaud,' I said, 'it is *nothing*.' 'Jump,' cried the others, 'jump.' But he turned round, as far as one can do such a thing in an ice-step, and covered his face with his hands, ejaculating, 'Upon my word, it is not possible. No! no!! no!!! it is not possible.'

How he came over I do not know. We saw a toe — it seemed to belong to Moore; we saw Reynaud a flying body, coming down as if taking a header into water; with arms and legs all abroad, his leg of mutton flying in the air, his bâton escaped from his grasp; and then we heard a thud as if a bundle of carpets had been pitched out of a window. When set upon his feet he was a sorry spectacle; his head was a great snowball; brandy was trickling out of one side of the knapsack, chartreuse out of the other — we bemoaned its loss, but we roared with laughter.

… I cannot close it without paying tribute to the ability with which Croz led us, through a dense mist, down the remainder of the Glacier de Pilatte. As an exhibition of strength and skill, it has probably never been surpassed in the Alps or elsewhere. On this almost unknown and very steep glacier, he was perfectly at home, even in the mists. Never able to see fifty feet ahead, he still went on with the utmost certainty, and without having to retrace a single step; and displayed from first to last consummate knowledge of the materials with which he was dealing. Now he cut steps down one side of a *sérac*, went with a dash at the other side, and hauled us up after him; then cut away along a ridge until a point was gained from which we could jump on to another ridge; then, doubling back, found a snow-bridge, across which he crawled on hands and knees, towed us across by the legs, ridiculing our apprehensions, mimicking our awkwardness, declining all help, bidding us only to follow him.

So our little campaign in Dauphiné came to an end. It was remarkable for the absence of failures, and for the ease and precision with which all our plans were carried out. This was due very much to the spirit of my companions; but it was also owing to the fine weather which we were fortunate enough to enjoy, and to our making a very early start every morning. By beginning our work at or before the break of day, on the longest days in the year, we were not only able to avoid hurrying when deliberation was desirable, but could afford to spend several hours in delightful ease whenever the fancy seized us.

I cannot too strongly recommend to tourists in search of amusement to avoid the inns of Dauphiné. Sleep in the chalets. Get what food you can from the inns, but do not as a rule attempt to pass nights in them. *Sleep* in them you cannot. M. Joanne says that the inventor of the insecticide powder was a native of Dauphiné. I can well believe it. He must have often felt the necessity of such an invention in his infancy and childhood.

On June 29th I crossed the Col du Galibier to St. Michel; on the 30th, the Col des Encombres to Moutiers; on July 1st, the Col du Bonhomme to Contamines; and on the 2nd, by the Pavilion de Bellevue to Chamounix, where I joined Mr. Adams-Reilly to take part in some expeditions which had been planned long before.

(Ibid., pp. 166–175)

ATTEMPT TO ASCEND MONT DOLENT, AIGUILLE DE TRÉ-LA-TÊTE AND AIGUILLE D'ARGENTIÈRE

1864 proved to be a fortunate year for Whymper. Having met a Mr Adams-Reilly a year earlier, the two men's goals appeared to compliment each other and between them they drew up a list of mountains to climb. This included Mont Dolent, 3,823m (12,543 ft), Aiguille de Tré-la-Tête, 3,930m (12,894 ft) and Aiguille d'Argentière, 3,901m (12,799 ft), all three in the Mont Blanc massif. For Reilly it was about gaining vantage points for mapping the area but for Whymper is was all about making the first ascent of each.

A few years ago not many persons knew from personal knowledge how extremely inaccurately the chain of Mont Blanc was delineated. In the earlier part of the century thousands had made the tour of the chain, and before the year 1860 at least *one* thousand individuals had stood upon its highest summit; but out of all this number there was not one capable, willing, or able, to map the mountain which, until recently, was regarded the highest in Europe.

Many persons knew that great blunders had been perpetrated, and it was notorious that even Mont Blanc itself was represented in a ludicrously incorrect manner on all sides excepting the north; but there was not, perhaps, a single individual who knew, at the time to which I refer, that errors of no less than 1000 feet had been committed in the determination of heights at each end of the chain; that some glaciers were represented of double their real dimensions; and that ridges and mountains were laid down which actually had no existence.

In 1863, Mr. Adams-Reilly, who had been travelling in the Alps during several years, resolved to attempt a survey of the unsurveyed portions of the chain of Mont Blanc. He provided himself with a good theodolite, and starting from a base-line measured by Forbes in the Valley of Chamounix, determined the positions of no less than 200 points. The accuracy of his work may be judged from the fact that, after having turned many corners and carried his observations over a distance of fifty miles, his Col Ferret 'fell within 200 yards of the position assigned to it by General Dufour!'

With very small hope that my proposal would be accepted, I invited him to take part in renewed attacks on the Matterhorn. He entered heartily into my plans, and met me with a counter-proposition, namely, that I should accompany him on some expeditions which he had projected in the chain of Mont Blanc. The unwritten contract took this form:—I will help you to carry out your desires, and you shall assist me to carry out mine.

Mr. Reilly presented his MS. map to the English Alpine Club. It was resolved that it should be published; but before it passed into the engraver's hands its author undertook to revise it carefully. To this end he planned a number of expeditions to high points which up to that time had been regarded inaccessible, and upon some of these ascents he invited me to accompany him. Before I pass on to these expeditions, it will be convenient to devote a few lines to the topography of the chain of Mont Blanc.

I believe it is correct to say that the Aiguille du Midi and the Aiguille de Miage were the only two summits in the chain of Mont Blanc which had been ascended at the beginning of 1864. The latter of these two is a perfectly insignificant point; and the former is only a portion of one of the ridges just now mentioned, and can hardly be regarded as a mountain separate and distinct from Mont Blanc. The really great peaks of the chain were considered inaccessible, and, I think, with the exception of the Aiguille Verte, had never been assailed.

The finest, as well as the highest peak in the chain (after Mont Blanc itself), is the Grandes Jorasses. The next, without a doubt, is the Aiguille Verte. The Aiguille de Bionnassay, which in actual height follows the Verte, should be considered as a part of Mont Blanc; and in the same way the summit called Les Droites is only a part of the ridge which culminates in the Verte. The Aiguille de Trélatête **[now Tré-la-Tête]** is the next on the list that is entitled to be considered a separate mountain, and is by far the most important peak (as well as the highest) at the south-west end of the chain. Then comes the Aiguille d'Argentière, which occupies the same rank at the north-east end as the last-mentioned mountain does in the south-west. The rest of the aiguilles are comparatively insignificant; and although some of them (such as the Mont Dolent) look well from low elevations, and seem to possess a certain importance, they sink into their proper places directly one arrives at a considerable altitude.

The summit of the Aiguille Verte would have been one of the best stations out of all these mountains for the purposes of my friend. Its great height, and its isolated and commanding position, make it a most admirable point for viewing the intricacies of the chain; but he exercised a wise discretion in passing it by, and in selecting as our first excursion the passage of the Col de Triolet.

We slept under some big rocks on the Couvercle on the night of July 7th, with the thermometer at 26·5 Faht., and at 4.30 on the 8th made a straight track to the north of the Jardin, and thence went in zigzags, to break the ascent, over the upper slopes of the Glacier de Talèfre towards the foot of the Aiguille de Triolet. Croz was still my guide, Reilly was accompanied by one of the Michel Payots of Chamounix, and Henri Charlet, of the same place, was our porter.

We occupied the 9th with a scramble up Mont Dolent. This was a miniature ascent. It contained a little of everything … The summit itself was little, — very small indeed; it was the loveliest little cone of snow that was ever piled up on mountain-top; so soft, so pure; it seemed a crime to defile it; it was a miniature Jungfrau, a toy summit, you could cover it with the hand.

But there was nothing little about the view from the Mont Dolent. **[Reilly recorded]** 'Situated at the junction of three mountain ridges, it rises in a positive steeple far above anything in its immediate neighbourhood; and certain gaps in the surrounding ridges, which seem contrived for that especial purpose, extend the view in almost every direction. The precipices which descend to the Glacier d'Argentière I can only compare to those of the Jungfrau, and the ridges on both sides of that glacier, especially the steep rocks of Les Droites and Les Courtes, surmounted by the sharp snow-peak of the Aig. Verte, have almost the effect of the Grandes Jorasses. Then, framed, as it were, between the massive tower of the Aig. de Triolet and the more distant Jorasses, lies, without exception, the most delicately beautiful picture I have ever seen — the whole *massif* of Mont Blanc, raising its great head of snow far above the tangled series of flying buttresses which uphold the Monts Maudits, supported on the left by Mont Peuteret and by the mass of ragged aiguilles which overhang the Brenva. This aspect of Mont Blanc is not new, but from this point its *pose* is unrivalled, and it has all the superiority of a picture grouped by the hand of a master … The view is as extensive, and far more lovely than that from Mont Blanc itself.'

We went down to Courmayeur, and on the afternoon of July 10th started from that place to camp on Mont Suc, for the ascent of the Aiguille de Trélatête; hopeful that the mists which were hanging about would clear away. They did not, so we deposited ourselves, and a vast load of straw, on the moraine of the Miage Glacier, just above the Lac de Combal, in a charming little hole which some solitary shepherd had excavated beneath a great slab of rock. We spent the night there, and the whole of the next day, unwilling to run away, and equally so to get into difficulties by venturing into the mist. It was a dull time, and I grew restless. Reilly read to me a lecture on the excellence of patience, and composed himself in an easy attitude, to pore over the pages of a yellow-covered book. 'Patience,' I said to him viciously, 'comes readily to fellows who have shilling novels; but I have not got one; I have picked all the mud out of the nails of my boots, and have skinned my face; what shall I do?' 'Go and study the moraine of the Miage,' said he. I went, and came back after an hour. 'What news?' cried Reilly, raising himself on his elbow. 'Very little; it's a big moraine, bigger than I thought, with ridge outside ridge, like a fortified camp; and there are walls upon it which have been built and loop-holed, as if for defence.' 'Try again,' he said, as he threw himself on his back. But I went to Croz, who was asleep, and tickled his nose with a straw until he awoke; and then, as that amusement was played out, watched Reilly, who was getting numbed, and shifted uneasily from side to side, and threw himself on his stomach, and rested his head on his elbows, and lighted his pipe and puffed at it savagely. When I looked again, how was Reilly? An indistinguishable heap; arms, legs, head, stones, and straw, all mixed together, his hat flung on one side, his novel tossed far away!

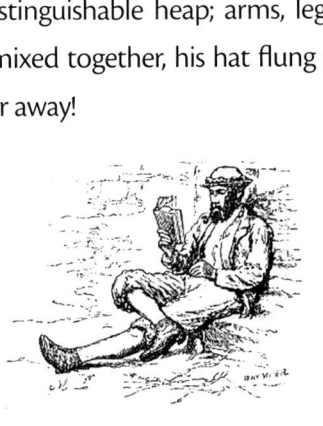

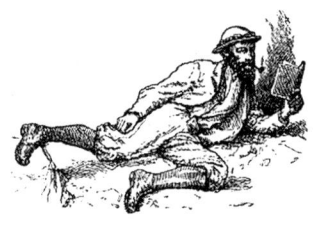

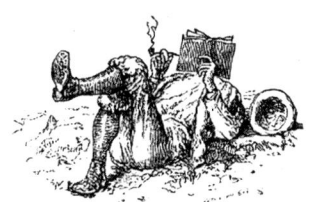

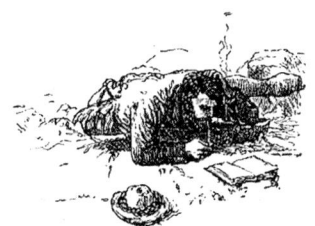

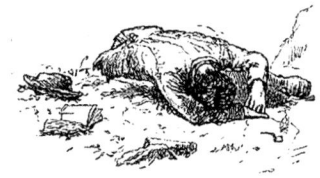

Bah! it was a dull time. Our mountain, like a beautiful coquette, sometimes unveiled herself for a moment, and looked charming above, although very mysterious below. It was not until eventide she allowed us to approach her; then, as darkness came on, the curtains were withdrawn, the light drapery was lifted, and we stole up on tiptoe through the grand portal formed by Mont Suc. But night advanced rapidly, and we found ourselves left out in the cold, without a hole to creep into or shelter from overhanging rock. We might have fared badly, except for our good plaids. When they were sewn together down their long edges, and one end tossed over our rope (which was passed round some rocks), and the other secured by stones, there was sufficient protection; and we slept on this exposed ridge, 9700 feet above the level of the sea, more soundly, perhaps, than if we had been lying on feather beds.

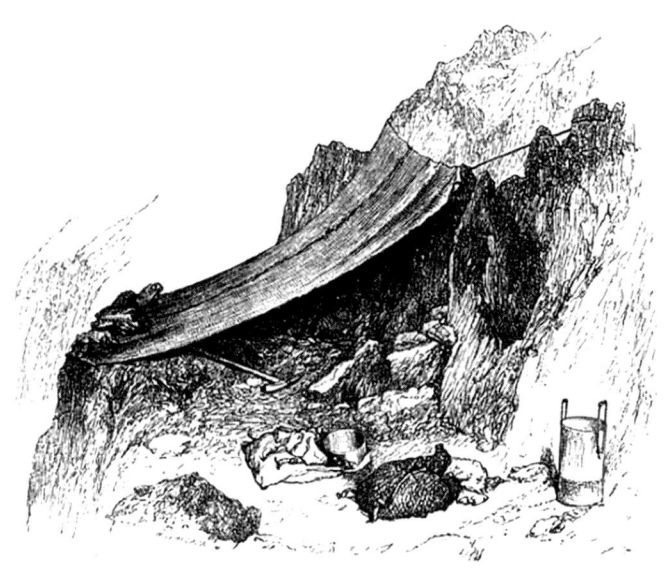

Our Camp On Mont Suc

We left our bivouac at 4.45 A.M. [**on 12th July**], and at 9.40 arrived upon the highest of the three summits of the Trélatête, by passing over the lowest one. It was well above everything at this end of the chain, and the view from it was extraordinarily magnificent. The whole of the western face of Mont Blanc was spread out before us; we were the first by whom it had been ever seen. I cede the description of this view to my comrade, to whom it rightfully belongs.

With just two days remaining of their excursions in the area, the party went on to attack the Aiguille d'Argentière.

… the evil spirit which prompts men to ascend mountains tempted us to stop, and to look back at the Aiguille d'Argentière. The sky was cloudless; no wind could be felt, nor sign of it perceived; it was only eight o'clock in the morning; and there, right before us, we saw another branch of the glacier leading high up into the mountain — far above the Col du Chardonnet — and a little couloir rising from its head almost to the top of the peak. This was clearly the right route to take. We turned back, and went at it.

The glacier was steep, and the snow gully rising out of it was steeper. Seven hundred steps were cut. Then the couloir became *too* steep. We took to the rocks on its left, and at last gained the ridge, at a point about 1500 feet above the Col du Chardonnet. We faced about to the right, and went along the ridge; keeping on some snow a little below its crest, on the Saleinoz side. Then we got the wind again; yet no one thought of turning, for we were within 250 feet of the summit.

The axes of Croz and Couttet went to work once more, for the slope was about as steep as a snow-slope could be. Its surface was covered with a loose, granular crust; dry and utterly incoherent; which slipped away in streaks directly it was meddled with. The men had to cut through this into the old beds underneath, and to pause incessantly to rake away the powdery stuff, which poured down in hissing streams over the hard substratum. Ugh! how cold it was! How the wind blew! Couttet's hat was torn from its fastenings, and went on a tour in Switzerland. The flour-like snow, swept off the ridge above, was tossed spirally upwards, eddying in tourmentes; then, dropt [sic] in lulls, or caught by other gusts, was flung far and wide to feed the Saleinoz.

'My feet are getting suspiciously numbed,' cried Reilly: 'how about frost-bites?' 'Kick hard, sir,' shouted the men; 'it's the only way.' *Their* fingers were kept alive by their work; but it was cold for the feet, and they kicked and hewed simultaneously. I followed their example too violently, and made a hole clean through my footing. A clatter followed as if crockery had been thrown down a well.

I went down a step or two, and discovered in a second that all were standing over a cavern (not a crevasse, speaking properly) that was bridged over by a thin vault of ice, from which great icicles hung in groves. Almost in the same minute Reilly pushed one of his hands right through the roof. The whole party might have tumbled through at any moment. 'Go ahead, Croz, we are over a chasm!' 'We know it,' he answered, 'and we can't find a firm place.'

In the blandest manner, my comrade inquired if to persevere would not be to do that which is called 'tempting Providence.' My reply being in the affirmative, he further observed, 'Suppose we go down?' 'Very willingly.' 'Ask the guides.' They had not the least objection; so we went down, and slept that night at the Montanvert.

Off the ridge we were out of the wind. In fact, a hundred feet down to windward, on the slope fronting the Glacier du Chardonnet, we were broiling hot; there was not a suspicion of a breeze. Upon that side there was nothing to tell that a hurricane was raging a hundred feet higher, — the cloudless sky looked tranquillity itself: whilst to leeward the only sign of a disturbed atmosphere was the friskiness of the snow upon the crests of the ridges.

We set out on the 14th, with Croz, Payot, and Charlet, to finish off the work which had been cut short so abruptly, and slept, as before, at the Chalets de Lognan. On the 15th, about midday, we arrived upon the summit of the aiguille, and found that we had actually been within one hundred feet of it when we turned back upon the first attempt.

To men who are sound in limb it may be amusing to arrive on a summit (as we did upon the top of Mont Dolent), sitting astride a ridge too narrow to stand upon; or to do battle with a ferocious wind (as we did on the top of the Aiguille de Trélatête); or to feel half-frozen in midsummer (as we did on the Aiguille d'Argentière). But there is extremely little amusement in making sketches and notes under such conditions. Yet upon all these expeditions, under the most adverse circumstances, and in the most trying situations, Mr. Reilly's brain and fingers were always at work.

(Ibid, pp. 176–192)

THE MOMING PASS

Reilly and Whymper then parted ways for a while and Whymper, with Croz, met up with their former companions, Moore and Almer. Moore believed he had seen a shorter way from Zinal to Zermatt than the two passes that were known, and was keen to discover whether this route could be crossed. As was the case with numerous other attempts to discover more direct mountain passes, this exploration was far from being hazard-free. On previous excursions, they had slept in hay barns, out in the open, on exposed ledges and beneath great boulders, but their next night was to be more unpleasant than any before.

… we immediately proceeded up the valley, and across the foot of the Zinal glacier to the Arpitetta Alp, where a chalet was supposed to exist in which we might pass the night. We found it at length, but it was not equal to our expectations. It was not one of those fine timbered chalets, with huge overhanging eaves, covered with pious sentences carved in unintelligible characters. It was a hovel, growing, as it were, out of the hill-side; roofed with rough slabs of slaty stone; without a door or window; surrounded by quagmires of ordure, and dirt of every description.

A foul native invited us to enter. The interior was dark; and, when our eyes became accustomed to the gloom, we saw that our palace was in plan about 15 by 20 feet; on one side it was scarcely five feet high, and on the other was nearly seven. On this side there was a raised platform, about six feet wide, littered with dirty straw and still dirtier sheepskins. This was the bedroom. The remainder of the width of the apartment was the parlour. The rest was the factory. Cheese was the article which was being fabricated, and the foul native was engaged in its manufacture. He was garnished behind with a regular cowherd's one-legged stool, which gave him a queer, uncanny look when it was elevated in the air as he bent over into his tub; for the making of his cheese required him to blow into a tub for ten minutes at a time. He then squatted on his stool to gain breath, and took a few whiffs at a short pipe; after which he blew away more vigorously than before. We were told that this procedure was necessary. It appeared to us to be nasty. It accounts, perhaps, for the flavour possessed by certain Swiss cheeses.

After a laborious trudge over many species of snow, and through many varieties of vapour — from the quality of a Scotch mist to that of a London fog — we at length stood on the depression between the Rothhorn and the Schallhorn. A steep wall of snow was upon the Zinal side of the summit; but what the descent was like on the other side we could not tell, for a billow of snow tossed over its crest by the western winds, suspended o'er Zermatt with motion arrested, resembling an ocean-wave frozen in the act of breaking, cut off the view.

Croz — held hard in by the others, who kept down the Zinal side — opened his shoulders, flogged down the foam, and cut away the cornice to its junction with the summit; then boldly leaped down, and called on us to follow him.

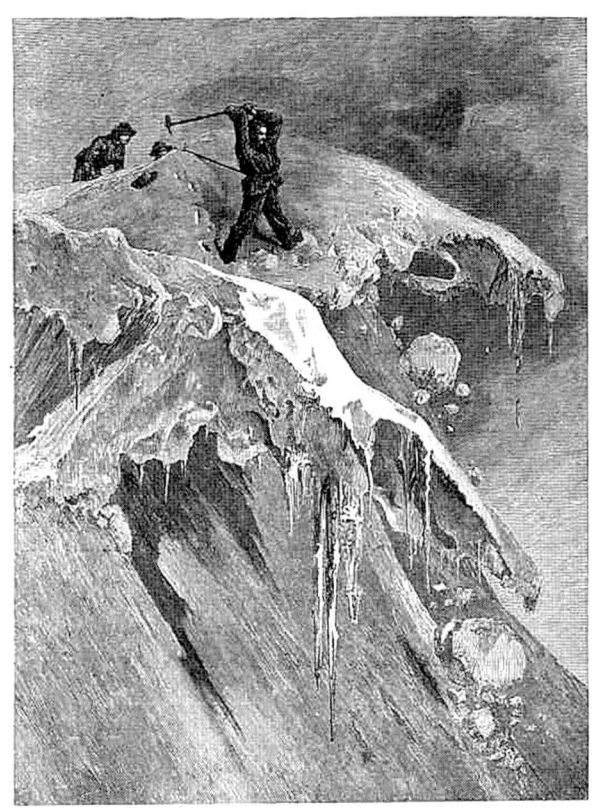

Summit Of The Moming Pass In 1864

It was well for us now that we had such a man as leader. An inferior or less daring guide would have hesitated to enter upon the descent in a dense mist; and Croz himself would have done right to pause had he been less magnificent in *physique*. He acted, rather than said, 'Where snow lies fast, there man can go; where ice exists, a way may be cut; it is a question of power; I have the power, — all you have to do is to follow me.' Truly, he did not spare himself, and could he have performed the feats upon the boards of a theatre that he did upon this occasion, he would have brought down the house with thunders of applause.

… after a most desperate and exciting struggle, and as bad a piece of ice-work as it is possible to imagine, we emerged on to the upper plateau of the Hohlicht glacier.

The glimpses which had been caught of the lower part of the Hohlicht glacier were discouraging, so it was now determined to cross over the ridge between it and the Rothhorn glacier. This was not done without great trouble. Again we rose to a height exceeding 12,000 feet. Eventually we took to the track of the despised Triftjoch, and descended by the well-known, but rough, path which leads to that pass; arriving at the Monte Rosa hotel at Zermatt at 7.20 P.M. We occupied nearly twelve hours of actual walking in coming from the chalet on the Arpitetta Alp (which was 2½ hours above Zinal), and we consequently found that the Moming pass was not the shortest route from Zinal to Zermatt, although it was the most direct.

Two dozen guides — good, bad, and indifferent; French, Swiss, and Italian — can commonly be seen sitting on the wall on the front of the Monte Rosa hotel: waiting on their employers, and looking for employers; watching new arrivals, and speculating on the number of francs which may be extracted from their pockets. The *Messieurs* — sometimes strangely and wonderfully dressed — stand about in groups, or lean back in chairs, or lounge on the benches which are placed by the door. They wear extraordinary boots, and still more remarkable head-dresses. Their peeled, blistered, and swollen faces are worth studying. Some, by the exercise of watchfulness and unremitting care, have been fortunate enough to acquire a fine raw sienna complexion. But most of them have not been so happy. They have been scorched on rocks, and roasted on glaciers. Their cheeks — first puffed, then cracked — have exuded a turpentine-like matter, which has coursed down their faces, and has dried in patches like the resin on the trunks of pines. They have removed it, and at the same time have pulled off large flakes of their skin. They have gone from bad to worse — their case has become hopeless — knives and scissors have been called into play; tenderly, and daintily, they have endeavoured to reduce their cheeks to one, uniform hue. It is not to be done. But they have gone on, fascinated, and at last have brought their unhappy countenances to a state of helpless and complete ruin. Their lips are cracked; their cheeks are swollen; their eyes are blood-shot; their noses are peeled and indescribable.

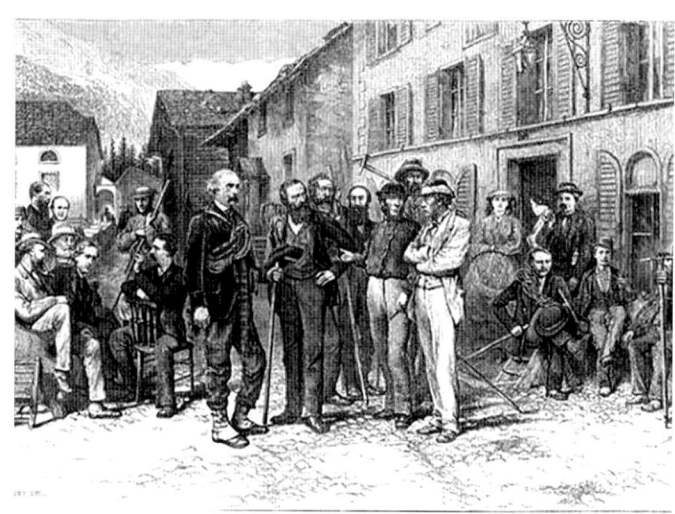

The Club-Room Of Zermatt, In 1864

Such are the pleasures of the mountaineer! Scornfully and derisively the last comer compares the sight with his own flaccid face and dainty hands; unconscious that he too, perhaps, will be numbered with those whom he now ridicules.

I left this agreeable society to seek letters at the post. They yielded disastrous intelligence. My holiday was brought to an abrupt termination, and I awaited the arrival of Reilly (who was convoying the stores for the attack on the Matterhorn) only to inform him that our arrangements were upset; then travelled home, day and night, as fast as express trains would carry me.

The family engraving business was working on an important commission that required great accuracy. Whymper felt it necessary to be there to ensure it was right.

(Ibid., pp. 193–203)

SUMMER 2015 (WEEK THREE)

AUTHOR'S LOG

Whymper's time and successes on the mountains above Chamonix were somewhat overshadowed by his ascent of the Matterhorn. This is understandable owing to the emphasis he placed on climbing it, and the tragedy that immortalised its first ascent. However, in 1864–65, Whymper spent a great deal of time around the popular town, and made the first ascent of numerous mountains within the sprawling Mont Blanc massif.

While the Matterhorn appears isolated and defiant, much of the Mont Blanc massif is a tangle of serrated ridges, pinnacles, spires and precipices. Rugged and precarious, they are no less a challenge, and in many cases, a greater one. In order to photograph the mountains up which Whymper made the first ascent, I embarked on a glacier trail to some of the most strategically placed mountain huts.

The first of these was the Couvercle Refuge at 2,687m. A cog train makes light work of the steep ascent from Chamonix to Montenvers, situated directly above the snaking Mer de Glace glacier that feeds off Mont Blanc. Then a series of vertical and near-vertical steel ladders ensures that only the competent climb down the 200m onto the glacier.

As a dry glacier, the crevasses were not hidden by snow, so it was considered relatively safe to cross it alone. With cramponed boots, I made my way up and around the glacier for several hours until reaching the point where another series of ladders allowed me to climb back up and off the glacier. Walking in crampons request care but soon feels natural enough. However, the first steps after they have been removed always feel particularly light, and the final walk to the refuge felt surprisingly easy.

Throughout the afternoon the cloud had gathered, and disappointingly, had hidden all the tops by the time I arrived at the hut. However, this was mountain weather and during the final hour of the day, the clouds swirled slowly like a magician's gloved hand to reveal one peak after another, as if out of nowhere, each with a more sun-warmed glow.

The morning brought a complete change with all the mountains displayed in their full glory. Immediately opposite the refuge, the massive bulk of Grand Jorasses caught the sun's rays, emphasising the towering walls along its huge north face (see page 220), while beyond it, Mont Blanc competed to be the star attraction as it loomed above all else, similarly catching the warming tones of the rising sun.

After the dramatic morning light show, I traversed up, down and around the ridge to the Charpoua Refuge. Perched on a precipice the tiny hut was surrounded by spiring rock pinnacles on three sides, and with a breathtaking 360-degree view, the remote hut is a true mountain refuge for climbers attempting the peaks to the south side of Aiguille Verte. A truly dramatic location, which I was reluctant to leave.

Several days later I was joined by my regular climbing partner – Mat and our good friend Ewan, and immediately, we made our way to the Argentière Refuge.

Although they had just arrived from Scotland, it was important for them to acclimatise as quickly as possible, so an initial night in a high hut had been planned. A gondola whisked us up to a very cold Grands Montets at 3,295m, requiring us to put on cold-weather gear before roping up and descending the icy mountainside to the glacier 500m below. All was going well until we reached the tangled moraine: a mass of shattered rock and boulders intertwined with deep crevasses and slippery ice. Picking our way through the danger we made very slow progress and soon realised the journey would take considerably longer than estimated.

Once on the glacier, we plodded up, over and across its crevassed surface, stopping frequently to photograph Mont Dolent 3,820m and the long serrated battlement of rock turrets leading to Aiguille de Triolet 3,870m. Guided over the frozen Antarctic-like landscape by an almost full moon, we arrived at the refuge at twilight, thankful for an excellent meal and comfortable bed.

As a result of a recent rock fall, the return was only a little less challenging, requiring constant vigilance to avoid crevasses and insecure debris along much of the glacier.

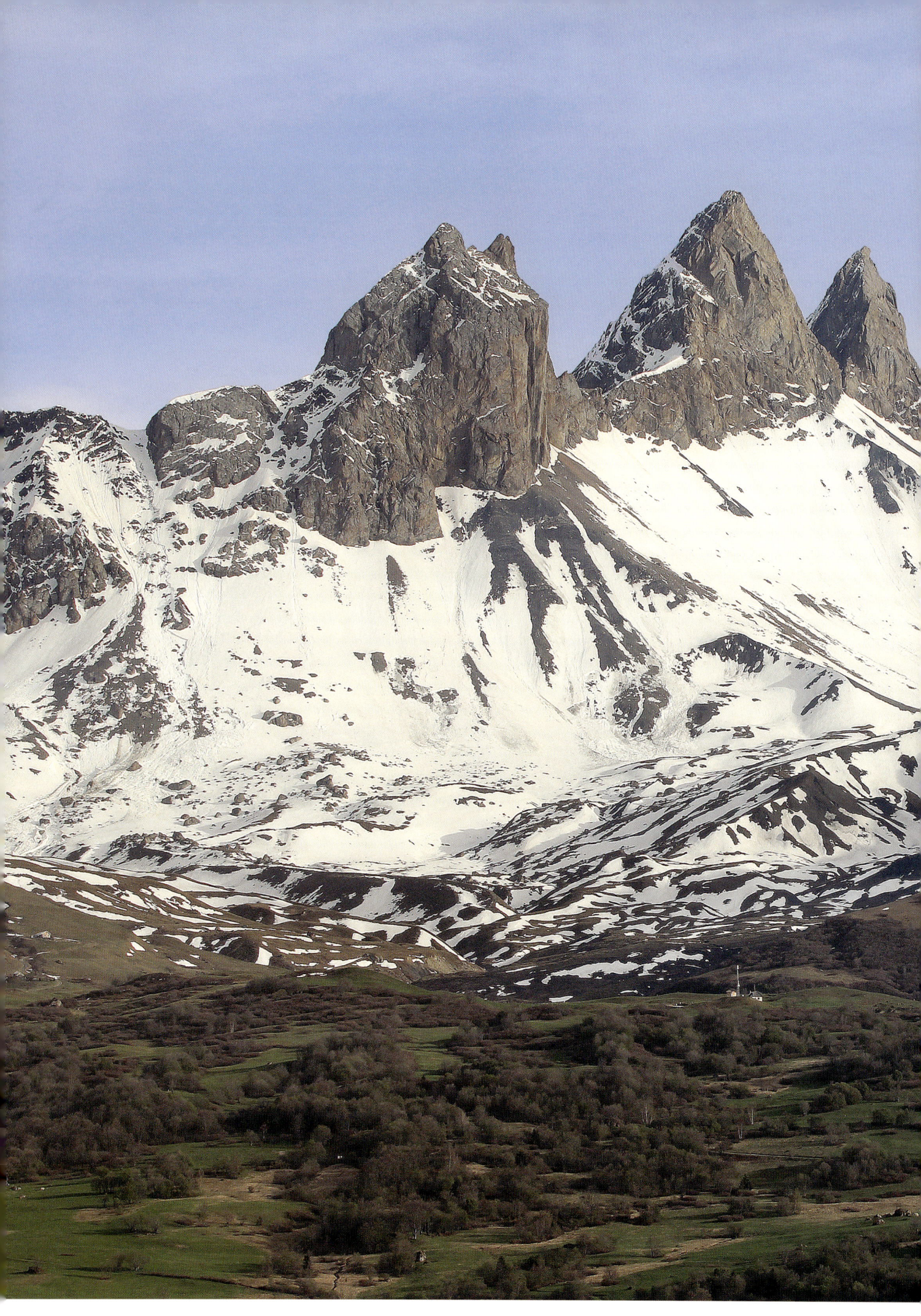

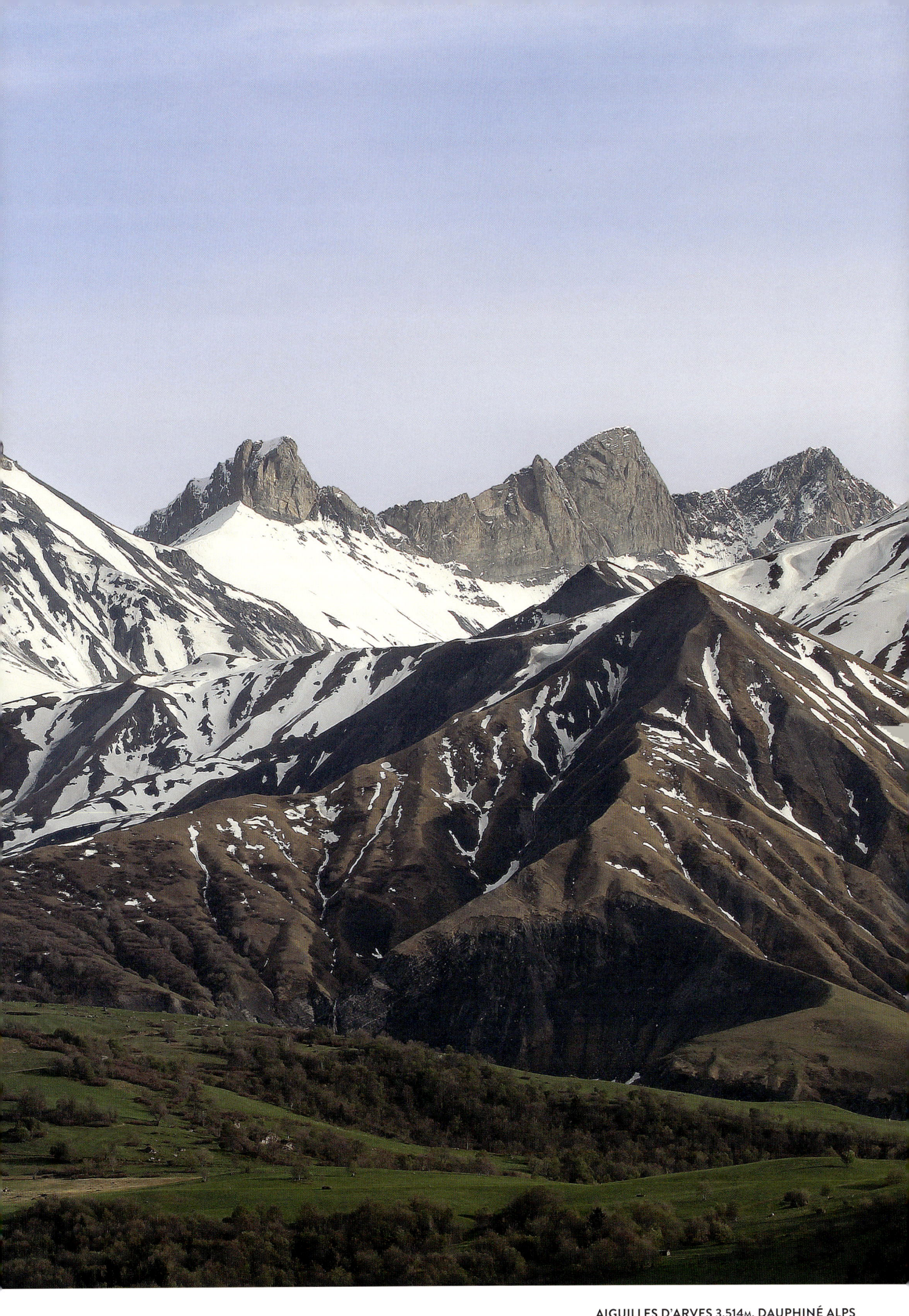

AIGUILLES D'ARVES 3,514M, DAUPHINÉ ALPS

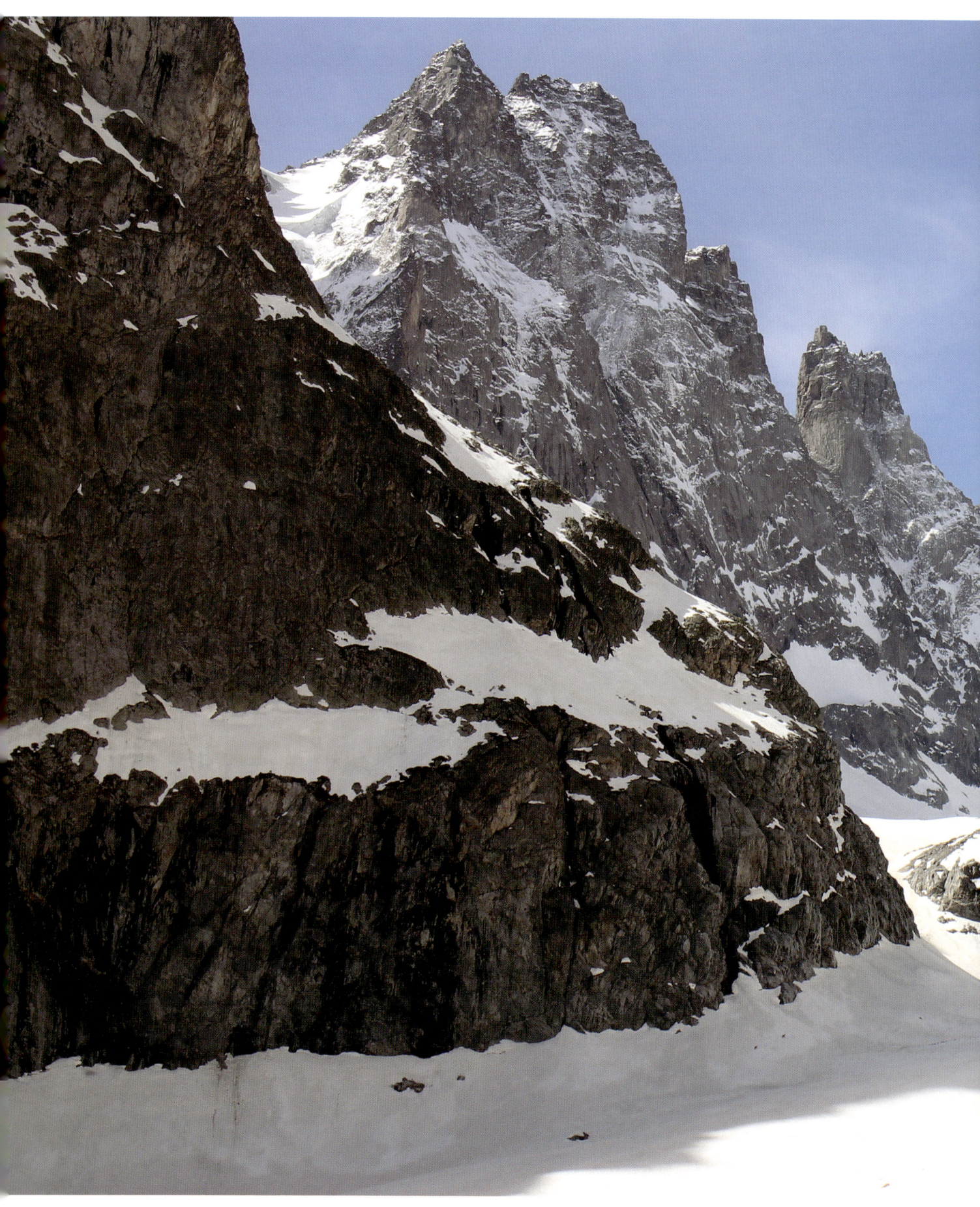

PIC SANS NOM 3,913M AND AILEFROIDE 3,954M FROM BARRE DES ÉCRINS, DAUPHINÉ ALPS

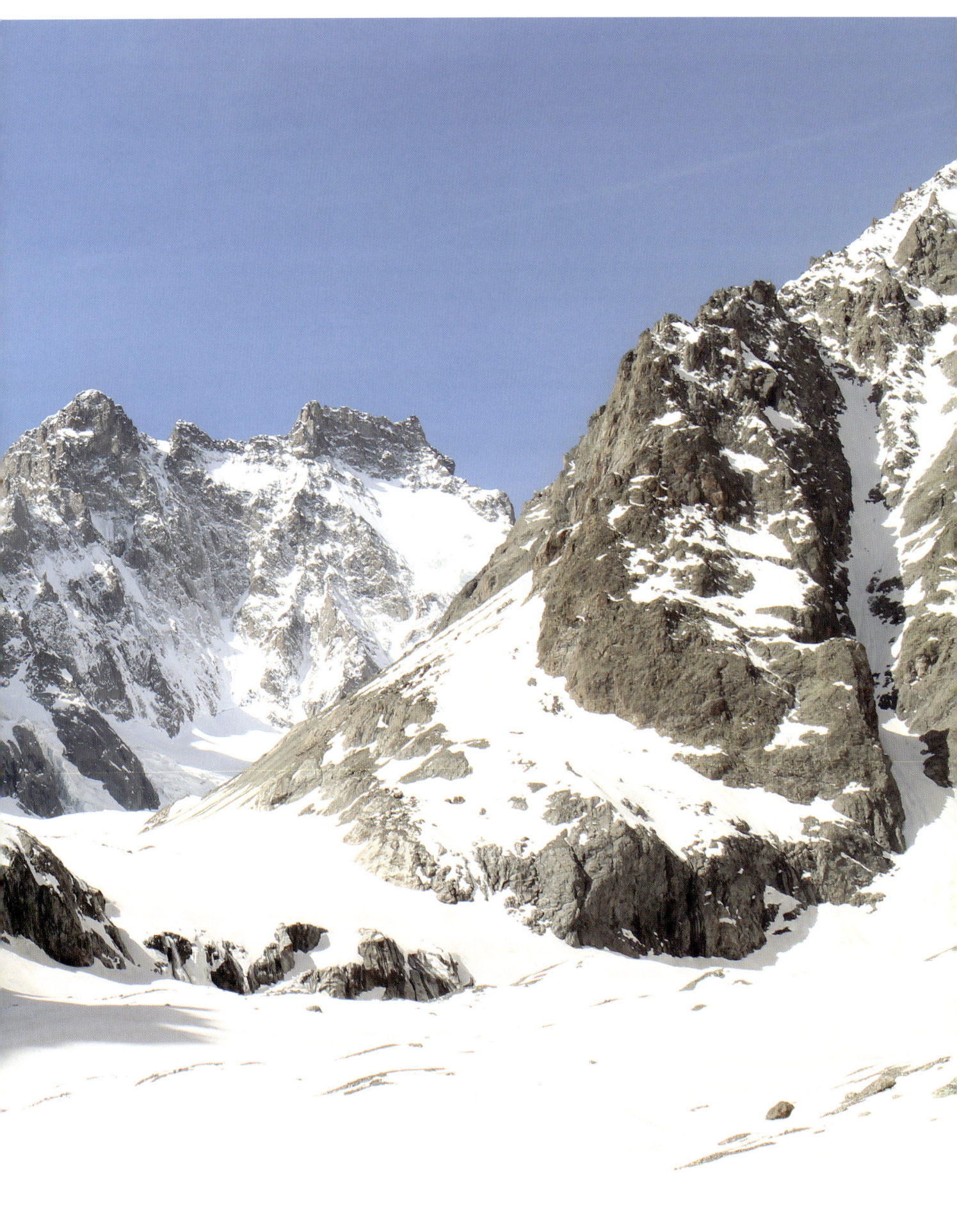

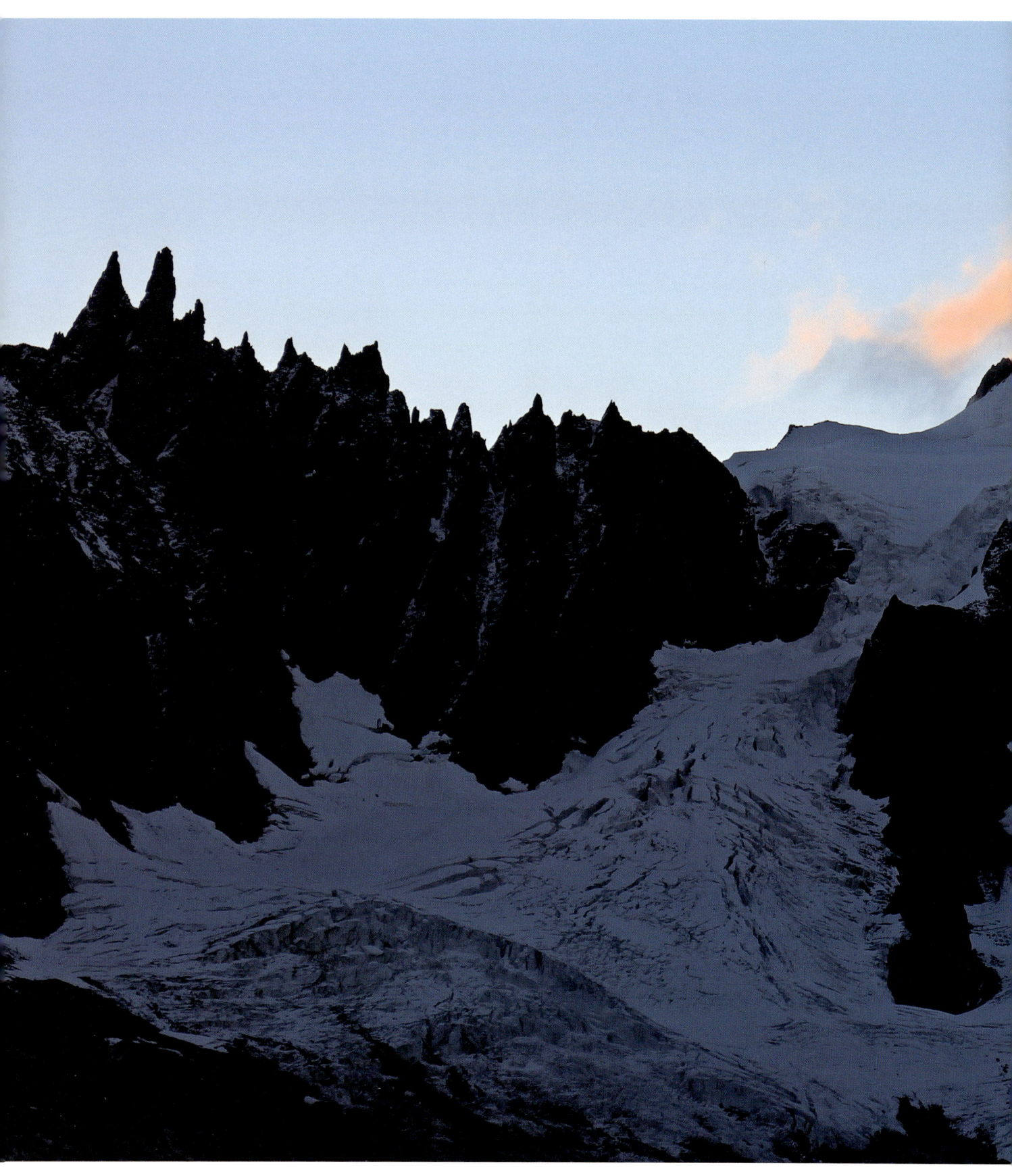
ARÊTE DES ROCHASSIERE AND POINT ISABELLE LEADING TO AIGUILLE DE TRIOLET 3,870M, MONT BLANC MASSIF

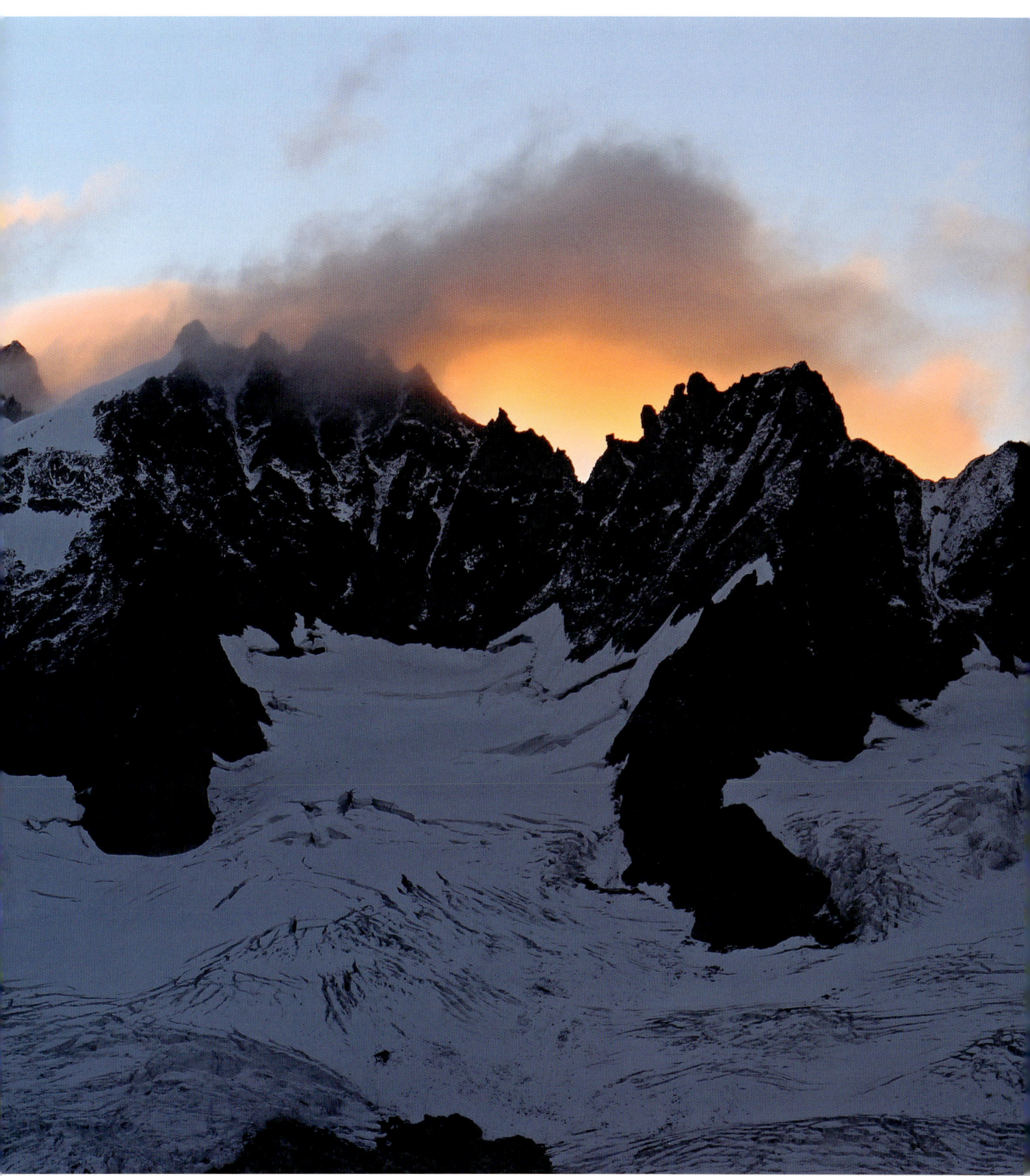

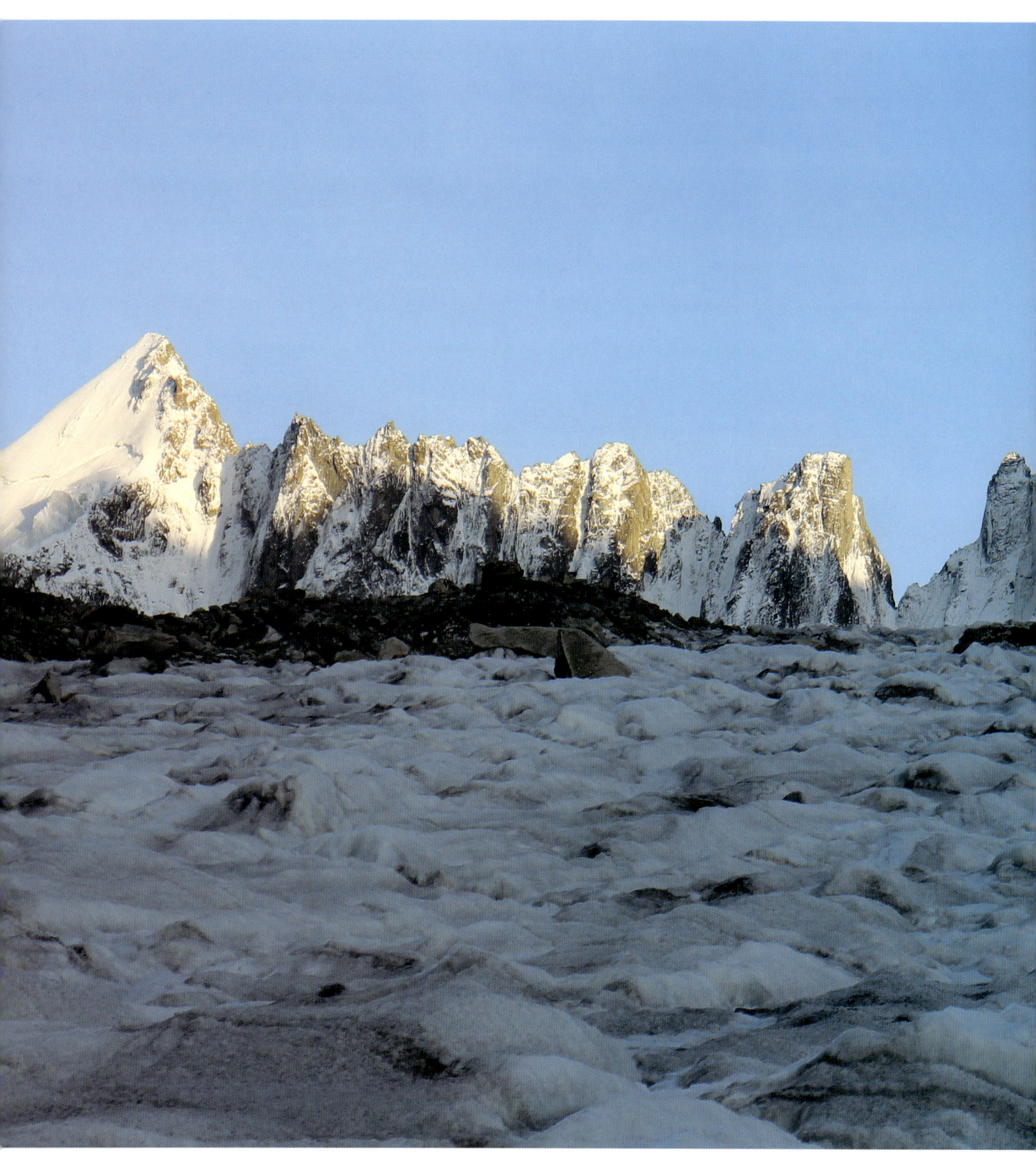

MONT DOLENT 3,820M TO AIGUILLE DE TRIOLET 3,870M, MONT BLANC MASSIF

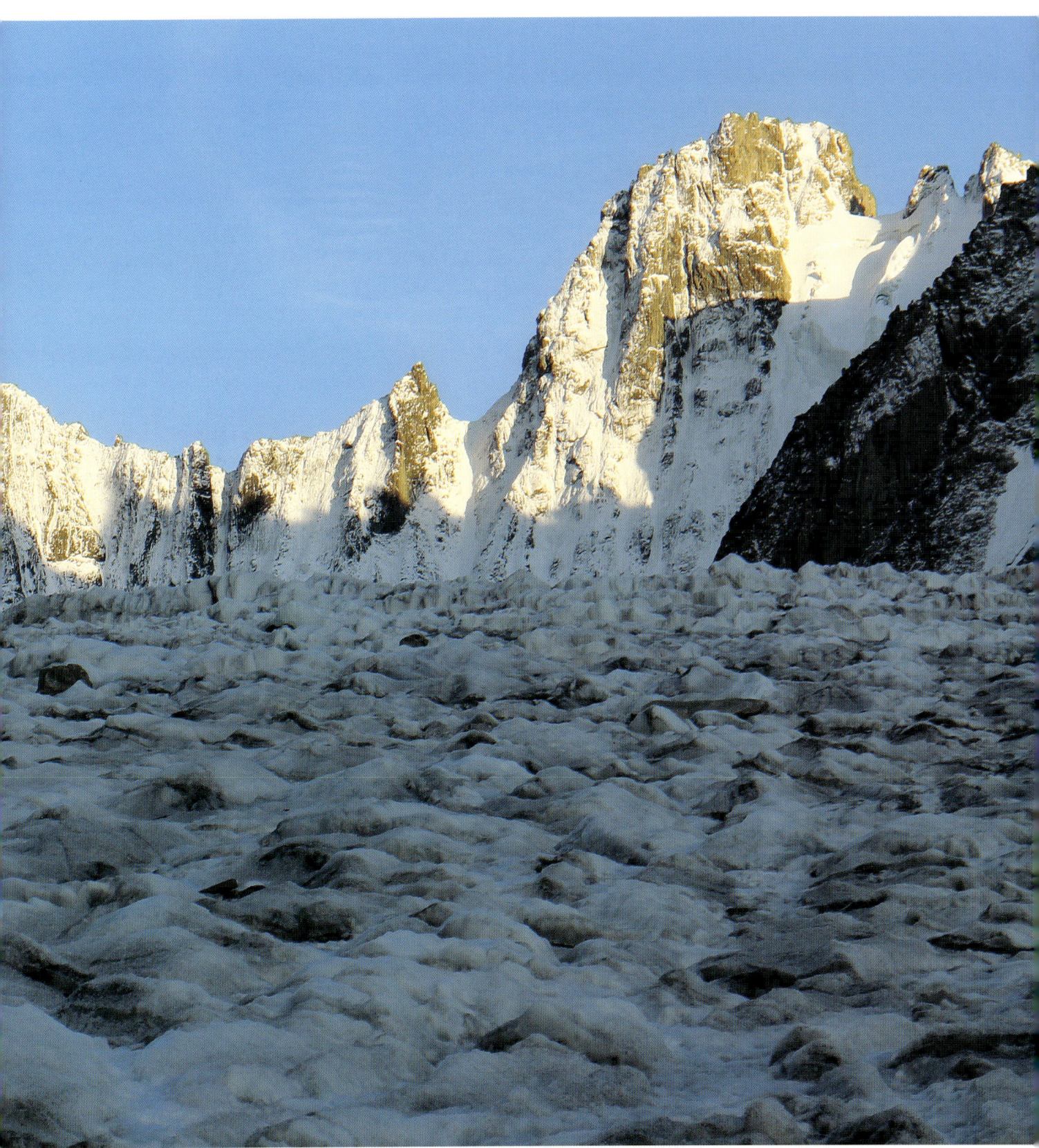

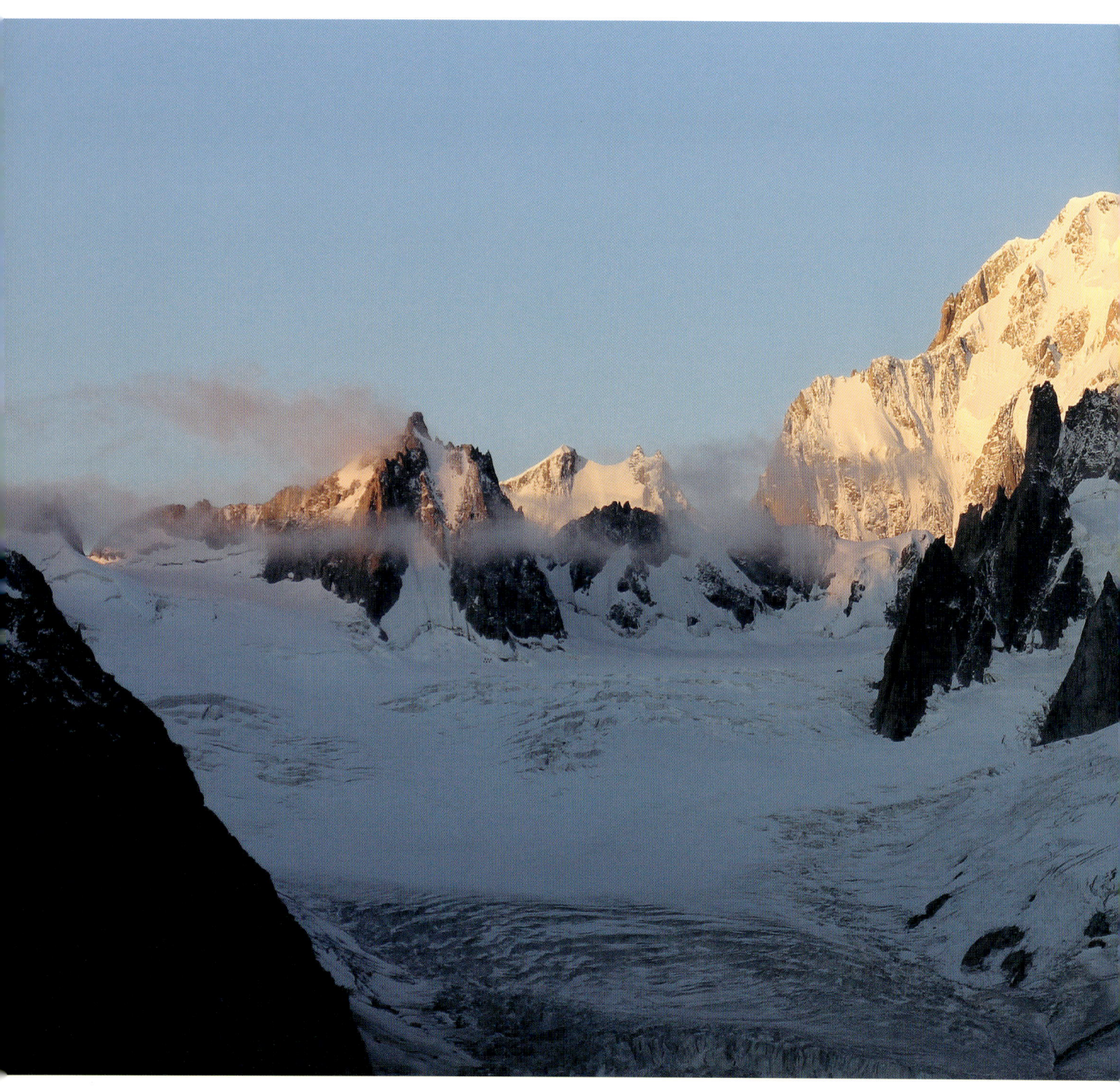

MONT BLANC 4,810M AND MONT BLANC DU TACUL 4,248M

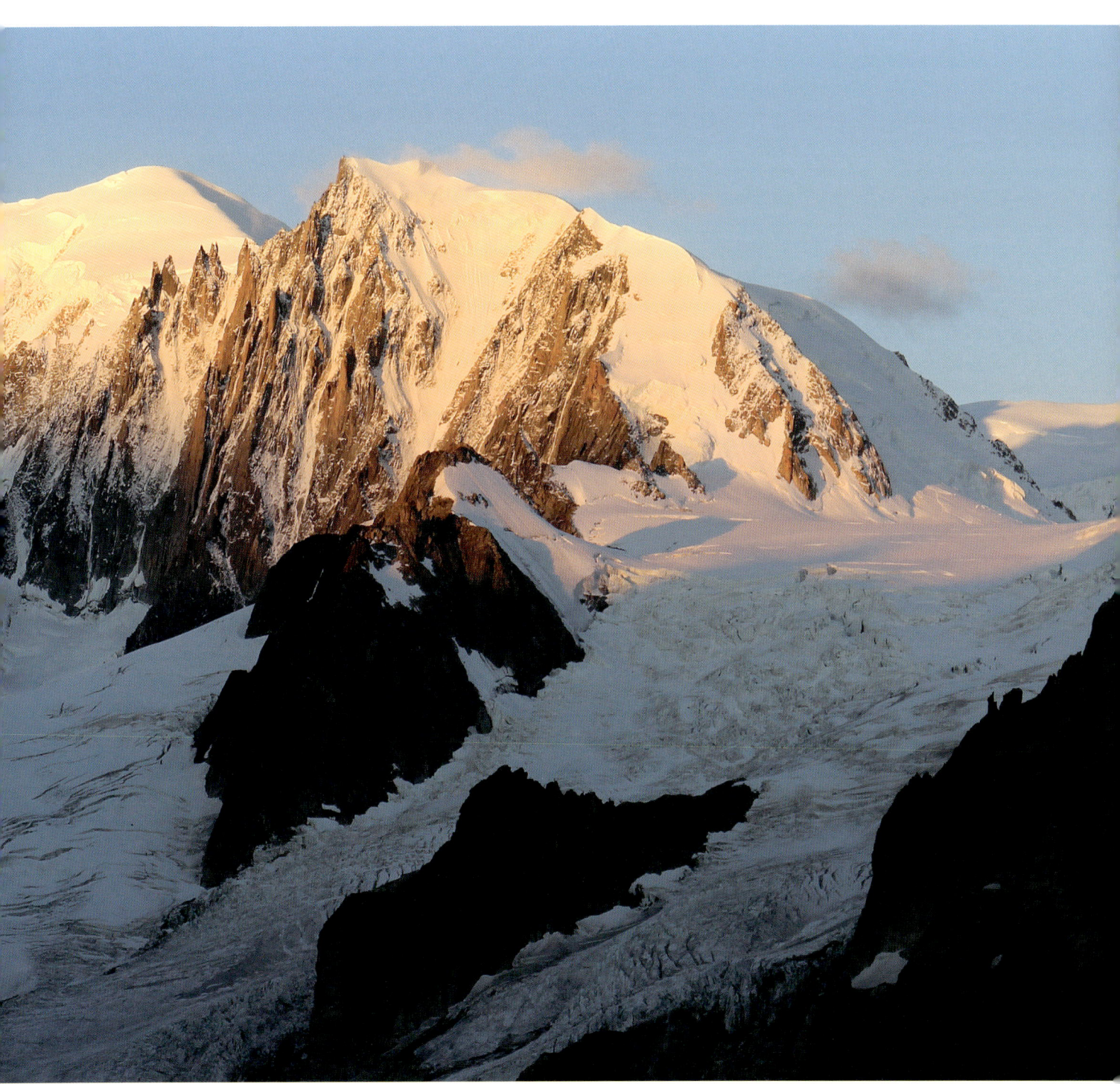

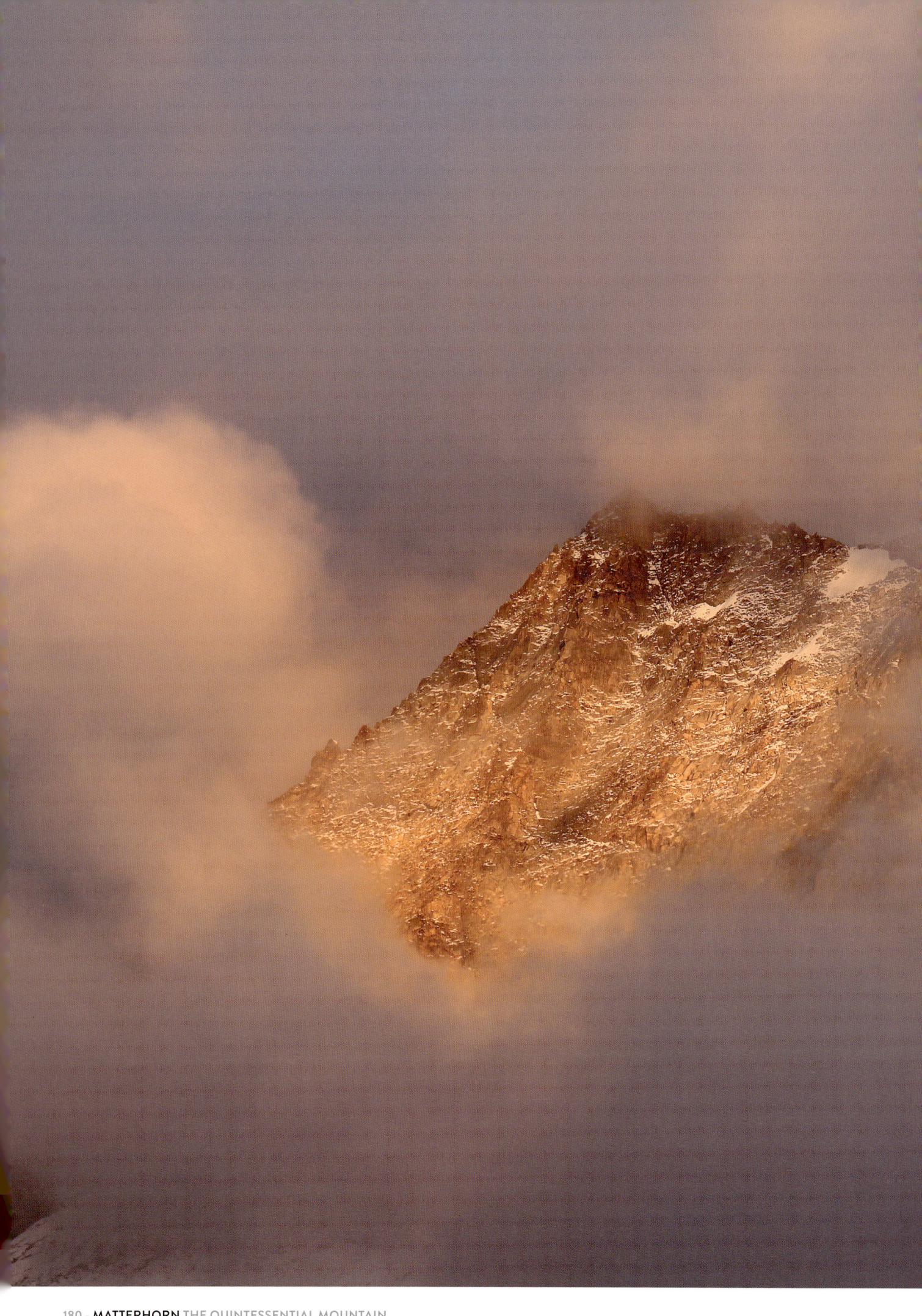

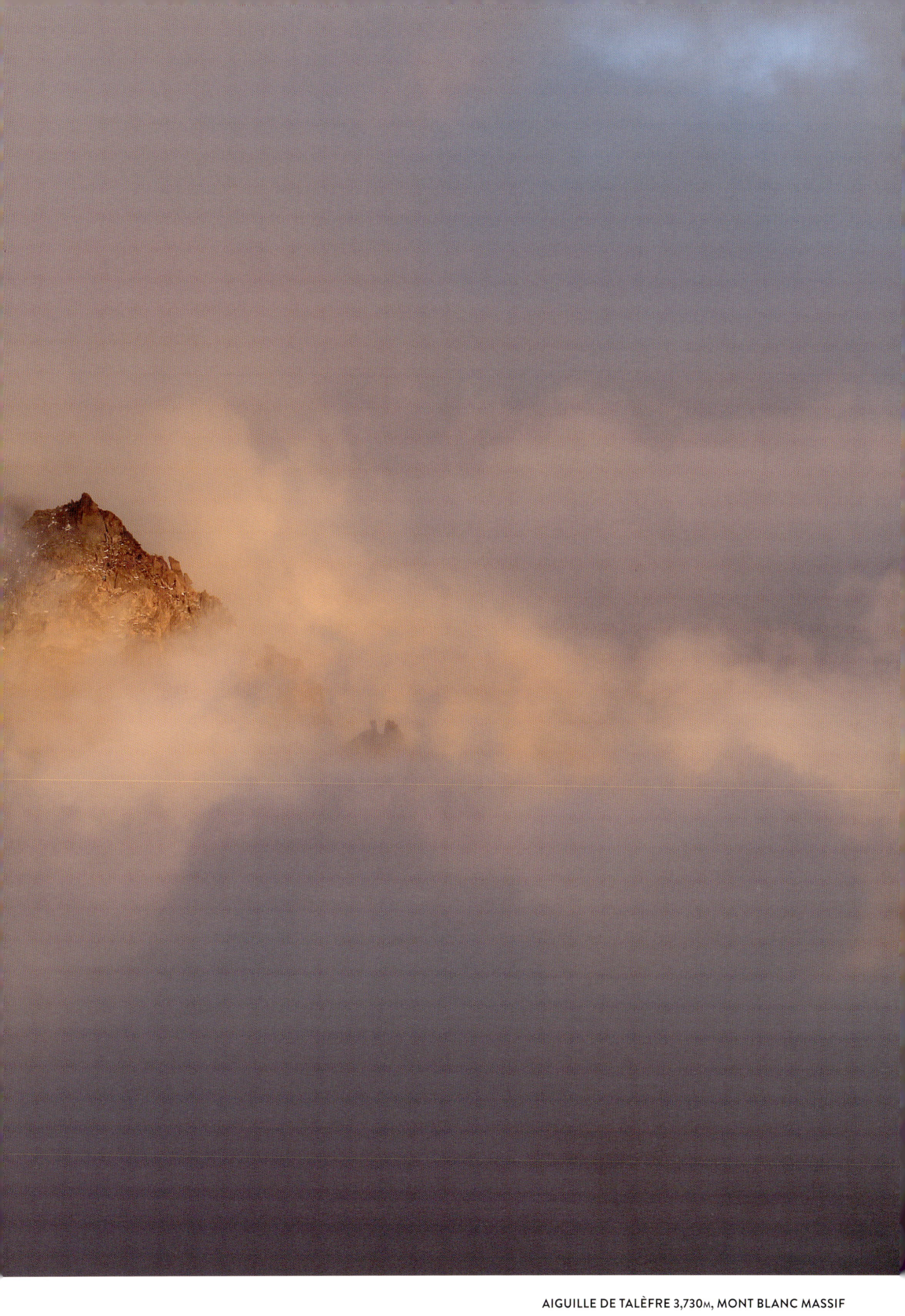

AIGUILLE DE TALÈFRE 3,730M, MONT BLANC MASSIF

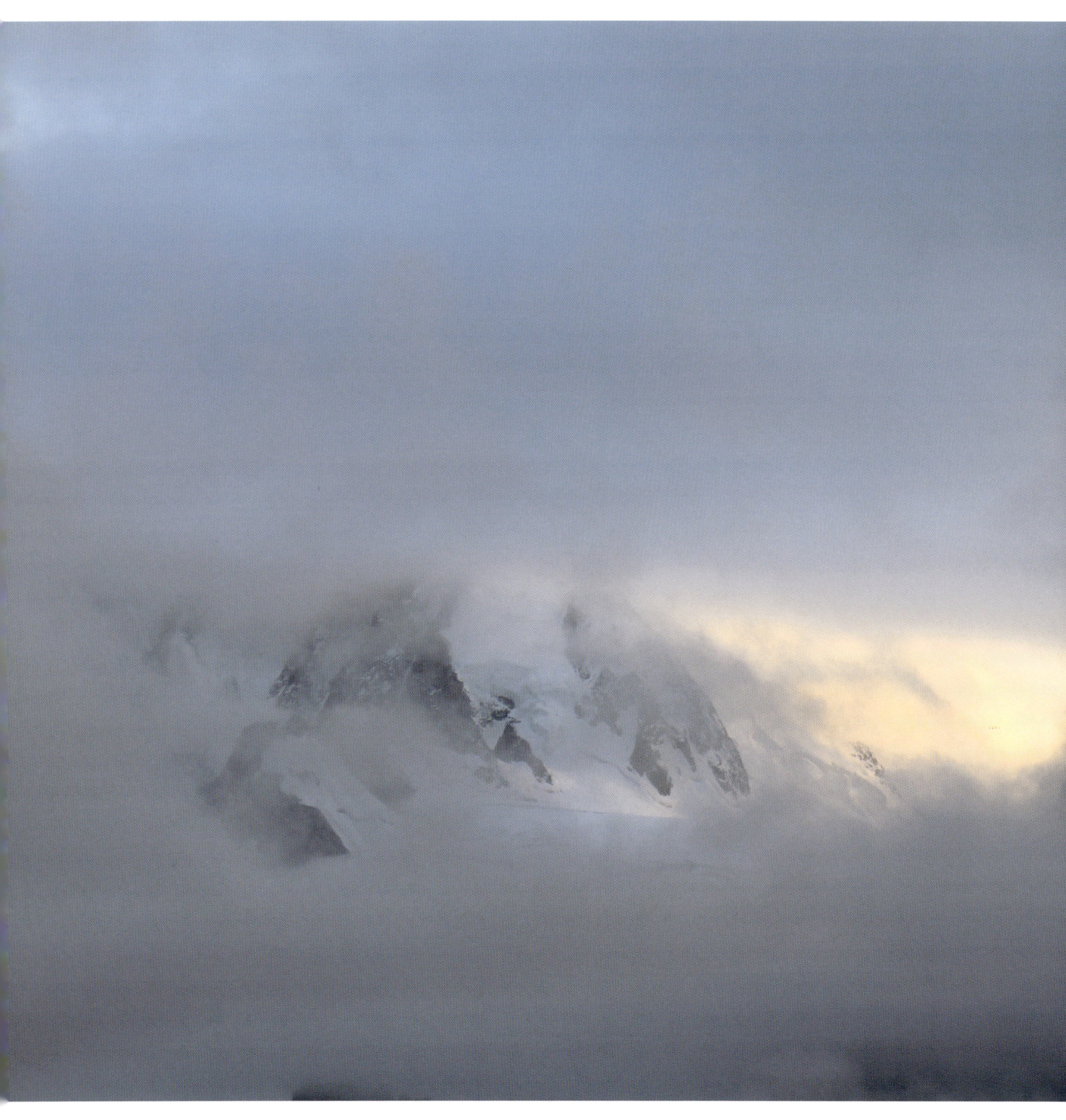

DENT DU REQUIN (SHARK TOOTH) 3,432M, MONT BLANC MASSIF

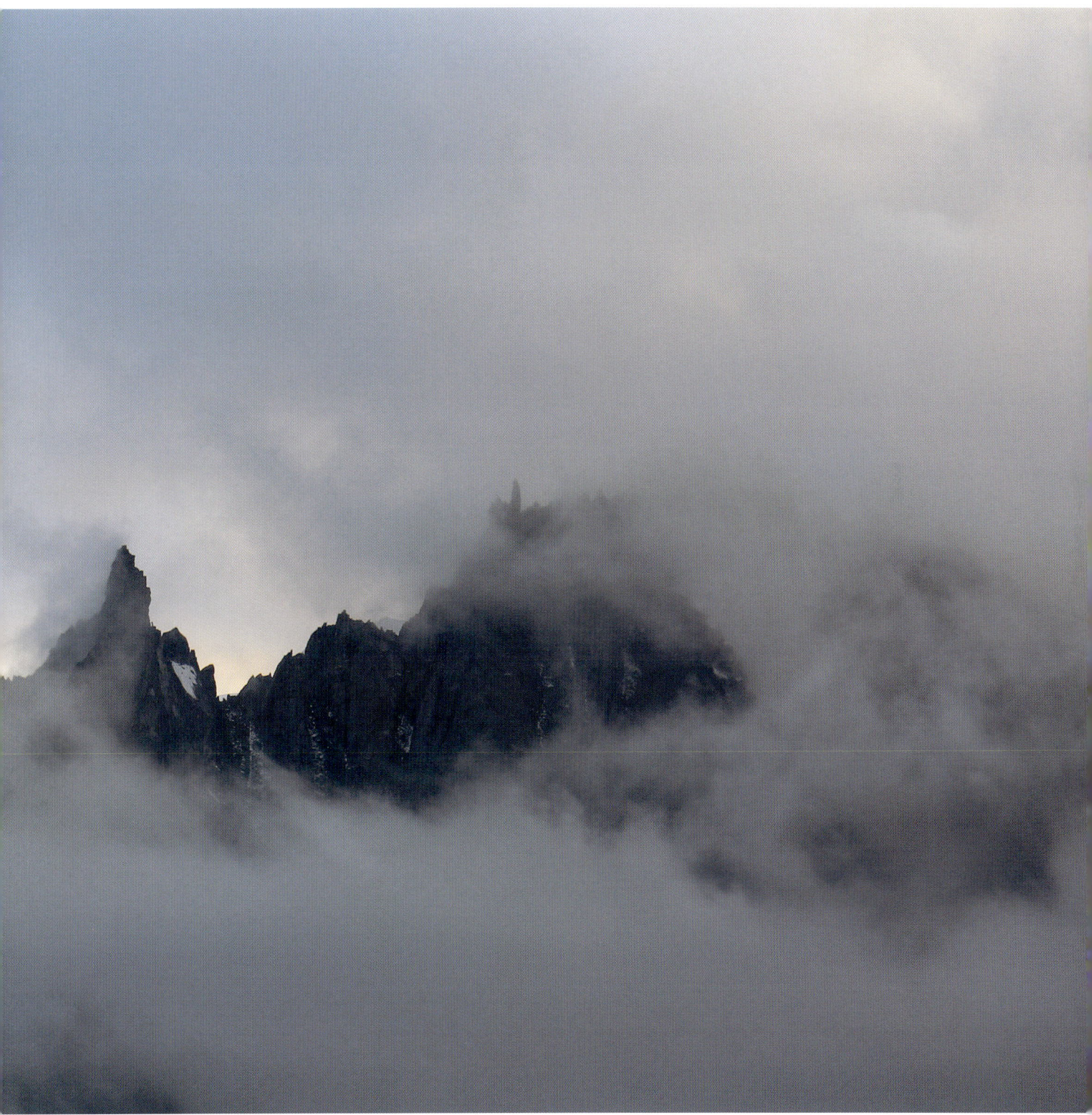

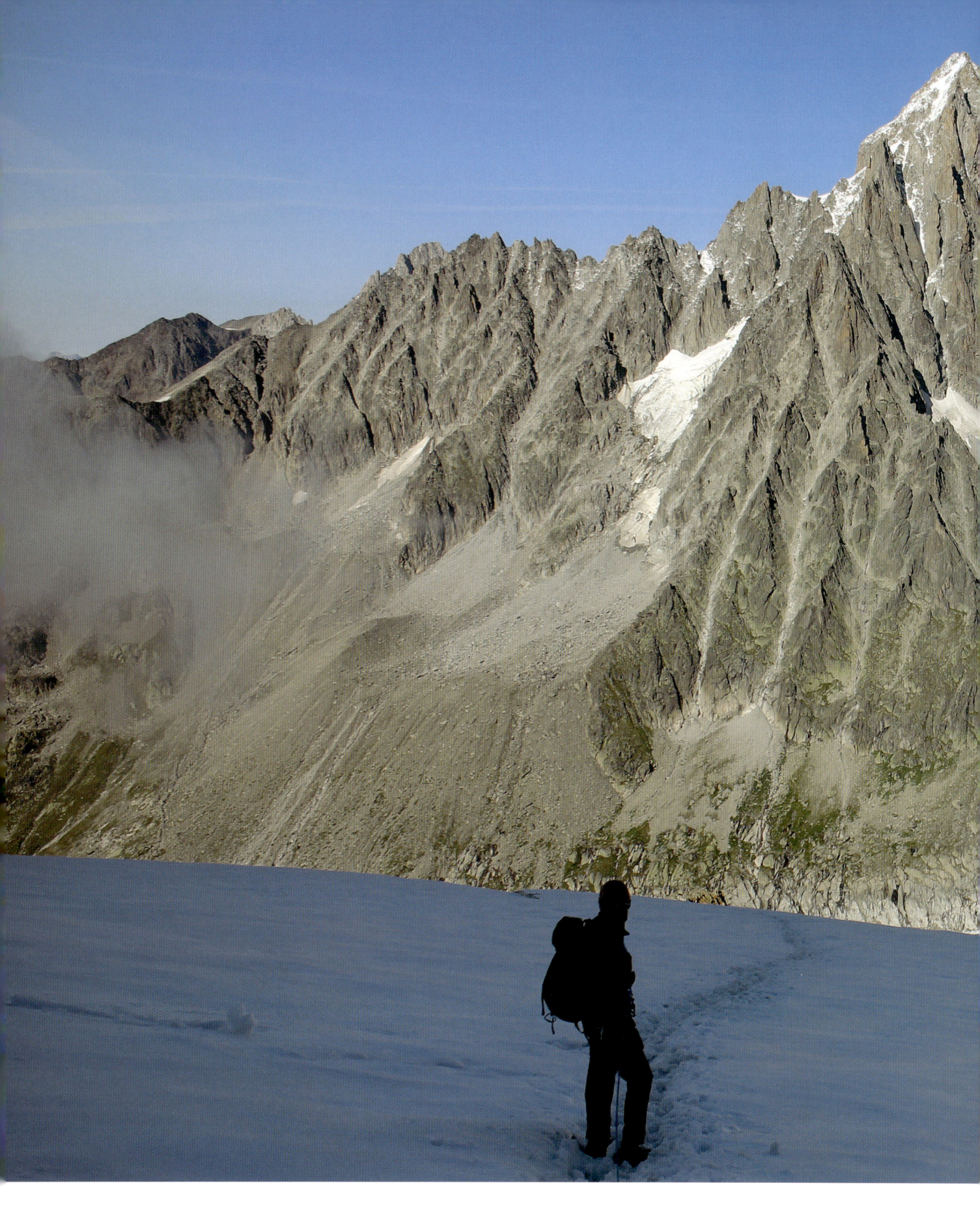

AIGUILLE D'ARGENTIÉRE 3,901M, MONT BLANC MASSIF

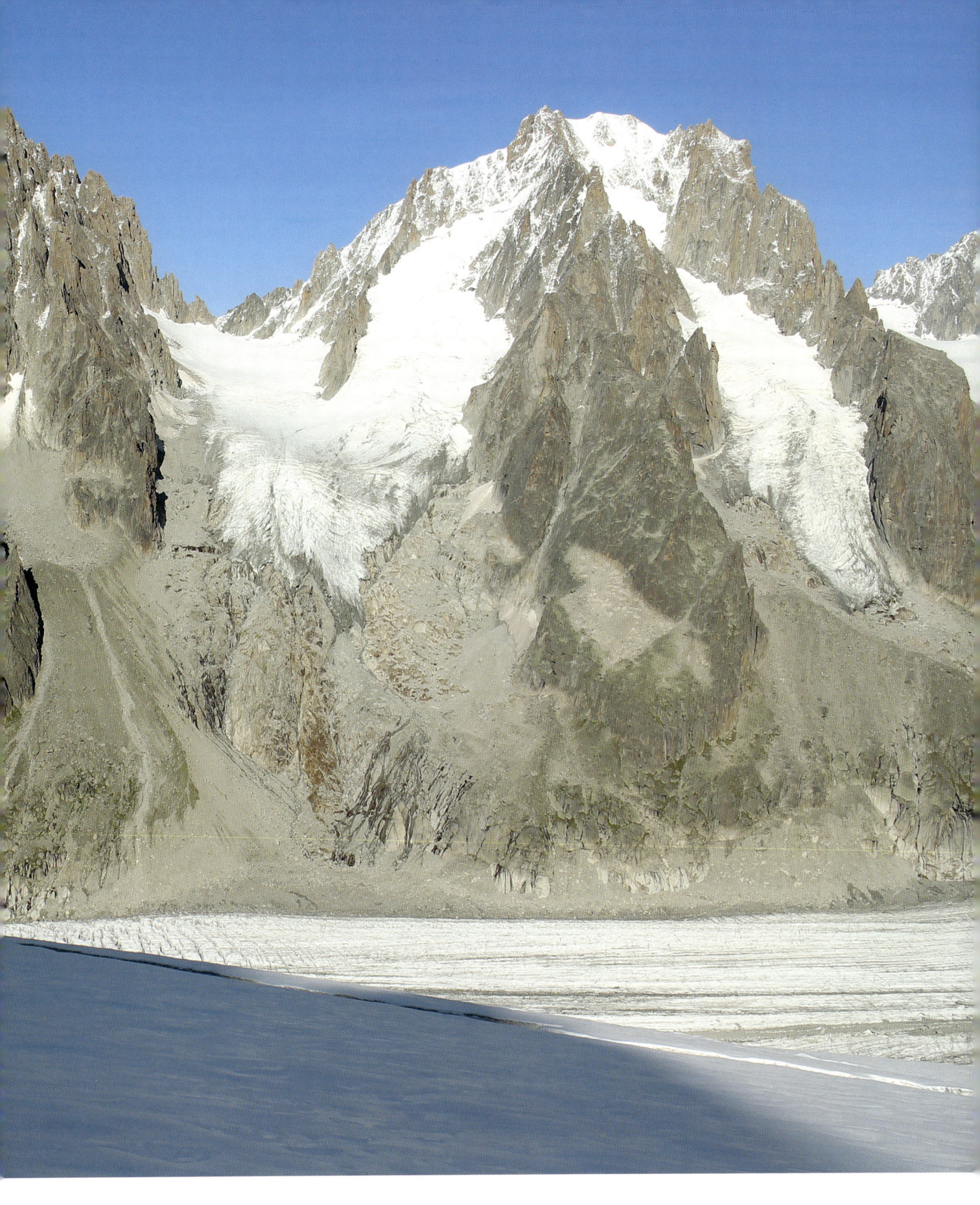

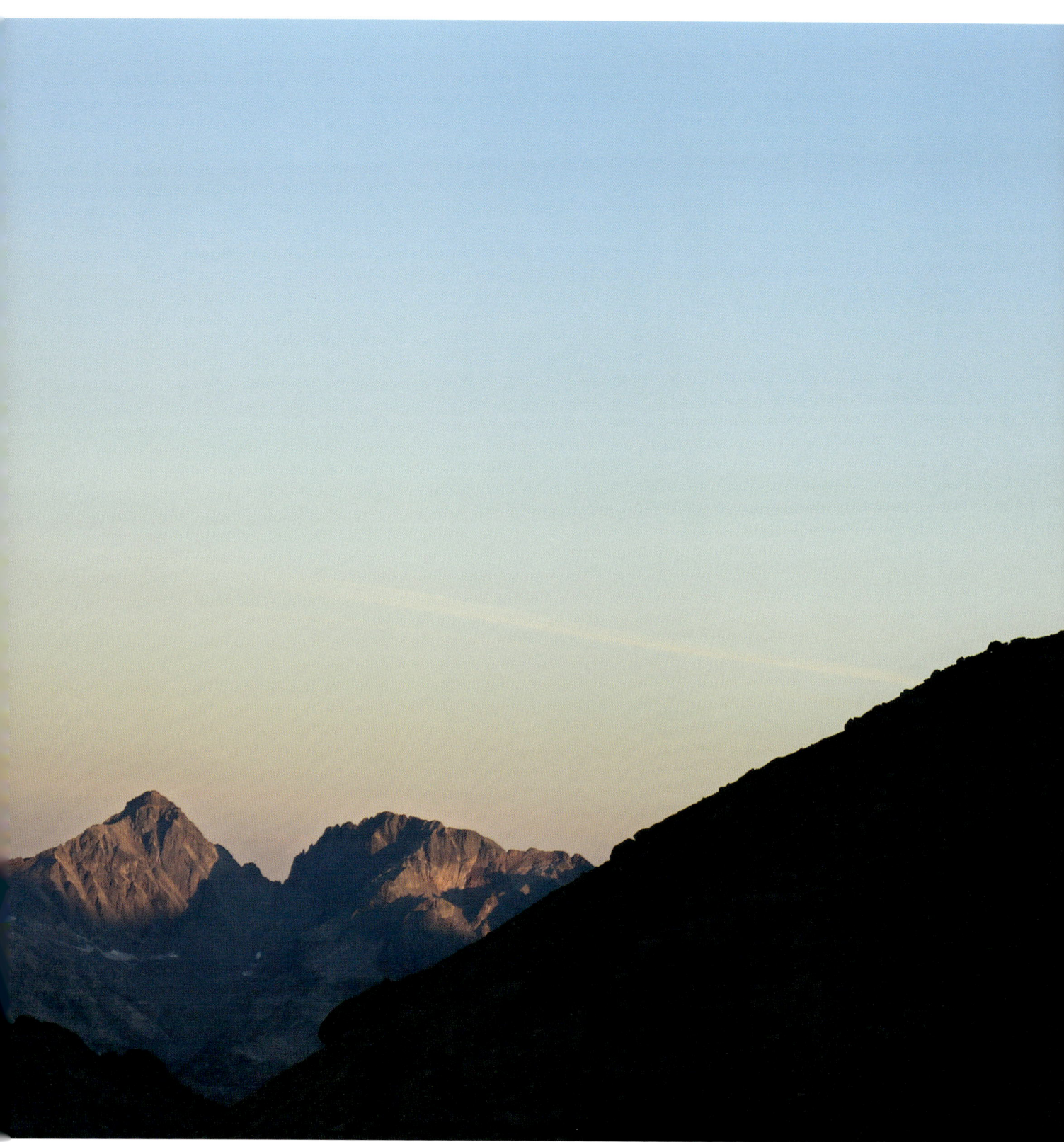

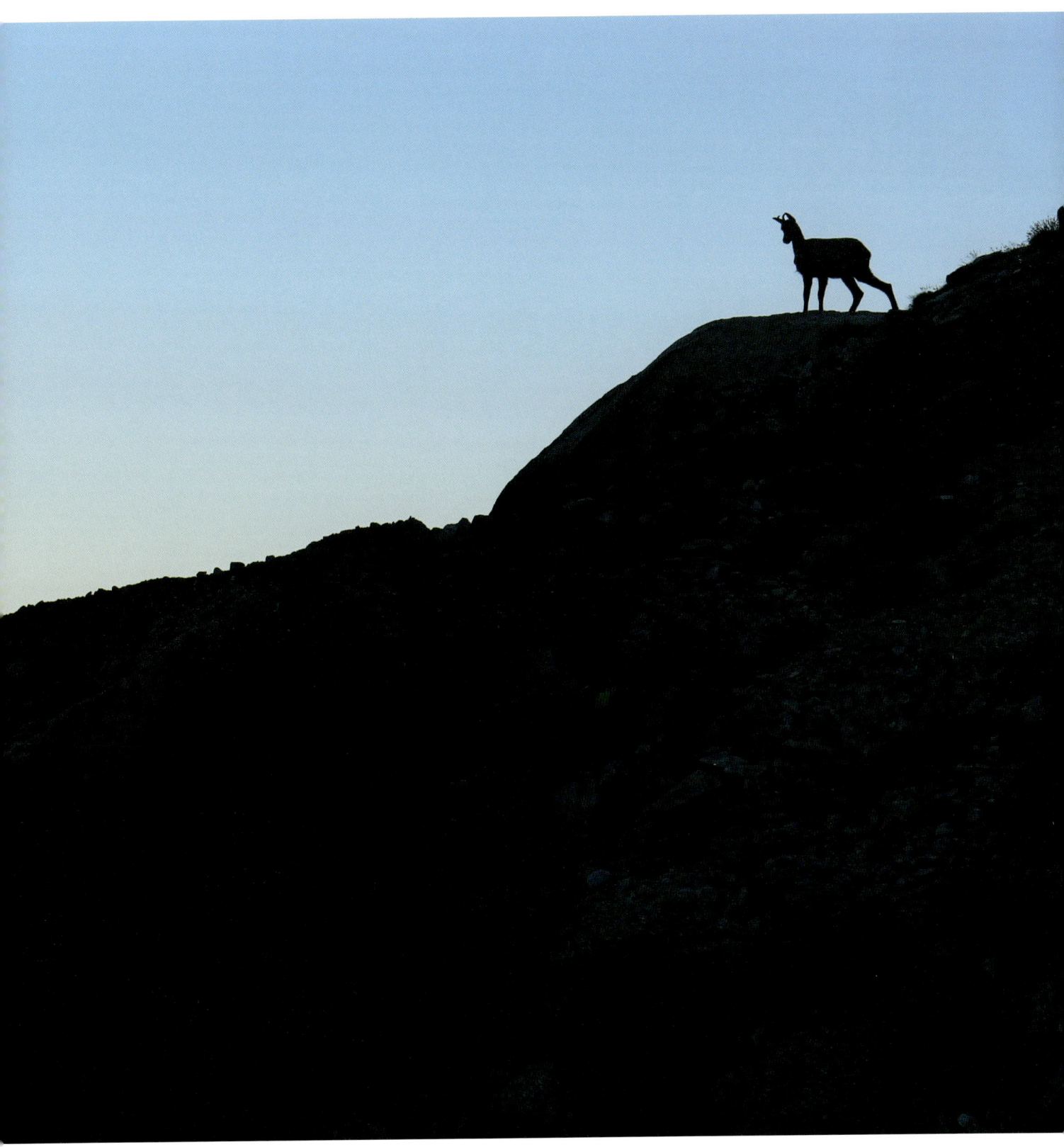

ALPINE CHAMOIS

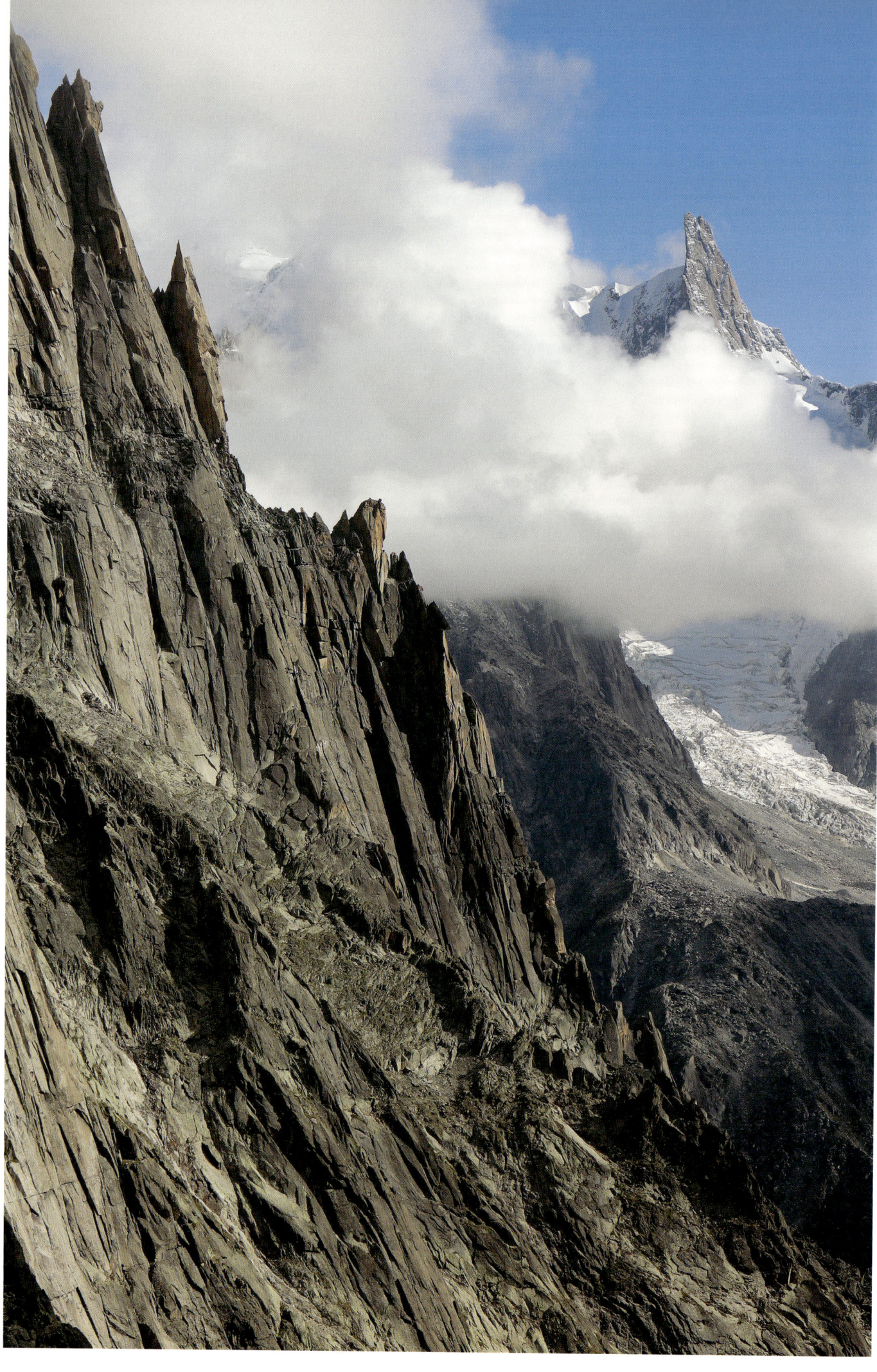

CHAPTER TEN

1865: GRAND CORNIER, DENT BLANCHE, GRANDES JORASSES, AIGUILLE VERTE, LA RUINETTE AND THE MATTERHORN

Whymper's ambition and self belief were now boundless, and he no doubt, spent every spare moment planning his 1865 assault, keen to develop his skills and most importantly to finally conquer the resilient Matterhorn. While there was no doubt about his highest objective, Whymper was still keen to attain more summits, including Dent Blanche 4,357m (14,291 ft), and to make the first successful summits of Grand Cornier 3,962m (12,999 ft), Grandes Jorasses 4,208m (13,806 ft), Aiguille Verte 4,122m (13,523 ft) and La Ruinette 3,875m (12,713 ft).

Supported with three excellent guides for much of this trip, including Michel Croz, Christian Almer and Franz Biener; anything must have appeared possible to Whymper. Conquest after conquest, he was riding high, but ironically, when the eventual opportune time came to climb the Matterhorn, Whymper found himself guideless.

Our career in 1864 had been one of unbroken success, but the great ascent upon which I had set my heart was not attempted, and, until it was accomplished, I was unsatisfied. Other things, too, influenced me to visit the Alps once more. I wished to travel elsewhere, in places where the responsibility of direction would rest with myself alone. It was well to know how far my judgment in the choice of routes could be relied upon.

The journey of 1865 was chiefly undertaken, then, to find out to what extent I was capable to select paths over mountainous country. The programme which was drawn up for this journey was rather ambitious, since it included almost all of the great peaks which had not then been ascended; but it was neither lightly undertaken nor hastily executed. All pains were taken to secure success. Information was sought from those who could give it, and the defeats of others were studied, that their errors might be avoided. The results which followed came not so much, perhaps, from luck, as from forethought and careful calculation.

For success does not, as a rule, come by chance, and when one fails there is a reason for it. But when any notable, or so-called brilliant thing is done, we are too apt to look upon the success alone, without considering how it was accomplished. Whilst, when men fail, we inquire why they have not succeeded. So failures are oftentimes more instructive than successes, and the disappointments of some become profitable to others.

In selecting the routes which were taken in 1865, I looked, first, for places where glaciers and snow extended highest up into the mountains which were to be ascended, or the ridges which were to be crossed. Next, for gullies filled with snow leading still higher; and finally, from the heads of the gullies we completed the ascents, whenever it was practicable, by faces instead of by arêtes. The ascent of the Grand Cornier (13,022), of the Dent Blanche (14,318), Grandes Jorasses (13,700), Aiguille Verte (13,540), Ruinette (12,727), and the Matterhorn (14,780), were all accomplished in this way; besides the other excursions which will be referred to by and by. The route selected, before the start was made, was in every case strictly followed out.

We inspected all of these mountains from neighbouring heights before entering upon their ascents. I explained to the guides the routes I proposed to be taken, and (when the courses were at all complicated) sketched them out on paper to prevent misunderstanding. In some few cases they suggested variations, and in every case the route was well discussed. The *execution* of the work was done by the guides, and I seldom interfered with, or attempted to assist in it.

It was not possible to find two leading guides who worked together more harmoniously than Croz and Almer. Biener's part was subordinate to theirs, and he was added as a convenience rather than as a necessity. Croz spoke French alone, Almer little else than German. Biener spoke both languages, and was useful on that account; but he seldom went to the front, excepting during the early part of the day, when the work was easy, and he acted throughout more as a porter than as a guide.

The importance of having a reserve of power on mountain expeditions cannot be too strongly insisted upon. We always had some in hand, and were never pressed, or overworked, so long as we were together. Come what might, we were ready for it. But by a series of chances, which I shall never cease to regret, I was first obliged to part with Croz, and then to dismiss the others; and so, deviating from the course that I had deliberately adopted, which was successful in practice because it was sound in principle, became fortuitously a member of an expedition that ended with the catastrophe which brings this book, and brought my scrambles amongst the Alps, to a close.

(Ibid, pp. 204–208)

ATTEMPT TO ASCEND GRAND CORNIER

On the 16th [June] we left Zinal at 2.5 A.M., having been for a moment greatly surprised by an entry in the hotel-book, and ascending by the Zinal glacier, and giving the base of our mountain a wide berth in order that it might be better examined, passed gradually right round to its south, before a way up it was seen. At 8.30 we arrived upon the plateau of the glacier that descends towards the east, between the Grand Cornier and the Dent Blanche, and from this place a route was readily traced. We steered to the north ... over the glacier, towards the ridge that descends to the east; gained it by mounting snow-slopes, and followed it to the summit, which was arrived at before half-past twelve. From first to last the route was almost entirely over snow.

The ridges leading to the north and to the south from the summit of the Grand Cornier, exhibited in a most striking manner the extraordinary effects that may be produced by violent alternations of heat and cold. The southern one was hacked and split into the wildest forms; and the northern one was not less cleft and impracticable ... Some small blocks actually tottered and fell before our eyes, and, starting others in their downward course, grew into a perfect avalanche, which descended with a solemn roar on to the glaciers beneath.

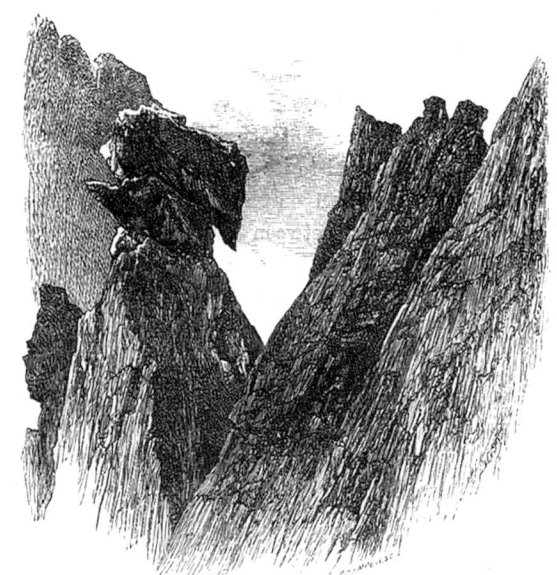

Part Of The Southern Ridge Of The Grand Cornier

It is natural that the great ridges should present the wildest forms — not on account of their dimensions, but by reason of their positions. They are exposed to the fiercest heat of the sun, and are seldom in shadow as long as it is above the horizon. They are entirely unprotected, and are attacked by the strongest blasts and by the most intense cold. The most durable rocks are not proof against such assaults. These grand, apparently solid — eternal — mountains, seeming so firm, so immutable, are yet ever changing and crumbling into dust. These shattered ridges are evidence of their sufferings. Let me repeat that every principal ridge of every great peak in the Alps amongst those I have seen has been shattered in this way; and that every summit, amongst the rock-summits upon which I have stood, has been nothing but a piled-up heap of fragments.

There are two primary causes for the disintegration of the mountains. First, from the heat of the sun detaching small stones or rocks which have been arrested on ledges or slopes and bound together by snow or ice. I have seen such released many times when the sun has risen high; fall gently at first, gather strength, grow in volume, and at last rush down with a cloud trailing behind, like the dust after an express train. Secondly, from the freezing of the water which trickles, during the day, into the clefts, fissures, and crannies.

What can one conclude, then, but that sun, frost, and water, have had infinitely more to do than glaciers with the fashioning of mountain-forms and valley-slopes?

My reverie was interrupted by Croz observing that it was time to be off. Less than two hours sufficed to take us to the glacier plateau below (where we had left our baggage); three quarters of an hour more placed us upon the depression between the Grand Cornier and the Dent Blanche (Col du Grand Cornier), and at 6 P.M. we arrived at Abricolla. Croz and Biener hankered after milk, and descended to a village lower down the valley; but Almer and I stayed where we were, and passed a chilly night on some planks in a half-burnt chalet.

(Ibid., pp. 209–214)

ATTEMPT TO ASCEND DENT BLANCHE

Croz and Biener did not return until past 5 A.M. on June 17th, and we then set out at once for Zermatt, intending to cross the Col d'Hérens. But we did not proceed far before the attractions of the Dent Blanche were felt to be irresistible, and we turned aside up the steep lateral glacier which descends along its south-western face.

The Dent Blanche is a mountain that is little known except to the climbing fraternity. It was, and is, reputed to be one of the most difficult mountains in the Alps. Many attempts were made to scale it before its ascent was accomplished. Even Leslie Stephen himself, fleetest of foot of the whole Alpine brotherhood, once upon a time returned discomfited from it.

It was not climbed until 1862; but in that year Mr. T. S. Kennedy, with Mr. Wigram, and the guides Jean B. Croz and Kronig, managed to conquer it.

Mr. Kennedy described his expedition in a very interesting paper in the *Alpine Journal*. His account bore the impress of truth; yet unbelievers said that it was impossible to have told (in weather such as was experienced) whether the summit had actually been attained, and sometimes roundly asserted that the mountain, as the saying is, still remained virgin.

I did not share these doubts, although they influenced me to make the ascent. I thought it might be possible to find an easier route than that taken by Mr. Kennedy … I halted my little army at the foot of the glacier, and inquired, 'Which is best for us to do? — to ascend the Dent Blanche, or to cross to Zermatt?' They answered, with befitting solemnity, 'We think Dent Blanche is best.'

From the chalets of Abricolla the south-west face of the Dent Blanche is regarded almost exactly in profile. From thence it is seen that the angle of the face scarcely exceeds thirty degrees, and after observing this I concluded that the face would, in all probability, give an easier path to the summit than the crest of the very jagged ridge which was followed by Mr. Kennedy.

We zigzagged up the glacier along the foot of the face, and looked for a way on to it. We looked for some time in vain, for a mighty *bergschrund* effectually prevented approach, and, like a fortress' moat, protected the wall from assault. We went up and up, until, I suppose, we were not more than a thousand feet below the point marked 3912 metres; then a bridge was discovered, and we dropped down on hands and knees to cross it.

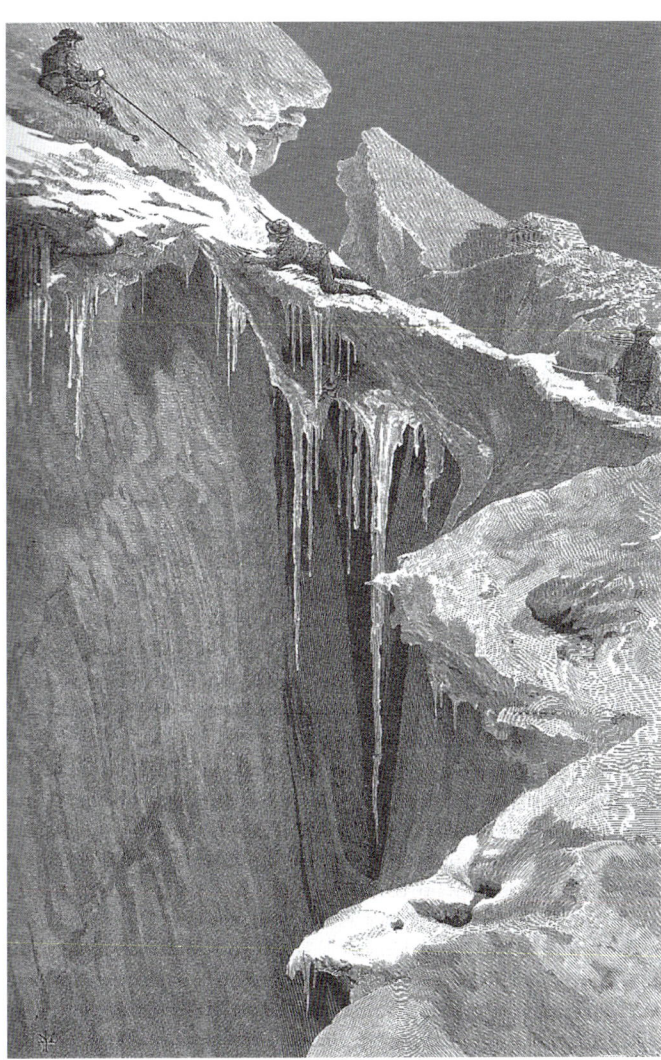

The Bergschrund On The Dent Blanche In 1865

A bergschrund is frequently, although not always, a big crevasse ... Sometimes it is *very* large, but early in the season (that is to say in the month of June or before) bergschrunds are usually snowed up, or well bridged over, and do not give much trouble. Later in the year, say in August, they are frequently very great hindrances, and occasionally are completely impassable.

We crossed the bergschrund of the Dent Blanche, I suppose, at a height of about 12,000 feet above the level of the sea. Our work may be said to have commenced at that point. The face, although not steep in its general inclination, was so cut up by little ridges and cliffs, and so seamed with incipient couloirs, that it had all the difficulty of a much more precipitous slope. The difficulties were never great, but they were numerous, and made a very respectable total when put together. We passed the bergschrund soon after nine in the morning, and during the next eleven hours halted only five-and-forty minutes. The whole of the remainder of the time was occupied in ascending and descending the 2400 feet which compose this south-western face; and inasmuch as 1000 feet per hour (taking the mean of ascent and descent) is an ordinary rate of progression, it is tolerably certain that the Dent Blanche is a mountain of exceptional difficulty.

The hindrances opposed to us by the mountain itself were, however, as nothing compared with the atmospheric obstructions. It is true there was plenty of, 'Are you fast, Almer?' 'Yes.' 'Go ahead, Biener.' Biener, made secure, cried, 'Come on, sir,' and *Monsieur* endeavoured. 'No, no,' said Almer, 'not there, — *here*,' — pointing with his bâton to the right place to clutch. Then 'twas Croz's turn, and we all drew in the rope as the great man followed. 'Forwards' once more — and so on.

Five hundred feet of this kind of work had been accomplished when we were saluted (not entirely unexpectedly) by the first gust of a hurricane which was raging above. The day was a lovely one for dwellers in the valleys, but we had, long ago, noted some light, gossamer clouds, that were hovering round our summit, being drawn out in a suspicious manner into long, silky threads. Croz, indeed, prophesied before we had crossed the schrund, that we should be beaten by the wind, and had advised that we should return. But I had retorted, 'No, my good Croz, you said just now 'Dent Blanche is best'; we must go up the Dent Blanche.'

I have a very lively and disagreeable recollection of this wind. Upon the outskirts of the disturbed region it was only felt occasionally. It then seemed to make rushes at one particular man, and when it had discomfited him, it whisked itself away to some far-off spot, only to return, presently, in greater force than before.

My old enemy — the Matterhorn — seen across the basin of the Z'Muttgletscher, looked totally unassailable. 'Do you think,' the men asked, 'that you, or any one else, will ever get up *that* mountain?' And when, undismayed by their ridicule, I stoutly answered, 'Yes, but not upon that side,' they burst into derisive chuckles. I must confess that my hopes sank; for nothing can look more completely inaccessible than the Matterhorn on its northern and north-west sides.

'Forwards' once again ... 'Not a thousand feet more; in three hours we shall be on the summit.' 'You mean *ten*,' echoed Croz, so slow had been the progress. But I was not far wrong in the estimate. At 3.15 we struck the great ridge followed by Mr. Kennedy, close to the top of the mountain. The wind and cold were terrible there. Progress was oftentimes impossible, and we waited, crouching under the lee of rocks, listening to 'the shrieking of the mindless wind,' while the blasts swept across, tearing off the upper snow and blowing it away in streamers over the Schönbühl glacier — 'nothing seen except an indescribable writhing in the air, like the wind made visible.'

Our goal was concealed by mist, although it was only a few yards away, and Croz's prophecy, that we should stay all night upon the summit, seemed likely to come true. The men rose with the occasion, although even *their* fingers had nearly lost sensation. There were no murmurings, nor suggestions of return, and they pressed on for the little white cone which they knew must be near at hand. Stopped again; a big mass perched loosely on the ridge barred the way; we could not crawl over, and scarcely dared creep round it. The wine went round for the last time. The liquor was half-frozen, — still we would more of it. It was all gone; the bottle was left behind, and we pushed on, for there was a lull.

The end came almost before it was expected. The clouds opened, and I saw that we were all but upon the highest point, and that, between us and it, about twenty yards off, there was a little artificial pile of stones. Kennedy was a true man, — it was a cairn which he had erected. 'What is that, Croz?' '*Homme des pierres*,' he bawled. It was needless to proceed farther; I jerked the rope from Biener, and motioned that we should go back. He did the same to Almer, and we turned immediately. *They* did not see the stones (they were cutting footsteps), and misinterpreted the reason of the retreat. Voices were inaudible, and explanations impossible.

We commenced the descent of the face. It was hideous work. The men looked like impersonations of Winter, with their hair all frosted, and their beards matted with ice. My hands were numbed — dead. I begged the others to stop. '*We cannot afford to stop; we must continue to move*,' was their reply. They were right; to stop was to be entirely frozen. So we went down; gripping rocks varnished with ice, which pulled the skin from the fingers. Gloves were useless; they became iced too, and the bâtons slid through them as slippery as eels. The iron of the axes stuck to the fingers — it felt red-hot; but it was useless to shrink, the rocks and the axes had to be firmly grasped — no faltering would do here.

We turned back at 4.12 P.M., and at 8.15 crossed the bergschrund again, not having halted for a minute upon the entire descent. During the last two hours it was windless, but time was of such vital importance that we pressed on incessantly, and did not stop until we were fairly upon the glacier. Then we took stock of what remained of the tips of our fingers. There was not much skin left; they were perfectly raw, and for weeks afterwards I was reminded of the ascent of the Dent Blanche by the twinges which I felt when I pulled on my boots. The others escaped with some slight frost-bites; and, altogether, we had reason to congratulate ourselves that we got off so lightly. The men complimented me upon the descent, and I could do the same honestly to them. If they had worked less vigorously, or harmoniously, we should have been benighted upon the face, where there was not a single spot upon which it was possible to sit; and if that had happened, I do not think that one would have survived to tell the tale.

We made the descent of the glacier in a mist, and of the moraine at its base, and of the slopes below, in total darkness, and regained the chalets of Abricolla at 11.45 P.M. We had been absent eighteen and a half hours, and out of that time had been going not less than seventeen. That night we slept the sleep of those who are thoroughly tired.

(Ibid., pp. 215–222)

SEVENTH ATTEMPT TO ASCEND THE MATTERHORN

We should have started for Zermatt about 7 A.M. on the 18th, had not Biener asked to be allowed to go to mass at Evolène, a village about two and a half hours from Abricolla. He received permission, on the condition that he returned not later than mid-day, but he did not come back until 2.30 P.M., and we thereby got into a pretty little mess.

The pass which we were about to traverse to Zermatt — the Col d'Hérens — is one of the few glacier-passes in this district which have been known almost from time immemorial. It is frequently crossed in the summer season, and is a very easy route, notwithstanding that the summit of the pass is 11,417 feet above the level of the sea.

We tied ourselves in line, of course, when we entered upon the glacier, and placed Biener to lead, as he had frequently crossed the pass; supposing that his local knowledge might save us some time upon the other side. We had proceeded, I believe, about half-way up, when a little, thin cloud dropped down upon us from above. It was so light and gauzy, that we did not for a moment suppose it would become embarrassing, and hence I neglected to note at the proper moment the course which we should steer, — that is to say, to observe our precise situation, in regard to the summit of the pass.

For some little time Biener progressed steadily, making a tolerably straight track; but at length he wavered, and deviated sometimes to the right, and sometimes to the left. Croz rushed forward directly he saw this, and taking the poor young man by his shoulders gave him a good shaking, told him that he was an imbecile, to untie himself at once, and to go to the rear. Biener looked half-frightened, and obeyed without a murmur. Croz led off briskly, and made a good straight track for a few minutes. Then, it seemed to me, he began to move steadily round to the left. I looked back, but the mist was now too thick to see our traces, and so we continued to follow our leader. At last the others … thought the same as I did, and we pulled up Croz to deliver our opinion. He took our criticism in good part, but when Biener opened his mouth that was too much for him to stand, and he told the young man again, '*You* are imbecile; I bet you twenty francs to one that *my* track is better than *yours*; twenty francs, now then, imbecile!'

Almer went to the front. He commenced by returning in the track for a hundred yards or so, and then started off at a tangent from Croz's curve. We kept this course for half-an-hour, and then were certain that we were not on the right route, because the snow became decidedly steep. We bore away more and more to the right, to avoid this steep bank, but at last I rebelled, as we had for some time been going almost south-west, which was altogether the wrong direction. After a long discussion we returned some distance in our track, and then steered a little east of south, but we continually met steep snow-slopes, and to avoid them went right or left as the case might require.

We were greatly puzzled, and could not in the least tell whether we were too near the Dent Blanche or too close to the Tête Blanche. The mists had thickened, and were now as dense as a moderate London fog. There were no rocks or echoes to direct us, and the guidance of the compass brought us invariably against these steep snow-banks. The men were fairly beaten; they had all had a try, or more than one, and at last gave it up as a bad job, and asked what was to be done. It was 7.30 P.M. and only an hour of daylight was left. We were beginning to feel used up, for we had wandered about at tip-top speed for the last three hours and a half, so I said, 'This is my advice; let us turn in our track, and go back as hard as ever we can, not quitting the track for an instant.' They were well content, but just as we were starting off, the clouds lifted a little, and we thought we saw the Col. It was then to our right, and we went at it with a dash. Before we had gone a hundred paces down came the mist again. We kept on nevertheless for twenty minutes, and then, as darkness was perceptibly coming on, and the snow was yet rising in front, we turned back, and by running down the entire distance managed to get clear of the Ferpècle glacier just as it became pitch dark. We arrived at our cheerless chalet in due course, and went to bed supperless, for our food was gone; all very sulky — not to say savage — agreeing in nothing except in bullying Biener.

The following day, they set off again with an earlier start and better visibility. In the clear conditions they could see their earlier tracks and discovered that Biener had not done as badly as they had thought. Croz on the other hand, had gone completely off-course and in a semi-circular direction, leading them in the opposite direction, while Almer had corrected the error. They had, in fact, been on the summit of the pass at the time they decided to retreat.

On the 20th we crossed the Théodule pass, and diverged from its summit up the Théodulhorn (11,391) to examine a route which I suggested for the ascent of the Matterhorn. Before continuing an account of our proceedings, I must stop for a minute to explain why this new route was proposed, in place of that up the south-western ridge.

The main peak of the Matterhorn may be divided into three sections. The first, facing the Z'Muttgletscher, looks completely unassailable; the second, facing the east, seems inaccessibility itself; whilst the third, facing Breil, does not look entirely hopeless. It was from this last direction that all my previous attempts were made. It was by the south-western ridge, it will be remembered, that not only I, but Mr. Hawkins, Professor Tyndall, and the chasseurs of Val Tournanche, essayed to climb the mountain. Why then abandon a route which had been shown to be feasible up to a certain point?

I gave it up for four reasons. 1. On account of my growing disinclination for arêtes, and preference for snow and rock-faces. 2. Because I was persuaded that meteorological disturbances (by which we had been baffled several times) might be expected to occur again and again. 3. Because I found that the east face was a gross imposition — it looked not far from perpendicular; while its angle was, in fact, scarcely more than 40°. 4. Because I observed for myself that the strata of the mountain dipped to the west-south-west.

When one looks at the Matterhorn from Zermatt, the mountain is regarded (nearly) from the north-east. The face that fronts the east is consequently neither seen in profile nor in full front, but almost half-way between the two; it looks, therefore, more steep than it really is. The majority of those who visit Zermatt go up to the Riffelberg, or to the Gornergrat, and from these places, the mountain naturally looks still more precipitous, because its eastern face (which is almost all that is seen of it) is viewed more directly in front. From the Riffel hotel the slope seems to be set at an angle of 70°. If the tourist continues to go southwards, and crosses the Théodule pass, he gets, at one point, immediately in front of the eastern face, which then seems to be absolutely perpendicular. Comparatively few persons correct the erroneous impressions they receive in these quarters by studying the face in profile, and most go away with a very incorrect and exaggerated idea of the precipitousness of this side of the mountain, because they have considered the question from one point of view alone.

Several years passed away before I shook myself clear of my early and false impressions regarding the steepness of this side of the Matterhorn. First of all, I noticed that there were places on this eastern face where snow remained permanently all the year round ... Such beds as these could not continue to remain throughout the summer, unless the snow had been able to accumulate in the winter in large masses; and snow cannot accumulate and remain in large masses, in a situation such as this, at angles much exceeding 45°. Hence I was bound to conclude that the eastern face was many degrees removed from perpendicularity; and, to be sure on this point, I went to the slopes between the Z'Muttgletscher and the Matterhorngletscher ... whence the face could be seen in profile. Its appearance from this direction would be amazing to one who had seen it only from the east.

A great step was made when this was learnt. This knowledge alone would not, however, have caused me to try an ascent by the eastern face instead of by the south-west ridge. Forty degrees may not seem a formidable inclination to the reader, nor is it for only a small cliff. But it is very unusual to find so steep a gradient maintained continuously as the general angle of a great mountain-slope, and very few instances can be quoted from the High Alps of such an angle being preserved over a rise of 3000 feet.

I do not think that the steepness or the height of this cliff would have deterred climbers from attempting to ascend it, if it had not, in addition, looked so repulsively smooth. Men despaired of finding anything to grasp. Now, some of the difficulties of the south-west ridge came from the smoothness of the rocks, although that ridge, even from a distance, seemed to be well broken up. How much greater, then, might not have been the difficulty of climbing a face which looked smooth and unbroken close at hand?

A more serious hindrance to mounting the south-west ridge is found in the dip of its rocks to the west-south-west. The great mass of the Matterhorn, it is now well ascertained, is composed of regularly stratified rocks, which rise towards the east. It has been mentioned in the text, more than once, that the rocks on some portions of the ridge leading from the Col du Lion to the summit dip outwards, and that fractured edges overhang ... Fig. 1 ... It will be readily understood that such an arrangement is not favourable for climbers, and that the degree of facility with which rocks can be ascended that are so disposed, must depend very much upon the frequency or paucity of fissures and joints. The rocks of the south-west ridge are sufficiently provided with cracks, but if it were otherwise, their texture and arrangement would render them unassailable.

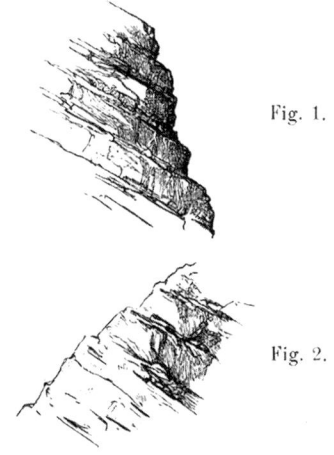

Fig. 1.

Fig. 2.

It was not until after my repulse in 1863, that I referred the peculiar difficulties of the south-west ridge to the dip of the strata; but when once persuaded that structure and not texture was the real impediment, it was reasonable to infer that the opposite side, that is to say the eastern face, might be comparatively easy. In brief, that an arrangement should be found like Fig. 2, instead of like Fig. 1. This trivial deduction was the key to the ascent of the Matterhorn.

The point was, did the strata continue with a similar dip throughout the mountain? If they did, then this great eastern face, instead of being hopelessly impracticable, should be quite the reverse. — In fact, it should be a great natural staircase, with steps inclining inwards; and, if it were so, its smooth aspect might be of no account, for the smallest steps, inclined in this fashion, would afford good footing.

It was not, therefore, from a freak, that I invited Mr. Reilly to join in an attack upon the eastern face, but from a gradually-acquired conviction that it would prove to give the easiest path to the summit; and, if we had not been obliged to part, the mountain would, doubtless, have been ascended in 1864.

My guides readily admitted that they had been greatly deceived as to the steepness of the eastern face, when they were halted to look at it in profile, as we came down the Z'Muttgletscher, on our way to Zermatt; but they were far from being satisfied that it would turn out to be easy to climb, and Almer and Biener expressed themselves decidedly averse to making an attempt upon it. I gave way temporarily before their evident reluctance, and we made the ascent of the Théodulhorn to examine an alternative route, which I expected would commend itself to them in preference to the other, as a great part of it led over snow.

There is an immense gully in the Matterhorn, which leads up from the Glacier du Mont Cervin to a point high up on the south-eastern ridge. I proposed to ascend this to its head, and to cross over the south-east ridge on to the eastern face. This would have brought us on a level with the bottom of the great snow-slope shown upon the centre of the eastern face ... This snow-slope was to be crossed diagonally, with the view of arriving at the snow upon the north-east ridge ... The remainder of the ascent was to be made by the broken rocks, mixed with snow, upon the north side of the mountain. Croz caught the idea immediately, and thought the plan feasible; details were settled, and we descended to Breil. Luc Meynet, the hunchback, was summoned, and expressed himself delighted to resume his old vocation of tent-bearer; and Favre's kitchen was soon in commotion preparing three days' rations, for I intended to take that amount of time over the affair — to sleep on the first night upon the rocks at the top of the gully; to make a push for the summit, and to return to the tent on the second day; and upon the third to come back to Breil.

We started at 5.45 A.M. on June 21st, and followed the route of the Breuiljoch for three hours. We were then in full view of our gully, and turned off at right angles for it. The closer we approached, the more favourable did it look. There was a good deal of snow in it, which was evidently at a small angle, and it seemed as if one-third of the ascent, at least, would be a very simple matter. Some suspicious marks in the snow at its base suggested that it was not free from falling stones, and, as a measure of precaution, we turned off on one side, worked up under cover of the cliffs, and waited to see if anything should descend. Nothing fell, so we proceeded up its right or northern side, sometimes cutting steps up the snow and sometimes mounting by the rocks. Shortly before 10 A.M. we arrived at a convenient place for a halt, and stopped to rest upon some rocks, immediately close to the snow, which commanded an excellent view of the gully.

While the men were unpacking the food I went to a little promontory to examine our proposed route more narrowly, and to admire our noble couloir, which led straight up into the heart of the mountain for fully one thousand feet. It then bent towards the north, and ran up to the crest of the south-eastern ridge. My curiosity was piqued to know what was round this corner, and whilst I was gazing up at it, and following with the eye the exquisitely drawn curves which wandered down the snow in the gully, all converging to a large rut in its centre, I saw a few little stones skidding down. I consoled myself with thinking that they would not interfere with us if we adhered to the side. But then a larger one came down, a solitary fellow, rushing at the rate of sixty miles an hour — and another — and another. I was unwilling to raise the fears of the men unnecessarily, and said nothing to them. They did not hear the stones. Almer was seated on a rock, carving large slices from a leg of mutton, the others were chatting, and the first intimation they had of danger was from a crash — a sudden roar — which reverberated awfully amongst the cliffs, and, looking up, they saw masses of rocks, boulders and stones, big and little, dart round the corner eight hundred feet or so above us, fly with fearful fury against the opposite cliffs, rebound from them against the walls on our side, and descend; some ricochetting from side to side in a frantic manner; some bounding down in leaps of a hundred feet or more over the snow; and others trailing down in a jumbled, confused mass, mixed with snow and ice, deepening the grooves which, a moment before, had excited my admiration.

The men looked wildly around for protection, and, dropping the food, dashed under cover in all directions. The precious mutton was pitched on one side, the wine-bag was let fall, and its contents gushed out from the unclosed neck, whilst all four cowered under defending rocks, endeavouring to make themselves as small as possible. Let it not be supposed that their fright was unreasonable, or that I was free from it. I took good care to make myself safe, and went and cringed in a cleft until the storm had passed. But their scramble to get under shelter was indescribably ludicrous. Such a panic I have never witnessed, before or since, upon a mountain-side.

There would have been singularly little amusement, and very great risk, in mounting this gully, and we turned our backs upon it with perfect unanimity. The question then arose, 'What is to be done?' I suggested climbing the rocks above us, but this was voted impossible. I thought the men were right, yet would not give in without being assured of the fact, and clambered up to settle the question. In a few minutes I was brought to a halt. My forces were scattered; the little hunchback alone was closely following me — with a broad grin upon his face, and the tent upon his shoulder; Croz, more behind, was still keeping an eye upon his *Monsieur*; Almer, a hundred feet below, sat on a rock with his face buried in his hands; Biener was nowhere, out of sight. 'Come down, come down,' shouted Croz; 'it is useless,' and I turned at length, convinced that it was even as he said. Thus my little plan was knocked on the head, and we were thrown back upon the original scheme.

We at once made a straight track for Mr. Morshead's Breuiljoch (which was the most direct route to take in order to get to the Hörnli, where we intended to sleep, preparatory to attacking the eastern face), and arrived upon its summit at 12.30 P.M. We were then unexpectedly checked. The pass, as one, had vanished! and we found ourselves cut off from the Furggengletscher by a small but precipitous wall of rock; — the glacier had shrunk so much that descent was impracticable. During the last hour clouds had been coming up from the south; they now surrounded us, and it began to blow hard. The men clustered together, and advocated leaving the mountain alone. Almer asked, with more point than politeness, 'Why don't you try to go up a mountain which *can* be ascended?' 'It is impossible,' chimed in Biener. 'Sir,' said Croz, 'if we cross to the other side we shall lose three days, and very likely shall not succeed. You want to make ascents in the chain of Mont Blanc, and I believe they can be made. But I shall not be able to make them with you if I spend these days here, for I must be at Chamounix on the 27th.' There was force in what he said, and his words made me hesitate. I relied upon his strong arms for some work which it was expected would be unusually difficult. Snow began to fall; that settled the matter, and I gave the word to retreat. We went back to Breil, and on to the village of Val Tournanche, where we slept; and the next day proceeded to Chatillon, and thence up the Valley of Aosta to Courmayeur.

(Ibid., pp. 223–236)

ATTEMPT TO ASCEND GRANDES JORASSES

On June 23 we mounted to the top of Mont Saxe, to scan the Grandes Jorasses, with the view of ascending it. Five thousand feet of glacier-covered precipices rose above us, and up all that height we tracked a way to our satisfaction. Three thousand feet more of glacier and forest-covered slopes lay beneath, and *there*, there was only one point at which it was doubtful if we should find a path. The glaciers were shrinking, and were surrounded by bastions of rounded rock, far too polished to please the rough mountaineer. We could not track a way across them. However, at 4 A.M. the next day, under the dexterous leading of Michel Croz, we passed the doubtful spot. Thence it was all plain sailing, and at 1 P.M. we gained the summit. The weather was boisterous in the upper regions, and storm-clouds driven before the wind, and wrecked against our heights, enveloped us in misty spray, which danced around and fled away, which cut us off from the material universe, and caused us to be, as it were, suspended betwixt heaven and earth, seeing both occasionally, but seeming to belong to neither.

The mists lasted longer than my patience, and we descended without having attained the object for which the ascent was made … The slopes were steep and covered with new-fallen snow, flour-like and evil to tread upon. On the ascent we had reviled it, and had made our staircase with much caution, knowing full well that the disturbance of its base would bring down all that was above. In descending, the bolder spirits counselled trusting to luck and a glissade; the cautious ones advocated avoiding the slopes and crossing to the rocks on their farther side. The advice of the latter prevailed, and we had half-traversed the snow, to gain the ridge, when the crust slipped and we went along with it. 'Halt!' broke from all four, unanimously. The axe-heads flew round as we started on this involuntary glissade. It was useless, they slid over the underlying ice fruitlessly. 'Halt!' thundered Croz, as he dashed his weapon in again with superhuman energy. No halt could be made, and we slid down slowly, but with accelerating motion, driving up waves of snow in front, with streams of the nasty stuff hissing all around. Luckily, the slope eased off at one place, the leading men cleverly jumped aside out of the moving snow, we others followed, and the young avalanche which we had started, continuing to pour down, fell into a yawning crevasse, and showed us where our grave would have been if we had remained in its company five seconds longer. The whole affair did not occupy half-a-minute. It was the solitary incident of a long day, and at nightfall we re-entered the excellent house kept by the courteous Bertolini, well satisfied that we had not met with more incidents of a similar description.

Despite making a successful ascent, the point reached was not actually the summit. Whymper and his team had climbed the second highest point, which is now known as Pointe Whymper 4,184m (13,727 ft). The summit, 24m (78 ft) higher, was first climbed by Horace Walker three years later.

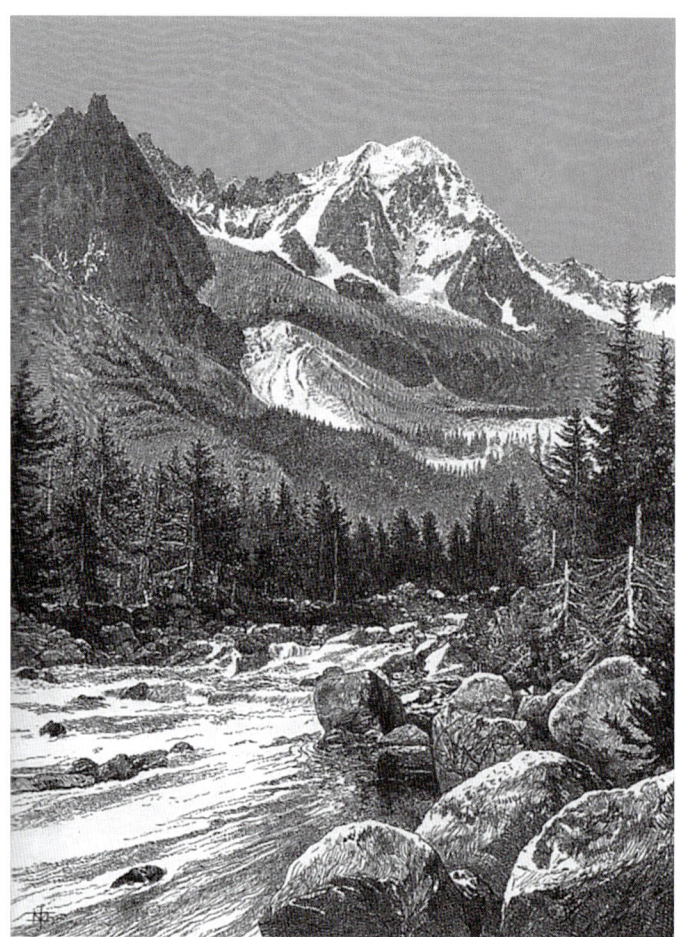

The Grandes Jorasses And The Doire Torrent, From The Italian Val Ferret

(Ibid., pp. 236–239)

ATTEMPT TO ASCEND AIGUILLE VERTE

Aiguille Verte was Chamonix's most illustrious mountain and making its first summit would be an enviable prize, particularly for 'outsiders'. Michel Croz now parted from us. His new employer had not arrived at Chamounix, but Croz considered that he was bound by honour to wait for him, and thus Christian Almer, of Grindelwald, became my leading guide.

Before recrossing the chain to Courmayeur, we ascended the Aiguille Verte. In company with Mr. Reilly I inspected this mountain from every direction in 1864, and came to the conclusion that an ascent could more easily be made from the south than upon any other side. We set out upon the 28th from Chamounix to attack it, minus Croz, and plus a porter (of whom I will speak more particularly presently), leaving our comrade very downcast at having to kick his heels in idleness, whilst we were about to scale the most celebrated of his native Aiguilles.

We camped on the Couvercle (7800) under a great rock, and at 3.15 the next morning started for our aiguille, leaving the porter in charge of the tent and of the food. Two hours' walking over crisp snow brought us up more than 4000 feet, and within about 1600 feet of the summit. From no other direction can it be approached so closely with equal facility. Thence the mountain steepens. After his late severe piece of ice-work, Almer had a natural inclination for rocks; but the lower rocks of the final peak of the Verte were not inviting, and he went on and on, looking for a way up them, until we arrived in front of a great snow couloir that led from the Glacier de Talèfre right up to the crest of the ridge connecting the summit of the Verte with the mountain called Les Droites. This was the route which I intended to be taken; but Almer pointed out that the gully narrowed at the lower part, and that, if stones fell, we should stand some chance of getting our heads broken; and so we went on still more to the east of the summit, to another and smaller couloir which ran up side by side with the great one. At 5.30 we crossed the schrund which protected the final peak, and, a few minutes afterwards, saw the summit and the whole of the intervening route. 'Oh! Aiguille Verte,' said my guide, stopping as he said it, 'you are dead, you are dead;' which, being translated into plain English, meant that he was cock-sure we should make its ascent.

Almer is a quiet man at all times. When climbing he is taciturn — and this is one of his great merits. A garrulous man is always a nuisance, and upon the mountain-side he may be a danger, for actual climbing requires a man's whole attention. Added to this, talkative men are hindrances; they are usually thirsty, and a thirsty man is a drag.

At the top of the small gully we crossed over the intervening rocks into the large one, and followed it so long as it was filled with snow. At last ice replaced snow, and we turned over to the rocks upon its left. Charming rocks they were; granitic in texture, gritty, holding the nails well. At 9.45 we parted from them, and completed the ascent by a little ridge of snow which descended in the direction of the Aiguille du Moine. At 10.15 we stood on the summit (13,540), and devoured our bread and cheese with a good appetite.

Even upon this mountain-top it was impossible to forget the world, for some vile wretch came to the Jardin and made hideous sounds by blowing through a horn. Whilst we were denouncing him a change came over the weather; cumulous clouds gathered in all directions, and we started off in hot haste. Snow began to fall heavily before we were off the summit-rocks, our track was obscured and frequently lost, and everything became so sloppy and slippery that the descent took as long as the ascent … as we rounded our rock a howl broke simultaneously from all three of us, for the porter had taken down the tent, and was in the act of moving off with it. 'Stop, there! what are you doing?' He observed that he had thought we were killed, or at least lost, and was going to Chamounix to communicate his ideas to the *guide chef*. 'Unfasten the tent, and get out the food.' Instead of doing so the porter fumbled in his pockets. 'Get out the food,' we roared, losing all patience. 'Here it is,' said our worthy friend, producing a dirty piece of bread about as big as a halfpenny roll. We three looked solemnly at the fluff-covered morsel. It was past a joke, — he had devoured everything. Mutton, loaves, cheese, wine, eggs, sausages — all was gone — past recovery. It was idle to grumble, and useless to wait. We were light, and could move quickly, — the porter was laden inside and out. We went our hardest, — he had to shuffle and trot … We had our revenge, and dried our clothes at the same time, but when we arrived at the Montanvert the porter was as wet as we had been upon our arrival at the Couvercle. We halted at the inn to get a little food, and at a quarter past eight re-entered Chamounix, amidst firing of cannon and other demonstrations of satisfaction on the part of the hotel-keepers.

The local guides were less celebratory and refuted that the summit had been reached, asking for evidence and for sighting of a flag. The dispute escalated almost in to a brawl before being diffused.

My friend Kennedy, who was on the spot, heard of the disturbance and rushed into the fray, confronted the burly guide, and thrust back his absurdities into his teeth.

There were the materials for a very pretty riot; but they manage these things better in France than we do, and the gendarmes — three strong — came down and dispersed the crowd. The guides … retired to cabarets to take little glasses of absinthe and other liquors more or less injurious to the human frame. Under the influence of these stimulants, they conceived an idea which combined revenge with profit. 'You have ascended the Aiguille Verte, you say. *We* say we don't believe it. *We* say, do it again! Take three of us with you, and we will bet you two thousand francs to one thousand, that you won't make the ascent!'

This proposition was formally notified to me, but I declined it, with thanks, and recommended Kennedy to go in and win. I accepted, however, a hundred franc share in the bet, and calculated upon getting two hundred per cent on my investment. Alas! how vain are human expectations! **[The main instigator]** Zacharie Cachat was put into confinement, and although Kennedy actually ascended the Aiguille a week later, with two Chamounix guides and Peter Perrn, the bet came to nothing.

The weather arranged itself just as this storm in a teapot blew over, and we left at once for the Montanvert, in order to show the Chamouniards the easiest way over the chain of Mont Blanc, in return for the civilities which we had received from them during the past three days.

(Ibid., pp. 247–255)

ATTEMPT TO ASCEND LA RUINETTE

All of the excursions that were set down in my programme had been carried out, with the exception of the ascent of the Matterhorn, and we now turned our faces in its direction, but instead of returning *via* the Val Tournanche, we took a route across country, and bagged upon our way the summit of the Ruinette.

There is not, I suppose, another mountain in the Alps of the same height that can be ascended so easily. You have only to go ahead: upon its southern side one can walk about almost anywhere.

Though I speak thus slightly of a very respectable peak, I will not do anything of the kind in regard to the view which it gives. It is happily placed in respect to the rest of the Pennine Alps, and as a stand-point it has not many superiors. You see mountains, and nothing but mountains. It is a solemn — some would say a dreary — view, but it is very grand. The great Combin (14,164), with its noble background of the whole range of Mont Blanc, never looks so big as it does from here. In the contrary direction, the Matterhorn overpowers all besides. The Dent d'Hérens, although closer, looks a mere outlier of its great neighbour, and the snows of Monte Rosa, behind, seem intended for no other purpose than to give relief to the crags in front. To the south there is an endless array of Bec's and Becca's, backed by the great Italian peaks, whilst to the north Mont Pleureur (12,159) holds its own against the more distant Wildstrubel.

We gained the summit at 9.15, and stayed there an hour and a half. My faithful guides then admonished me that Prerayen, whither we were bound, was still far away, and that we had yet to cross two lofty ridges. So we resumed our harness and departed …

The part of the glacier that we traversed was overspread with snow which completely concealed its numerous pitfalls. We marched across it in single file, and, of course, roped together. All at once Almer dropped into a crevasse up to his shoulders. I pulled in the rope immediately, but the snow gave way as it was being done, and I had to spread out my arms to stop my descent. Biener held fast, and said afterwards, that his feet went through as well; so, for a moment, all three were in the jaws of the crevasse. We now altered our course, so as to take the fissures transversely, and changed it again after the centre of the glacier was passed, and made directly for the summit of the Col d'Olen.

A committee of the English Alpine Club was appointed in 1864 to test, and to report upon, the most suitable ropes for mountaineering purposes, and those which were approved are probably as good as can be found. One is made of Manilla and another of Italian hemp. The former is the heavier, and weighs a little more than an ounce per foot (103 ozs. to 100 feet). The latter weighs 79 ozs. per 100 feet; but I prefer the Manilla rope, because it is more handy to handle. Both of these ropes will sustain 168 lbs. falling 10 feet, or 196 lbs. falling 8 feet, and they break with a dead weight of two tons. In 1865 we carried two 100 feet lengths of the Manilla rope, and the inconvenience arising from its weight was more than made up for by the security which it afforded. Upon several occasions it was worth more than an extra guide.

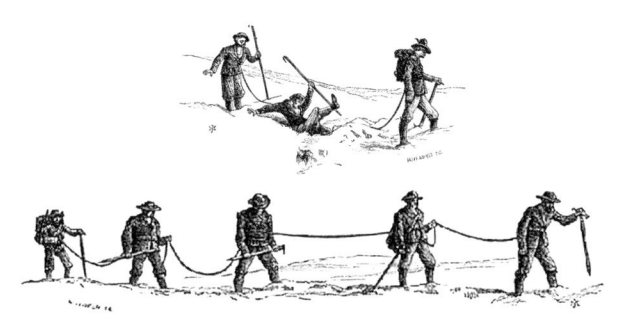

On the 7th we crossed the Va Cornère pass, *en route* for Breil. My thoughts were fixed on the Matterhorn, and my guides knew that I wished them to accompany me. They had an aversion to the mountain, and repeatedly expressed their belief that it was useless to try to ascend it. '*Anything* but Matterhorn, dear sir!' said Almer; '*anything* but Matterhorn.' He did not speak of difficulty or of danger, nor was he shirking work. He offered to go *anywhere*; but he entreated that the Matterhorn should be abandoned. Both men spoke fairly enough. They did not think that an ascent could be made; and for their own credit, as well as for my sake, they did not wish to undertake a business which, in their opinion, would only lead to loss of time and money.

I sent them by the short cut to Breil, and walked down to Val Tournanche to look for Jean-Antoine Carrel. He was not there. The villagers said that he, and three others, had started on the 6th to try the Matterhorn by the old way, on their own account. They will have no luck, I thought, for the clouds were low down on the mountains; and I walked up to Breil, fully expecting to meet them. Nor was I disappointed. About half-way up I saw a group of men clustered around a chalet upon the other side of the torrent, and, crossing over, found that the party had returned.

I explained the situation to Carrel, and proposed that we, with Cæsar and another man, should cross the Théodule by moonlight on the 9th, and that upon the 10th we should pitch the tent as high as possible upon the east face. He was unwilling to abandon the old route, and urged me to try it again. I promised to do so provided the new route failed. This satisfied him, and he agreed to my proposal. I then went up to Breil, and discharged Almer and Biener — with much regret, for no two men ever served me more faithfully or more willingly.

Although he was a climber with his own ambitions, including to summit the Matterhorn, Carrel made some of his living as a mountain guide and could not afford to turn down work. Agreements between guides and clients were often fluid, as clients, including Whymper, could not afford to contract a guide for the entire summer. Therefore, it would not have been uncommon for a guide to have various commitments and clients lined up.

Meanwhile, Felice Giordano was busy organising the extensive supply of provisions for the Italian Alpine Club and no expense was spared. Writing to Quintino Sella on the 7th he advised – 'I am starting off, heavily armed, for the destination you wot of. I sent off the day before yesterday the first tent, 300 metres of rope, and some iron hoops and rings, besides various kinds of provisions for ourselves, a spirit-lamp for heating water, tea, etc. All these things together weigh about 100 kilos. I have also sent Carrel 200 fcs., in order that he may meet these articles at Châtillon and transport them to Valtournanche and Breuil at once.'

'I am taking with me a second tent, three barometers, your own among them, and the *Annuaire du Bureau des Longitudes*. As soon as I reach the scene of the operations I will write to you again.'

'You need only trouble about your own personal requirements, viz., your headgear, a few rugs, etc., and – some good cigars; if possible, also a little good wine and a few shekels, because I have only been able to bring about 300 fcs. With me.'

'Let us, then, set out to attack this Devil's mountain, and let us see that we succeed, if only Whymper has not been beforehand with us.'

It was going to be a slow relentless push for the Italians, which, fortunately for Whymper, would give him crucial time to regain the initiative, ensuring a climatic international race for the summit.

The 8th was occupied with preparations. The weather was stormy; and black, rainy vapours obscured the mountains. Towards evening a young man came from Val Tournanche, and reported that an Englishman was lying there, extremely ill. Now was the time for the performance of my vow; and on the morning of Sunday the 9th I went down the valley to look after the sick man. On my way I passed a foreign gentleman, with a mule and several porters laden with baggage. Amongst these men were Jean-Antoine and Cæsar, carrying some barometers. 'Hullo!' I said, 'what are you doing?' They explained that the foreigner had arrived just as they were setting out, and that they were assisting his porters. 'Very well; go on to Breil, and await me there; we start at midnight as agreed.' Jean-Antoine then said that he should not be able to serve me after Tuesday the 11th, as he was engaged to travel 'with a family of distinction' in the valley of Aosta. 'And Cæsar?' 'And Cæsar also.' 'Why did you not say this before?' 'Because,' said he, 'it was not settled. The engagement is of long standing, but *the day* was not fixed. When I got back to Val Tournanche on Friday night, after leaving you, I found a letter naming the day.' I could not object to the answer; but the prospect of being left guideless was provoking. They went up, and I down, the valley.

The sick man declared that he was better, though the exertion of saying as much tumbled him over on to the floor in a fainting fit. He was badly in want of medicine, and I tramped down to Chatillon to get it. It was late before I returned to Val Tournanche, for the weather was tempestuous, and rain fell in torrents. A figure passed me under the church porch. '*Qui vive?*' 'Jean-Antoine.' 'I thought you were at Breil.' 'No, sir: when the storms came on I knew we should not start to-night, and so came down to sleep here.' 'Ha, Carrel!' I said; 'this is a great bore. If to-morrow is not fine we shall not be able to do anything together. I have sent away my guides, relying on you; and now you are going to leave me to travel with a party of ladies. That work is not fit for *you* (he smiled, I supposed at the implied compliment); can't you send some one else instead?' 'No, monsieur. I am sorry, but my word is pledged. I should like to accompany you, but I can't break my engagement.' By this time we had arrived at the inn door. 'Well, it is no fault of yours. Come presently with Cæsar, and have some wine.' They came, and we sat up till midnight, recounting our old adventures, in the inn of Val Tournanche.

Carrel had indeed found himself in a predicament as he had made two separate, albeit, not conflicting commitments. It is possible that he may have preferred to accompany Whymper but had to honour the agreement with the Italian Alpine Club. Giordano clarifies this in his telegram to Stella sent on 11th July – 'I reached Valtournanche on Saturday at midday. There I found Carrel, who had just returned from a reconnoitring expedition on the Matterhorn, which had proved a failure, owing to bad weather.'

'Whymper had arrived two or three days before; as usual, he wished to make the ascent, and had engaged Carrel, who, not having yet had my letters, had agreed, but for a few days only. Fortunately the weather turned bad. Whymper was unable to make his fresh attempt, and Carrel left him and came with me, together with five other picked men who are the best guides in the valley. We immediately sent off our advance guard, with Carrel at its head. In order not to excite remark we took the rope and other materials to Avouil, a hamlet which is very remote and close to the Matterhorn, and this is to be our lower base.'

'I have taken up my quarters at Breuil for the time being. The weather, the god whom we fear and on whom all will depend, has been hitherto very changeable and rather bad. As lately as yesterday morning it was snowing on the Matterhorn, but yesterday evening it cleared. In the night the men started with the tents, and I hope that by this time they will have reached a great height; but the weather is turning misty again, and the Matterhorn is still covered; I hope the mists will soon disperse.' 'Carrel told me not to come up yet, until he should send me word; naturally he wishes personally to make sure of the last bits.' '… it is also necessary to ascertain whether we can bivouac at a point much higher than Whymper's highest.' 'Meanwhile, on receipt of the present, please send me a few lines in reply, with some advice, because I am head over ears in difficulty here, what with the weather, the expense, and Whymper.'

'I have tried to keep everything secret, but that fellow, whose life seems to depend on the Matterhorn, is here, suspiciously prying into everything. I have taken all the competent men away from him, and yet he is so

enamoured of this mountain that he may go up with others and make a scene. He is here, in this hotel, and I try to avoid speaking to him.'

The weather continued bad upon the 10th, and I returned to Breil. The two Carrels were again hovering about the above mentioned chalet, and I bade them adieu. In the evening the sick man crawled up, a good deal better; but his was the only arrival. The Monday crowd did not cross the Théodule, on account of the continued storms. The inn was lonely. I went to bed early, and was awoke the next morning by the invalid inquiring if I had 'heard the news.' 'No; what news?' 'Why,' said he, 'a large party of guides went off this morning to try the Matterhorn, taking with them a mule laden with provisions.'

I went to the door, and with a telescope saw the party upon the lower slopes of the mountain. Favre, the landlord, stood by. 'What is all this about?' I inquired, 'who is the leader of this party?' 'Carrel.' 'What! Jean-Antoine?' 'Yes; Jean-Antoine.' 'Is Cæsar there too?' 'Yes, he is there.' Then I saw in a moment that I had been bamboozled and humbugged; and learned, bit by bit, that the affair had been arranged long beforehand. The start on the 6th had been for a preliminary reconnaissance; the mule, that I passed, was conveying stores for the attack; the 'family of distinction' was Signor F. Giordano, who had just despatched the party to facilitate the way to the summit, and who, when the facilitation was completed, was to be taken to the top along with Signor Sella!

I was greatly mortified. My plans were upset; the Italians had clearly stolen a march upon me, and I saw that the astute Favre chuckled over my discomfiture, because the route by the eastern face, if successful, would not benefit his inn. What was to be done? I retired to my room, and soothed by tobacco, re-studied my plans, to see if it was not possible to outmanœuvre the Italians.

'They have taken a mule's load of provisions.' 'That is *one* point in my favour, for they will take two or three days to get through the food, and, until that is done, no work will be accomplished.' 'How is the weather?' I went to the window. The mountain was smothered up in mist. 'Another point in my favour.' 'They are to facilitate the way. Well, if they do that to any purpose, it will be a long job.' Altogether, I reckoned that they could not possibly ascend the mountain and come back to Breil in less than seven days. I got cooler, for it was evident that the wily ones might be outwitted after all. There was time enough to go to Zermatt, to try the eastern face, and, should it prove impracticable, to come back to Breil before the men returned; and then, it seemed to me, as the mountain was not padlocked, one might start at the same time as the Messieurs, and yet get to the top before them.

The first thing to do was to go to Zermatt. Easier said than done. The seven guides upon the mountain included the ablest men in the valley, and none of the ordinary muleteer-guides were at Breil. Two men, at least, were wanted for my baggage, but not a soul could be found. I ran about, and sent about in all directions, but not a single porter could be obtained. One was with Carrel; another was ill; another was at Chatillon, and so forth. Even Meynet, the hunchback, could not be induced to come; he was in the thick of some important cheese-making operations. I was in the position of a general without an army; it was all very well to make plans, but there was no one to execute them. This did not much trouble me, for it was evident that so long as the weather stopped traffic over the Théodule pass, it would hinder the men equally upon the Matterhorn; and I knew that directly it improved company would certainly arrive.

About midday on Tuesday the 11th a large party [came] in sight from Zermatt, preceded by a nimble young Englishman, and one of old Peter Taugwalder's sons. I went at once to this gentleman to learn if he could dispense with Taugwalder. He said that he could not, as they were going to recross to Zermatt on the morrow, but that the young man should assist in transporting my baggage, as he had nothing to carry. We naturally got into conversation. I told my story, and learned that the young Englishman was Lord Francis Douglas, whose recent exploit — the ascent of the Gabelhorn — had excited my wonder and admiration. He brought good news. Old Peter had lately been beyond the Hörnli, and had reported that he thought an ascent of the Matterhorn was possible upon that side. Almer had left Zermatt, and could not be recovered, so I determined to seek for old Peter. Lord Francis Douglas expressed a warm desire to ascend the mountain, and before long it was determined that he should take part in the expedition.

Lord Francis Douglas was the younger brother of the Marquess of Queensberry. At just eighteen years old, Lord Douglas had served in the military and had made the second recorded ascent of the Ober Gabelhorn, 4,063m (13,330 ft) a few days earlier. The climb had been made just one day following the first ascent and was via a different route, so a notable achievement. With ample time to determine Douglas's physical and mental ability, Whymper was able to satisfy himself of his new companions suitability.

Favre could no longer hinder our departure, and lent us one of his men. We crossed the Col Théodule on Wednesday morning the 12th of July, rounded the foot of the Ober Théodulgletscher, crossed the Furggengletscher, and deposited tent, blankets, ropes, and other matters in the little chapel at the Schwarzsee. All four were heavily laden, for we brought across the whole of my stores from Breil. Of rope alone there was about 600 feet. There were three kinds. First, 200 feet of the Manilla rope; second, 150 feet of a stouter, and probably stronger rope than the first; and third, more than 200 feet of a lighter and weaker rope than the first, of a kind that I used formerly (stout sash-line).

We descended to Zermatt, sought and engaged old Peter, and gave him permission to choose another guide. When we returned to the Monte Rosa Hotel, whom should we see sitting upon the wall in front but my old *guide chef*, Michel Croz. I supposed that he had come with [**his last employer, a Mr Birkbeck**], but I learned that that gentleman had arrived in ill health, at Chamounix, and had returned to England. Croz, thus left free, had been immediately engaged by the Rev. Charles Hudson, and they had come to Zermatt with the same object as ourselves — namely, to attempt the ascent of the Matterhorn!

Lord Francis Douglas and I dined at the Monte Rosa, and had just finished when Mr. Hudson and a friend entered the *salle à manger*. They had returned from inspecting the mountain, and some idlers in the room demanded their intentions. We heard a confirmation of Croz's statement, and learned that Mr. Hudson intended to set out on the morrow at the same hour as ourselves. We left the room to consult, and agreed it was undesirable that two independent parties should be on the mountain at the same time with the same object. Mr. Hudson was therefore invited to join us, and he accepted our proposal. Before admitting his friend — Mr. Hadow — I took the precaution to inquire what he had done in the Alps, and, as well as I remember, Mr. Hudson's reply was, 'Mr. Hadow has done Mont Blanc in less time than most men.' He then mentioned several other excursions that were unknown to me, and added, in answer to a further question, 'I consider he is a sufficiently good man to go with us.' Mr. Hadow was admitted without any further question, and we then went into the matter of guides. Hudson thought that Croz and old Peter would be sufficient. The question was referred to the men themselves, and they made no objection.

Reverend Charles Hudson was an Anglican chaplain and a well-known climber. At thirty-six years of age, and the oldest member of the party (Whymper was twenty-five), Hudson also had a number of first ascents to his name and was considered a pioneer of guideless climbing, being the first to ascend Mont Blanc without a guide. The son of the chairman of the P&O shipping company, Douglas Hadow was Hudson's protégé and although young and inexperienced for the Matterhorn terrain, was considered, by Hudson, to be strong and sufficiently able.

So Croz and I became comrades once more; and as I threw myself on my bed and tried to go to sleep, I wondered at the strange series of chances which had first separated us and then brought us together again. I thought of the mistake through which he had accepted the engagement to Mr. Birkbeck; of his unwillingness to adopt my route; of his recommendation to transfer our energies to the chain of Mont Blanc; of the retirement of Almer and Biener; of the desertion of Carrel; of the arrival of Lord Francis Douglas; and, lastly, of our meeting at Zermatt; and as I pondered over these things I could not help asking, 'What next?' If any one of the links of this fatal chain of circumstances had been omitted, what a different story I should have to tell!

(Ibid., pp. 259–272)

EIGHTH ATTEMPT TO ASCEND THE MATTERHORN

Two days behind the well-equipped Italian team, the hastily consolidated British party set off with French and Swiss guides, up the opposite side of the mountain, along which very few men had set foot more than part way, and a route up which Whymper had never ventured. Their hopes of still beating the Italians was based on, either that the poor weather in the preceding days had hampered their progress, the scale of the Italian expedition was cumbersome, or that there was still some unknown insurmountable obstacle on the south side. There was still reason for optimism.

We started from Zermatt on the 13th of July, at half-past 5, on a brilliant and perfectly cloudless morning. We were eight in number — Croz, old Peter and his two sons, Lord F. Douglas, Hadow, Hudson, and I. To ensure steady motion, one tourist and one native walked together. The youngest Taugwalder fell to my share, and the lad marched well, proud to be on the expedition, and happy to show his powers. The wine-bags also fell to my lot to carry, and throughout the day, after each drink, I replenished them secretly with water, so that at the next halt they were found fuller than before! This was considered a good omen, and little short of miraculous.

On the first day we did not intend to ascend to any great height, and we mounted, accordingly, very leisurely; picked up the things which were left in the chapel at the Schwarzsee at 8.20, and proceeded thence along the ridge connecting the Hörnli with the Matterhorn. At half-past 11 we arrived at the base of the actual peak; then quitted the ridge, and clambered round some ledges, on to the eastern face. We were now fairly upon the mountain, and were astonished to find that places which from the Riffel, or even from the Furggengletscher, looked entirely impracticable, were so easy that we could *run about*.

Before twelve o'clock we had found a good position for the tent, at a height of 11,000 feet [**About 200m above where the Hörnli hut stands today**]. Croz and young Peter went on to see what was above, in order to save time on the following morning. They cut across the heads of the snow-slopes which descended towards the Furggengletscher, and disappeared round a corner; and shortly afterwards we saw them high up on the face, moving quickly. We others made a solid platform for the tent in a well-protected spot, and then watched eagerly for the return of the men. The stones which they upset told that they were very high, and we supposed that the way must be easy. At length, just before 3 P.M., we saw them coming down, evidently much excited. 'What are they saying, Peter?' 'Gentlemen, they say it is no good.' But when they came near we heard a different story. 'Nothing but what was good; not a difficulty, not a single difficulty! We could have gone to the summit and returned to-day easily!'

We passed the remaining hours of daylight — some basking in the sunshine, some sketching or collecting; and when the sun went down, giving, as it departed, a glorious promise for the morrow, we returned to the tent to arrange for the night. Hudson made tea, I coffee, and we then retired each one to his blanket-bag; the Taugwalders, Lord Francis Douglas, and myself, occupying the tent, the others remaining, by preference, outside. Long after dusk the cliffs above echoed with our laughter and with the songs of the guides, for we were happy that night in camp, and feared no evil.

We assembled together outside the tent before dawn on the morning of the 14th, and started directly it was light enough to move. Young Peter came on with us as a guide, and his brother returned to Zermatt. We followed the route which had been taken on the previous day, and in a few minutes turned the rib which had intercepted the view of the eastern face from our tent platform. The whole of this great slope was now revealed, rising for 3000 feet like a huge natural staircase. Some parts were more, and others were less, easy; but we were not once brought to a halt by any serious impediment, for when an obstruction was met in front it could always be turned to the right or to the left. For the greater part of the way there was, indeed, no occasion for the rope, and sometimes Hudson led, sometimes myself. At 6.20 we had attained a height of 12,800 feet, and halted for half-an-hour; we then continued the ascent without a break until 9.55, when we stopped for 50 minutes, at a height of 14,000 feet. Twice we struck the N.E. ridge, and followed it for some little distance, — to no advantage, for it was usually more rotten and steep, and always more difficult than the face. Still, we kept near to it, lest stones perchance might fall.

We had now arrived at the foot of that part which, from the Riffelberg or from Zermatt, seems perpendicular or overhanging, and could no longer continue upon the eastern side. For a little distance we ascended by snow upon the arête — that is, the ridge — descending towards Zermatt, and then, by common consent, turned over to the right, or to the northern side. Before doing so, we made a change in the order of ascent. Croz went first, I followed, Hudson came third; Hadow and old Peter were last. 'Now,' said Croz, as he led off, 'now for something altogether different.' The work became difficult, and required caution. In some places there was little to hold, and it was desirable that those should be in front who were least likely to slip. The general slope of the mountain at this part was *less* than 40°, and snow had accumulated in, and had filled up, the interstices of the rock-face, leaving only occasional fragments projecting here and there. These were at times covered with a thin film of ice, produced from the melting and refreezing of the snow. It was the counterpart, on a small scale, of the upper 700 feet of the Pointe des Ecrins, — only there was this material difference; the face of the Ecrins was about, or exceeded, an angle of 50°, and the Matterhorn face was less than 40°. It was a place over which any fair mountaineer might pass in safety, and Mr. Hudson ascended this part, and, as far as I know, the entire mountain, without having the slightest assistance rendered to him upon any occasion. Sometimes, after I had taken a hand from Croz, or received a pull, I turned to offer the same to Hudson; but he invariably declined, saying it was not necessary. Mr. Hadow, however, was not accustomed to this kind of work, and required continual assistance. It is only fair to say that the difficulty which he found at this part arose simply and entirely from want of experience.

This solitary difficult part was of no great extent. We bore away over it at first, nearly horizontally, for a distance of about 400 feet; then ascended directly towards the summit for about 60 feet; and then doubled back to the ridge which descends towards Zermatt. A long stride round a rather awkward corner brought us to snow once more. The last doubt vanished! The Matterhorn was ours! Nothing but 200 feet of easy snow remained to be surmounted!

You must now carry your thoughts back to the seven Italians who started from Breil on the 11th of July. Four days had passed since their departure, and we were tormented with anxiety lest they should arrive on the top before us. All the way up we had talked of them, and many false alarms of 'men on the summit' had been raised. The higher we rose, the more intense became the excitement. What if we should be beaten at the last moment? The slope eased off, at length we could be detached, and Croz and I, dashing away, ran a neck-and-neck race, which ended in a dead heat. At 1.40 P.M. the world was at our feet, and the Matterhorn was conquered. Hurrah! Not a footstep could be seen.

It was not yet certain that we had not been beaten. The summit of the Matterhorn was formed of a rudely level ridge, about 350 feet long, and the Italians might have been at its farther extremity. I hastened to the southern end, scanning the snow right and left eagerly. Hurrah! again; it was untrodden. 'Where were the men?' I peered over the cliff, half doubting, half expectant. I saw them immediately — mere dots on the ridge, at an immense distance below. Up went my arms and my hat.

'Croz! Croz!! come here!' 'Where are they, Monsieur?' 'There, don't you see them, down there?' 'Ah! the *coquins*, they are low down.' 'Croz, we must make those fellows hear us.' We yelled until we were hoarse. The Italians seemed to regard us — we could not be certain. 'Croz, we *must* make them hear us; they *shall* hear us!' I seized a block of rock and hurled it down, and called upon my companion, in the name of friendship, to do the same. We drove our sticks in, and prized away the crags, and soon a torrent of stones poured down the cliffs. There was no mistake about it this time. The Italians turned and fled.

While the hurling of rocks has been misinterpreted by some as trying to injure their competitors, the rockslide was created further along the summit so as to gain the attention of the Italian team and not to cause any harm. Indeed, despite the frustration that Carrel had made this attempt without Whymper, there was no animosity, and Whymper truly wished that Carrel could have been on the summit to share the moment with them.

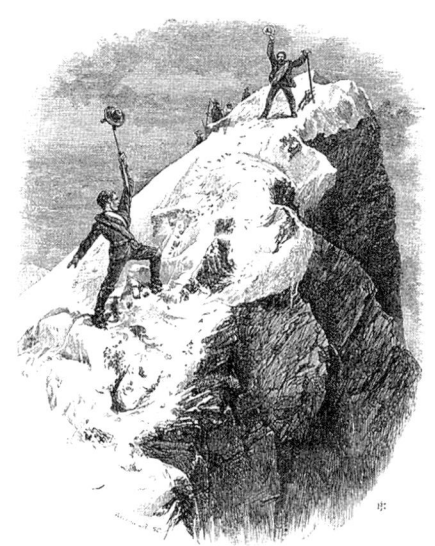

'Croz! Croz!! Come Here!'

Still, I would that the leader of that party [**Carrel**] could have stood with us at that moment, for our victorious shouts conveyed to him the disappointment of the ambition of a lifetime. He was the man, of all those who attempted the ascent of the Matterhorn, who most deserved to be the first upon its summit. He was the first to doubt its inaccessibility, and he was the only man who persisted in believing that its ascent would be accomplished. It was the aim of his life to make the ascent from the side of Italy, for the honour of his native valley. For a time he had the game in his hands: he played it as he thought best; but he made a false move, and he lost it. Times have changed with Carrel. His supremacy is questioned in the Val Tournanche; new men have arisen; and he is no longer recognised as *the* chasseur above all others: though so long as he remains the man that he is to-day, it will not be easy to find his superior.

The others had arrived, so we went back to the northern end of the ridge. Croz now took the tent-pole, and planted it in the highest snow. 'Yes,' we said, 'there is the flag-staff, but where is the flag?' 'Here it is,' he answered, pulling off his blouse and fixing it to the stick. It made a poor flag, and there was no wind to float it out, yet it was seen all around. They saw it at Zermatt — at the Riffel — in the Val Tournanche. At Breil, the watchers cried, 'Victory is ours!' They raised 'bravos' for Carrel, and 'vivas' for Italy, and hastened to put themselves *en fête*. On the morrow they were undeceived. 'All was changed; the explorers returned sad — cast down — disheartened — confounded — gloomy.' 'It is true,' said the men. 'We saw them ourselves — they hurled stones at us! The old traditions are true, — there *are* spirits on the top of the Matterhorn!'

We returned to the southern end of the ridge to build a cairn, and then paid homage to the view. The day was one of those superlatively calm and clear ones which usually precede bad weather. The atmosphere was perfectly still, and free from all clouds or vapours. Mountains fifty — nay a hundred — miles off, looked sharp and near. All their details — ridge and crag, snow and glacier — stood out with faultless definition. Pleasant thoughts of happy days in bygone years came up unbidden, as we recognised the old, familiar forms. All were revealed — not one of the principal peaks of the Alps was hidden … First came the Dent Blanche, hoary and grand; the Gabelhorn and pointed Rothhorn; and then the peerless Weisshorn: the towering Mischabelhörner, flanked by the Allaleinhorn, Strahlhorn, and Rimpfischhorn; then Monte Rosa — with its many Spitzes — the Lyskamm and the Breithorn. Behind was the Bernese Oberland governed by the Finsteraarhorn, and then the Simplon and St. Gothard groups; the Disgrazia and the Orteler. Towards the south we looked down to Chivasso on the plain of Piedmont, and far beyond. The Viso — one hundred miles away — seemed close upon us; the Maritime Alps — one hundred and thirty miles distant — were free from haze. Then came my first love — the Pelvoux; the Ecrins and the Meije; the clusters of the Graians; and lastly, in the west, gorgeous in the full sunlight, rose the monarch of all — Mont Blanc. Ten thousand feet beneath us were the green fields of Zermatt, dotted with chalets, from which blue smoke rose lazily. Eight thousand feet below, on the other side, were the pastures of Breil. There were black and gloomy forests, bright and cheerful meadows; bounding waterfalls and tranquil lakes; fertile lands and savage wastes; sunny plains and frigid *plateaux*. There were the most rugged forms, and the most graceful outlines — bold, perpendicular cliffs, and gentle, undulating slopes; rocky mountains and snowy mountains, sombre and solemn … There was every combination that the world can give, and every contrast that the heart could desire.

We remained on the summit for one hour —

'One crowded hour of glorious life.'

It passed away too quickly, and we began to prepare for the descent.

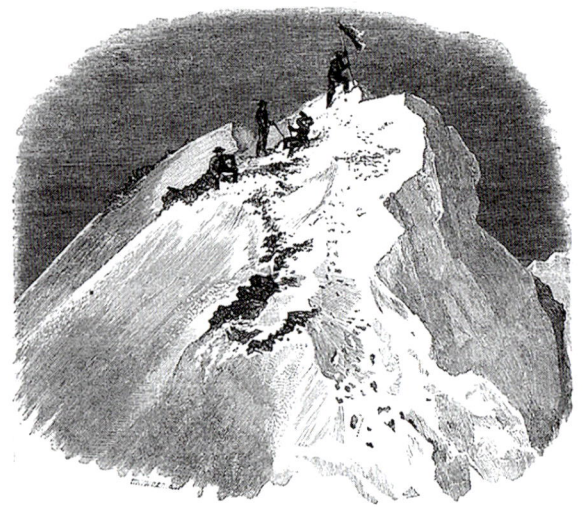

The Summit Of The Matterhorn In 1865 (Northern End)

Sadly, Giordano mistook the sighting of the men on the summit to be his Italian team and wrote on the 14th – 'At 2 p.m. to-day I saw Carrel and Co. on the top peak of the Matterhorn … so success seems certain.' 'If you do not come or telegraph by to-morrow evening I shall go and plant our flag up there, that it may be the first.' 'Whymper has gone off to make an attempt on the other side, but I think in vain.' **How galling, the reality must have been received when Carrel returned.**

(Ibid., pp. 273–284)

DESCENT OF THE MATTERHORN

Hudson and I again consulted as to the best and safest arrangement of the party. We agreed that it would be best for Croz to go first, and Hadow second; Hudson, who was almost equal to a guide in sureness of foot, wished to be third; Lord F. Douglas was placed next, and old Peter, the strongest of the remainder, after him. I suggested to Hudson that we should attach a rope to the rocks on our arrival at the difficult bit, and hold it as we descended, as an additional protection. He approved the idea, but it was not definitely settled that it should be done. The party was being arranged in the above order whilst I was sketching the summit, and they had finished, and were waiting for me to be tied in line, when some one remembered that our names had not been left in a bottle. They requested me to write them down, and moved off while it was being done.

A few minutes afterwards I tied myself to young Peter, ran down after the others, and caught them just as they were commencing the descent of the difficult part. Great care was being taken. Only one man was moving at a time; when he was firmly planted the next advanced, and so on. They had not, however, attached the additional rope to rocks, and nothing was said about it. The suggestion was not made for my own sake, and I am not sure that it even occurred to me again. For some little distance we two followed the others, detached from them, and should have continued so had not Lord F. Douglas asked me, about 3 P.M., to tie on to old Peter, as he feared, he said, that Taugwalder would not be able to hold his ground if a slip occurred.

Down in Zermatt, Taugwalder's young son had been looking up to the summit in the hope of seeing the climbers. What he saw was a considerable rock fall and had rushed into the Monte Rosa hotel to notify the owner and guests that he had seen an avalanche fall from the summit down the north face of the mountain. He was dismissed for telling 'idle stories', but he had indeed seen a terrible rock fall … and no ordinary fall at that. For 150 years, people have debated the accuracy of the following account, but on the basis that Whymper appears to have striven to be as accurate and as detailed as possible throughout the rest of his text, the following conjecture must be viewed in the same context.

Michel Croz had laid aside his axe, and in order to give Mr. Hadow greater security, was absolutely taking hold of his legs, and putting his feet, one by one, into their proper positions. As far as I know, no one was actually descending. I cannot speak with certainty, because the two leading men were partially hidden from my sight by an intervening mass of rock, but it is my belief, from the movements of their shoulders, that Croz, having done as I have said, was in the act of turning round to go down a step or two himself; at this moment Mr. Hadow slipped, fell against him, and knocked him over. I heard one startled exclamation from Croz, then saw him and Mr. Hadow flying downwards; in another moment Hudson was dragged from his steps, and Lord F. Douglas immediately after him. All this was the work of a moment. Immediately we heard Croz's exclamation, old Peter and I planted ourselves as firmly as the rocks would permit: the rope was taut between us, and the jerk came on us both as on one man. We held; but the rope broke midway between Taugwalder and Lord Francis Douglas. For a few seconds we saw our unfortunate companions sliding downwards on their backs, and spreading out their hands, endeavouring to save themselves. They passed from our sight uninjured, disappeared one by one, and fell from precipice to precipice on to the Matterhorngletscher below, a distance of nearly 4000 feet in height. From the moment the rope broke it was impossible to help them.

So perished our comrades! For the space of half-an-hour we remained on the spot without moving a single step. The two men, paralysed by terror, cried like infants, and trembled in such a manner as to threaten us with the fate of the others. Old Peter rent the air with exclamations of 'Chamounix! Oh, what will Chamounix say?' He meant, Who would believe that Croz could fall? The young man did nothing but scream or sob, 'We are lost! we are lost!' Fixed between the two, I could neither move up nor down. I begged young Peter to descend, but he dared not. Unless he did, we could not advance. Old Peter became alive to the danger, and swelled the cry, 'We are lost! we are lost!' The father's fear was natural — he trembled for his son; the young man's fear was cowardly — he thought of self alone. At last old Peter summoned up courage, and changed his position to a rock to which he could fix the rope; the young man then descended, and we all stood together. Immediately we did so, I asked for the rope which had given way, and found, to my surprise — indeed, to my horror — that it was the weakest of the three ropes. It was not brought, and should not have been employed, for the purpose for which it was used. It was old rope, and, compared with the others, was feeble. It was intended as a reserve, in case we had to leave much rope behind, attached to rocks. I saw at once that a serious question was involved, and made him give me the end. It had broken in mid-air, and it did not appear to have sustained previous injury.

For more than two hours afterwards I thought almost every moment that the next would be my last; for the Taugwalders, utterly unnerved, were not only incapable of giving assistance, but were in such a state that a slip might have been expected from them at any moment. After a time we were able to do that which should have been done at first, and fixed rope to firm rocks, in addition to being tied together. These ropes were cut from time to time, and were left behind. Even with their assurance the men were sometimes afraid to proceed, and several times old Peter turned with ashy face and faltering limbs, and said, with terrible emphasis, *'I cannot!'*

About 6 P.M. we arrived at the snow upon the ridge descending towards Zermatt, and all peril was over. We frequently looked, but in vain, for traces of our unfortunate companions; we bent over the ridge and cried to them, but no sound returned. Convinced at last that they were neither within sight nor hearing, we ceased from our useless efforts; and, too cast down for speech, silently gathered up our things, and the little effects of those who were lost, preparatory to continuing the descent. When, lo! a mighty arch appeared, rising above the Lyskamm, high into the sky. Pale, colourless, and noiseless, but perfectly sharp and defined, except where it was lost in the clouds, this unearthly apparition seemed like a vision from another world; and, almost appalled, we watched with amazement the gradual development of two vast crosses, one on either side. If the Taugwalders had not been the first to perceive it, I should have doubted my senses. They thought it had some connection with the accident, and I, after a while, that it might bear some relation to ourselves. But our movements had no effect upon it. The spectral forms remained motionless. It was a fearful and wonderful sight; unique in my experience, and impressive beyond description, coming at such a moment.

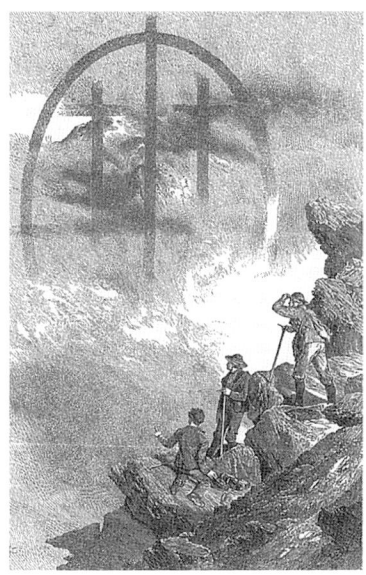

Fog-Bow Seen From The Matterhorn On July 14th, 1865

I was ready to leave, and waiting for the others. They had recovered their appetites and the use of their tongues. They spoke in patois, which I did not understand. At length the son said in French, 'Monsieur.' 'Yes.' 'We are poor men; we have lost our Herr; we shall not get paid; we can ill afford this.' 'Stop!' I said, interrupting him, 'that is nonsense; I shall pay you, of course, just as if your Herr were here.' They talked together in their patois for a short time, and then the son spoke again. 'We don't wish you to pay us. We wish you to write in the hotel-book at Zermatt, and to your journals, that we have not been paid.' 'What nonsense are you talking? I don't understand you. What do you mean?' He proceeded — 'Why, next year there will be many travellers at Zermatt, and we shall get more *voyageurs*.'

Who would answer such a proposition? I made them no reply in words, but they knew very well the indignation that I felt. They filled the cup of bitterness to overflowing, and I tore down the cliff, madly and recklessly, in a way that caused them, more than once, to inquire if I wished to kill them. Night fell; and for an hour the descent was continued in the darkness. At half-past 9 a resting-place was found, and upon a wretched slab, barely large enough to hold the three, we passed six miserable hours. At daybreak the descent was resumed, and from the Hörnli ridge we ran down to the chalets of Buhl, and on to Zermatt. Seiler **[the hotelier,]** met me at his door, and followed in silence to my room. 'What is the matter?' 'The Taugwalders and I have returned.' He did not need more, and burst into tears; but lost no time in useless lamentations, and set to work to arouse the village. Before long a score of men had started to ascend the Hohlicht heights, above Kalbermatt and Z'Mutt, which commanded the plateau of the Matterhorngletscher. They returned after six hours, and reported that they had seen the bodies lying motionless on the snow. This was on Saturday; and they proposed that we should leave on Sunday evening, so as to arrive upon the plateau at daybreak on Monday. Unwilling to lose the slightest chance, the Rev. J. M'Cormick and I resolved to start on Sunday morning. The Zermatt men, threatened with excommunication by their priests if they failed to attend the early mass, were unable to accompany us. To several of them, at least, this was a severe trial. Peter Perrn declared with tears that nothing else would have prevented him from joining in the search for his old comrades. Englishmen came to our aid.

We started at 2 A.M. on Sunday the 16th, and followed the route that we had taken on the previous Thursday as far as the Hörnli. From thence we went down to the right of the ridge, and mounted through the *séracs* of the Matterhorngletscher. By 8.30 we had got to the plateau at the top of the glacier, and within sight of the corner in which we knew my companions must be. As we saw one weather-beaten man after another raise the telescope, turn deadly pale, and pass it on without a word to the next, we knew that all hope was gone … They had fallen below as they had fallen above — Croz a little in advance, Hadow near him, and Hudson some distance behind; but of Lord F. Douglas we could see nothing. We left them where they fell; buried in snow at the base of the grandest cliff of the most majestic mountain of the Alps.

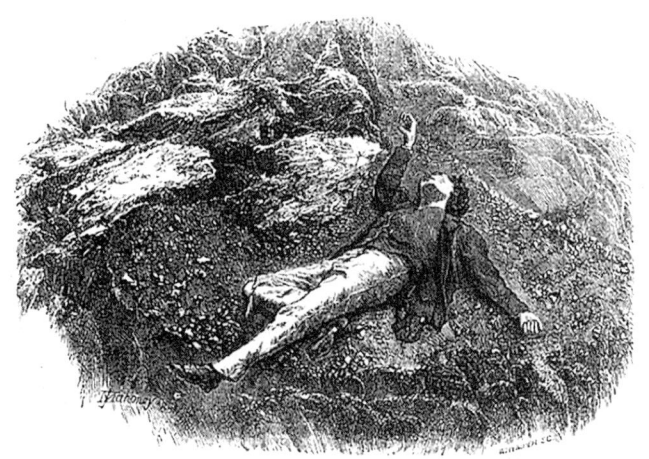

For over a century and a half, people have looked to find fault for the deaths of the four climbers. Were the deaths the fault of Old Peter Taugwalder for using an inferior rope? Was the rope cut by those who survived? Should Whymper have taken command and changed the order of the decent? Was it really Hadow who slipped first? Should Hadow have even been there? Some early reports claimed he was uncomfortable descending on the simplest of rocky routes.

What should be born in mind is that had a stronger rope been used to link all seven men, they would have undoubtedly *all* fallen to their death, and today, seven experienced mountaineers would never link up together in one chain. Furthermore, while no single man appeared

to have been in charge, the group had been functioning democratically, as had been the case with every other climb in which Whymper had been involved in the past. These were still early days in mountaineering and it would be wrong to judge their decisions with hindsight.

Whymper suffered badly as a result of the tragedy, not only from the criticism of other climbers and the media, but psychologically too. Maybe he had been hasty to team up with Rev. Hudson's team, but in climbing with Croz, his chance of success had been considerably improved. Whymper had sought to determine the ability of his newly unacquainted companions and had been assured of their aptitude. Considering the circumstances of the day, it is doubtful others would have done things differently. He and his party had conquered a mountain that most believed unconquerable. To do that, self-belief, resilience and an understanding of ones ability were vital. The Alps were not a playground, although many treated them as such, and surmounting the peaks then, as now, requires each individual to make a self-assessment of the risk against their own competence.

All those who had fallen had been tied with the Manilla, or with the second and equally strong rope, and, consequently, there had been only one link — that between old Peter and Lord F. Douglas — where the weaker rope had been used. This had a very ugly look for Taugwalder, for it was not possible to suppose that the others would have sanctioned the employment of a rope so greatly inferior in strength when there were more than 250 feet of the better qualities still remaining out of use. For the sake of the old guide (who bore a good reputation), and upon all other accounts, it was desirable that this matter should be cleared up; and after my examination before the court of inquiry which was instituted by the Government was over, I handed in a number of questions which were framed so as to afford old Peter an opportunity of exculpating himself from the grave suspicions which at once fell upon him. The questions, I was told, were put and answered; but the answers, although promised, have never reached me.

Meanwhile, the administration sent strict injunctions to recover the bodies, and upon the 19th of July, twenty-one men of Zermatt accomplished that sad and dangerous task. Of the body of Lord Francis Douglas they, too, saw nothing; it is probably still arrested on the rocks above. The remains of Hudson and Hadow were interred upon the north side of the Zermatt Church, in the presence of a reverent crowd of sympathising friends. The body of Michel Croz lies upon the other side, under a simpler tomb; whose inscription bears honourable testimony to his rectitude, to his courage, and to his devotion.

So the traditional inaccessibility of the Matterhorn was vanquished, and was replaced by legends of a more real character. Others will essay to scale its proud cliffs, but to none will it be the mountain that it was to its early explorers. Others may tread its summit-snows, but none will ever know the feelings of those who first gazed upon its marvellous panorama; and none, I trust, will ever be compelled to tell of joy turned into grief, and of laughter into mourning. It proved to be a stubborn foe; it resisted long, and gave many a hard blow; it was defeated at last with an ease that none could have anticipated, but, like a relentless enemy — conquered but not crushed — it took terrible vengeance. The time may come when the Matterhorn shall have passed away, and nothing, save a heap of shapeless fragments, will mark the spot where the great mountain stood; for, atom by atom, inch by inch, and yard by yard, it yields to forces which nothing can withstand. That time is far distant; and, ages hence, generations unborn will gaze upon its awful precipices, and wonder at its unique form. However exalted may be their ideas, and however exaggerated their expectations, none will come to return disappointed!

With the Ascent of the Matterhorn, my mountaineering in the Alps came to a close. The disastrous termination, though casting a permanent cloud over otherwise happy memories, and leaving a train of life-long regrets, has not altered my regard for the purest, healthiest and most manly of sports; and, often, in grappling with every day difficulties, sometimes in apparently hopeless tasks, encouragement has been found in the remembrance of hard-won victories over stubborn Alps.

We who go mountain-scrambling have constantly set before us the superiority of fixed purpose or perseverance to brute force. We know that each height, each step, must be gained by patient, laborious toil, and that wishing cannot take the place of working; we know the benefits of mutual aid; that many a difficulty must be encountered, and many an obstacle must be grappled with or turned, but we know that where there's a will there's a way: and we come back to our daily occupations better fitted to fight the battle of life, and to overcome the impediments which obstruct our paths, strengthened and cheered by the recollection of past labours, and by the memories of victories gained in other fields.

I have not made myself an apologist for mountaineering, nor do I now intend to usurp the functions of a moralist; but my task would have been ill performed if it had been concluded without one reference to the more serious lessons of the mountaineer. We glory in the physical regeneration which is the product of our exertions; we exult over the grandeur of the scenes that are brought before our eyes, the splendours of sunrise and sunset, and the beauties of hill, dale, lake, wood, and waterfall; but we value more highly the development of manliness, and the evolution, under combat with difficulties, of those noble qualities of human nature — courage, patience, endurance, and fortitude.

Some hold these virtues in less estimation, and assign base and contemptible motives to those who indulge in our innocent sport.

Others, again, who are not detractors, find mountaineering, as a sport, to be wholly unintelligible. It is not greatly to be wondered at — we are not all constituted alike. Mountaineering is a pursuit essentially adapted to the young or vigorous, and not to the old or feeble. To the latter, toil may be no pleasure; and it is often said by such persons, 'This man is making a toil of pleasure.' Let the motto on the title-page be an answer, if an answer be required. Toil he must who goes mountaineering; but out of the toil comes strength (not merely muscular energy — more than that), an awakening of all the faculties; and from the strength arises pleasure. Then, again, it is often asked, in tones which seem to imply that the answer must, at least, be doubtful, 'But does it repay you?' Well, we cannot estimate our enjoyment as you measure your wine, or weigh your lead, — it is real, nevertheless. If I could blot out every reminiscence, or erase every memory, still I should say that my scrambles amongst the Alps have repaid me, for they have given me two of the best things a man can possess — health and friends.

Still, the last, sad memory hovers round, and sometimes drifts across like floating mist, cutting off sunshine, and chilling the remembrance of happier times. There have been joys too great to be described in words, and there have been griefs upon which I have not dared to dwell; and with these in mind I say, Climb if you will, but remember that courage and strength are nought without prudence, and that a momentary negligence may destroy the happiness of a lifetime. Do nothing in haste; look well to each step; and from the beginning think what may be the end.

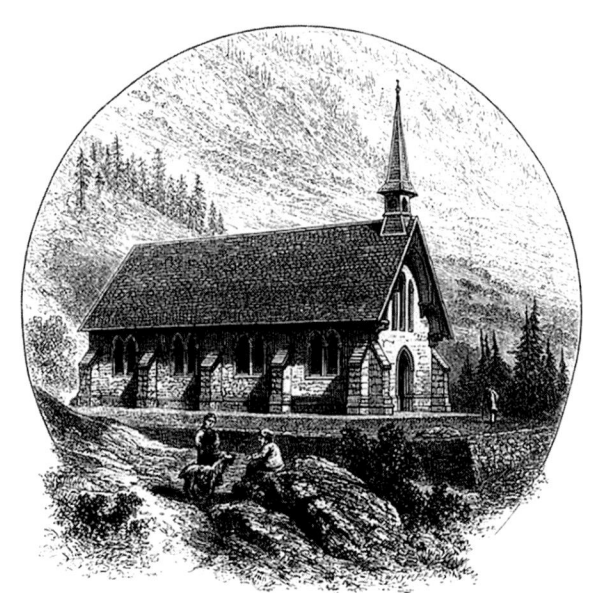

The English Church At Zermatt

(Ibid., pp. 285–298)

SUMMER 2015 (THE NADELHORN 4,327M) AUTHOR'S LOG

Although our intention had been for a steady increase in the demands of our climbing over a two-week period, culminating with the Matterhorn, a message from the Italian guide office a few days into our trip, advised that while the Lion Ridge route was now open, wet and snowy conditions were forecast and expected to last for most of the second week. We therefore needed to drop the first 'warm-up' mountain and go straight to the Nadelhorn. At 150m lower than the Matterhorn, the Nadelhorn requires a similar length of time to climb, so we considered it as ideal for acclimatisation and preparation.

To complicate matters further, the guide office was struggling to find guides for us for the new dates, so I made an urgent cry for help to a Swiss-based guide office to see if they could source guides for the Hörnli Ridge route (eerily reminiscent of Whymper's experience in 1865).

While waiting for news from both companies, unsure of whether we would be able to take advantage of the only weather window available to us, we set off for the Nadelhorn. The hut from which the climb commences is the Mischabelhütte, which at 3,329m is the third highest hut in Switzerland. The 1,000m climb to it started out at a steady pace but soon steepened, eventually becoming a series of metal steps, staples and rope-ways up a rocky ridge right to the front door. Sadly, rather than relaxing and enjoying the comfortable accommodation, the few hours prior to going to bed were taken up trying to resolve our guide dilemma, for which at least we had a mobile phone signal to make calls.

First, the Swiss company replied saying they had sourced two British guides, then the Italian office said they too had been successful. We now had two options, and owing to the shortened time scale and the fact that we were considerably closer to the Hörnli Ridge side, we reverted to the British guides. Pleased to have a date and guides in place, we retired to bed, apprehensive of what else might arise to prevent us from achieving our goal.

Having little, if any, sleep, a very quick breakfast and heading out at 4:30 a.m. was not the ideal start to a big climb, but excitedly and somewhat drowsily we headed out into the dark. An immediate 200m scramble up a ridge behind the hut soon had us alert and it was not long before we dressed and roped-up to cross the main glacier. Taking a wide arc, we avoided crossing all but one of the big crevasses; the latter crossed by a broad snow bridge just as the arriving sun set the horizon ablaze in a blood-red hue. Once across the glacier, we climbed steadily up snow ridges, working our way every now and then around rocky outcrops until the summit became clear.

Recent snow meant the ground was soft and liable to giving way at any time, which made for slower progress than we would have liked. A few slow-paced groups ahead of us further impacted our speed. The final 100m to the summit seemed to be particularly challenging for some ahead of us, as they appeared to be moving neither up nor down. As a result, more time was lost waiting for them to tentatively inch their way. After five hours, we were within a metre of the summit, but once again lost more time, waiting for a group to enjoy their lunch on the very small peak.

Following a disappointingly brief time on the summit, but not without taking in the panoramic view across to the Matterhorn, we made our decent, conscious that, by now, the snow and the snow bridges would be softening in the late-morning heat. Descending more rapidly than ideal, frequently stumbling and sliding as the snow gave way, we eventually reached the snow bridge, which now had a hole in the middle of it. We tentatively crossed over the crevasse and an hour later, arrived back at the hut.

By now, I was beginning to suffer from a long-term knee problem, but was unable to rest at the hut as there were just two hours before the cable car closed. Scampering down the ridge as quickly as we could, albeit slower than required, it soon became obvious that we were not going to make the cable car, and ended up walking all the way down to the village — 2,500m from the summit.

Parched and drained, we quenched our thirst, while I pondered on the Matterhorn.

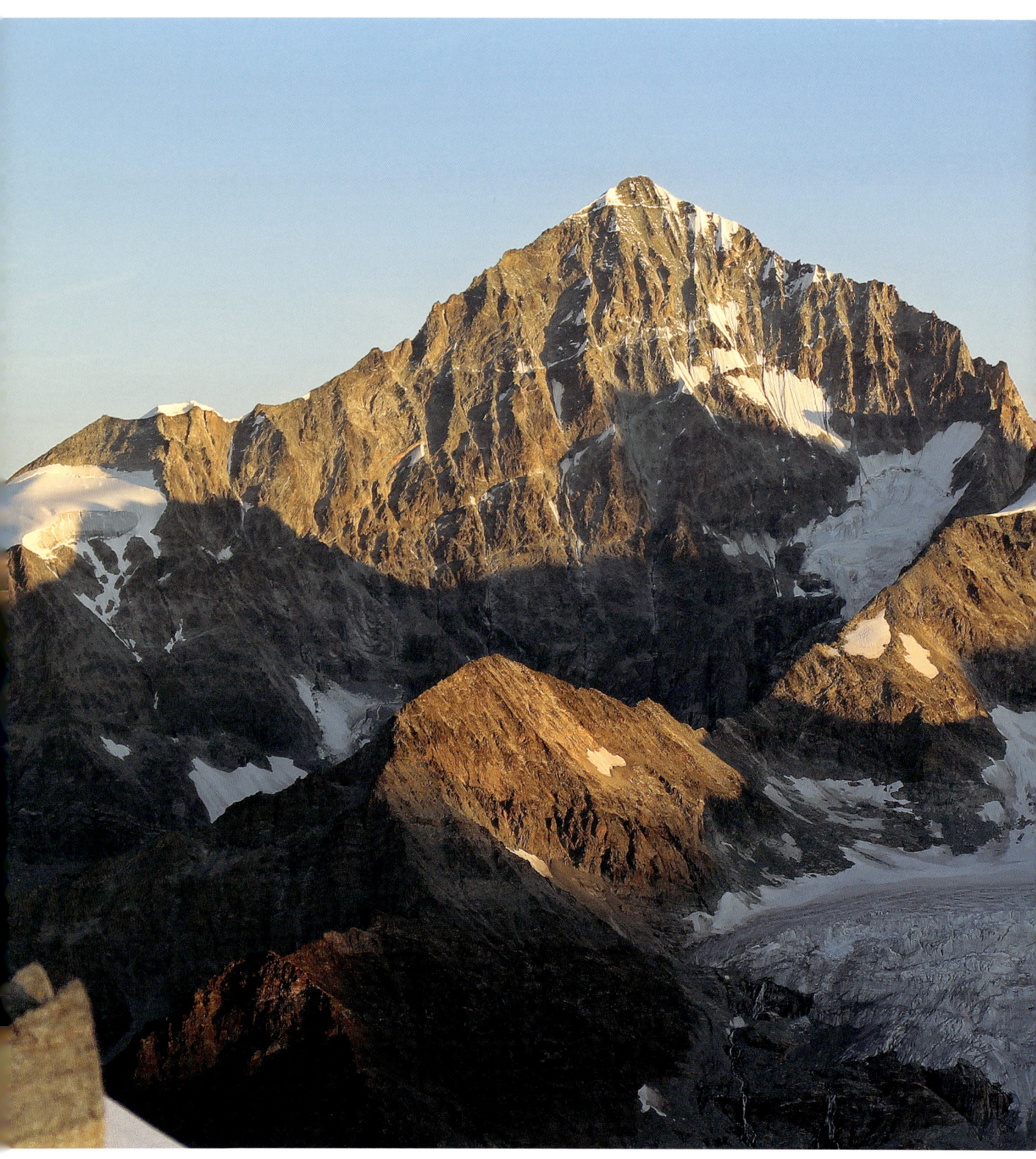

DENT BLANCHE 4,356M AND GRAND CORNIER 3,962M

Grand Cornier

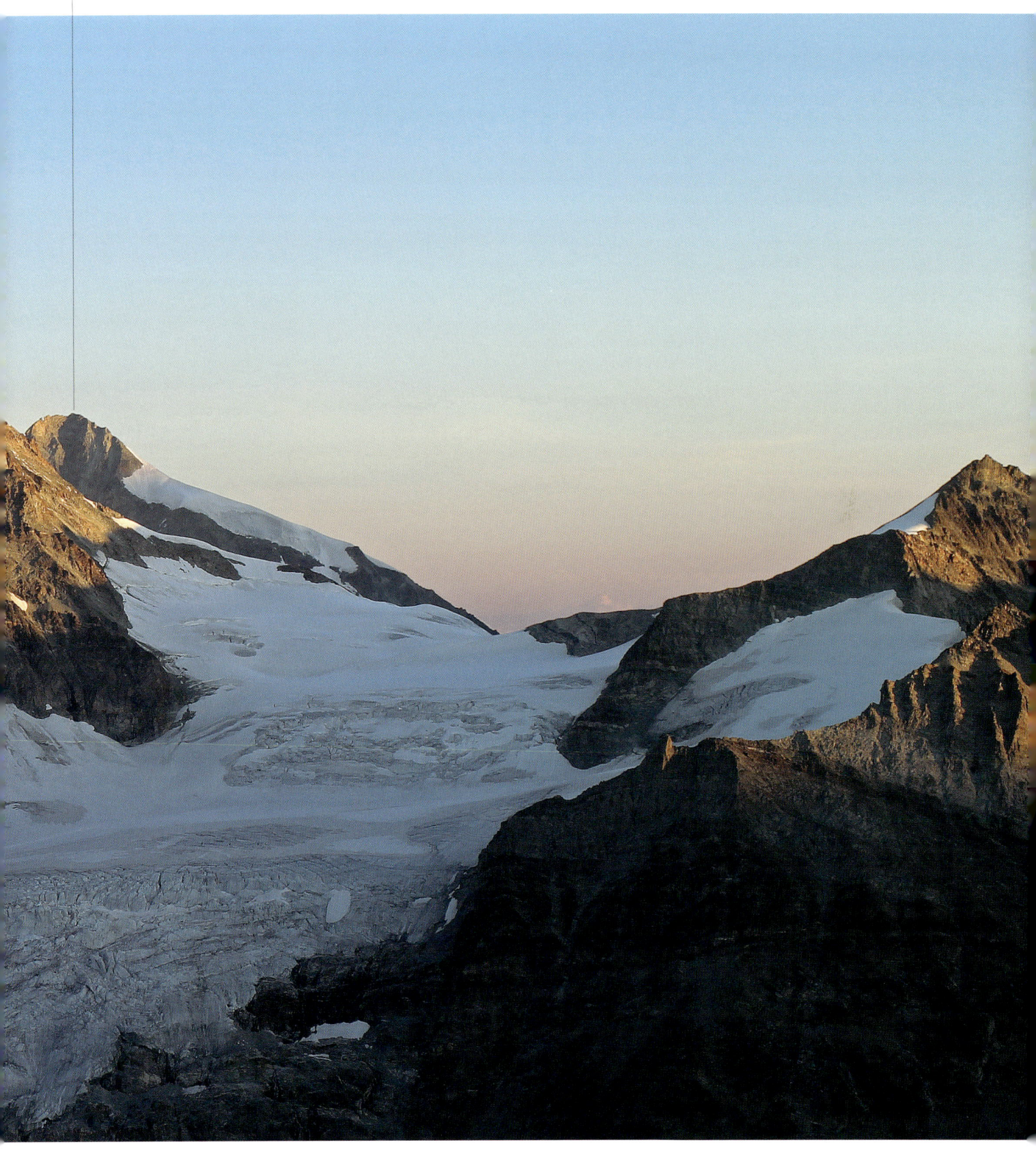

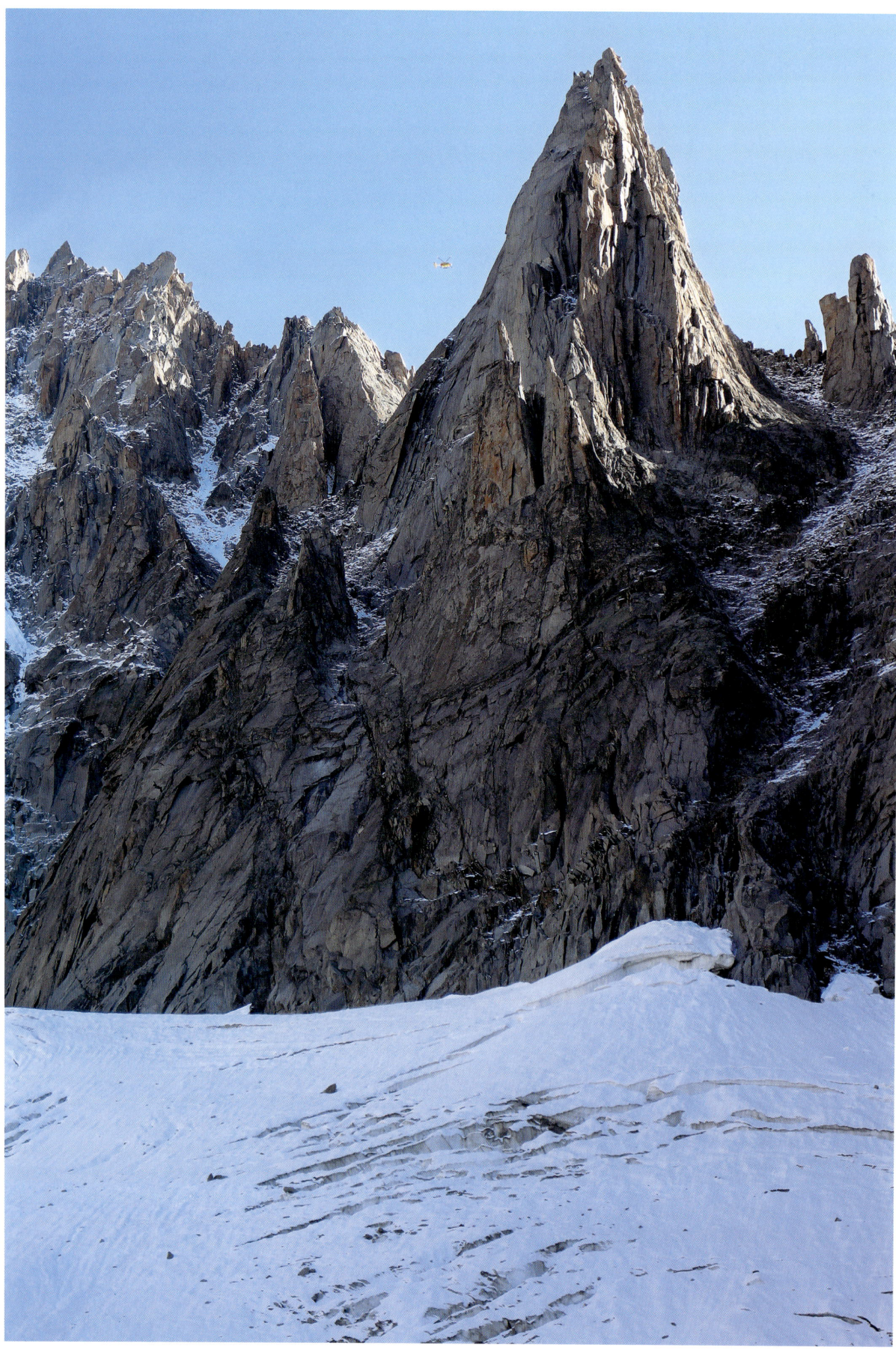

LE CARDINAL 3,647M, BELOW AIGUILLE VERTE, MONT BLANC MASSIF

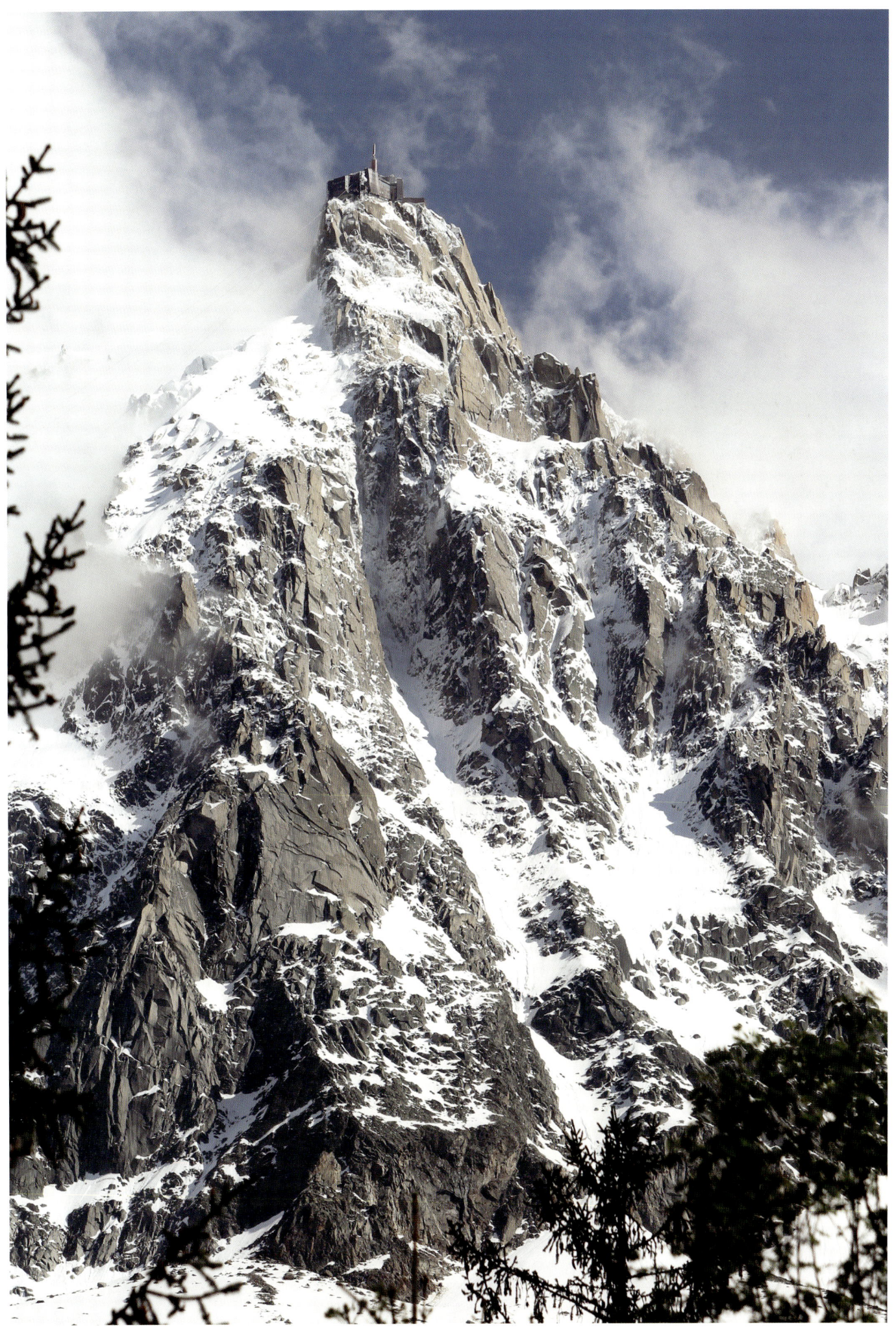

AIGUILLE DU MIDI 3,842M, MONT BLANC MASSIF

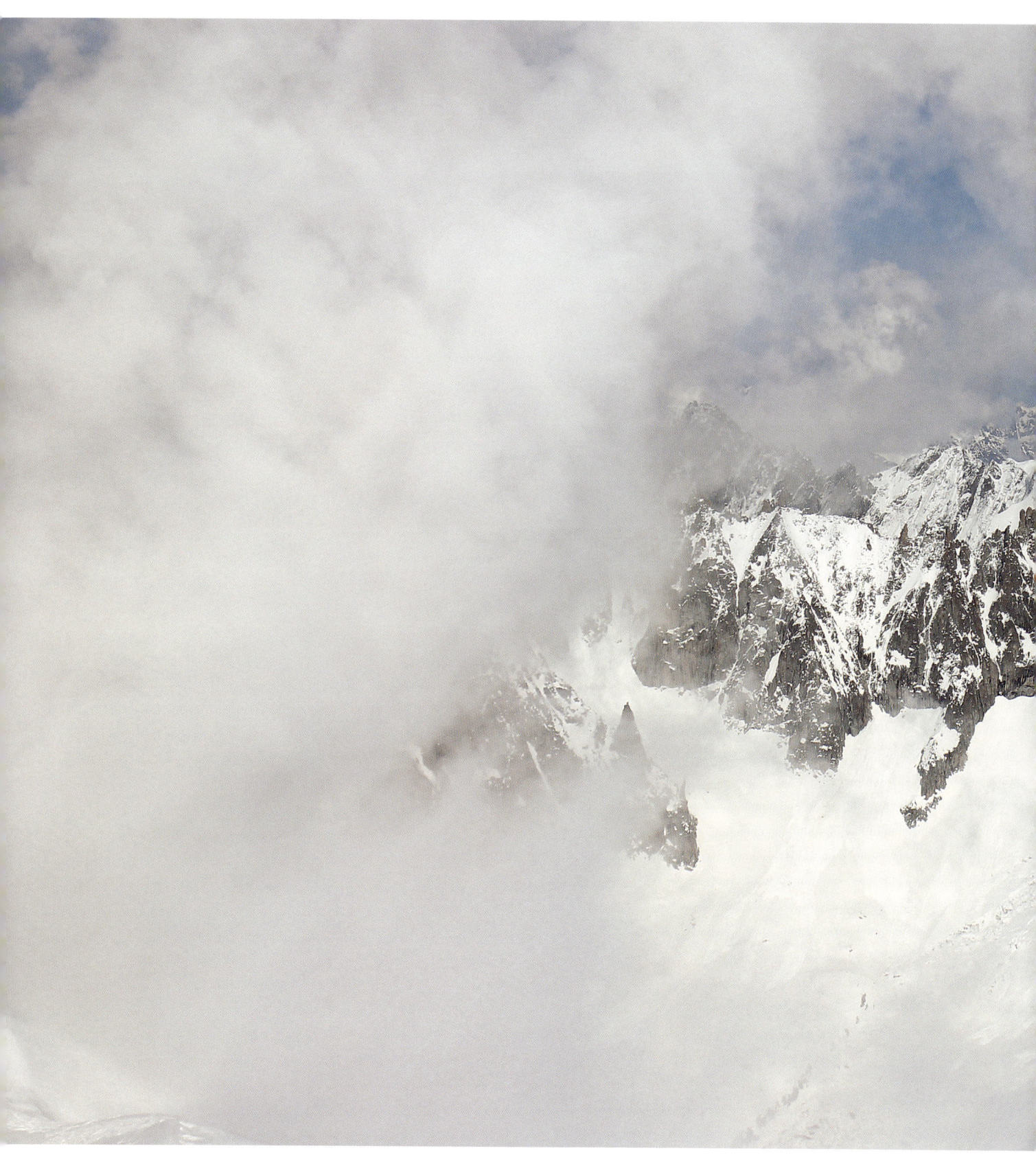

THE ROCHEFORT ARETE TO GRANDES JORASSES 4,208M, MONT BLANC MASSIF

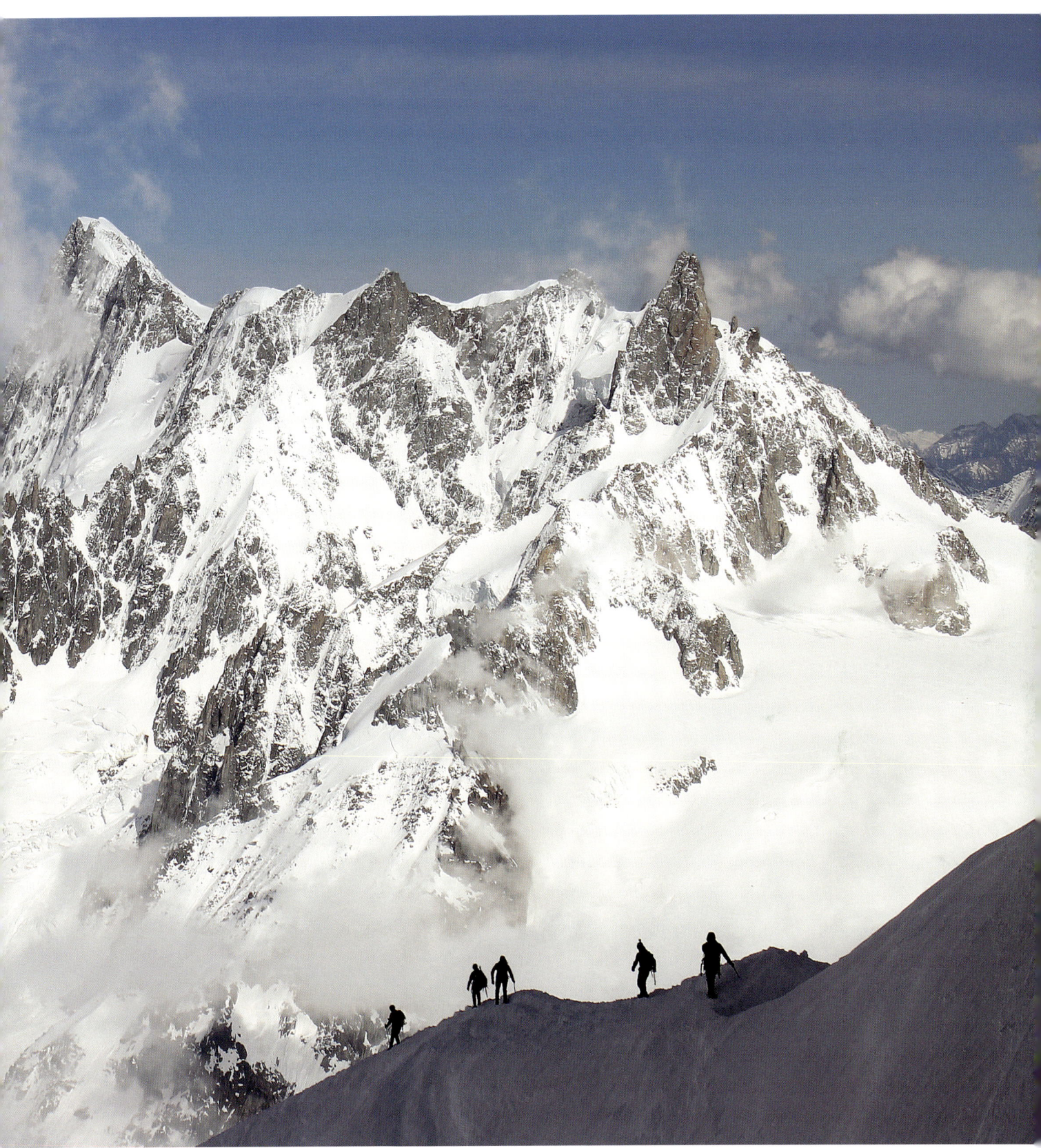

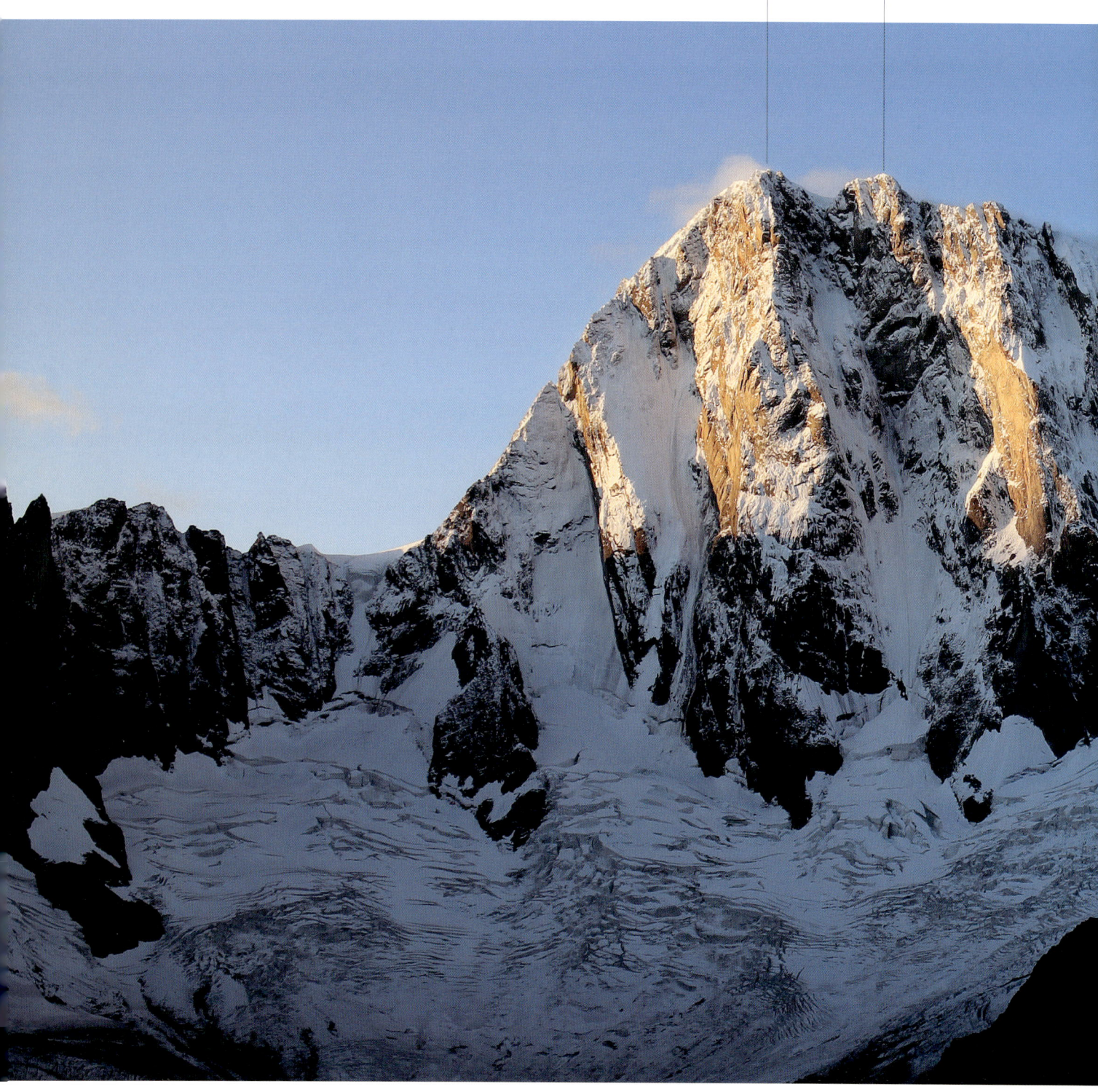

Grandes Jorasses 4,208m   *Pointe Whymper 4,184m*

GRANDES JORASSES 4,208M, MONT BLANC MASSIF

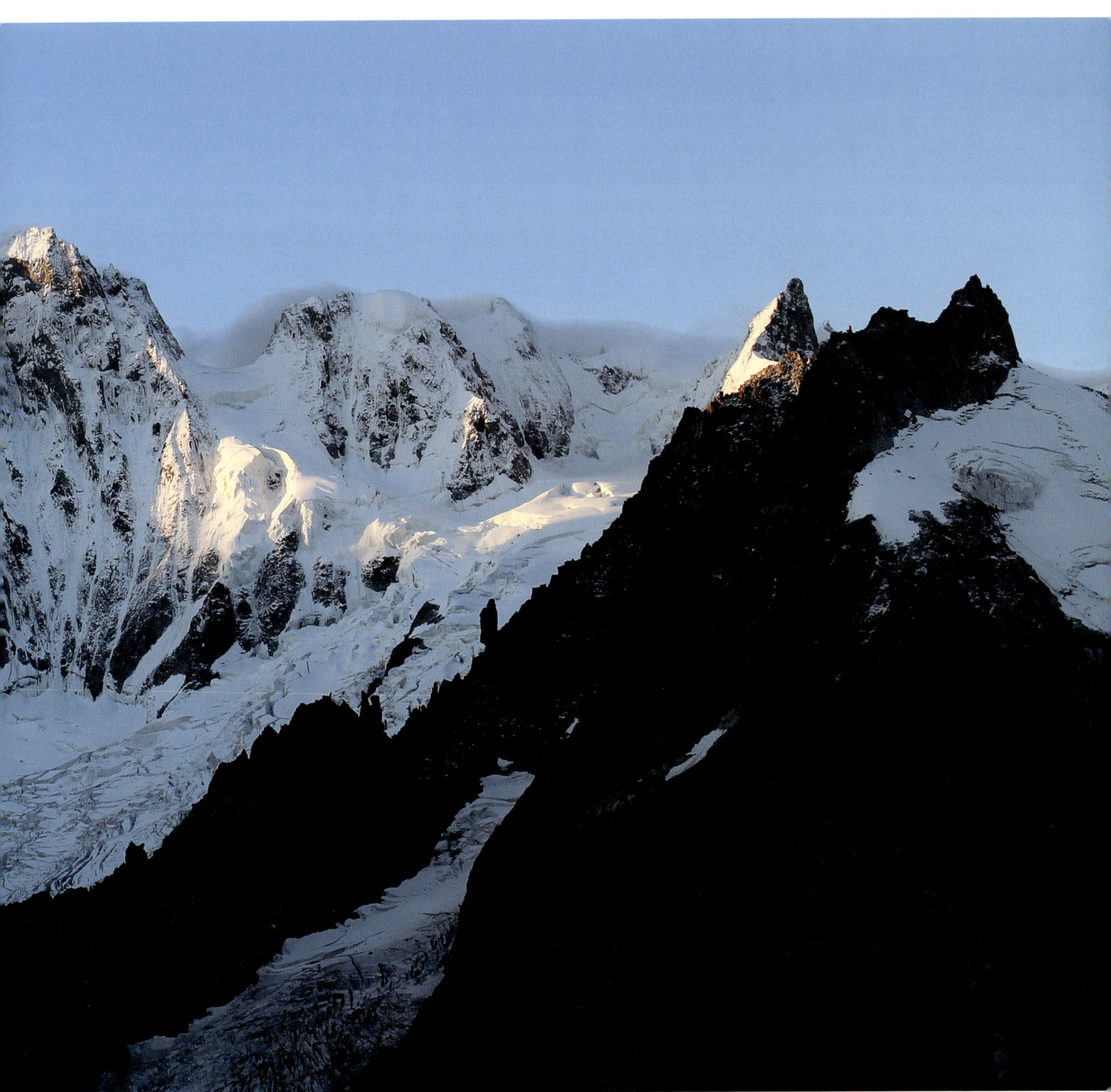

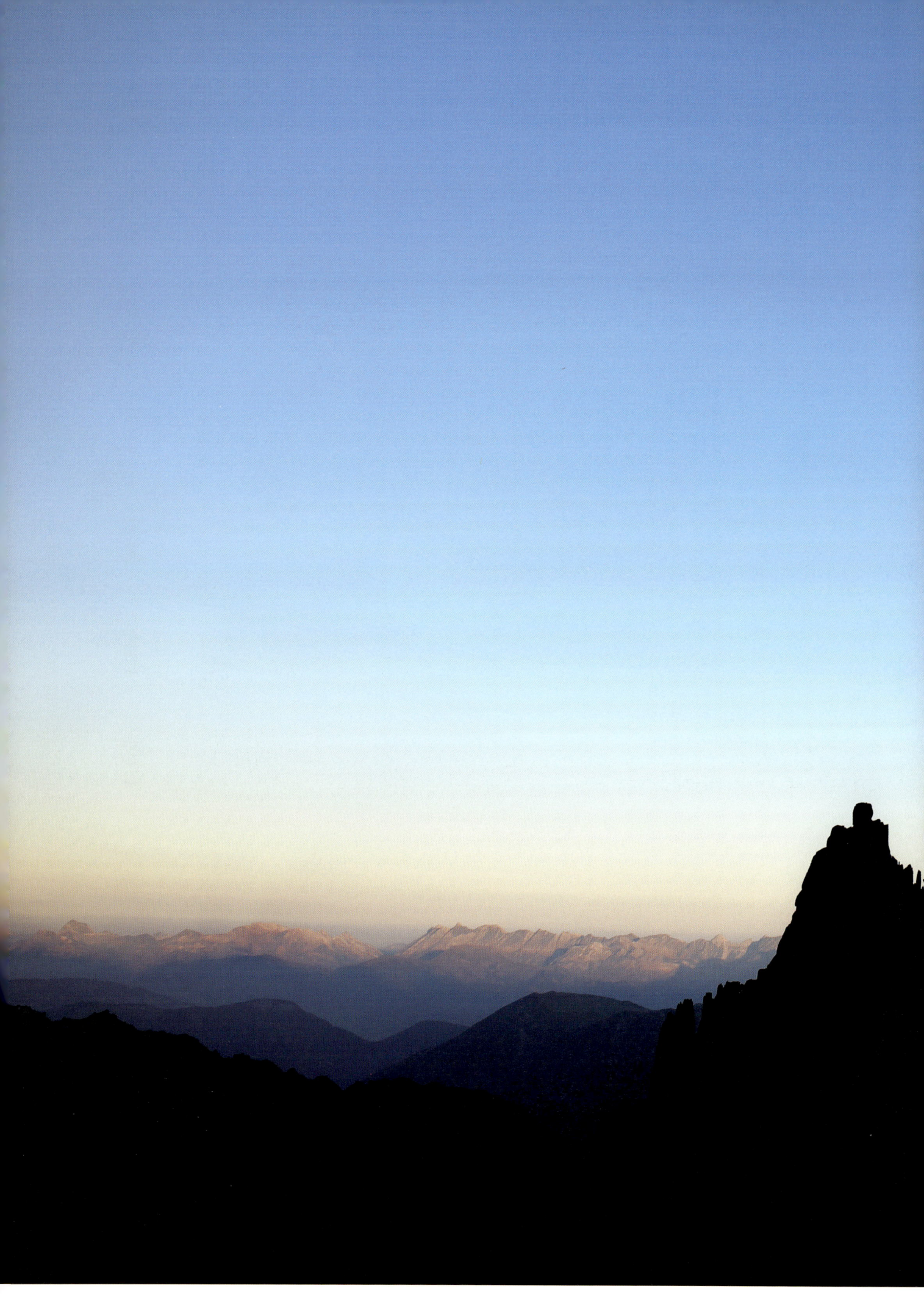

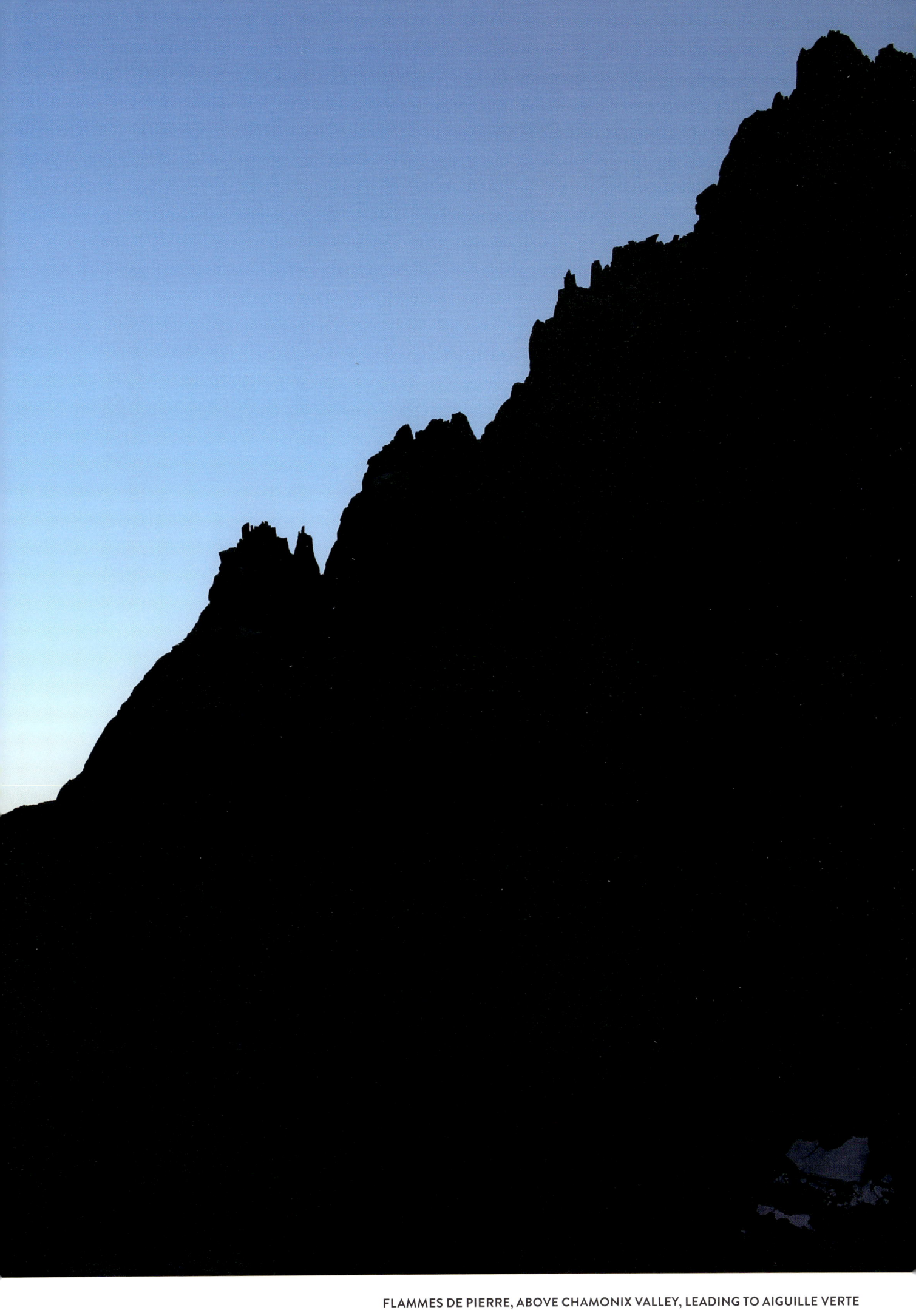
FLAMMES DE PIERRE, ABOVE CHAMONIX VALLEY, LEADING TO AIGUILLE VERTE

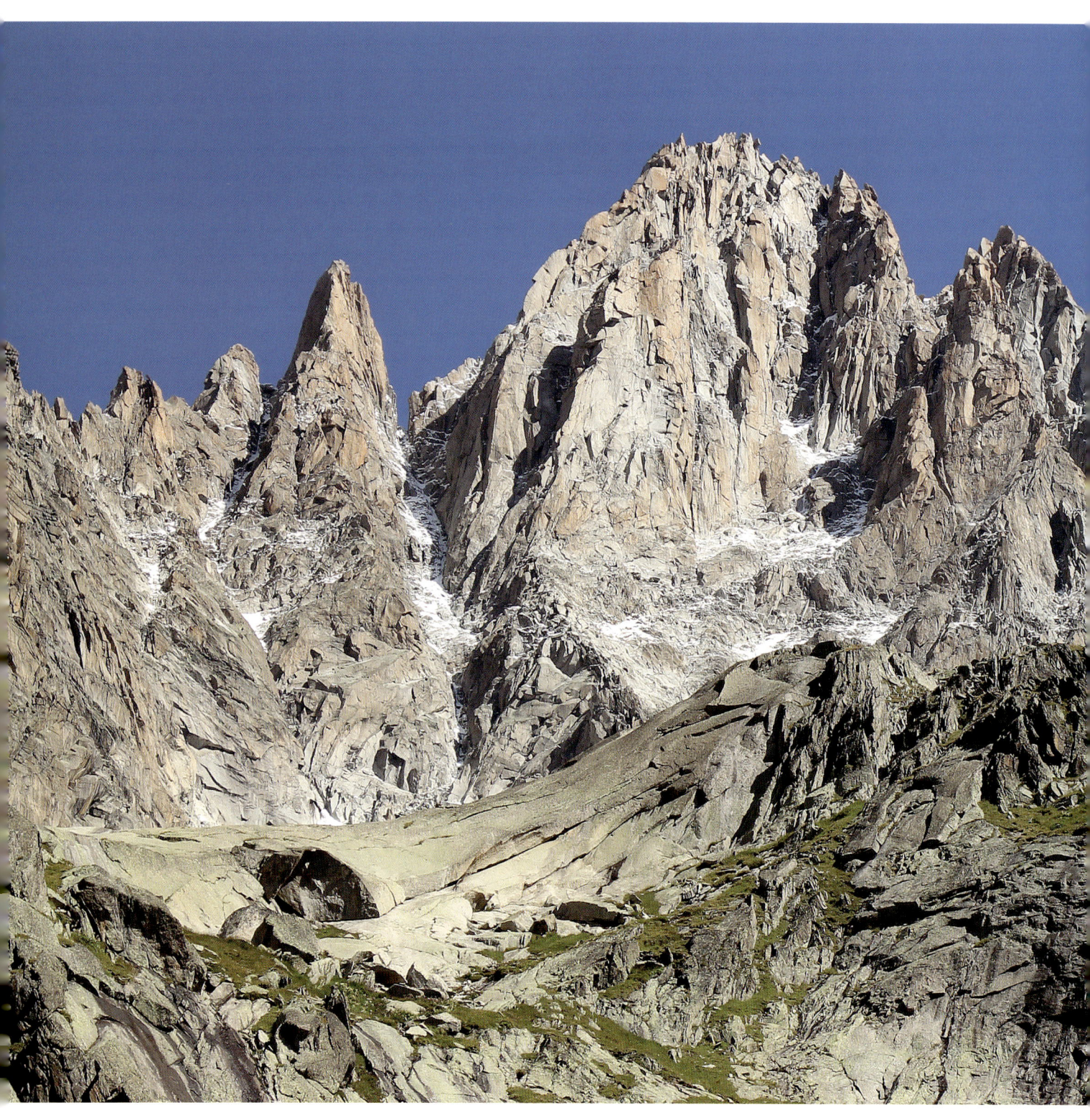
AIGUILLE SANS NOM 3,982M AND LE CARDINAL 3,647M, BELOW AIGUILLE VERTE

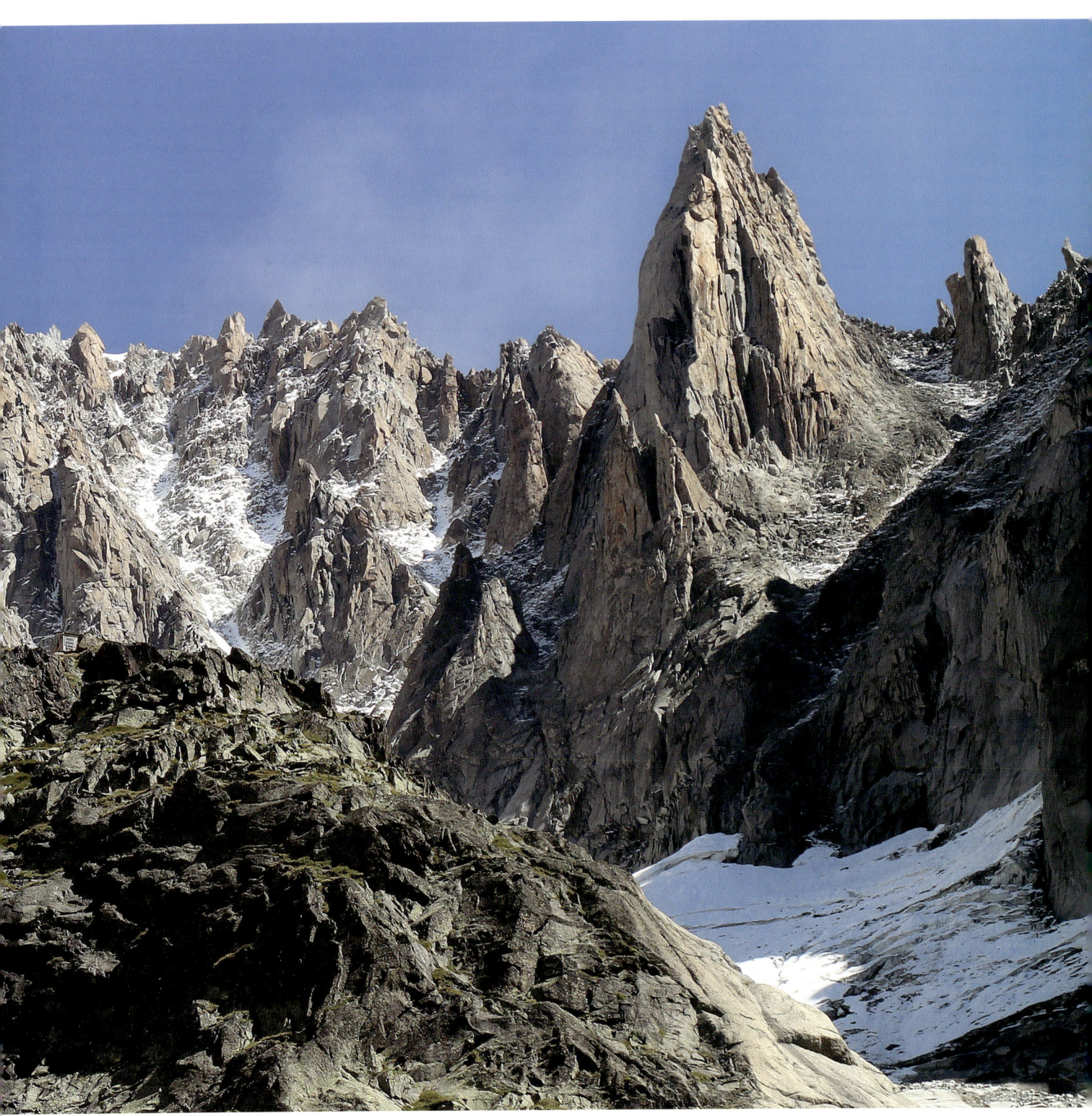

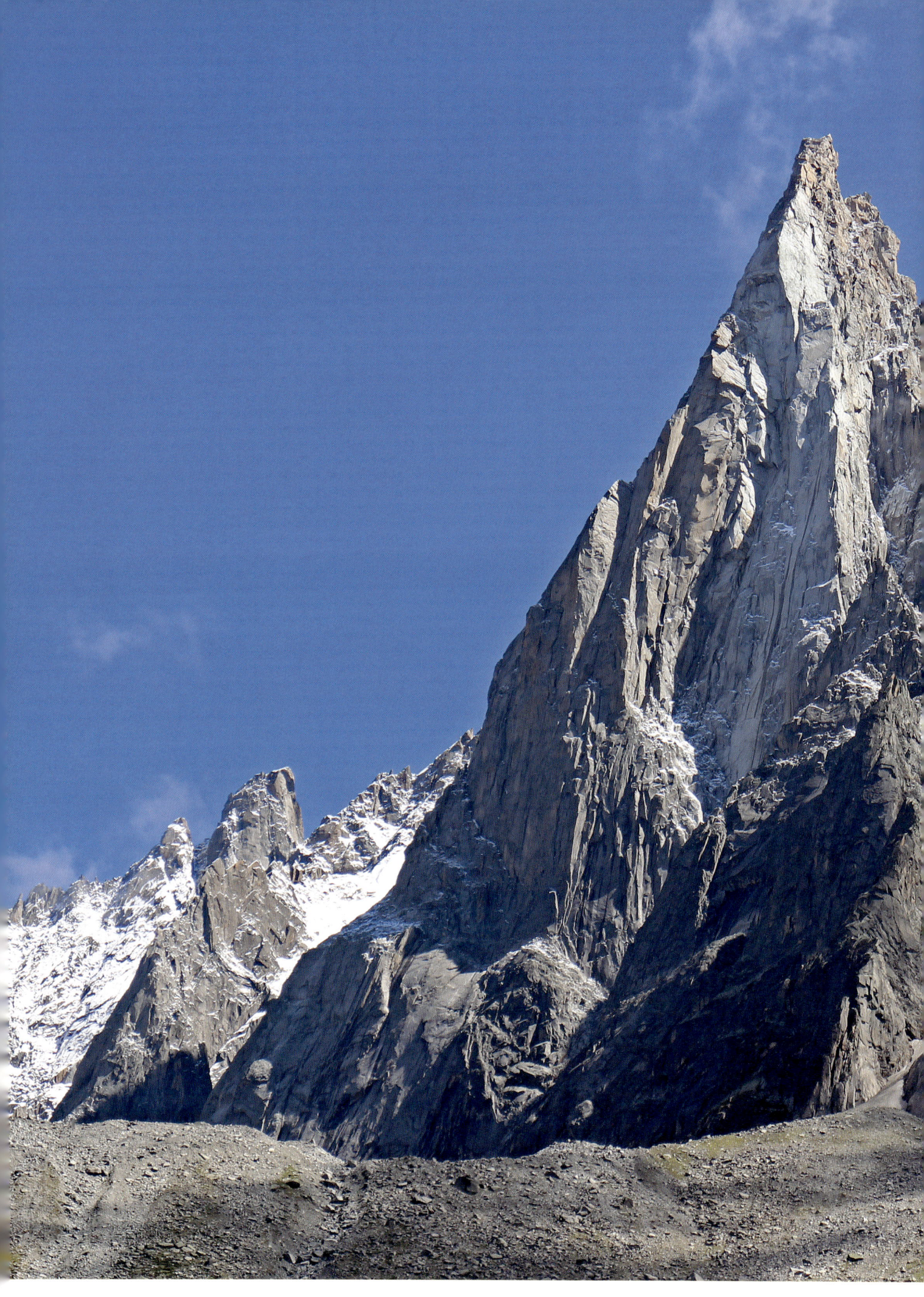

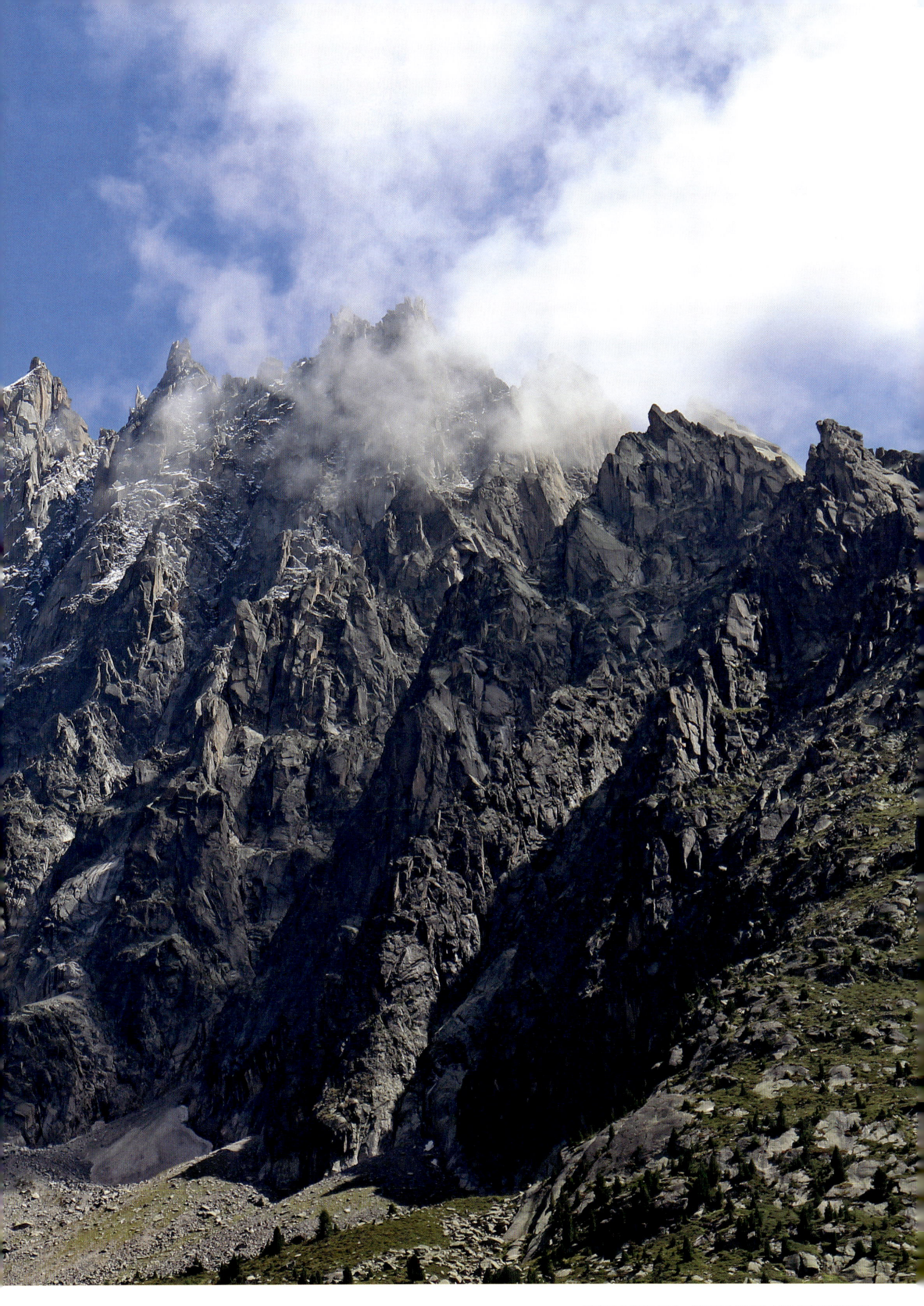

PETIT DRU 3,754M, LEADING TO AIGUILLE VERTE

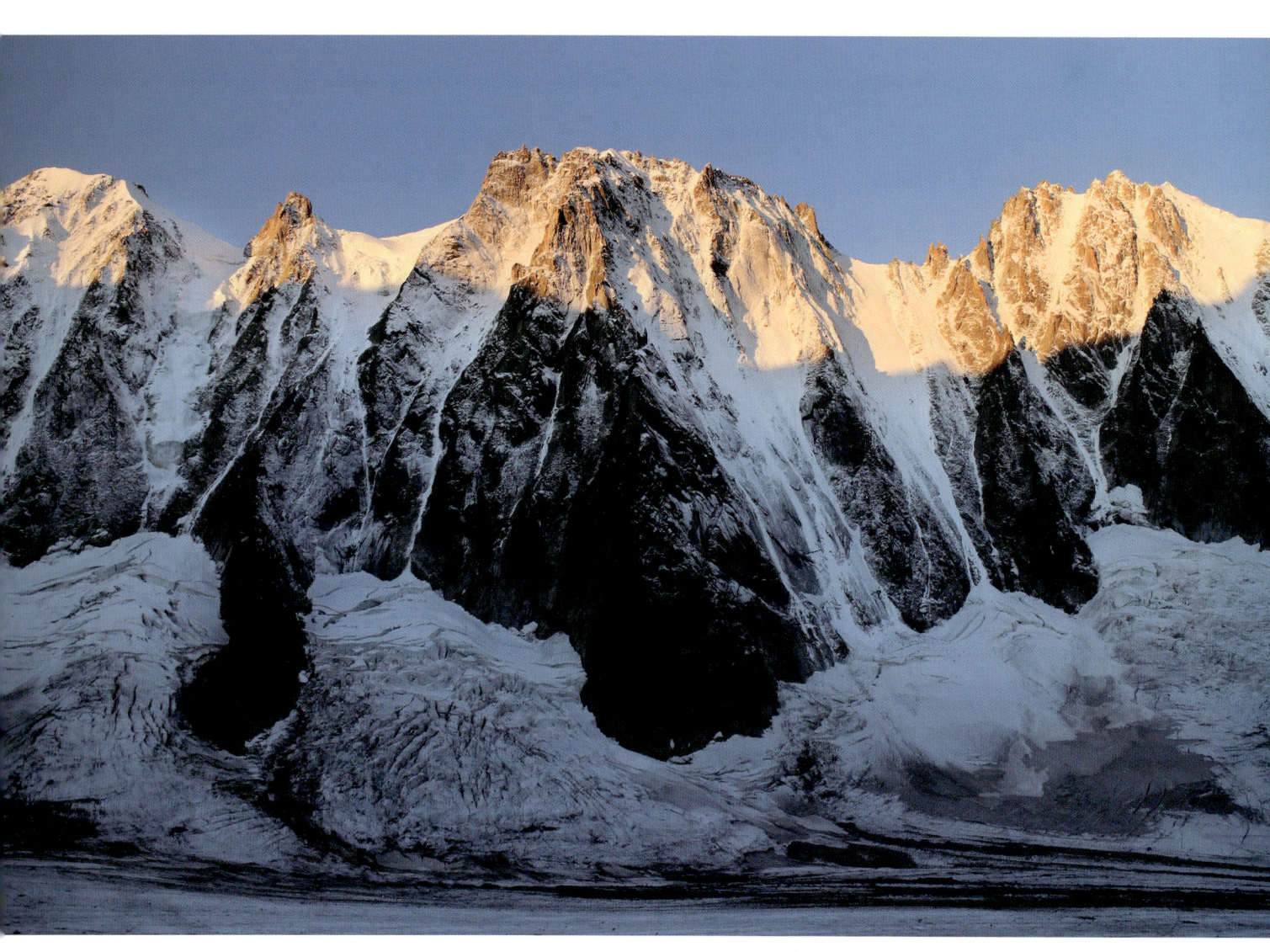
LES COURTES 3,856M, LES DROITES 4,000M AND AIGUILLE VERTE 4,122M, MONT BLANC MASSIF

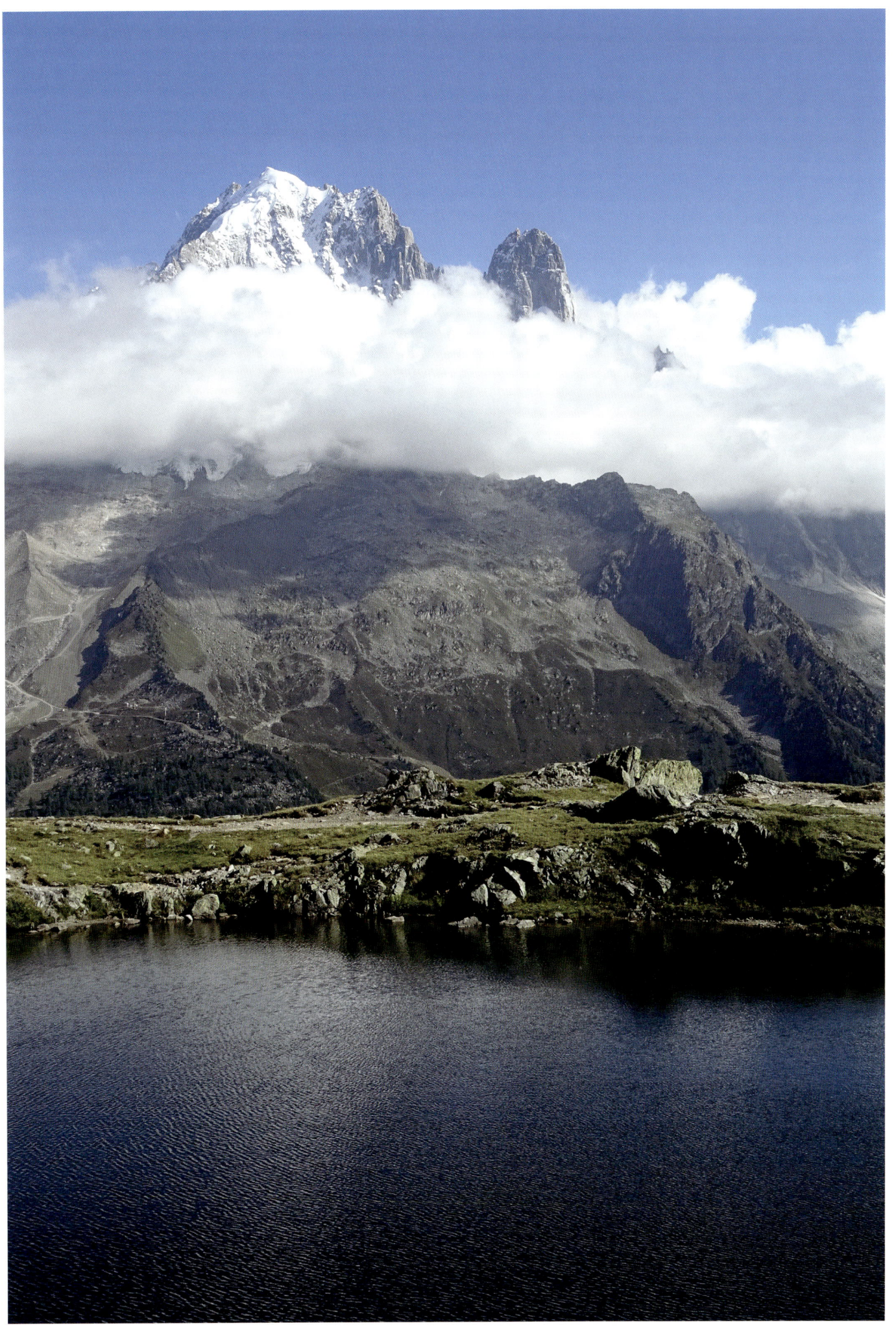

AIGUILLE VERTE FROM LAC DES CHÉSERYS

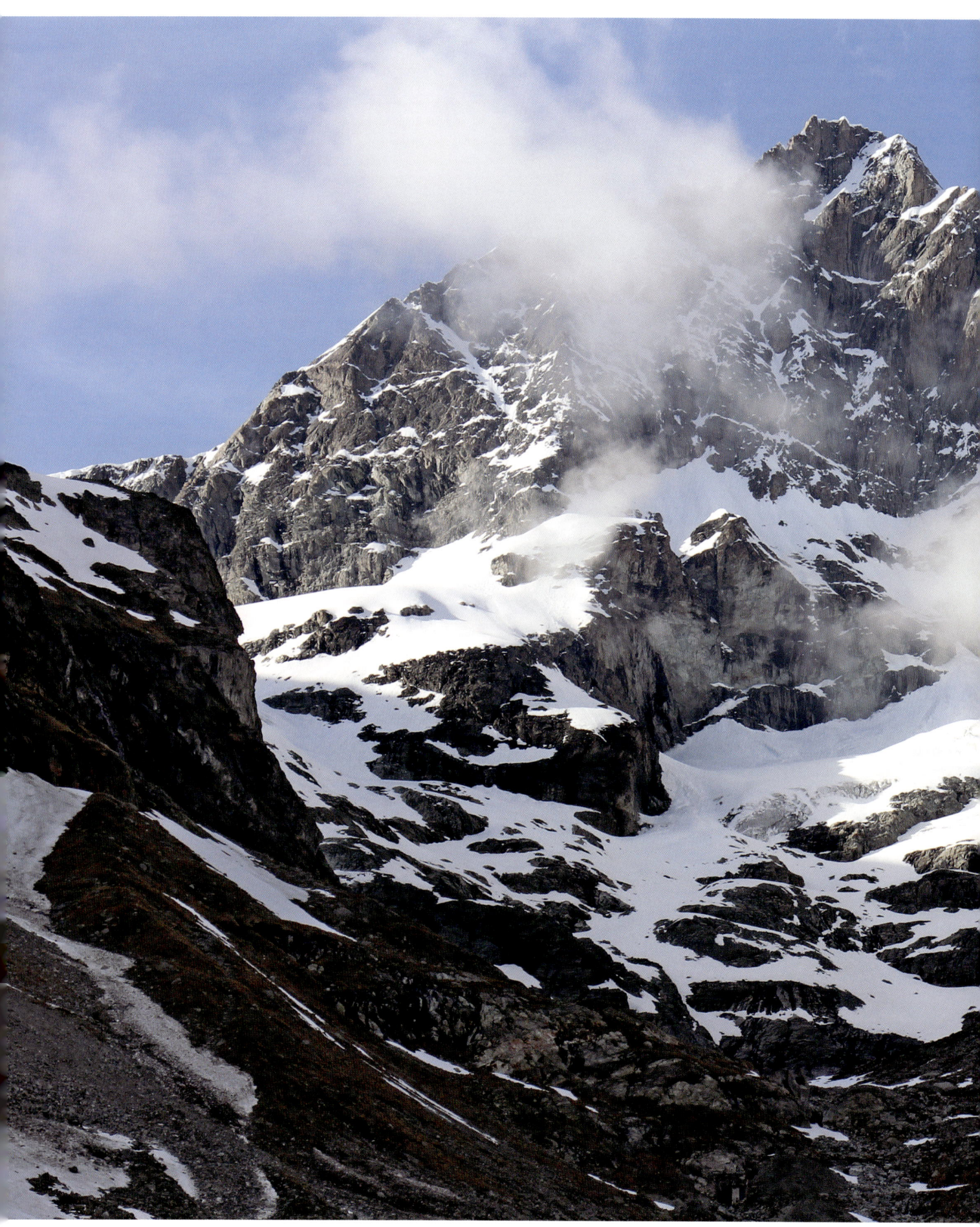
OBER GABELHORN 4,063M, PENNINE ALPS

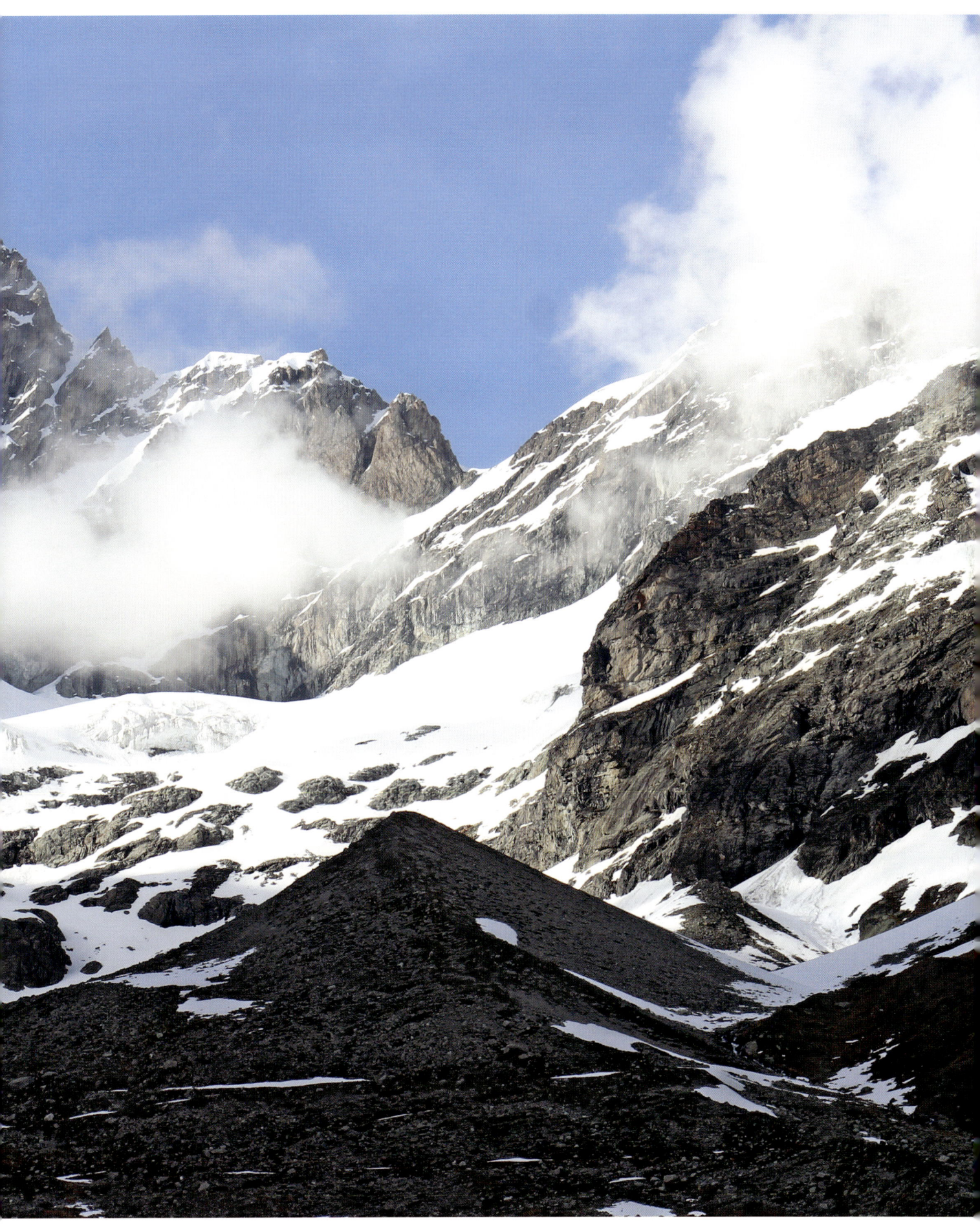

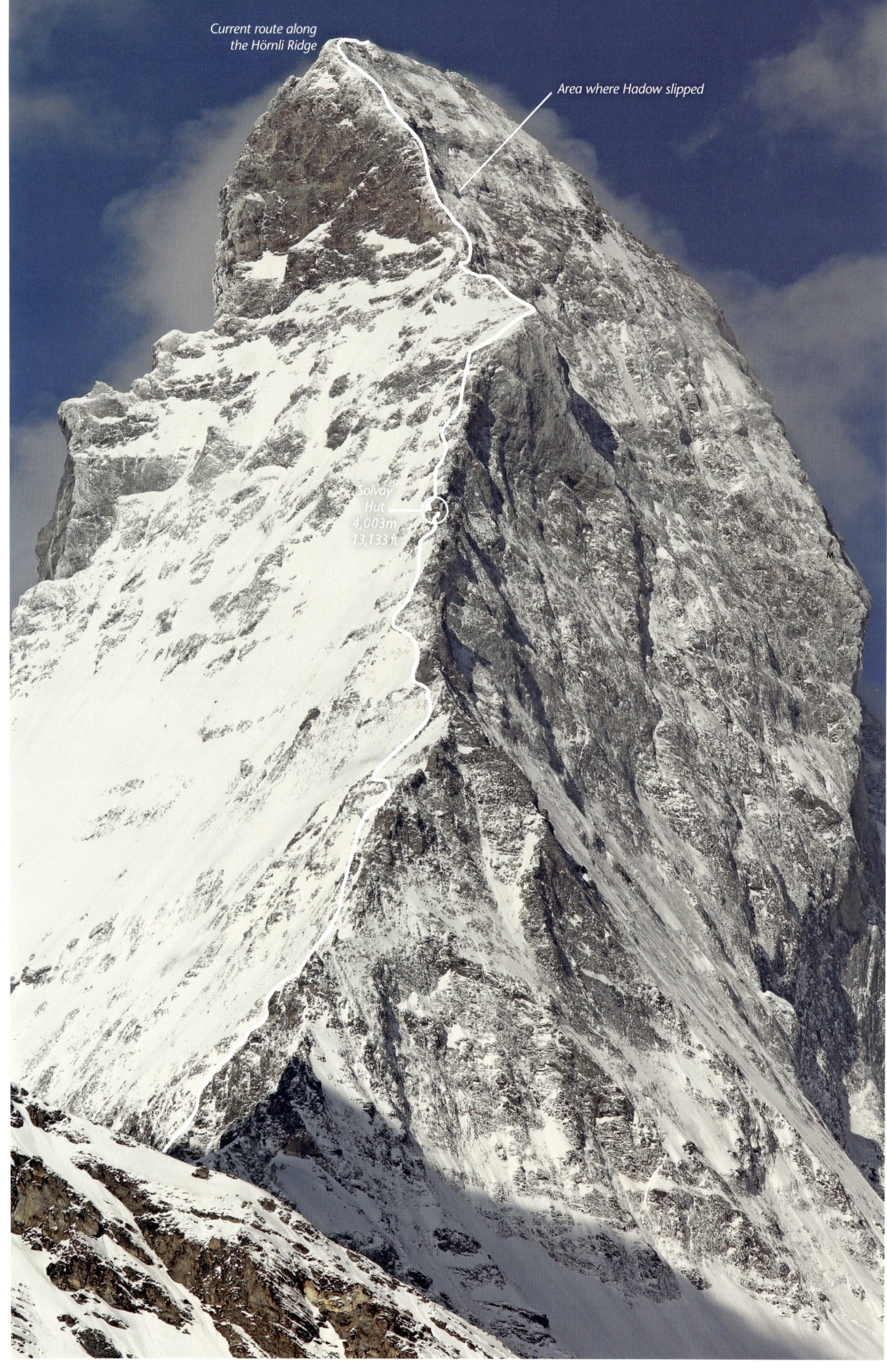

SUMMER 2015 (THE MATTERHORN; 4,478m)

AUTHOR'S LOG

It is well known that climbing the Matterhorn requires considerably more than technical climbing ability, and that the weather plays a significant part in achieving success. Despite the best planning and preparation, we were always going to be at the mercy of the elements. Two days of calm conditions, ideally during the second week, were what we were hoping for in order to give us time to acclimatise and settle in.

A month prior to our planned dates, no one was able to climb the Matterhorn from Italy, owing to the Carrel hut being closed as a result of a rockfall that had damaged the roof and dislodged some fixed ropes. Ironically, this had been caused by a prolonged spell of particularly warm, sunny weather, which had thawed the rock, allowing it to crumble. Too much of a good thing!

With two weeks to go, we received notification that the route was open and it looked like our decision to climb at the beginning of September had paid off. Then, with just one week to go, we were advised that an unsettled front was moving in and that climbing the Matterhorn on our intended dates would not be possible. We were encouraged to move them forward by three days, which we were potentially able to do, but that meant we would have less time to acclimatise and rest prior to our big day.

To complicate matters further, the Italian guide office was experiencing difficulty in finding guides for the revised dates, and we only learnt this on the morning on which we were heading out to climbed the Nadelhorn; a trip requiring all our attention and which could have done without the distraction. Remarkably, we found alternative guides at very short notice, but needed to amend our route and climb up and down the Hörnli Ridge instead of doing the international traverse that we had been so keen to do.

A final weather check confirmed that we did, indeed, have the perfect weather window and that the Italian guide office was accurate in warning of a long period of unsettled and snowy weather to arrive immediately after our climb. A week earlier the temperature had dropped and the freezing conditions had helped to stabilise the mountain, while the snow that had already fallen had settled and compacted, making travelling on it easier. The conditions could not have been better and waiting would most likely have resulted in no attempt being made. So, after so much uncertainty, the climb was on.

Having had only a day's rest after our marathon on the Nadelhorn, the morning of our walk up to the Hörnli hut arrived. We met our British guides: Sandy was a veteran and had climbed the north face in his teens, while John was coming to the end of a full summer in the Alps, and had just come down off Mont Blanc.

Following an introductory briefing we headed up to Schwarzsee by gondola, then started out by walking past the small lake and chapel where Whymper had stashed his equipment before his attempt up the Hönli Ridge. The two-hour walk up to the Hörnli hut was uneventful but gave us an opportunity to get to know each other and to gaze up at the ever-looming challenge immediately ahead.

Arriving at the refurbished Hörnli hut, we found it considerably busier than expected, which was somewhat alarming as this meant that there would be up to fifty pairs of people setting out in the morning with the same goal. At least the dormitories were relatively small and comfortable, increasing our chances of getting some sleep. A pleasant hour was spent on the terrace before a couple of hours on the Matterhorn to demonstrate our ability to our guides. It was immediately obvious how route-finding could be problematic and that the heavily fragmented rock would be a constant hazard. Assured of our competence, we returned for dinner and an early night.

As our guides were not local, we were given a 4 a.m. breakfast slot, which meant that despite getting up at 3:30 a.m. the corridors were already buzzing and there was a huddle of bodies at the exit waiting to be released. A calm but anxious mood filled the hut as ice axes clanked and ropes were coiled, securing climber to guide. Following one of the quickest breakfasts I've ever had, it was our turn and we exited the building with head-torch beams piercing the morning darkness, just sufficient to avoid stumbling over the scattered rocks.

Within minutes, a rope climb was required to get on to the ridge and we were immediately presented with what seemed to be one of the most frustrating aspects of climbing in the Alps: a line of people ahead waiting their turn on the fixed rope, leaving us no choice but to stand in the cold for over twenty minutes. Eventually, we ascended the rope and, despite going at a relatively easy and steady pace, started to pass climbers who were struggling on the broken and icy rock. Travelling in the dark within feet of the guides, we progressed in an almost hypnotic state for a couple of hours, until the rising sun provided some illumination, spectacularly revealing the landscape below.

Despite making good progress it was clear that Mat and his guide were quicker, and not wishing to impact on his chances of success, I suggested that they go on at a speed with which they were comfortable. Although the Solvay hut at 4,003m is more than halfway up the ridge, it is generally considered the halfway point and the place at which guides calculate whether their clients can reach the summit in time and have the ability to complete the day. Conscious of my own pace, the need for my guide to catch the last gondola car, and the ongoing concern that I could be slower in descending, I decided to abort my climb a little way below the hut. Saddened at making such a decision when I had not been faced with any technical or physical challenge beyond my ability, I knew that a second night at the Hörnli hut would have almost certainly guaranteed success.

Meanwhile, Mat made easy progress until the Lower Mosely Slab, which required climbing a vertical, then a horizontal rope section that proved particularly hard-going, having not rested since the start of the relentless climb. Jumping ahead of several groups by not stopping at the Solvay hut, the Upper Mosely Slab proved easier, but led to a narrowing of the ridge, with increased exposure requiring even greater alertness. From there, crampons were necessary to cross the mixture of snow and rock up to the Shoulder.

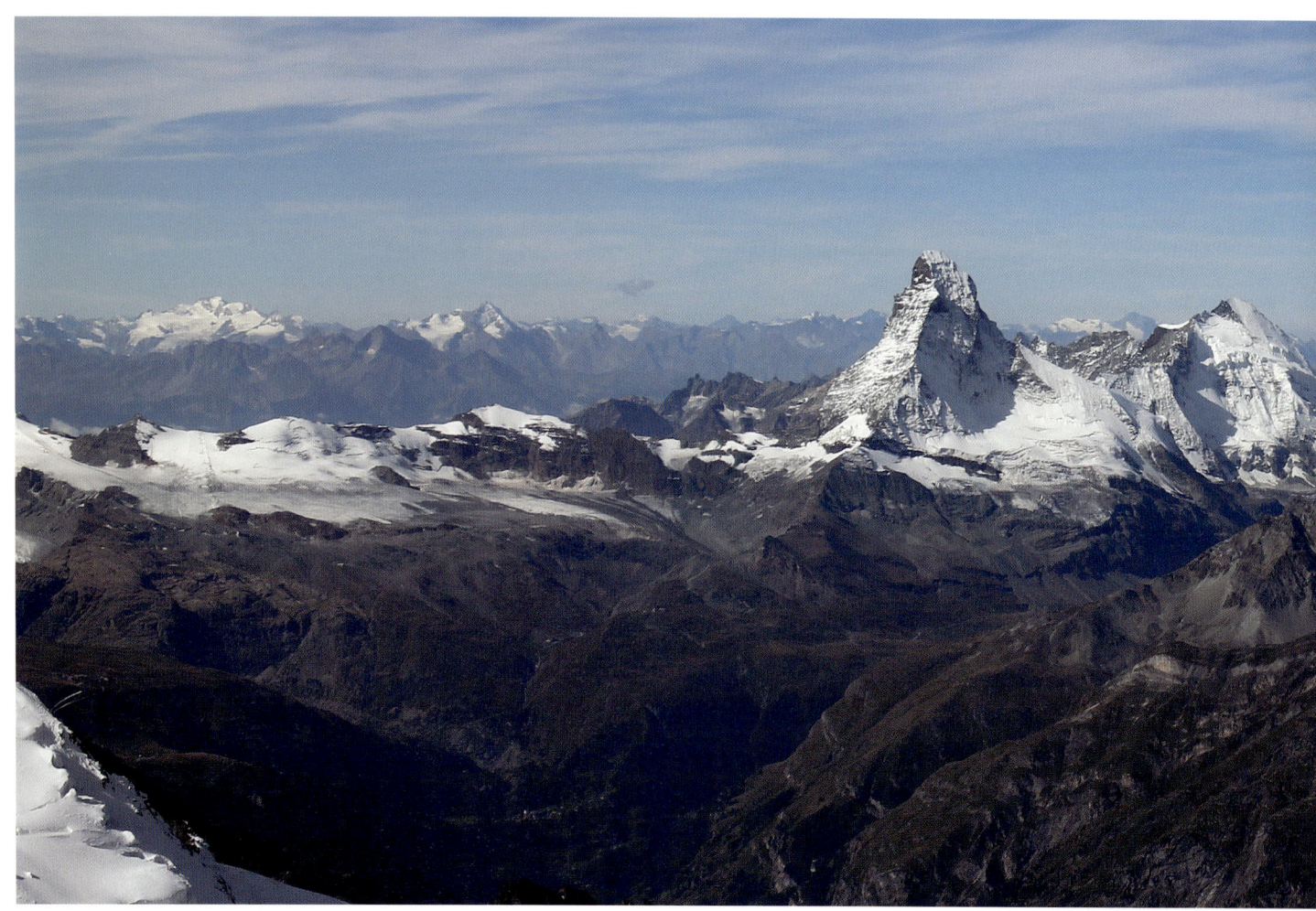

Another vertical fixed-rope section again proved strenuous and particularly challenging, as part of it was buried in frozen snow. This led to the 'roof', which, although not especially difficult at 35–40 degrees, was the most demanding part for Mat, felling at his weakest since the start. However, the sight of the summit crest spurred him on, and at 9:45 a.m. he was on the summit of the Matterhorn … seven years after his first attempt.

The all-too-brief time on the summit was filled with a mixture of emotions: relief at having accomplished a climb that had truly tested his ability; at the fulfilment of a long-held goal that meant so much to him; and knowing how much it would mean to his family, who had believed in him for so long.

The return takes an equal amount of time, if not longer, so there were still nearly five hours of down-climbing to the Hörnli hut. With a greater and more dangerous period ahead, alertness was crucial in finding the safest and most solid ground over which to descend.

Safely off the north face and below the Lower Mosley Slab, just as fatigue was setting in and adrenaline taking over, they found themselves unexpectedly on very loose rock and immediately realised they had deviated off route. Following some especially challenging and anxious down-climbing, and by lowering and traversing they managed to regain the right line without incident and proceeded on down more familiar territory.

After 9½ hours on the mountain, they reached the hut, exhausted, relieved, parched, thrilled and elated.

As forecast, the following day witnessed an immediate deterioration in the weather, which remained unsettled with very low cloud, rain and snow for the whole week. Prior to returning home, there was a distinctive autumnal feel in the air and even when the settled conditions returned, we felt sure the fresh snow would prevent any further attempt on the Matterhorn for the remainder of the 2015 season.

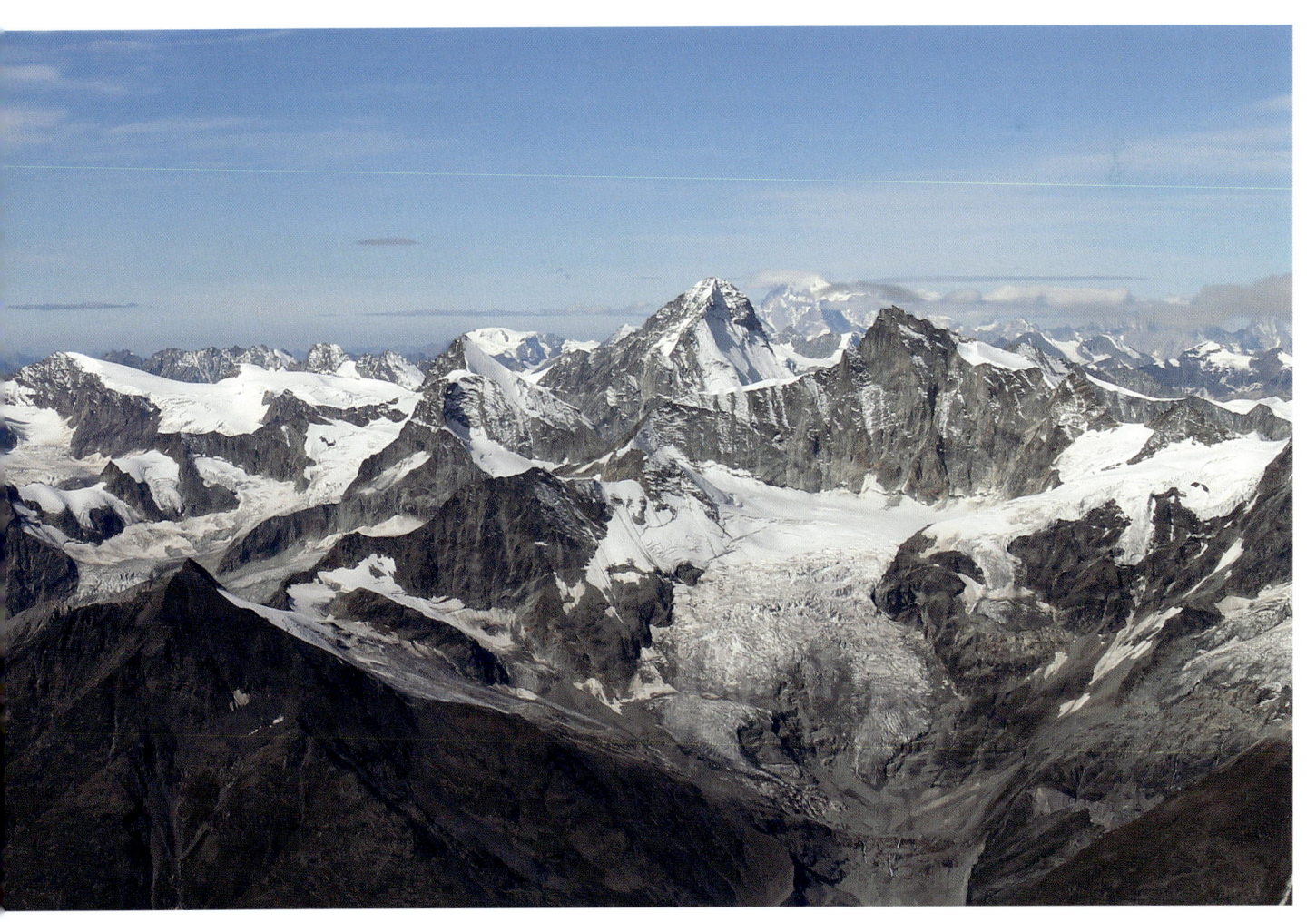

THE MATTERHORN AND WESTERLY PEAKS FROM THE NADELHORN

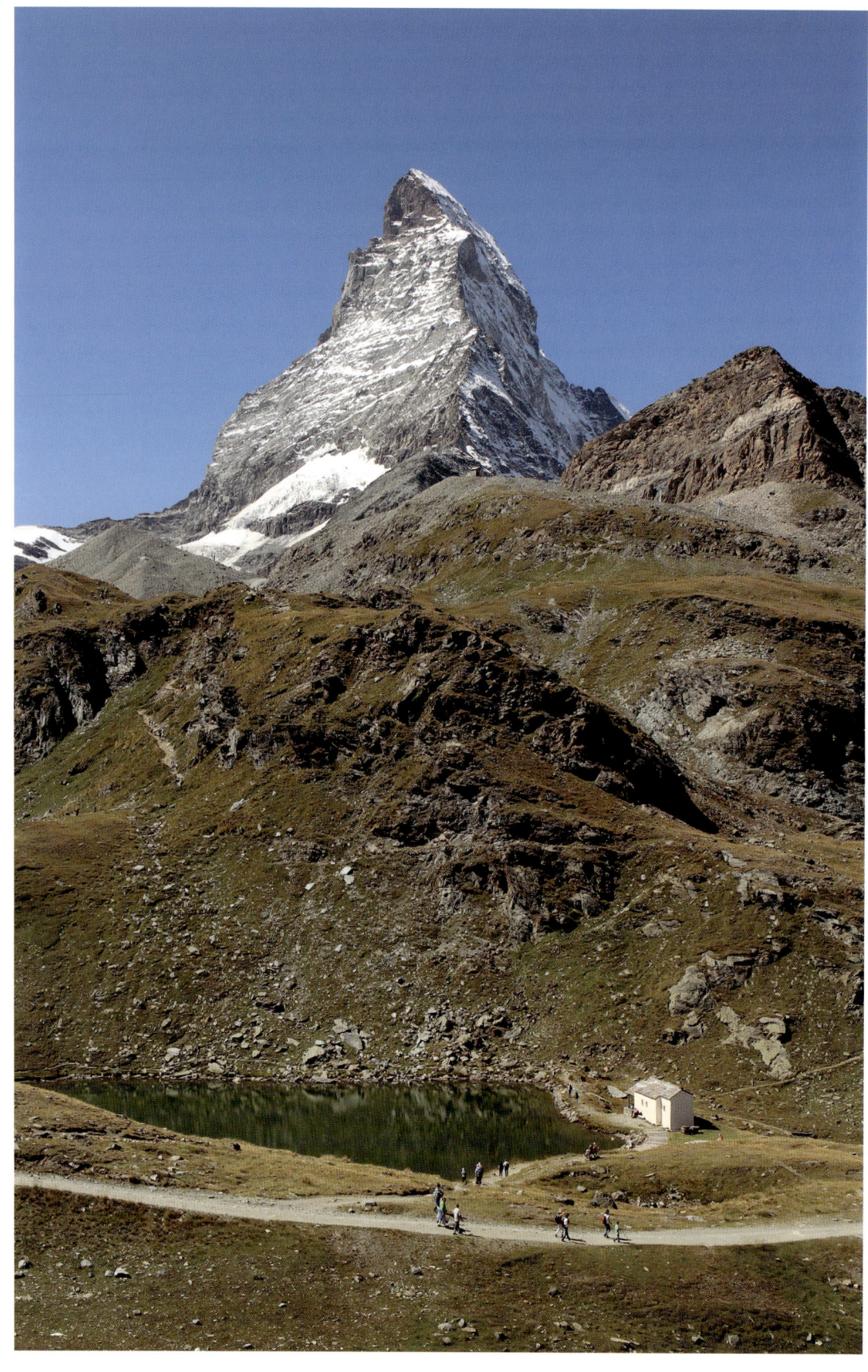

SCHWARZSEE LAKE

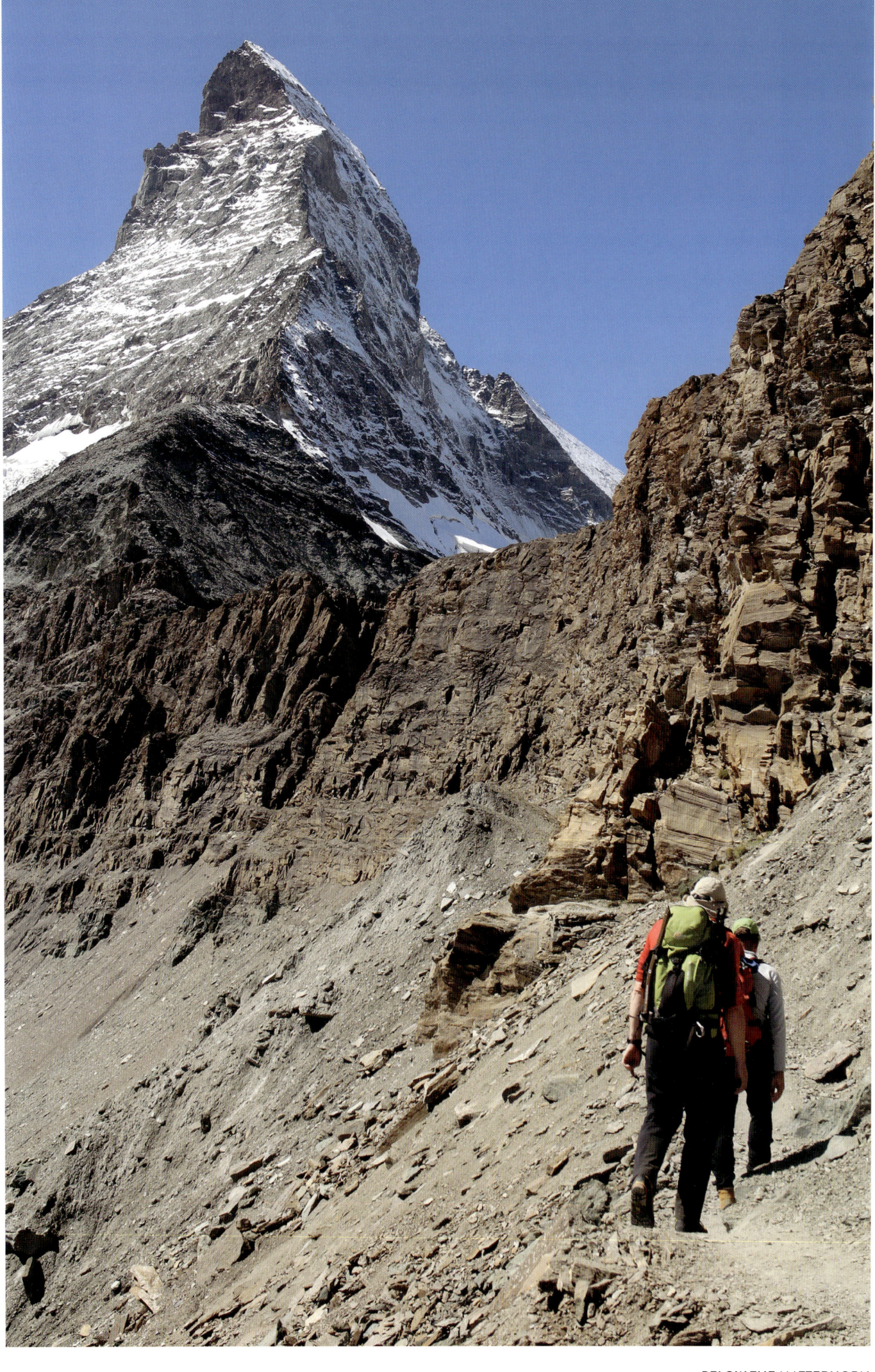

BELOW THE MATTERHORN

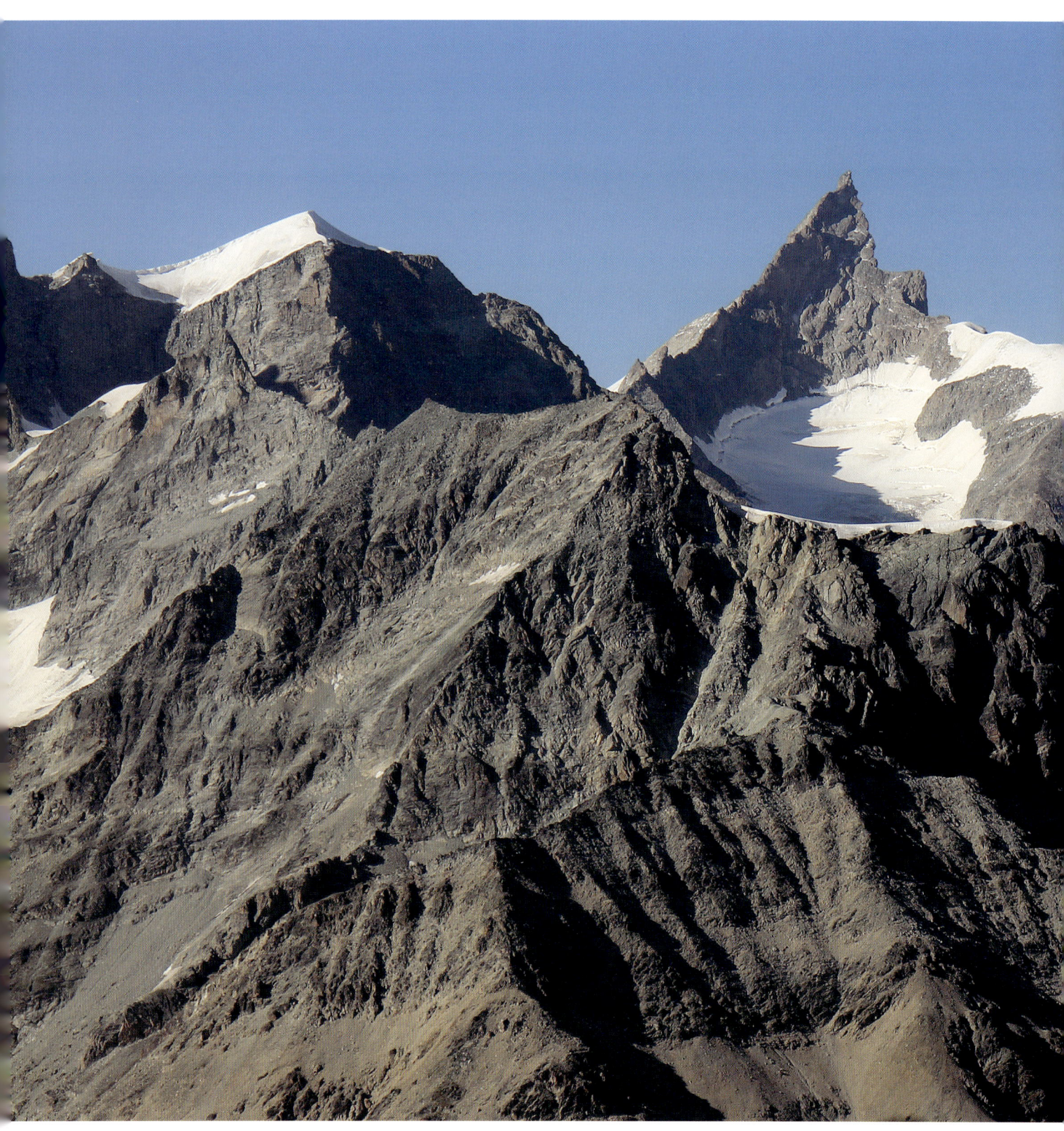

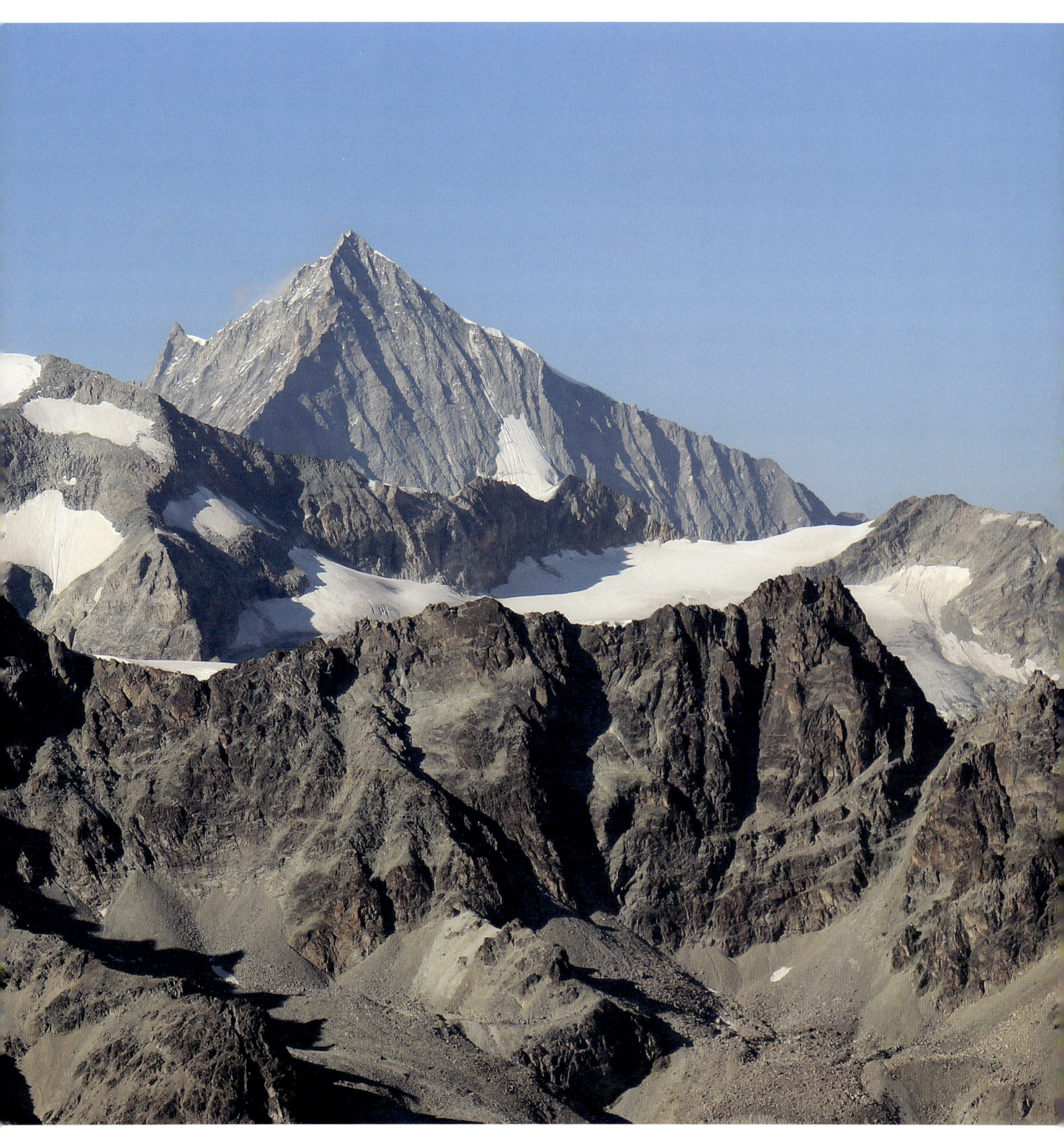

ZINALROTHORN 4,221M AND WEISSHORN 4,506M

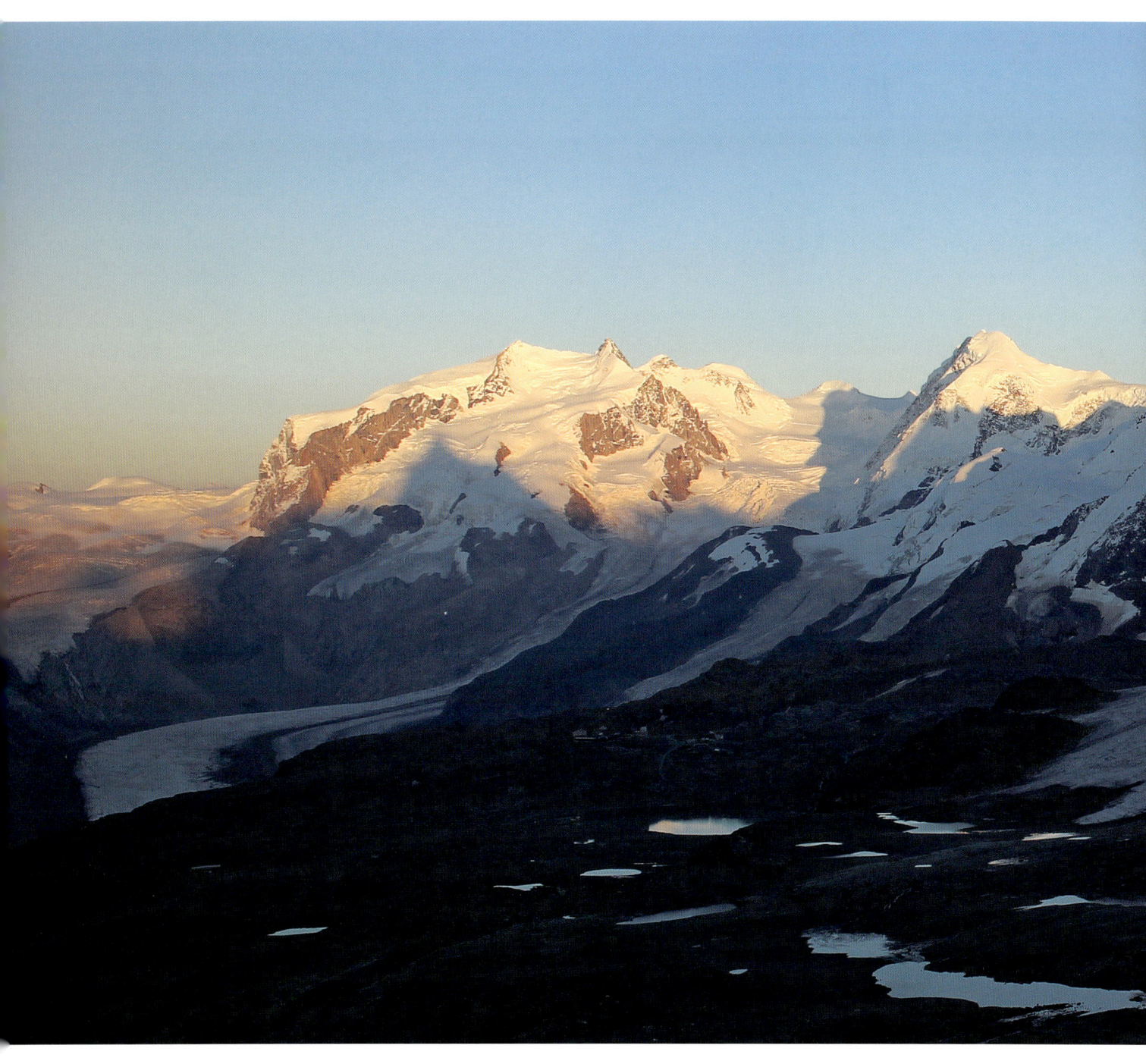
THE MONTE ROSA RANGE, PENNINE ALPS

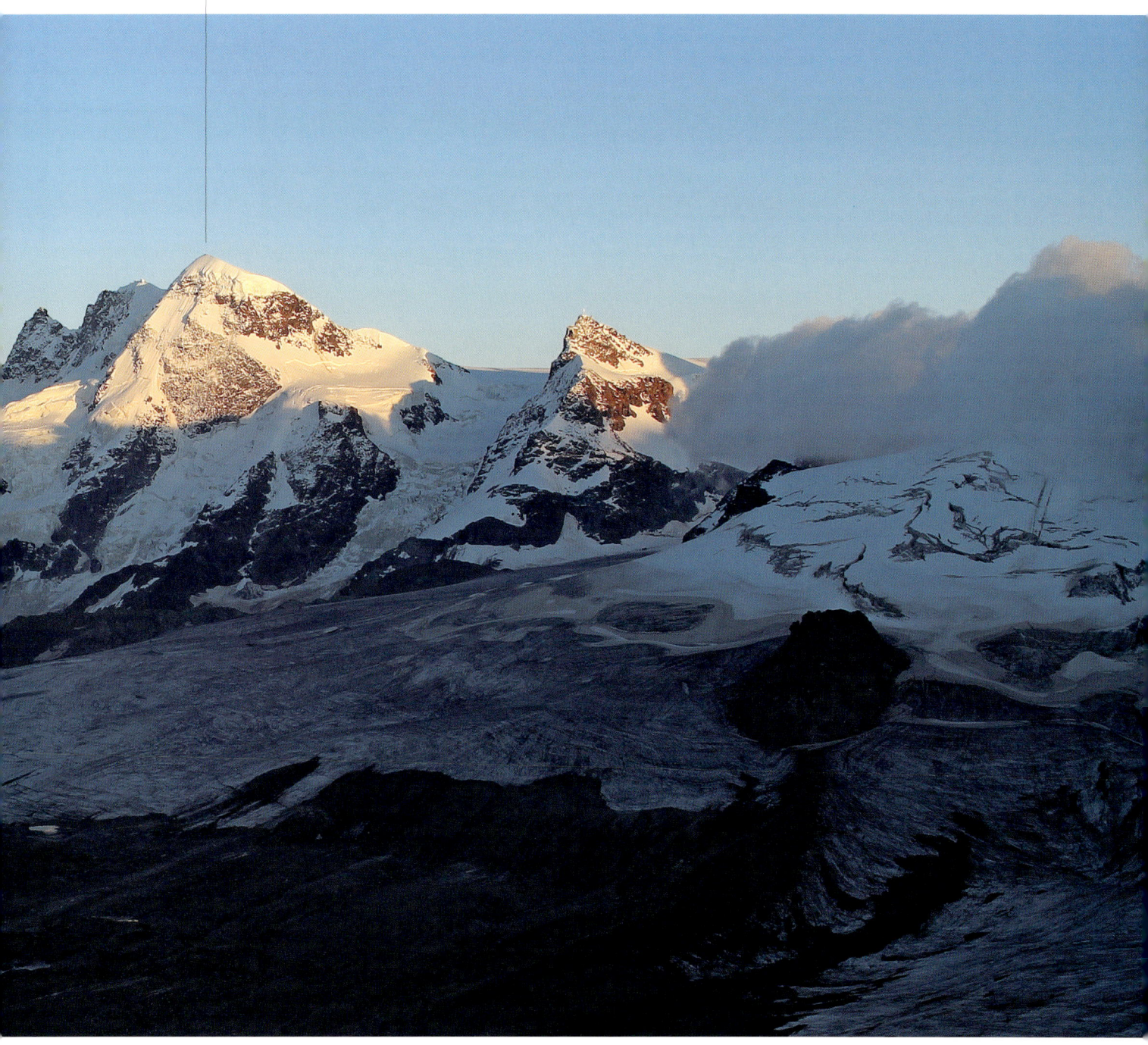

Monte Rosa
4,634m

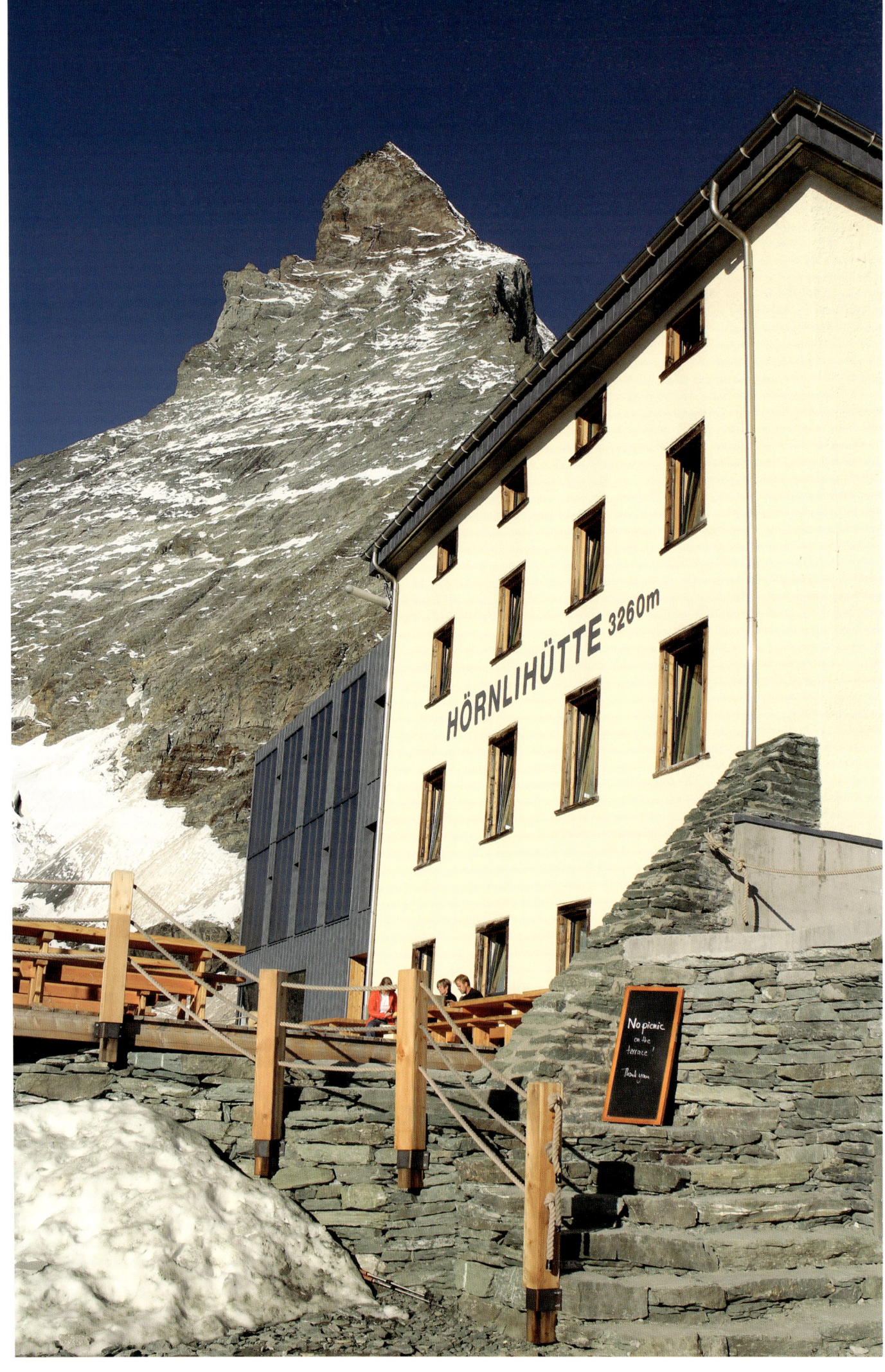

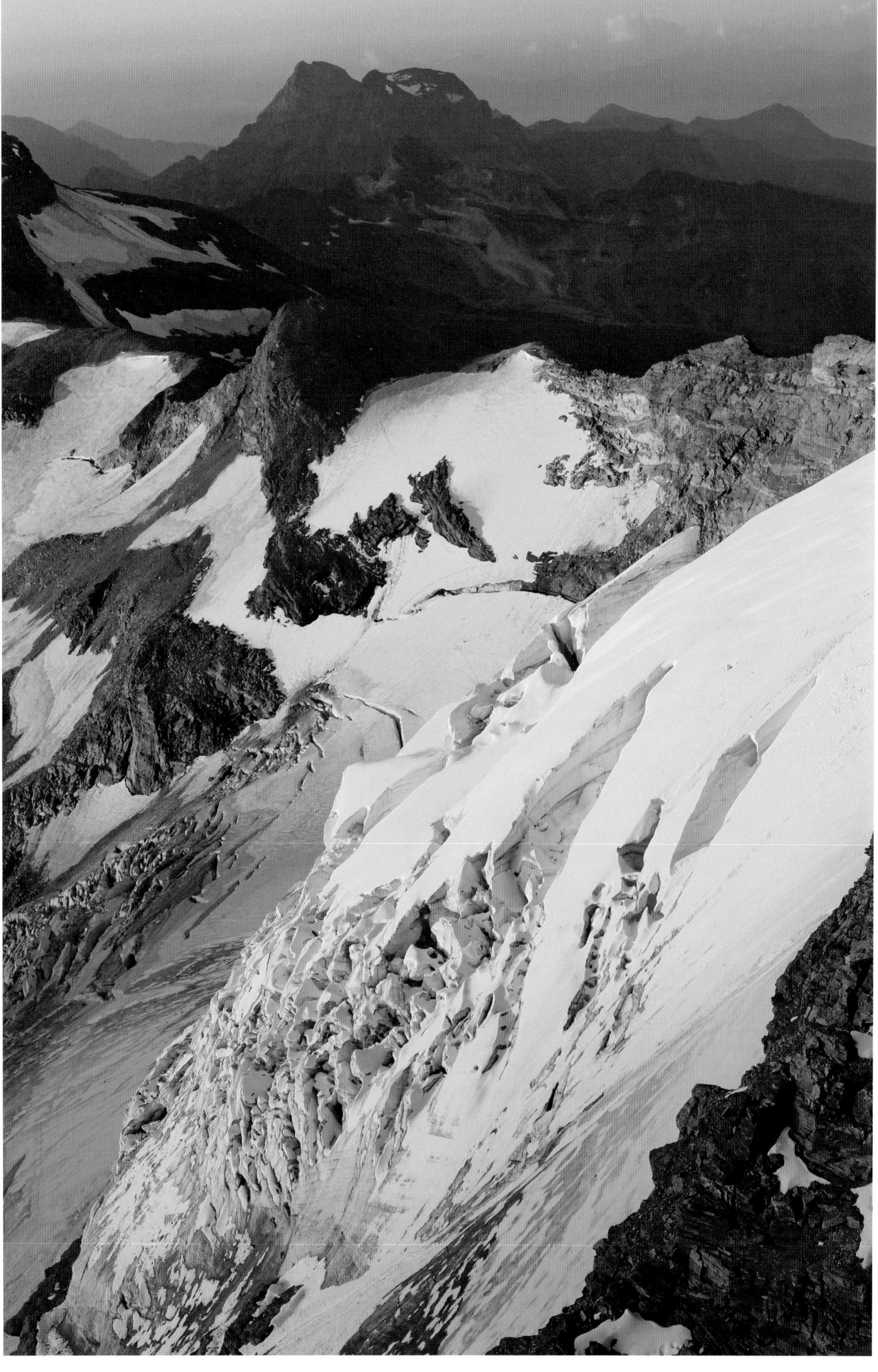

THE THEODUL PASS

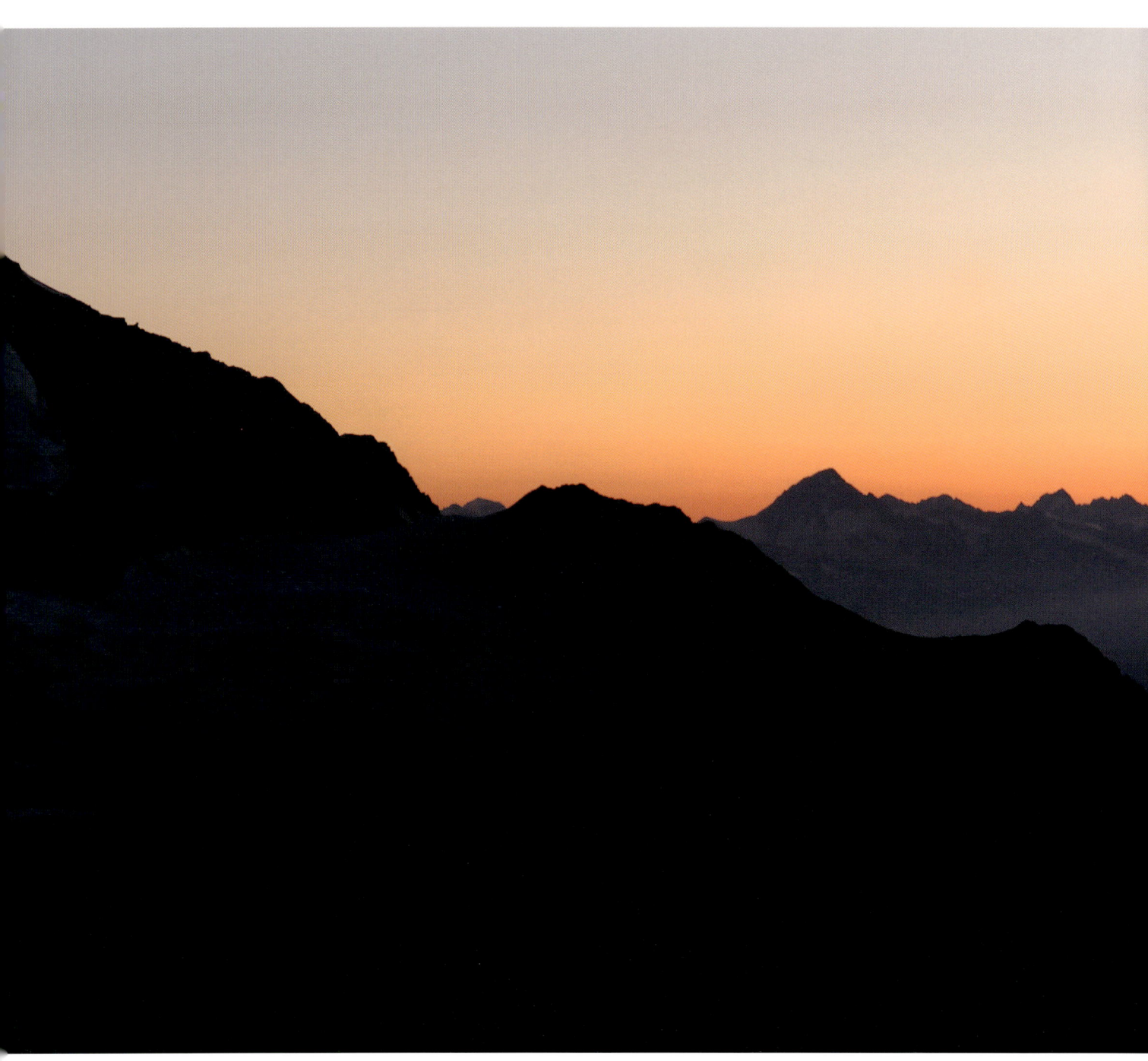

ALPENGLOW FROM THE HÖRNLI RIDGE

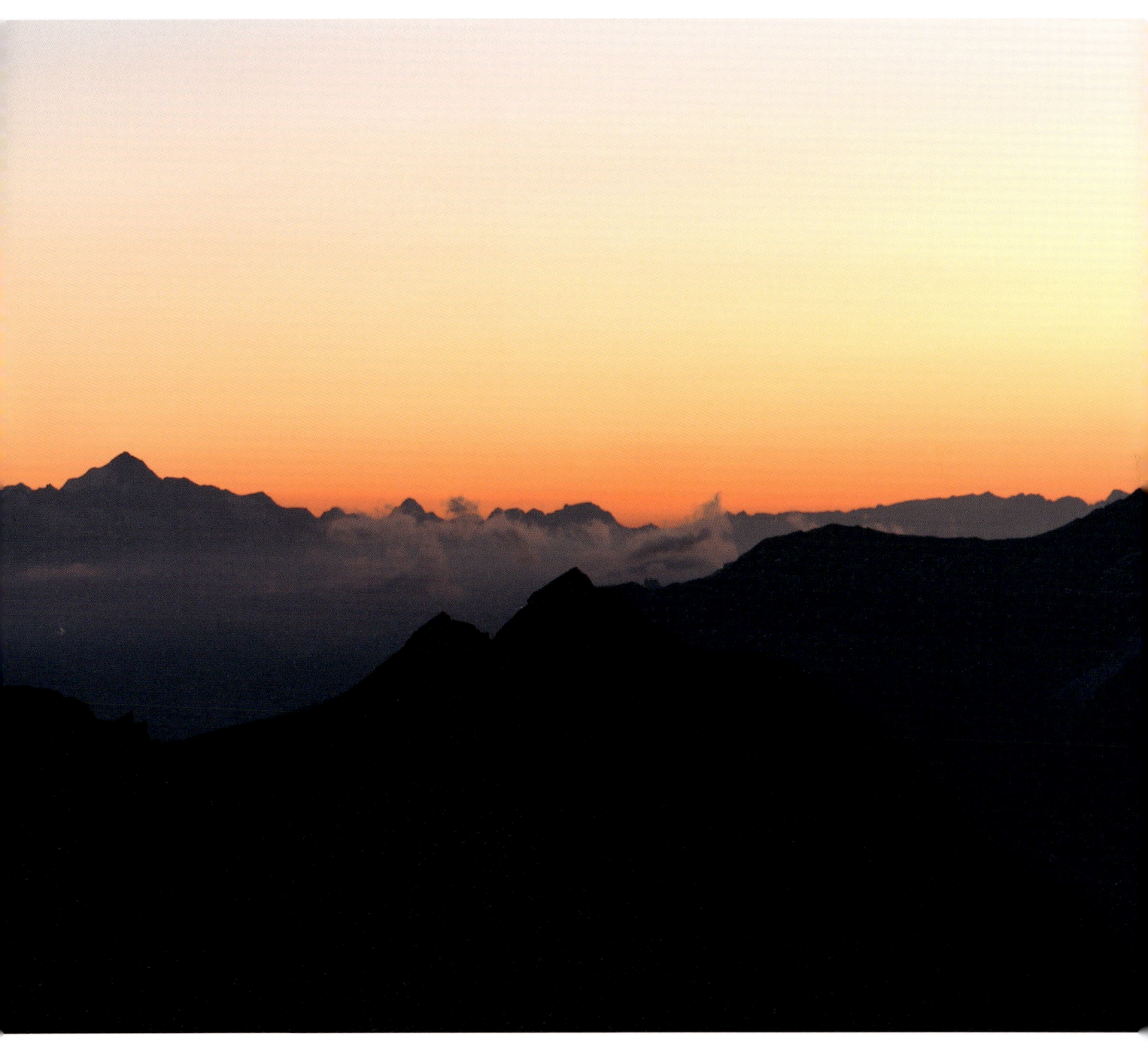

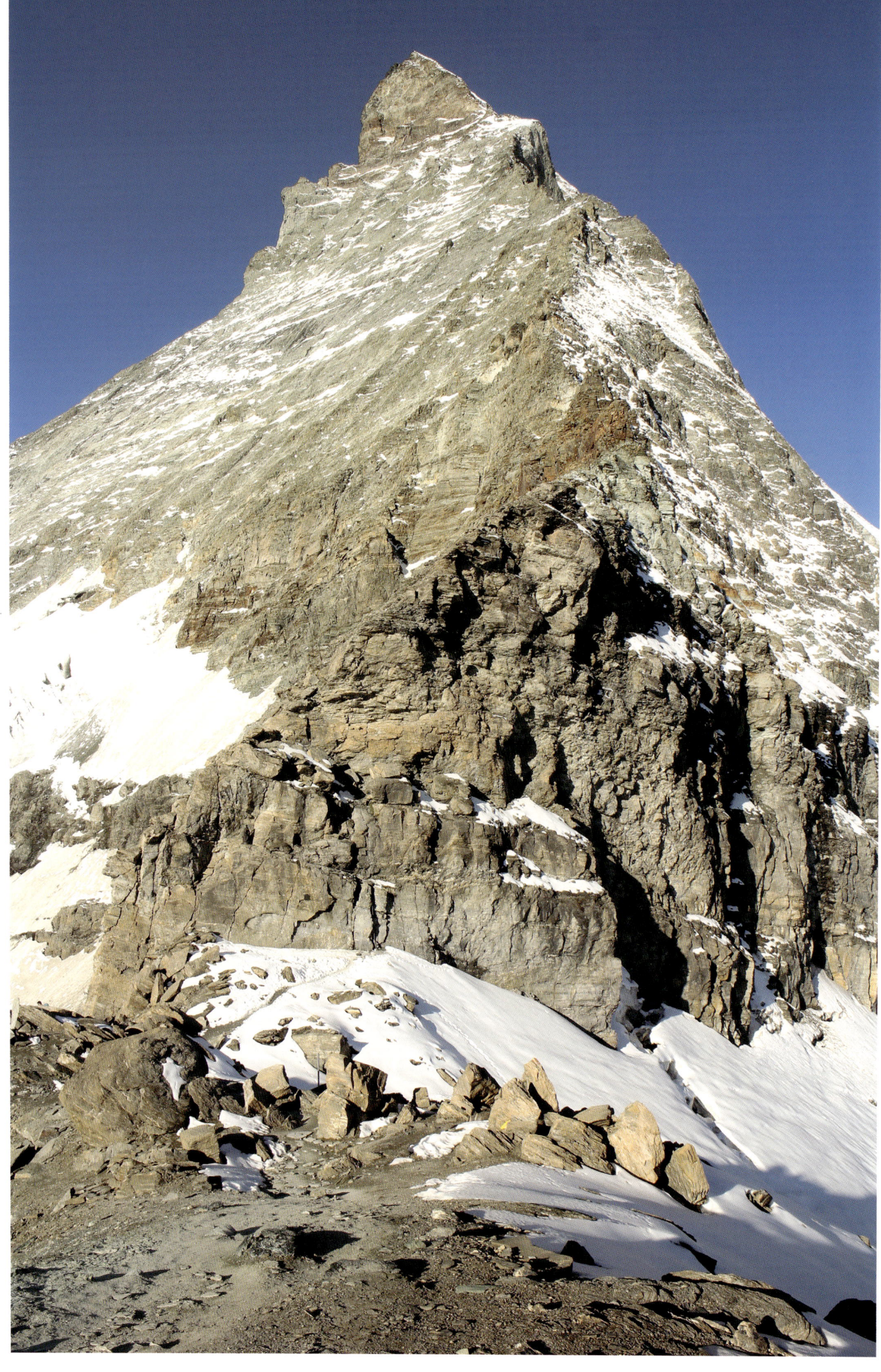

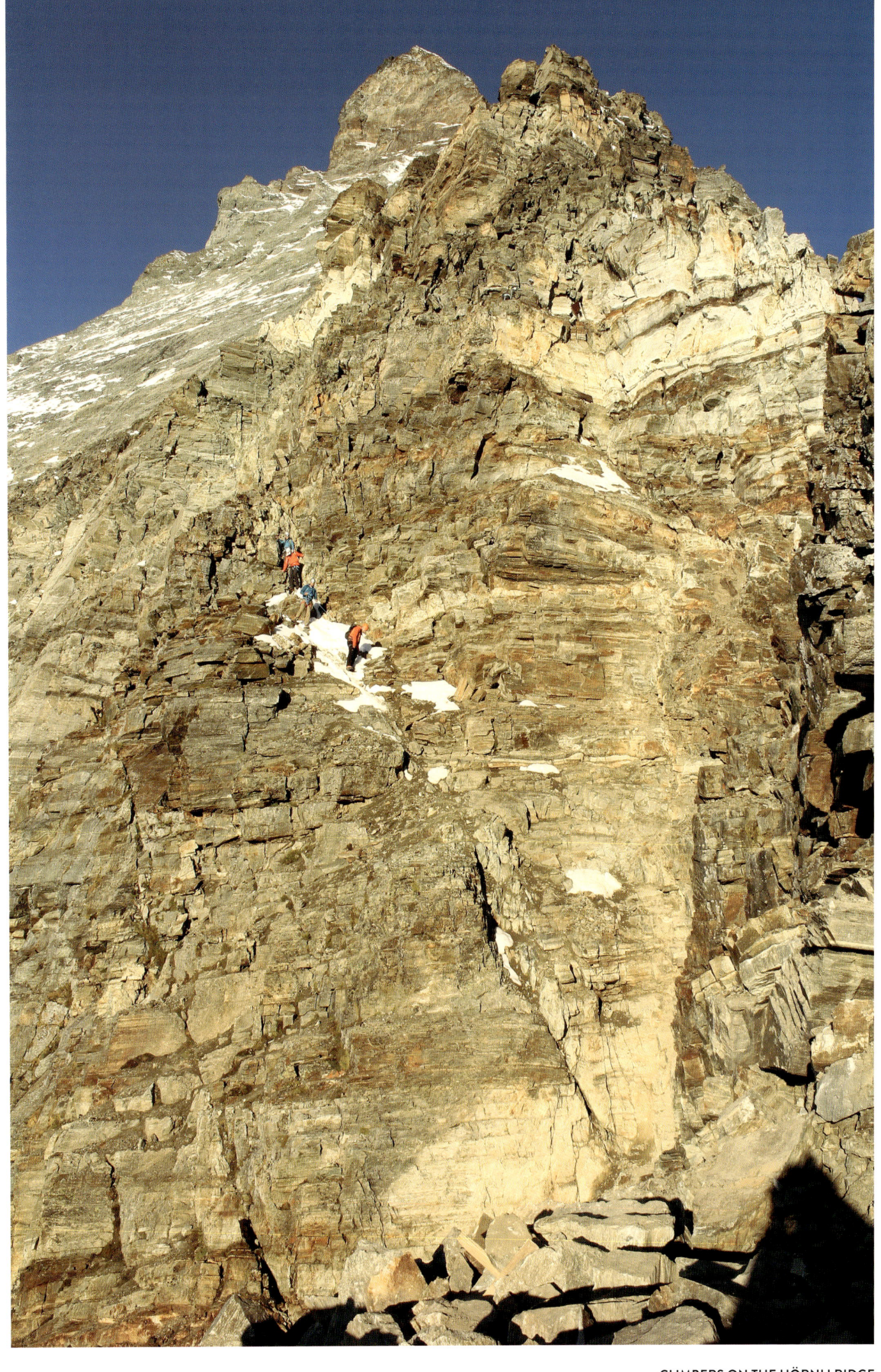

CLIMBERS ON THE HÖRNLI RIDGE

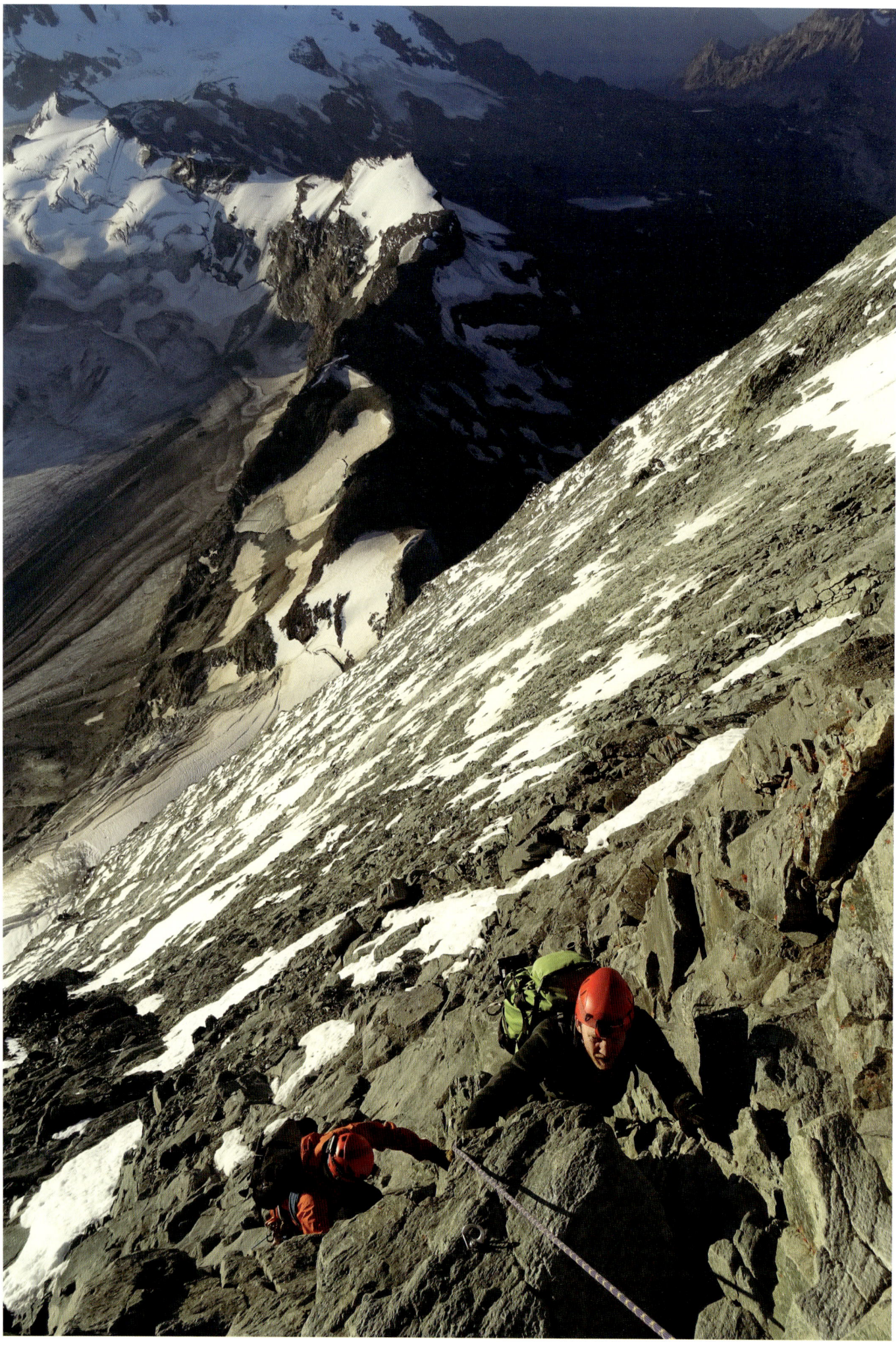

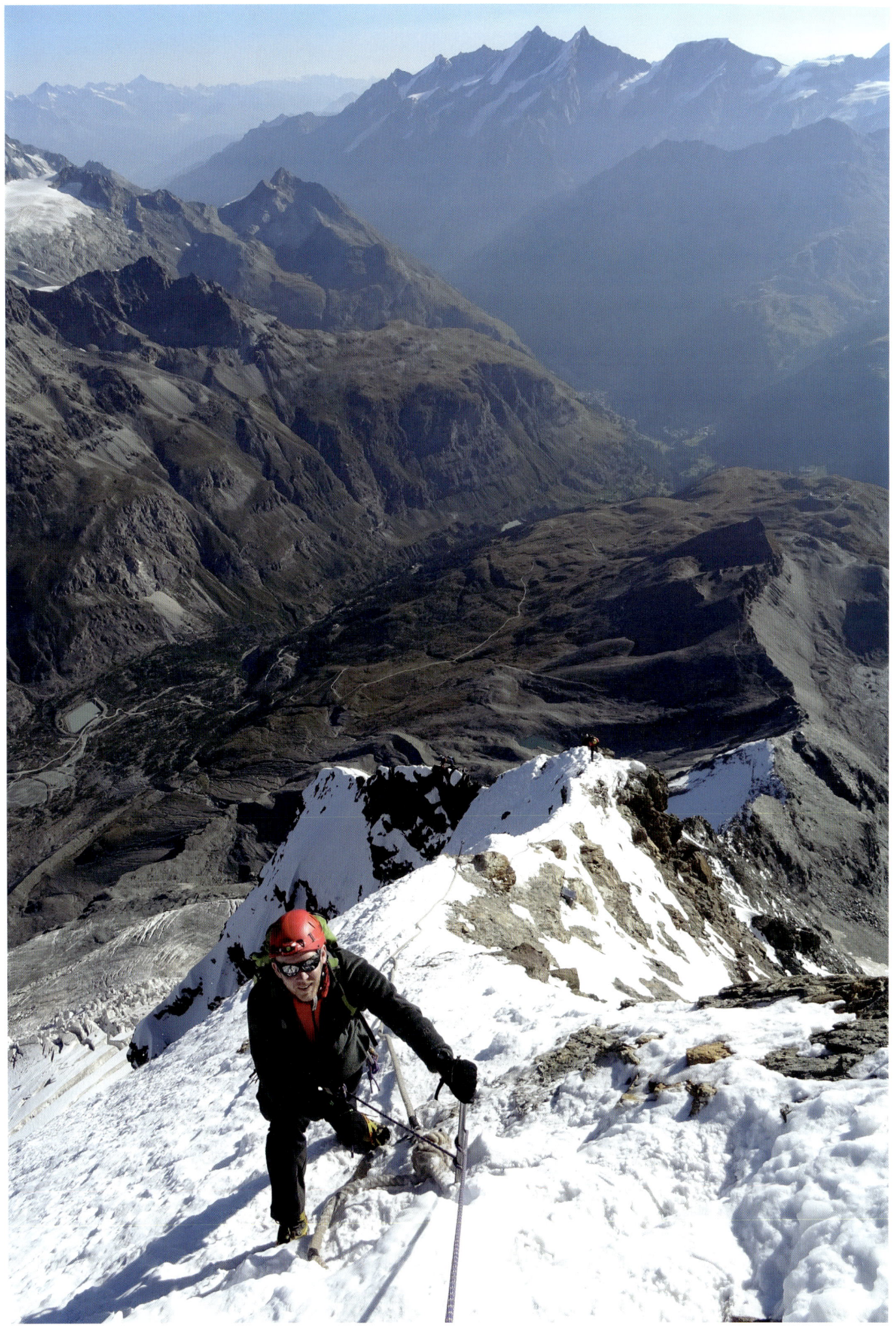

ABOVE THE SHOULDER

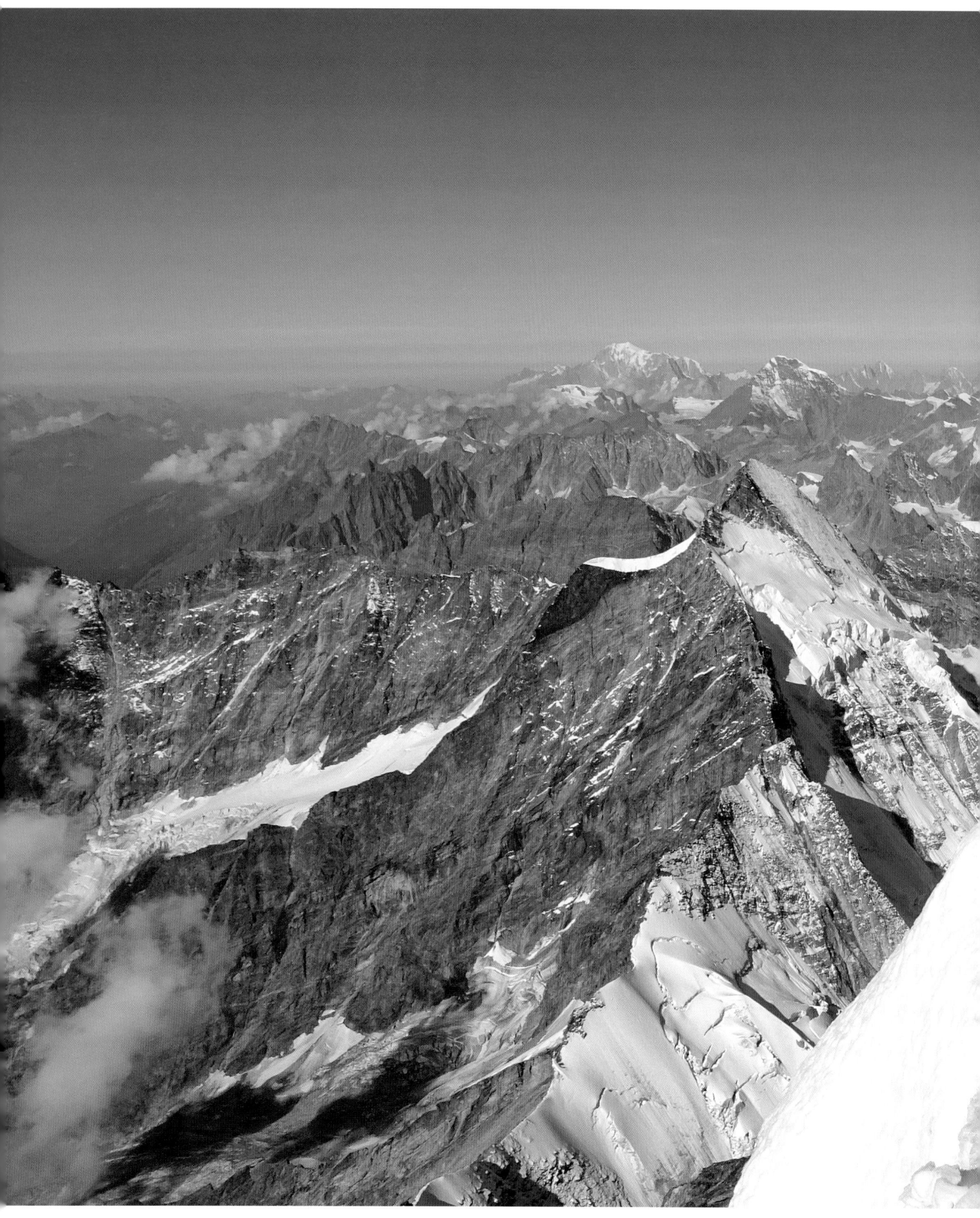

SUMMIT RIDGE OF THE MATTERHORN

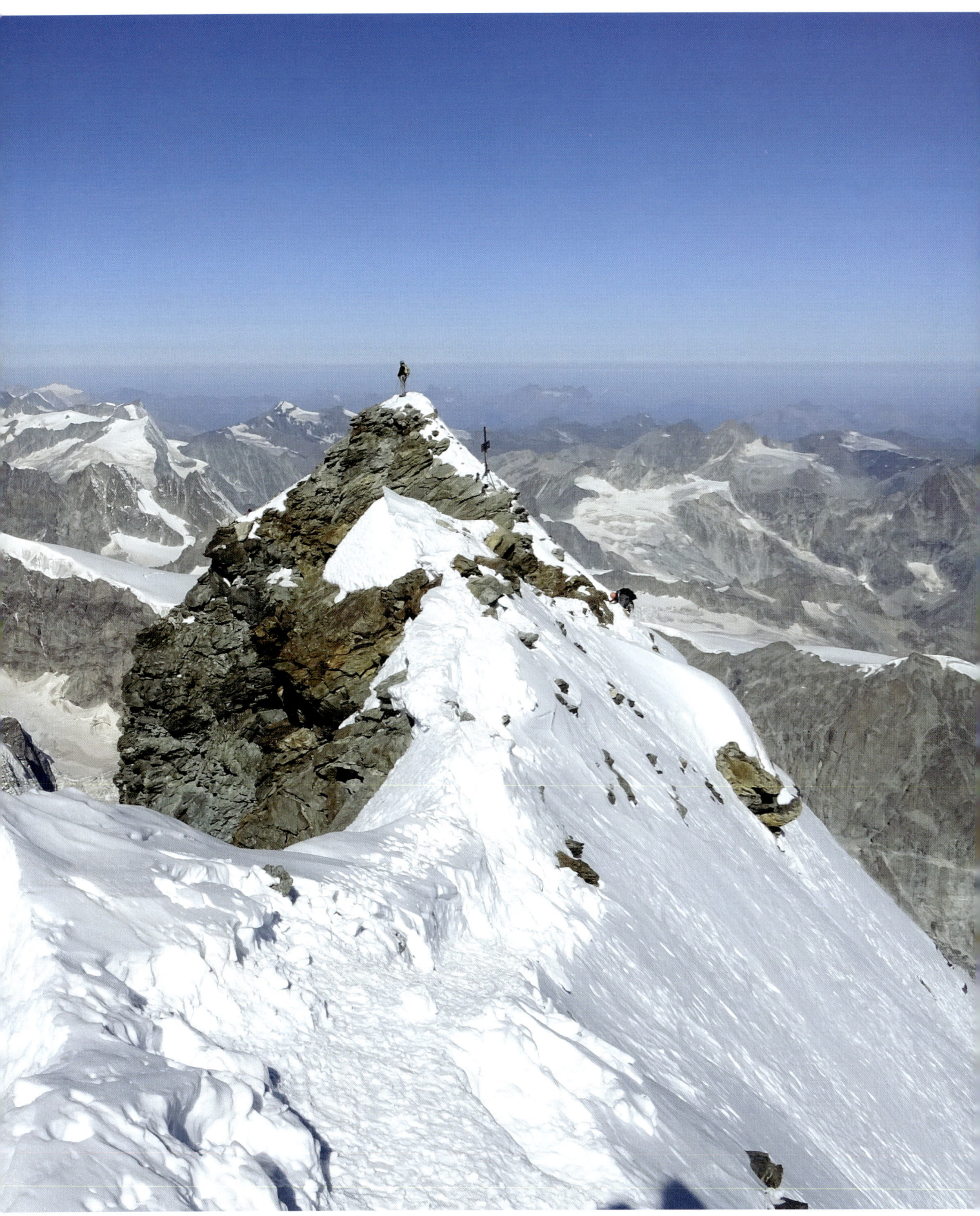

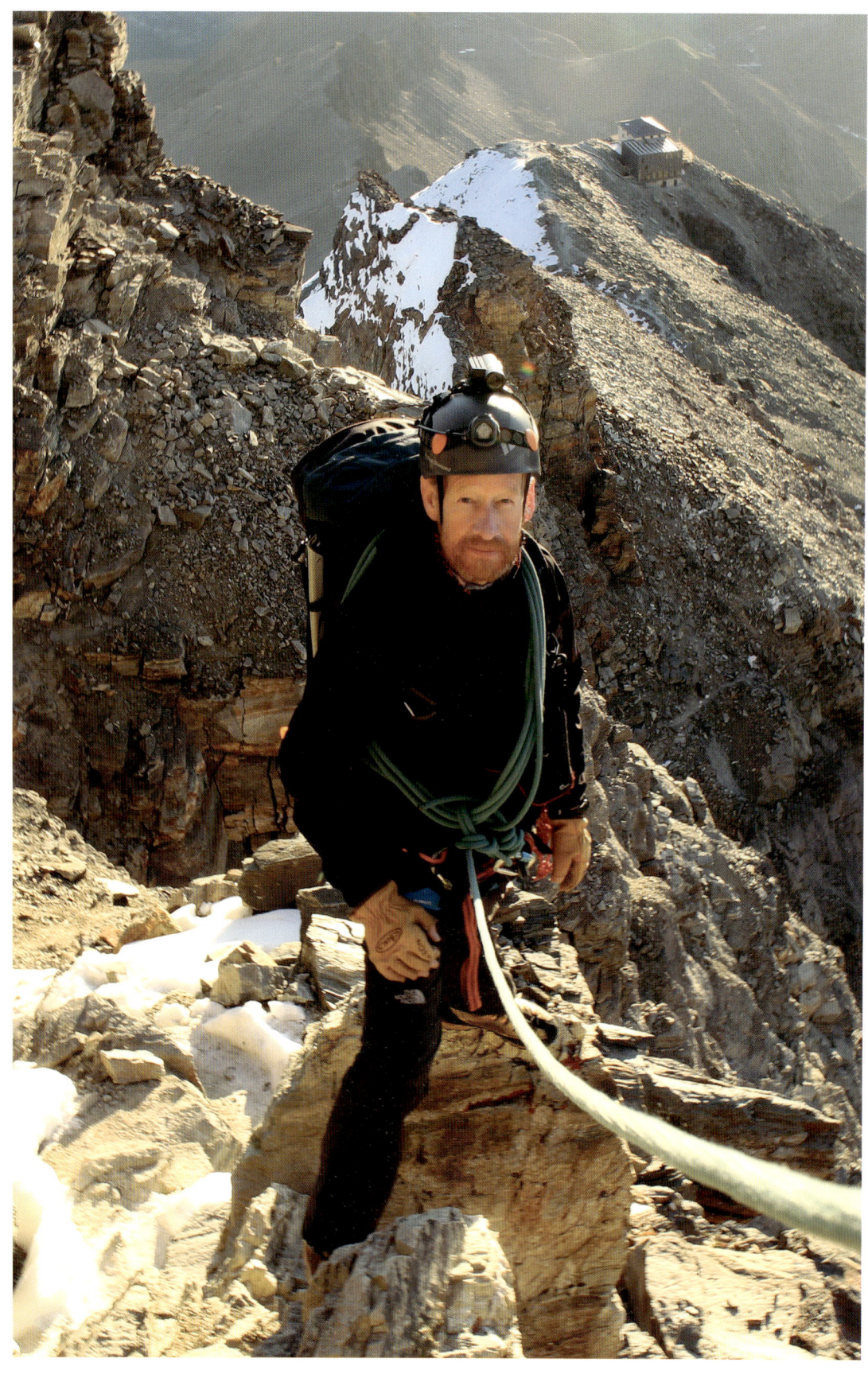

THE AUTHOR ON THE MATTERHORN

CHAPTER ELEVEN
AFTERWORD

RENEWED ATTEMPT BY CARREL TO ASCEND THE MATTERHORN FROM THE SOUTH

Carrel's judgement had failed him, both in respect to the difficulty of the Hörnli Ridge and in Whymper's resolve, resulting in victory slipping from his grasp. Nevertheless, another victory, which in one sense was a greater endeavour, soon presented itself. Giordano's telegram sent on 15th once again completes the story. 'Yesterday was a bad day, and Whymper, after all, gained the victory over the unfortunate Carrel. Whymper, as I told you, was desperate, and seeing Carrel climbing the mountain, tried his fortune on the Zermatt slope. Everyone here, and Carrel above all, considered the ascent absolutely impossible on that side; so we were all easy in our minds.' 'On the 13th little work was done, and yesterday Carrel might have reached the top, and was perhaps only about 500 or 600 feet below, when suddenly, at about 2 p.m., he saw Whymper and the others already on the summit.' 'Although every man did his duty, it is a lost battle, and I am in great grief.'

'I think, however, that we can play a counter-stroke by someone's making the ascent at once on this side, thus proving at any rate that the ascent is feasible this way; Carrel still thinks it possible.'

'At any rate, in order not to return ridiculous as well as unsuccessful, I think that we ought at least to plant our flag on the summit. I at once tried to organise a fresh expedition, but hitherto, with the exception of Carrel and another, I have not found any men of courage whom I can trust.'

The Val Tournanche natives who started to facilitate the way up the south-west ridge of the Matterhorn for [Messrs] Giordano and Sella, pitched their tent upon my third platform, at the foot of the Great Tower (12,992 feet), and enjoyed several days of bad weather under its shelter. On the first fine day (13th of July) they began their work, and about midday on the 14th got on to the 'shoulder,' and arrived at the base of the final peak (the point where [Tyndall] stopped on July 28th, 1862). The counsels of the party were then divided. Two [of them,] Jean-Antoine Carrel and Joseph Maquignaz — wished to go on; the others were not eager about it. A discussion took place, and the result was they all commenced to descend, and whilst upon the 'cravate' (13,524) they heard our cries from the summit. Upon the 15th they went down to Breil and reported their ill-success to Mr. Giordano ... [who] was naturally much disappointed, and pressed the men to set out again ... 'Until now I have striven for the honour of making the first ascent, — fate has decided against me, — I am beaten. Patience! Now, if I make further sacrifices it will be on your account, for your honour, and for your interests. Will you start again to settle the question, or, at least, to let there be no more uncertainty?' The majority of the men (in fact the whole of them with the exception of Jean-Antoine) refused point-blank to have anything more to do with the mountain. Carrel, however, stepped forward, saying, 'As for me, I have not given it up; if you (turning to the Abbé Gorret) or the others will come, I will start again immediately.' 'Not I!' said one. 'No more for me,' cried a second. 'If you would give me a thousand francs I would not go back,' said a third. The Abbé Gorret alone volunteered. This plucky priest was concerned in the very first attempts upon the mountain, and is an enthusiastic mountaineer. Carrel and the Abbé would have set out by themselves had not J. B. Bich and J.-A. Meynet ... come forward at the last moment. M. Giordano also wished to accompany them, but the men knew the nature of the work they had to undertake, and positively declined to be accompanied by an amateur.

These four men left Breil at 6.30 A.M. on July 16, at 1 P.M. arrived at the third tent-platform, and there passed the night. At daybreak on the 17th they continued the ascent by the route which had been taken before; passed successively the Great Tower, the 'crête du coq,' the 'cravate,' and the 'shoulder,' and at 10 A.M. gained the point at the foot of the final peak from which the explorers had turned back on the 14th. They had then about 800 feet to accomplish …

The passage of the cleft which stopped [Tyndall] was accomplished, and then the party proceeded directly towards the summit, over rocks which for some distance were not particularly difficult. The steep cliffs down which we had hurled stones (on the 14th) then stopped their way, and Carrel led round to the left or Z'Mutt side. The work at this part was of the very greatest difficulty, and stones and icicles which fell rendered the position of the party very precarious; so much so that they preferred to turn up directly towards the summit, and climb by rocks that the Abbé termed 'almost perpendicular.' He added, 'This part occupied the most time, and gave us the greatest trouble.' At length they arrived at a fault in the rocks which formed a roughly horizontal gallery. They crept along this in the direction of a ridge that descended towards the north-west, or thereabouts, and when close to the ridge, found that they could not climb on to it; but they perceived that, by descending a gully with perpendicular sides, they could reach the ridge at a lower point. The bold Abbé was the heaviest and the strongest of the four, and he was sacrificed for the success of the expedition. He and Meynet remained behind, and lowered the others, one by one, into the gully. Carrel and Bich clambered up the other side, attained the ridge descending towards the north-west, shortly afterwards gained an 'easy route, they galloped,' and in a few minutes reached the southern end of the summit-ridge.

The time of their arrival does not appear to have been noticed. It was late in the day, I believe about 3 P.M. Carrel and his comrade only waited long enough to plant a flag by the side of the cairn that we had built three days previously, then descended at once, rejoined the others, and all four hurried down as fast as possible to the tent.

The four Italians who started from Breil on the 16th of July were absent during 56½ hours, and as far as I can gather from the published account, and from conversation with the men, excluding halts, they took for the ascent and descent 23¾ hours. The hotel at Breil is 6890 feet above the sea, so they had to ascend 7890 feet. As far as the end of the 'shoulder' the way was known to Carrel, and he had to find the way over only about 800 feet. All four men were born mountaineers, good climbers, and they were led by the most expert cragsman I have seen … I know the greater part of the ground over which they passed, and from my knowledge, and from the account of Mr. Grove, I am sure that their route was not only more difficult, but that it was *much* more difficult than ours.

This was not the opinion in the Val Tournanche at the end of 1865, and the natives confidently reckoned that tourists would flock to their side in preference to the other … The indefatigable Carrel found a natural hole upon the ledge called the 'cravate' (13,524), and this, in course of time, was turned, under his direction, into a respectable little hut. Its position is superb, and gives a view of the most magnificent character.

Whilst this work was being carried out, my friend Mr. F. Craufurd Grove consulted me respecting the ascent of the Matterhorn. I recommended him to ascend by the northern route, and to place himself in the hands of Jean-Antoine Carrel. Mr. Grove found, however, that Carrel distinctly preferred the southern side, and they ascended accordingly by the Breil route. Mr. Grove has been good enough to supply the following account of his expedition.

> *In August 1867 I ascended the Matterhorn from Breil, taking as guides three mountaineers of the Val Tournanche — J. A. Carrel, J. Bich, and S. Meynet, — Carrel being the leader. At that time the Matterhorn had not been scaled since the famous expedition of the Italian guides mentioned above.*
>
> *Our route was identical with that which they followed in their descent when, as will be seen, they struck out on one part of the mountain a different line from that which they had taken in ascending. After gaining the Col du Lion, we climbed the south-western or Breil arête by the route which has been described in these pages, passing the night at the then unfinished hut constructed by the Italian Alpine Club on the 'cravate.' Starting from the hut at daylight, we reached at an early hour the summit of the 'shoulder,' and then traversed its* arête *to the final peak of the Matterhorn.*

The passage of this arête *was perhaps the most enjoyable part of the whole expedition. The ridge, worn by slow irregular decay into monstrous and rugged battlements, and guarded on each side by tremendous precipices, is grand beyond all description, but does not, strange to say, present any remarkable difficulty to the climber, save that it is exceedingly trying to the head. Great care is of course necessary, but the scramble is by no means of so arduous a nature as entirely to absorb the attention; so that a fine climb, and rock scenery, of grandeur perhaps unparalleled in the Alps, can both be appreciated.*

It was near the end of this arête, *close to the place where it abuts against the final peak, that Professor Tyndall's party turned in 1862, arrested by a cleft in the ridge. From the point where they stopped the main tower of the Matterhorn rises in front of the climber, abrupt, magnificent, and apparently inaccessible. The summit is fully 750 feet in vertical height above this spot, and certainly, to my eye, appeared to be separated from me by a yet more considerable interval; for I remember, when at the end of the* arête, *looking upward at the crest of the mountain, and thinking that it must be a good 1000 feet above me.*

When the Italian guides made their splendid [first] *ascent, they traversed the* arête *of the shoulder to the main peak, passed the cleft which has been mentioned, clambered on to the tremendous north-western face of the mountain ... and then endeavoured to cross this face so as to get on to the Z'Mutt* arête. *The passage of this slope proved a work of great difficulty and danger. I saw it from very near the place which they traversed, and was unable to conceive how any human creatures managed to crawl over rocks so steep and so treacherous. ... Passing on to the Z'Mutt* arête *without further difficulty, Carrel and Bich climbed by that ridge to the summit of the mountain. In returning, the Italians kept to the ledge for the whole distance across the north-western face, and descended to the place where the* arête *of the shoulder abuts against the main peak by a sort of rough ridge of rocks between the north-western and southern faces. When I ascended in 1867, we followed this route in the ascent and in the descent. I thought the ledge difficult, in some places decidedly dangerous, and should not care to set foot on it again; but assuredly it neither is so difficult nor so continuously dangerous as those gaunt and pitiless rock-slopes which the Italians crossed in their upward route.*

(Ibid., pp. 305–309)

A DECAYING MOUNTAIN

I made an ascent of the mountain in 1874 to photograph the summit, in order that I might see what changes had occurred since our visit of ten years before. The summits of all high mountains vary from time to time, and I was not surprised to find that the Matterhorn was no exception to the general rule. It was altogether sharper and narrower in 1874 than 1865. Instead of being able 'to run about,' every step had to be painfully cut with the axe; and the immediate summit, instead of being a blunt and rounded eminence, was a little piled-up cone of snow which went to a very sharp point.

The light was not favourable for photographing the *Cabane* when we returned from the summit, and I stopped alone with Carrel in it for a second night in order to get the morning light on the next day. Whilst quietly reposing inside, I was startled to hear a rustling and crackling sound, and jumped up, expecting that the building was about to take itself off to lower quarters; and presently I perceived that the hut had a tenant to whom I certainly did not expect to be introduced. A little, plump mouse came creeping out over the floor, being apparently of opinion that there ought not to be any one there at that time of day. It wandered about picking up stray fragments of food, occasionally crunching a bit of egg-shell, totally unaware of my presence, for I made out that the little animal was both blind and deaf. It would have been easy to capture it, but I would not do so, and left it there to keep company with other solitary tourists.

Whilst stopping in the *Cabane* we had the insecurity of its position forcibly impressed upon us by seeing a huge block break away from the rock at its side, and go crashing down over the very route which is commonly pursued by tourists.

(Ibid., pp. 312f)

A CONCLUDING THOUGHT

The ascent of the Matterhorn has now taken its place amongst those which are considered fashionable, and many persons get upon it who ought not to be upon a mountain at all. Although much has been done on both sides of it to facilitate the routes, and although they are much easier to traverse than they were in years gone by, it is still quite possible to get into trouble upon them, and to come utterly to grief. Considering how large a number of entirely incompetent persons venture upon the mountain, it is surprising so few meet with accidents; but if the number of accidents continues to increase at its present rate it will, ere long, not be easy to find a place of interment in the English churchyard at Zermatt.

(Ibid., pp. 314)

Putting the Matterhorn and Alps behind him, Whymper turned his attention to South America. While climbing with his former guide and adversary Jean-Antoine Carrel he researched the effects of altitude on the human body. He then spent time in the Canadian Rockies, acting as an advisor and ambassador for the Canadian Pacific Railway.

During this time Whymper remained single, but did eventually marry in 1906. His wife, forty-five years his junior was Edith Mary Lewin, the daughter of his landlady. Having spent sixty-six years living alone, it will have come as no surprise that the marriage ended after just four years, despite the birth of their daughter Ethel.

One year later, in Sept 1911, Whymper died surrounded by his first and true love – the Alps. Taken ill while in Chamonix, he locked himself in his room and refused any medical assistance. There is little doubt that, for the forty-five years of his life following the accident, Whymper was tormented by the tragedy on the Matterhorn; a sentiment made harder to bear by the on going criticism of some, and the failure of his peers to give him the acknowledgement he deserved.

'Every night, do you understand, I see my comrades of the Matterhorn slipping on their backs, their arms outstretched, one after the other, in perfect order at equal distances - Croz the guide, first, then Hadow, then Hudson, and lastly Douglas. Yes, I shall always see them...'

One can only hope that the memories of his time atop the mountains gave him a sense of fulfilment and comfort throughout his life, and that he died content in the knowledge that he had achieved the impossible.

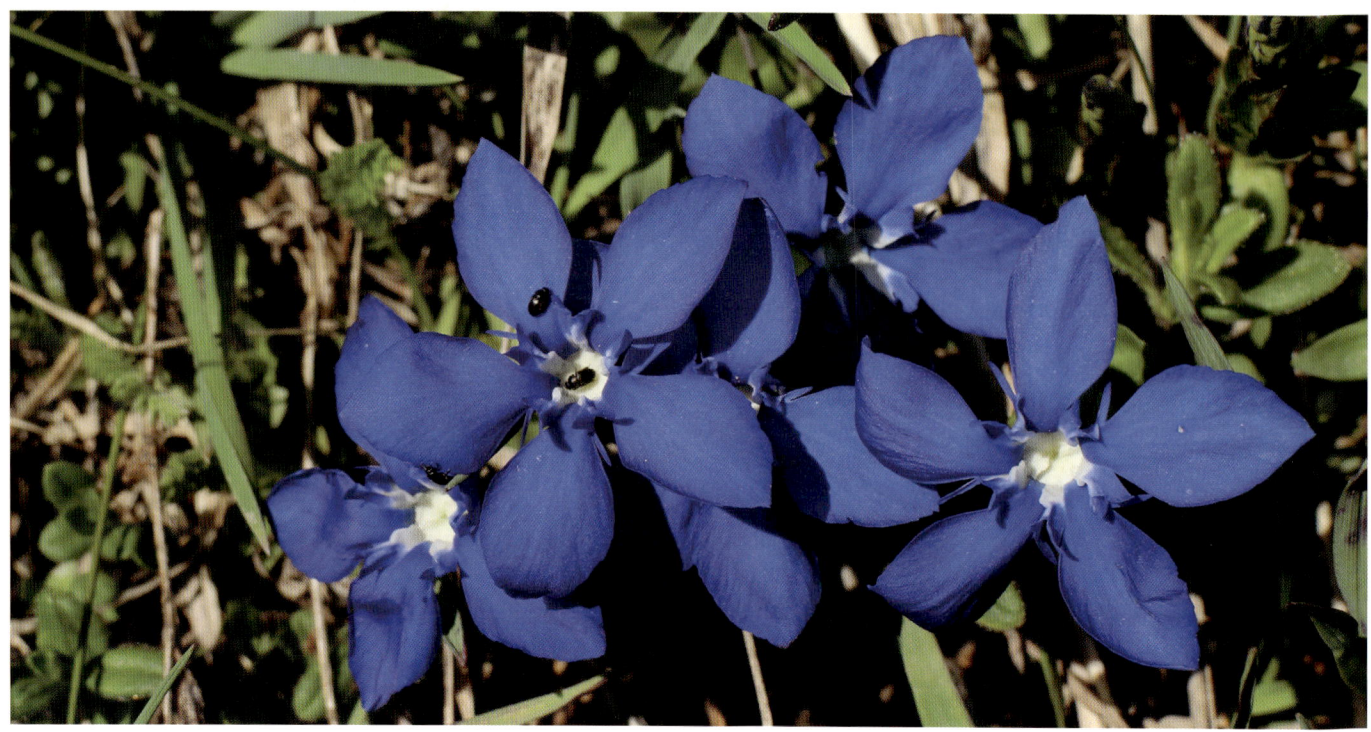